Marketing: The Encyclopedic Dictionary

Marketing: The Encyclopedic Dictionary

David Mercer

First published 1999

First published in USA
2 4 6 8 10 9 7 5 3 1

Blackwell Publishers Ltd
108 Cowley Road
Oxford OX4 1JF
UK

Blackwell Publishers Inc.-
350 Main Street
Malden, Massachusetts 02148
USA

British Library Cataloguing in Publication Data

A CIP catalogue record for this book is available from the British Library.

Library of Congress Cataloging-in-Publication Data

Mercer, David (David Steuart)
    Marketing: the encyclopedic dictionary / David Mercer.
      p. cm.
    Includes bibliographical references and index.
    ISBN 0-631-19107-0 (alk. paper). – ISBN 0-631-21126-8 (pbk.: alk. paper)
    1. Marketing – Dictionaries. 2. Marketing – Encyclopedias. I. Title.
HF5412.M47   1998
658.8'003 – dc21
                                                              98-26085
                                                                CIP

Typeset in 9 on 11 pt Ehrhardt MT
by Best-set Typesetter Ltd, Hong Kong
Printed in Great Britain by MPG Books Ltd, Bodmin, Cornwall

This book is printed on acid-free paper

Contents

Preface

This is a *reference* book intended to provide *practical* help to marketing practitioners and to managers in general; as well as to students, especially those on undergraduate and MBA courses. The emphasis, though, is on *practical*. It does inevitably provide *comprehensive* cover of all the theories (many minor ones as well as all the major ones), but it does this from the viewpoint of the practitioner, not the academic. In addition, the heart of the book is the large number of long articles which explore topics (of interest to practitioners and managers) in considerable depth – justifying its claim to be an encyclopedia – and on the basis that you are retrieving the information to make practical use of it in a specific situation. At the same time, it covers literally thousands of other terms in brief, fulfilling its role as a dictionary, and there are also thousands of cross-references to help you find these topics.

The content of the book has been developed over the past half-decade on the basis of direct contributions, to Open University Business School course teams, by dozens of marketing experts, and indirect contributions from the literally thousands of organizations who have helped us in our research. I extend my thanks to all of them.

Acknowledgements

Every attempt has been made to trace copyright holders. The author and publishers would like to apologize in advance for any inadvertent use of copyright material. Acknowledgements are presented in entry order.

Illustration on p. 49 reprinted from *Business Horizons*, December 1980, copyright © 1980 by the Foundation for the School of Business at Indiana University – use with permission.

Illustration on p. 69 reproduced from Booz, *New Products Management* for the 1980s, Allen and Hamilton Inc., 1981.

Illustration on p. 90 reproduced from S. Makridakis and S. C. Wheelwright, *Forecasting Methods for Management* (5th edn). Copyright © 1989. Reprinted by permission of John Wiley & Sons, Inc.

Illustration on p. 91 reproduced from Thomas J. Peters and Robert H. Waterman, Jr., *In Search of Excellence*, copyright © 1982 by Thomas J. Peters and Robert H. Waterman, Jr., reprinted by permission of HarperCollins Publishers.

Illustration on p. 105 reprinted by permission of *Harvard Business Review*: An exhibit from 'Automation to boost sales and marketing' by Rowland T. Moriarty et al., January–February 1989. Copyright © 1989 by the President and Fellows of Harvard College, all rights reserved.

Illustration on p. 151 reproduced from the *European Management* Journal by permission of Elsevier Publishers Ltd.

Illustration on p. 226 reproduced from *Planning for Social Change*, Henley Centre for Forecasting.

Illustration on p. 344 reproduced from S. J. Lyonski and E. M. Johnson, 'The Sales Manager as a boundary spanner: a role theory analysis', *Journal of Personal Selling and Sales Management*, November 1983.

Illustration on p. 364 reproduced from M. J. Thomas (ed.) *Marketing Handbook*, by permission of Gower Publishing Company.

Top illustration on p. 386 reproduced from Robert F. Lusch and Virginia N. Lusch, *Principles of Marketing*, PWS–Kent Publishing Company, Boston, 1987, p. 55.

Top illustration on p. 403 reproduced from S. Makridakis and S. C. Wheelwright, *Forecasting Methods for Management* (5th edn). Copyright © 1989. Reprinted by permission of John Wiley & Sons, Inc. Lower illustration reproduced from J. Hull, J. Mapes and B. Wheeler, *Model Building Techniques for Management*, Saxon House, 1976.

A

à la carte   The approach whereby advertisers use a range of service companies for each part of their advertising needs rather than giving their overall business to just one agency.
See also ADVERTISING AGENCY ELEMENTS; SPECIALIST AGENCIES

ABC analysis   This powerful technique simply requires that reports are sorted with the most 'important' customers (or products, or whatever is the subject of the report) at the beginning. Typically this will be in terms of volume (or value) of sales, so that the customers are ranked in order of their sales offtake – with the highest-volume (and hence most 'important') customers at the top of the list and the many low-volume customers at the bottom (since it matters less if they are not taken into account in decisions). As the 80:20 rule says that the top 20 per cent of customers on such a list are likely to account for 80 per cent of total sales, this approach can, in effect, be used to help reduce the data to be examined by a factor of five.
See also PERFORMANCE ANALYSIS

ABC (Attention, Benefits, Close)   *see* CALL STRUCTURE

above the line   *see* PUSH VERSUS PULL PROMOTION

absolute advantage   The economic term that describes the ability of a country to produce a good more efficiently than another country – though not necessarily to sell against a comparative advantage.
See also COMPARATIVE ADVANTAGE, GLOBAL

absorption costing   *see* MARGINAL COSTING, NEW PRODUCTS

absorption of overheads, pricing   *see* COST-PLUS PRICING

A–B split run testing   *see* SPLIT RUNS

access, segment viability   The producer must be able to get at the segment that has been found. If tapping that segment is too difficult, and accordingly too expensive, it clearly will not be viable. In the case of the car market there might, for the sake of the argument, be a small segment of the general low-priced market that could be met by a small manufacturer using hand-building techniques. If the consumers within the segment were, however, diffused evenly throughout the population, the producer might face difficulties on two levels. The first would be in obtaining national distribution on the low volumes. Setting up a separate dealership network, to provide the maintenance facilities, would be almost impossible – even some of the smaller existing manufacturers, such as Peugeot and Fiat, have incomplete networks. The second would be finding the means of delivering the promotional message to these potential buyers. If there can be no concentration of promotional resources, then segmentation may often not be justified.
See also SEGMENT VIABILITY

accessibility, filtering unsuitable foreign markets   The potential that a foreign market offers may be placed on one side of the scale, but the costs of tapping that potential (of providing the necessary exporting infrastructure) must be put on the other side before any sensible decision can be made. Key factors may be as follows.

Distance
With the advent of the Boeing 747 airliner and container ships, the world can now sometimes be thought of as a 'global village'. Trade between many countries is now an easy matter in physical terms (so that, for example, UK supermarkets can stock fresh vegetables from Israel, fish from the Seychelles, strawberries from California and apples from Chile), and (with modern voice and computer networks) communication is even easier in terms of remote contacts. There are, however, still many places (and indeed whole countries) which are not tied into the trade routes, and where the transport of goods (and even of visiting businessmen) may impose significant problems.

Language and culture

The problems of language should not be neglected. It may be quite possible to obtain a local agent who speaks good English (or to find an interpreter), but an ignorance of the local language can bar an exporter from many of the 'signals' that he or she could expect to use in interpreting a market (or the agent's performance). 'Aesthetic' considerations also must not be ignored; for example, certain colours are a sign of mourning in some cultures! In Japan, for instance, the McDonalds 'clown' advertising failed, because a white face signifies death! Of course, taste varies considerably. Heinz Ketchup is a global brand, but its formulation is different in different countries: to account for local tastes it is sweeter in the UK and Canada, spicier in continental Europe, and more tart and vinegary in the USA. Similarly, a lack of understanding of the culture can pose immeasurable barriers between an exporter and the market.

It is obvious, from this list of constraints, that the decision whether or not to enter a foreign market is not to be taken lightly! Even then, Vern Terpstra (1987) advises, 'In a sense, the language problem in foreign markets is beyond the capabilities of the international advertiser, it can be solved only with the help of local expertise.'

Business infrastructure

The support available to assist import business in a given market can vary widely; and needs to be taken into account. First, are there suitable agents – a sufficient number to offer alternatives should the first choice fail – to handle the product or service? Does your own government have a sound trade department in its local embassy, to provide accurate information and advice? What is the 'bureaucracy' like, in terms of importing: Will its incompetence (or its corruption) lead to shipments sitting on the quayside for months on end? What is the business etiquette? Punctuality, for instance, may vary considerably across national boundaries; and may wreak havoc with carefully crafted schedules for visits.
See also EXPORT MARKET ELIMINATION

Reference: Terpstra, Vern (1987) *International Marketing*. New York: The Dryden Press.

accordion fold   A small, inexpensive leaflet that is pleated (like an accordion) so that it can immediately be pulled out to full size.

account conflict   This happens when an advertising agency acquires two different accounts that are competing in the same market. It may be dealt with

by ensuring that the accounts are handled by different groups, but this may still be unacceptable to the clients. Problems were caused in the 1980s when mergers of agencies took place, and a number of clients changed agency because of the resulting conflicts.
See also CLIENT/AGENCY RELATIONSHIP

account planning   The most important activity in developing key relationships with customers, the organization's 'accounts', is the development of a sound plan – the account plan. Unlike the overall sales plan, however, which will deal with groups of customers, each account plan (or 'key account plan') deals quite specifically with a single customer. For each of these key accounts, a unique plan should be developed, which matches (at least in its scope of content) the overall marketing plan. It should detail the specific objectives, which will be individually related to the customer's needs and wants. It should detail the activities that are planned to meet these objectives, and to build the 'relationship'. If such a plan is produced internally within the selling organization, it will be a productive exercise. If it is produced in co-operation with the customer, so that the resulting plan becomes a shared plan, it may make a major contribution to the development of that business relationship; so that it becomes a genuine peer-to-peer relationship. Such an account plan was the basis of much of IBM's success in selling to its large accounts. Account management (in its most general sense, covering prospects as well as customers) is the essence of professional salesmanship. Customer account management, in particular, is the epitome of this. It is probably the most important single skill (apart from selling itself) required of a sales professional – and yet, perhaps typically, it is almost entirely neglected by sales trainers.
See also CALLS AVAILABLE ANNUALLY; COMPLEX SALE; MANPOWER PLAN, SALES; ORGANIZATIONAL BUYING SITUATIONS; RELATIONSHIP (MARKETING) MANAGEMENT; SALES PROFESSIONAL; SELLING; TERRITORY MANAGEMENT; TERRITORY SALES PLAN; WIN–WIN

accounts selection   *see* TERRITORY SALES PLAN

accuracy, of marketing research results   From time to time, much theoretical effort has been expended on calculating the (statistical) accuracy of marketing research (typically using the theoretical statistics of random samples, but applied to the actual quota samples). What has rarely been examined, however, is the accuracy of the results themselves.

For example, much criticism is levelled at techniques such as mail surveys, because of the poor response rate. What is rarely discussed is the response rate in quota samples, since this is not normally recorded; although the indications are that it may often be below 50 per cent (and the non-respondents, in these cases, might arguably be quite different in their responses). Accordingly, a particularly important piece of research was carried out by O'Brien and Ford. As part of another project, they compared the results, from exactly the same questionnaire on the same respondents (400 out of the 677 in the original sample), separated by ten months.

This research showed that no less than 41 per cent of these 400 respondents had changed their social class between the two surveys! It should be noted that, in fact, this means that the 'error' rate was 20 per cent on each survey (not quite as bad as the 40 per cent error rate which seems to be apparent at first sight). On the other hand, this research was carried out by one of the most respected (and reliable) marketing research agencies, which is well known for the control that it exercises over its field force – and this suggests that the level of error might be significantly higher yet for less well managed research!

These figures are much higher than most researchers allow for. Of these errors, O'Brien and Ford (1988) attributed 56 per cent to 'interviewer miscoding': the interviewer simply made a mistake, in an area in which, unlike much of routine marketing research, he or she has to use judgement. In addition, 29 per cent was due to 'depth of probing': the interviewer simply did not ask enough questions. Finally, 24 per cent derived from 'change in details given by correspondent': the respondent changed his or her mind.

These rates of 'error', for highest-quality research, should serve to alert you to the dangers of research that is of a more dubious quality – as much of it is. Far too much research is, being driven by the search for lower costs, of much lower quality! On the other hand, the 20 per cent 'error' should not stop you undertaking marketing research. For one thing, much of the research is concerned with 'facts' that do not require the interviewer to apply his or her judgement (the 'error' rate for age grouping/life stage, for example, was only 8 per cent per stage). Even the higher error rate was made up of errors that were in effect random, and hence cancelled each other out – so that the overall results were not distorted to anywhere near the same degree. In any case, marketing research has, over many years, shown its power to provide powerful predictions for the marketer.

See also DATA COLLECTION; SAMPLING; SURVEY RESEARCH

Reference: O'Brien, Sarah and Ford, Rosemary (1988) Can we at last say goodbye to social class? *Journal of the Market Research Society*, 30(3) July.

accuracy, of research reports Having established that the material in a research report is both relevant and reliable, the next step is to decide what the accuracy might be. The researcher should tell you this, but all too often this is a technicality which is buried deep in technical appendices that never reach the general reader. However, it is important to appreciate that underneath what appears to be a conclusive result showing, say, a preference for brand A of 55 per cent versus one for brand B of 45 per cent could in fact (and within a 65 per cent level of probability if, for instance, the sample is a small one) be an identical preference! Accuracy is not the same as reliability. As long as it is allowed for, low accuracy may be quite reliable; and useful in decision-making. The problem is in establishing what that accuracy may be. In marketing research the answer can normally be deduced from the sample size. If the sample size is over 500 the results are likely to be accurate to within 2–3 per cent (always assuming that the research has been well run). If the sample is over 1,000 it may be within 1 per cent. Below 100 though – as many of the more dubious pieces of 'quantitative' research may be – any statistical accuracy may be almost non-existent!
See also RESEARCH REPORTS, USAGE; SAMPLING STATISTICS

acetates *see* OVERLAY; PRESENTATION MEDIA

ACORN *see* BRANCH MARKETING; DATA AVAILABILITY, PRECISION MARKETING; DATA MANIPULATION, PRECISION MARKETING; DOOR-TO-DOOR; MARKETING RESEARCH, PRECISION MARKETING; RESIDENTIAL NEIGHBOURHOODS; SAMPLING

acquisitions *see* TAKEOVER BIDS

acquisition studies A specialized form of marketing research designed to obtain information to aid merger or acquisition activity. It is usually based on desk research, but the prime requirement is security – since leaks might cause movements in share prices.
See also MARKETING RESEARCH; RESEARCH DIAMOND; TAKEOVER BIDS

action plans *see* MARKETING PLAN BENEFITS; MARKETING PLAN STRUCTURE; MARKETING PLAN USE; PLANNING PROCESS

Activities, Interests, Opinions (AIO)   *see* AIO
(ACTIVITIES, INTERESTS, OPINIONS)

activity targets, territory   *see* CONTROL, OF
SALES PERSONNEL; TERRITORY SALES PLAN

actor   A person, group, or organization with an
interest in a particular issue.

ad   Advertisement.

adaptation   *see* CORPORATE OBJECTIVES; MARKET
PENETRATION

adaptation versus standardization   *see*
STANDARDIZATION VERSUS ADAPTATION

adaptive filtering   *see* TIME-SERIES ANALYSES

adaptive strategy   One of three strategic styles,
suggested by Henry Mintzberg (1973) – one suited to
large not-for-profit organizations. Strategy emerges
from a negotiated consensus.

Reference: Mintzberg, H. (1973) Strategy making in three
modes. *Californian Management Review*, 16(2).

added-value diagram   Michael Porter divides
the elements of the value chain into nine parts:

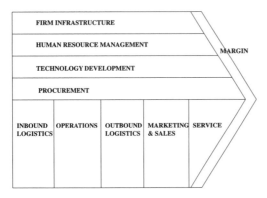

Each of these is to be investigated separately, to
optimize the value that it adds to the product or
service, but he also suggests that you look at the links
between them. Although Porter (1985) carefully
stresses that the investigation should look at added
value in terms of 'differentiation' (his word for those
activities which improve the customer's perceived
value of the product or service, by making it seem
different from its competitors) as much as in terms of

reduced costs, it is the latter aspect (that of 'cost
reduction') which tends to dominate his work – and
certainly dominates that of many of his followers.

Another type of diagram can be used to look even
more directly at the added value (which can simply
be in financial terms or – with greater difficulty – in
terms of customer value or perceived value):

See also MAKE OR BUY; PRACTICAL VALUE CHAINS;
PURCHASING

Reference: Porter, Michael (1985) *Competitive Advantage*.
New York: The Free Press.

added-value promotions   *see* NON-PRICE
PROMOTIONS

additive opportunities   *see* ANSOFF MATRIX

***ad hoc* database enquiries and reports**   If data is
suitably organized, on a computer database, it may be
possible to access it from terminals. The abstracted
data can then be processed from a variety of perspectives. This means that *ad hoc* reports or enquiries
may be easily prepared. Unfortunately, as yet, few
organizations have their data structured in such a
way that it can be used for analysis in more than
a very limited fashion. When such information is
made available via the manager's personal computer
(linked to the organization-wide network), it will
add an order of magnitude to the productivity of
the average personal computer (which is as yet
under-utilized). However, this element of designing
a Marketing Information System is the province of
the experts. In setting up such computer systems it is
all too easy to make mistakes that may corrupt the
data in the reports. More importantly – and a valid
reason for not letting managers loose on the raw
accounting systems data – corruption of the main
files may destroy the validity of the organization's
accounting systems.
See also INFORMAL (ORAL) REPORTS; WRITTEN REPORTS

administered marketing systems *see* VERTICAL MARKETING

administered pricing *see* LIST PRICES

adoption process The part of consumer buying behaviour theory that focuses on the consumer's mental processes.
See also BUYING DECISION, ADVERTISING MODELS

Advantage Matrix (Boston Consulting Group) In addition to the Boston Matrix, the Boston Consulting Group subsequently developed another, much less widely reported, matrix which approached the 'economies of scale' decision rather more directly. This is their 'Advantage Matrix'.

This takes as its 'axes' the two contrasting 'alternatives'; 'Economies of scale' (sometimes shown as 'Potential size advantage') against 'Differentiation' (sometimes shown as 'Numbers of approaches to achieving advantage'). In essence, the former category covers the approach described by Porter (1985). The result is four quadrants, examples being:

• fragmented businesses
• specialized businesses
• stalemated businesses
• volume businesses

Apart from the fact that it has not suffered as badly at the hands of later popularizers, the particular advantage of this matrix is that it highlights the assumptions that are hidden in the Boston Matrix. It may also give a better feel for the optimum strategy and the likely profits, but it does not give any feel for the cash flow, which was the main feature of the original matrix.
See also BOSTON MATRIX; GE (GENERAL ELECTRIC) MATRIX; THREE CHOICE BOX

Reference: Porter, Michael (1985) *Competitive Advantage.* New York: The Free Press.

adversarial mode *see* PLANNING PITFALLS

adversarial (win–lose) bargaining *see* SUPPLIERS

advertisement manager The person who is responsible for selling space in the media.
See also ADVERTISING MANAGER; MEDIA BUYING, ADVERTISING AGENCY

advertisement potency *see* MEDIA SELECTION

advertisement response *see* COUPON RESPONSE

advertisement size *see* AWARENESS, ADVERTISING

advertisement testing *see* ADVERTISING RESEARCH; COUPON RESPONSE

advertising Most contacts with consumers or end-users, which are individually relatively low in value, must inevitably be handled by indirect means. Of these, the main process used to 'talk' to consumers is advertising. Indeed, the 1979 research by Farris and Buzzell concluded (largely without any great surprises) that advertising/promotion ratios were higher when

– The product is standardized, rather than produced to order
– There are many end-users (e.g. almost all households)
– The typical purchase amount is small
– Sales are made through channel intermediaries rather than direct to users

These items represent almost the classical definition of where advertising should apply. More tellingly, however, Farris and Buzzell found that the ratios were also higher where

– Auxiliary services are of some importance
– The product is premium priced (and, probably, premium quality)
– The manufacturer has a high contribution margin per dollar of sales

Again, this emphasis on higher-quality/higher-margin products is not totally unexpected. Rather more unexpectedly, but perhaps reflecting the tactical use of advertising as a weapon for buying share and volume (especially at the time of new product launches), they also concluded the ratios were higher where

– The manufacturer has a relatively small share of market, and/or has surplus production capacity
– A high proportion of the manufacturer's sales come from new products

The question that has long been asked is 'Just how effective is advertising?' Lord Leverhulme (the founder of the Unilever empire) was supposed to have been the first to make the famous comment that

he was sure that half his advertising didn't work –
but the problem was that he didn't know which half!
This view is reinforced by Abraham and Lodish,
whose research apparently showed that only 46 per
cent of advertising campaigns for established brands
showed a positive impact on sales (although the ratio
was slightly higher, at 59 per cent, for new products)!
Clearly, it is important that organizations understand
what they are doing in this field.

As with any 'conversation', there may be many
topics that could be addressed, and many different
styles of delivery; as is shown by the many different
creative devices used by advertising agencies. In
general, though, there are three main groups of
activities:

- *Building awareness (informing)*. The first task of
  any advertising campaign is to make the audience
  appreciate that the product or service exists, and
  to explain exactly what it is.
- *Creating favourable attitudes (persuasion)*. The
  next stage, and the one that preoccupies most
  advertisers, is to create the favourable attitudes to
  the brand that will eventually lead the consumers
  to switch their purchasing patterns and take up
  the new brand.
- *Maintenance of loyalty (reinforcement)*. Just one of
  the tasks that is often forgotten is that of maintaining the loyalty of existing customers, who will
  almost always represent the main source of future
  sales.

See also BUDGETS; PROMOTIONAL LOZENGE; SELLING

Reference: Farris, Paul W. and Buzzell, Robert D. (1979)
Why advertising and promotional costs vary: some cross-
sectional analyses. *Journal of Marketing*, Fall.

advertising agency   *see* AWARENESS, ADVERTISING;
ADVERTISING PLAN; MESSAGE SELECTION

advertising agency creative department   *see*
CREATIVE DEPARTMENT, ADVERTISING AGENCY

advertising agency elements   There are many
variations on the general theme, of course, but the
traditional agency is structured around three main
functions:

- account handling
- creative
- media buying

The support functions behind these might be:

- production
- control
- administration

Administrative support in an agency is very much
the same as in any other service organization, with
the 'sales ledger' being particularly important – and
complex in terms of the transactions that it will
record. Agencies used to be paid exclusively by the
media, who traditionally gave them a 15 per cent
discount on the 'space' bought. This covered their
costs and, in the case of a large account, brought a
nice profit. Recently, though, agencies have also been
charging a separate fee for handling clients' business.
In the case of the smaller accounts, this has become
necessary to cover the additional costs incurred. In
the case of the large accounts, the intention may be to
cover all the costs, the larger spenders having now
learned that they can demand that the 15 per cent, or
larger, discount be passed on to them!

One specialist support function which is of particular importance is that of production. When the
client has approved the creative treatment, the ideas
need to be turned into artwork or commercials, and
then into blocks (to meet the correct specification for
the individual publication) or copies of the finished
commercials. These materials also then have to be
delivered to the media. Each medium, and often each
publication, has its own special peculiarities, and
knowledge of these is essential in producing the final
advertisements, so that they match the intentions of
their creators: for example, it is all too easy for a
sharp image to be muddied by poor handling in the
production processes. The management of these
many activities is, therefore, a specialist, and ultimately very important, activity.

With these activities and many more under way
at the same time within the agency and its
suppliers, the 'control' (sometimes called 'traffic')
function within an agency is also an essential
component.

In addition, the agency might offer specialist
support functions (closely paralleling those of the
advertiser), such as

- market research
- marketing
- public relations
- direct mail
- promotions

Apart from market research and marketing, which
are as important for the agency as for its clients, these

other functions typically operate as autonomous groups within the agency.

See also ADVERTISING; CLIENT/AGENCY RELATIONSHIP; CREATIVE DEPARTMENT, ADVERTISING AGENCY; MEDIA BUYING, ADVERTISING AGENCY

advertising agency media buying   *see* MEDIA BUYING, ADVERTISING AGENCY

advertising believability   There is, in general, one dimension of advertising which is often forgotten – that of believability:

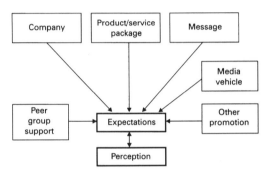

The inputs to the believability equation are many, and – as can be seen from the diagram – often lie outside of the advertising itself, so that the whole process is complex and difficult to manage. These outside factors can place quite constricting limitations on what may reasonably be said within the advertisement itself.

Most important of all is that the equation does not just cover pre-purchase belief. The most significant element is how that belief (the 'expectation') is satisfied in practice by the actual offering: a highly believable message may cause serious problems if the product or service package fails to live up to it.

As David Maister (1988) points out, 'Satisfaction equals perception minus expectation. If you expect a certain level of service and perceive the service received to be higher, you will be a satisfied customer. If you perceive this same level where you had expected a higher one, you will be disappointed and therefore a dissatisfied customer. The point is that both what is perceived and what is expected are psychological phenomena – not reality' – and it is the relative level that is important, not the absolute one.

See also ADVERTISING; CREATING THE CORRECT MESSAGES; CREATIVE DEPARTMENT, ADVERTISING AGENCY

Reference: Maister, David H. (1988) The psychology of waiting lines. In *Managing Services: Marketing, Operations*

and Human Resources. Englewood Cliffs, NJ: Prentice-Hall.

advertising budgets   Ideally, advertising should be set on the basis of profit-maximization models. Thus, in theory, the demand curve for a product or service against advertising expenditure is plotted, in much the same way as is that of the more traditional demand against price, so beloved of economists. Needless to say, however, there are very few products or services for which this ideal can be achieved. Where it is an option, where there are lengthy series of historical data and competitors are consistent in their actions, the ideal is sometimes attained by sophisticated (computerized) 'regression analyses'. Sometimes, and more pragmatically, the shape of the curve is guessed, judgementally, by the experts involved. Then 'marginal analysis' (the same principle as marginal costing) can be applied; and advertising can be increased just up to the point at which the additional income just offsets the additional costs. Unfortunately, due to the inherent complexities of promotion (and its long-term 'investment' impact), such calculations are rarely possible. Where they are possible (such as in the case of their use by Gallahers in the 1960s) they are remarkably effective; largely because they can justify significantly higher budgets than discretion would otherwise dictate.

More generally, the advertising budget is determined by even more basic means. Thus, for example, some of the more popular ways in which the advertising 'spend' is decided may be as follows:

- *Affordable.* The management may decide what they think is a 'reasonable' figure, often just on the basis of last year's spend, or whatever is left over when the expected revenue is offset against the projected costs and the required profits; implying that advertising is one of the unavoidable cost centres!
- *Percentage of sales.* This is almost the classical method, in which a fixed percentage of sales revenue is allocated. It is fast and easy to calculate, but it does not take into account any changes in conditions in the market – and implies perhaps that sales create advertising, rather than the other way round.
- *Competitive parity.* In competitive markets, the share of the advertising spend is often equated with the share of the market. There is evidence (from the UK car industry, for example) that advertising shares do broadly follow market shares (although the work shows that it is the

advertising share that positively creates the market share, rather than the other way round), but the approach still suggests that the competitors know better what they are doing!

- *Objective and task.* This approach simply asks what needs to be done (but with carefully calculated and quantified objectives), and then costs it. Unfortunately, it is rarely applied.

It would be ideal if a general model could be found that allowed the advertiser to forecast the sales outcomes of his spending, but in most markets the complexity of the other factors involved precludes this. So there is, perhaps, some excuse for the 'rules of thumb' described above; and, in practice, many marketers use all of these techniques – weighting the budget by whichever one seems most applicable to the task in hand. Keith Crosier (1987) comments that only three approaches are in common use. Aggregating the results of six surveys covering the period 1970–85, he reports the usage as follows:

Advertising/sales ratio	44 per cent
Executive judgement	21 per cent
Objective and task	18 per cent
All others	17 per cent

More subversively, perhaps, Thomas Bonoma (1986) reports, on the basis of his research, that 'the egalitarianism in resource allocation creates "global mediocrity": marketing that is excellent at nothing. Because the company spreads its resources thinly over many programs, the most vital marketing projects don't get the funding and attention they need. The creative marketing manager subverts this parody of equality by allocating resources on the basis of merit, often through budget switching of loose "shoebox" money.' The wise marketer also monitors what is happening throughout the year, as the various campaigns progress, to see if the budgets need to be reviewed; and, in any case, conducts formal reviews on a quarterly basis.

See also ADVERTISING; ADVERTISING AGENCY ELEMENTS

References: Bonoma, Thomas V. (1986) Marketing subversives. *Harvard Business Review*, November–December.

Crosier, Keith (1987) Promotion. In Michael J. Baker (ed.), *The Marketing Book*. London: Heinemann.

advertising by association   *see* MESSAGE, ADVERTISING

advertising campaign, recruitment   *see* RECRUITMENT, OF SALES PERSONNEL

advertising, direct mail   *see* DIRECT MAIL ADVERTISING

advertising expenditure   *see* MARKETING AUDIT

advertising, industrial   *see* INDUSTRIAL ADVERTISING

advertising investment   *see* LONGER–TERM COMPETITIVE SAW

advertising manager   The manager responsible for advertising within an organization, possibly as part of another role, such as marketing services manager (who is responsible for all of the services that support the main marketing management – who are possibly organized as brand or product managers) or publicity manager (an earlier title, which may also encompass public relations).
See also ADVERTISING

advertising, model   *see* DIALOGUE MODEL OF COMMUNICATION; ENCODING

advertising obsolescence   What you need to achieve with the advertising message determines not just its content but also the medium that conveys it. Most important, though, will be the message itself – how well it relates to the existing positioning and how well it achieves the planned repositioning (or maintains the existing one). This is not a simple task: see diagram p. 9.

The most obvious feature is that of the general decline that the investment in brand position experiences over time; as evidenced by the competitive saw, for instance, and as is reflected by the current 'appreciation level'. In the diagram below, this arises from two main components. One, referred to as 'depreciation', simply represents the attrition that the brand suffers as customers' attention is distracted by all the other stimuli that continuously inundate them. It also reflects the drift away from optimal positioning over time, as tastes change. The second, 'external obsolescence', reflects the attrition caused by the activities of competitors. Their promotion will reshape the market, so that your own brand's positioning again drifts away from the optimum.

The diagram below shows one further element, 'internal obsolescence'. This is a polite description for the self-inflicted wounds – often caused by overly anxious creative departments – where the brand positioning is actively moved away from the optimum

ADVERTISING INVESTMENT

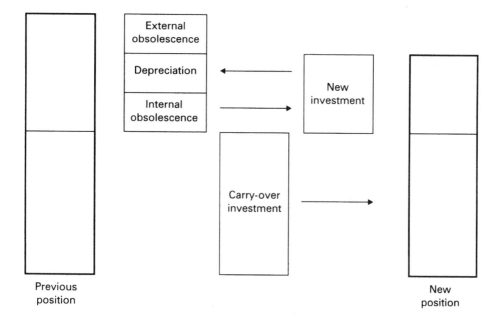

Previous position

New position

position by new advertising! It reflects the work that needs to be carried out before a combative advertising campaign can even start to work.

So far, we have looked at the message, and the campaign overall, in isolation; as if there is no influence on the customer beyond what he or she is exposed to in the media. But it is often argued that, especially in the case of a new product, the effect of promotion may occur in two stages. The promotion itself (usually advertising) persuades the more adventurous opinion leaders in the population to try the product or service. These opinion leaders then carry the message to those who are less exposed to it, and in the mass markets this often means to those who may be less exposed to the mass media.

This is not the same as the trickle-down theory, much favoured in certain parts of the social sciences, which assumes that patterns of consumption are led by the upper classes and then 'trickle down' to the lower classes. It is important to note that 'opinion leaders', rather, influence members of their own class – horizontally, in terms of class groupings.

As a result, it is clear that the impact of media advertising may be much more complex than many of its practitioners allow for. Thus, a more generalized aspect of communications within the community as a whole is 'word of mouth'. Much of advertising theory concentrates upon the 'direct'

receipt of advertising's 'indirect' communications; it assumes that the consumer receives the message directly from the media, and only from the media.

In practice, the message may well be received by word of mouth from a contact (who may have seen the advertising – or may, in turn, have received it from someone else). Equally, even if the consumer had previously seen the advertising, word-of-mouth comments may reinforce (or undermine) what this has achieved directly.

See also ADVERTISING; CREATING THE CORRECT MESSAGES; CREATIVE DEPARTMENT, ADVERTISING AGENCY

advertising plan This follows much the same approach as the overall marketing plan. First, as with all marketing activities, objectives must be set for advertising. These should include the following:

• *Who and where.* It is critical to define the target audience as exactly as possible, since this allows the 'media buyers' in the advertising agency to plan to achieve an economical coverage of this audience; to build up the media schedule (maybe across television, radio, press and magazines) to give a cumulative coverage (from all the elements, the commercials and advertisements, included) of the desired audience. It is also important to agree what percentage coverage of this desired audience will be acceptable.

- *When*. The timing factors need to be balanced with the requirement for each separate campaign to have sufficient impact; probably with upwards of five OTS ('Opportunities To See' the advertisement) for each.
- *What and how*. The message that the creative team (the copywriters and art directors, as well as television producers) from the agency will encapsulate, in interesting (and hopefully attention-getting) advertising, has to be the right message for the product and the audience; and the impact required may also determine the medium used.

The most important aspect of an advertising plan is that, as far as possible, it should be quantified, so that the subsequent performance of the advertising itself can be measured against it. The typical quantities which, if affordable, should always be measured after each campaign are:

- *Awareness*. Unless awareness levels are already very high, the advertising should have achieved a measurable increase in these.
- *Attitude*. It should also have created the planned attitude shifts.

See also ADVERTISING; ADVERTISING AGENCY ELEMENTS; MARKETING RESEARCH

advertising platform   *see* AGENCY CHOICE; MARKETING STRATEGIES

advertising processes   As seen by the client, the typical process in the creation of an advertisement will follow a number of stages.

Brief
The client's brief to the agency, and how that is translated within the agency, are the key determinants of a successful advertisement. No matter how brilliant the creative treatment may be, it will not succeed if it fails to meet the marketing objectives – unless, as is sometimes the case, the marketing objectives have been poorly thought out. From the brief, the agency creative team will, by a variety of techniques ranging from brainstorming to simply staring out of the window, slowly develop some creative ideas.

Roughs
After being developed by the creative team as 'thumbnail sketches', these ideas will be brought together as 'roughs' – relatively crude, roughly sketched, impressions (albeit usually laid out as advertisements) of the concepts being considered. Eventually, a number of these will be presented to the client, for discussion. From these alternatives one (or maybe several) will be chosen for further development. In the case of a commercial, this 'rough' will typically be in the form of a script accompanied by a 'storyboard'. Further stages of 'roughs', with both visuals and copy development (usually in consultation with the client, and certainly with the account executive), will gradually approach what is finally agreed to be the ultimate concept. The client should then formally approve these final roughs (sometimes referred to as 'finished layouts'). Indeed, the client should make certain that he or she is completely happy with what is being proposed at this stage, because changes from this point on can be very expensive, with new artwork often costing thousands of pounds/dollars (and new commercials usually being, literally, prohibitively expensive).

Artwork
The concept, by this time in the form of a 'working layout' in which all the elements are accurately positioned, will then usually be turned into finished artwork by specialist, external, suppliers. There are experts for almost everything; photographers who can produce ravishing pack shots, artists who can paint the very glossy colour work that is often demanded, television directors who can produce mini soap-operas, and so on. All are available for hire on the open market. The agency's skill is in knowing which of them will produce the best results in terms of the desired advertisement; and, to a certain extent, in knowing – even at the 'roughs' stage – just what might be achievable. The finished artwork will, once more, be presented for the client's approval. It is unusual, and expensive, for the basic materials to be altered; but it is quite normal for the details to be changed – usually in the 'body copy' (the descriptive paragraphs in the advertisement, as opposed to the headlines) or the detailed arrangement of the visual elements (which will just require 'cut and paste' treatment).

Proofs
The final stages of approval will take place when the blocks for the press advertisement, or the final cut of the commercial – with its matched soundtrack – have been produced, and the client can see exactly what has been paid for. It is very rare and inordinately expensive, but not unheard of, for changes to be made at this stage. It is worth noting that while the

'closing date' – the date by which the blocks must be provided to the publisher – may be only a few days before publication in the case of a newspaper, it may be as much as two or three months ahead in the case of magazines, which can extend the lead times for the whole creative process quite significantly.

Research

The impact of advertising should always be checked. If substantial sums are to be committed to media, this research may be run at each and any stage from the concept (the 'rough') through to the final proofs – when it is most usual to test these, to ensure that the required attitude shifts are achieved; and, perhaps more importantly, to ensure that unwanted side-effects are not observed. If it is affordable, research should always take place when the final advertisement is run in the media. If they convey nothing else, the resulting 'awareness' ratings will give a first indication of the 'creative' impact of the campaign.

See also ADVERTISING; ADVERTISING AGENCY ELEMENTS

advertising reach   *see* CUMULATIVE AUDIENCE

advertising research   This is one branch of marketing research in general, and it follows the same rules as the rest of such research. At the beginning of the development phase of a campaign, advertising concepts can be tested in advance of investment in production of the finished advertisements. This process is also frequently used to test individual pieces of advertising, press advertisements and (in particular) commercials, when they have been completed but before they are used, to ensure that they actually meet the objectives that have been set for them – for not all advertising turns out to be successful. The coverage achieved by the advertising will almost certainly be tracked directly if television commercials are used, since the BARB research monitors the performance of all television advertising (by each individual time slot). In the case of press advertising, it is sometimes considered worthwhile to conduct separate research to measure the proportion of the target audience that has actually seen the advertisement – and, more importantly, can remember seeing it! The same techniques can also be used for commercials (the UK BARB results being limited to which television sets are switched on and who is in the room at the time, which may not always give the result that the advertiser is seeking). It is also normal to monitor any advertising campaign's performance against the objectives set for it, typically in the following areas:

- *Awareness.* 'Spontaneous awareness' is measured as the proportion of those who can remember the brand without any prompting. 'Prompted awareness', which is usually much higher, measures the proportion who can recognize the brand when a prompt card (listing its name, amongst other competitive brands) is shown to the respondents. 'Recall' tests, on the other hand, explore what consumers can remember about the elements within the advertising (in the case of 'aided recall', with the benefit of being shown the advertisement).
- *Attitudes.* Most advertisements are normally designed to have an impact upon specific attitudes. This should be measurable, and should therefore be measured – to check that these objectives have been met. Ideally, in the most sophisticated approaches, the research should check that the brand has achieved the new (multidimensional) 'position' that was set as the objective.
- *Sales offtake.* The acid test of advertising, though, should be the additional sales generated. Due to the multitude of other factors usually involved, this is normally a difficult, if not impossible, measurement to make. It is an exercise that should, however, be undertaken – no matter how approximate the results – because a campaign that results in reduced sales, no matter how inaccurately measured, is unlikely to be judged a success!

'Test markets' can also be used, to compare different campaigns (with different spending levels or creative treatments, for example) in different regions, but in view of difficulties of comparison between regions and the urgency of most advertising campaigns, they are rarely utilized.

See also ADVERTISING; ADVERTISING AGENCY ELEMENTS; COPY TESTING; COUPON RESPONSE; MARKETING RESEARCH

advertising spend   *see* ADVERTISING BUDGETS

advertising threshold   The minimum point (awareness) at which a consumer is likely to make a first response to advertising.

See also ADVERTISING; ADVERTISING RESEARCH

advertising-to-sales ratio   *see* MONITORING, PROGRESS

advertising wearout   The time in a campaign when the consumer loses interest in the message.

See also ADVERTISING; ADVERTISING RESEARCH; INVENTORY CONTROL

advocacy advertising   Advertising by a company that promotes a particular view on an issue; such as the McDonalds advertising that seeks to persuade people not to drop litter.
See also ADVERTISING

affective stage   The middle stage of a three-stage marketing communications model, which moves from cognitive through affective to conative. In this affective stage, the supplier attempts to create a preference.
See also COGNITIVE STAGE; CONATIVE STAGE

affordable   *see* ADVERTISING BUDGETS; BUDGET; MANPOWER PLAN, SALES

after-sales service   Maintenance of a product (or sometimes a service) after it has been purchased.

age group   All those in a population who fall between the specified ages.

age influences, on the purchase decision   The demands of individuals and families vary over time. William D. Wells and George Gubar (1966) have identified a number of stages in an adult's life; each of which has characteristic patterns of earning and consumption:

1. Bachelor stage: young, single people not living at home.
2. Newly married couples: young, no children.
3. Full nest I: youngest child under six.
4. Full nest II: youngest child six or over.
5. Full nest III: older married couples with dependent children.
6. Empty nest I: older married couples, no children living with them.
7. Empty nest II: older married couples, retired, no children living at home.
8. Solitary survivor I: in labour force.
9. Solitary survivor II: retired.

These stages may have important implications for marketing strategies. Those in stage 1, for example, are recreation-oriented, and hence are prospective purchasers of Club 18–30 holidays. Those in stage 2 have high joint incomes, and spend them; amongst

them are the 'yuppies' who are so beloved of the suppliers of luxury goods. Stage 3 members are the typical first-time house buyers (buying at the same time all of the other durables and household goods that get dragged along with house purchase). Stages 3 and 4 are often the target of the mass consumer advertisers; they represent the archetypal housewife with a family to feed. By stage 5, the pattern of buying may have become more selective, as income increases. Stages 6 and 7 are once more able to spend on luxuries, although of a different type. Finally, stages 8 and 9 pose different support requirements.

Clearly, each marketer, in the consumer field, will target those age groups that are most relevant to his product or service. Financial service organizations selling insurance, for example, may perhaps tend to ignore stages 1 and 2, and concentrate on stage 3.

The demography of these age groups is not static, and there are peaks and troughs. Most notable in recent years was the 'baby boom' of the 1960s, which was reversed in the 1970s, when there was a comparable drop in birth rates. These changes had significant marketing impacts.

For the record, some important research work by O'Brien and Ford (1988) has found that, in the UK at least, 'life stage' (defined in broadly the same 'age group' terms as those above) was the best discriminator of all the factors normally used to classify consumers; measured in terms of the penetration (the percentage of consumers 'using') across a range of 20 typical consumer items.
See also DECISION-MAKING PROCESS, BY CUSTOMERS; REPEAT PURCHASING PROCESS

References: O'Brien, Sarah and Ford, Rosemary (1988) Can we at last say goodbye to social class? *Journal of the Market Research Society*, 30(3), July.
    Wells, William D. and Gubar, George (1966) Life cycle concepts in marketing research. *Journal of Marketing Research*, November.

agencies, data   *see* LOCAL AGENCIES, DATA; NATIONAL AGENCIES, DATA

agencies, PR   *see* PUBLIC RELATIONS AGENCIES

agencies, specialist   *see* SPECIALIST AGENCIES

agencies, telesales   *see* TELESALES AGENCIES

agency   *see* ADVERTISING AGENCY ELEMENTS; ADVERTISING PLAN; AWARENESS, ADVERTISING

agency account group *see* CLIENT/AGENCY RELATIONSHIP

agency briefing Having made the all-important advertising agency selection decision, the next most important act is to brief the agency. Sufficient time and effort must be devoted to this, inasmuch as it determines what the agency will produce – the computing adage, 'garbage in garbage out (GIGO)', applies equally to agency briefings. The briefing needs to be succinct and well thought out, concentrating on what the agency needs to know in order to undertake its assignment. This inevitably means that the brief should have been very well prepared, and fully documented, in advance. This is often an enlightening experience for the advertiser, because it highlights those issues which are – usually unexpectedly – ill defined. However, for such a briefing, all the issues must be defined with the utmost clarity. The better the briefing, and the clearer it is, the better will be the eventual advertising. Indeed, ideally, the heart of the brief should be contained on a single A4 page! Beware of those agencies that ask for 'open' briefs. It is true that this may allow them to make better use of their creative talents, which is what they want; especially since their creative 'portfolio', of pretty advertising, is what they use to attract other clients. Without clear direction, however, those creative talents may not be moving in the direction that the marketing strategy calls for; and changing the direction of such a team which is already committed to a full-blooded creative treatment (which they will undoubtedly have convinced themselves is comparable with the work of Da Vinci or Rembrandt) is well beyond the capacity of most clients!
See also ADVERTISING; ADVERTISING AGENCY ELEMENTS

agency choice Many promotional activities, especially those in the area of advertising, demand specialist skills which – as experience in both the UK and the USA indicates – few suppliers are likely to find in-house (though in France, for example, it is reported that almost half of all advertising is handled within the advertiser's own organization). This almost certainly means that you will have to employ a specialist agency to deal with these aspects of your business. The choice of such an agency represents a major, strategic, decision for any organization. That agency will be almost solely responsible for a number of key marketing activities. The success of the organization will thus come to depend upon the success of that agency; and on the relationship with it. It is a

decision that must, therefore, be very judiciously taken.

In terms of finding a suitable agency, there are directories that list advertising agencies; the most generally available, in the UK at least, being the *Advertisers' Annual*. The equivalent for direct mail organizations is the *Direct Mail Databook*. Unfortunately, although the listings in these may be very meaningful to those experts who are already working in the field, they offer relatively little help to the uninitiated. As a result, probably the wisest move is to find someone who has had first-hand experience of any agency that you might be considering. If all else fails, you should consider contacting some of their existing clients. But beware: for legal and other reasons, few clients will criticize their suppliers, even if they are so dissatisfied that they are about to move to another agency. David Ogilvy (1983) is much more pragmatic. He suggests, 'Start by leafing through some magazines. Tear out the advertisements you envy, and find out which agencies did them.' Kenneth Runyon (1984) offers (the larger account) an even more pragmatic approach: 'or discreetly disclose your intention to one or more media representatives. The grapevine in the advertising industry is a miracle of modern communications. Regardless of how the word gets out, within twenty four hours your intentions will be common knowledge in every centre in the industry.'

The next step depends upon the size of your budget. If you have one of the relatively few multi-million pound/dollar accounts, then you can expect the agencies to make the running. It is not unreasonable, in these circumstances, to expect half a dozen agencies to compete for the business (although it is normally recommended that you limit the numbers that finally make a formal presentation to three or four). Each will put considerable effort, and possibly a great deal of financial investment, into producing their idea of what your new advertising platforms should be – although the client may well be expected to fund the direct costs of such presentations (and with a number of competing agencies, this can make a substantial hole in even very large budgets). The client's role in this scenario is to examine the material, together with the personnel involved, and determine which package best meets the marketing needs of the organization, as well as which group the client's marketing staff will be happiest working with. As Kenneth Runyon again says, 'Screen the applicants. If your account is an important one, you will be deluged by agencies. If the account is less prominent, you will still be deluged, but by smaller agencies. Eliminate the agencies that do not meet the established criteria; tell them they have been eliminated and why.'

A client with a smaller budget may find the onus on him or her to persuade an agency to take an interest; and anything less than, say, $100,000 per year (of which $50,000 will go in service charges alone) may be almost impossible to place. Given that the business is minimally attractive, though, most smaller agencies will be prepared to send the potential account team along to deliver their standard presentation; and this typically will cover what they have achieved, especially in terms of creative treatments, for their existing clients. Again it might be wise, and fairer to the contenders, to limit the numbers who commit their resources to such a presentation to just three or four agencies. The match of this 'house style', along with the rapport with the account team (and, hopefully, the reports from other clients who have been contacted), will form the basis of the selection in this case.

One important element in any discussions will be, of course, exactly what charges will be incurred. Where agencies charge on a fee basis, as well as receiving their traditional media discounts, as many now do, it is well worth having spelt out exactly what these fees will be. Will there be an overall service charge? There will almost certainly be charges for the production of the blocks for press advertisements, and sometimes even for the finished artwork; and, understandably, the cost of commercials (which may run into six figures) will almost always be passed on.

David Ogilvy somewhat subversively recommends, 'If it [the agency commission] is 15 per cent, insist on paying 16 per cent. The extra one per cent won't kill you, but it will double the agency's normal profit, and you will get better service.'

This comment points the way to a more general point. The cost of the creativity is small compared with the cost of the media, and minute compared with the rewards that you hope the advertising will bring. It is, therefore, very worthwhile indeed to obtain the best 'creativity' that money can buy. The main practical advice must be to invest the time and effort necessary to make the best choice; learning, if necessary, exactly how each of the agencies on the shortlist operates – so that you can be sure that they will match your own requirements and style of management. They may, after all, largely determine your own marketing success. More rigorously, John Winkler (1983) suggests that there should be six stages to agency selection:

1. *Define the need* – a one page summary of what is needed, and what tasks are to be performed.
2. *Desk research* – checking the opinions of others, including existing clients (and references in the advertising trade press, as well as trade organizations such as 'The Incorporated Society of British Advertisers' – ISBA).
3. *Formulate a shortlist* – eliminate those handling competitive business or not offering the services wanted.
4. *Evaluation* – decide on the check-list (detailing the key questions to be asked) to be used in the evaluation.
5. *Narrowing the selection* – assessing each agency, and reducing the shortlist to two or three; before visiting each of these several times.
6. *Final selection and appointment* – agreeing the terms with the agency chosen.

See also ADVERTISING; ADVERTISING AGENCY ELEMENTS; MARKETING RESEARCH

References: *Advertisers' Annual.* London: British Media Publications.
  Durlacher, Jennifer (ed.) (1983) *Direct Mail Databook* (4th edn). Aldershot: Gower Press.
  Ogilvy, David (1983) *Ogilvy on Advertising.* London: Pan Books.
  Runyon, Kenneth (1984) *Advertising* (2nd edn). New York: Charles E. Merrill.
  Winkler, John (1983) Marketing and the function of advertising within it. In Norman A. Hart and James O'Connor (eds), *The Practice of Advertising.* London: Heinemann.

agency/client relationship   *see* CLIENT/AGENCY RELATIONSHIP

agency commission   *see* AGENCY CHOICE

agency selection   *see* AGENCY CHOICE

agent decisions   In appointing export agents or distributors, the questions involved may include the following.

What are they to do?
The 'export marketing plan' should parallel that of the 'domestic' one, and will potentially parallel the complexity of this, depending upon the exact requirements and complexity of the product or service – although the way in which this is presented to an agent may, for example, depend just as much on how sophisticated his or her organization is, and what it can handle in terms of planning information! The special questions to be asked of an agent (for

example) may include: What is the agent responsible for in terms of marketing (and finance)? What targets are to be set, again for marketing volumes (and financial results)? How is performance to be assessed against these? How long is the agreement to run for (short, medium or long term)? These are important questions, especially when many exporters, in their rush to get into a market, forget to design a system whereby they can monitor (and ultimately supervise) the performance of the agent or distributor (or even of their local office – although that is easier to rectify).

How can they be found?

The process of finding, and in particular of selecting, an agent or distributor is much like that of selecting any other agency; often, it depends upon personal relationships as much as upon legally binding agreements – the deal has to be in both parties' interests. First, it is up to the exporter to know what is wanted of an agent, and this may vary quite widely from one situation to another. Then, it is necessary to determine whether or not the agent meets the criteria. Sources of information on potential agents or distributors may include the following:

- *Other exporters.* Suppliers in related (but not competitive!) fields, who may have agents, can be contacted – and these agents will then have the advantage of being known quantities.
- *Trade publications.* Agents may advertise (or the exporter may choose to do so), or the editorial staff of such publications may know of them – and of their reputations, though typically indirectly!
- *Export departments.* Banks, as well as airlines and other service institutions, wish to develop export trade, to increase their own business; and they may accordingly have departments that will provide support for exporters, including advice on local agents – which should be reasonably reliable in the larger markets.
- *Governments.* Government departments (such as the British Overseas Trade Board in the UK) have a similar interest; and their local offices (in the embassy in the foreign country) should be able to provide advice on suitable partners – although they will need a precise brief of the requirements if they are to be most productively used.
- *Trade fairs.* Exporters often attend trade fairs, as do agents, and the latter may well have their own stands, which will give an indication of their existing clients.

How can their integrity be validated?

The two main aspects to be checked are *marketing ability* and *financial integrity*. In the first instance, the export departments of the 'service providers' (the banks, etc.), along with government departments, should be able to provide reports on the prospective agents. This should allow you to shortlist, say, three agents and/or distributors (if you are lucky enough to have as many suitable partners to choose from). The first formal step is usually to write to those on the shortlist. This letter has to perform two functions. That of eliciting information will be discussed below, but the letter (and its enclosures, of your sales literature) will also have to sell to the agent your own organization and its products or services. This selling aspect should not be forgotten: you may have to work hard to persuade a good agent to take your business rather than that of someone else. The questions you should ask will concern: their client list (and the products and/or services that they carry); their organization (branches, etc.) and staff (in particular, the number of sales personnel and their level of expertise, although you should not place too much reliance on any responses without checking them out yourself); and their published accounts (if they are a public company – but remember that foreign accounting 'conventions' may vary).

Banking and trade references

All of the banking and trade references should be taken up – preferably by telephone, where possible, as well as by letter, since people are often more forthcoming on the telephone, whereas they may hesitate to formalize doubts in a letter. In any case, many governments run export guarantee schemes, which effectively insure against foreign losses, and these should also be investigated as a final fall-back!

It is at this stage that, armed with all this information, you can at last make your first foray into the foreign market – to check out their claims in face-to-face consultations, and to set up exploratory meetings with, for example, potential customers. There is no substitute for such face-to-face meetings.

See also CHANNEL DECISIONS; MIDDLEMEN/AGENTS

agent (personal) selling Where a direct sales force can be afforded, it is usually the optimal approach. The problem is the cost involved. This has been nicely avoided by some 'direct selling' organizations that have recruited part-time agents (typically housewives) at rates of 'pay' that would probably be deemed scandalous if offered to full-time employees! This approach is most often associated with selling

from a 'catalogue'; not infrequently providing a range of goods comparable with those found in a department store (and offering, as payment to the agent, a discount). This has been most effectively handled by Avon Cosmetics; who have developed it to near perfection; with reportedly around a million 'representatives' worldwide . It is, indeed, surprising that nobody else has come close to their standard of practice, which uses the 'friendly' relationship between seller and buyer (who often know each other socially) to reinforce the sale (and also to motivate both seller and buyer). More 'formally' perhaps, Amway have used the same approach, albeit less widely (and with a more pedestrian range of 'cleaning' products), as have, for many years, *Encyclopaedia Britannica*.
See also PARTY SELLING; PRECISION MARKETING

agent's balance   Most agency agreements are not open-ended. The result is, therefore, an 'incentive balance' for the local agent, which the exporter should be aware of (although few are!):

- *Volume too low*. If the agent does not put in sufficient effort and sales are low (if, that is, the exporter can determine what sales should be!) then the exporter will become dissatisfied and switch to another agent.
- *Volume too high*. On the other hand, if sales get too high the exporter will be tempted into entering the market directly. This is an aspect that is at the forefront of many agents' minds, but is rarely considered by exporters.

See also MIDDLEMEN/AGENTS

agents or distributors   In many respects, these two different forms of legal entity operate, from the exporter's point of view, in much the same way. They will both handle all of the exporter's local operations, from import through to the customer. The legal distinctions between them (which can become important in certain litigation – so, obtain expert legal advice!) are as follows:

- *Agents* are independent intermediaries, between buyer and seller, who may act in the name of, and for, their client organization; receiving, in return,

commission on business transacted. Their contracts usually define exactly how, and where (in terms of territory), they may act for the organization.
- *Distributors* sell in their own name, and on their own behalf ('taking title' to the goods that they purchase from the exporting organization for the purpose of resale). Their territory may also be defined, but their compensation comes from the profit margins that they can create on the sales made.

See also ACCESSIBILITY, FILTERING UNSUITABLE FOREIGN MARKETS; MIDDLEMEN/AGENTS; WHOLESALERS AND DISTRIBUTORS

age profile   *see* MEDIA BUYING, ADVERTISING AGENCY

aggregate demand   A macroeconomic term that applies to the total demand for all goods and services in the economy at any one time.
See also MACRO- AND MICRO-FORECASTS; MACROECONOMICS

aggressive close   *see* CLOSING TECHNIQUES

agreement, interviewing/questioning   In many situations (and certainly in the sales situation) by far the most important closed questions (and arguably the most important questions of all) are those where you check for agreement. As the discussion progresses, it is imperative that you establish whether or not you are taking the other person with you. Or is the other party, as is all too often the case, politely acting out the role of audience to you as orator?

agreements   *see* ORDER PROCESSING; PROPOSALS

agricultural markets   *see* MARKET ENTRY TACTICS

AIDA   *see* BUYING DECISION, ADVERTISING MODELS; CALL STRUCTURE

aided recall   *see* ADVERTISING RESEARCH

AIO (Activities, Interests, Opinions)   This approach to lifestyles seeks, via long questionnaires (such as those proposed by Joseph T. Plummer in 1974), to measure respondents' positions on a number of dimensions spread across these categories (as well as the more usual demographic groupings). On the basis of their responses, they are then allocated (using sophisticated computer analysis techniques) to the AIO (Lifestyle) Groups.

See also LIFESTYLE INFLUENCES, ON THE PURCHASE DECISION; VALS (VALUE LIFESTYLES)

Reference: Plummer, Joseph T. (1974) The concept and application of life-style segmentation. *Journal of Marketing*, January.

airbrush An accurate paint spray used for producing artwork and retouching illustrations (photographs).

air date The date of first transmission of a commercial.

See also MEDIA BUYING, ADVERTISING AGENCY

airtime The amount of transmission time allocated to (and/or the actual time of) an advertisement on television or radio.

air transport *see* GLOBALIZATION

AIUAPR (Awareness, Interest, Understanding, Attitudes, Purchase, Repeat purchase) model In the more traditional forms of marketing, the search for information about customers is narrowed down to those facts which are of most direct use, by using models that map just the purchase process. This approach focuses on the aspect of the customer's life that is of particular interest to the marketer. There is a range of alternative models, but that of AIUAPR, which most directly links to the steps in the marketing/promotional process, may often be the most generally useful:

AWARENESS

↓

INTEREST

↓

UNDERSTANDING

↓

ATTITUDE

↓

PURCHASE

↓

REPEAT

- *Awareness.* Before anything else can happen, the potential customers must become aware that the product or service exists. Thus, the first task must be to gain the attention of the target audience. Predictably, all of the different models are in agreement on this first step. If the audience never hears the message they will not act on it, no matter how powerful it is.

- *Interest.* But it is not sufficient just to grab their attention. The message must interest them and persuade them that the product or service is relevant to their needs. The content of the message(s) must therefore be meaningful and clearly relevant to that target audience's needs, and this is where marketing research can come into its own.

- *Understanding.* Once an interest is established, the prospective customer must be able to appreciate how well the offering may meet his or her needs, again as revealed by the marketing research. This may be no mean achievement where the copywriter has just 50 words, or ten seconds, to convey everything there is to say about it.

- *Attitudes.* But the message must go even further; to persuade the reader to adopt a sufficiently positive attitude towards the product or service that he or she will purchase it, albeit as a trial. There is no adequate way of describing how this may be achieved. It is simply down to the magic of the copywriter's art, based on the strength of the product or service itself.

- *Purchase.* All of the above stages might take place in a few minutes, while the reader is considering the advertisement, in the comfort of his or her favourite armchair. The final buying decision, on the other hand, may take place some time later – perhaps weeks later, when the prospective buyer actually tries to find a shop that stocks the product.

- *Repeat purchase.* But in most cases this first purchase is best viewed as just a trial purchase. Only if the experience is a success for the customer will it be turned into repeat purchases. These repeats – not the single purchase, which is the focus of most models – are where the vendor's focus should be, for it is here that the profits are generated. The earlier stages are merely a very necessary prerequisite.

This is a very simple model, and as such applies quite generally. Its lessons are that you cannot obtain repeat purchasing without going through the stages of building awareness and then obtaining trial use – which has to be successful. This is a pattern that applies to all repeat-purchase products and services – to industrial goods just as much as to baked beans.

See also CALL STRUCTURE; DECISION-MAKING PROCESS, BY CUSTOMERS; ENHANCED AIUAPR MODEL; KISS ADVERTISING; MODELS; PEER PYRAMID; REPEAT PURCHASING PROCESS; THREE PILLARS OF THE PURCHASING PROCESS

alienation   *see* SYNTHESIS AND ASSIMILATION, OF MARKETING RESEARCH DATA

alliances   *see* STRATEGIC (INTERNATIONAL) ALLIANCES

alternative choice close   *see* CLOSING TECHNIQUES

alternatives evaluation, repeat purchasing
For most products or services, there are likely to be a number of competing brands in the market, ranging from internationally distributed brands, such as Coca Cola, down to those which can only be obtained in a few local shops. The process of choosing between these can be represented – possibly in an arbitrary way – as the result of a number of 'filtering' processes, where the consumer evaluates and chooses between alternatives. Some of these filtering processes are under the consumer's control and some are under the producer's control:

- *Availability.* The first consideration in the purchase process is whether the consumer has access to the product or service, and this is mainly under the control of the producers, and their distribution chains – which is why producers put so much emphasis on obtaining high levels of distribution. How far the consumer is prepared to venture in search of a difficult-to-obtain product is, of course, dependent upon the characteristics of the market. The tin of beans may have to be on the specific supermarket shelf just when needed. On the other hand, some consumers will wait several months and travel more than a hundred miles to see a star-studded musical in the West End of London, or even further to a Broadway show.
- *Awareness.* If the consumer is not aware of the brand, it will not be on the shopping list. Aware-

ness is to a large degree under the control of the supplier, reflecting the amount spent and the success of the promotional strategy.

- *Suitability.* Not all brands will be identical in the eyes of the consumer (except in pure commodity markets), at least in terms of how the various suppliers have presented them. Some will clearly be more suitable, at least from the consumer's viewpoint; and some will definitely seem unsuitable (in the UK, a *Guardian* newspaper reader is unlikely to buy *The Sun*, even if the former is unavailable). The producer may, for instance, use 'segmentation' as a means of targeting the brand on a specific segment of the market. This device matches the brand specification to the needs of that segment, so that it is seen to be more suitable – but in the process this probably makes it less suitable to buyers in other segments of the market.
- *Consumer choice.* It is perhaps only at the last stage of the purchase decision that the consumer's choice is asserted, to select from the brands that remain after the previous filtering stages. Such a choice is, however, not to be ignored. The consumer is not totally at the mercy of the advertiser. In the final analysis, the consumer will make his or her choice based on whatever good reasons he or she has in mind at that moment in time. Even if those reasons can be seen to be irrational, to the consumer at that moment in time they are absolutely rational, and so the brand best meets his or her perceived needs.

See also DECISION-MAKING PROCESS, BY CUSTOMERS; PURCHASE DECISION, MATCHING; REPEAT PURCHASING PROCESS

ambush marketing   Linking promotion to an event, such as the Olympics, without paying a fee.
See also SALES PROMOTION; SPONSORSHIP

Amdahl   *see* MARKET ENTRY TACTICS

American Tobacco   *see* MARKETING PLAN STRUCTURE

Amstrad   *see* CORPORATE PROMOTION VERSUS BRAND PROMOTION; MARKETING PLANNING, ANALYSIS

Amway   *see* AGENT (PERSONAL) SELLING

analogy   One approach to long-term forecasting, described in some detail by Joseph Martino (1972), is to look for an analogy. This may, for instance, come from history, or from another field or from another country. If the analogy matches the 'parameters' involved, it can offer a useful insight into the processes at work. It may be a simple (indeed simplistic) approach, but under the right circumstances it can be a powerful one.

See also QUALITATIVE FORECASTING METHODS; SYNECTICS®

Reference: Martino, Joseph P. (1972) *Technological Forecasting for Decisionmaking.* New York: American Elsevier.

analogy of natural (human) lives   *see* PRODUCT LIFE CYCLE (PLC)

analysis of marketing research data   The statistical data collected by survey research can be analysed in a wide variety of ways (as can that which is already available in the results emerging from desk research – and, in particular, those from performance data). Increasingly, these analyses use the availability of massive computing power to cut through the superficial results in order to try to see what lies beneath. The mathematics of these various techniques is beyond the scope of this volume; and the practical skill needed is that of finding the best expert to implement them – and knowing how much reliance to place on his or her judgement. Some examples of the techniques now used include the various forms of analysis listed below.

See also CLUSTER ANALYSIS; CONJOINT ANALYSIS; DISCRIMINANT ANALYSIS; FACTOR ANALYSIS; MARKETING PLANNING, ANALYSIS; MARKETING RESEARCH; MARKETING RESEARCH STAGES; MULTIPLE REGRESSION ANALYSIS; SURVEY RESEARCH

Analytical 4-Step   This simply outlines the stages that may help you to deploy your own judgement in any given marketing situation:

```
THE ANALYTICAL 4-STEP -

Step Zero - START - with nothing more than a blank sheet of paper
Step One - SEARCH - without any preconceptions as to the outcome
             - but based upon your own knowledge and experience
             write down what you think are the key factors involved
Step Two - SELECT - then progressively discard the least essential
             until you have reduced the number to six
Step Three- PRIORITIZE - these six factors
Step Four - SYNTHESIZE - identify what relationships and patterns exist,
             if necessary returning to Step 1, to reduce the six factors
             to no more than two 'prime directives'
             which encapsulate these.
```

This process, which may be used in a variety of management situations, but is especially suited to handling the complexities and uncertainties to be found in marketing, is deliberately kept as simple as possible. The hallmark of effective marketing practice is often simplicity.

The most powerful starting point for analysis is, thus, the simplest – a blank sheet of paper! Without any preconceptions about what to expect, without any artificial frameworks to bias your views, without any tick-lists to limit your horizons, you simply write down the key factors about the situation that faces you. Then the selection process begins, following much the same process as in the 'critic's charter': delete all those that will not be absolutely crucial to the marketing strategy or tactics that you are planning. Even so, it is likely that few factors will disappear at this stage, since most will seem essential – so you must be more ruthless and progressively discard the least important, until you have no more than six factors left (although these may be modified to encompass some aspects of the deleted items – as long as this does not dilute their impact).

Then prioritize these six factors (from one to six, in descending order of importance) and note *why* you have chosen these priorities (since, at a later stage and as conditions change, you may want to change the order of these items).

Finally, try to identify the relationships that exist between these factors. Some may be trade-offs (price against quality, say), while some may be complementary (support levels and image, say). This is also a stage at which the 'rules' which are featured in marketing texts may help. But, whatever aids you use, simply try to see what patterns emerge. At one extreme, this is a process of synthesis – trying to combine the components to produce something bigger, and better, than the individual parts. Ideally, you should reduce the six factors to no more than two 'prime directives' (the concepts or philosophies on which managers are able to focus, but which still encapsulate the key elements). At the other, it revolves around 'dilemmas', where there are several options that are apparently in conflict with each other. The management of the dilemma, so that apparently conflicting options may need to be simultaneously applied – with synergy rather than friction – is the route to success in these cases. The classic example is that of the Japanese, who simply would not accept that raising quality standards would cost more, and who went on to show that in practice it actually reduced overall costs.

Depending upon the outcome of this final stage, it may then be necessary to return to the first step, to add in extra factors that may be relevant. The whole process is then repeated. In many marketing planning activities, iteration is the key to progressive optimization of the final output.

This, then, is the 'Analytical 4–Step' approach to analysis, but to make it a little more memorable, there are actually five steps – and step zero is perhaps the most important of all! In the present context, this is referred to as 'zero-level marketing'.
See also CRITIC'S CHARTER; ZERO-LEVEL MARKETING

Reference: Mercer, D. S. (1997) *New Marketing Practice.* London: Penguin.

Analytical 4–Step, applied to core competences
The isolation of the core competences represents by far the most productive use of the Analytical 4–Step across the whole of marketing:

- *Step zero.* Start with nothing more than a blank sheet of paper. Try to isolate what makes your product or service unique, and what special 'competitive advantages' it – and your organization – has.
- *Step one.* Without any preconceptions as to the outcome, write down what you think are the key factors involved – those that best describe what you have found in step zero, but also including those from other inputs.
- *Step two.* Progressively discard the least essential until you have reduced the number to six; the least essential in this context being defined as those least important to the long-term survival of the product, service or organization.
- *Step three.* Prioritize these six, so that you end up with the absolutely key competence(s) at the top of your list.
- *Step four.* Identify what relationships and patterns exist – and if necessary return to step one – and then start to combine these competences to define, in outline, the product/service package (with no more than two prime directives or key concepts). Finally, as new ideas emerge from this process, repeat the whole 4–Step, until you have a well-formed outline.

See also ANALYTICAL 4–STEP; CORE COMPETENCES

analytical techniques   *see* MARKETING PLANNING, ANALYSIS

Andreasen model A model, based on an information-processing cycle, of consumer behaviour.
See also MODELS

animatic (storyboard)   *see* ADVERTISING PROCESSES

animation (cartoon)   *see* ADVERTISING PROCESSES

annual forecast   *see* FORECASTING DYNAMICS

annual plan   *see* MARKETING PLANS AND PROGRAMMES; PLANNING PROCESS; SHORT- VERSUS LONG–TERM FORECASTS

annual reports   *see* CORPORATE PUBLIC RELATIONS

annualized This term applies to statistics – for instance, rates of interest – that are calculated on an annual basis from those applying to shorter periods of time.

ANOVA A variance test of hypotheses, widely used by academics.

ANSI American National Standards Institute.

Ansoff Matrix Based on the work of Igor Ansoff (1957), the four basic product strategies (market penetration, product development, market extension and diversification) are often shown as the 'Ansoff Matrix', which is sometimes referred to as the 'directional matrix'. The four alternatives are simply the logical combinations of the two available 'positioning variables' (products and markets):

		Product	
		Present	New
Present	Present	Market penetration	Product development
Mission (market)	New	Market development	Diversification

In this context, the matrix illustrates, in particular, that the element of risk increases the further the strategy moves away from known quantities – the existing product and the existing market. Thus, product development (requiring, in effect, a new product) and market extension (a new market) typically involve greater risk than 'penetration'; and diversification (both new product and new market) generally carries the greatest risk of all. Polaroid, for example, lost $300 million on its ill thought out diversification of Polavision (instant home movies), but was later successful with its Polaroid Palette product for producing slides from computer displays.

In his original work, which did not use the matrix form, Igor Ansoff stressed that

> The diversification strategy stands apart from the other three. While the latter are usually followed with the same technical, financial, and merchandising resources which are used for the original product line, diversification usually requires new skills, new techniques, and new facilities. As a result it almost invariably leads to physical and organizational changes in the structure of the business which represent a distinct break with past business experience.

For this reason, amongst others, most marketing activity revolves around penetration; and the Ansoff Matrix, despite its fame, is usually of limited value – although it does always offer a useful reminder of the options that are available.

Most recently, Ansoff (1987) has shifted the emphasis to a three-dimensional matrix, which adds an extra dimension for 'geography' (region/nation):

> With the perspective of twenty years experience, a somewhat more complex description of the growth vector alternatives [his name for the matrix] becomes apparent. Instead of the two dimensions of the original matrix (product and mission), it is more realistic to describe the geographical growth vector . . .

In a similar vein to the original Ansoff Matrix, Peter Drucker (1964) has identified three kinds of opportunities:

- *Additive*. The 'additive opportunity more fully exploits already existing resources'. In terms of Ansoff, it is the new product in an existing market or the existing product in a new market. As Drucker says, 'it does not change the character of the business'.
- *Breakthrough*. This, typically, 'changes the fundamental economic characteristics and capacity of the business'. It is the extreme, of diversification, of which Ansoff in effect warns (at least in terms of the necessity of recognizing the high risks involved). This warning (which lay at the heart of Ansoff's categorization) has, though, been largely ignored by the teachers who subsequently transmitted his ideas to a generation of marketing managers.
- *Complementary*. This is a category that has not been separately explored by Ansoff (although, in practice, it could possibly lie in either of the two development quadrants, but is most likely to lie in that of diversification). As Drucker has said, 'The complementary opportunity will change the structure of the business. It offers something new which, when combined with the present business, results in a new total larger than the parts.' But he also emphasizes that it 'always carries considerable risk . . . It is therefore not a big opportunity unless it promises to multiply the wealth-producing capacity of the entire business.'

Complementary diversification is called 'convergent diversification' by Lusch and Lusch (1987), since it utilizes at least some part of the skills and knowledge of the organization. IBM's diversification into the telephone switching market, via the purchase of Rolm, would be considered to fall into this category; but IBM's subsequent failure to build successfully upon this investment – followed by its wise divestment of it – shows how risky even the apparently safest diversifications may be. Lusch and Lusch describe the riskiest diversification of all, that of going into a completely new area (the 'pure' Ansoff diversification, usually achieved by merger or acquisition of another organization), as 'conglomerate diversification'. This has been fashionable from time to time (as the periodic emergence of global conglomerates has evidenced), but these global conglomerates have rarely been as profitable as organizations focused on a single market (the quadrant which can be highlighted as the first choice – although this part of his message has rarely been passed on!).

Mergers and acquisitions of this 'conglomerate' type should not, however, be confused with those of the complementary type, which, despite the considerable amount of financial justification that often accompanies them, are frequently undertaken to build more-secure trading groups – as an 'insurance' to reduce risk by bringing more factors under the control of management.

See also CORPORATE PLAN; EXISTING PRODUCT CHANGES; MARKETING STRATEGIES; MATRICES

References: Ansoff, Igor (1957) Strategies for diversification. *Harvard Business Review*, September–October.
   Ansoff, Igor (1987) *Corporate Strategy* (revised edn). London: Penguin.
   Drucker, Peter F. (1964) *Managing for Results*. London: Heinemann.
   Lusch, Robert F. and Lusch, Virginia N. (1987) *Principles of Marketing*. Boston, MA: Kent Publishing.

answer print   The first print of the edited commercial.

anti-tobacco campaigns   *see* MARKETING OBJECTIVES

anti-trust laws   Laws passed in the USA, which may also apply to US organizations in terms of their operations outside of the USA, that make it illegal to do anything (especially in terms of unfair competition) to restrain trade.
See also EXPORTING; EXPORT MARKET ELIMINATION

apparent-agreement technique   *see* OBJECTION HANDLING

appeal   The basis of the advertising message; the reason why it will appeal to the consumer.
See also CREATING THE CORRECT MESSAGES; CREATIVE DEPARTMENT, ADVERTISING AGENCY

Apple   *see* CONVICTION MARKETING TYPES

applicants   *see* RECRUITMENT, OF SALES PERSONNEL

appointing a marketing research agency
Having decided your budget for a marketing research programme, the process of selecting the best market research agency may run along the following lines:

* short-listing – select three likely agencies
* briefing – send a detailed brief to each, and brief them personally if necessary
* proposal – receive the detailed proposal, including costs
* selection – select the proposal to best match your needs

See also MARKETING RESEARCH; SUBCONTRACTORS, MARKETING RESEARCH; SURVEY RESEARCH

appreciation (advertising impact)   *see* KISS ADVERTISING

appreciation level   *see* ADVERTISING OBSOLESCENCE

appropriation   An allocation (budget) of funds set aside for a particular purpose; especially, in the context of marketing, for advertising.
See also ADVERTISING; ADVERTISING BUDGETS

approval list   *see* PRICE, PURCHASE

approved list   *see* SUPPLIER SELECTION

approvers   *see* DECISION-MAKERS AND INFLUENCERS

arbitrage   The non-speculative transfer of resources (funds) between markets (especially as applied to financial markets) to take advantage of more favourable prices or terms and conditions that may apply.

arbitration   The settlement of a dispute by reference to an agreed third party rather than by a court of law.

archetype   A typical specimen, or – occasionally – the original model.

ARMA (Auto-Regressive Moving Average)   A computerized method of determining the best line of fit to a set of results.
See also FORECASTING TECHNIQUES; TIME-SERIES ANALYSES

armchair research   *see* RESEARCH DIAMOND

arousal method   *see* PSYCHOGALVANOMETER

art directors   *see* ADVERTISING PLAN; CREATIVE DEPARTMENT, ADVERTISING AGENCY

Arthur Andersen   *see* CONSULTANTS

artificial intelligence, precision marketing
see DATA MANIPULATION, PRECISION MARKETING

artists   *see* ADVERTISING PROCESSES; CREATIVE DEPARTMENT, ADVERTISING AGENCY

arts sponsorship   *see* POLITICAL CONTACTS; SPONSORSHIP

artwork   *see* ADVERTISING AGENCY ELEMENTS; ADVERTISING PROCESSES; CREATIVE DEPARTMENT, ADVERTISING AGENCY

asking price The price that the seller is hoping a product will make.

aspiration groups *see* PEER PRESSURE INFLUENCES, ON THE PURCHASE DECISION

assortment, retail *see* RETAIL 'PRODUCT' DECISIONS

assumptions *see* CONTINGENCY PLAN; MARKETING AUDIT; MARKETING PLAN BENEFITS; MARKETING PLAN STRUCTURE; POTSA PLANNING

assumptions, forecast *see* SENSITIVITY ANALYSIS, NEW PRODUCTS

assumptions, marketing plan It is essential to spell out the assumptions that lie behind the marketing plan. Most companies, however, do not even realize that they make such assumptions. IBM's key product marketing document is titled 'Forecast Assumptions'; and the agreement on what the assumptions are is often the key to understanding the marketing plan. You should, however, make as few assumptions as possible – and very carefully explain those you do make. As an extension to this process, when you estimate the results expected from your strategies, you should also explore a range of alternative assumptions, each meeting different needs. For example, if you have assumed the market will go up by x per cent, you might estimate sales from your chosen strategy at $£y$. You should, however, also estimate sales at a lower and higher rate of growth in the market; for example, 'At rate of growth of $(x - 2)$ per cent, sales will be $£(y - 3)$. At a growth rate of $(x + 2)$ per cent, . . .'. The most useful component of this part of the exercise may well be a 'sensitivity analysis', since this determines which factors have the most influence over the outcomes – and hence which factors should be most carefully managed.
See also PLANNING PROCESS

assumptive (joint) close *see* CLOSING TECHNIQUES

asterisk law A law that requires telemarketers not to contact those who have formally indicated that they do not wish to be approached by telephone sales personnel (marked by an asterisk on the list).
See also TELESALES

atmospherics Tailoring the designed environment, especially in retailers, to achieve the desired marketing impacts.

attainable average usage *see* USAGE GAP

attendances *see* EXHIBITIONS

Attention, Benefits, Close (ABC) *see* CALL STRUCTURE

attention-getting *see* AWARENESS, ADVERTISING

attention, in advertising models *see* BUYING DECISION, ADVERTISING MODELS

Attention, Interest, Desire, Action model *see* AIUAPR (AWARENESS, INTEREST, UNDERSTANDING, ATTITUDES, PURCHASE, REPEAT PURCHASE) MODEL

attention, of target audience *see* AWARENESS, ADVERTISING

attitude research *see* MOTIVATION RESEARCH

attitudes *see* ENHANCED AIUAPR MODEL; PEER PYRAMID; THREE PILLARS OF THE PURCHASING PROCESS

attitudes, advertising The advertising message must persuade the reader to adopt a sufficiently positive attitude towards the product or service that he or she will purchase it, albeit as a trial. There is no adequate way of describing how this may be achieved. It is simply down to the magic of the copywriter's art; based on the strength of the product or service itself.
See also ADVERTISING

Reference: Ogilvy, David (1983) *Ogilvy on Advertising.* London: Pan Books.

attitudes, customer *see* MONITORING, PROGRESS

attitude shifts *see* ADVERTISING PLAN; ADVERTISING PROCESSES

attitudes, inner market *see* INNER MARKETING CAMPAIGN

attitudes tracking *see* ADVERTISING RESEARCH; CONVICTION MARKETING FACTORS; MEDIA BUYING, ADVERTISING AGENCY; MEDIA SELECTION

attitudes tracking, behaviour   *see* COGNITIVE
DISSONANCE

attitudes tracking, location   *see* PROMOTIONAL
MIX FACTORS

attitudes tracking, profile   *see* MEDIA BUYING,
ADVERTISING AGENCY

attribute listing   A technique of idea generation
(for new products), which capitalizes on incremental
steps, is that of listing all the key attributes of the
product or service and then modifying each of them
to see if the result might be an improved version.
This approach has, in effect or by default, been the
dominant one in the personal computer market. Over
a period of less than a decade, the 'chip' has been
incrementally improved (from the original 8088 to
the 8086 and 80186, and then progressively the
80286, the 80386 and subsequently the 80486 and
beyond). In between these various stages the file storage has also been incrementally improved (from 360
kB floppy diskettes to versions storing hundreds of
megabytes, and to hard disks starting at 10 MB and
then reaching into the thousands of megabytes each).
Monitors were monochrome at first, then coloured
and then high-resolution colour. The printers too
have moved from dot matrix to laser. In each of these
individual stages just one of the overall attributes was
changed. Yet, over the decade, these many hundreds
of individual changes have added up to nothing short
of a revolution.
See also GENERATING IDEAS

auction   *see* PRICE, PURCHASE

audience   *see* INTEREST, ADVERTISING

audience research   The process of finding out
exactly who is the readership for a particular newspaper, or who watches which channel at a given time
on television, is a specialized form of market research; which – for obvious reasons – is usually conducted on behalf of the media owners, and is
published under horrendously complicated titles
(the reason for which is less obvious, unless it is to
give an air of authority!). Two examples from the
UK are as follows:

• *Press*. The Joint Industry Committee for
NAtional Readership Surveys (JICNARS): a
twice-yearly survey of 30 000 individuals, estab-

lishing the readership of more than 100 national
newspapers and magazines.
• *Television*. The Broadcasters Audience Research
Board (BARB): a weekly report on a panel of 3000
homes equipped with metered television sets.

The press figures are slightly complicated by the
fact that there are two measures. There is that of
readership, which represents the total number of
readers of a publication, no matter where they read it
– even in the doctor's waiting room – this information being obtained from market research (such as
JICNARS). Then there is also circulation, which is
the number of copies sold (mostly independently
validated by the Audit Bureau of Circulation, ABC).
Each printed copy may, of course, be read by a
number of readers; typically around three per copy
for a newspaper, but in excess of six per copy for the
magazine *Good Housekeeping*! The latter measure is
the only one which is normally available for specialist
magazines.
See also ADVERTISING; MARKETING RESEARCH; MEDIA
SELECTION

Audit Bureau of Circulation (ABC)   *see*
AUDIENCE RESEARCH

audit, marketing   *see* MARKETING AUDIT

audit (SWOT) analysis   *see* MARKETING PLAN
STRUCTURE

audit trail   This originally applied to records of
computer transactions which enabled the history of
activities (especially those relating to financial accounts) to be traced. Nowadays, it may be more generally applied to any record of events, or decisions,
that allows these to be investigated retrospectively.

autarky   An economic policy that aims to prevent
a country from becoming involved in international
trade.
See also EXPORT MARKET ELIMINATION

authority for claims   *see* REFERENCES

autocue   The prompting device, earlier called a
teleprompter, that is attached to the front of a television camera, or is placed in front of a lectern (and is
usually reflected to the speaker by a half-silvered
mirror, so that its presence is not obvious), which
rolls through the speech as the speaker delivers it.
See also PRESENTATIONS; PRESENTATION STYLE

automatic selling Selling a product by means of a vending machine.
See also DISTRIBUTION CHAIN; RETAILING

autonomous units *see* STRATEGIC BUSINESS UNIT (SBU)

Auto-Regressive Moving Average *see* ARMA

availability percentage *see* SERVICE LEVELS

avoidance of forecasting Forecasting is not the only answer to handling the uncertainties posed by the future. Robert Fildes (1987) suggests that there are a number of alternatives that can reduce risk – including that due to poor forecasting – if not the need for some kind of formal planning:

- *Insurance.* Future movements in exchange rates, for instance, may be covered by 'hedges' on the financial futures market.
- *Portfolios.* Risk can be spread across a number of areas that are unlikely to share the same 'downturns'.
- *Flexibility.* The Japanese, and to a lesser extent IBM, have developed means (particularly in manufacturing) for rapidly coping with unexpected changes.
- *Gearing.* The impact of changes can be reduced (at least in financial terms) by reducing the gearing of the operation. Highly leveraged companies may make very high profits in a boom, but be at risk in a downturn.

Of the alternatives listed above, the one that is emerging as the most important is that of flexibility. This is most evident in the development, mainly by Japanese corporations, of flexible manufacturing and dramatically reduced development lead times for high-technology goods. However, similarly accelerated timescales can be even more easily applied where technological development is less demanding and it is the promotional activities that need to be changed rapidly. This approach, while not superseding the others, simply requires that once change has been detected (probably by some form of environmental analysis) the speed of reaction will be so fast that the response may be implemented before the change reaches a significant level. More importantly, the speed of response should be faster than that of competitors, who might otherwise be able to take advantage of the change.

See also FORECASTING TECHNIQUES

Reference: Fildes, Robert (1987) Forecasting: the issues. In Spyros Makridakis and Steven C. Wheelwright (eds), *The Handbook of Forecasting* (2nd edn). Chichester: John Wiley.

Avon Cosmetics *see* AGENT (PERSONAL) SELLING

awareness *see* AIUAPR (AWARENESS, INTEREST, UNDERSTANDING, ATTITUDES, PURCHASE, REPEAT PURCHASE) MODEL; ENHANCED AIUAPR MODEL; PEER PYRAMID; REPEAT PURCHASING PROCESS; THREE PILLARS OF THE PURCHASING PROCESS

awareness, advertising The first task of advertising must be to achieve awareness, to gain the attention of the target audience. Predictably, all of the different models are in agreement on this first step. If the audience never hears the message they will not act on it, no matter how powerful it is. According to David Ogilvy (1983), one of the great gurus of advertising, 'On average, five times as many people read the headlines as read the body copy. It follows that unless your headline sells your product, you have wasted 90 per cent of your money.' Achieving awareness means, therefore, that the messages must first of all be seen and 'read'. They must grab the audience's attention. Advertising agencies have spent decades of their time honing the techniques involved; from challenging headlines in the press to mini soap-operas on television. On the other hand, you should be aware that there is often a tendency by advertising agencies to concentrate almost exclusively on this element – of awareness – so that they can produce attention-grabbing advertisements, which suitably impress the copywriter's peers in other agencies, but do not necessarily achieve the end result of 'making the sale'. David Ogilvy, again, puts the point in a forthright fashion: 'There have always been noisy lunatics on the fringes of the advertising business. Their stock-in-trade includes ethnic humor, eccentric art direction, contempt for research, and their self-proclaimed genius. They are seldom found out, because they gravitate to the kind of clients who, bamboozled by their rhetoric, do not hold them responsible for sales results.' 'Attention-getting' is in part a function of 'size'. A full-page advertisement is more likely to command attention than one that occupies a quarter page, and a two-minute commercial more than a 15 second one. In part it is, as suggested above, having some feature which breaks through the apathy of the reader or viewer; using a 'visual' or a headline which is out of the ordinary and demands attention – always remembering that it has to achieve this in an environment in which every other advertiser is attempting the same trick. This is one area, at least, in which a good advertising agency's creative department earns its keep! Indeed, this may be so successful that the advertising becomes almost 'generic'; as has that for Benson and Hedges cigarettes. Arguably, then, creativity (of the copywriters and visualizers in the advertising agency) is the key to this first stage.

See also ADVERTISING; ADVERTISING PLAN; MEDIA SELECTION; PROMOTIONAL MIX FACTORS

Reference: Ogilvy, David (1983) *Ogilvy on Advertising*. London: Pan Books.

awareness building   *see* BUILDING AWARENESS

awareness ratings   *see* ADVERTISING PROCESSES

awareness tracking   *see* ADVERTISING RESEARCH

B

baby boom   *see* AGE INFLUENCES, ON THE PURCHASE DECISION

back bench   Senior members of the editorial team on a newspaper.

back-checks   Supervisory recalls on calls that interviewers have made.
See also FIELDWORK QUALITY CONTROL

backdoor selling   Going round the organization's purchasing function to sell direct to the decision-maker.
See also SALES CALL

back-end performance, mailing   *see* RESPONSE RATES, MAILING

backloading   Scheduling a campaign so that costs are incurred later, in order that if the response should be poor, the campaign can be discontinued and money saved.
See also ADVERTISING PLAN; BUDGETS

back room operations   In service industries, one solution of productivity versus service has been to decouple the two. The 'back room' operations (such as order processing, 'component' production and inventory holding) have been hidden from the customer, and subjected to as rigorous a search for productivity improvements as elsewhere in industry. The personal contact ('front office') elements have, however, been developed in terms of the total marketing content rather than in terms of their narrower search for efficiency gains.

back-up plans   *see* CONTINGENCY PLAN

backward integration   *see* VERTICAL MARKETING

bad debts   *see* PROMOTIONAL PRICING

badging, local distributors   *see* MARKET ENTRY TACTICS

bait (loss leader)   *see* PROMOTIONAL PRICING

balancing under the influence   One aspect of the complex sale that may be neglected is the balance between all the actors involved. This is illustrated by the diagram below:

CUSTOMERS   **POLICE**

**DECISION
MAKERS**

The customers, in this context usually the users of the product or service, typically are the real decision-makers; the formal decision-maker typically has no option but to support their decision. Indeed, it is very unusual for permission to be refused – unless it is controversial, or especially important or cannot be resourced. But always waiting to pounce are the 'police'. These are the individuals (or departments) with veto power which, if brought into play, may outweigh even substantial amounts of customer protest (hence their considerable leverage on the balance shown above, which may go far beyond their apparent power in the organization). Accordingly, they may sometimes become an unexpected stumbling block; even a minor resource decision is likely to be policed by the finance department, not the formal decision-maker. You should be aware, though, that there are many other forms of police waiting to see if you overstep the mark (including, sometimes, 'secret police', whose involvement you do not even know about until they veto your pet project). These may range from the experts who check the technical specifications to those charged with guarding labour practices. The rule is, therefore, that the widest possible range of customer contacts should be made. They may turn out to be the secret police themselves (or they may be able to warn you who these are). If you recognize who they are, it is often easy to defuse potential problems in advance, but it is rarely so easy after the event.

See also SAFETY IN NUMBERS

banded free gift   *see* PROMOTION OBJECTIVES

banded offers   *see* PROMOTIONAL PRICING

banded sampling   *see* SAMPLING

bandwagon effect   *see* DELPHI TECHNIQUE; GROWTH STAGE, PRODUCT LIFE CYCLE

bankers   *see* FORECASTS OF SALES BUSINESS

bankers customer set   *see* TERRITORY SALES PLAN

banking and trade references, agents   *see* AGENTS OR DISTRIBUTORS

banks   The provision of a high-street service by any financial services organization, be they, for example, one of the UK clearing banks, a building society or an insurance company, follows much the same pattern as for any other retailer. Almost all of the factors apply, with some changed emphases:

- *'Product'*. As a bank is a 'service provider', the 'product' is largely intangible. As such, it is subject to all the problems that apply to services in general. The main remedy used is to brand the offering strongly.
- *Branding*. As with product branding, there are various approaches. The most frequently used is that of branding the company name or its logo. Occasionally, separate products (or product packages) may be branded, usually under the overall 'house brand'.
- *Place*. As a result of the 'product' intangibility, other means are used to convey the sense of quality. The premises, in particular, are often used to this end. This is most monumentally evident, perhaps, in the very prestigious bank premises constructed in the UK and elsewhere during the 1930s, when visible evidence of the bank's stability was especially important.
- *Technology*. Above all, the main weapon of competition is now that of the IT employed by the banks. In the UK, Barclays Bank goes as far as to say that it is in the 'IT Business' (rather than the money business!). Services to the customer, in this service industry, are now largely dependent upon this technology. This poses one ultimate problem for the high-street banks: Will the technology make their expensive premises (and staff) unnecessary? This has been compounded, perhaps, by the emphasis upon the technology used to deliver the services and (as a cost-cutting measure) the reduction of face-to-face service – the 'friendly branch manager' is often no longer available to talk to personal customers (or even to small business customers!). The disappearance of the branches would, however, pose even greater problems in terms of making tangible the intangible 'quality'!
- *Promotion*. This has become very important to banks, and a number of them are now at the leading edge of marketing; using research techniques and promotional methods (particularly that of precision marketing – an ideal vehicle, where they own massive customer databases) which are ahead of those in other sectors.

The worldwide changes in financial markets have ensured that many leading banks are, indeed, very active marketers – where previously few considered marketing to be relevant. Legal & General, for example, have reported that their views as to what products they were really offering (as opposed to what they should have been offering) have been turned upside down.

See also RETAILING

banner   A large expanse of (fabric) advertising material stretched across an open space.

See also POSTERS

BARB   *see* ADVERTISING RESEARCH; AUDIENCE RESEARCH

bar chart   *see* GRAPHS, AND FORECASTING

bar code   The now almost universally applied (to packaging) combination of lines and spaces, recognized by optical readers attached to computers, that uniquely identifies the product.

See also RETAIL PRODUCT OR SERVICE CATEGORIES

barons   *see* GLOBAL MARKETING

barons, managers   *see* PLANNING PITFALLS

BARS *see* BEHAVIOURALLY ANCHORED RATING SCALE (BARS)

barters *see* COUNTERTRADING; REGULATORY CONSIDERATIONS, FILTERING UNSUITABLE MARKETS

base line Material at the bottom of an advertisement or leaflet which gives the details of the organization.
See also CREATING THE CORRECT MESSAGES; CREATIVE DEPARTMENT, ADVERTISING AGENCY

Battelle Institute *see* INTERNATIONAL MARKETING RESEARCH

Bayesian decision theory The most sophisticated application of the network (or tree-structured) approach to long-term forecasting is to apply probabilities to each of the decisions; Bayes' Theorem offers a 'simple' formula (but one which is still somewhat incomprehensible to non-statisticians!) for dealing with conditional probability. The 'branches' at each level (or at each of the nodes of a network) are, in this approach, weighted by the probability of their occurring; a probability that is set by the forecaster (or by the group in the jury or Delphi techniques). The resulting probabilities of all of the possible outcomes can then be calculated. This process can be taken even further by calculating the composite 'pay-offs' (the product of the calculated value of the outcome multiplied by the probability) for each alternative. With computing power now easily available, these quantified outputs can help to give a good measure of the optimum outcomes; as long as, once more, it is recognized that all of the input factors are opinions rather than hard facts.

The wise forecaster also tries to understand how the various elements interact. The same 'pay-off' may be achieved by low risks on low-return activities or high risks on high returns – and most organizations (following 'risk-averse' strategies) would probably favour the former.
See also QUALITATIVE FORECASTING METHODS; TREE STRUCTURES, FORECASTING

Bay of Pigs *see* GROUPTHINK

bear market A market (especially a financial market) in which prices tend to fall as a result of persistent selling.

before-and-after research The most usual approach to experimental research in marketing is to test the 'subject' before he or she is exposed to the 'stimulus' (typically a product or commercial, or whatever is being tested) and again after exposure to it. The performance of the product or commercial, say, is judged by the change in the 'measurements' taken of the subject (normally in terms of attitudes).
See also EXPERIMENTAL RESEARCH

Behaviourally Anchored Rating Scale (BARS) A scale of observed behaviour (patterns) which is based on a comparison with earlier analysis of critical incidents. It is especially used in (employee) performance appraisal.
See also CRITICAL INCIDENT TECHNIQUE; MARKETING RESEARCH; SURVEY RESEARCH

behaviourgraphic classification *see* MARKETING RESEARCH, PRECISION MARKETING

behaviour patterns *see* DATA MANIPULATION, PRECISION MARKETING

belief, in product *see* CONVICTION MARKETING

belief, pre-purchase *see* ADVERTISING BELIEVABILITY

believability, advertising *see* ADVERTISING BELIEVABILITY; CONVICTION MARKETING FACTORS

bell-shaped frequency curve *see* NORMAL CURVE

below the line *see* PUSH VERSUS PULL PROMOTION

benchmark The standard against which other results are judged. 'Benchmarking' has now become a management process whereby an organization's results are compared with those of its competitors, and with the industry as a whole (and sometimes with key performers outside of the industry). It then typically sets itself the objective of matching 'best practice' – implementing the lessons to be learned from the top performers.
See also MARKETING RESEARCH

beneficial arrangement *see* INTER-ORGANIZATIONAL RELATIONS

benefit analysis The questions in a product audit can be addressed in the form of a benefit analysis. This is a more rigorous analysis of the benefits that the product(s) offers, in terms of what the customer needs and wants. In sales-oriented organizations this is often described as feature/benefit analysis; but this too frequently substitutes a mechanistic, product-oriented set of supplier-determined 'benefits' to match the chosen list of product 'features'. What is really needed is an appreciation of what the customer sees as the relevant benefits, and these may be unrelated to the product features that rule the supplier's life.

The list of customer benefits must, therefore, be very carefully compiled; preferably using market research to see it from the customer's viewpoint (and using techniques such as 'repertory grids' to ensure that these benefits are described in the customer's own terms). The list also needs to be clearly prioritized, to be ranked in order of what the customer considers most important; otherwise, the temptation is for the supplier to concentrate on the items where the organization can excel, regardless of the fact that these are relatively unimportant to the customer. On the other hand, the differential benefits that the supplier can offer, as against the competitive offerings, may be very important; if most of the other benefits, particularly the most important ones, are offered by all brands – and do not differentiate between brands in the market. Equally, the benefits offered by the organization itself should not be ignored; it is often these 'service' and support elements, rather than the product, which are the final influence on the customer's buying decision.

This review may be a salutary experience. Such awareness may be painful, but it is the necessary foundation for sound product planning.

The review may be more problematic for some organizations in the non-profit sector. As Keith Blois (1987) very perceptively states:

members of not-for-profit organizations often have a core product which is unchangeable because of their beliefs, convictions, training or the law. Often their commitment to supply the product is based upon a genuine desire to serve the public. However, without marketing, two things can and do happen which lessen the value of what they do. First, their pre-occupation with their core product (and its importance to them) can blinker them to the overall needs of their customers and ways in which the product can be augmented to increase customer satisfaction. Second, when additions and alternatives are made they sometimes, over time, become rigidly associated with the core products even though they are not

essential to the achievement of the organization's prime goal.

See also PRODUCT AUDIT

Reference: Blois, Keith (1987) Marketing for non-profit organisations. In Michael J. Baker (ed.), *The Marketing Book*. London: Heinemann.

benefits   *see* INTEREST, ADVERTISING; MESSAGE, ADVERTISING; SEGMENTATION; UNDERSTANDING, ADVERTISING

benefits versus products   *see* PRODUCTS VERSUS BENEFITS

Benetton, Luciano   *see* GLOBAL MARKETING

Benson and Hedges cigarettes   *see* AWARENESS, ADVERTISING

BERI (Business Environment Risk Index) This is a panel-based (subscription) service that offers an evaluation of country risk.
See also COUNTRY RISK

best-fit line   *see* TECHNOLOGICAL FORECASTING

best practice   *see* BENCHMARK

beta testing   *see* TEST MARKET

biased samples   *see* RANDOM SAMPLES

bias, of research reports   Most (survey) research reports contain bias, whether conscious or unconscious. It is very difficult for even the most professional researcher to remove all of his or her biases, and you would be wise to assume that the material still contains such elements of distortion. This bias may not be without value. The best research starts with a strong thesis as to what is likely to be found. While this will inevitably colour the results, it also ensures that the research is focused and provides meaningful insights – just as long as you recognize what that focus (or bias) is! The question to ask, so that you can discount its effect on the results, is what assumptions (biases) are implicit. Once you have written down what these are (or at least what you might reasonably believe that they are), you will be much better placed to understand the real implications of the figures.
See also RESEARCH REPORTS, USAGE

bidding against tenders *see* MARKET ENTRY TACTICS

bids *see* PRICE, PURCHASE

bilateral trade *see* COMPARATIVE ADVANTAGE, GLOBAL; COUNTERTRADING

billboard (poster) *see* ADVERTISING; ADVERTISING PROCESSES

billing The total value of an advertising agency's business; the total amount that it places with the media.

binding The means by which publications (books, brochures, etc.) are held together. Generally, it may be by glue, by staples, by stitching or by rings.

bipolar scale (Likert) *see* QUESTIONNAIRE DESIGN

bivariate analysis The form of quantitative analysis in which pairs of variables are analysed together. The (product–moment) correlation coefficient measures the strength of the relationship between them.

'black box' models *see* MODELS

bleed To run the advertisement up to the edge of the paper, to that part of a printed page which is guillotined off (or hidden in the trough between bound pages) so that the reader does not see it.
See also ADVERTISING; ADVERTISING AGENCY ELEMENTS

blind advertisement An anonymous advertisement; for instance, one that just gives a box number for reply.

blindness *see* GROUPTHINK; PARADIGM SHIFT, STRATEGY

blind testing Consumer preference testing, usually of new products or new versions of existing ones, in which the products are unidentified.
See also PRODUCT TEST

blink meter A machine that measures the rate of a test subject's blinking, as a test of their response to, say, an advertisement.
See also PSYCHOGALVANOMETER

blister pack Display packaging, sometimes referred to as a bubble pack, with a stiff cardboard backing sheet but a moulded transparent plastic front.
See also PACKAGING

blitz A very intensive, and short, marketing campaign – typically using advertising and/or (especially) sales.
See also SALES PROMOTION; SALES TEAM MANAGEMENT

blocks The metal 'plates' traditionally used in printing, made by specialist suppliers. The term refers especially to those that used to be provided by advertisers when letterpress printing was used by almost all newspapers. They have now been largely replaced by camera-ready artwork, which is transferred, by photographic reproduction, onto litho plates by the printer.
See also ADVERTISING AGENCY ELEMENTS; ADVERTISING PROCESSES; CREATIVE DEPARTMENT, ADVERTISING AGENCY

blocks for press advertisement *see* ADVERTISING AGENCY ELEMENTS; ADVERTISING PROCESSES

blow-up An extra large enlargement of an illustration.

body copy The text in the body of an advertisement, as opposed to the headlines.
See also ADVERTISING PROCESSES; CREATING THE CORRECT MESSAGES; CREATIVE DEPARTMENT, ADVERTISING AGENCY

body language *see* BUYING SIGNALS

Body Shop and PR *see* PUBLIC RELATIONS

Boeing airliners *see* GLOBALIZATION; GLOBAL MARKETING

boilerplate Standard copy (now typically held on word-processors or computers) and used, for instance, to insert standard paragraphs into direct mail letters.
See also DIRECT MAIL

bonuses, sales personnel *see* TERRITORY PLANS

bonus offer *see* PROMOTIONAL PRICING

Bon Viveurs *see* MARKETING RESEARCH, PRECISION MARKETING

book clubs *see* PRECISION (DIRECT) MARKETING, RETAIL

booking system A specialized variant of order processing is used by some service providers. In this case all of the future 'bookings' or spaces are held on the computer system and allocated, or sold, via terminals. The classic use of this is in the travel industry. The airlines' booking systems are now their most valuable assets (more important than the aeroplanes), since they control the whole flow of the airlines' resources.
See also DATA PROCESSING, LOGISTICS

booklet *see* BROCHURE

Boolean algebra A form of (algebraic) processing of logic statements; based, for instance, on 'false', 'true', 'and', 'or' and 'not' statements. It is used, for example, in some forms of computer analysis.

boost core competences This is the most positive statement that follows from the Pareto 80:20 rule. It merely says that, in any reallocation of resources, they should be diverted to those activities that have the most beneficial impact on the development of, or application of, the core competences.
See also CORE COMPETENCES; PARETO, 80:20, EFFECT

booth *see* SHELL SCHEME

bootleggers *see* SKUNKWORKS

Boston Consulting Group *see* ADVANTAGE MATRIX (BOSTON CONSULTING GROUP); BOSTON MATRIX; CONSULTANTS; ECONOMIES OF SCALE; EXPERIENCE CURVES; MARKETING MYOPIA

Boston Matrix As a visual tool for managing portfolios, the Boston Consulting Group, a leading management consultancy, has developed its well-known matrix:

For each product or service, the area of the circle represents the value of its sales. The Boston Matrix thus offers a very useful 'map' of the organization's product (or service) strengths and weaknesses – at least in terms of current profitability, as well as the likely cash flows.

The need that prompted this idea was, indeed, that of managing cash flow. It was reasoned that one

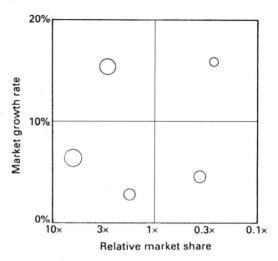

of the main indicators of cash generation was relative market share, and one that pointed to cash usage was that of market growth rate.

Relative market share
This indicates likely cash generation, because the higher the share the more cash will be generated. As a result of 'economies of scale' (a basic assumption of the Boston Matrix), it is assumed that these earnings will grow faster as the share increases. The exact measure is the brand's share relative to its largest competitor. Thus, if the brand had a share of 20 per cent, and the largest competitor had the same share, the ratio would be 1:1. If the largest competitor had a share of 60 per cent, however, the ratio would be 1:3, implying that the organization's brand was in a relatively weak position. If the largest competitor only had a share of 5 per cent, the ratio would be 4:1, implying that the brand owned was in a relatively strong position – which might be reflected in profits and cash flow. If you are using this technique in practice, it should be noted that this scale is logarithmic, not linear!

Exactly what constitutes a high relative share is, on the other hand, a matter of some debate; and its interpretation can cause problems in the use of the matrix in practice. The best evidence, as shown by my own research, is that the most stable position is (at least in FMCG markets) for the brand leader to have a share double that of the second brand, and treble that of the third. Brand leaders in this position tend to be very stable – and profitable.

The reason for choosing relative market share, rather than just profits, is that it carries more information than just cash flow. It shows where the brand is positioned against its main competitors, and indicates where it might be likely to go in the future. It can also show what type of marketing activities might be expected to be effective.

Market growth rate

Rapidly growing brands, in rapidly growing markets, are what organizations strive for, but the penalty is that they are usually net cash users – they require investment. The reason for this is often that the growth is being 'bought' by the high investment, in the reasonable expectation that a high market share will eventually turn into a sound investment in future profits. Thus, in part, the investment may be needed to cover the additional marketing costs. In the main, at least according to the theory, it is required to cover the high costs of increasing the capital employed; additional plant capacity, stocks and (customer) debtors. The theory behind the matrix assumes, therefore, that a higher growth rate is indicative of accompanying demands on investment. The cut-off point is usually chosen as 10 per cent per annum. Determining this cut-off point, the rate above which the growth is deemed to be significant (and likely to lead to extra demands on cash), is a critical requirement of the technique; and one that, again, makes the use of the Boston Matrix problematical in some product areas. What is more, the evidence, as again shown by my own research in FMCG markets at least, is that the most typical pattern is of very low growth, less than 1 per cent per annum. This is outside the range normally considered in Boston Matrix work, which may make application of this form of analysis unworkable in many markets.

Where it can be applied, however, the market growth rate says more about the brand position than just its cash flow. It is a good indicator of that market's strength, of its future potential (of its 'maturity' in terms of the 'market life cycle') and also of its attractiveness to future competitors.

The development of the theory is that, in common with other four quadrant matrices, products or services lying in each of the quadrants will behave differently, and will require different marketing strategies. As is often the case with such techniques, however, the quadrants have since been given rather exotic names (presumably to improve their memorability – though causing considerable confusion):

- star (top left)
- cash cow (bottom left)

- problem child (or 'question mark') (top right)
- dog (bottom right)

In theory, the cash flow is generated almost exclusively in the 'cash cow' quadrant; and is transferred in part to the stars but mainly to the problem children. The matrix can also be used diagrammatically to plot forecasts of future developments; and these can then indicate what the related future cash flows may be – again highlighting any pitfalls.

See also ADVANTAGE MATRIX (BOSTON CONSULTING GROUP); BUDGETS; ECONOMIES OF SCALE; GE (GENERAL ELECTRIC) MATRIX; INVESTMENT MULTIPLIER; EXPERIENCE CURVES; MARKETING MYOPIA; THREE CHOICE BOX

Boston Matrix, and the product life cycle   A basic, but hidden, assumption behind the Boston Matrix is the product life cycle. Thus, following the PLC, successful products will steadily process around the quadrants in anticlockwise fashion; starting as problem children, then moving through stars to cash cows, where hopefully they will dwell for some time, and then on to dogs and eventual extinction. Unsuccessful ones will never become cash cows, and will probably move from problem children directly to dogs, if they are allowed to live that long – for, no matter what the emotional investment in them (and it is often substantial), they must be ruthlessly culled if they are not to bleed the organization. Use of the matrix is most evident in those markets which, for special reasons, show clear product life cycles, such as the pharmaceuticals industry. Thus, Glaxo used at least part of the massive profits from its Zantac anti-ulcer drug (a cash cow whose life, protected by patents, was running out) to develop two new products: Summatriptan (a migraine treatment) and Salmeterol (an asthma treatment).

See also BOSTON MATRIX

Boston Matrix, criticisms   As originally practised by the Boston Consulting Group, the matrix was undoubtedly a useful tool, in those situations in which it could be applied graphically to illustrate cash flows. If used with this degree of sophistication, its use would still be valid. Later practitioners have, however, tended to over-simplify its messages. In particular, the later application of the names ('problem child', 'star', 'cash cow' and 'dog') has tended to overshadow all else – and is often what most students, and practitioners, remember.

This is unfortunate, since such simplistic use suffers from at least two problems:

- *Minority applicability.* The cash flow techniques are only applicable to a limited number of markets (where growth is relatively high, and a definite pattern of product life cycles can be observed, such as that of Ethical Pharmaceuticals). Use in the majority of markets may give misleading results.
- *Milking cash cows.* Perhaps the worst implication of the later developments is that the (brand leader) cash cows should be milked to fund new brands. This is not what my own research into the FMCG markets has shown to be the case. The brand leader's position is the one, above all, to be defended – not least since brands in this position will probably outlive any number of newly launched brands. Such brand leaders will, of course, generate large cash flows; but they should not be 'milked' to such an extent that their position is jeopardized. In any case, the chance of the new brands achieving similar brand leadership may be slim – certainly far less than the popular perception of the Boston Matrix would imply!

Almost alone amongst textbook authors, Igor Ansoff (1984) issues the warning, about the need to understand what is being measured, that 'before the BCG matrix is used, it is essential to make sure that the future prospects are adequately measured by volume growth and the firm's relative competitive position by its relative market share. When the conditions are right, the BCG has the advantage of simplicity . . .'.
See also BOSTON MATRIX

Reference: Ansoff, H. Igor (1984) *Implanting Strategic Management.* Englewood Cliffs, NJ: Prentice-Hall.

BOTB (British Overseas Trade Board)   *see* AGENTS OR DISTRIBUTORS; INTERNATIONAL *AD HOC* RESEARCH; INTERNATIONAL MARKETING RESEARCH

bottom-up planning   *see* PLANNING PROCESS

bounded rationality   *see* CORPORATE OBJECTIVES

Box and Jenkins   *see* TIME-SERIES ANALYSES

brainstorming   This well-known technique for generating new ideas is normally based upon a group of 6–10 individuals, preferably from dissimilar backgrounds and with some history of 'creativity', who are brought together to suggest the new (product)

ideas. The group should be briefed on the problem before the meeting starts. In the meeting itself the emphasis is on producing new ideas, no matter how silly they sound. Edward de Bono (1970) describes it thus: 'The brainstorming session provides a formal opportunity to make suggestions they would not otherwise dare make for fear of being laughed at. In a brainstorming session anything goes. No idea is too ridiculous to be put forward.' The secret is to keep ideas flowing, so that there is no time to worry about practicalities, and the ideas tabled can then proliferate – one idea often leading to a torrent of related ones. Vincent Nolan (1989) stresses the general point: 'Every idea has some merit, and it is worth taking the trouble to search out all its possible benefits and articulate them . . . This principle is the opposite of the way we behave in our society.' A relatively short session, of about half an hour, seems to be the generally recommended length; but even such a session may produce as many as a hundred ideas – not a few of which may prove potentially useful. Peter Sampson (1986) suggests going to the other extreme, with 3–4 hour long sessions, but this does seem rather long, taking into account the intensity of such sessions.
See also ADVERTISING PROCESSES; GENERATING IDEAS; VALUE ANALYSIS

References: De Bono, Edward (1970) *Lateral Thinking.* London: Ward Lock.
   Nolan, Vincent (1989) *The Innovator's Handbook.* New York: Sphere Books.
   Sampson, Peter (1986) Qualitative and motivation research. In Robert Worcester and John Downham (eds), *The Consumer Market Research Handbook.* Maidenhead: Pan Books.

brainwriting   *see* NOMINAL GROUP TECHNIQUE (NPT)

branching questions, telesales   *see* TELESALES AGENCIES

branch management   *see* RETAIL ORGANIZATION

branch marketing   One alternative, as a device for precision marketing, is that based upon branches. This is typically only open to those in the service sector (especially those in retailing), but for these fortunate few it represents a particularly powerful form of marketing, and is likely to grow considerably in use over the next few years – as the service sector learns to make use of marketing in general, and of precision marketing in particular. The 'precision' enters this marketing in a number of ways:

- *Location*. In the first instance, the actual site of the branch can be chosen to optimize its catchment area, so that the maximum number of potential customers (with the characteristics of those who patronize its other branches) can be attracted. This is normally carried out using a geographical database, such as ACORN or PIMS in the UK, to locate the clusters of potential customers; and then to optimize (by Monte Carlo or other statistical method) the number covered.
- *Range*. The exact range of products or services to be offered can be matched to the profile of the exact catchment area; and subsequently modified by practice, as shown by the actual sales.
- *Direct mail*. By targeting precisely those promotions that might be most attractive, direct mail can be used very effectively to attract new prospects, and to rejuvenate lapsed customers. A less direct (since they would not be personalized) but very cost-effective approach would be neighbourhood door-to-door drops.
- *Personal contact*. Once in the branch, and in a face-to-face sale (albeit only with a sales assistant at a cashpoint or check-out), the feedback from the EPOS system could allow personalization; even if only to allow the assistant to say 'Thank you, Mrs Smith', but possibly also to say 'We have just received a shipment of the perfume you particularly like, and which was out of stock the last time you called'.
- *Experimentation*. As with direct mail, branches have the luxury of being able to try out new ideas, and measure how effective they are. These ideas may encompass new lines, or new promotional devices (or just location in the store) or reflect different pricing policies. This is the most powerful form of research; testing exactly the factors that the question demands, rather than extrapolating from indirect indicators.

See also FACILITY DECISIONS, LOGISTICS MANAGEMENT; PRECISION MARKETING

branch/subsidiary office *see* LOCAL SALES ORGANIZATION

brand attrition/depreciation *see* ADVERTISING OBSOLESCENCE

brand extension This occurs when an existing strong brand name is used as a vehicle for new or modified products; for example, after many years of running just one brand, Coca Cola launched 'Diet Coke' and 'Cherry Coke'. Procter & Gamble, in particular, has made regular use of this device, extending its strongest brand names (such as Fairy Soap) into new markets (the very successful Fairy Liquid and, more recently, Fairy Automatic).

Leo Burnett (1988) report this as a trend, illustrating it (under the title of *Mega-Brand, Micro-Varieties*) with the following figures:

Summary of 25 brands handled by Leo Burnett:
Total number of micro-varieties = 1682
(Average number per brand = 67)
TREND OVER TIME (subsample of five brands)

	1983	1988	% change
Old Cutlass	11	19	+73%
Cocktails for Two	32	42	+31%
Maytag	72	93	+29%
Glad Food Service	13	28	+115%
Mrs. Smith's Pies	41	45	+10%
TOTAL	169	227	+34%

They note, for instance, that the 54 varieties of Glad Food Service Products included:

30 count Large Garbage Bags
15 count Large Trash Bags
30 count Deodorant Bags
Glad Microwave Wrap
40 count gallon Family Pack

According to David Aaker (1990), 'Each year from 1977 to 1984, 120 to 175 totally new brands were introduced into America's supermarkets. In each of these years, approximately 40 percent of the new brands were actually brand extensions.'
See also BRANDING; BRANDING POLICIES; MULTIBRANDS; OWN BRANDS AND GENERICS

References: Aaker, David (1990) Brand extensions: the good, the bad and the ugly. *Sloan Management Review*, Summer.
  Leo Burnett Inc. (1988) *Mega-Brand, Micro-Varieties*. New York: Leo Burnett, Research Department.

brand identity *see* CONVICTION MARKETING FACTORS

branding *see* BRAND EXTENSION; BRANDING POLICIES; BRAND MONOPOLY; MULTIBRANDS; OWN BRANDS AND GENERICS; PRODUCT (OR SERVICE) POSITIONING; SEGMENTATION

branding and differentiation *see* DIFFERENTIATION AND BRANDING

branding policies   There are a number of possible branding policies:

- *Company name*. Often, especially in the industrial sector, it is just the company's name that is promoted (leading to one of the most powerful statements of 'branding' – the well-known saying 'No one ever got fired for buying IBM').
- *Family branding*. In this case, a very strong brand name (or company name) is made the vehicle for a range of products (for example, 'St Michael', Mercedes or Black & Decker) or even a range of subsidiary brands (such as Cadbury's Dairy Milk, Cadbury's Flake and Cadbury's Wispa; or Mr Kipling cakes and the Kellogg brands).
- *Individual branding*. Each brand has a separate name (such as Seven-Up or McDonalds), which may even compete against other brands from the same company (for example, Persil, Omo and Surf are all owned by Lever Brothers).

A specialized form of branding is 'own label', where a retail chain (such as Sainsbury's in the supermarket sector, or Marks & Spencer in the clothing sector) applies its own 'brand name'.
See also BRAND EXTENSION; BRANDING; BRAND MONOPOLY; MULTIBRANDS; OWN BRANDS AND GENERICS

branding, services   Suppliers of services have considerable difficulty in differentiating their 'product' from all others. Even if they do manage to find a unique feature, it is likely to be copied within a matter of weeks (such 'product' lead times in the service sector are very short – often just the length of time it takes to produce new promotional material). As a result, the bigger service suppliers tend to rely on 'branding'; typically using the company name: Barclays Bank, Prudential (now property services as well as assurance), Thomson Holidays, Amex, Compuserve, etc.

brand investment   *see* ADVERTISING OBSOLESCENCE; LONGER–TERM COMPETITIVE SAW

brand leader spend   *see* BUDGETS; INVESTMENT MULTIPLIER

brand management   *see* MICROECONOMICS; PRODUCT/BRAND MANAGEMENT

brand monopoly   In economic terms the 'brand' is, in effect, a device to create a 'monopoly' – or at least some form of 'imperfect competition' – so that the brand owner can obtain some of the benefits that accrue to a monopoly, particularly those related to decreased price competition. In this context, most 'branding' is established by promotional means. There is, however, also a legal dimension, for it is essential that the brand names and trademarks are protected by all means available. But the monopoly position may also be extended, or even created, by patents and intellectual property (or copyright, as it used to be called in a narrower context). In all of these contexts, 'own-label' brands (the brands of a retailer, for example) can be just as powerful; and indeed some of these (such as those of Marks & Spencer or Sainsbury's) are perceived by consumers as the 'brand leaders' in certain market segments (as Marks & Spencer is the leading UK brand for women's underwear). However, the 'brand' – whatever its derivation – is a very important investment for any organization. RHM (Rank Hovis McDougall), for example, value their international brands at anything up to 20 times their annual earnings!
See also BRAND EXTENSION; BRANDING; BRANDING POLICIES; BRAND 'MONOPOLY' PRICING; COMPETITIVE PRICING; MULTIBRANDS; OWN BRANDS AND GENERICS

brand 'monopoly' pricing   Most of the economic thinking that lies behind the theory of price elasticity of demand revolves around 'perfect competition' (which in the economic context usually means exclusively price-based competition). On the other hand, it can be argued that one of the main objectives of the marketer, as exemplified by the brand manager, is to create a monopoly for the brands that he or she manages. The ideal outcome would be that the brand was so differentiated from its competitors that the customer would not choose these other brands even if the first choice brand was not available. The marketer wants to see the consumer enter the supermarket determined to buy Heinz Baked Beans, not just a suitable variety of ordinary baked beans. In a similar way, many Coca Cola purchasers have been persuaded that they are not in the market for an ordinary soft drink.

Although unbranded goods with patent protection may enjoy similar benefits, it is the development of a strong brand (with a unique identity and image) that usually allows the best vehicle for differentiating the product or service from its competitors; so that it becomes a virtual monopoly in its own unique 'market segment'.

A variation on this process, in the industrial purchasing sector, is described by Webster and Wind (1972): 'The constrained choice model concentrates on the fact that most supplier selection decisions involve choosing from a limited set of potential vendors. Potential suppliers in this set are "in" while all other potential suppliers are "out". Constraints on the set of possible suppliers can be imposed by any member of the buying organisation which has the necessary power ... The source loyalty model assumes that inertia is the major determinant of buying behaviour and stresses habitual behaviour.'

See also PRICE FACTORS

Reference: Webster, Frederick E., Jr and Wind, Yoram (1972) *Organizational Buying Behaviour*. Englewood Cliffs, NJ: Prentice-Hall.

brand (or market) share   This is the share of overall market sales taken by each brand. In the consumer field, it is usually measured by audit research on panels of retail outlets, such as that undertaken by A. C. Nielsen, and hence represents consumer purchases and not necessarily usage – although the distinction is usually not an important one. In the industrial field it is usually a 'guesstimate' based on research on a limited number of customers; although in some fields government departments audit total output. However, there are some complications. The share can be quoted in terms of volume (for example, the brand has a 10 per cent share of the total number of units sold) or in terms of value (for example, at the same time the brand took 15 per cent of the total money being paid out for such products, since it was a higher-priced brand). This difference can sometimes be dramatic. At one time, Amstrad claimed to have achieved the same market share as IBM, which was then the market leader in the PC market; but this was in *volume* terms: in terms of *value*, Amstrad had less than one-third of IBM's share, and was in fourth or fifth place (behind Compaq, Apricot and Olivetti). The measure of share is important because it delineates what extra business a producer can reasonably look for; and where he might get it. On the other hand, the evidence in many markets is that most business comes from repeat purchasing by existing customers. This is a fact which too many producers, in the grip of their understandable enthusiasm to recruit new users, ignore at their peril. It was a lesson learned the hard way by Coca Cola when it decided to change its basic formulation to attract new users – only to discover that it had alienated its existing customers!

See also CUSTOMERS; MARKETS; PENETRATION; USERS

brand perceptions   *see* SALES PROMOTION ADVANTAGES AND DISADVANTAGES

brand performance   *see* LONGER-TERM COMPETITIVE SAW

brand persona   *see* CONVICTION MARKETING FACTORS

brand position   *see* ADVERTISING OBSOLESCENCE; PURCHASE DECISION, MATCHING

brand proliferation   *see* MULTIBRANDS

brand promotion   *see* CORPORATE PROMOTION VERSUS BRAND PROMOTION

brand promotion versus corporate promotion   *see* CORPORATE PROMOTION VERSUS BRAND PROMOTION

brand reference book   *see* MARKETING AUDIT

brand senility strategies   *see* DECLINE STRATEGIES

brands, national/transnational   *see* GLOBAL MARKETING

brand-switching model ('Markov')   One particular form of forecasting is based upon projections of brand switching. Thus, in the 'Markov' model of the process, the current probabilities of brand switching (measured from consumer intentions) by existing users of each of the brands are known and, as these 'switches' actually come about over time, this will lead to a new levels of brand share (based upon a cumulative historical build-up) – which can, accordingly, be calculated. As can be seen from the matrix below (an example taken from Gordon Bolt), 50 per cent of the users of brand A will remain with it, and it will gain (looking down the related vertical column) 40 per cent from B and 30 per cent from C:

If, as shown, brand A had an existing share of 20 per cent (with B holding 30 per cent and C 50 per cent) this will result in a growth in share to 37 per cent.

Although apparently simple, this is actually an extremely sophisticated forecasting process. Even though it is much discussed in academic circles, where it is also greatly appreciated due to its mathematical elegance, it is of dubious practical value, since brand-switching intentions are rarely known with the degree of accuracy demanded (and, indeed, such brand switches can usually only be barely meas-

Probability that consumers will switch
brands

	A	B	C
	A	*B*	*C*
A	stay	change	change
	0.5	0.3	0.2
B	change	stay	change
	0.4	0.4	0.2
C	change	change	stay
	0.3	0.3	0.4

The application of probabilities to the existing brand shares to determine
the post-switch market shares

				New brand shares anticipated
A	0.5 of 20% = 10%	0.4 of 30% = + 12%	0.3 of 50% = + 15%	= 37%
B	0.4 of 30% = 12%	0.3 of 20% = + 6%	0.3 of 50% = + 15%	= 33%
C	0.4 of 50% = 20%	0.2 of 20% = + 4%	0.2 of 30% = + 6%	= 30%

ured – and then very expensively so – to this accuracy after the event!).

See also DERIVED FORECASTS; LONG-TERM FORECASTS;
MACRO- AND MICRO-FORECASTS; MEDIUM-TERM FORE-
CASTS; SHORT-TERM FORECASTS; SHORT- VERSUS LONG-
TERM FORECASTS

Reference: Bolt, G. J. (1981) *Marketing and Sales Forecasting: a Total Approach.* Kogan Page.

brand transference   *see* BRAND EXTENSION

brand value   There have been a number of attempts to 'capitalize' the consumer franchise into the
balance sheet, as the 'brand value' – literally what the
(brand) name was worth to the organization. In
the late 1980s, there was a fashion for hostile takeovers of organizations that owned major brands, particularly where the book value, and the market
capitalization, did not reflect the real trading value of
the brands. This reached a peak with the Nestlé bid
of £2.5 billion for Rowntrees – a bid of six times

Rowntrees' reported asset value – and the leveraged
buy-out of RJR Nabisco for $25 billion. As a result,
some organizations with especially strong brands
wrote a corresponding (goodwill) valuation into their
balance sheets, to make such takeovers that much
more difficult. Rank Hovis McDougall, for instance,
put a balance-sheet value on their brands of £678
million, and Grand Metropolitan one of £588
million. This practice has since been discouraged by
the various accounting bodies, and indeed the
Accounting Standards Committee in the UK has
called a halt to it. It does, though, have the very
positive advantage of concentrating the minds of
senior management, and making them realize just
how important these assets are.

See also CUSTOMER FRANCHISE; USAGE AND LOYALTY

break   The time when transmission of television
(or radio) programmes is broken off to allow the
commercials to be transmitted; also known as a commercial break or station break.

break-even analysis, new products   The essential requirement for a new 'product' is that it should, at the very least, 'break even'. In other words, the net operating profit, after deduction of both variable and fixed costs, over the projected life of the product or service should at least recover the initial investment. This is demonstrated, and practically calculated, by the use of a simple diagram:

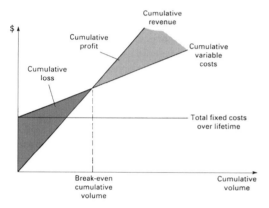

The revenue will typically be drawn as a straight line starting at the origin, and this will probably reflect the reality where the price is unchanged. The variable costs will also, in the simplest form, be shown as a straight line. This is something of a simplification; for, in practice, there may be steps in the line as new plant capacity has to be added. More importantly, this cost line will start at a height above the origin that allows for the fixed costs which will occur even if no product is sold – including all of the development and launch investments. Assuming that the product does break even, this will be shown where the two lines cross (and the cumulative revenue covers all of the cumulative costs), at the 'break-even point'. The (shaded) area between the lines above this point represents the overall profit. The diagram is a very simple way of demonstrating the volumes that are needed to recover all of the costs and initial investments.
See also PRODUCT DEVELOPMENT PROCESS; SENSITIVITY ANALYSIS, NEW PRODUCTS STRATEGIC SCREENING, NEW PAODUCTS

break-up value   The asset value of a company on the assumption that it will not continue trading.

breakthrough opportunities   *see* ANSOFF MATRIX

breakthrough, scientific   *see* CREATIVE IMITATION; LEAPFROG

Brecht, Bertolt   *see* SYNTHESIS AND ASSIMILATION, OF MARKETING RESEARCH DATA

bribery   *see* CHANNEL MOTIVATION; SOCIAL AND BUSINESS STRUCTURES, FILTERING UNSUITABLE MARKETS

brief, advertising   *see* ADVERTISING PROCESSES

brief, consultants   *see* CONSULTANTS

briefing a marketing research agency   The content of the marketing research brief will vary, depending upon your own organization's expertise in the field. An expert internal research department will be able to bring considerable expertise to bear; defining the methodology in detail, and leaving the agency just to provide the related costs. At the other extreme, many clients will simply know the type of information that they want and, more importantly, why they want it. In this latter case, it is important that – despite their lack of expertise – the client has a clear idea to be tested of what information is wanted. The brief should include outline details of the product or service (so that the agency can 'flesh out' the ideas behind the research – and gain some idea of what may, inevitably, be missing from the brief!). It should also include a clear description of the target audience, since much of the cost of such research comes from finding the respondents. The brief should be concise – preferably running to three or four pages only – but it must be comprehensive (at least in terms of what is specifically wanted). If the overall questions are not indicated in the brief, you will not receive the answers to them! Preferably, though, the written brief should be followed by a personal visit to each of the agencies. The team in the agency can then ask the questions that are necessary for them to establish your exact needs, in their terms. At the same time, you can judge their capabilities, and how well they will be able to work alongside your own organization.
See also APPOINTING A MARKETING RESEARCH AGENCY

briefing, agency   *see* AGENCY BRIEFING

British Overseas Trade Board   *see* BOTB (BRITISH OVERSEAS TRADE BOARD)

Broadcasters Audience Research Board   *see*
ADVERTISING RESEARCH; AUDIENCE RESEARCH

broadcasting   *see* NARROWCASTING

broadsheet   The large newspaper format (size),
typically used by the quality press, as opposed to the
tabloid (small) format used by the popular press.
See also MEDIA IMPACT; MEDIA SELECTION; MEDIA
TYPES

broadside   (US) A publicity leaflet.
See also ADVERTISING PROCESSES; PROMOTIONAL MIX

brochure   A publicity booklet, as opposed to a
leaflet.
See also ADVERTISING PROCESSES; INSERTS, DIRECT
MAIL; PROMOTIONAL MIX

brown goods   Electrical/electronic (consumer
durables) goods (housed in 'brown' cabinets), as
opposed to white goods which are used in the kitchen.
See also PRODUCT OR SERVICE CATEGORIES

browsing   *see* SCANNING, AND MIS

bubble pack   *see* BLISTER PACK

bucket-shop   A dealer or agent that may be of
dubious standing and resources.
See also DISTRIBUTION CHAIN

budgetary periods   *see* DERIVED FORECASTS

budgetary planning process   *see* PLANNING
PROCESS

budget available, promotional mix   *see*
PROMOTIONAL MIX FACTORS

budgeted costs   *see* MONITORING, PROGRESS

budget maximization   *see* NOT-FOR-PROFIT
ORGANIZATIONS, OBJECTIVES

budgets   The classic quantification of a marketing
plan appears in the form of budgets. Because these
are so rigorously quantified, they are particularly
important. They should, thus, represent an un-
equivocal projection of actions and expected results.
What is more, they should be capable of being monitored accurately; and, indeed, performance against
budget is the main (regular) management review

process. The purpose of a marketing budget is thus
to pull together all of the revenues and costs involved
in marketing into one comprehensive document. It is
a managerial tool that balances what is needed to be
spent against what can be afforded and helps to make
choices about priorities. It is then used in monitoring
performance in practice. The marketing budget is
usually the most powerful tool by which you think
through the relationship between desired results and
available means. Its starting point should be the marketing strategies and plans, which have already been
formulated in the marketing plan itself; although, in
practice, the two will run in parallel and will interact.
At the very least, the rigorous, highly quantified,
budgets may cause a rethink of some of the more
optimistic elements of the plans.

Approaches to budgeting
Many budgets are based on history. They are the
equivalent of 'time-series' forecasting. It is assumed
that next year's budgets should follow some trend
that is discernible over recent history. Other
alternatives are based on a simple 'percentage of
sales' or on 'what the competitors are doing'. There
are, however, many other alternatives, as set out
below.

Affordable
This may be the most common approach to budgeting. Someone, typically the managing director acting
on behalf of the board, decides what is a 'reasonable'
promotional budget, what can be afforded. This
figure is most often based on historical spending.
The amount for this year will be based on what was
spent last year, suitably modified (or not) to allow for
the current conditions. If the organization's profit
forecast is pessimistic, the budget may be cut. If it is
good, then the budget may be maintained in line with
inflation – or, if the marketing manager is very persuasive, it may actually be increased in real terms!
This approach assumes that promotion is a cost, and
it is sometimes seen as an avoidable cost (for example, when even IBM, of all companies, ran into difficulties with the profit performance of its personal
computer division, the first thing that it cut out was
almost all advertising!).

Percentage of revenue
This is a variation of the 'affordable' approach, but at
least it forges a link with sales volume, in that the
budget will be set at a certain percentage of revenue,
and thus follows trends in sales. It does, though,
imply that promotion is a result of sales, rather than

the other way round. Both of these first two methods are seen by many managements to be 'realistic', in that they reflect the reality of the business strategies as those managements see it. On the other hand, neither makes any allowance for change. They do not allow for the development to meet emerging market opportunities and, at the other end of the scale, they continue to pour money into a dying product or service (the 'dog').

Competitive parity

In this case, the organization relates its budgets to what the competitors are doing. For example, it matches their budgets, or beats them or spends a proportion of what the brand leader is spending. At its most sophisticated, the relative share of spending may be matched to the relative brand share. It is argued, by its adherents, that this approach can avoid promotional wars – and that it benefits from the 'wisdom' of the overall market. On the other hand, it assumes that the competitors know best, in which case the service or product can expect to be nothing more than a follower.

Zero-based budgeting

In essence, this approach takes the objectives, as set out in the marketing plan, together with the resulting planned activities, and then costs them out. At the end of the day there has to be some check on the total size of the budget, since it is fair to say that most if not all marketing managers ask for more than is really needed – on the basis that overkill makes certain of achieving the goal and, more politically, because they have long since learnt that as a matter of principle all budgets are cut back by top management! The essence is what is to be achieved. Looking at the advertising budget, for example, the following steps may need to be taken:

- *Determine advertising objectives*. The organization decides what it needs to achieve: What is the target audience? What (percentage) coverage is acceptable? What is the average number of advertising impressions (or Opportunities To See, OTS) that is required? What pattern (how many and when) of advertisements is needed to achieve these targets?
- *Calculate the cost*. The media schedule is then costed (by hand or, increasingly, using a computer model). This (together with the related production costs, for the creation of the press advertisements or the making of the television commercials) gives the advertising budget.

The other elements of the total promotional budget (sales team costs, sales promotion offers, public relations, staff costs, etc.) are all aggregated to give the final budget total.

Life cycle budgeting

This is based on the principle that the budget should take into account, perhaps as its major element, the stage of the appropriate life cycle at which the product or service is currently positioned. What portion of the expenditure needed over the whole life cycle should be allocated to this current budgeting period? This will be particularly relevant to portfolio management, where product life cycles have to be viewed in relation to the investment in new products and the 'milking' of those that have reached maturity or decline. On the basis of the 'Boston Matrix', this will also allow for a balance between the development of new products and the projected cash-generation life of cash cows.

See also CORPORATE OBJECTIVES; FORECASTS INTO BUDGETS; MARKETING PLANS AND PROGRAMMES; MARKETING STRATEGIES; PLANNING PROCESS; PR PLANS AND BUDGETS

Reference: McDonald, Malcolm H. B. (1993) *Marketing Plans*. London: Heinemann.

budgets, advertising   *see* ADVERTISING BUDGETS

buffer stock   *see* FACILITY DECISIONS, LOGISTICS MANAGEMENT; INVENTORY CONTROL; PRODUCTION DECISIONS, LOGISTICS MANAGEMENT

building awareness   A major requirement for any brand, especially newly launched ones, is to let consumers, the end-users, know that the brand exists. Even the Bible made the sound marketing point that 'hiding your light under a bushel' does nothing for brand awareness. These days, the classical vehicle for this, at least in theory and in the consumer markets, is a heavy television campaign, using simple short commercials – since the main aim is to build awareness that the brand exists. In industrial markets, where it may take months for the sales force to complete coverage of all potential prospects, the awareness may be built more rapidly by mailing campaigns or by telesales. These are often backed up by 'seminars', at which the message can be delivered to larger numbers of prospects at the same time.

See also AIUAPR (AWARENESS, INTEREST, UNDERSTANDING, ATTITUDES, PURCHASE, REPEAT PURCHASE) MODEL; PENETRATION; PRODUCT LIFE CYCLE (PLC)

building distribution In a well-managed campaign, this process will probably start before the brand is formally launched. Considerable emphasis, usually based initially on sales management activity but followed up by involvement of the whole sales force, will be placed on achieving the widest distribution through the major outlets, if distribution channels are used, or pilot installations (or 'reference sites') with the major buyers in the industrial markets. In many sectors, therefore, the sales force spends a disproportionate amount of its time on new brands. This is also the time when vast sums may be spent on trade shows. IBM, for example, can spend millions of dollars worldwide just on the half-day shows that are set up to introduce its dealers to new ranges of personal computers.

See also PENETRATION; PRODUCT LIFE CYCLE (PLC)

building society *see* BANKS

bulk transport *see* FACILITY DECISIONS, LOGISTICS MANAGEMENT

bulletin A short newsletter, produced regularly.

bulletin board A general facility on a computer network that allows participants to leave messages to be seen (as on a notice board) by everyone using the service.

See also COMPUTER-MEDIATED COMMUNICATIONS (CMC); DIRECT MAIL

bundling Giving away one product with another.
See also SALES PROMOTION

Burger King *see* CONVICTION MARKETING FACTORS; SALES PROMOTION ADVANTAGES AND DISADVANTAGES

bursts of advertising *see* MEDIA SELECTION

business as usual, sales manpower budget *see* MANPOWER PLAN, SALES

business cycles In the 1950s and 1960s, there was a fairly regular pattern to business levels, with recession leading to a slump, followed by recovery and then boom – and then recession again. The length of the cycle was believed to be, as demonstrated by the observed results, between four and five years (linked, some claimed, to the political, electoral cycle): confusingly for marketers, this was much the same length as was expected for many product life cycles!

In the 1970s and 1980s, the cycle was less regular, and less predictable; in line with the growing uncertainty. Even so, the varying levels of business – higher in recovery and boom, and lower in recession or slump – pose real problems for marketers. A manager should ideally forecast the start of a recession so that costs can be reduced (and inventories reduced). Similarly, the onset of recovery needs to be forecast so that inventories may be built up – and resources put in place to exploit the growth in sales volumes. There are many bodies, and individuals, ready to offer you forecasts of economic activity, with varying degrees of success – and, unfortunately, a rather poor track record on average!

See also DERIVED FORECASTS; KONDRATIEFF WAVE

business definition *see* MISSION

business environment *see* INTER-ORGANIZATIONAL RELATIONSHIPS; SWOT ANALYSIS

Business Environment Risk Index *see* BERI (BUSINESS ENVIRONMENT RISK INDEX)

business forecasts *see* FORECASTS OF SALES BUSINESS

business infrastructure *see* ACCESSIBILITY, FILTERING UNSUITABLE FOREIGN MARKETS

business interest (shared) *see* PARTNERSHIP TRIANGLE

Business International *see* INTERNATIONAL MARKETING RESEARCH; MARKET ENTRY DECISION

business, international *see* GLOBALIZATION

business management (economics) *see* MICROECONOMICS; TRANSACTION COST ECONOMICS

business perspectives *see* MARKETING MYOPIA

business policy *see* MARKETING MYOPIA

business process re-engineering At the beginning of the 1990s, this was the most popular management fashion, whereby – in theory at least – the overall (system of the) organization was investigated (and challenged) to ensure that the needs of the customer were being met. In that respect, the process paralleled that of a rigorous marketing audit. In practice, it was often used as an excuse for 'downsizing' –

making workers redundant – and 'delayering' – making managers redundant.

business schools, consultants *see* CONSULTANTS

business structure *see* EXPORT MARKET ELIMINATION

business-to-business marketing *see* INDUSTRIAL ADVERTISING; INDUSTRIAL MARKETING RESEARCH; INDUSTRIAL MARKETS AND THE MARKETING MIX; INDUSTRIAL PRODUCT CATEGORIES

business unit, strategic (SBU) *see* STRATEGIC BUSINESS UNIT (SBU)

business unit strategies *see* PLANNING PITFALLS

butchers *see* RETAIL PRODUCT OR SERVICE CATEGORIES

buy-backs *see* COUNTERTRADING

buyer *see* DECISION-MAKERS AND INFLUENCERS; PRODUCT OR SERVICE, TO BE PURCHASED; SPECIFICATION

buyer dissatisfied *see* ORGANIZATIONAL BUYING SITUATIONS

buyer marketing *see* PURCHASING

buyer multiplicity *see* DECISION-MAKERS AND INFLUENCERS

buyer's choice *see* RELATIONSHIP (MARKETING) MANAGEMENT

buyer/seller relationship *see* SALESMAN STEREOTYPE; SUPPLIERS

buyers, losses *see* WIN–WIN

buyer's price *see* PRICE, PURCHASE

buyers; retail *see* RETAIL MANAGEMENT

Buygrid Analysis The Buygrid Analysis of Robinson et al. describes three different buying situations:

- *new task*, where a previous purchase has never been made and, accordingly, the customer has no prior experience

- *modified rebuy*, which happens where a prospect has an existing supplier, but is either dissatisfied or has altered requirements, and is accordingly open to tender
- *straight rebuy*, where the prospect already has an existing supplier and is happy with their performance (and hence is unlikely to change)

See also BUYING DECISION, ADVERTISING MODELS

Reference: Robinson, P. J., Faris, C. W., and Wind, J. (1967) *Industrial Buying and Geative Marketing.* Allyn & Bacon. *Handbook* (3rd edn). Aldershot: Gower.

buying behaviour, pricing *see* PRICING, PRODUCT POSITIONING

buying centre *see* DECISION-MAKERS AND INFLUENCERS

buying decision *see* AIUAPR (AWARENESS, INTEREST, UNDERSTANDING, ATTITUDES, PURCHASE, REPEAT PURCHASE) MODEL; COMPLEX SALE; ENHANCED AIUAPR MODEL; PEER PYRAMID; THREE PILLARS OF THE PURCHASING PROCESS

buying decision, advertising models Most of the stages of the overall advertising process might happen in a few minutes while the reader is considering the advertisement; in the comfort of his or her favourite armchair. The final buying decision, on the other hand, may take place some time later; perhaps weeks later, when the prospective buyer actually tries to find a shop that stocks the product. This means that the basic message will probably need to be reinforced, by repeats, until the potential buyer is finally in a position to buy. It also means that, above all, the product or service must be in wide enough distribution for the prospective buyer to be able to find it! These stages are most evident in the AIDA ('Attention', 'Interest', 'Desire', 'Action') model, which is frequently advocated as the structure for the selling process. Similar stages are also described in the 'Hierarchy of Effects' model (where 'interest' and 'desire' are paralleled by 'knowledge', 'liking' and 'preference'). After AIDA, the most often quoted model within the advertising industry is DAGMAR (Defining Advertising Goals for Measuring Advertising Results), which splits the process down to the four steps of 'awareness', 'comprehension', 'conviction' and 'action'. There are a number of other models in the literature, but they all tend to describe the same processes from differing viewpoints. 'Step-wise' models are limited, however. In particu-

lar, although they may work in a cold sales call, in other complex real-life marketing situations they do not take into account time and experience. The attitude changes are likely to be more gradual, and much of advertising succeeds by marginally increasing the frequency of purchase of the brand among existing consumers. Thus, one of the major weaknesses of much of advertising theory is that it fails to take into account the history of the brand. Buying decisions are rarely taken in isolation. They are an accumulation of months – indeed, probably years – of experience on the part of the buyer. Abraham and Lodish (1990) observe that 'On average, 76% of the difference observed in the test year persisted one year after the advertising increase was rolled back. Over a three year period, the cumulative sales increase was at least twice the sales increase observed in the test year.' On the other hand, they also say that 'If advertising changes do not show an effect in six months, then they will not have any impact, even if continued for a year'.
See also ADVERTISING

Reference: Abraham, Magid M. and Lodish, Leonard M. (1990) Getting the most out of advertising and promotion. *Harvard Business Review*, May–June.

buying entry into market   *see* ECONOMIES OF SCALE, GLOBAL

buying groups   *see* MARKET ENTRY TACTICS

buying influences   *see* DECISION-MAKERS AND INFLUENCERS

buying intention   *see* OBJECTION HANDLING

buying, new task or routine   *see* ORGANIZATIONAL BUYING SITUATIONS

buying offices   *see* MARKET ENTRY TACTICS

buying possibilities, pricing   *see* MARKET-BASED PRICING

buying processes   *see* ORGANIZATIONAL PURCHASING

buying, professional   *see* PRODUCT OR SERVICE, TO BE PURCHASED

buying share and volume   *see* ADVERTISING

buying signals   Signals (usually body language – the non-verbal form of communication in which people show their responses by physical movements), observed by a salesperson, indicating that the customer is about to buy.
See also SALES CALL CLOSE

buying situations, organizational   *see* ORGANIZATIONAL BUYING SITUATIONS

buy or make   *see* MAKE OR BUY

buy or make, new products   *see* STRATEGIC SCREENING, NEW PRODUCTS

by-product pricing   *see* PRODUCT-LINE PRICING

C

cable   This is the media industry shorthand for cable television.

See also NARROWCASTING; TELEVISION

call bird   An item in a retail outlet that is deliberately priced low to entice customers into the store, in the hope that they will then buy other items.

See also SALES PROMOTION

calls available annually   Perhaps the most important calculation, in preparing sales (manpower) resource plans, is quite simply how many calls the sales force will be able to make (typically over a year). It is a calculation that relatively few sales managers make. Its importance is not in the knowledge itself, but in subsequently tracking performance: in monitoring whether the actual call rate is too low, it is necessary to know just what is too low. The basic element of this measure will probably be the day. For many sales professionals, at least for those in the area of capital goods, it may be difficult to book more than two (or perhaps three) calls a day; it cannot be accurately predicted exactly how long the calls will last – and, hence, the sales professional has to reserve a full morning or afternoon for each. Even here it should be possible to supplement this by *ad hoc* or cold calls, to at least double this rate – and these extra calls will be allowed for in the wise sales manager's plans. On the other hand, there are retail salesmen who can easily achieve rates of ten times this level. However, this rate assumes an ideal sales day, and this rarely ever happens. Many sales professionals have to spend a great deal of time preparing for calls, supporting customers and writing proposals. IBM management realistically recognizes that sales professionals spend at least 50 per cent of their time at their desks in the branch office. There must also be an allowance made for holidays, training, etc. In IBM, it is assumed that a sales professional (or any member of staff) will be available for just 200 days a year. Allocating 50 per cent of this time for office work, and taking into account the maximum possible total of only 200 days, it only requires a simple calculation to show that the effective available time can be reduced to as little as 100 days a year of face-to-face selling. At perhaps two calls per day (which may be a reasonable target for someone selling capital goods, with typically 50+ miles between each call) this gives just 200 possible calls a year. It is a sobering experience for most sales managers when they first come face-to-face with the true figures. It makes them much more aware of how important each call is. They realize that they cannot afford to let their sales personnel miss any, or to achieve anything less than their optimum performance in each call that they do make.

See also MANPOWER PLAN, SALES; SELLING; TERRITORY PLANS

calls, cold   *see* CALLS AVAILABLE ANNUALLY

calls per order   *see* CONTROL, OF SALES PERSONNEL

calls, preparation   *see* CALLS AVAILABLE ANNUALLY

calls, simulated   *see* SALES TRAINING

call structure   Many different structures have been suggested as to how sales professionals should handle a call. Of these, perhaps the best known is AIDA:

- Attention
- Interest
- Desire
- Action

There are many other similar acronyms. Interestingly, Alfred Tack (1975) (who quotes AIDA) discounts such sales formulae: 'after many years of teaching and research we know that separate steps no longer apply'. However, he does add, 'nevertheless, a salesman must have guidelines if his presentation is not to lose impact' and goes on to produce his own (admittedly easier) acronym, 'ABC':

- Attention
- Benefits
- Close

Of all the suggestions, his is probably the best, but only because it is the simplest, and does not force too many unnatural activities on what should be a simple dialogue. The best advice to the sales professional is not to follow acronyms, but to follow his or her own judgement, and the logic of the call itself.

See also SALES CALL

Reference: Tack, Alfred (1975) *How to Succeed in Selling.* New York: Tadworth, World's Work.

call targets   The basic building block of any sales campaign has to be its calls. Generally speaking, a number of calls are needed to get the business; and it is certainly true that the more calls that are made, the more business will be booked. This is often described in sales circles as the 'numbers game'. Thus, for every 1000 mailshots sent out there will be a certain percentage of returns that justify a sales professional calling personally; and telesales and cold calling will also generate proportional results. From these subsequent calls, a proportion will turn into serious prospects (some of whom will progress to demonstrations and proposals) – and out of these serious prospects a proportion will place orders, and a proportion (hopefully a good proportion) will place those orders with the organization undertaking these activities rather than with its competitors. At each stage, therefore, there is a conversion ratio. It is clearly the sales professional's personal skills (backed by sound account management) that ensure that this conversion ratio is as high as it can be. Converting a good prospect into a customer requires all the skills a sales professional possesses (as does converting a reply-paid card from a mailshot into a prospect). But it is a basic fact of the sales game that providing the raw material, the numbers of prospects to feed into the 'machine' that eventually converts them into business, is just sheer hard work. The more mailshots sent out, the more teleselling done and the more cold calls made, the greater will the raw material be for the conversion process. The eventual outcome is almost directly proportional to the numbers that are fed in (in theory, there will be a slight effect due to the best prospects inevitably being fed into the mill first – but generally the results are directly proportional). Miller, Heiman and Tuleja (1985) report, for example, that 'a recent survey done by a national association of sales executives . . . concluded that 80 percent of the new sales in this country [the US] are made by ten percent of the sales representatives – and that they close their sales only after making five or more calls on the client'.

See also CALLS AVAILABLE ANNUALLY; MANPOWER PLAN, SALES; SALES PROFESSIONAL; SELLING; TERRITORY MANAGEMENT; TERRITORY SALES PLAN

Reference: Miller, Robert B., Heiman, Stephen E. and Tuleja, Tad (1985) *Strategic Selling.* New York: William Morrow.

camera-ready copy   Text, together with illustrations, in a form ready to be photographed for final printing. The term is now often also used to describe the use of 'desktop published' material, which is produced on the user's own personal computer rather than by professional design studios.

See also ADVERTISING PROCESSES; BLOCKS

campaigning bodies   *see* DEFENSIVE (CORPORATE) PR

campaigns   *see* LONGER-TERM COMPETITIVE SAW

campaigns in isolation   *see* MESSAGE CONSISTENCY

campaign tracking   *see* ADVERTISING RESEARCH

candidates for recruitment   *see* RECRUITMENT, OF SALES PERSONNEL

canned presentation   A standard presentation that is used regularly.

See also PRESENTATION CONTENT; PRESENTATIONS

cannibalism, new products   One factor, often neglected in new product screening, is how much of the new brand's business will come from those of existing brands. Such 'cannibalism' must be taken into account where there is any degree of overlap; and if the organization is building on its strengths there often will be (and should be) significant overlap.

canonical analysis   An extension of multiple regression analysis, designed simultaneously to measure relationships between a number of dependent and independent variables.

See also ANALYSIS OF MARKETING RESEARCH DATA; MULTIPLE REGRESSION ANALYSIS

canvass   *see* SALES CALL

capacity loading   *see* SHORT-TERM FORECASTS

capacity matching   *see* NOT-FOR-PROFIT ORGANIZATIONS, OBJECTIVES

capacity, service-sector *see* SERVICE-SECTOR LOGISTICS

capital costs *see* COMPARATIVE ADVANTAGE, GLOBAL

capital equipment *see* GLOBAL MARKETING

capital equipment sales *see* DECISION-MAKERS AND INFLUENCERS

capital goods or consumables In terms of the basic 'dimensions' on which marketing is often organized, if the product (or indeed the service) represents a major investment, such as a domestic appliance in the home or a new production line in the factory, and will have a life measured in years, then it usually can be assumed that the decision-making process will be an extended one; often the province of face-to-face selling, even in consumer markets. Consumables, cans of beer or typewriter ribbons, on the other hand, will be repeat purchases that may be undertaken almost automatically – even in industrial markets – and the marketer's job will typically be to change these repeat buying patterns via the messages delivered in the media. The timescales may be very different, but once again many of the basic theories and practices are shared.
See also ORGANIZATIONAL PIGEON-HOLES

capital goods, reference seeking In the case of 'capital goods' (washing machines for households as well as machine tools for companies), it is not realistically possible to indulge in a 'trial' (or in 'repeat buying' over anything less than very extended periods); although the experience of one purchase, such as that of a washing machine, may be extended to a similar purchase, such as that of a tumble drier. In these situations, therefore, the typical consumer will seek reassurance from other sources. The industrial buyer may seek 'reference customers', to check that their own 'trial' has been satisfactory. In consumer markets the prospective buyer (even with the 'protection' offered by guarantees) may have to resort to the 'reputation' of the vendor (or, more recently, in the UK, to *Which?* magazine), or be influenced by the 'word of mouth' experiences of his or her contacts.
See also CONTROL, OF SALES PERSONNEL; DECISION-MAKING PROCESS, BY CUSTOMERS; PURCHASE DECISION, MATCHING; REPEAT PURCHASING PROCESS

caption The description, sometimes called a legend, attached to an illustration; for instance, in an advertisement or brochure.
See also ADVERTISING PROCESSES; CREATING THE CORRECT MESSAGES; CREATIVE DEPARTMENT, ADVERTISING AGENCY

captive audience An audience that cannot escape the message that you are promoting, such as those in conference sessions.
See also SEMINARS

captive product pricing This happens where on-going supplies are, for example, required to be subsequently purchased by the customer in order to support the use of a product. The supplier may choose to price the initial product low and to make the profit on the follow-on supplies. The example usually quoted is that of cheap razors that are offered to lock purchasers into buying that supplier's razor blades.
See also PRICE; PRICING STRATEGY

card (of questions) *see* MULTIPLE CHOICE, ON QUESTIONNAIRES

cards, reply-paid *see* REPLY-PAID CARDS

card system inventory control The traditional standby for inventory control, before the development of computers, was to have a card for each product; although, unlike the 'kanban' system, these were usually held centrally, by the purchasing or inventory control department. Each stock movement was duly recorded on the relevant product/component card (in, as goods were received from the supplier; and out, as goods were despatched to the customer), and the resulting balance adjusted.
See also INVENTORY CONTROL

cartel A group of (independent) companies formed to regulate prices in a market. This practice is illegal in some countries, including the USA and the UK.

cash and carry *see* WHOLESALERS AND DISTRIBUTORS

cash and wrap, retail *see* RETAIL 'PRODUCT' DECISIONS

cash cow In the popular application of the Boston Matrix, this term refers to those products in the quadrant with high market share but low market growth rate. The brand has maintained its high share, and hence its cash-generation capabilities, but the market life cycle has now moved to maturity and the growth is slow (conventionally below 10 per cent per annum), if at all. Investment is not required to any significant extent, because there is little need to recruit new customers and almost no demand for new plant. A 'cash cow' is, therefore, the main generator of cash of the profit that will cover the on-going investment in new products; primarily in the 'problem child' quadrant, but possibly also in that of the 'star'. Most leading brands, in FMCG markets at least, fall into this category – but maintain this position over long periods (in excess of a decade), which is outside the timescales usually considered in the use of the Boston Matrix.
See also Boston Matrix; budgets; investment multiplier

cash crop A crop grown for sale.

cash discount *see* trade discounts

cash flow and the product life cycle The most important, and often unwelcome, message that the product life cycle can usually bring to management is that of cash flow. The model offers a clear reminder, if it is needed – and it often is – that the launch of a new brand requires significant investment, and that this can last right through from its launch to the end of the growth phase, a longer period than most organizations allow for. What is worse, the more successful the new brand is, the greater is the investment that is likely to be needed! In new organizations, failing to appreciate the problems of rapid growth – of success – is, paradoxically, responsible for a number of failures, simply because the owners cannot find the funds to cover the debts that they have incurred in 'overtrading' to meet the needs of rapid growth. The life cycle model is also a reminder that once the maturity phase is reached, profits must be generated at a rapid enough rate to recoup the investments, and probably also to fund the new brands that are under development. This may seem an obvious enough requirement, but it was a lesson that EMI, for one, learnt the hard way. Its development of the body scanner (the CAT scanner) was a technological masterpiece, that indeed won its inventor a Nobel prize. Unfortunately, however, EMI was still investing well into what should have been the maturity phase when its American competitors moved into the next life cycle. The cash drain was such that EMI was forced to offer itself for sale!
See also Boston Matrix

cash flow risk *see* market entry decision

cash generators *see* budgets; investment multiplier; transnationals/multinationals and exporters

cashpoint, branch precision marketing *see* branch marketing

cash refunds *see* promotional pricing

casting off Estimating the space needed by the words to be printed.

catalogue selling *see* agent (personal) selling; in-house data, precision marketing; retailing

catalogue store A retail outlet which sells from a catalogue that the customer examines in the store, but which then supplies from stock held in the store.
See also retailing; retail organization

catastrophe theory This theory is derived from science and technology; but it may be very applicable to conviction marketing. In a very simplified form (for it is the idea, not the detail, that is important), it states that some systems can be 'overstressed', so that they will support loads beyond the point at which other systems would obviously start to deteriorate. When they pass the final point of no return, however, their performance degrades (they fail) suddenly and catastrophically. This can be compared with most other systems where the fail point may reached much more quickly, but the subsequent degradation in performance is much more gradual – and, hence, predictable and controllable (allowing, perhaps, for the possibility of recovery).

This can be illustrated by an example of venture management, offered by Halal and Lasken (1980):

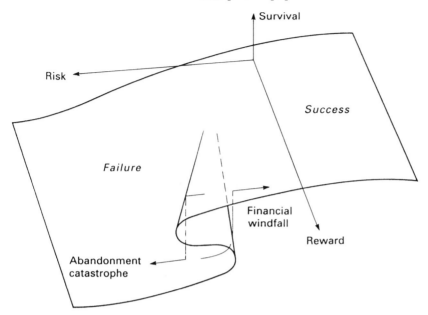

As risk is increased, along the left-hand line (labelled 'abandonment catastrophe') in this example, survival is not affected until the edge of the 'fold' in the surface is reached; whereupon there is a precipitous failure (leading to the 'abandonment catastrophe' – Halal and Lasken cite the example of RCA's eventual, and very hasty, exit from the computer industry in the 1970s). In theory, the reverse situation (here labelled 'financial windfall') can also happen; but, unfortunately, it is rather less probable. This phenomenon is characteristic of conviction marketing. The conviction marketer often persuades the customer (and the competitors) to defy the laws of 'marketing gravity' and slowly pushes them uphill! Often this is a process of incrementalism – making many, small, gradual changes, which are not individually noticed by the customers. This results in them achieving market positions, often of dominance, that are apparently unassailable, since their competitors cannot match this miraculous performance – which defies the 'laws of gravity'. IBM, for one, had in some respects achieved this feat at one time.

The problem is that once they are past the point of no return (and this can frequently be triggered by an apparently trivial change in circumstances), their position can be destroyed simply by their being forced – almost overnight – to obey the normal rules of the game (returning, in the graphical analogy illustrated above, to the bottom surface). This phenomenon has been most notable in the financial futures markets (the October 1987 crash, for instance), or in political circles (even Communism in Eastern Europe suffered this fate in 1989). Most recently it has been seen in the collapse of the East A sian economies. In a less dramatic manner, it might also be seen at work in those national industries (such as the UK motorcycle industry) that have been virtually destroyed by Japanese competition.

See also ADVERTISING; BUYING DECISION, ADVERTISING MODELS; CONVICTION MARKETING; PARADIGM SHIFT, STRATEGY

Reference: Halal, W. E. and Lasken, R. A. (1980) Management applications of catastrophe theory. *Business Horizons*, December.

catch–22 A situation in which conflicting requirements make resolution impossible.

catchment area, branch precision marketing   *see* BRANCH MARKETING

catchphrase   *see* SLOGAN

catch-up ball   *see* SERVICE QUALITY

category management   *see* PRODUCT/BRAND MANAGEMENT

category pricing   *see* SELECTIVE PRICING

Caterpillar Equipment   *see* GLOBALIZATION

CATI Computer Assisted Telephone Interviewing.

caveat emptor Let the buyer beware.

CBI survey of 'business confidence' *see* FORECASTING DYNAMICS; LEADING INDICATORS

CCN marketing *see* MARKETING RESEARCH, PRECISION MARKETING

CD-ROM The form of mass computer storage (based on the compact disk), attached to a personal computer, which is being increasingly used for storage of 'published' data.
See also DATABASES IN THE PUBLIC DOMAIN; EXTERNAL DATA; LIBRARIES

celebrity message Advertising based upon support from a celebrity.
See also CREATING THE CORRECT MESSAGES; CREATIVE DEPARTMENT, ADVERTISING AGENCY

censorship, self- *see* GROUPTHINK

census A survey of the whole 'population' involved; of users of a particular brand, for instance, but popularly of all of the inhabitants of a country.
See also DATA AVAILABILITY, PRECISION MARKETING; MARKETING RESEARCH, PRECISION MARKETING

central selling proposition *see* MESSAGE SELECTION

central shopping area *see* LOCATION, RETAIL

Centre for Interfirm Comparison *see* MONITORING, PROGRESS

centrespread The double-page spread at the centre of the magazine, which (if the magazine is staple-bound) does not have the gutter in the centre to spoil the layout.
See also BLEED; DOUBLE-PAGE SPREAD; GUTTER

ceteris paribus A term used, especially in economics, to describe the assumption that only the variables under investigation have any effect on the outcome – and that all other variables can be ignored.

chain of distribution *see* DISTRIBUTION CHAIN

chain store A retail outlet owned by a ('multiple' outlet) chain.
See also RETAILING; RETAIL ORGANIZATION

Chambers of Commerce *see* INTERNATIONAL MARKETING RESEARCH

champion *see* PRODUCT CHAMPION; PRODUCT/BRAND MANAGEMENT

champion, sales *see* CLOSING TECHNIQUES; PROSPECT QUALIFICATION

change agent, supplier's role A 'change agent' is an individual who personally stimulates change within an organization. In this context, much of the theory of industrial marketing would have the supplier assuming an almost passive role; and, indeed, an emphasis on subservience to the customer's needs and wants is a useful antidote to the widespread practice of selling to customers rather than marketing to them. Even in the marketing context, however, the supplier potentially has at least one very proactive role – as a change agent. It is true that innovation can diffuse both ways along the distribution chain – and many new products are the result of listening to customers. Some retailers, such as Marks & Spencer, will go so far as to invest considerable development in the products and processes of their smaller suppliers. More generally, however, innovation (and especially technological innovation) will diffuse forward along the chain; with the supplier offering new ideas which the customer, in turn, then passes on to the later members of the chain. This process is one of change, and the supplier (often unwittingly) adopts the role of change agent. To be in control of this process, though, the supplier needs to recognize what is happening – and to also realize that initiating change can be a difficult process, if ultimately a very powerful one. Some key elements of this process are as follows:

- *Customer perspective.* As always in marketing, the customer's viewpoint is all-important. It is even more important here; for a sales professional, blinded by the brilliance of the technological advance, may not stop to ask the critical question – which is, quite simply 'What benefit (if any) does this offer my customer?' Had Dupont stopped to ask themselves this question before they sallied forth with 'Corfam', for example, they might have saved themselves a considerable amount of money.

- *Education.* Introducing change is usually a process that requires education rather than just selling; it takes longer and requires considerably more explanation – and ultimately an understanding (not just an acceptance) by the customer.
- *Conviction marketing.* As major advances are something of a journey into the unknown, the techniques of 'conviction marketing' may need to be employed.

See also CONVICTION MARKETING; CUSTOMERS; INDUSTRIAL PURCHASING; WIN–WIN

channel   *see* DISTRIBUTION CHAIN

channel alternatives   A number of alternative 'channels' of distribution may be available. Organizations may, and often do, use a variety of such channels. The major ones are as follows:

- selling direct (via a sales force)
- mail order (including telephone sales)
- retailer
- wholesaler
- agent (who acts on behalf of the producer)

Distribution channels may not be restricted to physical products. They may be just as important for moving a service from 'producer' to consumer in certain sectors; since both direct and indirect channels may be used. Hotels, for example, may sell their services (typically rooms) direct or through travel agents, tour operators, airlines, tourist boards, centralized reservation systems, etc. There have also been some innovations in the distribution of services. For example, there has been an increase in franchising and in rental services, the latter offering anything from televisions to DIY tools. There has also been some evidence of service integration, with services linking together – particularly in the travel and tourism sector, where links now exist between airlines, hotels and car rental services, etc. In addition, there has been a significant increase in retail outlets for the service sector; where such outlets (estate agencies and building societies, for example) are now crowding out the traditional grocers and greengrocers from the high street.

See also AGENT (PERSONAL) SELLING; CHANNEL MEMBERSHIP; CHANNEL MOTIVATION; CHANNEL STRUCTURE; DISTRIBUTION CHAIN; MAIL ORDER; MONITORING AND MANAGING CHANNELS; RETAILER ORGANIZATION; SELLING; TELE-SALES; WHOLESALERS AND DISTRIBUTORS

channel captain   The most important member of the distribution chain. Traditionally this was the manufacturer, but now it is often the retailer.
See also DISTRIBUTION CHAIN

channel decisions   Which channel(s) to use is a major decision for most organizations. If the option of all sales being made direct, to the consumer or end-user, is chosen, there may be unacceptable cost penalties. On the other hand, the introduction of intermediaries can significantly reduce the amount of control that a producer has over the relationship with the end-user. The most likely factors to be taken into account in such a decision are the following:

- *Overall strategy.* The characteristics of the channel must be in line with the overall requirements of the marketing strategy. If very widespread distribution is called for, then the use of channels such as wholesalers may be almost inevitable. If quality of service – on the basis of selective distribution – is needed, then a specialist sales force may be the answer.
- *Product (or service).* The characteristics of the product itself will play a part. If it requires substantial support, and the strategy calls for widespread distribution, suitably qualified agents or dealers will need to be carefully selected. For example, if the product needs to be kept refrigerated, then a highly specialized distribution chain will be required.
- *Consumer location.* Where the end-users themselves are located will also have an influence. A diffuse, nationwide market for a consumer good will require a totally different chain to one for an industrial component sold, say, to the computer manufacturing industry in Scotland.
- *Cost.* Not least, of course, will be the comparative cost of the alternative channels.

See also CHANNEL MEMBERS; CHANNEL STRUCTURE; DISTRIBUTION CHAIN; INTERNAL MARKET

channel integration   *see* VERTICAL MARKETING

channel management   The channel decision is a very important decision for any company. In theory at least, there is a form of trade-off, in that the cost of using intermediaries to achieve wider distribution is supposedly lower. Indeed, most consumer goods manufacturers could never justify the cost of selling direct to their consumers; except by mail order. In practice, if the producer is large enough, the use of intermediaries (particularly at the agent and whole-saler level) can sometimes cost more than going direct. Many of the theoretical arguments about channels, therefore, revolve around cost. On the other hand, most of the practical decisions are concerned with control of the consumer. The small company has no alternative but to use intermediaries – often several layers of them – but large companies do have the choice. Many suppliers, however, seem to assume that once their product has been sold into the channel, into the beginning of the distribution chain, their job is finished. Yet that distribution chain is merely assuming a part of the supplier's responsibility; and, if he has any aspirations to be market-oriented, his job should in reality be extended to managing, albeit very indirectly, all the processes involved in that chain – until the product or service arrives with the end-user. This may involve a number of decisions on the supplier's part.

See also CHANNEL DECISIONS; CHANNEL MEMBERSHIP; CHANNEL MOTIVATION; DISTRIBUTION CHAIN; MONITORING AND MANAGING CHANNELS

channel members Distribution channels can have a number of 'levels'. Kotler defines the simplest level, that of a direct contact between the producer and the consumer – with no intermediaries involved – as the 'zero-level'. The next level, the 'one-level' channel, is that where there is just one intermediary; in consumer goods a retailer, for industrial goods a distributor, say. In recent years this has been the level that, together with the zero-level, has accounted for the greatest percentage of the overall volumes distributed in the UK; although the very elaborate distribution systems in Japan are at the other end of the spectrum, with many levels being encountered even for the simplest of consumer goods.

In the UK, the introduction of a second level – a wholesaler, for example – is now mainly used to extend distribution to the large number of small, neighbourhood retailers, which account for only a small part of the overall volume, but offer a local service to their customers.

See also CHANNEL STRUCTURE; DISTRIBUTION CHAIN

Reference: Kotler, P. (1991) *Marketing Monegement* (7th edn). Englewood Cliffs, NJ: Prentice-Hall.

channel membership To a degree, the supplier has some control over which organizations participate in (become the members of) the distribution chain, and what the structure of that channel might be. At one extreme, in mass consumer goods markets, where members of the chain merely offer a logistical service (making the product available, with varying levels of efficiency, to end-users), the supplier's main concern may be to maximize distribution levels; so that the maximum number of outlets 'stock' the product or service (where total sales may be proportional to total distribution) – thus making it easily available to consumers. At the other extreme, where dealers, for example, take over some of the supplier's responsibility for supporting sophisticated technical products, the supplier may be primarily concerned about the quality of the individual dealer. He or she will want to be sure that they will match his or her own quality of service. Under these circumstances, in particular, the choice of channel members becomes a very important activity; almost as if they were being hired as direct employees. These approaches can also be thought of as representing the intensity of the distribution:

- *Intensive distribution.* In this situation, the majority of resellers stock the 'product'; for example, with convenience products, and particularly the brand leaders in consumer goods markets – such as Camay in the soap market. Price competition may be evident as a factor.
- *Selective distribution.* This is the normal pattern – in both consumer and industrial markets – where 'suitable' resellers (less than 'all' resellers, but not rigorously controlled) stock the product; for example, the Revlon range of cosmetics.
- *Exclusive distribution.* Here, only specially selected resellers (typically only one per geographical area) are allowed to sell the 'product'; for example, Estée Lauder in cosmetics; where distribution is often deliberately limited to prestigious department stores.

See also CHANNEL DECISIONS; CHANNEL MOTIVATION; DISTRIBUTION CHAIN; MONITORING AND MANAGING CHANNELS

channel motivation Motivating direct employees to provide the necessary sales and service support is difficult enough. Motivating the owners and employees of the independent organizations in a distribution chain requires even greater effort. They, after all, will determine what the sales levels will be. There are many devices for achieving such motivation. Perhaps the most usual is 'bribery': the supplier offers a better margin, to tempt the owners in the channel to push the product rather than its competitors; or a competition is offered to the distributors' sales personnel, so that they are tempted to push the product. In some countries, indeed, it is normal practice to make payments to the customer's buyers (who are, in effect, acting as 'middlemen'). At the other end of the spectrum is the almost symbiotic relationship that the all too rare supplier in the computer field develops with its agents; where the agent's personnel, support as well as sales, are trained to almost the same standard as the supplier's own staff. Buying by channel members in general, and retailers in particular, exhibits two additional features:

- *Open to buy.* The buyer may have a budgeted total amount to divide between his or her purchases of all products. The current position that the suppliers face may, therefore, depend upon many factors outside their control; including existing stockholdings of other products that are over-stocked, forecast sales, product on order, and competing promotions from other suppliers. If the buyer does not have the money to spend (i.e. is in very much the same position as the consumer who has reached his or her credit limit!), no amount of persuasion will make any difference.
- *Forward buy.* On the other hand, when promotions or deals are particularly attractive, the same buyers may place orders for stocks that will last much longer than normal.

See also CHANNEL MEMBERSHIP; DISTRIBUTION CHAIN; MONITORING AND MANAGING CHANNELS

channels, as customers   The producer may not sell direct to the end-user, but may be forced to sell through distribution chains, 'channels', which act as intermediaries between producer and end-user. This may be as true of services as of products – for example, Commercial Union and the Prudential need their brokers to act as intermediaries – and even of the non-profit sector, where the universities, which are independent of government, have a major impact on the delivery of its higher education policy. The 'producer' thus has consumers, who are unseen, and customers, those in the distribution chain who are met face-to-face. These customers have different needs to those of the consumers; and, although they are conventionally seen as part of the same market, these marked differences have to be allowed for. One of IBM's few weaknesses is that it often sees the PC market in terms of what its dealers want; and not in terms of the needs of the all-important end-users, whom IBM does not meet face-to-face. This has resulted in an almost suicidally unprofitable concen-tration on price-cutting – whereas the original market research showed that, as might be expected for products of such complexity, support was what mattered to the end-user.

See also CUSTOMERS; DISTRIBUTION CHAIN

channel strategy   *see* CHANNEL DECISIONS

channel strip   The strip along the front edge of a shelf in a self-service store which carries details of the products.

See also RETAILING; SALES PROMOTION

channel structure   To the various 'levels' of distribution, which they refer to as the 'channel length', Lancaster and Massingham (1988) also add another element of its structure, the relationship between its members:

- *Conventional or free-flow.* This is the usual, widely recognized, channel, with a range of 'middlemen' passing the goods on to the end-user.
- *Single transaction.* A temporary 'channel' may be set up for one transaction; for example, the sale of property or a specific civil engineering project. This does not share many characteristics with other channel transactions, each one being unique.
- *Vertical Marketing System (VMS).* In this form, the elements of distribution are integrated.

See also CHANNEL MEMBERS; DISTRIBUTION CHAIN; INTERNAL MARKET

Reference: Lancaster, Geoff and Massingham, Lester (1988) *Essentials of Marketing.* New York: McGraw-Hill.

chaos   The mathematical theory of chaos has been espoused by some marketers as an answer to hand-ling random events. This is a mistake. The mathematical theory only describes the behaviour of a certain type of mathematical equation. Although relatively simple in form (to mathematicians at least), such equations produce wildly different outcomes depending on very small changes in the starting conditions. The resulting patterns may look like some of those experienced in marketing, but there is no easy way to determine the underlying relationships (the simple equations) – so this approach will not help prediction. On the other hand, it may be possible, by studying the observed patterns of outcome, to decide that these are genuinely chaotic (as opposed to being driven by underlying trends – or random, where they will at least follow some statistical probabilities); in which case you can at least understand the magnitude of the task facing your forecasters (who are, by definition, unable to forecast in this situation) and the high risks involved.

The technical limitations of forecasting are especially well illustrated by the 'mathematics of chaos'; first suggested by Edward Lorenz (1963). This has shown that even simple equations can lead to unpredictable results. Gordon and Greenspan (1988), for instance, show what happens in the case of the very simple non-linear equation

$$X_{next} = Xk(1 - X).$$

This is a recursive equation in which each subsequent value of X is calculated on the basis of its previous value; with the stability controlled by the constant k.

When $k = 3.15$, the pattern is stable; but when it is set to $k = 3.78$, the result is chaotic.

See also CATASTROPHE THEORY; FORECASTING TECHNIQUES QUANTITATIVE FORECASTING TECHNIQUES; UNCERTAINTY REDUCTION, FORECASTING

References: Gordon, Theodore J. and Greenspan, David (1988) Chaos and fractals: new tools for technological and social forecasting. *Technological Forecasting and Social Change*, 34.
Lorenz, Edward N. (1963) Deterministic nonperiodic flow. *Journal of Atmosphere Sciences*, March.

charismatic marketers   *see* CONVICTION MARKETING TYPES; LEADERSHIP, OF SALES PERSONNEL; PARADIGM SHIFT, STRATEGY; VISION, CORPORATE

charity voucher   *see* PROMOTIONAL PRICING

chat gap   *see* SALES CALL OPENING

chat mode   *see* COMPUTER-MEDIATED COMMUNICATIONS (CMC)

check editing   A means of controlling the quality of field surveys by checking (editing) a sample of questionnaires for mistakes.
See also SURVEY RESEARCH

checkout counter   *see* BRANCH MARKETING; RETAIL PRODUCT OR SERVICE CATEGORIES

checkweighing   Weighing a pack of product – typically as part of the production line – after filling, to ensure that it meets the required weight standard.

cherry-picking   Selecting bargains, typically by going from store to store to get the best deal.

See also RETAILING; SALES PROMOTION

Cheshire labels   Specially prepared (typically by a mailing house) continuous labels for affixing to the envelopes for mailings.
See also DIRECT MAIL

Reference: Jurick, Robert H. (1992) Lettershop processing. In Edward L. Nash (ed.), *The Direct Marketing Handbook*. New York: McGraw-Hill.

chicken   *see* PRISONER'S DILEMMA

Chinese wall   A barrier to information exchange which is deliberately created between different parts of an organization (especially in stockbroking), and which is usually intended to protect the confidentiality of customer or client information.

chi-square test   A statistical test, of survey research data, based on frequency distributions shown in two-way classification tables.
See also ANALYSIS OF MARKETING RESEARCH DATA

Reference: Harris, Paul (1986) Statistics and significance testing. In Robert Worcester and John Downham (eds), *Consumer Research Handbook* (3rd edn). New York: McGraw-Hill.

choice (constrained) model   *see* PRICING, PRODUCT POSITIONING

chronology   In marketing, this usually refers to arranging data by date sequence.

CIF (cost, insurance, freight)   The price for goods that includes their shipment to the port of destination.
See also EXPORTING

cinema   Although the numbers in the UK audience are now small, this may be the most effective medium for extending coverage to the younger age groups, since the core audience is aged between 15 and 24.
See also MEDIA TYPES

Cinzano   *see* STRUCTURE OF INTERNATIONAL MARKETING

circular   A non-personalized mailing, or door-to-door drop, of promotional literature.
See also DIRECT MAIL

circular distributors   *see* DOOR-TO-DOOR

circulation   *see* AUDIENCE RESEARCH; PRESS MEDIA; USERS

Citibank   *see* GLOBALIZATION

city-block model   *see* SAINT JAMES MODEL

civil servants   *see* POLITICAL CONTACTS

clarity   *see* CONVICTION MARKETING FACTORS

class   *see* SOCIAL CLASS INFLUENCES, ON THE PURCHASE DECISION

class groupings   The class groupings that have been traditionally used by the advertising agencies in the UK are as follows:

Percentage of UK population, 1988

AB, managerial and professional	17
C1, supervisory and clerical	23
C2, skilled manual	28
DE, unskilled manual and unemployed	32

UK government agencies use a rather more complicated class split, but the principle is much the same. Other countries use their own versions.
See also DECISION-MAKING PROCESS, BY CUSTOMERS; REPEAT PURCHASING PROCESS; SOCIAL CLASS INFLUENCES, ON THE PURCHASE DECISION

Classification Of Residential Neighbourhoods, A (ACORN)   *see* RESIDENTIAL NEIGHBOURHOODS

classified advertising   Groups, usually classified into categories, of small advertisements; typically consisting of text only, but sometimes with small, simple illustrations.
See also DISPLAY ADVERTISING; MEDIA SELECTION; SPECIALIST AGENCIES

classified data   Data that has been collected by using only different classifications or categories, rather than numerical measurements.
See also ANALYSIS OF MARKETING RESEARCH DATA

classified display advertising   A classified format advertisement, typically consisting of text only, run as a large-format (display) advertisement.
See also CLASSIFIED ADVERTISING; DISPLAY ADVERTISING; MEDIA SELECTION

class magazine   A journal for a group of readers, usually consumers rather than industrial readers, who have a special, shared interest.
See also MEDIA SELECTION; MEDIA TYPES

class profile   *see* MEDIA BUYING, ADVERTISING AGENCY; PRESS MEDIA

Clawson model   A model, of consumer behaviour, relating to the tensions (psychic conflicts) in a purchase decision.
See also MODELS

cleaning databases   *see* MARKET CLEARING

clearing banks   *see* BANKS

clearing, market   *see* MARKET CLEARING

client/agency relationship   Agencies are renowned for offering their clients excellent lunch facilities, and the afternoon meetings between agency personnel and their clients can, accordingly, be very convivial. It has to be recognized, however, that this is a business relationship – and one that is very important to the marketing success of the client. David Nylen (1986) offers six ground rules:

• *Admit the agency to full partnership*. The agency has a full stake in the success of the business, and the client is just as dependent on their success in handling the advertising. They must, accordingly, have the same 'access' (especially to senior management) as any other 'department' within the organization.
• *Be demanding of the agency*. The advertiser must demand high standards, and reward them.
• *Respect the agency's area of expertise*. This is probably the most difficult ground rule to implement, since everyone (from the shop-floor operatives to, most importantly of all, the chairperson's spouse) believes that they are experts on advertising – after all, they probably spend a significant part of each evening watching commercials! The only effective rule is to let the agency do what they are expert at, and are paid to do, without interference – which normally can only be counterproductive.
• *Reward superior performance*. The greatest reward for any agency is acceptance of the work done, and subsequent recognition of its effectiveness in practice – particularly if that recognition is de-

livered in glowing praise that they can use to attract other clients!

- *Be responsive to the agency profit position.* The agency has to make a profit too; although the advertiser has the right to expect that this should not be excessive.
- *Regularly evaluate the agency account group.* In the same way that any manager should regularly review the performance of his or her subordinates, those in charge of the organization's contacts with the agency should evaluate the performance of their 'subordinates' within that agency.

Even though the relationship is at heart a business one, it is still important to recognize its social aspects. Kenneth Runyon (1984) stresses that 'the client–agency relationship is a tenuous one, based on mutual respect and confidence. Unfortunately, confidence is a fragile commodity that is difficult to build and easy to destroy. Interpersonal relationships between client and agency are exceedingly important, and real or imagined slights of client personnel by agency representatives sometimes rupture the relationship. In addition, advertising agencies are not always selected for sound business or professional reasons. Friendship, rather than competence, is often the main criterion.'

There is much hype about accounts changing agencies but, as *The Economist* reports, 'clients are basically loyal ... only 10% of accounts change hands each year'. Thus, for instance, McCann Erickson have held the Coca Cola account for nearly 40 years.

See also ADVERTISING; ADVERTISING AGENCY ELEMENTS; MARKETING RESEARCH

References: Micklethwaite, John (1990) The advertising industry. *The Economist*, 9 June.
   Nylen, David W. (1986) *Advertising: Planning, Implementation and Control* (3rd edn). Houston, TX: South West Publishing.
   Runyon, Kenneth (1984) *Advertising* (2nd edn). New York: Charles E. Merrill.

client's brief   *see* MEDIA BUYING, ADVERTISING AGENCY

client services   *see* SALES PROFESSIONAL

cliff, in forecasting   *see* FORECASTS, LIMITING FACTORS

clinical interview   *see* INDIVIDUAL DEPTH INTERVIEWS

clipping service   A service that clips items about an organization (or about a subject specified by it) from the newspapers.
See also SCANNING, AND MIS; SCANNING TEAM

close   *see* CLOSING TECHNIQUES

closed questions   Questions of this kind, which typically require the answer 'yes' or 'no', have (justifiably) received a bad press. But it is still necessary to use them quite extensively, as part of the overall questioning process, to clarify points. The problem only comes about when they are used instead of open questions.
See also QUESTIONING

closed questions, on questionnaires   Most questionnaires are based on 'closed' questions, in which the respondent is asked to choose between a number of alternative answers; or the interviewer is asked – there and then – to code the respondent's answer to an apparently 'open' question against a number of pre-conceived answers. The advantage of such closed questions is that the answers are easy to analyse and are unambiguous. The obvious disadvantage is that this precludes the respondent from giving an answer outside these parameters; although one category is often 'other' (and a free-form explanation is requested), while another is 'don't know'. Beware of high numbers of 'don't knows'; particularly if you are an over-confident candidate in a parliamentary by-election!

Typical approaches to closed questioning are as follows.

Numbers
Many questionnaires ask the respondent questions such as 'How frequently do you purchase brand A?' or 'How much did you pay?', which prompt a numerical answer. On the other hand, this may be posing almost impossible feats of memory for some – indeed, perhaps most – respondents; unless the 'process' being investigated is a very regular one. Unfortunately, respondents are still quite willing to try to undertake these mental gymnastics, but this does not guarantee the accuracy of the results – so the use of such questions should be carefully reviewed.

Yes/no
With this type of question the respondent taking part in survey research is most simply asked to agree or disagree; for example, 'Have you ever used Nescafé? [yes/no]'.

Multiple choice

A basic yes/no question in survey research can be expanded to cover a number of alternative choices, from which the respondent is asked to select one (or sometimes more):

Which of these brands have you ever tried?

Red Mountain	☐
Maxwell House	☐
Nescafé	☐
Kenco	☐
None	☐
Other (please specify)	☐ ....
Don't Know	☐

In this approach, the respondent may be shown the list (sometimes referred to as a 'card', since this is the form in which it is shown), which is referred to as a 'prompted' answer. It is more likely that the interviewer will simply ask the question 'Which brands have you ever tried?' and code the free-form answer on to this pre-printed list in the questionnaire. This is referred to as a 'spontaneous' answer.

Semantic differentials

In this form of question, in survey research, the respondent is asked to choose where his or her position is on a (rating) scale between two bipolar words (or a range of words or numbers ranging across a bipolar position); for example,

Excellent	☐	Powerful	☐	5
Good	☐		☐	4
Adequate	☐		☐	3
Poor	☐		☐	2
Inadequate	☐	Weak	☐	1

As originally developed by Osgood (see Osgood et al., 1957), there were 20 specific rating scales that had a wide application. They have since been used more generally, as the above examples show.

One particularly widely used form of scaling (Likert, 1932) asks the respondent to rate opinion statements presented to him or her one at a time, in terms of his or her 'agreement' with it:

One decision that has to be made is the number of choices to be offered (five seems to be optimal, in terms of showing differentiation without confusing

Strongly agree

Agree

Neither agree nor disagree

Disagree

Strongly disagree

the respondent) and whether to offer an odd number (as is normally the case), so that the respondent can choose a central 'neutral' position, or an even one, which forces the respondent to choose between the alternatives.

See also LIKERT SCALES; QUESTIONNAIRE DESIGN

References: Likert, Rensis (1932) A technique for the measurement of attitudes. *Archives of Psychology*, No. 140.
Osgood, E. C., Succi, G. J. and Tannenbaum, P. H. (1957) *The Measurement of Meaning*. Urbana.

close, sales call   *see* CLOSING TECHNIQUES; SALES CALL CLOSE

closing probability   *see* TERRITORY SALES PLAN

closing techniques   As a result of the fear of closing, a whole range of techniques have been proposed to help the sales professional to ask for the order – psychological props to underpin the natural process. In this case, we will expand on the list of techniques, since an appreciation of these will give a flavour of the 'culture' that permeates much of selling. It is also the area where the uninitiated, on the receiving end of a 'sales call', may most clearly observe the rituals! The list that Alfred Tack gives is typical and seems succinctly to cover the main categories:

- *The alternative close*. This is often the standby in selling to retailers: 'Will 20 cases of baked beans be sufficient, or should we increase that to 30 cases?'
- *The summary close*. Having listed everything that has been done, the sales professional can justifiably say: 'Well, I guess all that remains is to sign the order.'
- *The fear close*. 'Our stocks are getting low, and I wouldn't want you to have to wait for your order, so can we get it signed now?'
- *The verbal proof close*. A good story, for example a good reference sell, can be used to lead to: 'Does that convince you that you should order?'

- *The isolation close*. Having listed the outstanding objections, the sales professional asks: 'If I am able to answer each of these points to your complete satisfaction, then can I assume we are in business?' This is sometimes referred to as the 'half-nelson close' (an analogy with the sport of wrestling), because it is a powerful but very aggressive technique.
- *The minor point close*. 'Shall we make the order out for red or blue?'
- *The concession close*. 'I'll add an extra 5 per cent discount if you order now.'

John Fenton (1984) also adds the 'trial use close', on the assumption that the prospect will not wish to be bothered to return the equipment when the invoice arrives at the end of the trial period. Interestingly, his research has shown that '74 percent of successful salesmen preferred the "Alternative Choice" close . . . In selling to retail 64 percent preferred the "Order Form" close'. It is clear, therefore, that most sales professionals use the 'alternative close' – that is, on the few occasions when they do get around to a positive close, rather than succumbing to the 'default close'! This result is not surprising, since the 'alternative close' is the easiest to use, and often follows most naturally out of the preceding discussion. It is not too difficult for the sales professional to change the informative question that is about to be asked, from 'Would you want the larger model?' into the closing 'Do you want the larger model?'; to be followed by the even more positive 'When do you want us to deliver?' There are, however, a number of more pragmatic 'closes' in real life, as follows.

The assumptive (joint) close

In line with the concept of the 'dialogue' (which can be developed as an analogy for the whole of marketing) the most natural technique, particularly in the context of management discussions, is simply to let the close develop naturally; to assume (right from the beginning of the call, and indeed from the beginning of the whole campaign) that the prospect will want to place an order. The 'close', therefore, is shared; it is a joint effort between the sales professional and the prospect (almost as if making the 'default close' work in their favour, by initiating and controlling it). The typical wording becomes: 'How do we now go about getting the order signed?'; in this context, 'we' being very clearly the prospect as well as the sales professional, making it a joint responsibility – and a shared 'win'. Alfred Tack (1975) quotes one saying that supports this view: 'There is an old selling tag: A GOOD SALE CLOSES ITSELF'.

The progressive (incremental) close

This also highlights one aspect of many professional sales (and of management negotiations); there is not one single close, but, rather, a steady progression through a series of increasingly committed intermediate closes. The 'close' here becomes the agreement to each of a series of steps that will eventually lead to the order. Each close, though, has to be as rigorously pursued as that which will result in the order. Each must be clearly agreed, and each must be accompanied by an action plan leading to the next step. This long-drawn-out process obviously has disadvantages, not the least being that there are that many more opportunities to lose – although there are also that many more opportunities to recover (unlike the eventual order, each of these steps is by no means final). For many sales professionals, who have difficulty facing one close, it is death by a thousand closes! It does, however, have the major advantage that it is an incremental process. Each decision escalates the commitment; but the prospect only has to make a number of small decisions, rather than one large one. This makes the process easier for you to control, as the decision develops its own momentum. The final close is just as small, and as easy to achieve, as any of the intermediate steps. It is also an ideal vehicle for the assumptive (joint) close. Indeed, it almost forces sales professionals into this mode; since, with so many steps, it is almost impossible not to work alongside the prospect. The routine question becomes: 'What do we need to do now?'

The trial close

Just about the most powerful sales technique, but one which is not widely used, is the 'trial close' (described by John Fenton as the 'pre-close'). It simply comprises a conventional close of any type (but most normally an assumptive one, probably as part of a progressive pattern) put at the earliest possible time that the sales professional believes that a close might be possible; or even earlier – most sales professionals are unduly pessimistic about how easy it is to close. It is then repeated at discreet intervals over succeeding calls, until it is finally successful. As it is, in essence, a repetitive close, it does need to be more subtle and discreet – of the 'What do we need to do?' type. As Tom Hopkins (1982) puts it, 'A Champion is closing most of the time. He's constantly trying test closes, and he'll go into his final closing sequence anytime he sniffs the sweet smell of success . . . the great ones usually close after their fifth attempt.' One of its main benefits is its 'trial' nature. It is not the 'life or death' final close. The chances are that the answer will be 'no', but the doors will not be closed. The downside risk is, thus, minimal. As such, it appears to be much easier for sales professionals to use; they do not have the same reluctance as they have over the final close, simply because the 'trial close' is usually not final – it is that much less 'important'. The psychological effort – the sheer courage needed – is much less, and the effect of a 'no' is not shattering to the ego (since it is expected). A not negligible benefit is that its use means that the final close, when a trial close actually results in an order, comes earlier in the campaign, close to the earliest possible moment. This has benefits for the flow of business but, more importantly, it minimizes the time during which the business is at risk (if Alfred Tack is right, at least 30 per cent of business goes to competitors because the close is not early enough – or is missing altogether). But, for me, the invaluable benefit comes when (as in most such trials, by definition) it results in a 'no'. The sales professional can then proceed to boldly (but discreetly) ask the question: 'Why?' For a sales professional, this combination of trial close and question ('Why?') is the most powerful analytical tool that I know of. The answer has to be (with very few exceptions indeed) a do-it-yourself guide to closing the business. The prospect is put on the spot, and typically has to give a completely honest answer; stating what he or she thinks are the best actions needed to win.

See also OBJECTION HANDLING; SALES CALL

References: Fenton, John (1984) *How to Sell Against Competition*. London: Heinemann.
  Hopkins, Tom (1982) *How to Master the Art of Selling*. London: Grafton.
  Tack, Alfred (1975) *How to Succeed in Selling*. New York: Tadworth, World's Work.

Club Méditerannée   *see* GLOBALIZATION

clubs   *see* PRECISION (DIRECT) MARKETING, RETAIL

cluster analysis   In analysis of survey research data, factors can be found by this set of methods (rather than by a single technique) that strongly differentiate, for example, certain customer groups from others; so that the 'cluster' is isolated (with high 'heterogeneity') from other clusters, while being internally cohesive (with high 'homogeneity' – that is, members of the cluster are similar). This is best demonstrated graphically, the 'clusters' being represented by higher densities of points in the space (the two dimensions) being mapped. Cluster analysis seeks to define the boundaries of these more dense regions. In the words of Punj and Stewart (1983), 'it is designed to identify groups and entities (people, markets, organizations) that share certain common characteristics (attitudes, purchase properties, media habits etc.) . . . segmentation research becomes a grouping task'. As this indicates, it is a particularly important technique in the case of 'segmentation'; where the aim is to split customers (and hence markets) into clearly differentiated groups. Cluster analysis is first used to discover the variables that offer the necessary degree of differentiation, and then – through a number of stages – to differentiate (with increasing definition) those in the sample under investigation. The methods used, and the boundary conditions chosen, can vary from researcher to researcher, so there is often some controversy over the results (to the extent that it is sometimes recommended that several methods are used to cross-check the results). Some statisticians, indeed, look askance at this method of analysis, since it was developed outside of the main disciplines of academic thought. As Punj and Stewart, again, comment: 'There are currently no clear guide-lines for determining the boundaries of clusters . . . The preferred definition of a cluster seems to vary with the discipline and purpose of the researcher.' They also make the important practical point that 'There should be some rationale for the selection of variables for cluster analysis . . . researchers must agree on those dimensions which are most relevant for classification for a particular purpose.' Indeed, much of the controversy has centred around the technique itself, whereas it is arguable that the real argument should have been about the selection of meaningful dimensions. The marketer, and the market researcher, must choose the dimensions that are meaningful to the consumer, and not just to the supplier. This is the reason for the use of techniques such as 'Kelly grids' in choosing the most suitable dimensions. Despite the controversy, cluster analysis – when properly used, and in full knowledge of its limitations – is one of the most powerful analytical techniques available to the marketer.

See also ANALYSIS OF MARKETING RESEARCH DATA; SEGMENTATION

Reference: Punj, Girish and Stewart, David W. (1983) Cluster analysis in marketing research: review and suggestions for application. *Journal of Marketing Research*, XX, May.

cluster approach   *see* EXPORT MARKET
ELIMINATION

clustered market segments   The most effective
'segmentation' of a market is usually based on sets of
characteristics that are specific to that market. The
spread of users across these characteristics may,
however, differ quite significantly. Both the homogeneous market (in which all of the users have similar,
closely grouped, preferences; for example, a commodity such as sugar) and the diffused market (the
theoretical opposite extreme; in which they have requirements that are evenly spread across the spectrum) tend to specify treatment of the market as one
single entity (but for very different reasons), and
segmentation is not relevant (unless competitors in a
diffused market have left part of it uncovered). It is
in the 'clustered' market – which is often encountered in practice; for example, with the purchasers of
chocolates – where segmentation can be used most
successfully. Ideally, the marketer would choose to
place the product exactly in the centre of the cluster
that he or she is aiming for; and would choose the
product or service characteristics to place the offering at exactly the right coordinates. Another approach, though, where the clusters may be too small
to justify a segmentation policy (or the marketer
simply wants to have a more general product/brand
which can be correspondingly larger), is to launch
the product or service so that it is equidistant from
several clusters that the marketer wishes to serve. It
may, thus, not exactly match the needs of any one
group, but is close to meeting those of several
groups. Such 'positioning', however, may be vulner-
able to attack from a competitor who positions his
brand exactly on one of the clusters.
See also CLUSTER ANALYSIS; PRODUCT (OR SERVICE)
POSITIONING; SEGMENTATION

cluster sampling   An alternative, and cheaper,
approach to random sampling in marketing research
– which may lose little of the accuracy if correctly
employed – is only to select the districts for interviewing on a random basis. Within these districts,
respondents can also be specified randomly (from the
local list of electors, for example) or could be obtained (albeit in this case only 'quasi-randomly') by
'random walk' (every tenth house on a given street,
say).
See also DATA COLLECTION; QUOTA SAMPLES; RANDOM
SAMPLES; SAMPLES; SAMPLING STATISTICS

cluster shift   *see* POSITION DRIFT

coach, buying influence   *see* DECISION-MAKERS
AND INFLUENCERS

coalitions   *see* CORPORATE OBJECTIVES

coarse marketing   Marketing was not developed,
nor dramatically advanced, in the laboratories of its
academic theorists. It was the outcome of the practical explorations by practitioners, gradually probing
the frontiers of what could be achieved by their activities. The academics usually came later and served
a very valuable function by documenting, in a form
that could be transferred to other managers, what
had been learned by this practice. Philip Kotler in
particular has made a massive contribution to the
advancement of marketing by collecting the techniques that had been developed by small groups of
very sophisticated marketers; ideas that had been
previously the province of just a few marketers, who
had been apprenticed in these centres of excellence.
Kotler and his contemporaries have offered this expertise to all managers. Even so, it is the practice of
marketing that is important; and the theory should
be in support of practice – a fact that some academics
may have begun to overlook.

In real life, the marketer does not face each decision with a copy of a textbook in his or her hand,
ready to work through the various lessons. The marketer starts with a quite specific environment –
which will immediately limit the range of factors to
be explored to a small subset of the hundreds explored in this volume. To the perceptive marketer,
the range of options to be explored will usually be
obvious. Beyond this, the position will be further
constrained by the resources that are available to deal
with them. For instance, theory always says that the
first step is marketing research, but if your competitor has just made a major change in strategy you may
have just days to react – whereas research may take
months. Real-life marketing, therefore, revolves
around the application of a great deal of common
sense, to handle a limited number of factors based on
imperfect information and limited resources (complicated by uncertainty and tight timescales). The
use of marketing techniques, in these circumstances,
is inevitably partial and uneven. Thus, for example,
new products will emerge from irrational processes,
and the rational development process may be used (if
at all) to screen out the worst non-runners. The
design of the advertising, and the packaging, will be
the output of the creative minds employed; this
management will screen, often by 'gut-reaction', to
ensure that it is reasonable. The successful marketer

will, in this context, be the one who trains his or her 'gut-reaction' to simulate that of the average customer! Waitrose (the supermarket part of the John Lewis Partnership), for example, see their market as the 'discerning customer'. This is fortunate, since they deliberately shun conventional marketing. Their marketing is, in effect, handled by their buyers, who buy to match their own tastes. As they are themselves people of 'discernment', this means that their 'gut-reaction' is very close to that of their customers – or at least of those potential customers who have chosen by self-selection to share their choices! The marketers who have to satisfy the needs and wants of consumers who are very different to themselves have a much more difficult job. The upper-class, middle-aged marketing manager who is trying to think himself under the skin of the young buyer of disposable nappies has as tough a job as any method actor ever had trying to work up a part under the gaze of Stanislavsky! It is possible, but this is where you really need the market research results to guide you around the psyche of that consumer. The one time, perhaps, when the marketing processes can be, and often are, thought through with the deliberation expected by writers of textbooks is during the annual planning process that leads to the overall marketing strategy. At that time, it may be possible to devote the necessary effort to thinking through all of the factors that impinge on the product or service. For most of his or her time, however, the marketing manager is likely to be using his or her considerable intelligence to analyse and handle the complex, and unique, situations being faced – without easy reference to theory. This will often be by 'flying by the seat of the pants', or 'gut-reaction'; where the overall strategy, coupled with knowledge of the customer, which has been absorbed almost by a process of osmosis, will determine the quality of the marketing employed. This, almost instinctive, management is called 'coarse marketing', to distinguish it from the refined, aesthetically pleasing, form favoured by the theorists. It is often relatively crude and would, if given in answer to a marketing examination, be judged a failure of marketing. On the other hand, it is the real-life world of most marketing!

See also ADVERTISING; BUYING DECISION, ADVERTISING MODELS; CONVICTION MARKETING

Coca Cola *see* CLIENT/AGENCY RELATIONSHIP; CONVICTION MARKETING; CONVICTION MARKETING FACTORS; GLOBALIZATION; GLOBAL MARKETING; INTERNATIONAL PRODUCT DECISION; MESSAGE, ADVERTISING; TRANSNATIONALS/MULTINATIONALS AND EXPORTERS

Coca Cola commercials *see* ECONOMIES OF SCALE, GLOBAL

Coca Cola local bottlers *see* LICENSING

coding of questionnaire answers *see* OPEN QUESTIONS, ON QUESTIONNAIRES

cognitive dissonance One, perhaps unexpected, feature of 'audience behaviour' was reported by Leon Festinger (1957). This is that interest in all forms of promotion, particularly of advertising, reaches a maximum after the consumer has made his or her purchase. The usual explanation for this apparently illogical behaviour is that the consumer is then searching for the proof that will justify his or her recent decision. In looking at the competitive advertising, say, the consumer is trying to seek out its flaws, in comparison with the chosen product or service, in order to obtain reassurance that the decision was the correct one. The importance from the advertiser's point of view is that advertising still has a job to do even after the sale has been made! In addition, the messages needed to address cognitive dissonance may be subtly different – they will provide reassurance, and will allow for the fact that these purchasers will also represent the main source of future sales.

See also ADVERTISING; BUYING DECISION, ADVERTISING MODELS

Reference: Festinger L. A. (1957) *A Theory of Cognitive Dissonance.* New York: Row, Peterson & Co.

cognitive mapping This is a graphical technique that provides a visual framework for setting down an individual's system of beliefs about a situation; and, in particular, the relationship between these beliefs.
See also NEW PRODUCT CREATION

cognitive stage The stage in the consumer decision process that draws his or her attention to the products or services offered and creates awareness.
See also AFFECTIVE STAGE; CONATIVE STAGE

cold calls *see* CALL TARGETS; CALLS AVAILABLE ANNUALLY; TELESALES

cold calls, prospects *see* SEMINARS; TERRITORY SALES PLAN

cold calls, telephone calls   *see* TELESALES

cold sales call in advertising models   *see* BUYING DECISION, ADVERTISING MODELS

colour separation   The process, now usually electronic, in which the full colour images are broken down separately into the primary colours that are needed for the plates to be used in, say, four-colour printing.

colour supplement   *see* MEDIA IMPACT

column   A (vertical) section of a newspaper, filled with printed editorial or advertisements.
See also MEDIA IMPACT; MEDIA SELECTION; MEDIA TYPES

combative repositioning   *see* LONGER-TERM COMPETITIVE SAW

combination   A block that combines both line and screen.
See also BLOCKS; SCREEN

combination door-to-door   *see* DOOR-TO-DOOR

commando selling   Intensive selling by a specialist sales team, typically over a short period and by an outside, contract sales force.
See also PROSPECT QUALIFICATION; SALES CALL

commercial break   *see* BREAK

commercial intelligence   *see* INTERNATIONAL MARKETING RESEARCH

commercials   *see* ADVERTISING AGENCY ELEMENTS; ADVERTISING PROCESSES; CREATIVE DEPARTMENT, ADVERTISING AGENCY

commercials, testing   *see* ADVERTISING RESEARCH

commercial traveller   An earlier name for a salesman, who travelled around his territory.
See also SALESMAN STEREOTYPE; SALES PROFESSIONAL

commission, agency   *see* AGENCY CHOICE

commission on business   *see* AGENTS OR DISTRIBUTORS

commission, sales personnel   *see* MOTIVATION, OF SALES PERSONNEL; TERRITORY PLANS

commitment   *see* CONVICTION MARKETING; MARKETING PLAN BENEFITS

commodity market   *see* COMPETITIVE PRICING; MARKET ENTRY TACTICS

commodity price   *see* EQUILIBRIUM PRICE; PRICE ELASTICITY OF DEMAND; PRICE FACTORS; PRICE, PURCHASE; PRICES, CUSTOMER NEEDS

Commodore Pet   *see* CONVICTION MARKETING TYPES

commoners   *see* GLOBAL MARKETING

common values   *see* CULTURE, ORGANIZATIONAL

communication   *see* MARKETING PLAN BENEFITS; SELLING

communication ability   *see* LEADERSHIP, OF SALES PERSONNEL; PLANNING PITFALLS

communication budget   *see* SELLING

communication model   *see* ENCODING

communication processes   *see* INADEQUACIES IN PLANNING

communication sources   *see* SECONDARY SOURCES OF COMMUNICATION

communications to 'stakeholders'   *see* CORPORATE PUBLIC RELATIONS

communicators   *see* CONVICTION MARKETING FACTORS

communist bloc   *see* MICROECONOMICS

community contact   *see* CORPORATE PUBLIC RELATIONS

community experience   *see* PEER PYRAMID

company magazines   *see* CORPORATE PUBLIC RELATIONS

company name   *see* BRANDING POLICIES

company officials and public relations   *see* PUBLIC RELATIONS company orientations   *see* ORGANIZATIONAL (MARKETING) ORIENTATIONS

comparative advantage, global Production can be located in those countries that have the most favourable cost or quality factors; just as the computer-component industries have established plants in Taiwan. Indeed, it should be noted in passing that conventional economic theory explains the whole of international trade on this basis. One country has a 'absolute advantage' over another in terms of producing a specific product, because the factors of production are more favourable (lower wage costs, material costs, capital costs, etc.). In bilateral trade, therefore, the country with the absolute advantage will export one product, in return for products for which another country has an absolute advantage. As with most economic theories, this is then overlaid with additional levels of complexity – to try to explain why real life is not the same as the basic theory describes! In practice, the patterns that emerge in the developed world are very much more complex; particularly where the now almost random fluctua-tions in the international money markets (often led by government intervention) make the scale of such 'absolute advantage' difficult to gauge. In any case, the global organizations seem to carry this 'absolute advantage' with them; and base their country-by-country allocations of production and other functions on factors other than simple price advantage.

On the other hand, management accounting in a multinational context has signally failed to reach the levels of useful information provision that are now deemed essential at the national level. As Kenneth Simmonds (1985) comments:

Rather than relying on transfer prices to signal cost information indirectly and inefficiently, a direct indication of short and long-term cost–volume–profit relationships would enable market units to propose actions that would fit an overall strategy. Management accounting has traditionally advocated the use of cost–volume–profit data within the single market firm. But management accounting within multinationals has not moved to provide system-wide cost–volume–profit relationships. There is no body of literature about how to transmit and use international cost–volume–profit data. In fact, there is nothing about how management accountants might construct cost–volume–profit calculations on a system basis for multi-plant multinationals with all the differences in costs and currencies this implies.

Thus, a comparative disadvantage may simply appear to occur because all the developmental (and/or head office) overheads are being charged against the home country. In any case, as IBM found with its PC, providing low-cost countries with experience in new technology can also very quickly lead to the creation of new international competitors!

Additionally, as Yoram Wind (1986) points out, 'there is no evidence that consumers are becoming universally more price conscious. In fact some of the products often viewed as global are fairly expensive – Cartier watches, Louis-Vuitton handbags or Canon cameras. Furthermore, the desirability of focusing on price positioning is very questionable.'

See also ECO-NOMIES OF SCALE, GLOBAL; GLOBALIZATION; GLOBAL MARKETING

References: Simmonds, Kenneth (1985) Global strategy: achieving the geocentric ideal. *International Marketing Review*, Spring.

Wind, Yoram (1986) The myth of globalization. *Journal of Marketing*, 3(2).

compensation plans   *see* MOTIVATION, OF SALES PERSONNEL

compensation trading   *see* COUNTERTRADING

competition   *see* COMPETITIVE SAW; NEW PRODUCT NEEDS; PROMOTIONAL MIX FACTORS

competition, global   *see* ECONOMIES OF SCALE, GLOBAL; GLOBALIZATION

competition, lack of   *see* SERVICE CULTURES

competition pricing   Apart from the competence of the supplier, in terms of the ability to match price to the consumers' 'perceived value', probably the major factor to affect price is competition. What the direct competitors, in particular, charge for their comparable products is bound to be taken into consideration by the consumers, if not by the producers. This, though, is just one aspect of managing competition. One response to price competition, therefore, should be to examine whether there are ways of 'managing' this to reduce its impact; and to signal to competitors that your response is not aggressive. Direct competition may be rare in the non-profit sectors, but indirect competition is not; and many of the same techniques can be applied. If, say, you are trying to attract people to keep-fit classes, you may have to persuade them that the 'value' of these is more than that of an alternative, which may be a session of bingo!

See also PRICE COMPETITION; PRICE FACTORS

competitions   *see* NON-PRICE PROMOTIONS; PROMOTION OBJECTIVES

competitions, sales incentive schemes   *see* MOTIVATION, OF SALES PERSONNEL

competition, third markets   *see* LICENSING

competitive advantage   *see* CONVICTION MARKETING TYPES; MAKE OR BUY; MARKET GAP ANALYSIS; MESSAGE, ADVERTISING; MISSION; POSITION DRIFT

competitive advantage, advertising   *see* COGNITIVE DISSONANCE

competitive advantage, global   *see* STANDARDIZATION VERSUS ADAPTATION

competitive gap   This is the gap between actual and potential sales resulting from your competitive performance. It typically represents what is left after the other 'gaps' (usage, distribution and product) have been taken into account. This is the share of business achieved among similar products, sold in the same market segment, and with similar distribution patterns; or at least, in any comparison, after such effects have been discounted. Needless to say, it is not a factor in the case of the monopoly provision of services by the public sector. It represents the effects of factors such as price and promotion – both the absolute level and the effectiveness of its messages. It is what marketing is popularly supposed to be about. But the product or service itself will still be the prime focus of marketing activity.

See also DISTRIBUTION GAP; GAP ANALYSIS; PRODUCT (OR SERVICE) GAP; USAGE GAP

competitive parity   *see* BUDGETS

competitive position   *see* GE (GENERAL ELECTRIC) MATRIX; THREE CHOICE BOX

competitive pricing   This form of pricing, which is most usually based on evidence from the market, is one in which product prices are determined by reference to the prices of competitive products. Where the product is a follower rather than a market leader, this may well be realistic. A sound appreciation of competitive actions – especially prices – is necessary for the most effective strategies to be formulated. The most effective marketing manager will, however, try to develop an understanding of the various competitive positions; based on an appreciation of the customer needs. A market leader should take advantage of the power that position offers, and a niche marketer should be able to use that uniqueness of positioning to gain some control over prices. In a 'brand monopoly' the marketer may have a significant degree of control over prices. In a commodity market, on the other hand, no control at all may be available. Once more, the marketer has to make a judgement as to the 'price elasticity of demand' (in this case in the context of competitors' prices). The position is usually more complex than participants allow for. Products or services, and, in particular, brands, are rarely identical. Each will have its special features; presumably developed by its management to meet some market need. Each, therefore, may justify a premium; a degree of differentiation in its pricing. Setting the optimal premium is the subject of considerable skill; and not a little bravery.

The 'easy' answer, chosen by many suppliers, is to match or preferably undercut their competitors. The problem is that all of the participants can only have the lowest price if they all have the same price; and that is usually a commodity based price – which is significantly lower than that which should be achieved where products or services are marketed effectively. Such 'commodity'-based markets do exist. Paradoxically, one of the most technically sophisticated markets, that of the IBM-compatible personal computer, has now to a degree become just such a commodity market; because many of the participants – in this case the dealers rather than the manufacturers – lacked the skills to handle any marketing approach other than price-cutting. In markets in which there are many suppliers, the skill is in knowing what 'premium' over the commodity price the chosen 'marketing mix' will justify. In markets in which there are a limited number of major products or services, it is arguable that an understanding of the psychology of the competitors is just as important. What will be their reaction to any price changes? If you put up your price, will they follow, taking advantage of the extra profit margin to be gained, or will they hold back, hoping to gain market share and volume? Again, it is all too easy to assume that all competitors will take the latter option, and aim for increased market share. The reality may be that a number of them, including the most sophisticated (who may offer the main competitive threat), will appreciate that their profit stands to gain more from a premium price than from marginally increased sales. A specific example of competitive pricing occurs in the retail sector, where 'leader pricing' is sometimes employed. The prices of certain lines are deliberately set low (perhaps even making a loss – when the line becomes a 'loss leader') to attract customers into the store. The intention is that these customers will then also buy other lines, on which the real profit will be made. You should note that the practice may be invalidated by customers realizing what is happening and, in any case, ethical objections have resulted in the 'loss leader' approach being made illegal in certain parts of the USA.

See also COMPETITION PRICING; COST-PLUS PRICING; MARKETING STRATEGIES; PRICE, PURCHASE; PRICING POLICIES, PRACTICAL

competitive relationships   *see* INTER-ORGANIZATIONAL RELATIONS

competitive saw   The product life cycle (PLC) is not effective at describing the changes that regularly occur in the stable market. The technique that has been developed for this is called the 'competitive saw':

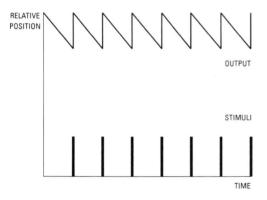

The principles involved are very simple, as is indicated by the chart above.

The first is quite simply that every 'stimulus' (every investment, be it an advertising or promotional campaign or a new feature added to the 'product') results, after a short delay, in a rapid improvement in 'output', the product or service's posi-

tion (typically directly in terms of its competitive position, and indirectly in terms of sales levels).

The second is that this advantage is then steadily diluted as competitors invest in their own activities, and the performance level (the competitive advantage or sales) slowly drops until the next stimulus is applied. Because of the competitive aspect and because it largely removes variations due to seasonality, etc., the measurements are usually in terms of relative share (although absolute figures may also be used).

This is a very simplified model of what actually happens, although something approaching it can be observed in practice (which is not the case with the PLC that it replaces), but even so it offers a number of benefits:

*   *Intimations of mortality*. It very effectively replaces the one important function of the PLC, that of reminding managers that there will be no future if they do not look after their brands, and continue to invest in them – but it does this more directly, and without the drawbacks of the other model.
*   *Timescaling*. On much the same theme, it is an ever-present reminder that you cannot neglect your brands, or stop investing in them, for too long.
*   *Linkage of inputs and outputs*. It encourages, and provides a framework for, managers to actively plan what inputs are needed, when, and what the outputs will be; and to determine the efficiency of conversion of inputs to outputs.
*   *Surfacing of investment*. It makes very clear the need for, and the results of, investment policies on brands. This is even more clear in the 'stepped saw'.

As the illustration below shows, there are two elements to performance. One is the average level. This is strategically most important, since it shows longer-term trends (a slowly decreasing average might be hidden by the variations in the saw):

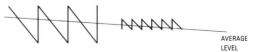

The other is the pattern of the saw itself, the time intervals and the performance variation per cycle, which determine the tactical approach.

The saw should not lull you into expecting regularity. Different stimuli will have different impacts, and will be more or less efficient, so the saw will be a jagged one:

As the saw is primarily an illustration of the impact of short-term investments, the main criterion will be which of the stimuli available will result in the most efficient investment pattern (which, advertising or new features say, will produce the greatest impact for the same amount of money), although a mix of stimuli will usually produce the highest efficiency overall.

The three main lessons of the competitive saw are the importance of relative performance, its time-related nature and the investments that lie underneath.

See also ADVERTISING OBSOLESCENCE; COMPETITION; INVESTMENT MULTIPLIER; PRODUCT LIFE CYCLE (PLC); STEPPED SAW

competitive strategy   *see* GLOBALIZATION

competitive structures   *see* MARKETING PLANNING, ANALYSIS

competitors   *see* BUDGETS; SWOT ANALYSIS

competitors, drift   *see* POSITION DRIFT

competitors, innovation   *see* CREATIVE IMITATION; LEAPFROG

competitors, price   *see* COMPETITIVE PRICING

complaints   Godley (1975) states that 'it is essential to record all complaints and the manner in which they are dealt with'. This may seem obvious, but even the Open University Business School found to its surprise, and dismay, that its students had no formal means of complaint; and this was only discovered when the students managed to find alternative, unofficial means. 'Customer complaints' is one of the most important aspects of business operations needing management control, yet it is often one of the most neglected. Such complaints are often treated as a nuisance by many organizations, and yet they have considerable value, for a number of reasons:

1. Although there will always be a small proportion of 'frivolous complaints', a complaint usually highlights something that has gone wrong with a part of the overall marketing operation; usually, the high quality, which should be a fundamental requirement for most organizations, has not been achieved. Whatever the reason, the sensible marketer will want to know exactly what has gone wrong, so that remedial actions may be taken.
2. The way in which a complaint is handled is often seen by customers, and their many contacts, as an acid test of the true quality of support. What is more, it is also a powerful reminder to the organization's own staff of just how important quality is.
3. Not least, customers who complain are usually loyal customers (those who are not loyal tend just to switch to another supplier), and will continue to be loyal (and valuable) customers, just as long as their complaint is handled well.

The first rule is that complaints should be positively encouraged. Theodore Levitt (1983) states that 'One of the surest signs of a bad or declining relationship [with a customer] is the absence of complaints from the customer. Nobody is ever that satisfied, especially over an extended period of time. The customer is not being candid or not being contacted.' That is not the same as saying that the reasons for complaints should be encouraged. However, assuming that despite your best efforts the problem has occurred, you should put nothing in the way of any customer who wants to complain; and, indeed, you should positively encourage such complaints – since the main difficulty lies with the many more customers who do not complain (and instead change to another supplier), rather than with the few who might abuse the complaints system.

Hart et al. (1990) report that, in the USA, 'Many businesses have established "800" numbers so customers can report problems easily and at the company's expense. American Express has installed such lines and estimates it achieves responses more quickly and at 10% to 20% of the cost of handling the correspondence.' General Electric has gone further still, by providing a centralized (expert), round the clock, general support service; which anyone who just has a query – not even a complaint – about one of its products may call free of charge.

The second rule is that all complaints should be carefully handled by painstakingly controlled, and monitored, procedures. Complaints must be handled well, and must be seen to be well handled – by the complainant, and by the organization's own staff.

The third, and most important rule, is that the complaint should then be fully investigated, and the cause remedied. Complaints are only symptoms – the disease needs to be cured. There may be an understandable temptation to overlook complaints until they reach a 'significant level' – but holding off until the complaints reach this 'pain level' usually means that they have already become damaging to the organization's image. It is far better to assume that 'one complaint is too many'!

So much for theory. The reality in most organizations is very different. The number of complaints are minimized, not by remedying the reasons for them but by evading the complainants! The assumption is usually made, wrongly so, that complainants are trouble-makers, and have to be handled in a confrontational manner!

See also MONITORING, PROGRESS; SERVICE LEVELS; SERVICE QUALITY

References: Godley, C. G. A. (1975) Marketing control. In E. F. L. Brech (ed.), *The Principles and Practice of Management*. London: Longman.
Hart, Christopher W. L., Heskett, James L. and Sasser, W. Earl Jr (1990) The profitable art of service recovery. *Harvard Business Review*, July–August.
Levitt, Theodore (1983) After the sale is over. *Harvard Business Review*, September–October.

complementary diversification *see* ANSOFF MATRIX

complementary relationships, brands *see* MARKETING RESEARCH, PRECISION MARKETING

complementary repositioning *see* LONGER-TERM COMPETITIVE SAW

complexity, role of sales personnel *see* CONTROL, OF SALES PERSONNEL; MOTIVATION, OF SALES PERSONNEL

complex sale The professional salesman is more likely to come into contact with a 'complex sale'. This is a sale where a number of individuals are involved in the buying decision, and the sales campaign is extended over a number of calls. Miller, Heiman and Tuleja (1975) define it as follows: 'A Complex Sale is one in which several people must give their approval before the sale can take place.' However, they go on to expand this comment: 'In a complex sale, you have short-term and long-term objectives. In the short term, you must close as many individual deals as you possibly can, and as quickly as possible. In the long term, you want to maintain healthy relations with the customers signing the deals, so they'll be willing to make further purchases in the months and years to come. It would be great if these two objectives always coincided, but you know that they don't.' Thus, in many ways, this environment is very different to that of the single call sale, which is the staple diet of many (if not most) sales trainers. Again, as Miller, Heiman and Tuleja put it: 'Because most sales-training programs emphasise tactical rather than strategic skills, even very good salespeople sometimes find themselves cut out of a sale at the last minute because they failed to locate or cover all the real decision makers for their specific sale.'

The complexity of the changing influences in a complex sale over time can be shown in the model below:

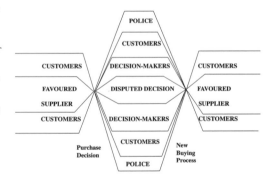

Here, in the period of the 'disputed decision' when the supplier is changing, three main groups are involved:

- *Customers*: the people who actually use the product or service and who, for most of the time, are the main contact with the supplier.
- *Decision-makers*: those in authority who have the formal responsibility for decision, and who may be quite separate from the customers.
- *Police*: the various departments (such as purchasing and quality control) who can veto the decision

if certain standards (such as price limits or quality levels) are not met.

This diagram overstresses the time devoted to such decision-making. For most of the time, probably more than 90 per cent of the total, the winner of the disputed purchase decision becomes the 'favoured supplier', dealing only with the 'customers' in the diagram above, usually the direct customers or end-users who make use of the product or service – with no serious challengers in sight. Perhaps the best way of looking at this simple on-going relationship is through the picture provided by the 'competitive saw', which also provides the necessary incentive to keep that relationship fresh – that is, until something undermines the customer's confidence in the arrangement (most usually as a result of a significant failure on the part of the supplier). Then, as shown above, the more complex – decision-making – phase is entered upon. In that phase, the other two sets of actors enter the scene.

See also COMPETITIVE SAW; CONTROL, OF SALES PERSONNEL; DECISION-MAKERS AND INFLUENCERS; DEMONSTRATIONS; PARTNERSHIP TRIANGLE; PROJECT MANAGEMENT; PROPOSALS; SAFETY IN NUMBERS; SALES PROFESSIONAL; SELLING; TERRITORY MANAGEMENT; TERRITORY SALES PLAN

Reference: Miller, Robert B., Heiman, Stephen E. and Tuleja, Tad (1985) *Strategic Selling*. New York: William Morrow.

computer conferences   *see* COMPUTER-MEDIATED COMMUNICATIONS (CMC)

computer database information   *see* IN-HOUSE DATA, PRECISION MARKETING

computer inventory control   This is now, generally speaking, the modern equivalent of the card systems of inventory control. It is, incidentally, usually a misnomer; since in most cases it is in reality only a stock-recording method. As with the card systems, it merely states (based on the movements in and out) what the balance of stock is. In the more sophisticated versions, it will also allow for on-order and back-order items. All of these are records of what has happened. The stock control – the decision as to what amount to reorder and when – remains the responsibility of the humans using the information; but the computer helps by providing a reminder when the stock falls below the minimum or reorder point, and provides assistance with some of the calculations, such as the economic order quantity

(EOQ). In the service industries it usually also shows the 'slots' (usually time-based, even in terms of theatre bookings) that are available at some time in the future.

See also INVENTORY CONTROL; MATERIALS REQUIREMENTS PLANNING (MRP)

computer listings   *see* DATA MANIPULATION, PRECISION MARKETING

computer mail   *see* ELECTRONIC DIRECT MAIL

computer marketing   *see* DELIVERY SYSTEMS, PRECISION MARKETING

computer-mediated communications (CMC)
One important vehicle for precision marketing, which is likely to emerge as the century draws to a close, is that of computer communication. The essential features of the more advanced CMC systems are described by Tony Kaye et al.:

> Most CMC systems provide an integrated range of facilities. These generally include:
>
> - electronic mail for one-to-one communications
> - one or more of asynchronous group communications (conferences)
> - a 'chat' mode for real-time exchange of short messages with other users
> - a directory of all users, with their resumés and information on when they last accessed the system
> - a directory of all listed conferences, and brief details of each one . . .

These technical characteristics give it, of course, many of the characteristics to make it the ideal vehicle for precision marketing. It can be used to 'talk' individually to thousands of contacts (simultaneously if necessary) – and all of the power of the accumulated database information is immediately available. More importantly, perhaps, it has the potential to be a new medium of communications, positioned midway between individual communications and the mass media; enabling thousands to talk together in one group. It is a future development that has implications for many organizations, and as such is well worth tracking.

See also PRECISION MARKETING

Reference: Mason, Robin (1989) An evaluation of COSY on an Open University course. In Robin Mason and Tony Kaye (eds), *Mindweave: Communications, Computers and Distance Education*. Oxford: Pergamon.

computer-readable data, precision marketing *see* DATA AVAILABILITY, PRECISION MARKETING

conative stage The last stage of the consumer decision-making process, which results in action. *See also* AFFECTIVE STAGE; COGNITIVE STAGE

concentrated marketing *see* NICHE; SEGMENTATION; SEGMENTATION METHODS

concentration ratio A measure of the extent to which a market is controlled by a small number of suppliers. *See also* COMPETITION

concept-based development *see* GLOBALIZATION

concept testing *see* ADVERTISING RESEARCH; COPY TESTING

concept test, new products This (marketing research) technique is used to test the viability of new product ideas (concepts), before any large investments have been made. Research has shown that more than 80 per cent of new product ideas fail. The proportion which never make it into development is probably at least as high; so that, overall, possibly less than 5 per cent of new product ideas are successful. It is important, therefore, that the 95 per cent of failures are culled as early as possible – before large sums are invested in them. The most widely quoted, and indeed definitive, research has been that conducted by Booz, Allen & Hamilton (1981). It showed that, in 1981, only one in seven (1:7) new product ideas resulted in a successful new product introduction. It is perhaps even more interesting that this was a dramatic improvement on their equivalent survey of 1968; when the success rate was only 1 in 58 (1:58). It appears that this dramatic improvement may have come about because of the improvement in screening procedures, at the earliest stage of the new product process – an improvement that may have been partly stimulated by that earlier report! Indeed, in the later report they note that, once launched, the success rate of new products had not varied (at 65 per cent). Beyond this, their research showed the following factors contributing to the success of new products:

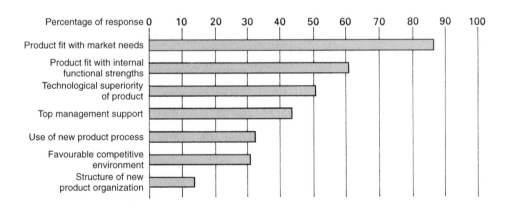

They also found a significant 'learning curve' ('experience effect'), where each doubling of the number of new products introduced apparently led to a decline in the cost of introduction by 29 per cent. John Stapleton (1989) illustrates graphically how the new ideas are progressively screened out (and the costs start to escalate) as they move through the overall new product process:

The 'concept test' is the first true consumer filter applied during the product development process. At least in theory, it should be applied before any significant amount of product development is undertaken; particularly as such development can be very expensive – perhaps running into hundreds of millions of dollars for a new pharmaceutical, and billions for a totally new airliner. The concept test is usually undertaken by conventional market research. It simply aims to find out from consumers what their attitudes to the new 'product' would be, and – the acid test – whether they would be likely to buy it. This is easier said than done, because consumers will not usually be able to draw upon existing experiences.

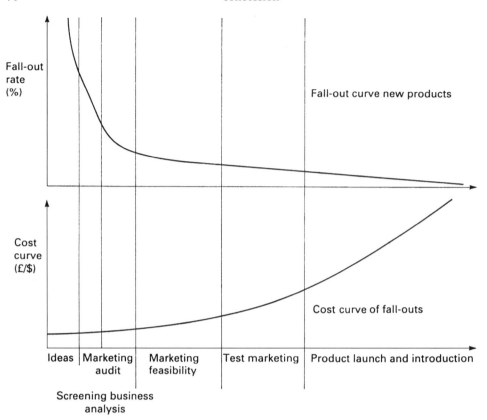

Fall-out
rate
(%)

Fall-out curve new products

Cost
curve
(£/$)

Cost curve of fall-outs

Ideas | Marketing | Marketing | Test marketing | Product launch and introduction
         audit   feasibility

Screening business
analysis

They have enough difficulty communicating how they feel about brands that they have actually purchased. Deciding how they might feel about future 'concepts' is obviously that much more difficult; particularly where the decision is divorced from the real-life situation.

Market researchers use a battery of different techniques to try to overcome the problem. They may produce dummy versions of the product. It is more likely that they may produce a rough commercial, perhaps just in 'storyboard' form; since this also reflects the difficulty of conveying the concept to the consumers – always a major consideration for a really innovative product. If you cannot describe it in an advertisement, you almost certainly will not be able to sell it! Be it a TV commercial or a press advertisement, the better finished the vehicle used to carry the concept is, the more representative are the responses from the consumers involved likely to be (although this obviously increases the cost – and may defeat the whole purpose of the concept test!). Despite the lack of precision in any of these techniques, they are useful in weeding out the products or services that

have little chance of success. This is potentially very valuable, since their creators, who have probably fought many hard battles to reach even this stage, usually can no longer be considered to be objective. In more sophisticated consumer markets, the 'concept' might be explored in the same way (and in almost as much detail) as any 'product'. In particular, it would be likely that the concept would be tested to see how it matched up to the required 'position' in the market. There are commercially available 'packages' that run very sophisticated concept tests, using these more complex (and computer-based) research techniques.

See also PRODUCT DEVELOPMENT PROCESS

References: Booz, Allen & Hamilton Inc. (1981) *New Products Management for the 1980s.*
Stapleton, John (1989) *How to Prepare a Marketing Plan* (4th edn). Aldershot: Gower Press.

concession   The right to be the only seller of a particular product or service in a location.
See also RETAILING

concession close *see* CLOSING TECHNIQUES

conditional probability *see* BAYESIAN DECISION THEORY

conferences and symposia Once there are more than, say, 20 attendees, a meeting ceases to be inter-active in any way. Even in the coffee breaks, the majority of prospects will be talking to each other rather than to one of the staff. As a result, the main requirement for larger 'conferences' (or symposia) is that the content of the presentations must carry the whole event. This means that you will have to very carefully select your speakers; for it is now their quality, and that alone, that delegates will remember – and judge you by. The sales messages becomes very indirect – unless it is a product launch meeting, which is a separate type of event. To a degree, it is the style of the meeting, which is often set almost as much by the details as by the overall importance of the subject matter, which is seen as your contribution. As such, the setting may become important. The main fact to keep in mind, though, is just how much effort needs to be put into such a conference. David Seekings (1981) stresses the point: 'Meetings are expensive. They absorb precious time and money. It is estimated that it takes over 300 executive man hours to arrange a two–day conference of about 200 people. Add to that secretarial time, administrative costs . . . it is sensible to ask whether a meeting is needed at all.'

See also DEMONSTRATIONS; PROMOTION; SELLING

Reference: Seekings, David (1981) *How to Organise Effective Conferences and Meetings*. London: Kogan Page.

conferences, computer *see* COMPUTER–MEDIATED COMMUNICATIONS (CMC)

conference style *see* PRESENTATION STYLE

confrontation *see* INTER–ORGANIZATIONAL RELATIONS

conglomerate diversification *see* ANSOFF MATRIX

conjoint analysis This technique looks, for example, at the combinations of product attributes (or groupings of them) that the customers would favour (and estimates the 'trade-offs' between them which the respondents are willing to make in the final purchase decision); in the process determining the im-portance of each and, hence, the most productive combinations. Indeed, its most important use is in sorting out the relative importance of a product's multidimensional attributes. The essence of the technique is that it overcomes the theoretical need to test for all of the combinations and permutations of possible attributes, by testing only a limited (but still large) number of these in pairs, to establish the level of interest in each element of these combinations, and then using sophisticated computer analysis to abstract/extrapolate the details relating to each of the individual factors. In this way, the final picture can be constructed without incurring totally exorbitant costs.

See also ANALYSIS OF MARKETING RESEARCH DATA

conquest marketing This term refers to pro-grammes, originally developed by the US automo-bile industry, aimed at acquiring market share and sales at the expense of your competitors, based on a marketing strategy that targets users or prospective users of a competitive product.

See also COMPETITION; GLOBALIZATION

consignment note This is the documentation (sometimes called a waybill) that accompanies a con-signment of goods from the supplier to the customer.

See also INVENTORY CONTROL

consistency, services *see* PROMOTION OF SERVICES

constrained choice model *see* PRICING, PRODUCT POSITIONING

constructive following *see* DEDICATED FOLLOWERS

constructs, outputs *see* HOWARD AND SHETH MODEL, OF CONSUMER BEHAVIOUR

consultancies, and marketing research Some large-scale surveys (such as the Taylor Nelson Monitor or MRB's Target Group Index (TGI) in the UK) are run to provide data for the research organization alone. The analysed output, in the form of reports (or computer-readable data), is then sold to a variety of buyers; and the cost of the survey is recouped in this way. These surveys may offer a very cost-effective way of building a database of survey information. TGI, for example, monitors some 5000 brands, as well as 200 attitude statements, across 45 000 interviews each year.

This data can provide a profile of an individual brand (in terms of its consumer profile, including sophisticated 'lifestyle' data derived from the attitude statements, as well as readership data and usage of complementary products, and the same data on competitive products) for as little as £20000 per annum.

See also CUSTOM RESEARCH; MARKETING RESEARCH; OMNIBUS SURVEYS; PANEL RESEARCH; RETAIL AUDITS; SUBCONTRACTORS, MARKETING RESEARCH

consultants   Although, ideally, you should use your own staff, who best know your organization and its environment, there may still be some reasons for buying in an outside viewpoint – that of a consultant. Leonard Guss (1986) summarizes the main reasons as follows:

> *Objectivity.* The consultant ideally is unencumbered by the conventional wisdom of the company or industry regarding what cannot be done or by previous postures and decisions which limit flexibility. This is the 'new broom' approach . . .
> *Broad point of view.* The management of a single company may become narrow in its viewpoint, entrapped in its knowledge of what had been done and did not succeed or what succeeded in the past, without recognizing that times have changed. Management views are also circumscribed by the 'culture' of the company, which has encouraged and revealed certain ways of perceiving and acting, while discouraging or punishing others. The marketing consultant can render valuable service by helping to redefine the nature of the business the client is in, and the changing nature of the competition.

In other words, outsiders can bring in new views to rejuvenate flagging or entrenched ideas. This outside viewpoint can, however, be obtained by a number of other means, which may sometimes offer better value:

- *Non-executive directors.* Hiring board members from outside, with suitable experience and knowledge (indeed, much the same as that of a consultant), can provide the organization with the alternative perspective – often at considerably less cost and on an on-going basis (such that the non-executive director becomes increasingly knowledgeable in the organization's affairs).

- *Customers and suppliers.* If the organization indulges in 'customer and supplier partnership', the same, broader (and challenging) viewpoints may be obtained from their directors – often, and very effectively indeed, for the price of a good lunch!
- *Educational institutions.* Many business schools welcome the opportunity to become involved with their local organizations. This may be on a consultancy basis (but usually at very competitive rates!), but the main benefit to the school, and especially to the organization, is the exchange of experience.

Consultants may also be hired to provide specialist skills that the organization does not possess. Leonard Guss, again, explains:

> *Overloaded internal staff . . .* It is good business practice not to have a staff as large as to be able simultaneously to attack every problem that can arise. This avoids large staff expenditures for make-work or trivial studies during off-peak periods . . .
> *Newer skills and techniques . . .* they offer expertise as a service, they can cultivate it to a greater degree than is often found with the smaller firm . . . No company can afford to maintain, continuously, skills and services of which it has infrequent needs . . .

The perils of using consultants
The use of consultants is not always without its problems, some of which derive from the fact that consultancy is a (profit-making) business like any other:

- *The next sale.* Having put their foot firmly in your door, the first task of any commercially oriented consultant is to find (and then to discreetly 'sell') the next piece of consultancy. Only then do such consultants feel comfortable enough to move on to what the client sees as the real work! The problem for that client is that there may, accordingly, be a significant, if not immediately obvious, mismatch of interests!
- *Gimmicks.* It is an unfortunate fact of life that some consultants (especially the less well-known ones) need the promotional benefits offered by a USP – in this context often better described as a gimmick! This 'technique' differentiates them from their competitors, in a valid marketing move with which you will no doubt sympathize. The

problem for you, the client, comes when the consultant then feels obliged to apply this technique regardless of its relevance to your specific problems.

- *Lack of knowledge.* The consultant will often start with relatively little knowledge of the organization and, with a few notable exceptions, will probably not have the time or resources to develop more than a perfunctory insight during the brief time of his or her commission. There is, therefore, a very real danger that they will offer the wrong solution(s), to misperceived problems and, even more importantly, they may overlook the real problems.
- *Management and staff commitment.* Much of the success of a new strategy depends upon obtaining the commitment of the whole range of management and staff who have been involved in its development, and are needed for its implementation. Apart from those given very extensive commissions, consultants can rarely afford (or are even afforded the opportunity) to become involved with such a wide range of management.

How to appoint consultants
The stages are much the same as those for appointing any outside agency:

1. *Define the need.* The most important stage of all is to determine exactly why the consultant is needed, and what their overall brief will be. The boundaries of the consultant's task must be clearly defined. Otherwise, at one extreme, they may (if they are enthusiastic, an otherwise commendable trait) take over the running of the whole business. At the other, they may even fail to address the problem which was the justification for their commission in the first place! It is fair to say, however, that you would be wise to apply the same care in defining the scope of the operation when you subcontract work to other departments within the organization.
2. *Sources.* It may not be too difficult to find the names of a number of consultants. The largest organizations are already well known (such as the Boston Consulting Group, McKinsey, etc.) or are part of the leading, and equally well-known, accountancy practices (such as Arthur Andersen, Coopers & Lybrand, DeLoitte Haskins & Sells, Peat Marwick Mitchell & Co.,

Price Waterhouse, Touche Ross, etc.). Others go to some lengths to make themselves known by writing for the leading management journals, or by conducting seminars that are widely advertised.

3. *Shortlist.* The problem lies in reducing the numbers to those suitable for shortlisting. In part, this will come about because of the specific tasks involved. If you simply want to 'subcontract' some work, which cannot be handled due to your limited resources, then it is unlikely that you will want to pay the fees of the major consultancies! If, on the other hand, you want to change the whole direction of your organization (at a cost running into millions), you probably would be ill advised simply to reach for your copy of Yellow Pages! Most consultancies will, in any case, ensure that their 'specialties' are made clear in their brochures. Beyond that, it is more a matter of deciding which consultants are – as described in their brochures – likely to match the needs, and style, of your own organization.
4. *Brief.* The brief has to give the best possible indication ('situation analysis') of what is expected of the consultants. In general, the more effort you put into preparing the brief, the better will be the consultancy work that will emerge at the end of the process.
5. *Personal visit.* Nothing beats meeting the personnel involved. They may well be on their 'best behaviour' but, at least, you will obtain some feel for how you are likely to be able to work together. This also provides the opportunity to ask whatever searching questions the written communications cannot address.
6. *The proposal.* The response from the consultants, which will often involve a presentation as well as the written report, will form the main 'evidence' for the final selection. It allows the competitors to say what they propose to offer; and, not least, to show that they have understood the brief. It will also detail their estimated charges – although the ultimate 'costs' to the organization of a failure by the consultants to resolve the problem are likely to be much higher.
7. *The decision.* Ultimately, the decision must be yours. It will be an important one, and needs to receive a corresponding amount of attention – using external consultants is rarely the 'easy option'.

Managing the relationship

The use of management consultants involves a very close business relationship. Senior management must accordingly clearly commit their support to them, and be seen to do so; otherwise, more junior staff will be tempted to withhold support – which will guarantee failure. At the same time, though, management must be in control, receiving regular progress reports, and aware of the dangers of over-commitment. The relationship should, however, be complementary; as, of course, as with any supplier.

The report

The report is ultimately what you have paid for, and the evidence on which you will take your decisions. Its receipt should, therefore, initiate some considerable analytical effort on your part (revolving around a degree of healthy scepticism), in order to take the decision(s) that had been predicated upon it. The employment of consultants does not abrogate your responsibility for taking that decision; even though, in effect, many managements may, foolishly, employ such consultants to take decisions that they are unwilling to take themselves!

See also AGENCY CHOICE; CORPORATE OBJECTIVES; MARKETING PLANS AND PROGRAMMES; MARKETING STRATEGIES; PLANNING PROCESS

Reference: Guss, Leonard M. (1986) Marketing consultants – when and how to select and use. In Victor P. Buell (ed.), *Handbook of Modern Marketing* (2nd edn). New York: McGraw-Hill.

consultants, and external data   There are a range of consultants who will take the whole information-gathering process off your hands, for a fee (usually quite a large one – so that this is, understandably, the most expensive solution).
See also EXTERNAL DATA; LIBRARIES

consumables   *see* GOODS OR CONSUMABLES

consumer   *see* CONSUMER OR CORPORATE CUSTOMER

consumer behaviour   *see* BUYING DECISION, ADVERTISING MODELS

consumer belief   *see* CONVICTION MARKETING FACTORS

consumer benefits   *see* INTEREST, ADVERTISING

consumer bodies   *see* DEFENSIVE (CORPORATE) PR

consumer bonus   *see* CREATIVE IMITATION; CUSTOMER BONUS; LEAPFROG

consumer drift   *see* POSITION DRIFT

consumer durables   These are consumer goods (such as refrigerators and cars) that have an extended life, and thus lie somewhere between consumables and investments.
See also GLOBAL MARKETING

consumer filter   *see* CONCEPT TEST, NEW PRODUCTS

consumer ideal brand   *see* SEGMENTATION METHODS

consumer, inherent characteristics   *see* SEGMENTATION

consumerism   The movement, led by activist pressure groups, which has emerged to 'champion' the rights of consumers against suppliers.

consumer or corporate customer   In terms of the basic 'dimensions' on which marketing is often organized, a fundamental split is that between sales made to individuals, the archetypal consumer in the television commercials, or to organizations, in this latter case often described as industrial sales or business-to-business selling. There may be significant differences in approach:

- *The individual consumer*, who is buying the product for his or her, or their family's, own use will typically spend less, but will be the sole decision-maker. Their suppliers, the mass consumer goods companies, will largely have to deal with such consumers by very indirect means. This requires that they listen to them, finding out about their needs as averages and in groups, by market research; and talking to them only via advertisements in the mass media.
- *Industrial sales* will, however, often be made by a face-to-face sales call, which can be afforded where the value of the individual sale is higher. The call will be made on someone who merely represents the buying organization – and who may not even be the only decision-maker. It is the nature (and extended length) of these negotiations, and the technical demands on the sales professionals involved, that frequently offer the most

characteristic difference compared with consumer goods marketing.

On the other hand, as Leslie Rodger (1984) says, 'There is no difference in principle between industrial and consumer products marketing. The difference is rather one of emphasis in the way in which the elements of the marketing mix are blended together to meet the particular needs of customers who may be a few specialized purchasers or a mass of consumers. The basic distinction lies in the purpose for which the goods are bought, i.e. goods bought for organizational purposes rather than for personal or family consumption.'

Wolf and Smith (1986) point out that the picture has become even more complex in recent years: 'In many respects the most important change may be described as the decline of the dichotomy [between consumer and capital goods] and the rise of the continuum . . . Today, garages and kitchens contain many items that bear a strong resemblance to industrial goods, both in terms of their investment and durability characteristics and in terms of the way in which we behave when we buy them. Similarly, a substantial and perhaps increasing number of industrial goods are moving to market through channels of distribution which bear a strong resemblance to the channels for consumer goods.'

See also ORGANIZATIONAL PIGEON-HOLES

Reference: Rodger, Leslie (1984) The marketing concept. In Norman A. Hart (ed.), *The Marketing of Industrial Products* (2nd edn). New York: McGraw-Hill.

Wolf, Jack and Smith, Wendell R. (1986) Market needs and market changes. In Victor P. Buell (ed.), *Handbook of Modern Marketing* (2nd edn). New York: McGraw-Hill.

consumer, product-related responses *see* SEGMENTATION

consumer recruitment *see* ENHANCED AIUAPR MODEL; PEER PYRAMID; THREE PILLARS OF THE PURCHASING PROCESS

consumer tastes *see* POSITION DRIFT

consumer trial *see* SAMPLING

consumption bundle, pricing *see* PRICES, CUSTOMER NEEDS

contact report A report of a meeting, usually between an agency and client, that summarizes the decisions taken.
See also CLIENT/AGENCY RELATIONSHIP

containerization The use of containers, packed at the supplier, for shipping overseas, on dedicated container vessels.
See also PHYSICAL DISTRIBUTION MANAGEMENT

container, reusable *see* NON-PRICE PROMOTIONS

content of messages *see* INTEREST, ADVERTISING

content, presentation *see* PRESENTATION CONTENT

contents page *see* MEDIA IMPACT

context for management activities *see* MARKETING PLAN USE

contingency plan In the context of the marketing plan, perhaps Malcolm McDonald's most interesting suggestion, and the one that is least often allowed for, is the 'contingency plan'. Few marketing plans are ever implemented exactly as intended; the marketing environment is a particularly uncertain one, so that it is essential to have full back-up plans to cover for the eventuality that some of the assumptions are proved to be incorrect. He suggests that the following questions are answered (for each assumption, in the form of a table):

Basis of Assumption
What event would have to happen to make this strategy unattractive?
Risk of such an event occurring (% or high/low etc.)
Impact if event occurs
Trigger point for action
Actual contingency action proposed

See also CORPORATE OBJECTIVES; CREATIVE IMITATION; LEAPFROG; MARKETING PLANS AND PROGRAMMES; MARKETING PLAN STRUCTURE; MARKETING STRATEGIES; PLANNING PROCESS

Reference: McDonald, Malcolm H. B. (1993) *Marketing Plans*. London: Heinemann.

continuity clubs Direct mail clubs, such as book clubs or the Reader's Digest, that maintain continuing, regular contact with their customers.
See also DIRECT MAIL; PRECISION (DIRECT) MARKETING, RETAIL

contours of equal travelling time *see* TERRITORY MANAGEMENT

contractible approach   *see* EXPORT MARKET
ELIMINATION

contract-out operations, and 'buy-in'   *see*
MAKE OR BUY

contracts   *see* LICENSING

contractual relationship   *see* STRATEGIC
(INTERNATIONAL) ALLIANCES

contractual systems channels   *see* VERTICAL
MARKETING

contra-deal   *see* RECIPROCAL TRADING

control department   *see* ADVERTISING AGENCY
ELEMENTS

controlled circulation publications   *see* PRESS
MEDIA; USERS

controlled price reduction   *see* PROMOTIONAL
PRICING

control, of sales personnel   The control of sales
personnel is complicated by factors listed under
LEADERSHIP, OF SALES PERSONNEL. All of these also
make direct control very difficult. There is one further complication:

* *Timespan.* Most sales campaigns, apart from
  those related to the simplest of consumer goods,
  now take a number of calls (especially where
  they are part of the 'complex sale'); and this process may extend over several months. The sales
  manager has to manage this process, controlling
  the interim stages without the measure of the
  final result to judge the effectiveness of these
  actions.

On the other hand, sales management does
have, in the final outcome (the sale itself), the
ultimate measure of performance. The performance
of sales personnel, more than that of almost any
other employees, can be measured with some
degree of accuracy; at least in the longer term.
Some specific techniques of control may be as
follows:

* *Regular (monthly) sales targets.* Where possible,
  performance against sales targets themselves (the
  ultimate measure) has to be monitored and con-

trolled. The shorter the timescale of this review,
always assuming that meaningful sales levels are
achievable in such an interval, the better is the
degree of control offered.
* *Regular activity targets.* As mentioned already,
  much of selling is a 'numbers game'. The numbers entering the 'sales funnel' will largely determine the results emerging at the other
  end. Controlling performance against these
  activity targets is, therefore, one way of effectively controlling the sales process between sales
  outcomes.
* *Personal contact.* Even so, the most effective
  management control remains that achieved by
  personal contact. The most productive environment for this control is often that in the sales call
  itself, with the manager accompanying (and
  listening to what happens, rather than running
  it!). The field sales manager, thus, should be
  'on the road' almost as much as his or her sales
  professionals.

The salesperson's performance is typically measured
by numbers, and in particular by sales volumes.
These numbers may be compared with:

* *Past sales.* One traditional approach is to see
  how a salesperson's sales have increased (or decreased) against the previous period (or, where
  sales are seasonal, a year ago). This makes no
  allowance, however, for the true potential of the
  territory.
* *Other personnel.* Perhaps the most prevalent approach, even if it is implicit rather then explicit, is
  to compare the performance of the individual
  with that achieved by other members of the sales
  team. This is, in any case, probably the main
  comparison that the individual him- or herself
  will make; peer pressure is a very strong motivator in sales teams. Once more, though, it does not
  take into account the relative strengths and weaknesses of the territories.
* *Targets.* Needless to say, the best measure is
  against target; which can, and should, take into
  account all the various differences between
  territories.

Marketing Improvements Limited (1988) suggest
ten key ratios for tracking sales productivity:

* sales : sales costs
* sales per salesman
* number of customers/contacts per salesman

- number of calls per day
- face-to-face time : total time
- orders : calls
- average order value
- field sales costs : total sales costs
- percentage of labour turnover
- most successful salesman : average salesman

Saul Gellerman (1990) suggests that, of these ratios, those of 'percentage of calls resulting in order' and 'average calls per order' may be the best indicators of productivity. In practice, many judgements are 'qualitative', not to say subjective. The sales manager judges his or her subordinates on the basis of what they seem to be doing and how they are doing it. This is particularly true of those involved in the sale of capital goods, where long periods may elapse between orders – and where 'management' becomes almost an act of faith. Such 'qualitative' judgements are, however, notoriously unreliable.

Hartley (1979), however, points out some of the problems in practical implementation of control procedures: 'Some salespeople are always tempted to falsify the information supplied in their reports, especially if they think the likelihood of being caught is remote. The reports most likely to be falsified are the sales call or activity reports . . . Rather than faking or falsifying a report . . . sales personnel find it more tempting to "manage" their activities so that they will look better on the report.'

See also LEADERSHIP, OF SALES PERSONNEL; PEOPLE (SALES) MANAGEMENT

References: Gellerman, Saul W. (1990) The tests of a good salesperson. *Harvard Business Review*, May–June.
    Hartley, R. F. (1979) *Sales Management*. Boston, MA: Houghton Mifflin.
    Marketing Improvements Limited (1988) *Salesplanner: 50 Forms for Systematic Sales Management*. Aldershot: Gower Press.

convenience sampling *see* QUOTA SAMPLES

convenience stores *see* LOCATION, RETAIL

convergence, global *see* GLOBALIZATION

convergent diversification *see* ANSOFF MATRIX

conversion rate, sampling *see* SAMPLING

conversion ratio *see* CALL TARGETS

conviction in advertising models *see* BUYING DECISION, ADVERTISING MODELS

conviction marketing An important – but little recognized – aspect of marketing, which is closely linked with 'message selection', is 'conviction marketing' or 'commitment marketing'. It is, in many respects, alien to most of the concepts of traditional marketing. Yet it is probably more prevalent than the genuine use of pure marketing; and arguably it is not infrequently more successful. It has a long and chequered history. The propaganda machines developed by the Nazis offered some of the most potent, and widely deplored, demonstrations of its power (and this represents one possible reason why discussion of this style of marketing is even now generally avoided). The religious 'marketing machines' had been even more effective in earlier generations (and can even now be very powerful, as is evidenced by the case of Islamic fundamentalism). In the commercial sector, though, its use has sometimes been just as powerful – and very productive! Indeed, the majority of the few truly global brands have embodied it to some degree: IBM, with its philosophy of 'Customer Service'; McDonalds, with Q. S. C. & V.; Coca Cola, with its embodiment of the American teenage dream; and Marlboro, and the wide open spaces of the frontier! In the earlier editions of his book, Philip Kotler (1976) referred to this as the 'propagandist model': 'manipulating words (rhetoric), feelings (atmospheres), and experiences (events) in a way that would capture one's devotion'. It is different to 'selling', which is conventionally seen as the main alternative to marketing, in that its focus is very firmly on the consumer – as all marketing is supposed to be – whereas the focus of 'selling' is internal (the customer is to be persuaded to take what the organization has to offer). On the other hand, conviction marketing's focus is still one-sided. There is little or no attempt to use market research to find out what the consumers need or want, although research is sometimes used to justify the organization's existing prejudices – and is frequently used, to great effect, to optimize the presentation of its chosen message. The powerhouse of such 'conviction marketing' is the powerful idea (the 'conviction' to which the organization has made its 'commitment'), to which the organization believes that the consumers are also committed (despite any evidence to the contrary!) or need (for their own good!). Despite the focus on the consumer, and frequent reference to the importance of that consumer, the real organizational commitment is to the overarching idea (or set of ideas, often a 'lifestyle'). Henry Mintzberg (1983) says 'We can refer to "stylistically rich" organizations as Missionaries, because they are somewhat akin to the religious

organizations by that name. Mission counts above all
– to preserve it, extend it, or perfect it. As a result of
their attachment to its mission, members of the organization resist strongly any attempt to change it, to
interfere with tradition. The mission and the rest of
the ideology must be preserved at all costs.' The
essence of, and the strength of, such 'conviction marketing' is the power that it gives to the marketing
organization to 'evangelize', where religious, as well
as political, parallels are often more relevant than
those of marketing theory.

See also ADVERTISING; BUYING DECISION, ADVERTISING
MODELS; CONVICTION MARKETING FACTORS; CONVIC-
TION MARKETING TYPES

References: Kotler, P. (1976) *Marketing Management* (3rd
edn). Englewood Cliffs, NJ: Prentice-Hall.
   Mintzberg, Henry (1983) *Power In and Around Organizations.* Englewood Cliffs, NJ: Prentice-Hall.

conviction marketing and myopia   The main
problem facing conviction marketers is that the necessary strength of their commitment may blind them
to the realities that face them and their customers. It
is difficult enough for any marketer to adopt the
unbiased perspective essential to understanding the
customer's needs and wants. It may be impossible
for a conviction marketer, whose 'vision' may be so
powerful that it precludes any doubts about the
'product'. The Concorde airliner development team
were convinced of the market for their 'baby', and
their market research supported that view – it was
only the market that disagreed. Even IBM can fall
foul of this problem, as it has done with its personal
computers; when its immensely strong corporate
'vision' got in the way of any meaningful recognition
of the scale of the problem posed by its wayward
dealers.

See also ADVERTISING; BUYING DECISION, ADVERTISING
MODELS; CONVICTION MARKETING

conviction marketing factors   The power of the
conviction marketing campaign(s) is dependent upon
the power of the idea(s) behind it. In turn, this power
derives from a number of factors:

   The concept being marketed must be distinctive.
Successful conviction marketing is not the province
of the marketer who is dedicated to pallid incrementalism. It has to be readily identifiable; as Coca Cola
was – in terms of the very powerful image of the
bottle, if not necessarily the product that it contained. Beyond that, however, it has to be based on
an identity, a brand personality. The beneficiaries of
conviction marketing are typically not products

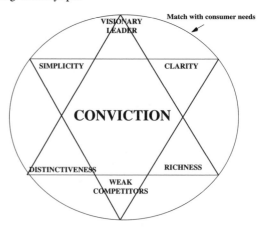

where the technical features are predominant. Coca
Cola and Marlboro are a matter of personal taste, but
it is the images associated with them, their brand
persona, which add the necessary richness to the
relatively mundane. Even in the case of IBM it was
the marketing and support (rather than the very
complex technology) which was its outstanding feature. The richness, the depth, to the identity seems
to be necessary (at least in the most successful examples), to give an almost human identity.

   Despite the richness of the concept, it has to be
instantly communicable, which demands that it be
clear – and preferably simple. It has to be conveyed
by simple messages, such as the shape of the bottle
(or now the graphics on the can) of Coca Cola, or the
cowboy and Marlboro. Where the product is complex, and none could be more complex than that of
IBM, it has to be enshrined in an associated philosophy, such as IBM, 'Customer Service' (personified
by the field personnel in the now rather outdated, but
very necessary, dark suits and white shirts). It is
frequently associated with a distinctive form of quality, as with McDonalds 'Hamburger University'.

   Conviction marketing is, above all, dependent
upon the consumer's belief in what its communicators say. Being somewhat unrelated to the basic
needs, the 'vision' of the 'product' (of its identity)
has to be conveyed to the target audience. They, in
turn, have to enter into a 'belief' in the 'product'
before they can fully appreciate it. This means that
the message being communicated has to be believed;
and that in turn means that the communicators
themselves need to believe.

   In some cases the 'communicators' can be those of
conventional marketing; the Marlboro cowboy in the
advertising, or the bright clean image of McDonalds'

outlets. But behind them there is often a human face. In IBM it was the sales force, immensely capable and imbued with (many would argue indoctrinated in) the IBM culture – and which of their customers could resist such evangelists? But, above all, it usually requires a strong (and almost obsessively dedicated) human personality at the centre, to make the vision work; the Watsons at IBM and Ray Kroc at McDonalds developed very rich cultures that were aimed more at their own employees (the 'communicators' that the public see) rather than at their markets.

See also ADVERTISING; BUYING DECISION, ADVERTISING MODELS; CONVICTION MARKETING; EMERGENT STRATEGY; GLOBALIZATION; INNER MARKETING CAMPAIGN; VISION, CORPORATE

conviction marketing types Conviction-marketed products can be broadly divided into two groups.

Product-based
These are products, or services – frequently in the high technology field – whose creator has a blinding faith in what product or service features are needed. Steve Jobs, at Apple, believed in the special technology of his products (even after IBM set new standards – and John Sculley had to be recruited from Pepsi, to inject more conventional marketing expertise), Alan Sugar believed in his personal ability to put together low-priced electronics packages. The problem with conviction-marketed products in this category is that they can be very rapidly overtaken by changes in the market. Typically, new technology supersedes them (just as the Commodore Pet, one of the original PCs, was displaced from the business market by Apple, which in turn was superseded as brand leader by IBM), or tastes change (as Woolworth found out as its traditional place on the high street was undermined).

Value-based
The strongest 'conviction-marketed' brands are those in very general markets where the distinctiveness comes from the image – from the intangible values associated with the brand. These brands are usually much more capable of change, since the identity is not usually locked into 'physical' features. The customers (and the organization's own employees) can easily accommodate the new features needed to cater for developments in technology and taste. IBM's 'Customer Service' carried it through decades of revolutionary change, and Disneyland is con-

stantly absorbing new rides – but still keeping them immaculately clean! Even McDonalds, which should perhaps be one of the most product-based of retailers, is in reality based on conviction marketing of values – 'Q. S. C. & V.' ('Quality, Service, Cleanliness & Value'). It has managed to change what it serves – adding a breakfast menu, and lines based on chicken and fish, as well as pizza in some outlets – and how it serves it; by increasing the size of its 'sit-down' sections it has become a restaurant rather than just a take-away outlet).

See also ADVERTISING; BUYING DECISION, ADVERTISING MODELS; CONVICTION MARKETING

cooling-off period The time (usually by law) allowed for hire purchase buyers to change their mind about the contract.

co-operation, world-scale ventures *see* STRATEGIC (INTERNATIONAL) ALLIANCES

co-operative distribution *see* MARKET ENTRY TACTICS

co-operatives, retail *see* RETAIL ORGANIZATION

Coopers & Lybrand, consultants *see* CONSULTANTS

coordination, inner market *see* INNER MARKETING CAMPAIGN

copy The text of an advertisement.
See also ADVERTISING PROCESSES; CREATING THE CORRECT MESSAGES; CREATIVE DEPARTMENT, ADVERTISING AGENCY; UNDERSTANDING, ADVERTISING

copy claim The claim made for the product or service in the copy.
See also CREATING THE CORRECT MESSAGES; CREATIVE DEPARTMENT, ADVERTISING AGENCY

copy date The date by which the advertisements (blocks) should reach the publisher for publication in a specific issue.

copy platform *see* PLATFORM

copyright *see* BRAND MONOPOLY; INTELLECTUAL PROPERTY

copy rotation The use of a rotating pool of advertisements to avoid reader boredom, or to present more messages than can be contained in one advertisement.

See also CREATING THE CORRECT MESSAGES; CREATIVE DEPARTMENT, ADVERTISING AGENCY

copy testing   A specialized form of testing is that relating to the content of the advertisement itself. This may take place at three stages:

- *Preliminary* – where parts of the advertising (including 'concepts') are tested before being incorporated in the finished advertisement.
- *Pre-testing* – where the finished advertisement is tested in its entirety (usually against its predecessor and/or its competitors) to ensure that it meets the objectives set by the advertising strategy.
- *Post-testing* – the actual consumer results, researched after exposure to the advertising.

All of these employ conventional marketing research techniques; measuring the specific factors that are judged to be important to the brand/advertising. In the case of the first two categories, however, the respondents are shown examples of the concepts or finished advertisements (or the finished commercial), and this requires the use of sophisticated, expert, techniques to compensate for the bias that this would otherwise introduce (and even then, with small sample sizes being typical, the results are often variable).

See also ADVERTISING; ADVERTISING AGENCY ELEMENTS; COUPON RESPONSE; MARKETING RESEARCH

copywriter   *see* ADVERTISING PLAN; ATTITUDES, ADVERTISING; AWARENESS, ADVERTISING; CREATIVE DEPARTMENT, ADVERTISING AGENCY; LETTER, DIRECT MAIL; UNDERSTANDING, ADVERTISING

core competences   These are the absolutely essential ingredients – which are unique to your products/services and/or to the organization and are just as likely to be intangible in nature – that will be responsible for the sustained success of your organization in the future.

See also ANALYTICAL 4-STEP; BOOST CORE COMPETENCES; CORE COMPETENCES PIE; DISCARD PERIPHERALS; ZERO-LEVEL MARKETING

core competences pie   These are four separate segments of the organization's internal and external environment that are used to stimulate separate ap-

proaches to the overall problem of determining what the organization's core competences are.

Using this intermediate approach, you develop your wider list of competences within these initial, broad categories. In the first place, this may stimulate your imagination, to unearth competences which – if you were to remain blinkered by the more conventional approaches – you might not have considered. Perhaps more importantly, it also shows you which competences appear in a number of slices; and – since they have wider impact – are more likely to be the crucial ones. The most useful segments in this context are as follows:

- *Historical resources*. This slice of the pie represents the traditional, inward-looking view of the organization. It reflects what the organization sees as being most important to itself, typically those competences in which it has most pride, the activities it believes it does better than anyone else – and, in general, what has succeeded in the past is an especially good indication of what will succeed in the future.
- *Competitive position*. This slice, however, requires you to look more dispassionately at its position, in relation to its 'competitors' (who are defined in the widest possible sense, including other government departments in the public sector just as much as commercial competitors in the private sector). Which competences give the organization a sustainable competitive advantage over those competitors? The key word here is sustainable. In this context, short-term advantage means little – to be a genuine core competence it has to be sustainable over the long term.
- *Customer benefits*. These are the competences that offer most to (or are most wanted by) your customers.
- *Future developments*. This is the aspect that is most often neglected, since most managers tend to look backward rather than forward. In a nutshell, it simply asks which competences will be important in five or ten years' time. This often turns out to be the most powerful contributor of all, because experience has been that managers find it easiest to widen their vision if the timescale they are talking about is (in their terms) very long – and this freedom acts as a potent stimulant for their, and your, imagination.

It has to be remembered that the whole point of the core competences pie lies in integrating the slices –

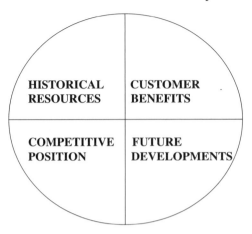

| HISTORICAL RESOURCES | CUSTOMER BENEFITS |
| COMPETITIVE POSITION | FUTURE DEVELOPMENTS |

the reverse of what might be expected – but it is to be hoped that this will, yet again, make it that much more memorable.

See also CORE COMPETENCES

core product *see* BENEFIT ANALYSIS

core schedule *see* SHARPENING THE CUTTING EDGE OF MEDIA

core services In many service sectors, a 'package' of services is offered. Within this package there will often be a range of core services, such as the provision of a bedroom for a hotel client, which the customer must use. But there will often be a range of optional services, such as the restaurant or leisure facilities, on which the provider may hope to make an extra profit (and indeed often hopes to make most of the profit – the core services only recovering the basic overheads!). This 'package' approach, which brings together a number of elements (some of which are optional), is a feature that is rarely evident in terms of pure products, but is prevalent in the service industries. The balance of the various elements of the package, and their management, is therefore a major aspect of marketing management in these industries.

corner shops *see* LOCATION, RETAIL

cornering by competitors, of 'buy-in' *see* MAKE OR BUY

corporate affairs *see* CORPORATE PUBLIC RELATIONS; DEFENSIVE (CORPORATE) PR; PROACTIVE PR

corporate citizen *see* CORPORATE PUBLIC RELATIONS

corporate financial services There is relatively little specific reference in this volume to the 'corporate financial services' market. This is partly because its suppliers publicly claim interests, and priorities, that take priority over marketing; although it must be noted that the most valued personnel are often those dealing with customers – as sales personnel! But it is also because, in many respects, the provision of corporate financial services follows the pattern of most other 'capital goods'! The process of making the sale – of negotiating the deal – follows that of any complex sale.

corporate interface *see* CORPORATE PUBLIC RELATIONS

corporate mission *see* MARKETING MYOPIA; MISSION

corporate objectives The overall objectives of commercial organizations are conventionally supposed to be financial; for example, *maximizing revenue* or *maximizing profit*, or *maximizing return on investment* or *minimizing costs*. But other aims are possible. Many companies choose long-term growth (which may be quite different from revenue maximization in the short term). Almost all have an implicit, and very powerful, aim of survival (which J. K. Galbraith (1958) spelled out so forcefully in his book *The Affluent Society*)!

One of the best known 'alternatives', that of 'satisficing' (rather than profit maximization), comes from Herbert Simon (1979): 'In one way or another, they [alternative theories] incorporate the notions of bounded rationality [rational decision-making limited by reality, including lack of information]: the need to search for decision alternatives, the replacement of optimisation [profit-based objectives] by targets and satisficing [minimal] goals, and mechanisms of learning and adaptation.'

If we accept the traditional assumption, as to the financial basis of the objectives behind the corporate plan, these objectives are ideally meant to be quantified in numerical and, in particular, financial terms.

In the most general terms, though, the 'objectives' behind a strategy address two questions: '*Where* do we want to be?' and '*When* do we expect to be there?'

A final caveat must be that the existence of a clearly defined, and formally stated, 'purpose' may still not explain what the organization's true objectives are.

It is important that you recognize the complexity that lies behind corporate objectives – and are not seduced by those who would argue that simplicity is the order of the day. Although the problems may have to be (artificially) simplified, to make them easier to handle, this should not blind you to their true nature. It should also alert you to the fact that, with so many variables which may be periodically in a state of flux, each new situation will be unique; and, despite the fact that rules of thumb will help, the solutions must be built anew for each problem.

See also CORE COMPETENCES; MISSION; PLANNING PROCESS; POTSA PLANNING; RULES OF THUMB

References: Galbraith J. K. (1958) *The Affluent Society*. London: Hamish Hamilton.
   Simon, Herbert A. (1979) Rational decision making in business organisations. *The American Economic Review*, September.

corporate plan   The starting point for the marketing plan, and the context within which it is set, is the corporate plan. In most marketing-oriented organizations, the contents of the corporate plan will closely match those of the marketing plan itself; but it will also include the plans for the disposition of the other internal resources of the organization. Thus, the corporate plan is likely to contain three main components:

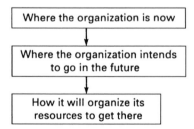

The first category is intimately involved with the customers. In marketing terms, although there are many other factors to take into account, the most important definition of where the company is positioned revolves around where it is in the market (and hence where it is with its customers). The same is largely true of the second stage as well; since, no matter how much its managers may wish otherwise, where the company can realistically expect to go is totally in the hands of its customers. It is only at the third stage that the four Ps come into

play as vehicles for moving the company to reach its objectives.

See also ANSOFF MATRIX; BOSTON MATRIX; GE (GENERAL ELECTRIC) MATRIX; INADEQUACIES IN PLANNING; MARKETING PLAN BENEFITS; MARKETING TRIAD; MISSION; PLANNING PROCESS; POTSA PLANNING; THREE CHOICE BOX

corporate promotion versus brand promotion   Most advertising, along with other forms of promotion, relates to specific brands. It is very direct in attempting to increase sales of that product or service. A growing element, however, has been that of corporate advertising. This promotes the overall organization rather than its individual brands. The rationale may be that it is the support to be obtained from the total organizational umbrella that ultimately sells the brands; and such a case can certainly be made for Marks & Spencer (whose corporate name is better known than its brand, St Michael) or for IBM. This may well be, however, because of a degree of nervousness induced by the increasing possibility of even very large corporations falling to hostile takeovers; and a corresponding attempt to raise the image of the company, and hence its share price – so that it might be able to conduct some takeovers of its own. The principles of corporate advertising, however, follow very closely those of brand advertising. In this context, the corporation is the brand writ large! The example of corporate advertising does, however, illustrate a more general point: the organization may conduct a number of different types of promotional campaign – often aimed at different audiences. That targeted on consumers is usually very evident, but there may also be a significant amount of promotion – often in the form of direct mail – directed at shareholders and other members of the financial community, again to protect the share price and reduce the risk of takeover activity. All of these different forms of promotion follow broadly similar rules, but each must be designed to meet the needs of its specific target audience. One word of caution, though: if these separate campaigns obviously come from the same supplier, they must also be consistent with each other – even if, as often happens, they are developed by different agencies.

See also ADVERTISING; SELLING

corporate public relations   PR is often used as a global term to cover a wider range of activities. Of these, one of the most important may be that of acting as the corporate interface with the outside world; sometimes referred to as 'corporate affairs'.

This aspect of PR is much more likely to be the province of corporate PR personnel. Some of the routine tasks are the following:

- *Communications to 'stakeholders'* – annual reports and newsletters (as well, possibly, as company magazines, sponsored journals, etc.) to the various stakeholders, from shareholders through to (most importantly) the workforce.
- *Speeches* – 'ghost-writing' the various speeches and presentations (both external and internal) in which senior management become involved.
- *Community contact* – acting as the channel for the 'corporate citizen' activities that organizations feel, usually with some justification, will help their image in the community

There may, however, be a 'strategic' element to corporate PR. This may operate from the two ends of the spectrum:

defensive PR ↔ proactive PR

See also DEFENSIVE (CORPORATE) PR; PROACTIVE PR; PUBLIC RELATIONS

corporate strategy and marketing In setting the context for marketing, it is important to understand how it fits into the organization's overall corporate strategy. The study of corporate strategy is now usually treated as a separate 'academic discipline', although it is closely related to the processes of marketing planning.

In a very simplified form, the corporate planning process might be represented as follows:

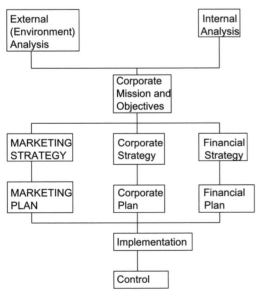

The input into the corporate strategy processes can thus be conveniently separated into two streams. The first, the internal elements (such as production and finance), are those upon which many organizations, and many people within each organization, concentrate their efforts. They, above all, are the object of much of the 'fire-fighting' that preoccupies even senior management.

The second element comprises the external elements, including 'marketing' in its broadest sense. There are, thus, a number of external, environmental, influences that can impinge on an organization; such as the prevailing social climate and, more directly, the accompanying legislation. For most commercial organizations, however, the predominant, most direct, features of the external environment are those that conventionally relate to the 'market', and to marketing.

In any organization that claims to be 'marketing-oriented', the market has to be the starting point for any process of strategic planning. Indeed, the strategic planning process in such organizations usually revolves around the marketing strategy and planning processes. It is for this reason that marketing planning processes are often almost indistinguishable from those of corporate strategy itself; in a way that the planning processes for the other functions are not.

See also ANSOFF MATRIX; BOSTON MATRIX; GE (GENERAL ELECTRIC) MATRIX; INADEQUACIES IN PLANNING; MARKETING PLAN BENEFITS; MARKETING STRATEGIES; MARKETING TRIAD; MISSION; PARADIGM SHIFT, STRATEGY; PLANNING PROCESS; POTSA PLANNING; THREE CHOICE BOX; VISION, CORPORATE

cost *see* BUDGETS; EXPERIENCE CURVES; MARKETING STRATEGIES

cost–benefit analysis A technique used, mainly in the public sector, to determine whether a project should go ahead; based on the costs compared with the potential benefits.

cost, insurance, freight *see* CIF (COST, INSURANCE, FREIGHT)

cost, marketing *see* MARKETING AUDIT

cost, new products *see* MARGINAL COSTING, NEW PRODUCTS

cost, overhead of order   *see* PRODUCTION
DECISIONS, LOGISTICS MANAGEMENT

cost per thousand   *see* DOOR-TO-DOOR; MEDIA
BUYING, ADVERTISING AGENCY; MEDIA SELECTION;
PROMOTIONAL MIX FACTORS; SHARPENING THE
CUTTING EDGE OF MEDIA

cost point   *see* FLEXIBLE MANUFACTURING

cost-plus pricing   The starting point for many
pricing exercises is an examination of the cost of the
product or service. For too many organizations, it is
also the finishing point. Such 'cost-plus' pricing may
be understandable where the price list contains hundreds of items: but, under those circumstances, it is
highly debatable whether the 'cost' for each item
represents anything more than an estimate. Paradoxically, cost-plus pricing seems to suggest that inefficiency (which would lead to a higher cost, and
hence via the same percentage mark-up to a higher
profit) should be rewarded!

The one area in which cost-plus pricing is possibly
justifiable is that where the supplier has a long-term
relationship, almost a partnership, with a customer
(often the government). In these circumstances, it is
sometimes agreed that a certain level of profit (as a
percentage of cost) is acceptable. But even here there
has to be a question as to the efficiency of such a
pricing policy – for the customer as well as for the
supplier, where profit is supposed to be the main
incentive – and the legal actions taken by government to recover unwarranted profits from some
defence contractors operating under these pricing
policies seem to argue for some dissatisfaction.

Exactly what 'cost' should be chosen is a matter of
debate, but few producers actually do conduct such a
debate, often selecting as their 'cost', by default, the
first one thrown up by their accounting system. If
you have studied accounting you will understand
that there can be a number of bases for cost figures,
each of which will give a different estimate – and
each of which will be as correct, in the specific context in which it is supposed to apply. Choosing which
cost to apply and, more importantly, understanding
the assumptions that lie behind it, is an art – and one
in which many marketers are unskilled.

The most critical element in this process is often
the most arbitrary; that of the allocation of overheads,
usually on the basis of 'absorption' of overheads
(whereby indirect overheads are allocated, on the
basis of 'judgement', to production departments and
then, combined with direct overheads, 'absorbed'

into the individual product costs, often on the basis of
labour content). Many stages in this process require
'judgements' as to where overheads are to be allocated (and add to the very arbitrary nature of the
whole process – and contribute a considerable degree
of indeterminacy to the final cost!).

'Marginal costs' (which avoid the problem of overhead allocation) may well be the most favourable
approach for new products; but may leave gaps in
terms of overhead recovery, as the older products
die. A judgement also has to be made as to the period
over which any initial investment is to be recovered.
It is as well to remember that a new 'product' does
not become profitable until it has at least recovered
all its overheads and its original investment.

Oxenfeldt and Kelly (1986) list a number of 'fundamental errors committed by business executives in
setting price':

1. The tendency to think in terms of averages
    . . . it ignores the particular and unusual
    circumstances under which the price move
    occurs and which call for the use of marginal
    or incremental costs . . . the assumption that
    all customers behave in the same way . . .
2. The reluctance to 'let bygones be bygones'
    . . . letting irrevocable and irretrievable past
    expenditures enter into the cost computations
    underlying price decisions . . . The vital con-
    cept to apply here is sunk costs. These are
    outlays already made that cannot be revoked
    and about which nothing can be done. Such
    costs must be ignored . . .
3. The tendency to ignore alternatives . . .
    business people frequently charge out these
    elements on the basis of what was paid for
    them in the past (book costs) rather than what
    they would yield in alternative use. The con-
    cept of opportunity costs has been developed
    to help highlight the constant need to think
    in terms of alternatives when arriving at the
    decision.
4. The tendency to emphasise cost considera-
    tions over demand considerations . . . This
    tendency reaches its pinnacle in cost-plus
    pricing where demand considerations are
    simply ignored.

See also PRICING POLICIES, PRACTICAL

Reference: Oxenfeldt, Alfred R. and Kelly, Anthony O.
(1986) Pricing consumer products and services. In Victor P.
Buell (ed.), *Handbook of Modern Marketing* (2nd edn). New
York: McGraw-Hill.

counter-advertising Advertising specifically designed to counter what has been said by a competitor in their advertising.
See also ADVERTISING; KNOCKING COPY

counter-jumper A salesperson who sells, over the counter, in a store.

counter-marketing In what is usually a public-sector activity (but is occasionally undertaken by the private sector, where some uses of a product are damaging the corporate image), there may be a marketing objective of stopping consumption completely. The anti-tobacco and anti-drug campaigns are the most obvious examples; but McDonalds' campaigns to stop its customers dropping litter, or the brewers' campaigns to stop drinking and driving, fall into this category.
See also CORPORATE OBJECTIVES; MARKETING OBJECTIVES; PLANNING PROCESS

counter-offer A higher offer made in response to another offer.

counter-purchasing *see* COUNTERTRADING

countersegmentation There is an argument that segmentation may have been taken too far in some areas. The response could, accordingly, be to consolidate several segments, by launching a brand (or repositioning a brand, or integrating several existing brands) to cover several segments. This may allow economies of scale, without major reductions in benefits; and, on balance, increased competitive advantage.
See also PRODUCT (OR SERVICE) POSITIONING; SEGMENTATION

countertrading This category of international trading – which includes barter deals, counter-purchasing, buy-backs, switch trades, offset deals and compensation trading – accounts for a significant proportion of international trade. The main forms are as follows:

• *Barter*. Payment for goods by goods, with no direct involvement of money, usually as a one-time exchange that leaves the supplier having to find a market for the goods that have been received in exchange.
• *Buy-backs* (sometimes called 'compensation agreements'). The supplier (usually of technology or capital equipment) agrees to buy back

some of the resulting product, to cover the cost of the deal.
• *Switch-trades*. These are deals involving various partners (usually specialist institutions) which aim to achieve a balance of trade.
• *Clearing arrangements*. These are bilateral trade agreements between countries rather than individual organizations.

Needless to say, most organizations would prefer cash, but if this is not available then a counter-trade may be better than nothing. However, it has to be recognized that it is difficult and time-consuming; and often leaves the vendor with products that are difficult to sell (sometimes more so than the original product sold!).

country portfolio Having entered and achieved an adequate level of sales in a number of countries, the transnational/global corporation will then need to consider how its 'portfolio' of country operations is balanced, how their different strengths (and weaknesses) complement the overall operation.
See also EXPORT MARKET ELIMINATION

country prices *see* INTERNATIONAL PRICE DECISION

country risk One of the factors that needs to be taken into account, particularly by the multinationals, is the risk that their investments in a particular country will be nullified; either by 'investment recovery risk', resulting from government action (such as expropriation or war), or 'cash flow risk', due to radically reduced economic returns (from strikes, debt and currency problems, etc.). These may be categorized as follows:

• *World system risk*. This is the risk to the whole system of international trade (posed by problems such as the 'North/South divide' and Third World debt).
• *Country risk*. This is the general risk of doing business in the particular country (which is often the only 'country risk' discussed – even though it may merely be of direct interest to international banks).
• *Project risk*. Most importantly, John Stopford identifies the fact that the specific risk of each project may vary considerably (an exploiter of raw material supplies may be in danger of nationalization, whereas, at the same time, a supplier of essential 'high-tech' equipment may be received

with open arms). This element is, though, not often taken into account.

There are a number of suppliers of 'country risk analysis', based on tracking political and other indicators in these countries (with an overall risk factor calculated from these), including Frost & Sullivan and Business International. Their reports are of most use to the large banks, whose country-level lending may be at risk. They may be of less direct use to corporations involved in specific sectors of markets, which are not addressed by such reports. The best advice is to include an assessment of such risks in the overall research, and then to monitor developments (including political developments) closely.
See also INTERNATIONAL MARKETING; MARKET ENTRY DECISION; RISK ANALYSIS

Reference: Stopford, J. (1989) *Personal Comunication.* London: London Business School.

coupon response One particularly effective measure of the effectiveness of press advertising, along with that of direct mail, can be implemented where the purpose of the advertising is to elicit a direct response, typically in terms of motivating the reader to ask for further information though a 'coupon' included in the advertisement or mailed material. Each such advertisement or mailing can then be given a code; the usual means being including a dummy 'department number' (which equates to the publication used, say) as part of the mailing address. The response obtained from each of the publications (or each of the mail packages) can then be measured accurately – at least in terms of the percentage coupon response rate – although, of course, that may not be an appropriate measure if what is primarily being attempted is a shift in attitudes. This technique can also be used to test, and directly compare, two or more advertisements where the media owner offers 'split runs', in which the overall print run is split (usually geographically) or the television is run by regions. Comparison of the results, for each part of the test (with its different advertisement or campaign), may give a good indication of performance, although geographical variations will need to be allowed for (and even this may be partly compensated for by 'flip-flop testing', in which the test is repeated with the regions reversed). More basically, you should be aware that coupon response may not be the best measure of the performance that you want to gauge; for instance, long-term

image building will not be demonstrated by this approach.
See also ADVERTISING; ADVERTISING AGENCY ELEMENTS; COPY TESTING; MARKETING RESEARCH; PROMOTIONAL MIX FACTORS; RESPONSE PATES, MAILING

coupons   *see* NON-PRICE PROMOTIONS; PROMOTIONAL PRICING; PROMOTION OBJECTIVES

coupons, drops   *see* EPOS AND EFTPOS, PRECISION MARKETING

coupons, redemption levels   *see* PROMOTIONAL PRICING

coupons, sales incentive schemes   *see* MOTIVATION, OF SALES PERSONNEL

courage   *see* LEADERSHIP, OF SALES PERSONNEL; VISION, CORPORATE

courtesy   In the marketing context, this often means free of charge.

courtship, sales   *see* RELATIONSHIP (MARKETING) MANAGEMENT

coverage   The percentage of a target audience (market) reached by the advertising campaign.
See also ADVERTISING PLAN; AUDIENCE RESEARCH; BUDGETS; CUMULATIVE AUDIENCE; ECONOMIES OF SCALE, GLOBAL; EFFECTIVE COVER; FACILITY DECISIONS, LOGISTICS MANAGEMENT; MEDIA BUYING, ADVERTISING AGENCY; MEDIA SELECTION; SHARPENING THE CUTTING EDGE OF MEDIA

CPT (cost per thousand)   *see* COST PER THOUSAND

creaming   *see* SKIMMING, PRICING

creating new products   *see* NEW PRODUCT CREATION

creating the correct messages   Clearly, the prime objective of most, if not all, promotion is to make the 'sale' (where the 'sale' in the case of a not-for-profit organization might, for example, be to persuade the target audience to adopt a different behaviour pattern; say, to give up smoking). To achieve this end-result, though, it will almost certainly need to communicate one or more messages (whether the promotion consists of face-to-face selling or advertising on television). The tasks that these messages must undertake include the following:

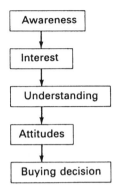

See also ADVERTISING; ATTITUDES, ADVERTISING; AWARENESS, ADVERTISING; BUYING DECISION, ADVERTISING MODELS; INTEREST, ADVERTISING; UNDERSTANDING, ADVERTISING

creative advertising   *see* MESSAGE, ADVERTISING

creative department, advertising agency   The *raison d'être* for most agencies is their creative skill. They, and often they alone, have the expert talent to take the mundane marketing objectives of the client and turn them into eye-catching, memorable advertisements. This is reflected in the importance ascribed to creativity by agency clients. A *Marketing Week* survey of the clients of the top UK advertising agencies showed that their average ratings of importance (on a ten-point scale from 'most important' downwards) in terms of their 'overall assessment of agency performance' were as follows:

creativity	8.7
value for money	8.3
attentiveness and adaptability	8.0
quality of account managers	8.0
media buying	7.7
marketing strategy	7.1
international coverage	3.3

To achieve this creative performance, the large agency may well have a number of creative specialists:

- *Copywriters*. The creative powerhouse of an agency is often its copywriters. They write the words for the advertisements, be these 'copy' in a press advertisement or the script for a television commercial. But they are often also expected to be the source of the original creative ideas, which turn the dull marketing objectives into sparkling advertising.
- *Artists*. The visual elements of press advertisements are provided by artists, usually called 'visualizers' (or, more grandly, in line with typical agency hype, 'art directors'). They work hand in hand with the copywriters, to the extent that it is frequently difficult to determine which member of this creative team has produced a specific creative idea. The visualizer, specifically, provides the various 'roughs' (the draft sketches) of the visuals, including 'storyboards' (the rough cartoons illustrating which visuals will be in the final commercial) that accompany the scripts. These visualizers do not usually produce the finished artwork: their input is purely creative, and there are specialist photographers and illustrators, subcontractors to advertising agencies, who do this very high quality finished work.
- *Producers*. For a commercial – television, radio or cinema – an outside production company and director will be chosen (to meet the needs of the specific commercial). The agency producer, in the mirror image of the account executive's role, will supervise relations with this outside team; to ensure that the finished commercial meets everyone's requirements.

See also ADVERTISING AGENCY ELEMENTS; ADVERTISING PLAN; ADVERTISING PROCESSES

creative imitation   The greatest threat usually comes from known competitors. It is important, therefore, to monitor their developments very closely. Any major new change that they introduce must be taken seriously, and immediately evaluated to see if it is a genuine threat to the (position of the) brand. At the same time, where time is the essence of such competition, contingency plans must be prepared (and development work on a response begun).

The main point to remember is that a brand/market leader with a strong position rarely loses that position to even a serious threat – as long as it delivers an effective counter (usually by imitation) fast enough.

Creative imitation, though, can offer wider benefits. Many ideas can be productively transferred from other fields of human activity.

Indeed, the major technique for finding major new product developments is (creative) scanning of the horizon – preferably a decade or more ahead, since such major developments take time as well as money. It is true to say that the seeds of major innovations can usually be sown a number of years (or even decades) ahead. The scientific breakthroughs that lead to new tech-nologies normally follow this rule; but so also do the changes in lifestyles that lead to new consumer demands.

See also CUSTOMER BONUS; EXISTING PRODUCT CHANGES; FEATURE MODIFICATION; GAP ANALYSIS; GENERATING IDEAS; LEAPFROG; NEW PRODUCT CREATION; NEW PRODUCT INNOVATION; PRODUCT CHURNING, NEW PRODUCTS

creative inspiration   *see* PRODUCT DEVELOPMENT

creative 'portfolio'   *see* AGENCY BRIEFING

creative 'portfolio', advertising   *see* MESSAGE, ADVERTISING

creativity   *see* AGENCY CHOICE; AWARENESS, ADVERTISING

credibility   *see* LOGICAL INCREMENTALISM

credit   *see* PROMOTIONAL PRICING

credit card, precision marketing   *see* DATA AVAILABILITY, PRECISION MARKETING

credit control   *see* MONETARY POLICY

critical incident technique   This technique focuses on the important incidents that affect an employee's work performance; as defined by the employee.
See also BEHAVIOURALLY ANCHORED RATING SCALE (BARS); MARKETING RESEARCH; SURVEY RESEARCH

critic's charter   The most important feature of this approach to analysing potential solutions to marketing problems is the rejection of anything and everything which does not directly help you solve your specific problem. This may sound trivial, for why should anyone think of offering solutions that are irrelevant or simply do not work? But, in their enthusiasm to help, many marketing experts will rush to do just that! The recognition of the individuality of each situation is normally a key requirement for sound marketing practice:

THE CRITIC'S CHARTER - the practical steps in evaluating a marketing theory for use in a given situation are;

1. Is it directly relevant to the specific needs of the situation?
   (if not, discard it)
2. What other theories attempt to explain the same phenomena?
   (check for alternatives)
3. Does it offer the (most) productive framework for meeting your specific needs?
   (discard any explanations which are clearly less effective)
4. How does it complement the theories you are using to examine other phenomena?
   (if it clashes with the main techniques to such an extent that it could cause confusion then discard it, after checking to see that it is not the only one 'in step')
5. What reliance can be put upon it and what evidence is there of its effectiveness?
   (discard all techniques which have no substantial, proven backing)
6. Is it 'original' or has it been distorted by later interpretation?
   (discard all theories which have been stripped of their meaning by popularization, or go back to the original)
7. Does it match with your own experience, and does it make sense?
   (discard anything which does not make sense, but only after you are sure you understand what it is trying to say)

8. THEN, AND ONLY THEN, USE IT - BUT ONLY AS A STARTING POINT *(AND AS A FRAMEWORK)* FOR FURTHER INVESTIGATIONS; TO FIND THE SOLUTION WHICH BEST MATCHES THE UNIQUE NEEDS OF THE SPECIFIC SITUATION. UNLESS PERSUADED OTHERWISE BY THE FACTS, ASSUME YOUR OWN JUDGEMENT IS BETTER THAN THAT OF ANY EXPERTS *(WHO CANNOT UNDERSTAND THE SPECIFIC SITUATION AS WELL AS YOU CAN)* !

This process will inevitably discard most of the theories and techniques you are investigating. Even so, there is a reasonable chance that, from the wide variety on offer, there should be at least one idea which can provide some new insight into the problems at hand.

What use you then make of such theory depends entirely upon the specific needs of the moment. The most important advice, however, is given by the last recommendation from the critic's charter: to use it as no more than a starting point. Indeed, its main value may be in terms of the new insights that it stimulates, which may in turn suggest new solutions. More generally, it should offer a productive framework within which answers may more easily be worked out.

However you use theory, though, you should only use it as an aid to your own judgement. In marketing you cannot delegate important decisions to outsiders. No matter how expert they are, they cannot have the amount of experience of the matter in hand that you do!
See also ANALYTICAL 4-STEP; ZERO-LEVEL MARKETING

Reference: Mercer, D. S. (1997) *New Marketing Practice.* London: Penguin.

crop   To cut down a photograph or illustration to the right size.

Crosby, P. B.   A very influential US guru of quality, who introduced some of the most important techniques as part of his work on the US Pershing Missile programme. These ideas were, however, taken up by the Japanese rather than the Americans! His main contributions are the concept of zero defects and his 14 Steps to Quality – of which the most influential in Japan, but virtually unknown outside, is that of Error Cause Removal (a 'suggestions scheme' approach).

See also QUALITY; SUGGESTIONS SCHEMES; ZERO DEFECTS; ZERO DEFECTS VERSUS AQL

Reference: Crosby, P. B. (1979) *Quality is Free*. New York: McGraw-Hill.

cross-border shopping   *see* INTERNATIONAL PRICE DECISION

cross-country market research   *see* INTERNATIONAL PRODUCT DECISION

cross-disciplinary teams   *see* PRODUCT/BRAND MANAGEMENT

cross-elasticity of demand   This is a concept from economics, which measures how demand for different products or services is interrelated. It is quite simply defined as being equal to

(percentage change in quantity of commodity X)/ (percentage change in price of commodity Y)

The effect here will be different if Y is a *substitute* for X (margarine against butter often being given as the example, in which case there will be a positive cross-elasticity; that is, the sales of X will increase if the price of Y increases) or if Y is a *complement* (say, bread against butter, where the cross-elasticity will be negative, since the sales of X will decrease with an increase in the price of Y). However, once more, in practice this becomes a very sophisticated technique. To remove the effects of the other factors involved, such as promotional activities, typically requires exact sales figures (usually obtained as a result of a pooling arrangement between manufacturers) covering an extended period; and the technique consumes significant amounts of computing power as the various regression analyses are run.

See also MARKETS; SEGMENTATION

cross-functional coordination/management
see PRODUCT/BRAND MANAGEMENT

cross-impact matrices   These matrices, the use of which is complex, look beyond the probabilities of

Development D	Probability P
1 One month reliable forecasts	4
2 Feasibility of limited weather control	2
3 General biochemical immunization	5
4 Elimination of crop damage from adverse weather	5

	Then the probability of			
If this development were to occur	D_1	D_2	D_3	D_4
D_1		—	—	⇧
D_2	⇧		—	⇧
D_3	—	—		—
D_4	—	—	—	

one event occurring, to see how combinations of events may reinforce each other. It takes all the events along one axis (or dimension) of the matrix, and the possibility of that event interacting with each of the other events (in other words, its effect on the others) along the other axis. This is best illustrated by the example described by Spyros Makridakis and Steven Wheelwright (1989):

The upward arrows, in this form of the cross-impact representation, show the combinations of events that will interact (leading to a higher overall probability).

The complications increase, however, when the interactions between more than two of these elements are considered – and when the degree of interaction also has to be forecast. A typical, practical, matrix (built using the most popular, KSIM, technique/language, developed by Kane – see Kane, 1972) may well involve 20–50 variables; and thus between 400 and 2500 cross-impacts. However, the cross-impact matrix provides a systematic means of combining separate forecasts of the parts (that is, for the discrete events listed).

See also QUALITATIVE FORECASTING METHODS

References: Kane, J. (1972) A primer for a new cross-impact language – KSIM. *Technological Forecasting and Social Change*, 4.

Makridakis, Spyros and Wheelwright, Steven C. (1989) *Forecasting Methods for Management* (5th edn). Chichester: John Wiley.

cross-impact matrices forecast   *see* SCENARIOS

cross-national segments   *see* INTERNATIONAL PRODUCT DECISION

cross-price elasticity of demand   *see* PRICE ELASTICITY OF DEMAND

cross-subsidization   *see* ECONOMIES OF SCALE, GLOBAL; TRANSNATIONALS/MULTINATIONALS AND EXPORTERS

cross-substitutes, price   *see* PRICE ELASTICITY OF DEMAND

cross-tabulation   The most widely used, and typically the most useful, form of presentation of research results. The key variables are split (usually by percentage) across the other selected variables in a table.

cross-technological components   *see* SUPPLIERS

crowding out   The economic concept that government spending, deficits or debt reduces the amount of business investment – and thus may be self-defeating in terms of stimulating the economy.

See also KEYNESIANISM; MONETARISM; RATIONAL EXPECTATIONS THEORY

crusaders   *see* GLOBAL MARKETING

cultural barriers   *see* SOCIAL AND BUSINESS STRUCTURES, FILTERING UNSUITABLE MARKETS

cultural constraints   *see* INTERNATIONAL PRODUCT DECISION

culture, organizational   In the ultimate extension of 'inner marketing', Peters and Waterman (1982) stress that the 'culture' of an organization (generally speaking, the common values that its employees share) can be a very important contributor to its success. Such 'culture' can be even more important in determining what 'customer service' is provided. They conceptualize this cultural element as 'shared values', which is central to their framework of the 'seven S's':

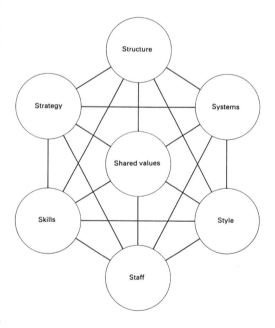

Even in the manufactured goods sector, the customer sees his 'customer service' in terms of all of his contacts with the company. He does not restrict his view to the narrow confines of product availability, or to just those members of the sales force who are supposed to be the 'ambassadors' of the company; even less is he influenced by advertisements that tell him how good the service is, if his own experiences are otherwise. He will also view the telephone operator and the invoice clerk as ambassadors, and will react badly if their 'customer service' is poor (as it all too often is).

The 'culture' of the company is often what conditions this 'customer service'. Both McDonalds and Disney have similarly strong cultures – and they show, not least, in their spotlessly clean premises and also in their bottom-line profits.

The problem of addressing the 'cultural dimension', even though this is an essential element that must be allowed for in any marketing operation, is that changes in the culture of an existing organization may literally take years to be completed. If existing cultures are strong, and the changes are major, the process may take decades. Both IBM and the Japanese corporations, who probably have the strongest cultures of all, needed as much as 15 years fully to develop all of the detailed aspects of the new, and rich, cultures that they were introducing.

Henry Mintzberg (1983) explains:

As the organization establishes itself, it makes decisions and takes actions which serve as commitments and establish precedents that reinforce themselves over time. Actions become infused with value. When the forces are strong enough ideology begins to emerge. Furthermore, stories – sometimes called 'myths' – develop around important events and the actions of great leaders in the organization's past. Gradually the organization develops a history of its own . . . Over time this tradition influences behaviour, and that behaviour in turn reinforces the tradition. Eventually, an ideology may become established.

Culture is not, therefore, a topic to be taken lightly; although more minor changes (particularly those that 'complement' the existing culture) may be accepted more rapidly – but, even then, not in days!
See also CONSULTANTS; CONVICTION MARKETING; INNER MARKETING

References: Mintzberg, Henry (1983) *Power In and Around Organizations.* Englewood Cliffs, NJ: Prentice-Hall.
Peters, T. J. and Waterman, R. H. (1982) *In Search of Excellence.* New York: Harper & Row.

cultures, influences on the purchase decision
Overall, culture is an increasingly important factor in the purchasing decision. It is most noticeable in terms of nations; that of the UK, with its remaining class consciousness, may be very different from that of the USA, with its money consciousness. The Mediterranean way of life, in the sun, may be quite different to the Nordic, in the cold. But cultures change. It has taken nearly a decade for the political parties to recognize it; and much of marketing has yet to recognize the fact.
See also DECISION-MAKING PROCESS, BY CUSTOMERS; PEER PRESSURE INFLUENCES, ON THE PURCHASE DECISION; REPEAT PURCHASING PROCESS; SOCIAL CLASS INFLUENCES, ON THE PURCHASE DECISION; SUB-CULTURES, INFLUENCES ON THE PURCHASE DECISION

cumulative audience Sometimes called cumulative reach, this is the cumulative number (or percentage) of homes or individuals reached by advertising contained in the whole schedule over the time period under consideration.
See also MEDIA BUYING, ADVERTISING AGENCY; MEDIA SELECTION

cumulative coverage *see* ADVERTISING PLAN; MEDIA SELECTION

cumulative image *see* CUSTOMER FRANCHISE

cumulative sales *see* EXPERIENCE CURVES

cumulative totals This is a measure that is normally used in the context of control – measuring how cumulative sales are performing against target, for example, to see how the organization is likely to fare against its year-end targets – rather than as a tool of forecasting.
See also QUANTITATIVE FORECASTING TECHNIQUES; Z CHARTS

currency exchange rates *see* INTERNATIONAL PRICE DECISION

currency problems *see* MARKET ENTRY DECISION

currency restrictions *see* REGULATORY CONSIDERATIONS, FILTERING UNSUITABLE MARKETS

customary pricing There is one situation in which the price is obvious. It is described by Kent Monroe (1973) as 'customary pricing', which 'excludes all price alternatives except a simple price point. The traditional example has been the five-cent candy bar or package of gum'. The supplier's choice here is the 'quantity' to offer against this fixed price – and 'price changes' become incremental 'size changes'.

See also COMPETITION PRICING; COST-PLUS PRICING; PRICING POLICIES, PRACTICAL

Reference: Monroe, Kent B. (1973) Buyer's subjective perceptions of price. *Journal of Marketing Research.*

customer bonus   Many strategies are suggested for finding and deciding on new products. Best of all, though, is to let the customer or consumer tell you how the product or service should be developed. This approach is most obvious in those industrial markets where some customers naturally undertake a substantial share of application development; that is, work on the uses to which the product or service is put. Sound development strategy in these cases may simply be based upon observing what these customers are doing, and selecting the best solution(s) that emerge – and then translating them to the wider customer set. In the process, the required changes to the product or service itself may also emerge – inherent in the demands posed by these new applications.

The same principle can just as successfully be applied to consumer products; after all, that is what much of marketing research aims to achieve. On the other hand, as for example practised by the Japanese, it can be approached more simply – and directly – and hence much better understood, intuitively, by the manager. Thus, the Japanese take enormous pains to find out what changes their customers want. Often, they launch multiple versions of the product or service, the ultimate test of consumer taste – those that sell best represent the customers voting with their wallets. On the other hand, they are fortunate (or wise) in having a Japanese public who are educated to try the many new products brought to market.

See also CREATIVE IMITATION; EXISTING PRODUCT CHANGES; FEATURE MODIFICATION; GAP ANALYSIS; GENERATING IDEAS; LEAPFROG; NEW PRODUCT CREATION; NEW PRODUCT INNOVATION; PRODUCT CHURNING, NEW PRODUCTS

customer care programmes   *see* SELLING SERVICES

customer-centred versus organization-centred, non-profit   In the specific context of not-for-profit organizations, Kotler and Andreasen (1987) distinguish 'customer-centred organizations' (those that meet the 'ideals' of marketing), defined by them as follows:

> A customer-centred organization is one that makes every effort to sense, serve, and satisfy the needs and wants of its clients and publics within the constraints of its budget.

They contrast these with those that are 'organization-centred', in which a number of attitudes exist, including the following:

1. The organization's offering is seen as inherently desirable.
2. Lack of organizational success is attributed to customer ignorance, lack of motivation, or both.
3. A minor role is afforded market research.
4. Marketing is defined primarily as promotion . . .

They advise:

> Indoctrinating a nonprofit organization from top to bottom with the proper marketing philosophy . . . recognizing that the introduction of a new philosophy is as much a political exercise as a matter of logic and persuasion. Allies must be sought and enemies deflected. Above all, it is essential to secure a top management commitment to the new way of thinking. Without it, a true marketing organization will not be achieved and customer-centred thrusts in one area will inevitably run afoul of organization-mindedness elsewhere.

See also NOT-FOR-PROFIT ORGANIZATIONS; SERVICE CULTURES

Reference: Kotler, Philip and Andreasen, Alan R. (1987) *Strategic Marketing for Nonprofit Organizations.* Englewood Cliffs, NJ: Prentice-Hall.

customer complaints   *see* COMPLAINTS; MONITORING, PROGRESS

customer contact forecasts   Where the 'market' comprises the customers and the supplier is one stage removed from the customers' own judgements (because the products or services are the subject of 'derived demand' or are delivered to consumers via third-party distribution channels), one key input to forecasts (but one that is rarely used!) is the comparable forecasts of the larger customers themselves. If you are selling steel to the car industry, you had better understand how that industry is forecasting its own future. The 'account planning' process is an ideal mechanism for this invaluable input.

See also ACCOUNT PLANNING; QUALITATIVE FORECASTING METHODS

customer database   *see* TERRITORY SALES PLAN

customer demand, pricing   *see* PRICES, CUSTOMER NEEDS

customer franchise   One of the most positive ways of consolidating the consumer as the most important focus of the organization is to look on this relationship as a prime asset of the business – one that has been built up by a series of marketing investments over the years. As with any other asset, this investment can be expected to bring returns over subsequent years. On the other hand, also like any other asset, it has to be protected and husbanded.

This 'asset' is often referred to as the 'customer franchise'. It represents all of the elements of the complex relationship that the organization has built up with its individual customers or clients (as well as, in aggregate form, its position in the markets).

At one extreme, it may come from the individual relationship developed face-to-face by the sales professional. At the other, it is the cumulative image, held by the consumer, resulting from long exposure to a number of advertising campaigns.

In some markets the customer franchise may be so strong as to be exclusive; in effect giving the supplier a monopoly with those customers. Microsoft holds just such a position with its Windows Operating System. Equally, until recently, the UK high street (clearing) banks could be reasonably confident that, once they had recruited a customer – as a teenager – he or she would generally remain loyal to them for the rest of his or her life!

The franchise may be much wider than this, however. Consumers may regularly switch brands, for variety, but they may still retain an image (hopefully a positive one) of the brand, which may swing the balance when their next purchase decision is taken. It may thus still have a value (upon which the advertiser can build) even if the current purchasing decision goes against it. A later decision may, once again, swing in its favour.

The customer franchise is, therefore, a very tangible asset, in terms of its potential effect on sales; even if it is intangible in every other respect.

It is based, though, on an accumulation of impacts over time. Unfortunately, too many marketers – particularly those in creative departments within advertising agencies – signally fail to recognize the importance, and long-term nature, of this investment. They treat each new campaign as if it could be taken in isolation – no matter how it meshes with previous messages that have been delivered to the consumer. The evidence is that the consumer, on the other hand, does not view the advertising and promotion in such lofty isolation; instead, he or she incorporates it into their existing image – to good or bad effect, depending upon how well the new campaign complements the old. Gallahers is still running very much the same advertising campaign for Condor pipe tobacco that it launched 20 years ago, and is still holding the lead that it then established. It takes courage, though, to resist the blandishments, and even threats, from the creative teams, who are thus denied the satisfaction of seeing their own special ideas emerge. Accordingly, many advertisers appear to be driven to accept a new advertising strategy every new budget year.

See also BRAND (OR MARKET) SHARE; BRAND VALUE; MARKETING MYOPIA; PENETRATION; USAGE AND LOYALTY

customer interface management   *see* SALES CALL; SALES PROFESSIONAL

customer loyalty   *see* PROMOTIONAL PRICING

customer panels   *see* MONITORING, PROGRESS

customer relationship   *see* INTERACTION, AND THE ORGANIZATIONAL PURCHASE; PARTNERSHIP TRIANGLE; SELLING

customer response to the brand   *see* USAGE AND LOYALTY

customers   In commercial markets it might seem an easy task to define who your customers are; they are simply the buyers of your brand. Those, coming out of the supermarket, who have just bought your brand clearly do fall into this category. But the dividing line is often not quite so clear. Where do those lie who have previously bought, but have now switched to another brand? Where do you put very loyal users who have most recently bought another brand just for a temporary change? How do you categorize a consumer of a particular durable, where the last purchase might have been half a decade ago? The boundaries are not so clear after all, and often need to be defined, typically by marketing research, for each product or service; and in terms that are meaningful for the actions being planned. In the public sector, the boundaries may be even more blurred: unemployment benefit is paid to those out of work, but is intended just as much to support their dependants.

See also MARKETS; PROSPECTS; USERS

customer satisfaction Most dissatisfied customers do not complain (97 per cent, according to one US survey), but they do tell their friends – the same survey showed that 13 per cent complained to more than 20 other people! On the other hand, as Philip Kotler (1988) points out, a satisfied customer:

1. Buys again
2. Talks favourably to others about the company [although, as reported in the survey quoted above, only to three others – compared with the average of 11 others when complaining!]
3. Pays less attention to competing brands and advertising
4. Buys other products that the company adds to its line

Clearly, if it was not already obvious, any organization should be highly motivated to make certain that its customers are satisfied. Yet, in practice, remarkably few do so! It is essential, therefore, that (as a first step in this process) an organization monitors the satisfaction level of its customers. If all else fails, this may be done at the global level, as measured by market research. Preferably, though, it should be at the level of the individuals or groups. IBM, for example, conducted a survey of all of its direct customers every year. The results were not just analysed to produce overall satisfaction indices, although that was done (and senior management viewed any deterioration with alarm), but they were also provided to field management so that they could rectify any individual problem situations where the customer was dissatisfied with any aspect of the IBM service and the IBM representative (presumably on 97 per cent of the occasions, if the above results hold true in this field) did not realize this to be the case.

It is possible that many retailers may not be able to use such information at the individual level, although some service providers may want to keep track of the satisfaction of their regular customers. They may, however, track satisfaction levels by branch, to detect unwelcome deteriorations before they do untold harm.

There are a number of advantages to conducting satisfaction surveys (particularly where any individual problems highlighted can be subsequently dealt with):

1. Like complaints, they indicate where problems lie; for rectification.
2. If they cover all customers, they allow the 97 per cent of non-complainers to communicate their feelings; and vent their anger.
3. They positively show even the satisfied customers that their supplier is interested in the customer.
4. They help to persuade the supplier's staff to take customer service more seriously.

See also MARKETING MYOPIA; MONITORING, PROGRESS; SERVICE LEVELS; SERVICE QUALITY; WIN–WIN

References: Albrecht, Karl and Zemke, Ron (1985) *Service America*. New York: Dow-Jones Irwin.
  Kotler, Philip (1988) *Marketing Management* (6th edn). Englewood Cliffs, NJ: Prentice-Hall.

customer satisfaction survey The intangible elements of quality can be, and should be, measured, simply by asking the customer (by market research surveys, such as the 'Customer Satisfaction Survey' that IBM conducts annually on every one of its mainframe customers). Asked the right questions, they will be only too happy to tell you what is right and, more importantly, what is wrong with your operations. And they are unlikely to worry about whether it is measurable – they will just worry about what is important to them!

See also CUSTOMER SATISFACTION

customer-satisfying process *see* MARKETING MYOPIA

customer service *see* INNER MARKETING CAMPAIGN; INVENTORY CONTROL; MARKETING STRATEGIES; TERRITORY SALES PLAN; VISION, CORPORATE

customer service categories There are a range of different approaches to (retail) service. The retail sale of products is now dominated by self-service (which did not feature to any significant extent much over three decades ago). That of services is, understandably, still the province of personal service:

- *Self-service*. In the now familiar manner, customers select their own goods and take them to the checkout in the supermarket; or to a cashpoint in other retail establishments, such as multiple chemists, bookstores or even fashion outlets. The sole contact with the staff of the retailer is the act of payment.
- *Self-selection*. Here the customers still select the item from the shelf (although they may ask for assistance from sales staff), but they then take it to a salesperson to pay.
- *Personal service*. In the product area this is a diminishing sector of the retail trade, although some customers are still willing to pay for such service; particularly where expert advice is needed, in high fashion or photographic outlets, for example. It is, by default, still the mainstay of the personal services sector. Estate agents and travel agents rely on the face-to-face contact; although banks, often the most obvious high-street presence, are increasingly looking to automate their mass 'money-shop' activities. Such personal service is also the essence of the food (and drink) sectors, in both restaurants and take-aways.

See also LOCATION, RETAILING; RETAILING; RETAIL ORGANIZATION; RETAIL PRODUCT OR SERVICE CATEGORIES

customer service levels *see* SERVICE LEVELS

customer service programmes *see* INNER MARKET

customer service quality *see* SERVICE QUALITY

customer set *see* TERRITORY SALES PLAN

customers, new product ideas By far the greatest sources of new product ideas are customers. They are, after all, the users of the product or service; and the new uses that they make of it, or the changes in specification that they demand, are both the most potent forces on the product development process and its richest source of ideas. This customer 'information' will normally be received via the sales force (or even through the medium of correspondence). This may be in the form of descriptions of what the customer is actually doing with the 'product' (which may indicate new uses for it), or requests from the customer for specific new products or services. As in most aspects of marketing, the key to success is, thus, a focus on the customer. But in this case it should

take the form of listening avidly to all of their suggestions; because, buried in the many trivia, will be some gems, which may become the cash cows of the future – if I may be allowed to mix my metaphors. Eric Von Hippel's research (into the rather specialized area of innovation in the scientific instruments market) reported that 'in 81 per cent of all the innovation cases studied, we found that it was the user who perceived that an advance in instrumentation was required; amended the instrument; built a prototype; improved the prototype's value by applying it; and diffused detailed information on the value of the invention . . .'. His team found that the pattern was repeated in the process equipment industry, but it was not universal (two of his students found that the reverse was true in parts of the polymers industry, where it would have been difficult for users to undertake the development). He continued, in the paper, to make a plea for separating 'All Users' into 'Routine Users' and 'Innovative Users', with extra effort devoted to the latter (in view of their importance for product innovation).

See also CREATIVE IMITATION; CUSTOMER BONUS; GENERATING IDEAS

Reference: Von Hippel, Eric A. (1978) Users as innovators. *Technology Review*.

customer/supplier relationships *see* INTER-ORGANIZATIONAL RELATIONS

customer value, pricing *see* PRICES, CUSTOMER NEEDS

customization of markets *see* IN-HOUSE DATA, PRECISION MARKETING

custom research This is the staple diet of the market research industry. The research organization is commissioned by a client to undertake a specific piece of research. The research company then accepts responsibility for all aspects of the research.

There are organizations that cover – or claim to cover – all types of market research. On the other hand, many organizations specialize in particular fields. For example, there is usually a quite distinct split between those that specialize in the consumer fields, the province of the large 'random' surveys, and those in the industrial field, where research often revolves around extended interviews with individual organizations. Equally, there are clear divisions between those involved in retail audits and those

conducting questionnaire surveys on individual consumers; and of those conducting group discussions or in-depth psychological interviews. Over the past two decades the most important factor in the market for such research has been its price. It has been traded as a commodity, and the emphasis has been on cost-cutting. Accompanying this trend has been, understandably, a reduction in quality – for the methods used have often been 'shaved' to reduce costs to the bare bone. In using market research results, therefore, this is a factor that must be allowed for.
See also CONSULTANCIES, AND MARKETING RESEARCH; MARKETING RESEARCH; OMNIBUS SURVEYS; PANEL RESEARCH; RETAIL AUDITS; SUBCONTRACTORS, MARKETING RESEARCH

cut and paste   *see* ADVERTISING PROCESSES

cut-pricing, retail   *see* RETAIL 'PRODUCT' DECISIONS

cutting edge of media   *see* SHARPENING THE CUTTING EDGE OF MEDIA

cutting edges (research time)   *see* RESEARCH DIAMOND

cycles, business   *see* BUSINESS CYCLES; DERIVED FORECASTS

cyclical ordering   *see* PRODUCTION DECISIONS, LOGISTICS MANAGEMENT

D

DAGMAR *see* BUYING DECISION, ADVERTISING MODELS

dailies *see* PRESS MEDIA

daily workload, salesman *see* TERRITORY PLANS

damaged goods *see* FAULTS

danger signals *see* SCANNING, AND MIS

dangers, inherent in use of marketing techniques Marketing techniques should be the servants of the marketer. They should be used as an aid to the creative decision-making processes, and can never be a substitute for these. Although they may frequently offer helpful insights, they rarely ever offer definitive answers in themselves. There is sometimes a desire to look for simple solutions to what are usually complex marketing problems; and, in particular, to look for solutions that incorporate the expertise of acknowledged masters in the field. These desires are not infrequently stimulated by the service providers who are offering such marketing panaceas.

data access problems All too often, access to key data is limited to a few people; for example, the circulation of a memo may be rarely to more than half a dozen people – especially from sales personnel in the field (where there are likely to be no carbon copies). The traditional system then requires that the recipient (say, the regional sales manager) recognizes the importance of any data and then abstracts this to incorporate in his or her own reports to higher management. The message thus travels hierarchically through the organization – being filtered and distorted at each stage. This inevitably incurs delays (reporting periods typically increase in length the higher in the organization the message reaches). More importantly, it demands that a number of intermediaries recognize the significance of the data. If just one of them ignores it (because he or she does not see its relevance, or even because he or she would prefer it to go no higher), that data is lost to those in the chain above. The increasing use of 'electronic mail' should have a dramatic effect on the availability of such information.
See also ELECTRONIC MAIL; ROUTING RULES; WRITTEN REPORTS

data analysis *see* ANALYSIS OF MARKETING RESEARCH DATA

data analysis, of verbal reports *see* VERBAL DATA ANALYSIS

data availability, precision marketing Until recently, suppliers in the mass markets were not allowed the luxury of interaction with their customers. The cost of a sales force for face-to-face contact was, and still is, prohibitive. The new factor, which can go some way to achieving the same impact, is the availability of much more detailed information on individual customers (or groups of these) together with the processing power (in terms of computing) to handle this data. In recent years an increasing amount of detailed data about consumers has become available from existing sources. The ACORN work, for example, is based upon census data which is now generally available in computer-readable form. In addition to this, many organizations are recognizing the value of what they hold on their own databases – membership lists, for example – and are making them available for sale. A more fundamental, and as yet little developed, approach is to consolidate these various databases; to provide a greater amount of information on, and a more 'three-dimensional' picture of, the individuals involved. To date, at least in the UK, this approach has been most effectively explored in terms of consolidating the 'warranty card' information (the 'market research' information provided by consumers who return warranty, or guarantee, cards) from different suppliers. In the longer term, the consolidation of the very large databases (including those of the credit card companies – always assuming that this will be allowable under legislation such as the Data Protection Act in the UK) will provide quite detailed information on at least some of the activities of most individuals in the population.

The main drivers for change, in addition to the general availability of more information about consumers, are:

- marketing research
- EPOS and EFTPOS
- in-house data

See also EPOS AND EFTPOS, PRECISION MARKETING; IN-HOUSE DATA, PRECISION MARKETING; MARKETING RESEARCH, PRECISION MARKETING

database cleaning *see* DATABASE, INVESTING IN YOUR OWN

database, customers and prospects *see* MAILING LIST

database, investing in your own The most productive database ('mailing list') is usually the one that you have built yourself. As Edward Nash (1986) comments, in the context of mail order operators, 'The single most valuable list used by the majority of advertisers is their own house list. Tragically, it is often the most neglected. For most direct marketing companies, it is the single most precious asset – the one whose loss could put them out of business. It is usually the most responsive list to a company's additional offers.' Even in organizations with more general fields of operation, the data obtained as a result of those operations (enquiries, face-to-face selling, exhibitions, direct mail, etc.) should all be treated as the precious resource that they are. They should be consolidated and protected (with the resulting database 'cleaned', for instance of duplicate entries – the bugbear of most mailing lists, and hated by recipients) so that they are usable, and useful, as a direct input to all marketing activities; and especially for precision marketing, which will make the most powerful use of them.
See also PRECISION MARKETING

Reference: Nash, Edward L. (1986) *Direct Marketing: Strategy, Planning, Execution* (2nd edn). New York: McGraw-Hill.

database marketing *see* EPOS AND EFTPOS, PRECISION MARKETING

database, precision marketing *see* DATA AVAILABILITY, PRECISION MARKETING

databases in the public domain A growing amount of information is being made widely available (mainly by commercial information providers, but also by government bodies) on computerized databases. This data covers almost every subject; with vast quantities of information on technical subjects, such as patents, as well as the marketing information with which this volume is primarily concerned. This data can be particularly easy to access; especially if it is available on the Web. A number of these databases (for example, ABI Inform, which is the main marketing abstracts database) are now also available on CD-ROM. Use of these databases will, of course, demand access to a computer terminal, or (these days more likely) a personal computer that can communicate with an external mainframe computer (that is, has a 'modem') or can handle the CD-ROM. This also requires some familiarity with the use of a PC – but not a great deal, because the database operators make access very easy once you have reached their computer. A range of services is already available. Perhaps the most comprehensive is 'Dialog'. This brings together a number of individual databases, covering several hundred subjects ranging from business news to science and technology and the social sciences (and including such esoteric topics as 'Chinese patent abstracts' and 'smoking and health'!). There are also a variety of more specialized financial databases (some of which are included on 'Dialog'), which give details of company performance, for example; and these are now widely used to check credit-worthiness. For the wider perspective, there are a number of news clipping databases; including 'Profile', which contains the text from several years of a range of quality newspapers and journals. On these, the data can be found by word search (or, more likely, a search for combinations of the key words).
See also EXTERNAL DATA; LIBRARIES

database, tree structure *see* MATERIALS REQUIREMENTS PLANNING (MRP)

data collection The logistically most resource intensive stage of survey research is when the army of interviewers descends on the unsuspecting public. There are, however, a number of possible methods of contacting respondents:

- mail surveys
- telephone surveys
- personal interviewing

See also MAIL SURVEYS; MARKETING RESEARCH; MAR-
KETING RESEARCH STAGES; PERSONAL INTERVIEWING;
SURVEY RESEARCH; TELEPHONE SURVEYS

data, information and intelligence These
words are used in quite specific ways when
marketing researchers (or at least those most exposed to Information Technology, IT) are being
'rigorous':

- *'Data'* are a collection of facts; for example,
  the 'demographic (census)' figures relating
  to neighbourhoods – although it could equally
  well be measurements of the attitudes of
  customers.
- *'Information'* is data that have been selected and
  ordered with some specific purpose in mind; for
  example, the overall profile of the neighbourhoods that make up the catchment area where a
  superstore chain is considering opening another
  branch.
- *'Intelligence'* is the interpretation that is then
  made, following analysis, of this information; for
  example, the resulting profile of the store's likely
  customers, and its optimal location(s).

In theory, these are important distinctions. Unfortunately, most marketers, and even many marketing researchers, tend to use them rather loosely; to
the extent that they are often interchangeable in conversation, if not in the learned journals! The important distinction to be made is that there is a gradation
of 'value' in the information as it is gradually processed from its original 'amorphous' form until it
becomes a finely honed tool; which will positively
help to answer the specific question facing the marketer. Its power as a tool increases as it goes through
this process, from raw data to selected prime information to analysed intelligence; but then, you must
also remember, so does the potential bias applied to
the data. At the first stage you can make errors of
omission, as relevant data are left out (perhaps
because they are inconvenient in terms of the end
justification wanted). At the second, the errors may
be those of commission (seeing things in the
information that are not really there, but that you
want to be there – much research information is very
much like the psychologists' 'Rorschach Blot', in
which the viewer can see anything which takes his or
her fancy).
See also MARKETING INTELLIGENCE SYSTEMS (MIS)

data, in-house, precision marketing *see* IN-
HOUSE DATA, PRECISION MARKETING

data manipulation, precision marketing The
theory of precision marketing is simple. It is merely
a matter of matching the requisite marketing
approach to the individual. Thus, for example,
Sears targets those of its customers who have purchased a number of domestic appliances without
any associated maintenance cover, for a drive to
sell them general maintenance contracts. A salesperson, in face-to-face contact, follows much the
same process. The problem comes in manipulating
the vast quantities of data involved. Until recently,
even starting on this task was near impossible,
just because of the amount of data involved, but
now commercial computers (which the larger
organizations already have) have developed to the
stage at which they can easily handle the amount
of this 'paperwork'. The problem has thus become
one of what to do with all this data; what decisions
to make on the basis of it. In theory, at least,
each store could hold more of those items that are
most demanded by its unique set of customers;
and it could provide the number of 'facings' (the
shelf space) justified by the sales of each of these
products – and it could even locate the product
where it could be most effectively promoted (in
association with the other products bought) to these
customers. The harsh reality is that such decisions
are still the prerogative of the individual manager,
a manager already inundated with more computer
listings than he or she knows what to do with. Needless to say, they only have the time to take these
decisions on a handful of items (and then probably
only on a national basis rather than branch by
branch). Even then, these decisions can be taken just
as effectively without the aid of the computer; the
bread and pastries buyer for Waitrose only needs to
talk to each of his six regional suppliers to find out
from them – on the basis of their very direct involvement – exactly which decisions are needed in each
one of his main stores.

Computers cannot (at least as yet) take decisions,
without being fed very elaborate sets of rules to
govern every possible situation. Unfortunately,
developing the rules to cover the many billions of
possible combinations and permutations of 5000
products across several hundred stores would tax the
brains of a large number of geniuses. So, as yet, the
power lies relatively dormant. The same problems
will potentially arise with precision marketing to

large numbers of individual customers, except that there may well be millions of these rather than just hundreds of stores! There are two main solutions to this dilemma.

Expert systems
The longer-term solution may well be to teach the computers how to make the necessary decisions, including some 'learning from experience, expert systems', using artificial intelligence, expert systems or expert systems based approaches.

Simplified approaches
In the shorter term, the answer may be to develop simpler ways of dealing with the data which, while not releasing the true potential of precision marketing, will still allow some of the benefits to be gained. There are two main routes:

* *Aggregation*. The individuals, or separate stores, can be aggregated with others that share broadly similar performance or behaviour patterns – this is the broad principle on which ACORN already works. The precision is limited, but at least 'individual' approaches are possible at the group level.
* *Simple decisions*. Instead of exactly matching the consumers' total purchasing profile, the decisions can be made to relate to relatively simple factors. Thus, the Sears (US) example – of just selling maintenance contracts to those who do not have them – can be made to work.

This approach can be developed incrementally, adding new decisions based upon simple combinations of factors as experience indicates that these work. It is even possible that this could grow into one form of expert system; but the chances are that it will just grow until its size results in chaos – by which time, hopefully, the genuine expert system should be available!
See also PRECISION MARKETING

data mining   With large amounts of electronic (computer) data now being created, and stored on vast databases, the new requirement is to retrieve this data – when needed – in a useful form. This is not a trivial problem, and much IT effort is going into solving it, and providing effective forms of such data mining.

data pools   *see* INDUSTRY DATA POOLS

data processing, logistics   Physical distribution (from supplier to end-user), be it of products or services, is now almost always intimately bound up with the systems (usually computer-based) that process the associated 'paperwork':

* order processing
* booking systems
* enquiry processing
* inventory control

See also BOOKING SYSTEM; ENQUIRY PROCESSING; INVENTORY CONTROL; ORDER PROCESSING

Data Protection Act   *see* DATA AVAILABILITY, PRECISION MARKETING

data reduction   *see* FACTOR ANALYSIS

data warehouses   This is the name now being given to the very large databases; or rather to the vast stores of data now emerging from computer systems which, due to their size and complexity, are not yet as usable as databases are supposed to be.
See also DATA MINING

dawn raid   *see* TAKEOVER BIDS

dealer brand   A brand owned by a retailer (dealer) other than the store-named (own) brand.
See also OWN BRANDS AND GENERICS

deal, special   *see* WIN–WIN

debugging   *see* TEST MARKET

DEC   *see* GLOBALIZATION

decay strategies   *see* DECLINE STRATEGIES

decentralized control   *see* STRATEGIC BUSINESS UNIT (SBU)

deciders   *see* DECISION-MAKERS AND INFLUENCERS

decision alternatives   *see* CORPORATE OBJECTIVES

decision-makers   *see* COMPLEX SALE

decision-makers and influencers   In the context of industrial goods marketing, it is perhaps the 'organizational' factors that may predominate. There is much theory – and even more opinion is expressed – about how the various 'decision-makers' and 'influencers' (those who can only influence, not decide, the final decision) interact. Decisions are frequently taken by groups, rather than individuals. Often, the official 'buyer' does not have authority to take the decision.

Webster and Wind (1972) identify six roles within the 'buying centre':

- users, who will actually use the product or service
- influencers, particularly technical personnel
- deciders, the actual decision-makers
- approvers, who formally authorize the decision
- buyers, the department with formal authority
- gatekeepers, those who have the power to stop the sellers reaching other members of the 'buying centre'

Thus, the most obvious way in which the complex sale is different is the complexity introduced by the multiplicity of 'buyers' involved. The convention is to split these 'buyers' into 'decision-makers' and 'influencers', the clear implication being that the small group of 'decision-makers' should be the prime target – although 'influencers' should not be neglected. This is a useful distinction, in that it correctly focuses the sales professional's attention on the key decision-makers, and forces him or her to contact them; for too many sales personnel remain bogged down amongst the 'influencers'. The problem with this two-way split is that both 'decision-makers' and 'influencers' are very general categories; probably too general (and too confined within the sales perspective) to best help the sales professional zero in on the exact decision structure. Miller, Heiman and Tuleja (1989) seem to offer a better (if at times much more complex) structure. They identify four 'buying influences', the first three of which relate to the more conventional structure:

- *Economic buyer.* The economic buyer is the ultimate decision-maker. This buyer is a single entity; usually a single person (but possibly a group, such as a board), who holds the purse strings, and must approve the decision. Clearly, this buyer is the most important in the whole structure: 'Almost by definition you don't find people who give final approval far down on the corporate ladder.'

- *User buyers.* These are the people who are going to use whatever is being offered. In the more conventional model they would lie uncomfortably between 'decision-makers' and 'influencers' – and a virtue of the more complex model is that it allows the sales professionals to handle this important group most effectively: 'The role of the User Buyer is filled by someone who will actually use (or supervise the use of) your product or service. The role of the User Buyer is to make judgements about the impact of that product or service on the job to be done.'

- *Technical buyers.* These are the true 'influencers' of the simpler model; but with a powerful veto power; which could still be fatal for the sale. They vet the specification for technical conformance. Paradoxically, in many complex sales situations (certainly in the case of computers of any sort), the purchasing department falls into this category: 'The Technical Buyers' role is to screen out. They're gate-keepers.'

Miller, Heiman and Tuleja make the important point that these categories are not a function of the titles on the doors; they are a result of specific relationships to the 'purchase'. Even more importantly, these authors emphasize the fact that the structure is not fixed. The relationships change for different purchases; and people move from one category to another. In practice, the decision-making process is normally deeply embedded in the 'user' process. The users have a great deal of delegated power. In many cases, although the final decision may have to be approved by higher authority, this is in reality only a veto power (any board that saddles its user departments with an unwelcome choice is asking for trouble). Miller et al.'s (1989) special contribution to this search is to identify a fourth category of 'buying influence' – the 'coach'. In essence, it says that the sales professional should identify one or more contacts who can (and are willing to) guide them through the complexities of the sale – to use the American sporting analogy, they can 'coach': 'The role of a coach is to guide you in the sale by giving you the information you need to manage it to a close that guarantees you not only the order, but satisfied customers and repeat business as well.'

See also COMPLEX SALE; CUSTOMERS; INDUSTRIAL PURCHASING; SAFETY IN NUMBERS; SALES PROFESSIONAL; SELLING; TERRITORY MANAGEMENT; TERRITORY SALES PLAN

References: Miller, Robert B., Heiman, Stephen E. and Tuleja, Tad (1989) *Strategic Selling*. London: Kogan Page.
Webster, Frederick E. and Wind, Yoram (1972) *Organizational Buying Behaviour*. Englewood Cliffs, NJ: Prentice-Hall.

decision-making process, by customers The question 'How do customers make their decisions?' is more difficult to answer than might be expected. Customers do not come to each buying decision with conveniently blank minds, and then rationally consider the options; even though much of economic theory, and not a negligible proportion of marketing theory, is predicated on such an approach. In such theory, often the only significant variable to be considered is the price! In reality, the decision-making process is an extended, and complex, one – and often a confused one. Even in the apparently simple case of buying a tin of baked beans, a purchaser in a supermarket, faced by the massed ranks of competing brands, may have a number of factors in mind. Just some of the factors might, for example, be:

- experience
- lifestyle
- peer recommendation
- price
- point of sale

Which of these factors, if any, will eventually swing the balance may depend upon the individual purchaser, the product or any one of a number of other factors. The process is usually not clear, least of all to the purchaser. As a result, there are a number of theoretical 'models' of the process. In the case of those products that are purchased frequently, and repeatedly, the simplest model breaks the process down into just three stages:

- awareness
- trial
- repeat purchase

See also AGE INFLUENCES, ON THE PURCHASE DECISION; CULTURES, INFLUENCES ON THE PURCHASE DECISION; ECONOMIC INFLUENCES, ON THE PURCHASE DECISION; FAMILY INFLUENCES, ON THE PURCHASE DECISION; GEOGRAPHICAL INFLUENCES, ON THE PURCHASE DECISION; LIFESTYLE INFLUENCES, ON THE PURCHASE DECISION; MASLOW'S HIERARCHY OF NEEDS; OCCUPATIONAL INFLUENCES, ON THE PURCHASE DECISION; PURCHASE DECISION, MATCHING; REPEAT PURCHASING PROCESS; SOCIAL CLASS INFLUENCES, ON THE PURCHASE DECISION

decision model, exporting This should be more than a checklist on which to base your decision as to whether it is profitable to export or not. It must achieve the following:

- Reference all of the variables that are known to have a significant effect on the marketing of the organization's products or services in existing markets.
- Prioritize these variables, in terms of their importance to the existing operation, and in terms of the proposed international operation – and add any other new factors that will become important in the new context.
- Specify the decision-making process itself: How are the decisions to be taken, in terms of the (performance) criteria that are to be applied to the variables?

Without such a model which – it must be admitted – few exporters use (although some might later regret the omission!), the decision-making process will be *ad hoc*; possibly, or even probably, reacting to only short-term considerations. A decision model is simply a means of structuring the information (in essence, a series of standard questions to be asked), so that the most rational, and best informed, decisions can be made.
See also COMPARATIVE ADVANTAGE, GLOBAL; ECONOMIES OF SCALE, GLOBAL; EXPORTING; GLOBALIZATION; GLOBAL MARKETING

decision protocol interview A specialized form of interviewing, typically in-store, that takes place immediately after purchase and seeks to determine why the purchase was made.
See also SURVEY RESEARCH

decision support systems Computer systems that enable management to access and manipulate data, to help them to make better decisions.
See also MARKETING INTELLIGENCE SYSTEMS (MIS)

decision trees *see* TREE STRUCTURES, FORECASTING

DE class *see* SOCIAL CLASS INFLUENCES, ON THE PURCHASE DECISION

decline stage, product life cycle   According to PLC theory, eventually the whole market may decline or other newer products may be introduced which are themselves a substitute for the established product. The product or service thus goes into a terminal decline – although this decline can last for years. Companies may 'milk' products or services at this stage (minimizing costs and maximizing price, to take maximum profit advantage of the reducing number of loyal customers who still support the brand).

decline strategies   Michael Porter (1980) identifies four possible organizational strategies for a market that is in decline:

- *Leadership*. If the market is still profitable it may be worthwhile temporarily investing to become one of the few leaders, before 'harvesting' profits.
- *Niche*. A segment may be identified that will decay slowly and still has high returns.
- *Harvest*. This is the 'milking' strategy, with cost cutting, no investment and, probably, reducing levels of customer service.
- *Divestment*. This consists of selling the business early in decline (or even at the end of the maturity phase, if the symptoms can be accurately detected – but the evidence suggests that few companies have this degree of expertise).

The biggest potential pitfall, into which many organizations have fallen, is that of simply failing to recognize that the market or the brand is in decline. Applying the strategies applicable to the maturity phase, or even those for the growth phase (to try to recover former glories), is not unusual, but is usually disastrous. It is a problem that besets many other fields of human endeavour. It has been said, for example, that the British Army has entered each war fully prepared for the previous war!

The major problem of such 'weak brands' is not the direct losses that they bring – it is the distraction of management attention away from the breadwinners. Philip Kotler (1965), who has spent a number of years pondering on this problem, states 'The fact is that as products and product lines increase numerically the range of management problems seems to grow geometrically . . . Every weak-selling product which lingers in a company's line constitutes a costly burden. Businessmen do not realize the magnitude of the burden because of a fixation with the more direct costs.' He later makes the more specific point that 'The main reason for harvesting a business entity is to pull out cash that can be put to better uses in the company.'

On the other hand, many brands (probably the majority) are discontinued early as a result of conscious marketing decisions – for reasons other than those of pure brand senility.
See also PRODUCT LIFE CYCLE (PLC)

References: Kotler, Philip (1965) Phasing out weak products. *Harvard Business Review*, March–April.
   Porter, Michael (1980) *Competitive Strategy*. New York: The Free Press.

decomposition models   *see* TIME-SERIES ANALYSES

decoy   A dummy name put into a mailing list (by the list supplier) to verify usage of that list.
See also DIRECT MAIL

dedicated followers   What often makes the task easier for conviction marketers is that their competitors seem even more mesmerized than their customers. Many organizations are 'dedicated followers'; they always look to their competitors to take the lead. Their adherence to this creed goes beyond that required of 'followers', the subsidiary brands in a market that are simply not in any position to set the pace. It goes beyond the IBM approach of 'constructive following', whereby that organization deliberately lets other, smaller, organizations explore (and take the risks inherent in) new developments, only to recapture the initiative (by deploying the vast resources at its command) when the markets prove viable – a strategy that usually proves successful. 'Dedicated followers', though, assume that the market leader always knows best; so that even IBM's mistakes, say, are ascribed to covert machinations, which must have some ultimate value, and these too are copied! 'Dedicated followers' represent a terminal case of myopia. They are organizations that, in effect, subcontract their policy-making to their competitors. As such, they deserve to – and usually do – pay the ultimate price.
See also ADVERTISING; BUYING DECISION, ADVERTISING MODELS; CONVICTION MARKETING

default close   *see* CLOSING TECHNIQUES; SALES CALL CLOSE

defensive (corporate) PR The organization will often be exposed to the activities of external pressure groups. The corporate PR department, if one exists, will typically be the one that 'defends' the organization against these onslaughts, and handles the external interface with such groups. The corporate PR group may, indeed, be the source of the organization's knowledge of such groups. Roger Haywood (1984) suggests, for instance, that 'It is the responsibility of the PR adviser to understand the position of all important external groups – particularly those trying to exert pressure for change, such as a campaigning consumer body, a group of dissident shareholders . . . What is their case? Is it factually based? Who are they trying to influence? How are they attempting this?' He goes on to suggest an important first line of defence, one which is often ignored in the heat of the moment, actually remedying what these groups are attempting to rectify themselves: 'Of course, if the PR adviser feels there is validity in their claims then, especially, it becomes his or her responsibility to advise management and try to institute appropriate policy changes within the organisation.' How the organization then responds to such pressure, usually in terms of its own submissions to the bodies that wield power (most often, via the media, and public opinion) is most clearly the responsibility of the corporate PR function. As Roger Haywood, again, comments, 'Certainly the organization should think very carefully before refusing to communicate in sensitive areas. Any communications should be through the same media used by the pressure groups and every critical comment or negative news story should be dealt with promptly with a properly counter-balanced company statement . . . lobbies have been more successful because of the inability of the opposition to handle their case properly.'

See also CORPORATE PUBLIC RELATIONS; PUBLIC RELATIONS

Reference: Haywood, Roger (1984) *All About PR: What to Say and When to Say It.* New York: McGraw-Hill.

Defining Advertising Goals for Measuring Advertising Results (DAGMAR) *see* BUYING DECISION, ADVERTISING MODELS

defining the objectives, of marketing research *see* MARKETING RESEARCH OBJECTIVES

definition of business *see* MISSION

definitions of marketing *see* MARKETING DEFINITIONS; REALISTIC MARKETING

delayering The removal of layers of management, typically as a result of developments in computer communications – but also often as an excuse for redundancies.

See also BUSINESS PROCESS RE-ENGINEERING

delegation *see* LEADERSHIP, OF SALES PERSONNEL

deliberate strategies *see* EMERGENT STRATEGY

delivery and support specification The support elements behind any 'product' (including their method of 'delivery' in general) are now likely to be as important as the 'product' itself. The main point to make, in the present context, is that the buyer is, once more, the guardian of those levels of support; he or she must ensure (initially, at least, by choosing the correct supplier) that the demanded level of support is feasible – and then is delivered.

See also PURCHASING; SPECIFICATION

delivery date *see* LEAD TIME

delivery organizations, door-to-door *see* DOOR-TO-DOOR

delivery, purchasing *see* PRODUCT OR SERVICE, TO BE PURCHASED

delivery systems, precision marketing The ultimate requirement of a precision marketing system is that it should be capable of being delivered, in terms of promotional effort. Many forms of media will claim to deliver tightly defined audiences (and some of the specialist magazines and trade magazines do exactly that), but in general the minimum size of group that can be targeted (often no smaller than an individual town) excludes them from precision marketing. The traditional approach, and probably still the cheapest and most effective in this context (until computer-based communications come into their own), is direct mail. Moriarty and Schwarz (1989), in the context of MSP (Marketing and Sales Productivity) systems, illustrate how the various systems may be integrated:

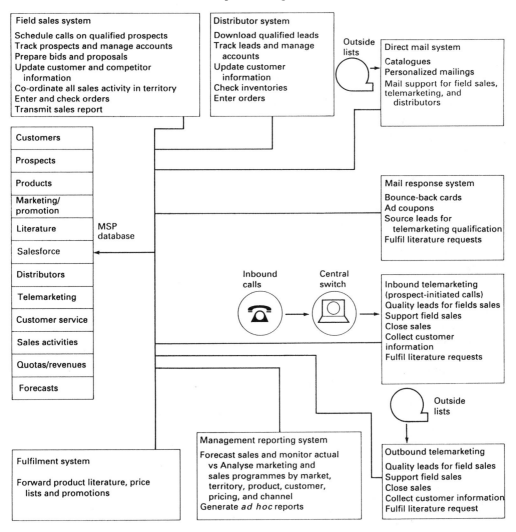

On the other hand, Shaw and Stone (1988) point out some of the dangers of computerization: 'Fully computerized marketing is powerful. If this power is misdirected, dramatic mistakes can be made. Millions of letters can and have been mailed in error, with the wrong offer or to the wrong customer. In a company with branch sales offices, branch management and staff may be alienated. The marketing organization and all its porches may need restructuring to deal with this new way of marketing . . .'.

See also PRECISION MARKETING

References: Moriarty, Rowland T. and Schwarz, Gordon S. (1989) Automation to boost sales and marketing. *Harvard Business Review*, January–February.

Shaw, Bob and Stone, Merlin (1988) Competitive superiority through database marketing. *Long Range Planning*, 21(5).

delivery vehicles   *see* FACILITY DECISIONS, LOGISTICS MANAGEMENT

Delphi technique   The opposite extreme to the jury method of combining expert opinion to produce a long-term forecast is the 'Delphi' technique, originally developed at the Rand Corporation. In this case the (anonymous) experts are quite deliberately not brought together; so as to avoid any 'bandwagon' effect. Instead, a questionnaire is circulated to the team. This initial questionnaire is quite general, asking only for predictions of the major changes that might impact the organization in the longer term. The collected replies – including, for example, predictions of changes in technology – are then distributed to the team, together with a further questionnaire which, this time, asks more pointed questions; for example, requesting predicted dates of introduction of the new technology, or forecasts of its impact on the organization – developing the ideas generated by the first questionnaire. The rounds of questioning progress, becoming increasingly specific, until a sufficiently detailed picture is obtained.

See also QUALITATIVE FORECASTING METHODS; SCENARIOS

demand   *see* MACROECONOMICS; MARKETING OBJECTIVES

demand and supply, laws   *see* NEOCLASSICAL ECONOMICS

demand curve   *see* SUPPLY AND DEMAND

demand curve estimation   Three main ways of measuring the demand curve (and the related price elasticity of demand) are suggested by theorists:

- *Statistical analysis of historical data.* This, at least in theory, uses historical data to 'plot' the curve. Unfortunately, there are very few situations in which this can be carried out directly, since there are too many variables in the normal complex market situation – and the 'environmental' factors, in particular, change over time. Even the use of 'regression analysis' may not be able to remove the effects of those other factors.
- *Survey research.* It might seem that market research should be able to find out what consumers would buy at various prices, allowing the curve to be plotted. In practice, as it turns out, the results from such research are generally so inaccurate that the curves cannot be plotted with any certainty.
- *Experiment.* The one successful device is to test prices, in a test market. For many manufacturers this may be of questionable value; for the costs of the test are not insignificant (especially where national retailers have to be involved) and the price effect measured may be relevant for just a short time. Retailers themselves, with the luxury of many branches in which to run such tests with minimal dislocation of activities, are much better

placed. The practical reality is that these techniques are rarely used!

See also PRICE ELASTICITY OF DEMAND; PRICE FACTORS; PRICES, CUSTOMER NEEDS; SUPPLY AND DEMAND

demand elasticity   *see* PRICE ELASTICITY OF DEMAND

demand function   *see* SUPPLY AND DEMAND

demarketing   Sometimes demand may exceed supply. In these circumstances, the marketing emphasis will be on rationing scarce supplies. Occasionally, the supplier, rather than bring on-stream expensive new plant, may seek to persuade customers to buy less (or be less dissatisfied with the scarcity). Some suppliers of electrical energy have heavily advertised energy conservation measures to achieve this end (for, otherwise, the cost of meeting the peak winter loads would be very high – and unprofitable).

See also CORPORATE OBJECTIVES; MARKETING OBJECTIVES; PLANNING PROCESS

Deming, W. Edwards   The US production management guru who introduced the (statistic and technologically based) concepts of quality control to the Japanese in the 1950s.

See also QUALITY

demographic data   *see* AGE INFLUENCES, ON THE PURCHASE DECISION; MARKETING RESEARCH, PRECISION MARKETING

demonstrations   Demonstrations are an activity at which the sales professional is expected naturally to excel; and one that he or she is typically less than well prepared for. To succeed in giving an excellent demonstration, you need to be expert in almost all areas of salesmanship. According to market research, no fewer than three-quarters of personal computer buyers expected to see a demonstration before buying, and nearly half of all the buyers rated such a demonstration as being the most influential marketing factor affecting their decision (twice the level of any other factor). There are a number of times in a sales campaign when a demonstration is likely to be most relevant; and, as such, the sales professional may even successfully run several demonstrations (each covering a different aspect) as the campaign progresses. The main excuses for a demonstration are as follows:

- *Exhibitions*. A demonstration is one excellent way of stimulating initial interest in the product or service. If the prospect sees the product doing things that he likes, and that he cannot do with his existing product, you may have made a convert. Clearly, this type of demonstration will be in a standard mould. It will also be given to a relatively large audience, not to an individual; since the cost of giving a demonstration (at least on a complex product) usually makes them inappropriate for single prospects.

- *Seminars*. Seminars featuring demonstrations are often used to open campaigns, but (depending on the exact subject matter) they can be used throughout the earlier stages of any campaign. In demonstration terms they offer the advantage of a captive audience; although this will usually be relatively small – eight is an ideal number. However, it is still a general audience; and the demonstration will need to be equally general.

- *Pre-closing*. The classic demonstration, however, is given for a single prospect; one who has been qualified as being worth all the effort. It is normally given in the closing stages of the campaign; as a final 'working' proof of the viability of a proposal.

See also CALL TARGETS; DESIGNING DEMONSTRATIONS; EXHIBITIONS; PROMOTIONAL MIX FACTORS; SELLING; SEMINARS; TELEVISION

demurrage Compensation paid when a shipment is delayed at a port.

department number *see* COUPON RESPONSE; RESPONSE RATES, MAILING

department stores *see* CHANNEL MEMBERSHIP; RETAIL PRODUCT OR SERVICE CATEGORIES

dependent demand *see* MATERIALS REQUIREMENTS PLANNING (MRP)

depot (warehouse) *see* FACILITY DECISIONS, LOGISTICS MANAGEMENT; PHYSICAL DISTRIBUTION MANAGEMENT

depreciation, advertising *see* ADVERTISING OBSOLESCENCE; LONGER–TERM COMPETITIVE SAW

depreciation, brand *see* ADVERTISING OBSOLESCENCE

depth This refers to the total number of products carried, across all the product lines, and thus relates to the market segments addressed. These may be very simply defined segments; where a range of pack sizes (from 'trial size' to 'jumbo economy') can address the differing value needs of consumers. Alternatively, they may be carefully targeted brands, such as Unilever uses in the detergent market, precisely aimed at different segments of a very large market.
See also PRODUCT (OR SERVICE) MIX

depth interview *see* INDIVIDUAL DEPTH INTERVIEWS

depth of identity *see* CONVICTION MARKETING FACTORS

deregulation *see* GLOBALIZATION; REGULATIONS

derived demand One clear difference about much of the demand for industrial products or services is that it is a 'derived demand'. It is derived, ultimately, from consumer demand. As a result, the industrial marketer (selling steel, say) may be just as concerned about the demand for the ultimate consumer product (the automobile, perhaps). In recent years this has led to the relationship between some industrial sellers and their customers being more akin to a 'partnership' – where both sides are in the same boat, in terms of being dependent upon the final product selling well to the consumer.
See also CUSTOMER CONTACT FORECASTS; INDUSTRIAL PURCHASING

derived forecasts All forecasts are based upon a series of assumptions (not least, in many cases, that the 'environmental factors' will remain unchanged). In practice though, in a different approach, lower-level forecasts can also be successfully derived from 'global' forecasts made at higher levels. The more sophisticated forecasters, and especially those whose organizations have large shares of their markets, may thus choose to split their forecasting process into a number of stages:

world and national economies > market > 'product' > by pack > by time

World and national economies
Sometimes called 'environmental forecasts', the highest level of all is that for the world economy; where the OECD (Organization for Economic Co-

operation and Development) usually provides the most widely respected forecasts. At the country level, the comparable figures are provided by government departments (in the UK, mainly by the Treasury), although other expert institutions (such as the London Business School and the Cambridge Group) also produce their own (sometimes conflicting) versions. Prior to the 1980s, these 'national' forecasts were often predicated upon the existence of 'cycles' of economic activity; moving from boom through to recession and back again over a 4–5 year period (matching, perhaps not without significance, the political cycles of the major economies) – although longer cycles of up to 60 years have been postulated (most notably by the Russian economist, Nicholai D. Kondratieff). These country-level forecasts are, however, often ignored by organization-level forecasters. This is less problematic than it may seem, though, as the national forecasters have a poor reputation for accuracy!

Market

The most important higher-level forecast, particularly for those organizations with high brand shares, is that of the market (or 'industry'). This will, of course, be affected by external factors. These may include the progress of the national economy, where a recession or boom (or the trade cycle in general) usually affects all markets, and demographic changes – for example, the 'baby boom' and the later 'baby bust' had major implications for organizations such as Mothercare. The market forecast will also take into account factors that are more specific to that market itself; whether it is relatively new, with large numbers of potential customers still to be recruited, or mature, with little further growth potential, say. Market forecasts tend to be based, as do individual product forecasts, on historical trends. However, they may also be based upon modelling the numbers of different customers (by type – possibly, in consumer markets, based on demographic changes) and predicting their changing usage patterns. This is particularly useful in new markets (where historical data is not available, except by analogy with existing similar markets), although it is not necessarily an easy technique to implement. Who are the potential users? How much will they each use? These may be very difficult questions to answer for a really innovatory new product or service.

'Product'

Most forecasting takes place at the product (or company) level, and is based on historical data. If, on the other hand, the market forecasts have already been completed (and calculated 'accurately') the alternative approach is to derive the product forecast from that of the market, by forecasting the changes in brand share. This is a rather different process, since it mainly focuses upon competitive positions (which may be under-weighted in other forecasts).

The wise forecaster will try to use both historical and derived forecasting methods, and see how the results compare. In general, the more forecasts (on different bases) that are undertaken, the more confidence can be placed in the final outcome. However, the comparison will often pose embarrassing problems for the forecaster, since the methods are quite likely to generate differing projections. But the process of explaining the differences (assuming that this is carried out with intellectual rigour, rather than just to reinforce existing prejudices) will often give the forecaster greater insight into the processes at work; and will, just as importantly, give a valuable indication of the likely accuracy of the forecast finally made.

By pack

From the product forecast it will often be necessary to forecast the sales of the individual packs, or variants, of the product (or service). These are frequently calculated as a simple percentage split, but the wise forecaster will also investigate any trends that may be present.

By time

The forecasts, or budgets, will also need to be expressed in terms of the budgetary periods (usually months), to take account of seasonality and special activities (promotions, for instance).

See also BRAND-SWITCHING MODEL ('MARKOV'); LONG–TERM FORECASTS; MACRO– AND MICRO–FORECASTS; MEDIUM–TERM FORECASTS; SHORT–TERM FORECASTS; SHORT– VERSUS LONG–TERM FORECASTS

design, and quality   *see* ZERO DEFECTS; ZERO DEFECTS VERSUS AQL

designer brands   *see* AESTHETICS

design fashions   Many of the most prevalent 'life cycles' relate to fashions in design. The television sets of the 1990s look very different (at least in the details) to those of the 1950s (or even those of the 1970s), although there has been no significant change in function that might explain this. Colour television, for instance, did not demand a different shape *per se*.

How the 'product' is packaged (the design of the retailer's store, and the outward shape of the product as much as the packing it comes in) reflects its time, and usually 'dates' the product far faster than the technology that it contains. 'Mid-life kickers' are, thus, often about redesign (of features as well as shape), to bring the product into line with current tastes (but without significantly changing its performance). As with technological life cycles there is, therefore, a design cycle – but, once more, it is largely under the control of the supplier.

designing demonstrations A demonstration is not about showing how your product works. It is about proving that it works. Above all, it is about selling your product, by showing it off to its best advantage. The general design of the demonstration, therefore, has to bring out the product's selling points. It also has to do this interestingly, understandably and even entertainingly: ideally, a demonstration should be a 'theatrical' performance (but not intrusively so). As theatre, the demonstration has to tell a story, building to a climax, with variations in pace to make it more interesting – very like a stage play. The design features, for instance, that you may need to consider in setting up the longer 'pre-closing' demonstration may include the following:

- *Demonstrate the basic needs.* In the rush to show all the benefits, there is a temptation to avoid showing the prospect the basic features that are essential to his needs. The basic needs will probably not be 'sexy', and may not be the factors that decide the sale – but if they are omitted they may lose it!
- *Be realistic.* In this context, the demonstration needs to be realistic, and believable. In meeting the prospect's needs, it has to do this in a way that simulates (at least) the real-life situation.
- *Be brief.* On the other hand, you should make these routine (mundane, and potentially boring) tasks as brief as possible – as long as you do demonstrate them.
- *Highlight the selling points.* The other objective of any demonstration is to sell your product. It is important, therefore, that your demonstration clearly highlights those aspects that are crucial to the main sales messages. However, such highlighting is best achieved by making it the focus of a logical structure: the demonstration should develop towards each of these points.

- *KISS.* The emphasis should be on keeping the demonstration simple. There have to be just a few clear points that you will want to make, and you will need to pare down your demonstration to its basic essentials, so that those key points are clear.
- *Structure.* To give the greatest clarity, the structure of the demonstration needs to be simple, clear and logical (to the extent that it should become self-evident to the prospect).
- *Invulnerability.* One key aspect of any demonstration is that it must be, as far as possible, 'idiot-proof'. If pressing the wrong button at the wrong time can ruin your demonstration, you can be certain that some idiot will push it with monotonous regularity.
- *Simplicity of use.* In addition to keeping the overall design simple, the actual use should be kept as simple as possible. This is so that even the proverbial idiot (in this case the sales professional) can run the demonstration. Ideally, it should be simple enough for the prospect – who you have to assume will have no previous experience – to run.
- *Preparation.* The one prerequisite for a successful demonstration is adequate preparation; and here, adequacy is a matter of putting in some considerable effort.

See also DEMONSTRATIONS; PROMOTION; SELLING

design of packaging *see* MARKETING STRATEGIES

design stage (research) *see* RESEARCH DIAMOND

desire in advertising models *see* BUYING DECISION, ADVERTISING MODELS

desk research *see* EXTERNAL DATA; WALKABOUT

desktop publishing (DTP) The use of special programs running on personal computers or workstations to produce near-typeset output, for small-scale publishing or reports.

destructive testing *see* TORTURE TESTING

detailed results, of research reports These should always be examined; preferably by looking at the original analyses (tables) as well as the written interpretation – since any interpretation distances you from the facts. These results should be examined critically. Do you agree with what the researcher has deduced from them? There is no reason why any researcher should be more capable than you – in terms of this analysis. It is true that he or she should be more experienced in the techniques involved, but you should be more experienced in the field being researched. 'Challenge' the results! Most often, you will find that you agree with the researcher. Occasionally, however, you will find new information which is worthwhile; and in all cases you will better understand what the research is about.

See also RESEARCH REPORTS, USAGE

detergent production   *see* ECONOMIES OF SCALE, GLOBAL

developing countries   *see* STANDARDIZATION VERSUS ADAPTATION

development cycle   *see* PRODUCT DEVELOPMENT

development investments   *see* BREAK-EVEN ANALYSIS, NEW PRODUCTS

development process   *see* PRODUCT DEVELOPMENT PROCESS

deviation from target   *see* MONITORING, PROGRESS

dialogue model of communication   This very simplified model of communication uses the specific analogy of the sales conversation to represent the whole range of communications processes available. Thus, market research is used to 'listen' to consumers:

Market research

'Promotion' comes in the other half of the dialogue, that of 'talking' to the consumer:

Promotion

The ideal form of promotion is, indeed, the conversation that takes place between the expert sales professional and his or her customer. It is ideal, when properly handled, because as well as being interactive, the communication in each direction (listening and talking) is specific to the needs of both – and, if successful, should end in the best possible solution, matching the needs of both. Other forms of promotion, which deal in the 'average' needs of groups of people, can only hope to approximate to this ideal.

See also ADVERTISING; SELLING

dialogue, relationships in marketing   *see* MARKETING TRIAD

diamond   *see* PROMOTIONAL LOZENGE

dichotomous question   One which can only be answered by 'yes' or 'no'.

See also QUESTIONNAIRE DESIGN

die stamping   Embossing, raising the surface in a pattern (a logo, for instance), of paper by compressing it between two dies.

difference (experimental research)   In some experimental research the objective is simply to see if the subject can tell the difference between the stimuli being presented. The usual method is to present two stimuli to the subject in a group of three, a 'triad' (where two are the same and one is different), and the subject is then asked to distinguish between them. If the subject cannot tell the difference, the results will be random.

See also EXPERIMENTAL RESEARCH

differentiation and branding   The epitome of the process of differentiation, making a product or service different from its competitors (so that a competitive advantage may be created), is 'branding'. The product is given a 'character', an 'image', almost like a personality. This is based first of all on a name (the brand), but then almost as much on the other factors that affect image; the packaging and, in particular, advertising. This all attempts to make the brand its own separate market, or at least its own segment; so that shoppers buy Heinz Baked Beans rather than ordinary baked beans. This sometimes succeeds to the extent that brands become generic (such as Kleenex, Hoover and Biro).

Trevor Watkins (1986) specifies it in the following terms:

The firm's strategy is to make its products different from its competitors in such a way that customers can be convinced that they are superior.

This can be done by making the physical product different or by making the way in which the customer perceives the product different, i.e. by psychological or emotional differences. These factors can be achieved by packaging differences, by having a range of sizes, shapes, qualities etc., by gimmicks, by after-sales service provision or perhaps most importantly by promotional activity – usually linked to at least one of the other differences. In monopolistic competition promotion is very often the main form of competition. The main aim of media advertising or 'above the line' promotion is to create a definite and distinct brand image.

In recent practice, it is also being applied to non-profit activities. In this case it is usually not for competitive reasons (although 'competition' between charities can sometimes be as cut-throat as any in the commercial sector), but as a means of improving awareness of what is available, and of differentiating between alternative offerings designed for different segments. It has even reached the stage at which government departments, such as the DTI, have adopted expensively created 'logos'! Gardner and Levy (1955) explain that 'a brand name is more than a label employed to differentiate among the manufacturers of a product. It is a complex symbol that represents a variety of ideas and attitudes. It tells the consumers many things not only by the way it sounds (and its literal meaning, if it has one) but, more important, via the body of associations it has built up and acquired as a public object over a period of time.'

See also BRAND EXTENSION; BRANDING; BRANDING POLICIES; BRAND MONOPOLY; MULTI-BRANDS; OWN BRANDS AND GENERICS; PRODUCT (OR SERVICE) POSITIONING; SEGMENTATION

Reference: Gardner, Burleigh and Levy, Sidney J. (1955) The product and the brand. *Harvard Business Review*, March–April.
Watkins, Trevor (1986) *The Economics of the Brand: A Marketing Analysis.* New York: McGraw-Hill.

diffused strategy *see* LOGICAL INCREMENTALISM

diffusion of innovation One particular aspect of consumer behaviour that has attracted considerable interest is that relating to the way in which new products, or new ideas, are taken up. As Gatignon and Robertson (1985) suggest:

The diffusion process can be characterized in terms of three dimensions; the rate of diffusion,

the pattern of diffusion, and the potential penetration level. The rate of diffusion reflects the speed at which sales occur over time. The diffusion pattern concerns the shape of the diffusion curve. Typically, the curve showing only decreasing returns and the S-shaped or sigmoid curve have been represented by exponential and logistic forms, respectively. The potential penetration level is a separate dimension indicating the size of the potential market – i.e. the maximum cumulative sales (or adoption) over time.

They also make the point that:

Marketing actions are important in influencing the speed of diffusion, as well as the process of diffusion by segment. Indeed, in most cases marketing actions are designed to achieve faster penetration, to block competition, and to establish a market franchise. Commitment of sizeable marketing expenditures . . . is likely to result in a diffusion function that is more similar to the exponential curve than to a sigmoid curve . . .

A final complication of the consumer decision-making process is that the adoption of new products is not necessarily uniform throughout the population. Everett Rogers (1962) found that there were five separate groups of consumers, each of which adopted different rates of new product adoption. They were, proceeding from the quickest adopters through to the laggards:

innovators	2.5 per cent
early adopters	13.5 per cent
early majority	34 per cent
later majority	34 per cent
laggards	16 per cent

The 'innovators' are seen by him to be venture-some, willing to take risks, whereas the 'early adopters' are the main opinion leaders in their community. This classification suggests that the marketer should perhaps take a particular interest in these two leading groups when a product launch is contemplated.

Adoption of innovation may not be without its costs. As Gatignon and Robertson also observe: 'This concept ["innovation or switching costs"] is more common in the adoption of production system innovations, but is also relevant for consumer innovations that have consequences or costs for the consumption system in which they are placed. For instance, the adoption of an innovation might require other changes in the consumption system or the adoption of ancillary services, which would raise the total cost of innovating . . .'. They add, 'New product innovators will be drawn from heavy users of other products within the product category . . . Heavy users have different knowledge structures – or ways to relate components of knowledge – such that improved predictions [by them] of outcomes can be made.'

In a wider context, Roy Amara gives the very important warning 'Don't be fooled by the diffusion curve', explaining that there are now:

> two familiar curves of 'percentage of adoption' of a technology with the passage of time. One of these – assumed to be actual – shows the long period of time over which some technologies diffuse to high levels of adoption and the many others which never go on to fulfil their early promise. The other curve – the perceived trajectory – is unfortunately the one we carry around in our heads in the early stages of new technologies. This perceived curve differs from the actual in two important respects – it is steadily increasing, and it grows in a much shorter period of time . . . The result is the usual hype gap in the early stages of a technology . . .

See also DECISION-MAKING PROCESS, BY CUSTOMERS; PRODUCT LIFE CYCLE (PLC); PURCHASE DECISION, MATCHING

References: Amara, Roy (1988) What we have learned about forecasting and planning. *Futures*, August.

Gatignon, Hubert and Robertson, Thomas S. (1985) A propositional inventory for new diffusion research. *Journal of Consumer Research*, 11, March.

Rogers, Everett M. (1962) *Diffusion of Innovations*. New York: The Free Press.

Digital Equipment Corporation   *see* GLOBALIZATION

Dilemma, Prisoner's   *see* PRISONER'S DILEMMA

diminishing marginal utility   *see* PRICES, CUSTOMER NEEDS

directional matrix   *see* ANSOFF MATRIX

directive questions   These are a form of closed (or partially closed) question, designed to steer the conversation in the direction you wish it to go. Typical examples open with 'If you could . . .', 'Do you . . .' and 'Would you . . .'.

See also QUESTIONING

direct mail   *see* CORPORATE PROMOTION VERSUS BRAND PROMOTION; COUPON RESPONSE; DELIVERY SYSTEMS, PRECISION MARKETING; ELECTRONIC DIRECT MAIL; PRECISION (DIRECT) MARKETING, RETAIL

direct mail advantages and disadvantages
The characteristics of direct mail give it certain advantages, and disadvantages, over most other means of promotion.

Advantages
- *Specific targeting.* Clearly, the most important aspect of direct mail (in common with all 'precision marketing', but to the greatest extent perhaps) is that it can be directed exactly at the specific, individual, customer.
- *Personalization.* It can address that customer personally. If the full benefits of precision marketing are exploited, it can be directly tailored to his or her needs (interactively based upon prior experience, as recorded on the database).
- *Optimization.* Because of its direct response nature, the marketing campaign(s) can be tested, and varied, to obtain the optimal results.
- *Cumulative.* Responses add to the database, allowing future mailings to be even better targeted.
- *Flexible.* A direct mail campaign can be mounted quickly on a wide variety of topics within an overall promotional campaign.

Disadvantages
- *Cost.* The cost per thousand will be higher than almost any other form of mass promotion (although the wastage rate may be much lower).
- *Poor quality lists.* The mailing lists may initially be of poor quality (with duplicate names etc.) which may be expensive to 'clean' or may even offend customers (by their duplication, for instance).
- *Relatively undeveloped.* The techniques of direct mail (at least in terms of precision marketing) are, as yet, relatively unsophisticated (as compared, say, with those applied to advertising), and this may mean that the medium is less effectively used.

Perhaps the greatest disadvantage, certainly in terms of consumer marketing, is the poor image that direct mail currently holds. Its popular description, as 'junk mail', is well deserved.

See also PRECISION MARKETING

direct mail advertising   Direct mail advertising is just one part, albeit a very large one, of direct marketing overall; but it can make an important contribution to closely targeted, precision-marketing campaigns – especially those in the industrial sector – as a way of generating numbers of prospects. The normal response rate for such mailings is often claimed to be as much as 1 or 2 per cent, but in practice rates can be much lower. On the other hand, mailing to specialized markets, with particularly powerful messages, they can reach almost 10 per cent. Even so, you will still have to distribute large numbers to obtain even reasonable numbers of prospects; it is a 'numbers game' with a vengeance. Pierre Passavant (1984) makes the point, which is not widely appreciated, that 'The direct marketer allocates a far larger proportion of the sales dollar to promotion than manufacturers or most sellers of packaged goods . . .'.

As with all forms of promotion, however, before conducting any mailing you have to be clear what your specific objectives are. Most mailings are designed to produce immediate sales leads – enquiries. Even then, you may decide to set your specific objective as attracting people to a free seminar, or to 'buy' enquiries by offering a free sample.

Reference: Passavant, Pierre A. (1984) Direct marketing strategy. In Edward L. Nash (ed.), *The Direct Marketing Handbook*. New York: McGraw-Hill.

direct mail coupons   *see* PROMOTIONAL PRICING

direct mail databook   *see* AGENCY CHOICE; MAILING LIST

direct mail houses   *see* IN-HOUSE DATA, PRECISION MARKETING

direct mail message   *see* DIRECT MAIL OFFER

direct mail offer   The basis for a mailing has to be an 'offer'. This may be simply a statement of the products or services, or it can be a specific promotion. As with all forms of promotion, you need to be very clear what your real offer is and, despite the apparent opportunity to convey large amounts of material, you will usually need it to be kept as simple as possible. The material will almost inevitably arrive on the prospect's desk at the same time as half a dozen other pieces of flotsam and jetsam – just when he or she wants to get on with more important things. Thus, as with all advertising, your direct mail message will have just a very few seconds to grab their attention – otherwise it will be consigned to the waste-basket, along with the rest of the rubbish that they receive. The much quoted sales acronym, KISS (Keep It Simple, Stupid), is nowhere more applicable than in mailings. Finally, as direct mail is almost always only a part of a wider campaign, there must be a clear action associated with the message. This may be just the suggestion (but a strong one) that the recipient should return the reply-paid card; or it may be a stronger action, telling the recipient to be prepared for a telephone call from a salesperson.

See also PRECISION MARKETING

direct mail sales   *see* PROMOTIONAL LOZENGE

direct mail sales force   *see* AGENT (PERSONAL) SELLING

direct mail sampling   *see* SAMPLING

direct mail selling   *see* CHANNEL DECISIONS; PRECISION (DIRECT) MARKETING, RETAIL

direct mail selling organizations   *see* AGENT (PERSONAL) SELLING

directories   These are a prime source of external data about organizations, typically providing lists that have been prepared in a variety of useful ways. The most important of these will be available in your central library; but the more specialized ones may only be found in the trade association libraries. The most useful, generally available, ones referred to in industrial marketing, for example, are:

- *Yellow Pages* – giving the widest coverage, but the least useful information
- *Kompass* – giving details of the larger companies (nation by nation), together with the products they produce

These may be supplemented by national directories, such as (in the UK):

- *Dunn & Bradstreet Key British Enterprises* – giving much the same information (but also regionally)
- *Kellys Manufacturers and Merchants* – providing wider coverage, but with less detail

For many marketers, these directories can be invaluable sources of potential customers, but they can also be almost as valuable (for managers in general) as a source of services: the cross-indices of *Kompass*, for example, show who supplies what service or product.
See also EXTERNAL DATA; LIBRARIES

direct response   *see* COUPON RESPONSE

dirty proof   One with many corrections to be made.

discard peripherals   This very simple rule, which follows from the Pareto 80:20 rule, works from the other extreme to that of 'boost core competences', and is even more ruthless. It demands that you do not just ignore the weaker elements of your operations, which some define as anything that is not central to the core competences, but that you actually discard them.
See also BOOST CORE COMPETENCES; CORE COMPETENCES; PARETO, 80:20, EFFECT

discontinuous innovation   *see* RADICAL INNOVATION

discount close   *see* CLOSING TECHNIQUES

discount outlets   *see* RETAIL PRODUCT OR SERVICE CATEGORIES

discounts   Having set the overall price, the supplier then has the option of offering different prices (usually on the basis of a discount) to cover different circumstances. The types of discount most often offered are as follows:

- *Quantity discounts.* Those who offer to buy larger quantities of the product or service (typically as part of the distribution chain, but also the larger industrial buyers) are frequently given incentives. In consumer markets this is more often achieved by larger pack sizes (or by banding together smaller packs) as 'family or economy' packs. It is often deemed more cost-effective to offer extra product ('30 per cent extra free' or '13 for the price of 12') instead of reducing price; because the extra product represents only a marginal increase in cost to the supplier – and may push the user into using more (and even finding new uses).
- *Cash discounts.* Where credit is offered, it is sometimes decided to offer an incentive for cash payment or for prompt payment (to persuade customers to pay their bills on the due date – although too often they take the discount anyway and still pay late).
- *Allowances.* In the durable goods market suppliers often attempt to persuade consumers to buy a new piece of equipment by offering allowances against trade-in of their old one. Generally speaking, these are simply hidden discounts targeted at a group of existing 'competitive' users.
- *Seasonal discounts.* Suppliers to markets that are highly seasonal (such as the holiday market) will often price their product or service to match the demand, with the highest prices at peak demand.
- *Promotional pricing.* Suppliers may, from time to time, wish to use a price discount as a specific promotional device.
- *Individual pricing.* Under certain circumstances it may be possible for a customer, even in a consumer market, to negotiate a special price; and such haggling is the essence of sales in some of the Mediterranean countries. It may also be the basis of some industrial and business-to-business selling. The pricing decision is here left to the sales professional, often with disastrous effects on profit.
- *Features, optional.* The reverse of discounts may be that customers are offered a basic product to which they can add features, at extra cost (and often, unlike discounts, with much higher profit margins).
- *Product bundling.* Instead of a discount, customers might be offered a 'bundle' of related products – a package of accessories with a camera, for instance; typically in this case at a reduced price, as compared with the prices of the separate items (although sometimes the separate items are not really sold apart from the special promotional 'bundle').
- *Psychological pricing.* Some suppliers deliberately set very high 'recommended' prices in order to be able to offer seemingly very high discounts ('massive savings') against them. This is a policy which may, however, rebound when consumers realize what is happening – and, in any case, such tactics are now often subject to regulation, and may even be illegal.

See also BUNDLING; COMPETITION PRICING; COST–PLUS PRICING; PRICE, PURCHASE; PRICING POLICIES, PRACTICAL; PROMOTIONAL PRICING; PSYCHOLOGICAL PRICING; SERVICE PRICES; TRADE DISCOUNTS

discriminant analysis This technique is used to test how reliable the variables used in data analysis are as predictors, by indicating how well they measure (and distinguish between) the factors. In effect, it is the reverse of regression analysis, where the aim is to maximize the ratio:

(variance between group means)/(variance within groups)

See also ANALYSIS OF MARKETING RESEARCH DATA; MULTIPLE DISCRIMINANT ANALYSIS

discriminating monopoly A monopoly where the supplier charges different prices to different segments; for example, charging one price to domestic consumers and another to industrial ones.

discussion meeting *see* PRESENTATION STYLE

diseased ego *see* VISION, CORPORATE

diseconomies of scale The opposite of economies of scale – the unit cost rises as volumes increase.
See also ECONOMIES OF SCALE

disintegration The decision to buy-in rather than make in-house.
See also MAKE OR BUY

Disney, Walt *see* CONVICTION MARKETING TYPES

disparaging copy *see* KNOCKING COPY

display advertising Advertising, usually based on a design of one form or another, which is not just text (typically classified) advertising.
See also CLASSIFIED ADVERTISING; CREATING THE COR-RECT MESSAGES; CREATIVE DEPARTMENT, ADVERTISING AGENCY; MEDIA BUYING, ADVERTISING AGENCY; MEDIA SELECTION

display outer An outer pack which, while providing the usual function of an outer in offering protection in transit, also opens out to offer a display at point of sale.
See also PACKAGING; SALES PROMOTION

dissatisfied buyer *see* ORGANIZATIONAL BUYING SITUATIONS

dissatisfiers *see* PSYCHOLOGICAL INFLUENCES, ON THE PURCHASE DECISION

dissident shareholders *see* DEFENSIVE (CORPORATE) PR

dissolve A process whereby one image is replaced by another by mixing them together; as compared with a fade, where the changeover is accomplished by fading to black between the two (or a jump cut, where the images are simply butted, resulting in a noticeable jump). The process orginated in filming, but is now often used (with two or more slide projectors) in sophisticated presentations.
See also PRESENTATION MEDIA

dissonance, cognitive *see* COGNITIVE DISSONANCE

distance *see* ACCESSIBILITY, FILTERING UNSUITABLE FOREIGN MARKETS

distinctive competence *see* MISSION

distinctive identity *see* CONVICTION MARKETING FACTORS

distortion of message *see* ENCODING

distress merchandise Stock sold off cheaply to reduce debts.
See also PRICING STRATEGY; SALES PROMOTION

distribution *see* LOCAL SALES ORGANIZATION; PROMOTIONAL MIX FACTORS

distribution battle *see* GROWTH STAGE, PRODUCT LIFE CYCLE

distribution building *see* BUILDING DISTRIBUTION

distribution centre A supplier's (regional) centre, which receives bulk deliveries for splitting into smaller deliveries for local distribution to retailers.
See also PHYSICAL DISTRIBUTION MANAGEMENT

distribution chain In the sale of goods there frequently may be a chain of intermediaries involved, each passing the product down the chain to the next organization, before it finally reaches the consumer or end-user. This process is known as the 'distribution chain' or as the 'channel' (of distribution). Each of the elements in these chains will have their own specific needs, which the producer must take into account, along with those of the all-important end-user. The ideal sales situation is that where the sup-

plier and the customer meet face-to-face for a dialogue. There are, however, many products and services where the value of the individual sale does not
justify such an approach, nor any other form of direct
approach from the producer. The sale then has to
made through intermediaries, who can spread their
costs across a range of products or services from
different producers. The most obvious examples of
these intermediaries are the retailers (rather than the
original manufacturers) from whom we buy our consumer goods. But such intermediaries can be found
in a wide variety of situations. These intermediaries
may also hold stock, provide service support and act
as information gatherers and business consultants to
the original producer. The exact relationship will
depend in part upon the legal, contractual implications of the specific type of intermediary; a dealer
will, for example, be totally independent of the producer, whereas an agent will be acting on behalf of
that producer – and will typically be operating the
same terms and conditions.
See also CHANNEL DECISIONS; CHANNEL MEMBERS;
CHANNELS, AS CUSTOMERS; CHANNEL STRUCTURE; PRO-
MOTIONAL MIX FACTORS

distribution channel, pricing   *see* PRICE AND
THE DISTRIBUTION CHANNEL

distribution company   *see* DOOR-TO-DOOR

distribution data   *see* MARKETING AUDIT

distribution gap   One gap between the actual and
potential sales of a brand is that posed by the limits
on the distribution of the product or service. If it is
limited to certain geographical regions as, for example, some draught beers are, it cannot expect to make
sales in other regions. At the other end of the spectrum, the multinationals may take this to the extremes of globalization – at which no part of the
globe can avoid exposure to their products. Equally,
if the product is limited to certain outlets – just as
some categories of widely advertised drugs are limited by law to pharmacies – then other outlets will
not be able to sell them.
See also COMPETITIVE GAP; GAP ANALYSIS; PRODUCT
(OR SERVICE) GAP; USAGE GAP

distribution levels   *see* CHANNEL MEMBERS

distribution management   *see* LOGISTICS
MANAGEMENT

distribution objectives   *see* MARKETING
OBJECTIVES

distribution of data   *see* ELECTRONIC MAIL

distribution of income   *see* EXPORT MARKET
ELIMINATION

distribution patterns, product screening   In
terms of proposed new products, if existing channels
of distribution can be used then costs will be minimized; and the product or service will be built on
existing strengths. If new channels are needed, then
development of these may pose significant costs, and
will lead to a learning curve in the handling of those
channels – a factor that is not necessarily understood
by managements.
See also NEW PRODUCT SCREENING, PRODUCT FACTORS

distribution processes   *see* LOGISTICS
MANAGEMENT

distributive trades   A collective term for wholesalers and retailers.
See also RETAILING; WHOLESALERS AND DISTRIBUTORS

distributors   *see* AGENTS OR DISTRIBUTORS;
MIDDLEMEN/AGENTS; WHOLESALERS AND
DISTRIBUTORS

divergent marketing   Setting up separate groups
for each of the organization's main lines, so that each
is a distinct profit centre.
See also PRODUCT (OR SERVICE) MIX; PRODUCT (OR
SERVICE) STRATEGY; PRODUCT PORTFOLIO

divergent thinking   *see* SYNECTICS®

diversification (strategy)   This involves a quantum leap, to a new product and a new market.
It consequently involves more risk, and is more
normally undertaken by organizations that find
themselves in markets that have limited, often
declining, potential. It can, however, be a positive
move to extend the application of existing expertise; Heinz, for instance, has steadily (and
successfully) extended beyond its '57 varieties' core
business (which revolved around baked beans and
soups).
See also ANSOFF MATRIX; MARKET ENTRY DECISION;
PRODUCT (OR SERVICE) STRATEGY

divestment strategies   *see* DECLINE STRATEGIES

dog   In the popular application of the Boston Matrix, the 'dog' is a product in the quadrant with low market share and low market growth rate. A product here has little or no future. It may not yet be making a loss, unless it is demanding a disproportionate use of overheads, but it will probably do so in the not too distant future. Hence it too should have its future regularly reviewed; so that it can be discontinued as soon as it becomes a burden. This perhaps ought to be sooner than the strict cash flows might demand, for the problems can too easily distract management's attention from more important, and more profitable, products.
See also BOSTON MATRIX

Dole Hawaiian pineapples   *see* GLOBAL MARKETING

domestic (home) market   *see* STRUCTURE OF INTERNATIONAL MARKETING

door-to-door   An alternative, and cheaper, approach to direct mail is to employ a door-to-door (of which, in the UK, the Royal Mail itself is one example) to drop unaddressed mailings (and through-the-letterbox material in general) to all addresses in a specific area (either as an individual operation, 'solus', or perhaps more frequently on a shared basis). This loses many of the personalized, and more directly targeted, advantages of direct mail. But where the area is tightly defined (as it can be by using 'residential neighbourhoods', such as ACORN), it can still offer a degree of precision. In particular, it now offers a very good vehicle for 'sampling' new users on a tightly targeted basis (and, once again, it can be optimized by testing). The maximum coverage by delivery organizations in the UK (such as Circular Distributors and Donnelly Marketplace) is 16.5 million homes (85 per cent of the total), but other levels are, for instance, 'Standard National' (15 million homes), 'Urban' (10 million homes) and 'Combination' (6 million homes in major cities). The cost per thousand reflects the ease of reaching these different addresses.
See also MARKETING RESEARCH; PRECISION MARKETING; PROMOTIONAL PRICING; PROMOTION OBJECTIVES; TEST MARKET

dormant   No longer active, typically used of a customer account that has stopped buying.
See also TERRITORY MANAGEMENT

double-decker   Two poster sites, one immediately above the other.
See also POSTERS

double-page spread   An advertisement that covers the whole of two facing pages, in a magazine or newspaper.
See also ADVERTISING PROCESSES, ON THE PURCHASE DECISION

down market   Appealing to a less wealthy segment of the population.
See also SOCIAL CLASS INFLUENCES, ON THE PURCHASE DECISION

downside   The negative aspect of a situation, especially that of making a loss.

downsizing   A polite term (and implied justification) for large-scale redundancies.
See also BUSINESS PROCESS RE-ENGINEERING

drawdown   The drawing of funds against a line of credit.

drift, position   *see* POSITION DRIFT

drill (2 mm)   *see* PRODUCTS VERSUS BENEFITS

drip   A long campaign, with advertisements appearing at long intervals.
See also ADVERTISING

drive time   The (peak) time during which radio listeners are driving to work.

driving forces   *see* GLOBALIZATION

dry-run   A final rehearsal, of a presentation, say.
See also PRESENTATIONS

DTP   *see* DESKTOP PUBLISHING (DTP)

dubbing   Superimposing a sound track over the completed film.

dummy calls   *see* SALES TRAINING

dummy 'department number'   *see* COUPON RESPONSE

dummy pack   An empty pack used for display purposes.

dumping   *see* ECONOMIES OF SCALE, GLOBAL; UNLOADING

dumping, of product   *see* INTERNATIONAL PRICE DECISION

Dun & Bradstreet   *see* INTERNATIONAL MARKETING RESEARCH

duplicate entries   *see* DATABASE, INVESTING IN YOUR OWN; MAILING LIST

durables   *see* PRODUCT OR SERVICE CATEGORIES

dustbin audit   *see* PANEL RESEARCH

Dutch auction   A form of bidding where the price starts high and comes down until someone accepts it.

duties payable on imported goods   *see* REGULATORY CONSIDERATIONS, FILTERING UNSUITABLE MARKETS

dying product   *see* BUDGETS

dynamic obsolescence   Deliberate obsolescence created by replacing a product with a new version. *See also* PRODUCT CHURNING, NEW PRODUCTS

dynamic or static models   *see* MODEL CATEGORIES

dynamics of forecasting   *see* FORECASTING DYNAMICS

E

early adopters   *see* DIFFUSION OF INNOVATION

early signals   *see* SCANNING, AND MIS; TEAM
SCANNING

earning the right   *see* SALES CALL OPENING

EC (EU) harmonization of standards   *see*
REGULATORY CONSIDERATIONS, FILTERING UNSUITABLE
MARKETS

econometric models   The models used by
forecasters can grow to be very large, and are not
necessarily limited to one equation. The very
large econometric models, which simulate the
workings of national economies, can contain
hundreds of factors spread across dozens of linked
equations – and requiring large amounts of computing power to run. Unfortunately, as a result, they
are barely understandable even to those running
them.
See also QUANTITATIVE FORECASTING TECHNIQUES;
TIME-SERIES ANALYSIS

economic batch quantity   The trade-off between (stock) holding cost and set-up cost which
determines the lowest overall cost per batch. One
great advantage of flexible manufacturing is that,
by reducing set-up times (and hence set-up costs),
the size of the economic batch can be significantly
reduced.
See also INVENTORY CONTROL; JUST IN TIME (JIT);
KANBAN; LOGISTICS MANAGEMENT; OPTIMIZED PRO-
DUCTION TECHNOLOGY (OPT); SET-UP TIMES

economic buyer   *see* DECISION-MAKERS AND
INFLUENCERS

economic buying influence   *see* DECISION-
MAKERS AND INFLUENCERS

economic influences, on the purchase decision
For many of the more theoretical marketers, especially those coming from the economic disciplines,
the main influence on the customer's purchase deci-

sion is seen to be economic; particularly in the case
of the industrial sale. The influence of economic
factors appears first of all in terms of the economic 'well-being' of the consumers. One of the
methods of categorization of consumers, therefore,
is by income group. This behaviour is modified
by the overall economic climate. If the climate is
optimistic and a boom is under way, the domestic
consumer will be likely to spend more money.
For many economists and not a few marketing
theorists, however, price is by itself by far the single
most important factor. This is the reason for its el-
evation to become, by itself, one of the four Ps. An
even larger group of marketers, on the other hand,
would contend that there may be many other factors
which are, depending on the situation, even more
important.
See also DECISION-MAKING PROCESS, BY CUSTOMERS;
REPEAT PURCHASING PROCESS

economic order quantity (EOQ)   *see* COMPUTER
INVENTORY CONTROL; PRODUCTION DECISIONS,
LOGISTICS MANAGEMENT

economies of scale   One of the major hidden
assumptions of some marketing theories, including
the Boston Matrix, is that there are 'economies
of scale'. The more that is sold, the more that is
produced, the lower (it is assumed) will be the unit
cost.
   This is a philosophy that used to be embraced
in particular by Japanese corporations. Kotler and
Fahey (1982) make the point that 'The Japanese
search for market segments that exhibit strong
economies of scale and strong experience curve
effects. Their strategy is to enter the market with
a low-priced improved product, capture a large
market share, and in the process bring down
manufacturing costs to allow real learning curve
effects to take place as well as the generation of substantial margins to be used elsewhere in the marketing arena.'
   Such economies of scale are widely believed
to apply in many industries. They may simply
result from the increased efficiencies to be ob-

tained from large-scale plants, or just from the effect of spreading fixed overheads across larger volumes.

Support from a rather different direction (and reflecting an 'economy of scale' which derives from position in the market) comes from Robert Buzzell (1981) who found, from an analysis of PIMS data, that 'market share distributions are highly skewed . . . a distribution in which each competitor's share is in constant proportion to the next higher ranked competitor's share . . . with about two thirds lying between 0.5 and 0.8 . . . It should come as no surprise, therefore, to find that sales of a given product category are highly concentrated among a few leading competitors, and that when competitors are ranked by size, each one is considerably larger than the next on the list.' This position is moderated by only one factor: 'businesses with very large market shares tend, on average, to lose share gradually over time'.

On the other hand, research undertaken by John Stopford et al. tends to indicate that, at least in the industries studied (which were dominated by organizations in the process of regenerating themselves), the volumes needed for optimal economies of scale have recently been reducing (possibly in part as a result of the introduction of microprocessing techniques).

More generally, though, as indicated by the Japanese example, 'experience' is now seen as the main source of economies of scale. The more that is 'produced', the more that is learned, and the more experience that is available to reduce costs. This element of economies of scale relates to experience over the total production run, not just the current production levels, so its effect is cumulative, potentially offering the early leaders a major competitive advantage – and creating substantial barriers against late entrants. Matsushita, for example, looks to very long term investments in order to build the economies of scale resulting from such experience.

See also EXPERIENCE CURVES; FLEXIBLE MANUFACTURING; PRODUCTION DECISIONS, LOGISTICS MANAGEMENT; VARIETY

References: Buzzell, Robert D. (1981) Are there 'natural' market structures? *Journal of Marketing*, Winter.

Kotler, Philip and Fahey, Liam (1982) The world's champion marketers. *The Japanese Journal of Business Strategy*, 3(1).

Baden Fuller, C. W. F., Dell'Osso, F. and Stopford, J. M. (1988) Competition dynamics behind the mask of matu-rity. Paper presented to the conference on Corporate Strategy and Industrial Organisation, London Business School, 12 December 1988.

economies of scale, entry barriers *see* EXPERIENCE CURVES

economies of scale, global Concentrating the total demands of a number of countries on a limited number of plants, and sharing the accumulated experience (as well as engaging in joint pur-chasing across these plants), should lead to economies of scale. Procter & Gamble, for example, successfully concentrated detergent production on fewer plants than Unilever, potentially gaining a cost advantage in the process (although this was undermined by the shift to liquid detergents, which were less susceptible to economies of scale). Similarly, there might be some economies to be achieved by global marketing (as recommended by the advertising agency Saatchi & Saatchi – before they found that their own economies of scale were less evident!); for example, expensive commercials could be used in several countries. McCann-Erickson (as reported by Quelch and Hoff, 1986) said that they saved $90 million in production costs, over 20 years, on Coca Cola commercials in this way. Hamel and Prahalad (1985), however, make the important point that the impacts of global organization may be complex: 'It is more difficult to respond to the new global competition than we often assume. A company must be sensitive to the potential of global competitive interaction even when its manufacturing is not on a global scale. Executives need to understand the way in which competitors use cross-subsidization to undermine seemingly strong domestic share positions.' In other words, a company's business may be destroyed by 'dumping' when a foreign competitor is determined to buy entry into the market.

See also COMPARATIVE ADVANTAGE, GLOBAL; GLOBALIZATION; GLOBAL MARKETING

References: Hamel, Gary and Prahalad, C. K. (1985) Do you really have a global strategy? *Harvard Business Review*, July–August.

Quelch, John A. and Hoff, Edward J. (1986) Customizing global marketing. *Harvard Business Review*, May–June.

economies of scope These exist if it is cheaper to produce two different products together rather than separately.

See also ECONOMIES OF SCALE

Economist Intelligence Unit *see* INTERNATIONAL MARKETING RESEARCH

economy packs *see* TRADE DISCOUNTS

ECR *see* ERROR CAUSE REMOVAL (ECR)

EDI *see* ELECTRONIC DATA INTERCHANGE (EDI)

edit To change text to improve it. In the case of promotion, this task is usually carried out by a professional editor.
See also CREATING THE CORRECT MESSAGES; CREATIVE DEPARTMENT, ADVERTISING AGENCY

editorial In the context of advertising, this is the material appearing in the media, especially the text and illustrations in newspapers and magazines, that is controlled by the editor (and publisher) rather than by advertisers.
See also MEDIA IMPACT; MEDIA SELECTION; MEDIA TYPES

editorial advertisement An advertisement (in a newspaper or magazine) that looks like editorial, but that will usually be labelled 'advertisement'.
See also ADVERTISING PROCESSES

editorial comment *see* SECONDARY SOURCES OF COMMUNICATION

editorial mention A mention of an organization (or individual) – good or bad – in the editorial content of a publication.
See also PUBLIC RELATIONS

education *see* INNER MARKETING CAMPAIGN

education level *see* SOCIAL AND BUSINESS STRUCTURES, FILTERING UNSUITABLE MARKETS

effective cover Coverage in terms of the percentage of the target audience who have seen the commercial four times (which is said to be the minimum number of impressions to have adequate impact) rather than just once (which is the case for 'coverage').
See also AUDIENCE RESEARCH; COVERAGE; CUMULATIVE AUDIENCE; MEDIA BUYING, ADVERTISING AGENCY; MEDIA SELECTION

effectiveness of press advertising *see* COUPON RESPONSE

effectiveness of test markets *see* TEST MARKET

efficiency of the production processes *see* ECONOMIES OF SCALE; EXPERIENCE CURVES

EFTPOS Electronic Funds Transfer at Point Of Sale, whereby the retailer has an electronic/computer link (at the checkout, for instance) that enables the customer's bank or credit account to be immediately debited for the purchase.
See also EPOS AND EFTPOS, PRECISION MARKETING

ego, diseased, monument to *see* VISION, CORPORATE

ego drift *see* POSITION DRIFT

EIU, marketing in Europe *see* INTERNATIONAL MARKETING RESEARCH

elasticity of demand *see* CROSS-ELASTICITY OF DEMAND; PRICE ELASTICITY OF DEMAND

electoral register *see* SAMPLES

Electrolux washing machines *see* GLOBAL MARKETING

electronic conferences *see* COMPUTER-MEDIATED COMMUNICATIONS (CMC)

electronic data interchange (EDI) A method – and a philosophy – of allowing organizations to communicate with each other (typically, to place orders for supplies) and with their banks, despite their having incompatible computer systems.
See also ORDER PROCESSING

electronic direct mail Some organizations have recently started to use telex and fax in the same way as direct mail. This is more expensive, but may be more likely to be read by the recipient (due to its, as yet, unusual nature). This approach is now being extended to 'E-mail'. All of these media follow the rules of 'direct mail', and are likely to become just as susceptible to being treated as 'junk mail', as greater use is made of them!
See also PRECISION MARKETING

electronic funds transfer *see* EFTPOS; EPOS AND EFTPOS, PRECISION MARKETING

electronic mail   The increasing use of 'electronic mail' should have a dramatic effect on the availability of information. Using this, it is almost as easy to send a memo to a hundred recipients as to one. Indeed if, as is the case with most such systems, 'standard' distribution lists are available, it is even easier! This has a number of important implications:

- *Speed of distribution.* The data now becomes available to everyone immediately (or, at least, as soon as they return to their terminal).
- *Breadth of distribution.* The key data is now, typically, distributed to ten times as many managers; providing them with data that they might previously have missed and yet needed for their work. More likely, but equally importantly, it provides them with a better perspective of what is happening throughout the organization.
- *Lateral communications.* These managers are now likely to be involved in a lateral transfer of information (between members of a department, and even across departmental boundaries) as well as (and often instead of) hierarchical communications through the normal management structure. This has implications for organizational structures, offering data flows that are much more like those of Japanese organizations than those of the traditional Western organization.

However, this is not an unmixed blessing. The fact that memos may be distributed to ten times as many managers also means that each of them will now receive ten times as many memos as before. It is not unknown for managers who are at the focus of activities to return to their desk after a couple of days' absence and find more than a hundred memos waiting for them (and this before the commercial distributors of 'junk mail' have found their way on to such networks). The obvious problem is that of data overload. If the manager is not to sink under the sheer torrent of such verbal data, he must learn new techniques:

- *Data senders.* In view of its rather different characteristics, the originators of data transmitted this way have to find means of making the content more immediately understandable. For example, the title of the memo will need to be meaningful in itself (and may have to be associated with an equally meaningful 'keyword abstract'). A brief summary or abstract will, in any

case, be needed for the reader who is skimming the mail to see which items are relevant and should be read in more detail. The verbal data itself will need to be clearly structured, so that the readers will be quickly able to select just those parts which are directly relevant to them. There will be every incentive to learn these new techniques, since those who send long, unstructured memos will soon find that they are not read.

- *Data receivers.* In view of its rather different characteristics, those receiving memos and reports by electronic mail will have to learn new skills; such as how to prioritize their use of incoming data – ruthlessly discarding the 80 per cent that is useless or irrelevant, and handling the remaining 20 per cent in the most appropriate way (selecting for immediate action, or filing for future attention, or adding it to an information database).

See also COMPUTER-MEDIATED COMMUNICATIONS (CMC); DATA ACCESS PROBLEMS ELECTRONIC DIRECT MAIL; ROUTING RULES; WRITTEN REPORTS

electronic point of sale   *see* EPOS AND EFTPOS, PRECISION MARKETING

electronic shopping   *see* PRECISION (DIRECT) MARKETING, RETAIL

7 Eleven   *see* GLOBALIZATION

elicitation interview   A specialized form of survey interview using open-ended questions to elicit the respondent's key determinants of their buying behaviour (typically six in number).
See also SURVEY RESEARCH

Reference: Sampson, Peter (1986) Qualitative research and motivation research. In Robert Worcester and John Downham (eds), *Consumer Research Handbook* (3rd edn). New York: McGraw-Hill.

E-mail   *see* ELECTRONIC DIRECT MAIL

embassy in the foreign country   *see* AGENTS OR DISTRIBUTORS

embassy trade department   *see* ACCESSIBILITY, FILTERING UNSUITABLE FOREIGN MARKETS

embossing   *see* DIE STAMPING

emergent strategy   The traditional theory relating to corporate strategy neglects one very important aspect, which is that a considerable amount of strategy emerges as a result of unpredictable changes in the environment rather than from rational control by management. This emergent strategy means that managers are forced to follow courses of action that they had not planned.

This is most clearly illustrated by a diagram:

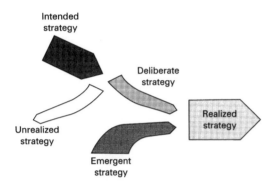

This diagram very clearly shows how the intended strategy, decided upon traditionally or incrementally, is overtaken by events in two main ways. One, which will probably be recognized by the organization, is that of unrealized strategy, where it proves impossible to implement the chosen strategy in practice.

Less obvious is the emergent strategy that is decided by events in the external environment – and, thus, forced upon the organization. This may not necessarily be recognized, in its totality, by the organization, since many of its implications may be hidden. As markets become more complex, however, such emergent strategies are becoming more common.

Many organizations see both of these processes in terms of failure: they have been forced, usually by unpredictable events, to abandon their own strategy. There is, accordingly, a tendency for these unwelcome facts to be ignored until they are so obvious that they cannot be avoided. This is a major error. Such deviations must be recognized (probably through one or other form of environmental analysis, coupled with networking) as soon as possible – so that the organization can react in good time.

A much more powerful approach, however, is to be proactive – to seize upon these deviations as the basis for future developments. What needs to be recognized is that emergent strategies are the most powerful strategies of all. They must, by definition, be directly derived from the needs of the market: even successful deliberate strategies may not ideally match market needs, but may achieve their targets by sheer force (especially where conviction marketing lies behind them). Emergent strategies are, thus, likely to be vigorous ones.

There are two main approaches to capitalizing on such emergent strategies. The first of these, favoured in the West, is the umbrella strategy. This is a form of very positive delegation, in that the overall strategies, the umbrella, are very general in nature – and allow the lower-level managers, who are closest to the external environment, the freedom to react to these changes.

A much more direct, and hence even more powerful, approach is that favoured by the Japanese corporations. They integrate emergent strategies with their own. Indeed, it is arguable that, in terms of marketing, to a large extent they use emergent strategies instead of deliberate strategy. This is evidenced as much by an attitude of mind as by any other feature. They deliberately go out to look for symptoms of such emergent trends that can be detected in the performance of their own products. More than that, though, they often deliberately launch a range of products rather than a single one, to see which is most successful. It is almost as if they deliberately seek out the emergent strategies by offering the best environment for them to develop – the very reverse of the Western approach, which seeks to avoid them! The Japanese then go on to build on these emergent strategies with a number of very effective tools, most of which are designed to overcome the major problem that accompanies emergent strategies – that they emerge on the scene much later than deliberate ones (and are likely to be visible to all the competitors at the same time), so that time is the essence. Thus, time management techniques (including parallel development, along with flexible manufacturing and JIT), which have been developed by the Japanese, offer them a significant competitive advantage in handling such emergent strategies.

See also CORPORATE PLAN; CORPORATE STRATEGY AND MARKETING; LOGICAL INCREMENTALISM; PARADIGM SHIFT, STRATEGY; PLANNING PROCESS

empirical data   Data obtained from direct observation.

employee attitudes   *see* INNER MARKET

employee motivations/wants   *see* INNER MARKET

employment agency   *see* RECRUITMENT, OF SALES PERSONNEL

employment by sector   *see* SOCIAL AND BUSINESS STRUCTURES, FILTERING UNSUITABLE MARKETS

employment levels   *see* SOCIAL AND BUSINESS STRUCTURES, FILTERING UNSUITABLE MARKETS

empty nest   *see* AGE INFLUENCES, ON THE PURCHASE DECISION

enclosures, mail   *see* LETTER, DIRECT MAIL

encoding   The most generally quoted model of the communication process stresses the element of 'encoding':

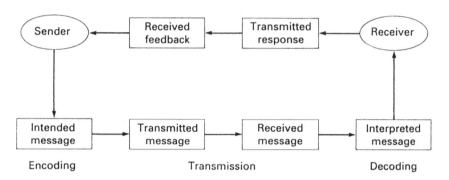

This is an elaborate way of saying that human-to-human communication is a very complex process, and that there is considerable latitude for misinterpretation. More fundamentally, it illustrates the need for considerable skill in creating the messages that the receiver (the consumer) finds persuasive – hence the justification for highly paid advertising agency copywriters. However, it also demonstrates the fact that the medium of transmission (press or television) can also change the message (although perhaps not to the extent claimed by Marshall McCluhan – that 'the medium is the message'), again justifying the need for the copywriters (and media buyers!).

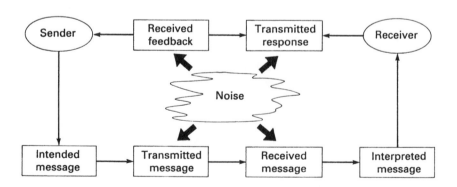

This 'electronic' metaphor does, however, illustrate the point that 'noise' is a major problem for any promotional message. The message itself may be distorted in transmission, in the few seconds that the reader spends on it before the page is turned, or before the viewer is distracted from the message of the commercial. The recipient may, accordingly, obtain a very fragmentary message (hence the emphasis on simplicity in advertising messages). Worst of all, though, will be the torrent of other 'noise', the potentially more interesting editorial matter that surrounds the advertisement or just the distractions of everyday life, through which the advertisers' messages have to be heard: hence the reliance on multiple 'Opportunities To See' – to 'turn up the volume' – to break through the noise barrier. There is also the investment in creative talent to optimize the impact of the individual message, and hence its chance of breaking through!

See also ADVERTISING; SELLING

Encyclopaedia Britannica   *see* AGENT (PERSONAL) SELLING

endgame strategy   *see* DECLINE STRATEGIES

end-of-life price reductions   *see* TECHNOLOGICAL LIFE CYCLE

end-of-life strategy   *see* TECHNOLOGICAL LIFE CYCLE

end-users   *see* INTERMEDIARIES OR END-USERS; PROMOTIONAL MIX FACTORS; SAFETY IN NUMBERS

enemies, stereotyped   *see* GROUPTHINK

Engel–Kollatt–Blackwell model, of consumer behaviour   This model follows a slightly more 'mechanistic' approach than the Howard and Sheth one.

See also HOWARD AND SHETH MODEL, OF CONSUMER BEHAVIOUR

Reference: Engel, D., Kollatt, D. and Blackwell, R. (1978) *Consumer Behaviour*. New York: The Dryden Press.

engineering specifications   *see* SPECIFICATION

Enhanced AIUAPR Model   Simple AIUAPR theory is rarely taken beyond the initial purchase, to look at the series of transactions that repeat purchasing implies. The consumer's growing experience over a number of such transactions is often the determining factor in the later – and future – purchases. All of the succeeding transactions are, thus, interdependent, and the overall decision-making process may, accordingly, be much more complex than most models allow for. Fortunately, the additional complexity has a logic to it. In the single dimension that the original model inhabits from top to bottom, there is a growing involvement of the customer with the product or service. The 'Enhanced AIUAPR Model' takes this and adds a further dimension that specifically reflects,

on one side, the attempts by the vendor to influence this process – which were implicit in the original model. It shows, however, the way in which the vendor's involvement changes from the most impactful advertising at the start of the process to the highest-quality support at the end – a progression that is not fully described in less complex models.

On the other side, however, it shows the involvement of the customer with his or her peer group; whose influence is not even hinted at in the original version:

The starting point is, in this case, earlier than in the original AIUAPR model:

- *Susceptibility.* Even before you can build awareness, the consumer's mind has to have been opened up to the concept behind the product or service. In line with the theories of 'diffusion' this acceptance of a new need may have emerged from the workings of the opinion leaders in the consumer's peer group. On the other hand, this is also the stage at which the supplier has to accept some form of market (or segment) building role; often making use of public relations as much as advertising. It should be noted, however, that the seemingly distinct steps often – indeed, usually – overlap. Thus, some sections of the population – the opinion leaders, say – could be well into the repeat purchasing stage, while other sections are only just beginning to perceive the need. Accordingly, promotion and advertising will often have to meet the requirements of all stages at the same time – a complex demand, which is one reason why very successful advertising campaigns are so rare!

- *Awareness.* In the original, AIUAPR, the role of high-impact advertising (or prospecting in industrial markets) was implicit rather than being a formal part of the model as here. The main difference, however, is that research shows that the stimulus is just as likely to come from an opinion leader in the peer group. These offer a hidden, and potentially very powerful, 'sales force' on behalf of the product or service; albeit that they in turn have necessarily been recruited by advertising (or by public relations activities – often a neglected medium, which is especially important in reaching this group).

- *Interest/understanding.* These two are coupled together, since it is difficult to conceive of one happening without the other being at least in part also involved; although they may offer

Enhanced AIUAPR

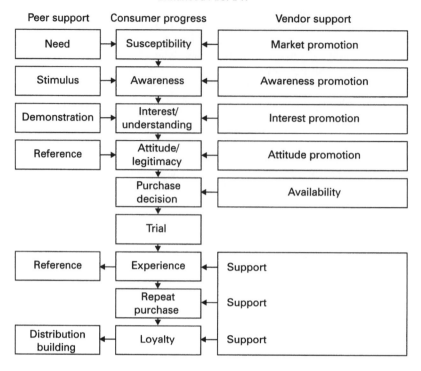

Peer support	Consumer progress	Vendor support
Need	Susceptibility	Market promotion
Stimulus	Awareness	Awareness promotion
Demonstration	Interest/ understanding	Interest promotion
Reference	Attitude/ legitimacy	Attitude promotion
	Purchase decision	Availability
	Trial	
Reference	Experience	Support
	Repeat purchase	Support
Distribution building	Loyalty	Support

very different challenges to the advertiser. Again, however, it is members of the peer group, already users, who may be most likely to be able to proffer the 'demonstration' of the product (or the results of the service) to the prospective consumer.

- *Attitude/legitimacy*. Although one further stage is added, that of 'legitimacy' (persuading the prospective purchaser that, backed by his or her favourable attitudes, a purchase may be justified), this is merged with the attitude-building process; and both may be dependent on the 'reference' support from members of the peer group, who are already loyal users, as much as upon advertising.

- *Purchase decision*. This should, by this stage of the process, be almost automatic; and, for once, the consumer is probably alone in making this particular decision. A key element, also featured in the original model but often (wrongly) taken for granted, is that the product or service must be easily available for the consumer to achieve that purchase.

- *Experience*. One stage ignored by the original model is that which happens when the consumer tries the product or service for the first time. This

may, or may not, be a favourable experience; but – wherever in the spectrum it lies – it represents a major discontinuity in the model. At this point, the nature of the accompanying processes changes. In the case of the vendor's promotional activities, the emphasis switches abruptly from recruitment to support (perhaps still involving advertising, but mainly by conventional support services). This is perhaps best illustrated by the switch from new account selling before to account management afterwards, in face-to-face selling. At the same time, the consumer switches from being a recipient of advice to one who can, from experience, give it to his or her peer group. This is hopefully of a positive nature, since a bad experience is typically reported to many more peers than a good one!

- *Repeat purchase*. In this development of the original model, this becomes almost a technicality.

- *Loyalty*. More important is the final step, that of creating a loyal user; based upon successive positive experiences (backed by sound support). These loyal users become, in turn, the 'references' for new users (or even the 'opinion leaders' who feature so strongly in this enhanced model).

A condensed version of this complex model is offered by the 'Three Pillars of the Purchasing Process'.

See also AIUAPR (AWARENESS, INTEREST, UNDERSTANDING, ATTITUDES, PURCHASE, REPEAT PURCHASE) MODEL; CALL STRUCTURE; DECISION-MAKING PROCESS, BY CUSTOMERS; MODELS; PEER PYRAMID; REPEAT PURCHASING PROCESS; THREE PILLARS OF THE PURCHASING PROCESS

enquiries   *see* DIRECT MAIL ADVERTISING

enquiries, handling   *see* INBOUND TELEMARKETING COMMUNICATIONS

enquiry processing   The real start of the order processing cycle, if the supplier wants to offer the best service and maintain the closest control, is the enquiry; for the enquiry conversion rate is usually a key statistic, and details of potential customers are an invaluable addition to the marketing database.

See also DATA PROCESSING, LOGISTICS

entertaining   *see* SUPPLIER EVALUATION

enthusiasm   *see* LEADERSHIP, OF SALES PERSONNEL

entrance fees   *see* SELECTIVE PRICING

entrenched competitors   *see* TRANSNATIONALS/ MULTINATIONALS AND EXPORTERS

entrepôt   A large international port dealing in re-exports.

entrepreneurship, of sales personnel   *see* CONTROL, OF SALES PERSONNEL; FACTORS OF PRODUCTION; MOTIVATION, OF SALES PERSONNEL

entry   *see* LICENSING

entry decision   *see* INTERNATIONAL PRODUCT DECISION

envelope curve extrapolation   The form of forecasting known as 'envelope curve' extrapolation expects technology to develop by quantum leaps, with new techniques gradually being improved until they reach the ceiling of their performance – at which point they are then overtaken by the next development.

See also QUALITATIVE FORECASTING METHODS

envelope stuffer   Promotional material that is stuffed into a direct mail envelope.

See also DIRECT MAIL

environment   *see* SWOT ANALYSIS

environmental analysis   *see* INERTIAL BALANCE; TEAM SCANNING

environmental factors   *see* MARKETING PLANNING, ANALYSIS

environmental forecasts   *see* DERIVED FORECASTS

environmental turbulence   *see* NOT-FOR-PROFIT ORGANIZATIONS, OBJECTIVES

EOQ (economic order quantity)   *see* ECONOMIC ORDER QUANTITY (EOQ)

EPOS (Electronic Point Of Sale)   The computerized technique of recording sales as they are made – now typically by the use of bar code readers linked to in-store computers.

EPOS and EFTPOS, precision marketing   The most immediate stimulus to precision marketing, albeit probably more in theory than in practice, is the introduction of EPOS (Electronic Point Of Sale), to be followed by EFTPOS (which adds Electronic Funds transfer), by the major retailers. With EPOS, details of an individual transaction (although, as yet, typically not the identity of the individual purchaser) can be tracked. With EFTPOS, it is possible to relate these transactions to any individual. In this way, retailers in particular will be able to build up a very detailed picture of the buying habits of individual customers. In the specific context of supermarket retailing, Cathy Bond (1990) comments that 'Database marketing is on the way, ushered in by the growth of EPOS and direct debit scanning tills. It is worlds away from the kind of mass coupon drops and mailers which typically herald a new store opening, or which try to drum up seasonal extra business. Database experts dream of a world where mailshots will look as if they were tailor-made for every recipient. Where grocery retailers will value individual customers and not think of them as just so many feet through the door each week. The attitude will be caring, but not patronising – and definitely not tainted with the intrusive commercialism that is conventional direct marketing's big drawback.'

See also BRANCH MARKETING; PRECISION MARKETING

Reference: Bond, Cathy (1990) Customer conscious. *Marketing*, 8 March.

equations   *see* MODELS

equilibrium price   According to 'neoclassical' economics, this is the price that will be set by the market. Begg's definition is as follows: 'The equilibrium price clears the market . . . It is the price at which the quantity supplied equals the quantity demanded.' In economics, therefore, the basis of price is this balance between supply and demand; and price itself is most often seen as the prime determinant of both supply and demand.

The body of this theory was largely developed in the nineteenth century, when the economic wealth of nations was still developing. At that time, most of the markets were still almost pure commodity markets, supplying basic essentials – which were undifferentiated – and the consumer's choice was accordingly based on price alone, their purchasing strategy being to use their very limited funds to obtain the maximum amounts of these basic essentials. This simple approach may still work in commodity markets, where professional buyers purchase identical commodities solely on the basis of price.
See also DEMAND CURVE ESTIMATION; PRICE ELASTICITY OF DEMAND; PRICE FACTORS; PRICES, CUSTOMER NEEDS; SUPPLY AND DEMAND

Reference: Begg, David, Fischer, Stanley and Dornbusch, Rudiger (1987) *Economics* (2nd edn). New York: McGraw-Hill.

equitable waits   *see* QUEUE

equity holding in local operation   *see* JOINT VENTURE

Error Cause Removal (ECR)   The quality control technique (introduced by Crosby) that lies at the heart of quality control in some Japanese firms (especially Toyota). It looks like a normal suggestions system, but the workers are only required to identify the problem (for which they are still rewarded), and the responsibility for finding and implementing a solution then rests with management.
See also CROSBY, P. B.; QUALITY; SUGGESTIONS SCHEMES

errors   *see* FAULTS

errors of commission   *see* DATA, INFORMATION AND INTELLIGENCE; MARKETING RESEARCH OBJECTIVES

errors of omission   *see* DATA, INFORMATION AND INTELLIGENCE; MARKETING RESEARCH OBJECTIVES

escalation clause   A clause in a contract, typically one applying to a long time period, that allows the contractor to raise its prices under certain conditions. *See also* PRICES, CUSTOMER NEEDS

ESOMAR   *see* INTERNATIONAL *AD HOC* RESEARCH

estate agents   *see* RETAIL PRODUCT OR SERVICE CATEGORIES

estates department, retail   *see* RETAIL MANAGEMENT

esteem needs   *see* MASLOW'S HIERARCHY OF NEEDS

estimated error   *see* GRAPHS, AND FORECASTING

estimation of 'price elasticity'   *see* DEMAND CURVE ESTIMATION

estimation of the demand curve   *see* DEMAND CURVE ESTIMATION

ethical belief   *see* GROUPTHINK

Euromonitor, *Market Research Europe*   *see* INTERNATIONAL MARKETING RESEARCH

Europe   *see* TRIAD POWER

European Society for Market Research   *see* INTERNATIONAL *AD HOC* RESEARCH

evaluation of alternatives   *see* REPEAT PURCHASING PROCESS

evaluation of supplier   *see* SUPPLIER EVALUATION

evaluation of the alternatives, repeat purchasing   *see* ALTERNATIVES EVALUATION, REPEAT PURCHASING

evangelism   *see* CONVICTION MARKETING

events, seasonal   *see* PROMOTIONAL PRICING

evil enemies   *see* GROUPTHINK

evolution   *see* INNOVATIVE IMITATION

excess capacity, price   *see* PRICE COMPETITION

excess demand   *see* PRICE INCREASES

excessive optimism   *see* GROUPTHINK

exchange   *see* COUNTERTRADING

exclusive   A story that is given to one publication only.
See also PUBLIC RELATIONS

exclusive dealing   *see* CHANNEL DECISIONS; CHANNEL MEMBERS

exclusive distribution   *see* CHANNEL MEMBERSHIP

executives and public relations   *see* PUBLIC RELATIONS

executive summary   *see* MARKETING PLAN STRUCTURE

ex gratia   Done as a favour, at no charge.

exhibitions   This area of promotional activity is generally related to 'selling', because many prospects expect to find their suppliers at such venues. For example, market research showed that just under 30 per cent of personal computer buyers expected to find their suppliers at exhibitions. Martyn Davies (1981) summarizes the main benefits when he says that 'Exhibitions afford you the double benefit of demonstration with personal contact . . . Prospective buyers can see and handle your product, try for themselves and ask questions.' These are powerful benefits but, like any other promotional activity, exhibitions demand careful planning – and not a little expertise – in order to reap these rewards. The main activities involved are as follows.

Selection
Every exhibition organizer thinks that his offering is essential, but very few of them really are; and most organizations will need to very carefully select those which they must attend. Clearly, the organizers should be able to provide statistics of attendances at previous events, and the exhibitor list for the upcoming show gives the best flavour of that show. The main question is, perhaps, 'Is it a major event, or one for also-rans?' If the main vendors in the industry are not attending, then ask yourself why.

Stand location and design
The main requirement, whatever the chosen size and shape, is to obtain the best location. As John Fenton (1984) stresses, the three main priorities are 'Position, position and position', echoing the well-known dictum about the location of retail outlets. The best positions are typically along the central aisles, as close as possible to the larger, more spectacular, stands. John Fenton insists on the use of a professional stand designer – understandably, where he is looking for the maximum impact – but, on a lesser scale, it is possible to use one of the many modular stand systems that are available and it will be possible to take that to a number of exhibitions; thus helping to recover the cost, since even the simplest set is likely to cost several thousand pounds. The costs do not stop with the stand system. This will only provide the framework for the graphics and photo 'blow-ups' that form the backdrop to the displays. A designer (although not necessarily a specialist stand designer) will also be needed to produce these; and, again, it can be expensive (the cost seeming to grow exponentially with the size of the material). The massive photo blow-ups that cover the whole back wall of stands are impressive, but hideously expensive. They might not even be productive. One IBM group spent a small fortune on a colour blow-up to cover the back wall of their stand at the Royal Show, the largest agricultural show in the UK. It showed a hillside, covered with a crop of corn; colourfully dappled with poppies and other wild flowers. It was a beautiful picture. Unfortunately, all that the farmers attending the show could see was a good crop ruined by weeds (poppies are pretty for town dwellers, but are an expensive mistake for a farmer – and, in that case, for IBM!).

Budgets
The establishment of budgets for an exhibition stand requires a considerable amount of experience, and should not be undertaken lightly.
See also DEMONSTRATIONS; MARKETING MIX; PROMOTIONAL MIX; SELLING

References: Davies, Martyn (1981) *The Effective Use of Advertising Media*. London: Business Books.
   Fenton, John (1984) *How to Sell Against Competition*. London: Heinemann.

exhibitions and conferences, and external data
The most important source of external data is likely to come from face-to-face contact. In the case of members of the sales force, this will largely be part of business as usual, in the form of sales calls. Else-

where, such opportunities have to be created. In most organizations, perhaps the most fruitful sources of such new material are those likely to be found at exhibitions and conferences. There is, of course, the 'formal' material, to be found in the exhibits themselves or in the papers presented – and these are, indeed, significant sources of information. But, just as importantly, there are the face-to-face conversations with the other participants. However, these do not just happen. To obtain the best information you must be prepared to seek it out; identifying suitable sources (from speakers, from the floor just as much as from the platform, and from key personnel on stands) and then creating the opportunity to talk to them.

See also EXTERNAL DATA; LIBRARIES

existing customers   *see* SELLING

existing (known risk) suppliers   *see* ORGANIZATIONAL BUYING SITUATIONS

existing (market) usage   *see* USAGE GAP

existing product changes   Gap analysis largely focuses on incremental changes of existing products in existing markets (just one part of the Ansoff four-part matrix – albeit by far the most important one, that of penetration). Even within this most important quadrant, however, the list of possible innovations can be expanded. Peter Drucker (1955), for example, suggests five possibilities:

1. New products or services that are needed to attain marketing objectives.
2. New products or services that will be needed because of technological change that may make present products obsolete.
3. Product improvements needed both to attain market objectives and to anticipate expected technological changes.
4. New processes and improvements in old processes needed to satisfy market goals – for instance, manufacturing improvements to make possible the attainment of pricing objectives.
5. Innovations and improvements in major areas of activity – in accounting or design, office management or labour relations – so as to keep up with advances in knowledge or skill.

Despite being more than 40 years old, this list offers sound advice. The last two categories, and in particular the emphasis on innovations in other areas of activity, are often neglected in the 'new product' development process. The focus is on the product itself; whereas changes in how it is manufactured, delivered or supported may in fact be the main areas in which 'competitive advantage' can be gained.

See also ANSOFF MATRIX; COMPETITIVE GAP; CREATIVE IMITATION; CUSTOMER BONUS; DISTRIBUTION GAP; GAP ANALYSIS; LEAPFROG; MARKET GAP ANALYSIS; NEW PRODUCT NEEDS; PRODUCT (OR SERVICE) GAP; USAGE GAP

Reference: Drucker, Peter (1955) *The Practice of Management*. London: Heinemann.

existing range(s), match   *see* MATCH WITH EXISTING RANGE(S), PRODUCT SCREENING

expansive approach   *see* EXPORT MARKET ELIMINATION

expectation   *see* ADVERTISING BELIEVABILITY; SERVICE QUALITY

expense analysis   *see* MONITORING, PROGRESS

expenses, sales personnel   *see* TERRITORY PLANS

experience   *see* ENHANCED AIUAPR MODEL; PEER PYRAMID; SALES TEAM MANAGEMENT; THREE PILLARS OF THE PURCHASING PROCESS

experience, accumulated   *see* ECONOMIES OF SCALE, GLOBAL

experience, and the (customer) decision-making process   At the time of buying a product or service, the purchaser will probably have already tried a number of the brands and decided, or (even more influentially) their family will have made their decision known, that some of these are acceptable and others are not. As part of this process, the purchaser may have had a bad experience with a brand, or a particularly good one. On the other hand, he or she may simply have become bored (albeit temporarily) with the taste of the brand to which they have been loyal for some time past.

See also DECISION-MAKING PROCESS, BY CUSTOMERS

experience curves   Experience is now seen as the main source of economies of scale. The more that is 'produced', the more that is learned – and the more experience that is available to reduce costs. This element of economies of scale relates to experience over the total production run, not just the current production levels, so its effect is cumulative; potentially offering the early leaders a major competitive advantage – and creating substantial barriers against late entrants. The definitive support for this theory was given by the Boston Consulting Group when it proposed (in 1970) a general observation, based upon its consultancy work, that the characteristic decline in the unit cost of value added 'is consistently 20 to 30 per cent each time accumulated production is doubled. This decline goes on in time without limit (in constant prices) regardless of the rate of growth of experience. The rate of decline is surprisingly consistent, even from industry to industry.' On the other hand, arguing the case for a more general approach to cost reductions, William Alberts records that most 'experience' costs savings do not actually materialize specifically in relation to 'experience' but derive from other advantages enjoyed by the benefiting organizations.

See also ECONOMIES OF SCALE; VARIETY

Reference: Alberts, W. (1989) The experence corve doctrine reconsidered, *Journal of Marketing*, July 1989. Boston Consulting Group (1970) *Perspectives on Experience.*

experience effect *see* CONCEPT TEST, NEW PRODUCTS

experimental research Exposing selected participants to different treatments, ranging from testing new products to viewing commercials and measuring their responses to them, represents one approach to marketing research. In theory, this approach may be used experimentally to establish the basic relationships involved. More frequently, in practice, it is just used to select the best solution (or product or advertising concept) from a range of alternatives; or even more pragmatically to check that the one already chosen is acceptable.

See also BEFORE-AND-AFTER RESEARCH; LATIN SQUARE; MARKETING RESEARCH; MARKETING RESEARCH STAGES; SPLIT RUNS

experimentation, branch precision marketing *see* BRANCH MARKETING

expert opinion, forecasts *see* INDIVIDUAL OR EXPERT OPINION, FORECASTS

expert systems These are computer systems that use forms of artificial intelligence, typically using rules of thumb derived from experts in the field, to support decisions in complex real-life situations that call for special expertise.

See also MARKETING INTELLIGENCE SYSTEMS (MIS)

expert systems, precision marketing *see* DATA MANIPULATION, PRECISION MARKETING

exponential smoothing This is a very impressive title for a simple, but useful, mathematical forecasting technique that can quite easily be handled manually. It allows greater weight to be given to recent periods. Instead of, for example, the average trend over the whole of the last year being calculated, the sales data for each of the months is given a weighting, depending on how recent that month was. In a manner somewhat akin to the moving annual total, it takes the previous figure, in this case the moving forecast, and adds on the latest 'actual' sales figure; except that it does this in a fixed proportion, which is chosen to reflect the weighting to be given to the latest period. The general form is

$$F_{t+1} = F_t + aE_t,$$

where F_{t+1} is the new forecast, F_t is the previous one and E_t is the deviation (or 'error') of the actual new performance recorded against the previous period forecast; and a is the weighting to be given to the most recent events. For example, if a weighting of 0.1 is to be given to the latest figure, then the new forecast will be (previous forecast) + (0.1 × deviation of last actual from the forecast). Note that as the last forecast had, in turn, been produced by the same process (as had the forecasts over the preceding periods), there is no need to subtract any further figures; since in this way all of the earlier sales figures are incorporated (but with 'exponentially' decreasing importance as they recede into the past). Clearly, the higher the proportion of the current month, the greater will be the weighting given to recent periods. Exponential smoothing will not, in this simple form, allow for seasonality; although more sophisticated (but less easily understood) versions can do this.

See also QUANTITATIVE FORECASTING TECHNIQUES

export consortium *see* MARKET ENTRY TACTICS

exporters *see* AGENTS OR DISTRIBUTORS

export guarantee schemes   *see* AGENTS OR
DISTRIBUTORS

export/import house   *see* MARKET ENTRY TACTICS

exporting   In general, are there are three main initial decisions in international marketing:

1. Should we undertake international marketing
    operations at all?
2. If yes, then in what individual country markets?
3. And by what means?

The first question to be asked therefore, of organizations that are currently limited to their national market, is quite simply whether they should export at all.
The reality is that, apart from the ubiquitous multinationals, probably very few organizations benefit
significantly, at least in financial terms, from their
'international operations'. There is, of course, one
major constraint on any organization's global ambitions: Will its products or services translate to other
markets?

Product or service constraints
Indeed, before progressing further, it would be as
well if any organization were to itemize the key characteristics of the products or services that are to be
considered for 'export':

1. What are the most important constituents
    of a product (and its related packaging) or
    service?
2. How specialized, sophisticated and expensive is
    it?
3. What 'infrastructure' (technical support, distri-
    bution, marketing support, etc.) is essential?
4. How adaptive is the organization, in terms of its
    ability to meet the differing needs of overseas
    markets?

Market entry decisions
Having, for whatever reason, taken the fateful deci-
sion to enter international markets, the next set of
decisions relate to which specific markets should, or
should not, be entered. It is wise, in this context, to
develop what is called a 'decision model'.
See also COMPARATIVE ADVANTAGE, GLOBAL; DECISION
MODEL, EXPORTING; ECONOMIES OF SCALE, GLOBAL;
GLOBALIZATION; GLOBAL MARKETING; INTERNATIONAL
MARKETING PITFALLS; INTERNATIONAL MARKETOING
RESEARCH

export market elimination   One approach to
targeting export markets is to select, for considera-

tion, just those countries in which 'experience' (or
hearsay) has suggested there may be worthwhile
business. This approach (sometimes called an
'expansive' one) starts with a 'cluster' of countries
(often those located, in geographical terms, close to
the original domestic market) which have (known)
characteristics similar to those that the organization
is familiar with.
    Another approach (sometimes described as 'con-
tractible'), and one that might be worth pursuing,
even if in parallel with the first one, is to start with all
countries and then eliminate (as rapidly as possible)
those that are proved to be unsuitable. The effect
may ultimately be the same, but this approach has
the virtue of not unnecessarily eliminating the potential markets which are less than obvious. There are a
number of methods that can be used to filter out
unsuitable markets, in addition to regulatory considerations, social and business structures and
accessibility:

*   *common sense*. In the elimination of export mar-
    kets, the first filter is the obvious one. For some
    products or services, there may be groups of
    countries that are clearly unlikely to buy signifi-
    cant quantities.

The next set of filters requires more information:

*   size of population
*   state of development
*   economic considerations
*   living standards

See also ACCESSIBILITY, FILTERING UNSUITABLE
FOREIGN MARKETS; COMPARATIVE ADVANTAGE, GLOBAL;
ECO-NOMIES OF SCALE, GLOBAL; GLOBALIZATION; GLO-
BAL MARKETING; REGULATORY CONSIDERATIONS, FIL-
TERING UNSUITABLE MARKETS; SOCIAL AND BUSINESS
STRUCTURES, FILTERING UNSUITABLE MARKETS

expositions   *see* EXHIBITIONS

exposure to advertising   *see* CUSTOMER
FRANCHISE

expropriation   *see* MARKET ENTRY DECISION

extended group interview   A longer form of the
group interview, typically lasting up to 6–7 hours.
See also GROUP RESEARCH

extended product   *see* PRODUCT PACKAGE

external data The main source of generally available external data is usually that offered by 'desk research'. This is based on 'published' data (in its widest sense), often referred to as 'secondary data' (because it has been generated in response to someone else's questions). In the context of marketing, the data can perhaps be split into three main areas:

- environmental intelligence
- competitive intelligence
- market intelligence

Once the data has been located, its handling follows the same processes as for internal data. It is the 'finding' that is different, and the key to sound desk research. Parts of this data may, in fact, already be available within the organization. On the other hand, it may be necessary to find this data the hard way, from external sources; and it will certainly be necessary to update the information from the original, external, sources. Some useful sources of data that might be considered in this search (by managers in general, not just those involved in marketing) are as follows:

- libraries
- directories
- national agencies
- local agencies
- commercial information providers
- databases
- trade associations
- exhibitions and conferences
- news media

See also DATABASES IN THE PUBLIC DOMAIN; DIRECTORIES; EXHIBITIONS AND CONFERENCES, AND EXTERNAL DATA; INFORMATION PROVIDERS, COMMERCIAL; LIBRARIES; LOCAL AGENCIES, DATA; NATIONAL AGENCIES, DATA; NEWS MEDIA, DATA; TRADE ASSOCIATIONS, AND EXTERNAL DATA

external diseconomies The results of actions, such as pollution, by an organization, that cause uncompensated costs to other actors (parties).

external environment *see* SWOT ANALYSIS

external factors *see* SWOT ANALYSIS

external groups *see* DEFENSIVE (CORPORATE) PR

external influence *see* DIFFUSION OF INNOVATION

extra free *see* PROMOTIONAL PRICING

ex-users *see* USAGE AND LOYALTY

ex-works The price set where the buyer has to take delivery at the supplier's works, and to arrange for carriage himself.

Exxon petroleum *see* STANDARDIZATION VERSUS ADAPTATION

eyeballing The simplest, and often the best, approach to forecasting (and certainly the best check on any more sophisticated technique) is 'eyeballing' the sales charts! With some practice you should be able to sort out the main features of what is happening – and that is better than most computer models achieve.
See also FORECASTING TECHNIQUES; FORECASTS OF SALES BUSINESS

F

face-lift Redesign of a product or corporate image.
See also EXISTING PRODUCT CHANGES; FEATURE MODIFICATION

face-to-face selling *see* PROMOTIONAL MIX FACTORS

facia *see* FASCIA

facility decisions, logistics management
After the decisions as to what product or service is to be provided, the decision of where to provide it is probably one of the most basic decisions for most organizations. Where, geographically, the markets are to be found, and which of these the organization will address, must be a key strategic decision. Even if, by tradition, national coverage is decided upon, this decision should be taken rationally and not simply by default. Having taken that basic 'distribution' decision, the question that follows is how these chosen markets can be best served, offering the best possible service for the lowest cost. Unfortunately, once again, these two factors are usually opposed. Service usually improves with the number of depots or branches. At one extreme, exemplified by retailing, this makes it easier for the customer to make a visit. At the other extreme, it minimizes the time that it takes to get a service engineer to the customer's own location. On the other hand, the more outlets there are, the higher will be the overhead costs to be carried, since each physical location will have basic running costs that cannot be avoided. Even in terms of service levels, there may be an optimum number of outlets; since service begins to fall if there are too many outlets, and if there are insufficient personnel with the range of expertise needed in each outlet.

The three main depot 'facility' decisions will be:

- numbers of warehouses
- size of warehouses
- locations of warehouses

See also INVENTORY CONTROL; LOGISTICS MANAGEMENT; PRODUCTION DECISIONS, LOGISTICS MANAGEMENT; TRANSPORT DECISIONS, LOGISTICS MANAGEMENT

facing Advertisements that face editorial matter.
See also ADVERTISING PROCESSES

facings The number of packs facing (side by side) the customer on a supermarket shelf. The more facings a product is given, the better is the chance that the customer will find it and buy it.

factor analysis This is a multivariate technique (typically used on survey research data) which is used to group together 'related' variables (by the detection of related patterns in the data, usually concerned with buying behaviour). Superficially, these may appear to be independent, but in fact can be shown (at least, statistically, in terms of the dependent outcomes) to be highly correlated. That is, there is an underlying relationship that means that they behave in much the same way and have a similar impact on the final results. The technique is primarily a tool used (in 'data reduction') to reduce a large number of possible variables to a lesser, aggregated or summarized, number – which can be more easily handled.
See also ANALYSIS OF MARKETING RESEARCH DATA; SEGMENTATION

factoring This is a means of raising money, whereby invoices are 'sold' to a credit organization (usually owned by a bank). It typically takes one of two forms:

1. *Invoice discounting*. In this case, the supplier sells the invoice to the factor at a discount, but continues to collect the money from the customer in the normal way (before paying off the factor, who will carry bad debts in addition to providing early release of the money).
2. *Factoring*. In this case, the factor takes over the whole sales ledger, including the collection of money from the customer.

factors of production The basic factors identified by classical economics as those needed to produce economic goods. They typically include land (which was simply that originally, and earned

rent, but is a category that now, more generally, also includes all natural resources), labour (which earned wages), capital (which earned interest) and – in some versions – entrepreneurship (which earned profit).
See also COMPARATIVE ADVANTAGE, GLOBAL

facts books One solution to handling verbal data, at least in terms of the top level of key facts, is to create a series of 'facts books' (or, if the volumes of key data are sufficiently large, facts libraries). These contain, for example, all of the key data about a particular product, and associated with them will be the supporting literature (perhaps in related files), such as reports and competitive brochures. It is sometimes sound practice to circulate a summary of the relevant facts book, to all those involved, before the start of the marketing planning process – so that the marketing plans themselves need only contain the planning decisions (and justifications), and are not lost in the torrent of background material that swamps the key details in many such planning documents.
See also MARKETING AUDIT; VERBAL (COMPUTER) DATABASES; VERBAL DATA RETRIEVAL; WRITTEN REPORTS

fad An extreme version of a fashion is a 'fad', where the rapid growth and decline phases are separated by only a very short maturity phase. It could be argued that some pop records fall into this category, but the usual examples given are those such as skateboards and hula-hoops. These are markets in which it may be difficult to make a significant profit. On the other hand, it is likely that there will be very little consumer resistance, and hence no need for investment to overcome this. So those who recognize what the phenomenon really is, and are quick into the market – and just as quick out of it (a much more difficult decision!) – may do well.

fade, images *see* DISSOLVE

failure rate curve Sometimes called the 'bathtub curve', this describes the reliability of a component, measured by the proportion of a sample failing, at various stages over the life of that component.

fairground trade *see* SERVICE QUALITY

faith, management *see* VISION, CORPORATE

faking sales reports *see* CONTROL, OF SALES PERSONNEL

falling brand share, price *see* PRICE COMPETITION

false economy *see* PRICE, PURCHASE

falsified sales calls *see* CONTROL, OF SALES PERSONNEL

familiar strange, making the *see* SYNECTICS®

family audiences *see* TELEVISION

family branding *see* BRANDING POLICIES

family influences, on the purchase decision Perhaps the most influential 'peer group' is that of the family; to the extent that it (rather than the individual) is often the focus of the marketer's activities.
See also CULTURES, INFLUENCES ON THE PURCHASE DECISION; DECISION-MAKING PROCESS, BY CUSTOMERS; PEER PRESSURE INFLUENCES, ON THE PURCHASE DECISION; REPEAT PURCHASING PROCESS; SOCIAL CLASS INFLUENCES, ON THE PURCHASE DECISION; SUBCULTURES, INFLUENCES ON THE PURCHASE DECISION

family packs *see* TRADE DISCOUNTS

fancy goods Small, attractive items.

fantasy *see* SYNECTICS®

fares *see* SELECTIVE PRICING

Farm Journal *see* PUBLICATIONS, PRECISION MARKETING

fascia The board over the front of a store that displays its name, but may also be used for advertising material.
See also ADVERTISING PROCESSES; RETAILING; SALES PROMOTION

fashion life cycle One of the more interesting of the patterns of life cycle is that of rapid penetration. This is the shape that can be ascribed to 'fashions' or 'fads' which come, and go, very quickly. Almost the whole life cycle is taken up with growth and then decline – with the latter often very rapid indeed. There is only a very brief 'maturity'. Judging these patterns may be a matter of commercial life and death for those in the fashion businesses! Thus, 'fashion'-oriented businesses (which may be in industries other than those in the clothing sector) may show something approaching the conventional curve but in compressed form; so that what takes several years for another product may be seen to happen in as many months (or weeks, or even days in the pop record business) in a fashion-dominated business. Such 'fashions' can also afflict industrial markets; it is arguable that certain features of the personal computer market, such as the concentration on 'chip' speeds, have at times responded in much the same way. In the case of fashion, it is unlikely that there will be significant investment in the introductory phase, since the suppliers involved are likely to be much more aware of how transitory such fashions may be. The decline phase too may be brief – sometimes spectacularly so. In some younger age groups, to be caught wearing an outdated fashion is to invite ridicule.

fashions/colours stocked, retail   *see* RETAIL 'PRODUCT' DECISIONS

fashions, design   *see* DESIGN FASHIONS

fashion shops   *see* RETAIL PRODUCT OR SERVICE CATEGORIES

Fast Moving Consumer Goods (FMCG)   *see* PRODUCT OR SERVICE CATEGORIES

faults   The measure that is perhaps most immediately obvious to the customer is the fault rate. This may be divided into two categories:

- *Errors* – the wrong 'product', or the wrong quantity (or the wrong price), or delivery to the wrong address. These errors should not happen; but they do – and far more frequently than you might expect.
- *Faulty or damaged goods* – this is usually what 'quality' is seen to be about; and customers, understandably, expect 100 per cent performance in this area (but rarely get it, except in the standardized mass consumer markets).

In many markets, this means that (in order to avoid delivery of out-of-date products, or offering those beyond their expiry date) the distribution chain has to operate a rigorous FIFO (First In First Out) control system; whereas LIFO (Last In Last Out) is more normal and natural, the latest addition to stock being loaded on to the front of the shelf, pushing the older stock to the back!
See also SERVICE LEVELS

favourable attitudes   *see* ADVERTISING

favoured supplier   *see* BALANCING UNDER THE INFLUENCE; COMPLEX SALE

fax   *see* ELECTRONIC DIRECT MAIL

fear   *see* MESSAGE, ADVERTISING; SALES CALL CLOSE

feasibility of objectives   *see* MARKETING STRATEGIES

feature   An editorial article or section of a magazine (along with the associated advertisements) that focuses on (features) one topic.
See also ADVERTISING PROCESSES; PUBLIC RELATIONS

features/benefits   *see* OBJECTION HANDLING

feature check   The promotions and other point of sale activity (in-store) recorded as part of retail audits.
See also RETAIL AUDITS

feature modification   Sometimes called 'functional modification', this approach to product development makes changes (usually minor ones) to what the product or service does. Frequently, the main element of the modification will simply be a change in packaging. However, it may be expanded into the major message needed to rejuvenate a jaded advertising campaign!
See also CREATIVE IMITATION; CUSTOMER BONUS; LEAPFROG; PRODUCT (OR SERVICE) MODIFICATION

features   *see* MESSAGE, ADVERTISING

fee basis   *see* AGENCY CHOICE

feed   To give tips and leads to another salesperson.
See also TERRITORY MANAGEMENT

feel–buy–learn model   One of the models of marketing communications, in which the learning element comes after purchase.

Feigenbaum, A. V.   The production management guru who introduced to the Japanese the concept that all parts of the company contribute to quality (TQM).
See also QUALITY; ZERO DEFECTS

fibre-board shipping outers   *see* PACKAGING

fidelity bonus The business practice whereby a supplier rewards loyal members of the distribution chain with favourable terms and conditions.
See also CHANNEL MOTIVATION; TRADE DISCOUNTS

field sales management *see* PEOPLE (SALES) MANAGEMENT

field sales manager contact *see* CONTROL, OF SALES PERSONNEL

field training *see* SALES TRAINING

field trials *see* TEST MARKET

fieldwork quality control In conducting survey research, a number of important questions need to be asked about how the work (of the interviewers) in the field is being controlled. These include the following: How will these interviewers be recruited? What instructions will be issued to them? How is the fieldwork to be monitored? How are the field force of interviewers supervised? It is normal practice for supervisors, in addition to regularly accompanying interviewers on their calls, to call back on 10 per cent of all calls made, to check the accuracy of the recorded responses – and to check that the calls have actually been made!
See also APPOINTING A MARKETING RESEARCH AGENCY; MARKETING RESEARCH; SAMPLING; SURVEY RESEARCH

FIFO (First In First Out) The inventory control procedure whereby the oldest stock is used first; and new stock is, for example, put at the back of the shelf.
See also FAULTS; INVENTORY CONTROL; LIFO (LAST IN FIRST OUT)

fighting brand *see* PRICE CHALLENGE REACTIONS

film rush *see* RUSH

filtering rules *see* ROUTING RULES

filtering unsuitable markets *see* EXPORT MARKET ELIMINATION

filter question An initial question in a survey, designed to determine which respondents are worth questioning further.
See also QUESTIONNAIRE DESIGN

final assembly *see* MATERIALS MANAGEMENT

final cut of commercial *see* ADVERTISING PROCESSES

final proof Sometimes called a final pull, showing the advertisement as it will appear.
See also CREATING THE CORRECT MESSAGES; CREATIVE DEPARTMENT, ADVERTISING AGENCY

financial analysis, new products *see* STRATEGIC SCREENING, NEW PRODUCTS

financial community advertising *see* CORPORATE PROMOTION VERSUS BRAND PROMOTION

financial projections *see* MARKETING PLAN STRUCTURE

financial ratios *see* MARKETING PLAN STRUCTURE

financial results *see* MONITORING, PROGRESS

financial services *see* BANKS

financial services industry *see* SERVICE–SECTOR LOGISTICS

finished artwork *see* ADVERTISING PROCESSES; CREATIVE DEPARTMENT, ADVERTISING AGENCY

finished goods *see* INVENTORY CONTROL

finished goods, warehouse parts kit *see* MATERIALS MANAGEMENT

finite waits *see* QUEUE

fire-fight To fight bad publicity.

First In First Out *see* FIFO (FIRST IN FIRST OUT)

first-time users *see* USAGE AND LOYALTY

fiscal policy A government's programme of spending (including its transfer payments – the amount, for instance, that it pays out in social security and hence transfers between one group of the population and another) and taxes. Fiscal policy and monetary policy together are the main tools used by governments to control the economy.
See also MONETARY POLICY

Fishbein model   A model of consumer behaviour that concentrates on the act of purchasing, and that also includes normative beliefs about how the consumer feels that he or she should behave.
See also BUYING DECISION, ADVERTISING MODELS; MARKETING RESEARCH; MODELS

fishbone diagram   As developed by Professor Kaoru Ishikawa of the University of Tokyo, this diagram lists the causes of a problem as spurs (diagonals) leading into a central (horizontal) backbone which points to the problem. It is used as an aid to identifying and listing all the possible causes (possibly using sub-spurs that branch off the main spurs).
See also NEW PRODUCT CREATION

fishbone effect   *see* MACRO- AND MICRO-FORECASTS

fishy-back freight   The transport of trucks or railcars on barges.

five-year plan   *see* FORECASTING DYNAMICS

fixed spot   A television commercial that is – for a premium fee – transmitted at a fixed time.
See also ADVERTISING PROCESSES

flagship   The key product or service on which the organization's reputation depends.
See also BRANDING POLICIES; CASH COW

flash pack   A pack with a promotional offer (typically a reduction in price) highlighted on the label.
See also SALES PROMOTION

flat scheduling   *see* JUST IN TIME (JIT); KANBAN

fleet operations   *see* TRANSPORT DECISIONS, LOGISTICS MANAGEMENT

flexible development   Taken to its limit, the flexible manufacturing process can be applied to all parts of an organization, with dramatic effects; particularly in the area of 'development'. The key improvements in this area seem to emerge from the implementation of development teams that cut across functional barriers (thus paralleling, for much the same reason, the brand manager structure). With this improved coordination, large parts of the development can proceed in parallel, rather than sequentially. As, in addition, development (in this context) is much closer to manufacturing (and is often physically relocated next to production, to ensure that this happens) implementation is handled in parallel – faster, and with fewer problems. The process is helped by the fact that the Japanese tend to concentrate on incremental development, which is much more clearly tied to existing manufacturing processes, rather than discontinuous leaps. The most important result is that the time to create the next product can be cut by a factor of two or three; allowing (as in the case of Honda, for example) a company to launch two or three 'generations' for every one announced by its competitors – in effect, making the competitors' products obsolete. It also means that an imitative product can be in the market before the competitors' products have become established.
See also FLEXIBLE MANUFACTURING; JUST IN TIME (JIT)

flexible manufacturing   The essence of this development was arguably that production lines could be more easily, and hence more gradually and economically, changed from one product to another. The use of this was, in fact, always a critical underlying assumption behind JIT. It was the reverse of the 'focused factories', based on reduced product ranges and dedicated to economies of scale resulting from long production runs, that drove Japanese companies in the 1960s. Flexible manufacturing allowed smaller production runs and wider ranges. It thus allowed them to move to 'variety', a greater number of product lines. Traditionally, there had been a trade-off between scale and variety (the breadth of the range had to be reduced, to increase the volume of individual sales on each line, before economies of scale could be enjoyed). Flexible manufacturing dramatically reduced the need for such trade-offs; so that factories could enjoy economies while still producing a greater variety. To quote George Stalk Jr, of the Boston Consulting Group, 'In a flexible factory system, variety-driven costs start lower and increase more slowly as variety grows. Scale costs remain unchanged. Thus the optimum cost point for a flexible factory then occurs at a higher volume and with greater variety than for a traditional factory . . . Very simply, a flexible production enjoys more variety with lower total costs . . .'
See also AVOIDANCE OF FORECASTING; ECONOMIC BATCH QUANTITY; EMERGENT STRATEGY; FLEXIBLE DEVELOPMENT; JUST IN TIME (JIT); SEGMENTATION APPROACHES; SET-UP TIMES

Reference: Stalk, George Jr (1988) Time – the next source of competitive advantage. *Harvard Business Review*, July–August.

flexography   A lower-quality, but cheaper, printing process using rubber plates, typically used to print cardboard outers.
See also BLOCKS

flier   A promotional leaflet, typically a simple one with just one page.

flipchart   *see* PRESENTATION MEDIA

flip-flop testing   *see* COUPON RESPONSE; SPLIT RUNS

flong   A sheet of paperboard that used to be used in newspaper letterpress to take the impression of the Linotype set type (which was then called a matrix), and then was filled with hot lead to produce the final printing plate.
See also LETTERPRESS

floor display   A separate free-standing display (in-store and not on the shelves) of goods (usually on promotion).
See also SALES PROMOTION

floorwalker   A more senior staff member in a department store, who supervises staff as well as advising customers.

flow diagram   *see* SYSTEMS APPROACHES

flyer   *see* LETTER, DIRECT MAIL

flying by the seat of the pants   *see* COARSE MARKETING

fly-posting   Placing posters, illegally, without permission and without payment.
See also POSTERS

FMCG (Fast Moving Consumer Goods)   *see* PRODUCT OR SERVICE CATEGORIES

FOB (Free On Board)   The price quoted for delivery to the port of shipment.

FOB pricing   *see* GEOGRAPHICAL PRICING

focus   *see* NEW PRODUCT INNOVATION

focused factories   *see* FLEXIBLE MANUFACTURING

folder test   A form of pre-test advertising undertaken by exposing the press advertisement under test to consumers, in a folder that also contains samples of competitive advertisements.
See also ADVERTISING RESEARCH; COPY TESTING

fold-out   A special advertisement in a magazine that folds out to form a larger advertisement.

folklore   *see* SALES TEAM MANAGEMENT

follower pricing   *see* BUDGETS; COMPETITIVE PRICING; DEDICATED FOLLOWERS

font   The complete set of type in a given typeface (design of type, for printing).

footage   The amount of movie film shot.

forced relationships   This is a technique used to extend product ideas that have already been generated. All of these existing ideas are considered in pairs, to see if the combination produces further new ideas.
See also ATTRIBUTE LISTING; GENERATING IDEAS

force field analysis   This creative technique lists the opposing forces (driving forces versus restraining forces) as lines on opposite sides of a horizontal backbone (with the length of line for each indicating its importance).
See also NEW PRODUCT CREATION

forcing distribution   *see* FULL-LINE FORCING

Ford Automobiles   *see* GLOBAL MARKETING; STANDARDIZATION VERSUS ADAPTATION

forecast assumptions   *see* ASSUMPTIONS, MARKETING PLAN; SENSITIVITY ANALYSIS, NEW PRODUCTS

forecasting assumptions, IBM   *see* POTSA PLANNING

forecasting avoidance   *see* AVOIDANCE OF FORECASTING

forecasting dos and don'ts   Roy Amara gives some very pragmatic 'dos and 'don'ts' of forecasting and planning:

1. Don't be a vacuum cleaner . . . avoid collecting every speck of information that crosses your field of view unless you know exactly how you are going to use it . . .
2. Don't substitute error for uncertainty . . . For those key variables with the greatest uncertainty, you should not try – however great the temptation – to be a hero . . .
3. At times lean against the wind . . . One of the most effective is to question conventional wisdom – at times . . .
4. Hedge forecasts with possible surprises . . . Surprises are by definition events or trends we perceive to be of low probability. We are particularly interested in identifying those surprises that could have a large impact if they were to occur. Identifying such possible surprises is simply another way of compensating for the fact that we are necessarily working with incompletely specified systems . . .
5. Look for breakpoints and discontinuities . . . however, [this] combines the elements of keen insight, high courage and considerable luck . . .
6. Focus on underlying driving forces . . . We need to discover and understand the underlying elements affecting variables of interest . . .
7. Look for clusters of drivers . . . Driving forces do not normally act singly but in clusters . . . it is precisely the interaction of drivers that provides clues on underlying structure . . .
8. Translate environmental forecasts into business issues, . . . into forms that have more direct meaning to business functions . . . in the form of a threat or opportunity . . .
9. Don't be fooled by the diffusion curve . . . the perceived curve differs from the actual in two important respects – it is steadily increasing, and it grows in a much shorter period of time . . . The result is the usual hype gap in the early stages of a technology . . .
10. Keep asking so what? . . .

Above all, though, treat forecasting seriously. Do not simply produce those optimistic targets which the 'short-termism' of financial stakeholders demands. Such targets may be achieved by heroic efforts on the part of management and staff, but usually at the expense of the long-term future of the organization. The important forecasts, respected by the world's most successful organizations but ignored by the less successful, are the long-term ones. If you do not know where you expect (or at least actively plan for) your organization to be five years in the future, then it will probably never get there!

See also FORECASTING TECHNIQUES; QUANTITATIVE FORECASTING TECHNIQUES

Reference: Amara, Roy (1988) What we have learned about forecasting and planning. *Futures*, August.

forecasting dynamics It is often assumed that forecasts are immutable and static. In practice, forecasts should be amended as and when the environment changes. Thus, the best-managed organizations probably have a quarterly review of their annual forecast (and associated budgets), so that forecasts for the remaining quarters can be based on the latest information. The most sophisticated indulge in 'rolling forecasts', whereby at each quarter a full year ahead is forecast; in other words, a new fourth quarter is added to the plan. More important, and less well recognized perhaps, is the fact that even the five-year forecasts may need to change quite dramatically each time they are reviewed; in this case typically on an annual basis. Over the preceding year it is more than likely that the external environment, as well as the organization's own internal environment, will have changed significantly – and in ways that were not predicted.

See also LONG–TERM FORECASTS; MEDIUM–TERM FORECASTS; SHORT–TERM FORECASTS; SHORT– VERSUS LONG–TERM FORECASTS

forecasting models *see* TIME–SERIES ANALYSES

forecasting of demand, service sector *see* SERVICE–SECTOR LOGISTICS

forecasting techniques In the business community, the term 'forecasting' is more normally associated with figures; the annual sales forecast, for example. In the social sciences, however, forecasts are frequently produced in a qualitative, verbal, form. Both of these are valid, and both offer useful insights. Thus, there are two general forms of forecasting – *qualitative* (verbal) and *quantitative* (numerical). In general, the qualitative forecasts come into their own in the long term (in strategic and macro-forecasting). In these cases, the process may also sometimes be globally described as 'technological forecasting' (since this is the 'discipline' in which many of the techniques were first developed – as well as now representing a specific subset of techniques). The short-term (tactical and micro-) forecasts are usually more quantitative.

See also DERIVED FORECASTS; EYEBALLING; INDIVIDUAL OR EXPERT OPINION, FORECASTS; LONG-TERM FORE-CASTS; MACRO- AND MICRO- FORECASTS; MEDIUM-TERM FORECASTS; QUALITATIVE FORECASTING METHODS; QUANTITATIVE FORECASTING TECHNIQUES; SHORT-TERM FORECASTS; SHORT- VERSUS LONG-TERM FORECASTS

forecasting uncertainty reduction   *see* UNCERTAINTY REDUCTION, FORECASTING

forecasts by sales team   *see* FORECASTS OF SALES BUSINESS

forecasts, derived   *see* DERIVED FORECASTS

forecasts into budgets   Assuming that forecasts have been kept separate from the budgets – and this is not often the case – the first, and most important, decision is what budgets to set. Amongst these will be budgets that parallel the forecasts themselves; with a sales budget (or target) paralleling the sales forecast, for example. These budgets may appear to be identical to the forecasts, but the difference is that, where the forecast is the best estimate of what might happen (given the best environmental information and making a number of general assumptions), the budget represents what the organization has decided to do. These planned (budget) figures are a commitment within the overall plans, and take into account the planned actions to be taken in terms of the controllable (internal) factors. In many organizations, a series of subtly different budgets (often high and low budgets) are produced for different audiences; in much the same way that there are two sets of accounts in some countries, one for the owner and one for the taxman! There always has to be the original forecast, which must be made as accurately as possible, but it should be recognized that there may be a number of budget variants based on this, although (confusingly) they are often also referred to as 'forecasts':

- *Profit forecast*. Every organization dreads not making its profit targets, so the forecast used in calculating these is often deliberately pessimistic.
- *Manufacturing forecast*. On the other hand, most organizations do not want to be out of stock, and will accept some spare capacity as the price to pay for this, so this forecast is usually somewhat optimistic.

- *Salesforce targets*. It is often reckoned that salesmen need very challenging targets, so these are set very optimistically. For sound motivational reasons, IBM, on the other hand, sets its salesforce targets (as opposed to forecasts) rather pessimistically, since it – quite deliberately – wants 80 per cent of its staff to be 'successful' and beat their targets.

See also LONG-TERM FORECASTS; MEDIUM-TERM FORE-CASTS; SHORT-TERM FORECASTS; SHORT- VERSUS LONG-TERM FORECASTS

forecasts, limiting factors   Joseph Martino (1972) identifies a number of 'personal' factors that can adversely affect the accuracy of forecasts:

- *Vested interest*. The forecaster's own commitment to what he or she is investigating can colour judgment
- *Narrow focus on a single technology or technical approach*. The technology, say, with which the forecaster is familiar tends to predominate
- *Commitment to a previous position*. Existing beliefs, and existing forecasts, have an inertia of their own.
- *Overcompensation*. On the other hand, recognizing the problems can lead to overreaction.
- *Giving excessive weight to recent evidence*. Recent events loom much larger in the mind.
- *Excessive emphasis on the troubles of the recent past*. The current problems will, almost inevitably, loom even larger.
- *Unpleasant course of action*. Sometimes the real alternatives may be too unpleasant to contemplate.
- *Dislike of the source of an innovation*. The forecaster may, irrationally, choose to ignore some sources.
- *Systematic optimism/pessimism*. Studies have shown that there is a systematic shift from optimism (for short-term forecasts) to pessimism (for long-term forecasts). According to Joseph Martino, 'A useful rule of thumb is that the shift from optimism to pessimism comes at a point about five years in the future.'

The most frequent mistake in practice is that of not learning from experience. This is sometimes called the 'hockey stick effect', since this is the distinctive shape of the forecast curve that frequently results. The explanation of this is that, when 'actuals' fail to live up to optimistic forecasts, the starting point of the new forecast is changed to allow for this – but the slope of the forecast line remains (still optimistically) unchanged. Nobody in the forecasting process asks why the forecast was missed: nobody learns from experience!

There is great virtue in simplicity in forecasting. Mick McLean (1977) comments, for instance, that 'The more simple the model is, the more easily it may be understood by the audience to whom it is addressed. This means that not only are any policy recommendations derived from the model more comprehensible, but their derivation from the underlying assumptions of the model can be more clearly traced.' Spyros Makridakis and Steven Wheelwright (1989) make much the same, very valid, point about forecasting in general, that 'users prefer simple, intuitive, easy-to-use, easy-to-comprehend methods'. It is these factors, rather than the accuracy that is ultimately desired, which determine when and how forecasting is used.

Practical use seems, therefore, to be possibly the best recipe for success! The practical effect of all these limitations often results (as described by Bernard Taylor) in a forecasting phenomenon (usually relating to long-range forecasting) known as the 'cliff'. In essence, management uses forecasting for a period of time (albeit often without fully understanding why and how it should be carried out) until the point at which problems arise – when all forecasting (at least that with any pretences to sophistication) is summarily dropped!

See also FORECASTING TECHNIQUES; QUANTITATIVE FORECASTING TECHNIQUES

References: Makridakis, Spyros and Wheelwright, Steven C. (1989) *Forecasting Methods for Management* (5th edn). Chichester: John Wiley.

Martino, Joseph P. (1972) *Technological Forecasting for Decisionmaking*. New York: American Elsevier.

McLean, Mick (1977) Getting the problem right – a role for structural modelling. In Harold A. Linstone and W. H. Clive Simmonds (eds), *Futures Research: New Directions*. Reading, MA: Addison-Wesley.

forecasks, monitoring   *see* MONITORING FORE-CASTS

forecasts of sales business   The most productive part of any sales planning usually starts with the forecasts of where the business – typically in the relatively short-term future – will come from.

Bankers
The easiest part of any forecast should be to deal with the 'bankers', those accounts that the sales personnel

know will soon complete the formality of signing the order. Even then, forecasting exactly when they will sign is not necessarily that easy. Paradoxically, it is somewhat more difficult to control if they have already stated that they will be placing the order. They have, as far as they are concerned, already given their sales contact the order; and see their formal signature as a petty administrative detail. Bankers are still, however, the easiest to predict, and should form the core of any forecast.

Probables versus possibles
Looking at sales professionals' forecasts, probables and possibles fall into three main groups. Those accounts labelled as 80 per cent chance of closing can (if the salesman is a professional) usually be counted as genuine 'probables'; sales professionals tend to be unduly optimistic, but an 80+ per cent confidence level is usually indicative of a good chance of success. Those falling below 50 per cent, however, are usually not the 'possibles' that most sales professional would like to think they are, but are more normally 'likely losers'. The main question to be asked of this category is 'Is it worth putting any more resources into these?' The experienced sales professional (and, in particular, his or her manager) will usually include in the overall forecast only the business with a better than 50 per cent chance. In any case, the wise sales manager will divide the aggregated forecasts of the sales team by a factor of two when making his or her own submission to senior management!

See also CALLS AVAILABLE ANNUALLY; EYEBALLING; MANPOWER PLAN, SALES; SALES PROFESSIONAL; SELL-ING; TERRITORY MANAGEMENT; TERRITORY SALES PLAN

foreign agencies   *see* INTERNATIONAL *AD HOC* RESEARCH

foreign buying groups   *see* MARKET ENTRY TACTICS

foreign government buying offices   *see* MARKET ENTRY TACTICS

foreign ownership   *see* REGULATORY CONSIDERATIONS, FILTERING UNSUITABLE MARKETS

forfaiting   A method of (medium-term) financing of exports by selling bills of exchange or promissory notes to a bank.

format franchise   *see* RETAIL ORGANIZATION

format of presentation   *see* PRESENTATIONS

forme   The frame into which letterpress type is locked for plate-making or printing.

forward buy   *see* CHANNEL MOTIVATION

forward delivery   Goods purchased for delivery at some time in the future.

forwarding agent   *see* SHIPPING AND FORWARDING AGENT

forward integration   *see* VERTICAL MARKETING

foul proof   The corrected proof from which a new proof has to be produced.

fount   *see* FONT

four-colour print   The use of the three primary colours and black ink in printing to give the impression of full colour. Even better quality may be obtained by use of six colours.
See also ADVERTISING; ADVERTISING AGENCY ELEMENTS

four Os   An aid to remembering the elements of a marketing operation: Objects, Objectives, Organization, Operations.

four Os of purchasing   These are a view of purchasing, typically as seen by marketers:

- *Objects*. What general uses will the product have?
- *Objectives*. What specific functions do buyers expect it to fulfil?
- *Organization*. Who within the organization can authorize the purchase?
- *Operations*. What are the procurement procedures?

four Ps   *see* 4 Ps

fractures and marketing research   There are some areas in which marketing research may not be particularly helpful. When there is a major discontinuity in the overall environment, described by Gareth Morgan as a 'fracture', this changes all of the factors to such an extent that market research may be largely useless.

In this situation, most marketing research is meaningless, since it essentially measures the historical position, unearthing data on what has gone before.

The discontinuity means that the future is decoupled from the past – it means that the future will be different. Even consumer research will be largely valueless when this happens, since the consumers asked their opinions will not know enough about the new developments to answer the questions accurately, but will base their answers (incorrectly) on their existing perspective – and this will, again, not offer the researcher a valid view of the future.
See also INERTIAL BALANCE; MARKETING RESEARCH

Morgan, G. (1988) *Riding the Waves of Change*. Jossey-Bass.

fragmented businesses   As represented by one quadrant in the Advantage Matrix (from the Boston Consulting Group), these organizations gain benefit from differentiation, particularly in the services sector, but little from economies of scale; examples being restaurants and job-shop engineering. Competition may be minimized by innovatory differentiation.

frame   One exposure on a photographic (or movie) film.

franchise channels   *see* VERTICAL MARKETING

franchise, customer   *see* CUSTOMER FRANCHISE

franchisees   *see* RETAIL ORGANIZATION

franchise, retail   *see* RETAIL ORGANIZATION

franchising   *see* CHANNEL DECISIONS

franking   Printing (or cancelling) postage on a letter.

freebie   Something provided for free, especially to journalists as part of PR.
See also PUBLIC RELATIONS; SALES PROMOTION

free credit   *see* PROMOTIONAL PRICING

free-flow channel   *see* CHANNEL STRUCTURE

free-form answer   *see* CLOSED QUESTIONS, ON QUESTIONNAIRES; OPEN QUESTIONS, ON QUESTIONNAIRES

free gifts   *see* NON-PRICE PROMOTIONS; PROMOTION OBJECTIVES

free goods   *see* PROMOTIONAL PRICING

free on board   *see* FOB (FREE ON BOARD)

free on board pricing   *see* GEOGRAPHICAL PRICING

freephone number   *see* INBOUND TELEMARKETING/COMMUNICATIONS

freepost card   *see* REPLY-PAID CARDS

free press   *see* PRESS MEDIA

free publications   *see* USERS

free sample   *see* DIRECT MAIL ADVERTISING

free-sheets   *see* PRESS MEDIA

free-standing inserts   *see* PROMOTIONAL PRICING

freight forwarder   A distribution service that offers only documentation and delivery to foreign destinations.
See also EXPORTING

frequency   *see* MEDIA SELECTION

frequency curve   *see* NORMAL CURVE

frequency distribution   The summarizing of data into categories or bands (defined by upper and lower limits) by reporting in tabular or graphical form the numbers of 'observations' (results) falling into each band.
See also ANALYSIS OF MARKETING RESEARCH DATA; GRAPHS, AND FORECASTING; NORMAL CURVE

frequency of purchase in advertising models   *see* BUYING DECISION, ADVERTISING MODELS

fringe accounts   Customers that are not very profitable.
See also ACCOUNT PLANNING

front office   *see* BACK ROOM OPERATIONS

Frost & Sullivan   *see* MARKET ENTRY DECISION

FSIs   *see* PROMOTIONAL PRICING

fudge   A second-colour machine on a newspaper printing line for adding the stop-press or the ears (advertisements) to either side of the masthead (the publications title) at the top of the front page.
See also MEDIA SELECTION

Fujitsu   *see* MARKET ENTRY TACTICS

full-cost pricing   *see* COST-PLUS PRICING

full cost recovery   *see* NOT-FOR-PROFIT ORGANIZATIONS, OBJECTIVES

full-function wholesaler   One that provides the whole range of services, including delivery to customers.
See also WHOLESALERS AND DISTRIBUTORS

full-line forcing   The practice, by a supplier, of compelling a stockist to take no competitive lines.

full nest   *see* AGE INFLUENCES, ON THE PURCHASE DECISION

functional plan   *see* MARKETING PLAN BENEFITS

function audit   *see* MARKETING AUDIT

funds providers   *see* NOT-FOR-PROFIT ORGANIZATIONS, OBJECTIVES

fustest with the mostest   *see* INNOVATIVE IMITATION

futurism   The process of 'forecasting' the very long range future was taken to its limits in the 1970s by the Rand Institute and, in particular, by the Hudson Institute (under Herman Kahn). That work has now fallen somewhat into disfavour – it tended to offer single, more confidently prescriptive, views of the future, which have more recently been replaced by multiple scenarios that better reflect the uncertainty. More recently, Spyros Makridakis (1989) has produced new material in a similar vein.
See also SCANNING, AND MIS; TEAM SCANNING; SCENARIOS

Reference: Makridakis, Spyros (1989) Management in the 21st century. *Long Range Planning*, 22(2).

G

Gallahers *see* ADVERTISING BUDGETS; MARKETING PLAN STRUCTURE

galley proof First proofs of typeset material, before it is split up into pages.

galvanometric response *see* PSYCHOGALVANOMETER

game plan *see* MARKETING STRATEGIES

game playing *see* PLANNING PITFALLS

game theory Theory, such as the Prisoner's Dilemma, based on the parallel with games of chance, which describes strategic situations in which the participants (small groups or organizations) have incomplete information about each other's intentions.
See also PRISONER'S DILEMMA; ROLE PLAYING

gap analysis A specific technique used to analyse where gaps may be; in marketing, rather than just cash flow, terms:

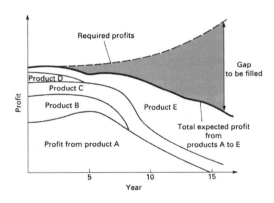

The bottom line shows what the profits are forecast to be, for the organization as a whole. The upper, dotted line, shows where the organization, and in particular its shareholders, want to be: almost inevitably, that will require an ascending line, implying growth in profit – success demands as much! The shaded area between these lines represents what is called the 'planning gap', and this shows what is needed of new activities in general and of 'new products' in particular.

In 'gap analysis', the gap is seen to come from four main causes:

* usage gap
* distribution gap
* 'product' gap
* competitive gap

The relationship between these is best illustrated by the following bar chart:

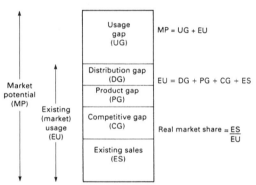

The usage gap is that between the total potential for the market and the actual current usage by all the consumers in the market. All other 'gaps' relate to the difference between the organization's existing sales (its market share) and the total sales of the market as a whole. This difference is the share held by competitors. These 'gaps' will, therefore, relate to competitive activity.
See also COMPETITIVE GAP; CREATIVE IMITATION; CUSTOMER BONUS; DISTRIBUTION GAP; EXISTING PRODUCT CHANGES; LEAPFROG; MARKETING PLANNING, ANALYSIS; PRODUCT (OR SERVICE) GAP; USAGE GAP

Garbage In Garbage Out *see* AGENCY BRIEFING; MARKETING AUDIT

gatefold *see* FOLD-OUT

gate-keepers   *see* DECISION-MAKERS AND INFLUENCERS

GATT   *see* GLOBALIZATION

GDP (gross domestic product)   *see* EXPORT MARKET ELIMINATION

GDP per capita   *see* EXPORT MARKET ELIMINATION

gearing   *see* AVOIDANCE OF FORECASTING

GE (General Electric) Matrix   This is a little-taught matrix, but one that is probably used more than others by practising corporate strategists. It can, though, only be used effectively at the business unit level and above, since it is a device for managing portfolios rather than individual products or services. On the other hand, the factors that it plots are more 'intuitive' than those used by some other approaches. Thus, the vertical axis simply plots the 'product/market attractiveness'; in other words, how worthwhile the business is. The horizontal axis covers 'business strength/competitive position'; what the organization's competitive advantage is. Equally, though, in its correct use, calculating these positions can be a long process and requires considerable explanation. (Although, in essence, the calculations still reflect judgements, these are carefully weighted. In unsophisticated hands, however, that can lead to a false sense of security!). If you want to use this approach with the correct precision, it is best to look up the details in a specialist text!

What seems, at first sight, to be even more complex is that it is a 3 × 3 matrix, whereas most others in management theory make do with 2 × 2 matrices. In practice, this adds little to the complexity – and

Business strength/competitive position

	strong		
high	invest	invest	evaluate
Product/ market attractiveness	invest	evaluate	disinvest
low	evaluate	disinvest	disinvest

much to the flexibility, as you will see below from the outcomes for the various boxes:

Thus, the addition of the 'grey' area, diagonally across the middle (where the instruction is to 'evaluate'), softens the harsh yes/no outcomes that are characteristic of 2 × 2 matrices.

See also ADVANTAGE MATRIX (BOSTON CONSULTING GROUP); BOSTON MATRIX; CORPORATE PLAN; CORPORATE STRATEGY AND MARKETING; MARKETING STRATEGIES; STRATEGIC BUSINESS UNIT (SBU); THREE CHOICE BOX

General Agreement on Trade and Tariffs   *see* GLOBALIZATION

General Electric Company   *see* MONITORING, PROGRESS

General Foods   *see* EXPORT MARKET ELIMINATION; INTERNATIONAL PRODUCT DECISION

general interest magazines   *see* PRESS MEDIA

General Mills   *see* STRUCTURE OF INTERNATIONAL MARKETING

generating ideas   In the absence of a new product idea, and to meet a planning gap, a number of techniques to stimulate the flow of new ideas have been described:

- brainstorming
- quality circles
- skunkworks
- attribute listing
- morphological analysis
- Synectics®
- customers
- innovative imitation

See also ATTRIBUTE LISTING; BRAINSTORMING; CREATIVE IMITATION; CUSTOMER BONUS; CUSTOMERS; INNOVATIVE IMITATION; LEAPFROG; MORPHOLOGICAL ANALYSIS; QUALITY CIRCLES; SKUNKWORKS; SYNECTICS®

generation leapfrogging   *see* CREATIVE IMITATION; LEAPFROG

generations, of products   *see* TECHNOLOGICAL LIFE CYCLE

generic robust strategies   There are some traditional 'investments', typically in intangibles, that can go some way to underwriting the long-term survival of most organizations regardless of what the future developments are. These are referred to as *generic robust strategies*. It should be noted that these are quite different to Michael Porter's generic strategies – which relate to the province of (shorter-term) corporate strategies.

In general, the main investments – in this category – relate to the *relationships* built up (invested in) with the main groups of *stakeholders*. In essence, the benefit of such investment is to create the *goodwill* (with customers, as relationship marketing does) that allows any organization the breathing space necessary for it to regroup – for instance, by carrying through a programme of creative imitation – in the face of changes that would otherwise be cataclysmic. Of course, the organization has to have sufficient speed of reaction to overcome the problems (demanding the creation of goodwill with its staff, as inner marketing does) before the goodwill runs out, but the goodwill itself is what allows the possibility of recovery.

See also ROBUST STRATEGIES

Reference: Porter, M. E. (1985) *Competitive Advantage.* New York: The Free Press.

generics   *see* OWN BRANDS AND GENERICS

geodemographics   A combination of geographical and demographic variables that typically are used to allow tight segmentation of consumers by local area (such as, in the UK, ACORN, A Classification Of Residential Neighbourhoods).
See also MARKETING RESEARCH, PRECISION MARKETING; SEGMENTATION

geographical clustering   *see* INTERNATIONAL PRODUCT DECISION

geographical coverage   *see* ECONOMIES OF SCALE, GLOBAL

geographical database   *see* BRANCH MARKETING

geographical growth vector   *see* ANSOFF MATRIX

geographical influences, on the purchase decision   For some products or services, geographical variations may be quite significant. Much has recently been made of the 'North/South divide' in the UK, but there may also be fundamental differences in taste between regions.

See also DECISION-MAKING PROCESS, BY CUSTOMERS; REPEAT PURCHASING PROCESS; RESIDENTIAL NEIGHBOURHOODS

geographical pricing   Where transport costs are important, and particularly where there are widely separated populations (as there are in the USA), then geographical location may become a factor in pricing. Some strategies to cope with this may be as follows:

- *Uniform pricing.* The same price is offered at all locations, regardless of delivery costs. This is the most widely applied policy in consumer goods markets; not least because it is easiest to apply, in terms of the paperwork created.
- *FOB.* 'Free on board' means that the cost of all transport is charged to the customer. This is more likely to be found in industrial markets, and particularly those, such as raw materials, where the item in question is bulky.
- *Zone pricing.* In this case the price is different for each geographical region, or 'zone', to incorporate the average transport costs incurred in shipping to that region.

There are, of course, other possible regional pricing policies. Not least of these are regional variations to allow for the strengths of local, regional, competitors.
See also PRICE FACTORS

geographical territories   *see* TERRITORY MANAGEMENT

geometric representation of consumers' perceptions   *see* SEGMENTATION METHODS

gestation period   The time between the first enquiry and the placing of the order. In the capital goods field, this may be many months.
See also ACCOUNT PLANNING; TERRITORY MANAGEMENT

ghosting   Showing part of the product by cutting away some of the packaging.

ghostwriting   *see* CORPORATE PUBLIC RELATIONS

Giffen goods   The economic name for goods for which demand increases as price increases (the opposite way to that predicted by the laws of supply and demand).

See also NEOCLASSICAL ECONOMICS; PRICE FACTORS

gifts, sales incentive schemes *see* MOTIVATION, OF SALES PERSONNEL

GIGO *see* AGENCY BRIEFING

giveaway *see* NON-PRICE PROMOTIONS

global acquisitions policy *see* GLOBALIZATION

global brands *see* CONVICTION MARKETING

global comparative advantage *see* COMPARATIVE ADVANTAGE, GLOBAL

global competition *see* ECONOMIES OF SCALE, GLOBAL

global convergence *see* GLOBALIZATION

global economies of scale *see* ECONOMIES OF SCALE, GLOBAL

global forecasts *see* DERIVED FORECASTS

globalization There has been much talk of 'globalization'; not least by the Saatchi & Saatchi advertising agency – possibly in defence of their own global acquisitions policy, which proved so problematical! Indeed, the impact of the transnationals and multinationals cannot be ignored – they often account for a major part of any nation's business activity.

Warren Keegan (1989) identifies a number of forces that have led to the expansion of international business:

- '*The International Monetary Framework*' – the rapid development of the international financial markets.
- '*The World Trading System*' – in particular, the influence of GATT.
- '*Global Peace*' – this was reinforced by 'perestroika'.
- '*Domestic Economic Growth*' – making these markets more receptive to imports.
- '*Communications and Transportation Technology*' – so that business can be carried out on a global basis.
- '*The Global Competition*' – one of the responses to the above factors.

Michael Marien (1989) offers a slightly different list, but with much the same message: 'An impressive array of current and potential driving forces propels this development. Among technologies, communications and computers are in the forefront in linking the world (and are themselves being linked), and air transport has facilitated physical movement of people. Leading idea-drivers include transnational corporations, "Europe 1992", the new capitalism of deregulation and global competition, and the thawing Cold War.' The theme has been reinforced by Theodore Levitt (1983): 'The result [of technology] is a new commercial reality – the explosive emergence of global markets for globally standardised products, gigantic world-scale markets of previously unimagined magnitudes'. At its most basic level, when one now walks into a supermarket, be it in Europe or the USA, one is immediately at home. The layout is much the same, the products are much the same (and are promoted in much the same way) – even the muzak sounds the same! As might be expected, in the light of his general work on competitive strategy, Michael Porter identified a range of factors that revolved around two main areas of activity; global comparative advantage and global economies of scale.

Only in a few markets has true globalization been achieved. These seem to require one or more of the following characteristics to be present.

Technological development
A number of these markets are driven by highly developed, and rapidly changing technology; and it is this technology itself that gives the cross-country and cross-cultural uniformity. At the same time, the expense of developing the technology also offers economies of scale to justify the globalization process. The classic examples are the organizations involved in the computer industry; such as IBM, Compaq and Microsoft. Even McDonalds has developed a special expertise in fast-food catering technology.

Innovation
Some markets have been conquered by the global organizations which first marketed an innovatory product (IBM, Sony or Boeing, for example) or service (McDonalds, 7 Eleven or Citibank), which they have then rolled out to the national markets before significant competitors have begun to emerge.

Concept-based
Some of the brands (such as Coca Cola, Marlboro, Levis, Timotei or Club Méditerannée) have developed such powerful concepts or images (verging on 'mini-cultures' in their own right) that they have

been able to overwhelm local cultures (at least in the field in which they hold sway).

Conviction marketing

Similarly, the owners of most of these brands have been so convincing (on the basis of 'conviction marketing') that they have been able to overpower, and often obliterate, local differences. Thus, Hunt et al. (1982) make the point, about the dramatic success of Honda in the motorcycle market, that 'Honda turned market preference around to the characteristics of its own products and away from those of American and European competitors'. It is also interesting, in this context, that some of the most successful global brands (such as IBM and Coca Cola and McDonalds, or Club Méditerannée and Perrier, or Toyota and Sony) seem to be able to embody a considerable (and very powerful) element of what is best in their original national cultures. This is perhaps most evident in the US brands, possibly because of the global dominance of the American media.

Conquest

There has been another driver for globalization of brands, and that has been 'conquest'. One of the legacies of the Second World War was the global distribution of certain brands. Perhaps the most notable was Coca Cola, which followed closely behind the advance of the US troops. There were other examples, though. Hunt et al. (1982), for instance, say (about the globalization of Caterpillar) that 'Navy Seabees who left their Caterpillar equipment in other countries following World War II planted the seeds of globalization. The company established independent dealerships to service these fleets and this base of units provided a highly profitable flow of revenue from spare parts, which paid for inventorying new units.'

Although the position in terms of individual brands is less clear, there is evidence of 'convergence' between the main markets.

See also COMPARATIVE ADVANTAGE, GLOBAL; CONVICTION MARKETING; ECONOMIES OF SCALE, GLOBAL; STANDARDIZATION VERSUS ADAPTATION; TRANSNATIONALS/MULTINATIONALS AND EXPORTERS

References: Hunt, Thomas, Porter, Michael and Rudden, Eileen (1982) How companies win out. *Harvard Business Review*, September–October.

Keegan, Warren J. (1989) *Global Marketing Management* (4th edn). Englewood Cliffs, NJ: Prentice-Hall.

Levitt, Theodore (1983) The globalisation of markets. *Harvard Business Review*, May–June.

Marien, Michael (1989) Driving forces and barriers to a sustainable global economy. *Futures*, December.

Parter, M. (1980) *Competitive Strategy*. Free Press.

global marketing   Gogel and Lareche (1989) look at company strengths across two dimensions, product strength and geographical coverage:

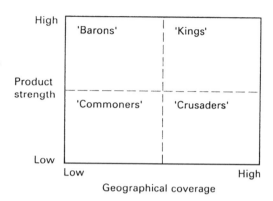

The four resulting archetypes range from 'kings' (which are in the strongest position – with a wide geographical coverage and strong product portfolio, giving them 'leverage') to 'commoners' (which are weak on both fronts, and thus need to adopt niche strategies). In between are 'barons' (with strong products – and hence well placed to expand – but concentrated in a limited number of countries) and 'crusaders' (which have expanded geographically, but from a weak product base, making them vulnerable to competition).

What is less clear is the degree to which the many multinationals (as opposed to the relatively few transnationals – or 'global corporations' as Levitt calls them) themselves actually see, and exploit, a global marketplace. Some of the suppliers of expensive industrial capital equipment – IBM in computer mainframes and Boeing in airliners, for example – may be able to bestride the world. To a lesser, usually continental, extent, suppliers of 'consumer durables', such as Ford in cars and Electrolux in washing machines, can also tap wider markets. What is interesting, in marketing terms, is how few truly global consumer brands there are. Coca Cola, Heinz, Kelloggs, Marlboro and McDonalds spring immediately to mind; representing, at least to some, symbols of US economic domination. But, beyond these and a few other similar examples, there are fewer global brands than might be expected. Unilever has run Lux soap as an international brand for decades, and has more recently promoted Timotei shampoo across a wide range of countries. But, like many other companies (including its main competitor, Proctor & Gamble), most of its brands are purely national, even when other national companies produce virtually identical products (but under different brand names!). On the other hand, many of the 'international brands' are national brands translated (often literally as exports) to the world stage. Thus Johnny Walker Scotch Whisky, Volkswagen German Cars and Dole Hawaiian Pineapples are firmly based on national identities.

There could, no doubt, be arguments made for a different categorization, and many would argue that the difference between transnational and international brands is not that significant. Even so, it should not be so surprising that there are so few genuinely global brands. Marketing theory assumes, correctly in most cases, that the product or service (and the whole marketing mix) has to be matched to customer needs and wants. The theory of global brands, on the other hand, assumes that 'global customers', with almost exactly the same 'global tastes' (and susceptible to the Saatchi's same 'global messages of persuasion'), can be found. But even Luciano Benetton, quoted in a Harvard Business School Case, said 'When speaking of "second generation" Benetton, I am thinking of a new business reality which is extra-European in scope. But we have to take into account the diverse requirements of the markets we are planning to enter.' The complication is that 'global marketing', in its purest sense, requires the differences between countries (compare, for instance, Japan with the USA, or Nigeria with Italy) to be negligible, or at least sufficiently small that they can be ignored in practice. In most instances, this is just not realistic; and each national market has to be approached separately – and often in a very specific way.

In a supermarket the products may look the same in Europe and the USA, but the brands will be very different. This will in part be due to genuine differences in the formulation, to match local tastes, but it will also reflect the comparative strengths of the corporations (and their history of acquisitions) in those markets. Philip Kotler (1986) gives the example of 'the impact of different laws governing advertising in different countries. A 30-second Kellogg cereal commercial would recognise the following changes if introduced in three European countries; in the Netherlands, deletion of references to iron and vitamins; in France deletion of the child actor; in Germany, deletion of the claim that "Kellogg make the corn flakes the best they've ever been".' The position on these specific issues may, at least in theory, have changed after the 'harmonization' of 1992 was complete, but the point remains valid (just written, perhaps, on a larger scale!). Perhaps the

most dramatic example of the failure of 'global marketing' was that of the Parker Pen Company. In the mid-1980s it set out to bring its marketing, across 154 countries, under a 'global marketing' umbrella – with the centralization of all major decisions and standards. Unfortunately, as it found, the markets were different. As a result, the single, worldwide campaign ('Make Your Mark With Parker') was a failure, and Parker Pen has apparently now lost much of that worldwide business.

See also COMPARATIVE ADVANTAGE, GLOBAL; ECONOMIES OF SCALE, GLOBAL; GLOBALIZATION

References: Gogel, Robert and Lareche, Jean-Claude (1989) The battlefield for 1992: product strategy and geographic coverage. *European Management Journal*, 7(2).

Heskett, James L. and Signorelli, Sergio (1988) Benetton. In Robert D. Buzzell and John A. Quelch (eds), *Multinational Marketing: Cases and Readings*. Reading, MA: Addison-Wesley.

Kotler, Philip (1986) Global standardization – courting danger. *Journal of Consumer Marketing*, 3(2).

global orientation   *see* STANDARDIZATION VERSUS ADAPTATION

global strategy   *see* TRANSNATIONALS/ MULTINATIONALS AND EXPORTERS

global undertakings   *see* STRATEGIC (INTERNATIONAL) ALLIANCES

GM Cars   *see* STANDARDIZATION VERSUS ADAPTATION

goals   *see* BUDGETS; MARKETING OBJECTIVES; MARKETING STRATEGIES; PLANNING PITFALLS

goals, ambiguous   *see* NOT-FOR-PROFIT ORGANIZATIONS, OBJECTIVES

goals, superordinate   *see* VISION, CORPORATE

Gold Blend   *see* MESSAGE, ADVERTISING

golden parachutes   *see* TAKEOVER BIDS

Gompertz curve   *see* TECHNOLOGICAL FORECASTING

gondola   An island display in a supermarket, where shoppers can reach both sides.

good, demand for   *see* SUPPLY AND DEMAND

goodwill valuation   *see* CUSTOMER FRANCHISE

government action   *see* MARKET ENTRY DECISION

government lobbying   *see* PROACTIVE PR

government subsidies   *see* FACILITY DECISIONS, LOGISTICS MANAGEMENT

government trade department   *see* ACCESSIBILITY, FILTERING UNSUITABLE FOREIGN MARKETS

grapevine, advertising industry   *see* AGENCY CHOICE

graphs, and forecasting   The use of graphs is important in forecasting, as it is in other parts of marketing. It is as well, therefore, that you understand what is involved. Raymond Willis (1987) starts from the very basic point that, in order to achieve the requisite accuracy, you must use the correct graph paper ('marked in small squares with heavier lines every fifth or tenth square', so that decimal figures are easy to plot). He adds the following hints:

1. 'Every graph should have a heading' – so that the reader understands what it is about (and so that it can later be retrieved from the files!).
2. 'Show your source' – so that the reader (and you) know where the data come from.
3. 'Make your scales easy to read and understand' – the vertical and horizontal scales should be clearly marked (at intervals that allow the reader easily to determine what the plotted figures are). Clear labelling is especially important in the case of logarithmic scales, where a wide range (perhaps covering a factor of 1000) may be shown on the same chart.
4. 'Show the baseline for the vertical scale' – unless the amount of change is so small that it would not be observable on the graph (in which case, Raymond Willis suggests that you show it in terms of percentage change or indexed figures rather than absolute ones), always include the 'zero point' on the graph (to avoid misleading the reader as to the relative size of the changes).
5. 'Make the intent of the graphs clear' – clearly show exactly what is being plotted (use bar charts, for instance, where a whole year's results are shown – so that lines joining the annual points do not imply a smooth growth, which might not have happened). Make the separate lines clearly different (and reproducible, by dotted/dashed lines etc., on black and white photocopies). In the context of forecasting, perhaps the most important distinction to highlight is that between historical and projected data.

To these sound guidelines, I would add just one more, where it is possible:

6. Show the scale of the estimated error – it is frequently possible to make an estimate of the error implicit in the historical figures (even if they are derived from one-off market research surveys) or in the forecasts (if the relevant statistical calculations have been carried out – albeit approximately). This additional evidence offers an important qualification to the graphs, and dramatically reduces the temptation for the reader to attribute a spurious degree of accuracy to them.

See also QUANTITATIVE FORECASTING TECHNIQUES

Reference: Willis, Raymond E. (1987) *A Guide to Forecasting for Planners and Managers*. Englewood Cliffs, NJ: Prentice-Hall.

gratis   Free, without cost.

gratuitous repositioning   *see* POSITION DRIFT

gravure   The printing process that uses small depressions in the printing plate to carry the ink to the paper. Traditionally, it has been used for large runs of (high-quality) journals.
See also ADVERTISING; ADVERTISING AGENCY ELEMENTS

green consumers   Those consumers who are influenced by (green) environmental issues when making their purchase decisions.
See also PURCHASE DECISION, MATCHING

green-field investment   The establishment of a completely new facility (typically applied to a factory) by the organization, which offers the benefit of being able to start everything from the ground up – following the most effective practices, rather than those dictated by history.
See also FACILITY DECISIONS, LOGISTICS MANAGEMENT

greengrocers   *see* RETAIL PRODUCT OR SERVICE CATEGORIES

greenmail   *see* TAKEOVER BIDS

Gresham's Law   The well-known saying, from the time of Elizabeth I, that 'bad money drives out good', which is less directly applicable amongst the complexity of modern financial dealings.

grey market A legal market for goods which are in short supply, or supplies obtained (by distributors) from another country that offers better prices.

gripe session A sales meeting at which demotivated sales personnel offer little but complaints and criticism – typically a sign of major problems in the sales force (and maybe with sales management).
See also SALES TEAM MANAGEMENT

gross audience Sometimes called 'gross impressions', this is the total number of times the advertisement/commercial has been seen across all the audience. It is called gross cover in the case of television and radio.
See also ADVERTISING RESEARCH

gross contribution *see* MONITORING, PROGRESS

gross cover *see* GROSS AUDIENCE

gross domestic product *see* EXPORT MARKET ELIMINATION

gross impressions *see* GROSS AUDIENCE

gross profit *see* MONITORING, PROGRESS

group commitment *see* MARKETING PLAN BENEFITS

group consensus *see* GROUPTHINK

group discussions *see* GROUP RESEARCH

group membership (shared) *see* PARTNERSHIP TRIANGLE

group pressure *see* GROUPTHINK

group research Typically used as the first (qualitative) stage of marketing research fieldwork, and often called 'group discussions' or 'focus group research', this technique requires that a selected, relatively homogeneous, group (typically containing 6–10 members) of participants is encouraged to discuss the topics that the researchers are investigating. The interviewer ('group leader' or 'moderator'), who has to be skilled in the technique and often is a trained psychologist, carefully leads the discussion;

ensuring that all of the group members are able to put forward their views. The interviewer's role is then an essentially passive one, where his or her prime concern is to foster group interaction (and, in the terms of William Wells, 'pest control' – including, most importantly, any one individual dominating the group).

The essence of such group discussions is indeed that the participants can develop their own ideas in an unstructured fashion – interacting with, and stimulating, others. The whole session is typically captured on a tape recorder for, most importantly, later analysis in depth. This often allows insights that are hidden by the preconceived questions posed in questionnaire surveys.

As Bellenger et al. (1976) state, 'The concept is based on the assumption that individuals who share a problem will be more willing to talk about it amid the security of others sharing the problem.' This reflects the clinical origins of the technique, but it also shows how powerful it can be in revealing hidden attitudes.

An added advantage (if carefully controlled) that sometimes applies is that the 'client' can also attend such sessions (usually watching from behind a two-way mirror). As Sidney Levy (1979) says, 'they feel they are getting quick results, the participation, stimulation, and sense of conviction gained from perceiving the live expression of opinions'.

Such group research is, in the words of William Wells (1974), 'a superb mechanism for generating hypotheses when little is known'; and is thus a particularly productive approach to piloting the first stage of larger research projects.

It is, however, increasingly being used as a cheaper and faster alternative for those organizations that cannot afford the full-scale research – and, in line with the move to 'low-cost' research, even for those that can (a feature that William Wells reported as early as 1974)! This is arguably better than nothing, but if such use is planned the 'researcher' should beware of attributing too much significance to it; and in particular to any such 'statistical' outcomes. The sample sizes are usually far too small to allow any statistical conclusions to be drawn and the conclusions are very dependent upon the researcher's interpretations. Unfortunately, some of the agencies commissioning this research do attribute something approaching statistical significance (or at least an unjustifiable degree of importance) to their results by themselves. In this case, unfortunately, it must be the client who has to recognize the very real limitations of the information that can be derived from them. Not least, you should take heed of Bellenger et al.'s warning that 'there are many charlatans in the business of conducting focus groups, and the marketer must exercise care in selecting the research firm to conduct the interviews'.

See also MARKETING RESEARCH; MARKETING RESEARCH STAGES; QUALITATIVE RESEARCH

Reference: Bellenger, D. N., Bernhardt, K. L. and Goldstucker, J. L. (1976) *Qualitative Research in Marketing.* American Marketing Association. Wells, William D. (1974) Group interviewing. In Robert Ferber (ed.), *Handbook of Marketing Research.* New York: McGraw-Hill.

groups　*see* MARKETING RESEARCH, PRECISION MARKETING

groups of actors　*see* NOT-FOR-PROFIT ORGANIZATIONS, OBJECTIVES

group technology　*see* JUST IN TIME (JIT)

groupthink　Whereas the current paradigm determines the perspective of everyone in the organization, 'groupthink' is a related process that only applies to a group of managers; although, as these are often the executive team, it may be difficult to separate the effects of the two.

Based upon his research into President Kennedy's 'Bay of Pigs' adventure, Irving Janis derived a number of symptoms that may be detected when groupthink is taking place. The first of these relate to how the group choose to see the outside world, and may be similar to those involved in a paradigm shift:

(a) *Invulnerability* – excessive optimism about their (illusory) position.
(b) *Blindness* – collective avoidance (rationalization) of unwanted warnings.
(c) *Moral superiority* – unquestioned (but unwarranted) belief in their ethical position.
(d) *Stereotyped enemies* – black and white, good versus evil.

The remainder, however, relate to how the group (and individuals within the group) organizes itself to combat these 'enemies':

(e) *Pressure* – on any group member who dissents
(f) *Self-censorship* – of anything which deviates from the group consensus.
(g) *Unanimity* – an illusion that there is no possible dissent within the group.
(h) *Mindguards* – some members of the group may set themselves up to police the rest.

The key impact of groupthink is the extent to which it divorces the group from reality. Once you have seen it in action, which fortunately is rare (in terms of a full manifestation), you will probably never forget this almost manic abandonment of reality (and the accompanying damage to the organization), but lesser manifestations can be seen in more humdrum management situations (the well-known 'yes-men' syndrome can have similar effects).

See also CORPORATE PLAN; CORPORATE STRATEGY AND MARKETING; EMERGENT STRATEGY; LOGICAL INCREMENTALISM; PARADIGM SHIFT, STRATEGY; PLANNING PROCESS

Reference: Janis, Irving L. (1972) *Victims of Groupthink.* Boston, Massachusetts: Houghton Mifflin.

group value　Prompted by the threat of hostile takeovers to break up groups into their component parts, some have considered ways of writing in an 'asset' value for the synergy that the group brings to its separate parts. Needless to say, this is controversial with the accountants – and no group has yet gone as far as trying to incorporate any such sums in its accounts. On the other hand, it offers a very powerful device for measuring what the group adds to the sum of the components.

See also BRAND VALUE

growth　*see* CORPORATE OBJECTIVES; PRODUCT LIFE CYCLE (PLC)

growth curves　*see* TECHNOLOGICAL FORECASTING

growth stage, product life cycle　According to PLC theory, by the beginning of this stage customers have become aware of the product or service and its benefits. Accordingly, usage is growing, often rapidly. More people want it, and want to use more of it. During this stage, the suppliers often have to increase the capacity of their plant, and run promotional campaigns to consolidate and extend their share of the new market. In the process they frequently make substantial investments, which usually absorb what profit is being made, so that this part of the life cycle is not normally expected to be a profit generator – and may even demand further net investment. As a result of these investments in new plant, and the increasing volumes, the prices usually reduce – assuming that a policy of 'skimming' had been adopted in the introductory phase. Attracted by the growth in the market, further competitors may enter; but, with the market growing, direct (price) competition is probably not a major factor. This growth of sales, customer numbers and, in particular, numbers of suppliers can sometimes be explosive – which is called the 'bandwagon effect'. As a result of awareness having been largely established, and in the light of growing competition, the emphasis at this stage may well be on promotion of the 'brand'; establishing the correct attitudes to the product. Promotion is still heavy, although it may sometimes be possible to start making a profit. In recent years, another feature of this phase has been the battle for distribution; where, in particular, there has been a concentration of retail distribution into the hands of a few major operators, especially those running supermarkets. It is vital to the success of a brand to obtain the widest possible distribution, so there will probably be much energy expended on negotiations with these key players.

growth vector alternatives   *see* ANSOFF MATRIX

guarantee cards, precision marketing   *see* DATA AVAILABILITY, PRECISION MARKETING

guarantees   *see* REPEAT PURCHASING PROCESS

guard book   *see* MESSAGE CONSISTENCY

guests   *see* SERVICE QUALITY

guidelines   *see* MARKETING STRATEGIES

guilt   *see* MESSAGE, ADVERTISING

gut-reaction   *see* COARSE MARKETING

gutter   Where the two facing pages join together in a magazine or book. It is usually left blank, but can be printed across to form a double-page spread.
See also BLEED; DOUBLE-PAGE SPREAD

Guttman cumulative scales   Cumulative questions, for questionnaires, such as 'Is your age over 60?', '. . . over 40?' or '. . . over 20?', each of which incorporates (cumulatively) the previous figures.
See also QUESTIONNAIRE DESIGN

H

habitual behaviour, pricing *see* PRICING, PRODUCT POSITIONING

haggling of the bazaar *see* SOCIAL AND BUSINESS STRUCTURES, FILTERING UNSUITABLE MARKETS

half-nelson close *see* CLOSING TECHNIQUES

halftone An image which represents shades of grey (as in a photograph) for printing by different sizes of dots.
See also LINE DRAWING; SCREEN

hall tests The name sometimes given to marketing research tests (typically product or packaging tests) where the respondents are brought together at a location (in a 'hall').
See also PRODUCT TEST

halo effect The measurement of 'attitudes' (or at least of specific elements of these 'attitudes') is complicated, in practice, by the 'halo effect'. Thus, respondents will tend to report more favourably on all of the separate elements (all of their likes and dislikes of specific aspects) of 'attitude' towards the brand(s) that they favour.
See also MOTIVATION RESEARCH; SERVICE QUALITY

Hamburger University *see* SERVICE QUALITY

Hamlet (cigar) commercials *see* AWARENESS, ADVERTISING; MESSAGE, ADVERTISING

handbill A leaflet or flyer designed to be handed out to the public at large.

handout, publicity *see* PUBLIC RELATIONS

hard-core loyals *see* USAGE AND LOYALTY

hard systems approach *see* SYSTEMS APPROACHES

harmonization of standards *see* REGULATORY CONSIDERATIONS, FILTERING UNSUITABLE MARKETS

Harvard Business School *see* MONITORING, PROGRESS

harvest strategies *see* DECLINE STRATEGIES

hawk To sell goods from door to door.

headhunter *see* RECRUITMENT, OF SALES PERSONNEL

head-in positioning *see* SEGMENTATION

headline Heading of an advertisement or article which is set in more prominent type.
See also ADVERTISING PROCESSES; AWARENESS, ADVERTISING; BODY COPY; DIRECT MAIL; KISS ADVERTISING

headspace The (apparently empty) portion of air in some packaged powdered products, which is caused by settlement of the powder after filling.
See also PACKAGING

heavy users *see* USAGE AND LOYALTY

heavy viewers *see* MEDIA SELECTION

Heineken lager *see* MESSAGE, ADVERTISING

Heinz *see* GLOBAL MARKETING

Heinz ketchup *see* ACCESSIBILITY, FILTERING UNSUITABLE FOREIGN MARKETS

Henley Centre for Forecasting *see* PROACTIVE PR

heresy *see* PARADIGM SHIFT, STRATEGY

heterogeneity A term used, usually in survey research or data analysis, to describe results/characteristics that show significant differentiation between the individuals involved.
See also ANALYSIS OF MARKETING RESEARCH DATA; CLUSTER ANALYSIS; HOMOGENEITY

heterogeneity of services   *see* VARIABILITY, SERVICES

heterogeneity within country   *see* INTERNATIONAL PRODUCT DECISION

hidden motivations   *see* MOTIVATION RESEARCH

hidden (research) time   *see* RESEARCH EIAMOND

hierarchy   *see* PLANNING PITFALLS

Hierarchy of Effects model   *see* BUYING DECISION, ADVERTISING MODELS; PURCHASE DECISION, MATCHING

Hierarchy of Needs   *see* MASLOW'S HIERARCHY OF NEEDS

high budget, diverse strategy   *see* NEW PRODUCT INNOVATION

high-impact advertising   *see* ENHANCED AIUAPR MODEL; THREE PILLARS OF THE PURCHASING PROCESS

high-involvement product   One where the customer takes time and effort to ensure that they make the correct purchase decision.
See also PURCHASE DECISION, MATCHING

high key   An illustration in which the majority of the tones lie at the white end of the grey scale.

high-street outlets   *see* LOCATION, RETAIL; RETAIL PRODUCT OR SERVICE CATEGORIES

high tech   In terms of the basic 'dimensions' on which marketing is often organized, it is arguable that the markets for high technology are rather different – and particularly in that they are characterized by rapid change and high uncertainty.
See also CONVICTION MARKETING TYPES; ORGANIZATIONAL PIGEON–HOLES

high-technology equipment ban   *see* REGULATORY CONSIDERATIONS, FILTERING UNSUITABLE MARKETS

hire purchase   *see* INSTALMENT PLAN

hiring   *see* OFF–BALANCE–SHEET FINANCING

historical precedent, sales manpower budget *see* MANPOWER PLAN, SALES

historical pricing   The normal extension of cost-plus pricing is to base today's prices on yesterday's. The annual round of price increases, for example, is based on last year's price uplifted by something approximating to the increase in the cost of living; or the true increase in costs – whichever is the higher!
See also COST-PLUS PRICING; PRICING POLICIES, PRACTICAL

history, budgets   *see* BUDGETS

history of advertising campaigns   *see* MESSAGE CONSISTENCY

history of marketing   It is important to recognize that marketing has been in existence for a number of millennia; ever since man first started to barter the surpluses he had accumulated. For most of that time, though, it has been seen as a peripheral activity – for such surpluses, almost by definition, represented a relatively small part of the total in subsistence economies!

Even after the Industrial Revolution made such surpluses more commonplace, the 'marketing' of them only became the province of the 'salesman' with his specialized skills.

Jones and Monieson (1990) suggest that the first academic discussions of 'marketing' can be traced back to the turn of the century; to, for instance, the E. D. James series of articles in *Mill Supplies* between 1911 and 1914.

However, in the wider sphere of practical business management, it was only after 1945 that the newly fashionable advertising agencies began to redefine the discipline in a way which came close to the modern concept of marketing. The 1950s, then, may be seen (in very general terms) as the decade of advertising. They were a period when the influence of the agencies peaked; and their clients appointed advertising managers to control this newly discovered resource.

Indeed, it was, arguably, only at the beginning of the 1960s that marketing in its modern form, based upon a customer focus (and, in particular, making extensive use of market research to investigate that customer's needs and wants), emerged on a large scale. This decade represented the heyday of the 'pure' marketing manager – and, especially, of the few pioneers who became brand managers (at the pinnacle of a new profession!). Almost all of these pioneers, however, practised a form of marketing that had been learned by a practical apprenticeship, rather than in the classroom. This was, perhaps, the headiest period of marketing; as the frontiers of the new discipline were daily pushed back by the development of new approaches (but led by practice rather than, as now, derived from theory).

Wolf and Smith (1986) reinforce this rather nostalgic view: 'Marketing probably achieved its greatest influence during the 1960s, a time of rapidly expanding markets. The marketing plan was a significant element in guiding a firm's product-market choices.'

The discipline matured in the 1970s as, led by Philip Kotler's seminal text *Marketing Management –* first published in 1967 – the ideas that had developed from practical experience were codified. Marketing became routinized, as an increasingly important function of management. Wolf and Smith, again, chart another aspect of marketing's progress during this time: 'the influence of the field waned in the turbulent 1970s when strategic planning ascended. This change forced management to concentrate on reacting to environmental changes and consolidating competitive positions to conserve scarce resources' – elements that have now been incorporated into modern marketing. In the 1980s, however, it lost much of its previous self-confidence; possibly in part as a reflection of the worldwide recession, which changed the emphasis from exploiting the potential of expanding markets to defending existing share of a static market from rapacious competitors. Not least in terms of the new ideas being developed, the attention moved to more aggressive techniques, with a more immediate pay-back – including derivatives of those developed by Michael Porter (1980) in his *Competitive Strategy*, derivatives which, however, conveniently ignored his longer-term perspectives.

Warren Keegan (1989) summarized the changes as follows:

By 1980 it was clear that the 'new' concept of marketing was outdated and that the times demanded a strategic concept. The strategic concept of marketing, a major evolution in the history of marketing thought, shifted the focus from the customer or product to the firm's external environment. Knowing everything there is to know about the customer is not enough. To succeed, marketers must know the customer in a context which includes the competition, government policy and

regulation, and the broader economic, social and political macro forces that shape the evolution of markets.

It is as yet too early to be certain, but the evidence is that since the early 1990s the 'paradigm' has been in the process of shifting once more, to a position somewhere between the two previous extremes. There is increasing use, once again, of the techniques of marketing (and increasing confidence in the outcome), but this is now an informed usage, which recognizes the inherent limitations.

In the 1980s the leading edge of marketing moved on also, at least in part, to the service industries – particularly to retailing and financial services – which were experiencing massive changes. Such very rapid and significant changes, 'fractures' as they are graphically termed by Gareth Morgan (1988), seem to be major catalysts for extensive change throughout the affected organization.

References: Drucker, Peter F. (1964) *Managing for Results.* London: Heinemann.

Jones, Brian D. G. and Monieson, David D. (1990) Early development of the philosophy of marketing thought. *Journal of Marketing,* 54.

Keegan, Warren J. (1989) *Global Marketing Management* (4th edn). Englewood Cliffs, NJ: Prentice-Hall.

Kotler, P. (1967) *Marketing Management* (1st edn). Englewood Cliffs, NJ: Prentice-Hall.

Morgan, Gareth (1988) *Riding the Waves of Change.* San Francisco: Jossey–Bass.

Porter, Michael E. (1980) *Competitive Strategy.* New York: The Free Press.

Wolf, Jack and Smith, Wendell R. (1986) Market needs and market changes. In Victor P. Buell (ed.), *Handbook of Modern Marketing* (2nd edn). New York: McGraw-Hill.

hit rate   The success rate, in terms, for instance, of contacting prospective buyers or obtaining responses from mailings.

hoarding   A large poster site.

hockey stick effect   *see* FORECASTS, LIMITING FACTORS; PLANNING PITFALLS

holdback   The negotiating strategy of holding back the final offer to close a sale.
See also SALES CALL CLOSE

holding cost   *see* ECONOMIC BATCH QUANTITY

holding stock   *see* INVENTORY CONTROL; LOGISTICS MANAGEMENT; PRODUCTION DECISIONS, LOGISTICS MANAGEMENT

Holiday Inns   *see* MARKETING MYOPIA

holistic approach to problems   *see* SYSTEMS APPROACHES

holistic evaluation   The evaluation of a marketing campaign as a whole rather than in parts.
See also ADVERTISING RESEARCH

homogeneity   A term used, usually in survey research or data analysis, to describe results/characteristics that show little differentiation between the individuals involved.
See also ANALYSIS OF MARKETING RESEARCH DATA; CLUSTER ANALYSIS; HETEROGENEITY

horizontal and vertical industrial markets   At a much less sophisticated level than consumer market segmentation, some markets for industrial products are described as either 'horizontal' or 'vertical'. 'Horizontal' markets are those where use of the product or service stretches across a wide range of industries. Thus, the use of word-processing or spreadsheet software is general, across most businesses, and is accordingly defined as a horizontal market (as would be that for business stationery or self-service coffee machines). 'Vertical' markets are those where use of the product or service is strictly limited to a single industry (or a limited number of them). Software designed to support dairy herd management, for example, has a very narrow ('vertical') market, that of dairy farmers, while word-processing based software for handling legal documents has a similarly 'vertical' market, in solicitors' offices.
See also INDUSTRIAL MARKETS AND THE MARKETING MIX; PRODUCT (OR SERVICE) POSITIONING; SEGMENTATION

horizontal marketing   In this form of distribution channel, two or more non-competing organizations agree on a joint venture – a joint marketing operation – because it is beyond the capacity of each individual organization. In general this is less likely to revolve around marketing synergy than investment.
See also CHANNEL DECISIONS; CHANNEL MEMBERSHIP; CHANNEL MOTIVATION; DISTRIBUTION CHAIN

horizontal publication   A magazine or journal aimed at readers across a range of industries and sectors.

horns (opposite to halo) effect   *see* SERVICE QUALITY

hostess (party) selling   *see* AGENT (PERSONAL) SELLING

hot metal   *see* FLONG; LINOTYPE

hot shop agencies   *see* SPECIALIST AGENCIES

house accounts   Customers that an organization keeps for itself when it appoints agents or distributors; who are not then allowed to call on these accounts.
See also DISTRIBUTION CHAIN

house brand   *see* OWN BRAND AND GENERICS

household 'impressions'   *see* MEDIA SELECTION

house journal   A magazine produced for stakeholders in an organization, usually mainly for employees.
See also PUBLIC RELATIONS

house list   *see* DATABASE, INVESTING IN YOUR OWN

house style   *see* AGENCY CHOICE

housewife agents   *see* AGENT (PERSONAL) SELLING

Howard and Sheth model, of consumer behaviour   One of the best known of the 'explanatory' models, which has been developed to explain the interactions between the various factors involved in marketing, is the Howard and Sheth model, of consumer behaviour. This contains a deal of common sense; although, as is often the case, the rather obscure terminology makes it appear more confusing than it is. It is divided into three main components:

Inputs
These are the inputs (stimuli) that the consumer receives from his or her environment:

- *Significative.* These are the 'real' ('physical') aspects of the product or service (that the consumer will make use of).
- *Symbolic.* These are the ideas or images attached by the supplier (for example, by advertising).
- *Social.* These are the ideas or images attached by 'society' (for example, by reference groups).

Outputs
These are what happens – the consumer's actions – as observable results of the input stimuli.

Constructs

Between the inputs and outputs are the processes that the consumer goes through to decide upon his or her actions. Howard and Sheth group these into two areas:

- *Perceptual.* Those concerned with obtaining and handling information about the product or service.
- *Learning.* These are the processes of learning that lead to the decision itself.

As has already been mentioned, even though this is one of the simpler models, the terminology is somewhat obscure, and the nature of the links not immediately obvious – and it takes the best part of a book to explain what is happening within it!

Such models can help theorists to better explain consumer behaviour but, generally speaking, it is more difficult to put them to practical use in specific marketing situations.

See also ENGEL–KOLLATT–BLACKWELL MODEL, OF CONSUMER BEHAVIOUR; MODELS

Reference: Howard, J. A. and Sheth, J. N. (1969) *The Theory of Buyer Behaviour.* New York: John Wiley.

HPC *see* MOTIVATION, OF SALES PERSONNEL

huckster *see* SALESMAN STEREOTYPE

Hudson Institute *see* FUTURISM

human factors, new products The availability of manpower may be a factor in the viability of new products, and will become an increasingly important one with the demographic changes that are taking place. The chances are that new developments will require skilled personnel, and these are becoming more and more difficult to recruit. It may just be possible for the existing workforce to be retrained, but this would mean that the marketing plans may have to take into account the organization's training capabilities!

See also NEW PRODUCT SCREENING, ORGANIZATIONAL FACTORS

Human Resource Management (HRM) *see* INNER MARKET; INNER MARKETING CAMPAIGN; QUALITY CIRCLES

humour *see* MESSAGE, ADVERTISING

Hundred Percent Club *see* MOTIVATION, OF SALES PERSONNEL

hybrid channels *see* MONITORING AND MANAGING CHANNELS

hygiene factors *see* PSYCHOLOGICAL INFLUENCES, ON THE PURCHASE DECISION

hype Over-inflated claims made, for example, by advertising.

hypermarkets *see* LOCATION, RETAIL

hypothesis testing The (academic) approach to testing relationships between variables, to see if these relationships are significant.

I

IBM *see* CONVICTION MARKETING FACTORS; CORPORATE PROMOTION VERSUS BRAND PROMOTION; DEDICATED FOLLOWERS; GLOBALIZATION; INTERNATIONAL PRODUCT DECISION; STANDARDIZATION VERSUS ADAPTATION; TRANSNATIONALS/MULTINATIONALS AND EXPORTERS

IBM account-planning sessions *see* RELATIONSHIP (MARKETING) MANAGEMENT

IBM culture *see* CONVICTION MARKETING FACTORS

IBM customer service *see* VISION, CORPORATE

IBM environmental factors *see* MARKETING PLANNING, ANALYSIS

IBM Forecast Assumptions *see* ASSUMPTIONS, MARKETING PLAN; POTSA PLANNING

IBM Hundred Percent Club (HPC) *see* MOTIVATION, OF SALES PERSONNEL

IBM planning meetings *see* MARKETING PLAN USE

IBM prices worldwide *see* INTERNATIONAL PRICE DECISION

IBM sales commission *see* MOTIVATION, OF SALES PERSONNEL

IBM sales force training *see* SALES TRAINING

IBM sales manpower planning *see* CALLS AVAILABLE ANNUALLY

IBM sales operation *see* TERRITORY MANAGEMENT

IBM sales success *see* PROSPECT QUALIFICATION

iceberg principle A model that suggests that people's real desires are buried deep under the surface

and are, accordingly, much more difficult to deal with.
See also MODELS

idea generation *see* GENERATING IDEAS

ideal brand *see* SEGMENTATION METHODS

idea power *see* CONVICTION MARKETING; GLOBALIZATION

identical products worldwide *see* INTERNATIONAL PRODUCT DECISION

identifiable concept *see* CONVICTION MARKETING FACTORS

identity, segment viability To be viable, a segment has to have characteristics which will enable it to be separately identified (and measured by market research), by both the producers and the consumers. It must be recognizable to both as a cohesive entity.
See also SEGMENT VIABILITY

ideology *see* CONVICTION MARKETING; CULTURE, ORGANIZATIONAL

idiot-proofing *see* DESIGNING DEMONSTRATIONS

illusory position *see* GROUPTHINK

illustrator *see* CREATIVE DEPARTMENT, ADVERTISING AGENCY

image *see* CONVICTION MARKETING FACTORS; CUSTOMER FRANCHISE; PRODUCT IMAGE, PACKAGING

image-building *see* PROMOTIONAL LOZENGE

image modification This may also be associated with style modification (or 'perceived quality' changes), but in essence the product or service itself remains unchanged; and some image modifications may actually stress this (Ovaltine and Bovril in the 1980s, for example). 'Image modification' concentrates on changing the 'non-product attributes', so that consumers feel that the 'total package' has changed. Image is often the most important element of that package.

See also PRODUCT (OR SERVICE) MODIFICATION

image pricing   *see* SELECTIVE PRICING

IMF, *International Financial Statistics*   *see* INTERNATIONAL MARKETING RESEARCH

imitation   *see* CREATIVE IMITATION; CUSTOMER BONUS; INNOVATIVE IMITATION; LEAPFROG

impact   *see* ADVERTISING PLAN; ADVERTISING PROCESSES; CUSTOMER FRANCHISE; ENHANCED AIUAPR MODEL; KISS ADVERTISING; MEDIA IMPACT; SHARPENING THE CUTTING EDGE OF MEDIA; TELEVISION; THREE PILLARS OF THE PURCHASING PROCESS

imperfect competition   *see* BRAND MONOPOLY; PRICE FACTORS

imperfect information   *see* COARSE MARKETING

IMP (International Marketing and Purchasing Group)   *see* INTERACTION, AND THE ORGANIZATIONAL PURCHASE

implementation phase   *see* RINGI

import   *see* AGENTS OR DISTRIBUTORS

import business support   *see* ACCESSIBILITY, FILTERING UNSUITABLE FOREIGN MARKETS

imported goods duties   *see* REGULATORY CONSIDERATIONS, FILTERING UNSUITABLE MARKETS

imports   *see* GLOBALIZATION; STRUCTURE OF INTERNATIONAL MARKETING

impression cover   The number of transmissions, or insertions, needed to achieve the required coverage.

impressions   *see* BUDGETS; MEDIA SELECTION

improvement, continuous   *see* KAISEN

impulse purchase   A product or service bought by a customer on the spur of the moment, but often persuaded to do so by sophisticated merchandising in the store.

See also PURCHASE DECISION, MATCHING

inadequacies in planning   The researches of Malcolm McDonald and his team at the Cranfield Business School have shown that there are ten main factors that lead to problems in the marketing planning process. The main messages deriving from this work are as follows:

* *Commitment.* The management involved – particularly top management, and above all the chief executive – must be committed to the planning process and to the implementation of the plans that it produces. They must be involved in the process and understand that it is highly relevant, and indeed essential, to their own management activities; and is not just a once-a-year ritual that they must endure.
* *Time.* Implementation of the planning process takes longer than people expect or wish. Malcolm McDonald (1984) suggests, realistically, that it should not be expected to be producing fully operational plans for perhaps three years, which is very much longer than the few weeks normally allowed! In part, this time is needed for all of the individuals to develop their communication processes (and understand each other's terminology), as well as to understand that there is more to planning than numbers and unconnected details.
* *Understanding.* The managers must also recognize what the various planning processes are; including operational planning, as opposed to strategic planning, how the marketing plan integrates into the corporate plan, what the role of the planner is, etc.

See also CORPORATE OBJECTIVES; MARKETING STRATEGIES; PLANNING PROCESS

Reference: McDonald, Malcolm H. B. (1984) *Marketing Plans.* London: Heinemann.

inbound calls   *see* TELESALES

inbound telemarketing/communications   This represents the other side of the telesales coin. A telesales (or 'enquiry handling') team receives calls from customers and prospects. These calls may be part of 'business as usual', in which case they may be handled by in-house teams (Hertz and Avis, for example, have large teams to handle telephone orders).

On the other hand, they may be part of a one-off promotional campaign (with, for instance, an advertised offer being directed to a standard 'freephone' number – 0800 in the UK or 800 in the USA). These are typically handled by specialist agencies (which have the computer systems and, especially, the extensive telephone lines necessary for these peak loads). 'Enquiry-handling' in general, though, is a weak link in most organizations' marketing operations. Very few organizations indeed have formally planned (and controlled/monitored) enquiry handling systems.
See also TELESALES

incentive schemes   *see* MOTIVATION, OF SALES PERSONNEL

income statement   *see* PROFIT-AND-LOSS STATEMENT

incremental close   *see* CLOSING TECHNIQUES

incremental development   *see* FLEXIBLE DEVELOPMENT; RADICAL INNOVATION

incremental development of services   *see* PRODUCT TEST

incrementalism   *see* CATASTROPHE THEORY; CONVICTION MARKETING FACTORS; LOGICAL INCREMENTALISM

incremental strategy   *see* EMERGENT STRATEGY; MARKETING STRATEGIES

indent   To put in an order for supplies, typically internally within the organization.
See also PURCHASING

independent business   *see* STRATEGIC BUSINESS UNIT (SBU)

independent intermediaries   *see* AGENTS OR DISTRIBUTORS

independents, retail   *see* RETAIL ORGANIZATION

independent variables   *see* MULTIPLE REGRESSION ANALYSIS

index-linked   Price or cost changes that are linked to the percentage changes in the index of inflation.

indicators, leading   *see* LEADING INDICATORS

indicators, long-term   *see* MONITORING, PROGRESS

indifference curve, pricing   *see* PRICES, CUSTOMER NEEDS

indirect advertising contact   *see* PROMOTIONAL LOZENGE

indirect channels   *see* CHANNEL DECISIONS

indirect communications   *see* OPINION LEADERS

indirect expenses, sales personnel   *see* TERRITORY PLANS

indirect export sales   *see* MARKET ENTRY TACTICS

individual depth interviews   These are sometimes called 'intensive' interviews or semi-structured interviews. They can last for an hour or more, and can follow a variety of formats; from an almost totally free form (which, like the true depth or clinical interview conducted by a psychologist, is so specialized as to be outside normal market research practice), through the non-directive form (where the interviewer, while still in control, allows the respondent to answer in whatever form he or she wants), to the semi-structured form (which is much closer to the conventional questionnaire interview, but which still allows the respondent some freedom of expression). The essence of all of these is that the answers are totally open-ended, and have to be analysed by skilled personnel – but the freedom of expression often leads to a less constrained view of their true attitudes.
See also MARKETING RESEARCH; QUALITATIVE RESEARCH

individually customized products   *see* SEGMENTATION APPROACHES

individual management of sales   The traditional view of selling has been that it is a 'professional' role (if even that) rather than a management one (very few sales professionals manage teams of subordinates). In practice, much of the sales professional's role is actually concerned with management. The typical, competent, sales professional should manage a number of resources and processes:

- *Territory.* The sales professional is typically solely responsible for his or her territory (which is usually geographically defined). He or she is responsible for everything that happens in this territory; for all activities, with a range of responsibilities (albeit on a smaller scale) comparable with those normally assumed by a brand manager, or even by the chief executive of a subsidiary.
- *Sales plan.* Within that territory, in particular, he or she has to create a sales plan, a 'cut down' version of the marketing plan (and probably a very simplified one – but a plan nonetheless). Performance against that plan will have to be monitored, and tactics changed to allow for deviations against target – just as in the overall organizational plan.
- *Organizational resources.* Every sales professional will have, to a greater or lesser extent, some organizational resources at his or her command – not least his or her own time, but also support resources (including service support, marketing support and, possibly, even budgeted amounts of territory-based promotional funding). All of these resources will have to be managed in exactly the same way as the rest of the organization's resources are managed by its team of managers.
- *Support personnel.* It is conventionally assumed that sales professionals do not manage people; and, indeed, very few do actually have formal responsibility for subordinates. Yet many indirectly control the activities of support personnel. What is more, they have to achieve this management control, often under difficult circumstances on customer premises, without any formal authority!
- *Customer interface.* Above all, the sales professional manages the 'customer interface', that most important asset of any organization, the relationship with the customer (and/or the customer organization) – the 'goodwill'.

See also CALLS AVAILABLE ANNUALLY; MANPOWER PLAN, SALES; SALES PROFESSIONAL; SELLING; TERRITORY MANAGEMENT

individual or expert opinion, forecasts In practice, most forecasts emerge from an individual. In the small company, it may be the owner. In the larger organization it may be the marketing manager. In the largest of all, it may be the brand manager, or even the manager of the forecasting department. The individual forecast is inevitably a personal judgement, an opinion. But, then, so are most of the other qualitative methods of forecasting (and, indeed, under their veneer of arithmetical respectability, so are many quantitative methods!). No matter how many historical facts are available to support the judgement, the act of forecasting is generally a creative art. *See also* QUALITATIVE FORECASTING METHODS

inducement   *see* STRATEGIES FOR INTENT BUYERS

industrial advertising   Whereas consumer goods advertising has to handle almost all of the 'contact' with the end-user audience, that of industrial advertising (often called 'business-to-business' advertising) typically only forms part of the overall communication. It is often designed just to create the initial awareness, and (frequently based on reply-paid 'coupons' included with the advertising) generate 'leads', before the face-to-face sales process (conducted by the producer's own sales force or, perhaps more likely, by its agents' and dealers' sales forces) takes over. Much of industrial advertising is, therefore, designed to elicit responses that will lead to a sales visit. It also often needs to convey more information than equivalent consumer advertising: for example, capital goods are significantly more complex than those of repeat purchase consumer goods. The advertising campaigns may also have to work over much longer periods, since purchases may be more infrequent; and the purchase process itself may be extended. The other major point is that the average advertising budget, which reflects the secondary importance of advertising compared with face-to-face selling, is usually much lower – normally less than seven figures, and often less than six figures – even for relatively large organizations. The average target audience is also much more specifically selected, and this has led to the emergence of a specialist group of media, pre-eminent amongst whom are the trade press. In this context, media buying has become a correspondingly specialist activity; frequently majoring on identification of the few publications that can reach the specialist target audience, rather than producing a balanced schedule for reaching them most economically – as is the task with consumer goods campaigns. *See also* ADVERTISING; SPECIALIST AGENCIES

industrial distributors   *see* WHOLESALERS AND DISTRIBUTORS

industrial goods markets   *see* PROMOTIONAL MIX
FACTORS

industrial marketing research   Marketing research in the industrial goods area is typically less
involved with survey research. On the one hand, the
output of statistics about the 'average customer' may
be less useful: each customer's needs often have to be
considered separately (the value of their business justifies this, and the contact with the salesperson makes
it a possibility). On the other hand, the difficulty and
cost of conducting such survey research on industrial
customers is much higher. For one thing, the 'lists'
(which define the 'sampling frames', the population
from which the sample is drawn) are often not available, or are inaccurate and incomplete. The result is
that desk research is even more prevalent – and even
more important – than in consumer research; and
this is often conducted by 'experts' (typically outside
agencies) rather than by the individual manager.
Much of the survey work that is done tends to
revolve around in–depth (unstructured) interviews
with relatively few respondents. In any case, the total
population, the 'universe', may be just a few hundred
organizations (especially if consideration is governed
by the value of purchases). The interviews are usually conducted between 'experts' and senior managers (and the views of the 'organization' sought
rather than those of the individual). Mail, and telephone, surveys are often used for larger exercises,
since the cost of face-to-face interviewing is usually
prohibitive. Response rates may be poor, however;
figures of as low as 20 per cent are quoted as being
typical.
See also MARKETING RESEARCH; SAMPLING, INDUSTRIAL
MARKETS

industrial markets and the marketing mix
While the differences between consumer markets
and industrial markets are usually more apparent
than real, and most of the theories, and techniques,
apply equally to both, the balance of the marketing
mix is one factor that is likely to be significantly
different for each. The elements involved may be the
same, but the blend will probably be different; with,
for example, more emphasis given to direct contact
(revolving around face-to-face selling) in industrial
markets, as opposed to the indirect techniques (of
marketing research and advertising) that are used in
most consumer markets. Even so, there are far more
similarities than differences; and those differences
that remain arise largely because of the disparity in
costs of contacting the customer personally – and not

because of any more basic differences in approach.
See also MARKETING MIX; ORGANIZATIONAL PIGEON-
HOLES; 4 Ps

industrial product categories   The industrial
products that are sold to industrial businesses and
institutional, or government, buyers – to be incorporated in their own products, resold or used within
these organizations – are often allocated different
'pigeon-holes'. These buying processes are often
categorized, at the most basic level, by the broad
product type. The principal types are as follows:

*   *Basic raw materials* (such as steel, for a car manu-
    facturer) are usually sold on a contractual basis to
    a tight specification. Sales are often achieved by
    competitive pricing, credit terms and delivery
    reliability.
*   *Component markets* (such as radiators) differ from
    basic materials because of their wider variation,
    and product quality and reliability become ex-
    tremely important.
*   *Capital goods markets* (such as lathes) are normally
    dominated by high technical capability on both
    sides.
*   *Maintenance, repair and operating goods* (such as
    detergents for floor cleaning) are consumable
    items, usually of low unit value, often sold
    through distributors.

See also INDUSTRIAL PURCHASING

industrial purchasing   *see* CHANGE AGENT,
SUPPLIER'S ROLE; DECISION-MAKERS AND
INFLUENCERS; DERIVED DEMAND; INDUSTRIAL
PRODUCT CATEGORIES; INTERACTION, AND THE
ORGANIZATIONAL PURCHASE; JOINT DEMAND

industrial sales   *see* CONSUMER OR CORPORATE
CUSTOMER

industrial selling   *see* SALES CALL

industry associations and public relations   *see*
PUBLIC RELATIONS

industry data pools   The collection of shared information on sales volumes via trade associations or
other groups of suppliers.

industry territories   *see* TERRITORY MANAGEMENT

inelastic demand   *see* PRICE ELASTICITY OF
DEMAND

inertial balance   Stability is the natural state of a market, but there is still a risk of sudden and dramatic change – which is compounded by myopic management:

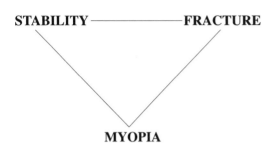

STABILITY ———————— FRACTURE

MYOPIA

- *Stability*. Although this 'steady state' may be the natural state, maintenance of this position will often require significant investment.
- *Fracture*. Outside events can occasionally destroy stability, sometimes so completely that its most important characteristics are changed completely (and the market is overturned – hence the precarious balance shown above).

See also FRACTURES AND MARKETING RESEARCH; SCANNING, AND MIS

inertia markets   Markets in which customers make repeat purchases and generally – due to inertia – use the same brand.
See also BRAND MONOPOLY; BRAND (OR MARKET) SHARE

inertia of consumers   *see* PEER PYRAMID

inertia, pricing   *see* PRICING, PRODUCT POSITIONING

inertia selling   A method of selling, usually by mail, whereby goods are sent unsolicited in the hope that the recipient will not return them, but will pay for them.
See also DIRECT MAIL

inflation   *see* BUDGETS

influencers   *see* BALANCING UNDER THE INFLUENCE; DECISION-MAKERS AND INFLUENCERS

infomercials   These are paid-for announcements on television (typically on special channels or during unsocial hours) that last 15–30 minutes. They are also typically linked to a direct response.
See also DIRECT MAIL

informal (oral) reports   Informal (oral as opposed to written) contacts are the staple diet of management. However, while it is difficult enough to abstract useful data from written paperwork, it is not usually even considered worthwhile to mention oral data. Yet this probably represents the most important source of data available to any manager, particularly to one involved in the sales and marketing functions. Johansson and Nonaka (1987) make the point that 'Japanese-style market research relies heavily on two kinds of information, soft data obtained from visits to dealers and other channel members and hard information about shipments, inventory levels, and retail sales. Japanese managers believe that these data better reflect the behaviour and intentions of flesh-and-blood consumers.' In any case, every meeting – be it a formally organized meeting of a group or an informal one between two individuals – is potentially rich with useful data. To take advantage of this, a number of techniques need to be employed:

- questioning
- listening
- recording and organizing

See also LISTENING; QUESTIONING; RECORDING AND ORGANIZING INFORMAL DATA; VERBAL (COMPUTER) DATABASES; VERBAL DATA RETRIEVAL; WRITTEN REPORTS

Reference: Johansson, Johny K. and Nonaka, Ikuiiro (1987) Market research the Japanese way. *Harvard Business Review*, May–June.

informant (respondent)   *see* SURVEY RESEARCH

information   *see* DATA, INFORMATION AND INTELLIGENCE

information-gathering   *see* SALES CALL; SELLING

information officer   *see* PUBLIC RELATIONS

information providers, commercial   In addition to those commercial organizations that provide data in published form, typically as directories, there are others who specialize in providing information (from their files, libraries or databases) against specific requests. In addition, there is a range of agencies (for example, Dun & Bradstreet) that will provide credit ratings on particular organizations.
See also EXTERNAL DATA; LIBRARIES

information search, repeat purchasing In the case of most products and services, the consumer will obtain information about them passively; absorbing messages from the media – both advertising and editorial – and from friends and contacts. The consumer will not usually even be aware that such information is being absorbed. For some, particularly important, decisions the information search will be active. The consumer will discuss the matter with friends and 'experts', and will seek out information from sources such as *Which?* magazine. The 'information search' stage is generally where the marketer comes into his or her own. In both of the above cases, the marketer must make certain that suitable 'information', usually in the form of advertising, is available, at the right time, which usually demands continuous or burst patterns of advertising, in the right place, which is a matter of spending what can be afforded to obtain the best media coverage, and with the right information or message, which usually means that based upon the best possible market research.

See also DECISION-MAKING PROCESS, BY CUSTOMERS; PURCHASE DECISION, MATCHING; REPEAT PURCHASING PROCESS

information seeking *see* OPINION LEADERS

information sharing *see* OPINION LEADERS

information systems *see* DATA PROCESSING, LOGISTICS

information unit A group of staff, or a department, set up to provide information (especially marketing research) to managers.

informed buyer, price *see* EQUILIBRIUM PRICE

informing customers *see* ADVERTISING; SELLING

infrastructure *see* EXPORT MARKET ELIMINATION

in-house data, precision marketing A number of organizations – direct mail houses (especially those in the general catalogue business), domestic appliance retailers (where the customer's name and address is usually taken), etc. – already have detailed customer information available on their existing records. Even organizations in the FMCG field – such as Heinz, Nestlé, Pedigree Petfoods and Kraft General Foods – are also consolidating data they accumulate about their consumers. In the USA, for example, Sears (US) uses the computerized database

information on its 40 million customers to promote special offers to specific target segments. The classic example is now the loyalty cards (or clubs) that are offered by the leading supermarkets and other retailers. The result is described by Stanley Davis (1987): 'Mass customization of markets means that the same large number of customers can be reached as in the mass markets of the industrial economy, and simultaneously they can be treated individually as in the customized markets of the pre-industrial economies.'

See also PRECISION MARKETING

Reference: Davis, Stanley M. (1987) *Future Perfect.* Reading, MA: Addison-Wesley.

in-house production, and ' buy-in' *see* MAKE OR BUY

initial call *see* SALES CALL

inner market By definition, marketing is primarily concerned with the world *outside* the organization. On the other hand, if it is to optimize the use of the resources, it also has to be concerned with what lies *inside* the organizational perimeter. Increasingly, indeed, the most valuable resource of any organization (and particularly those in the service sector) is its people, and the skills that they possess. In tapping this internal resource, so that the organization can face up to its external environment, it turns out that many of the traditional tools of marketing can be used to great effect – especially in the very important areas of internal communication and motivation, of harnessing and focusing this (people) resource to meet the objectives of the marketing plan.

 What is increasingly being recognized is that the marketing function may effectively be distributed widely across the whole organization, not just concentrated in the marketing department. Christian Grönroos (1989) makes the point that 'This [marketing] function is not the same as the marketing department's. The latter's is an organisational solution only, whereas the size and diversity of the former depends on the nature of the customer relations. Hence, the marketing function is spread over a large part of the organisation outside the marketing department, and all of the activities which have an impact on the current and future buyer behaviour of the customer cannot be taken care of by marketing specialists only.'

 Many organizations in the service sector, and not a few in the manufacturing sector, have 'customer service programmes'. These use many of the promotional devices of marketing – advertising, incentives, seminars, etc. – to persuade employees (particularly those in contact with customers) to adopt the correct attitude to those customers.

Piercy and Morgan (1990) explain that 'In working with a variety of organisations we have identified this problem as the internal marketing strategy gap. Our thinking is simply that in addition to the development of strategies aimed at the external marketplace, in order to achieve the organisational change needed to make these strategies work, it is necessary to carry out exactly the same process for the internal marketplace in companies – in short, we have both internal and external customers.'

Such campaigns have received a mixed response.
See also INNER MARKETING; INNER MARKETING CAMPAIGN; INTERNAL MARKET; SERVICE QUALITY

References: Grönroos, Christian (1989) Defining marketing: a market-oriented approach. *European Journal of Marketing*, 23(1).
Piercy, Nigel and Morgan, Neil (1990) Making marketing strategies happen in the real world. *Marketing Business*, February.

inner marketing   The first requirement of the process of inner marketing, and the one that distinguishes it from almost all other 'customer service programmes', is some form of marketing research; exactly as with any other marketing programme – but here conducted on the organization's own employees! Only with this basic information on employee attitudes can the 'inner marketer' start to devise the programmes that are necessary to create the new attitudes that will deliver the requisite service to the external customers.
See also INNER MARKET; INNER MARKETING CAMPAIGN; INTERNAL MARKET; SERVICE QUALITY

inner marketing campaign   The actions needed to achieve the end-result of inner marketing follow the well-trodden path of any marketing campaign; although they are alien to much of human resource management. Even in the marketing context, it should be recognized that it may take far longer to achieve the desired results than in a traditional consumer marketing campaign – because, frequently, the requirement is to make fundamental shifts in attitude. The campaign may, then, have a number of different objectives:

Information
At the most basic level, the staff will need to understand what is expected of them – by their own man-

agement and, in particular, by their customers.

Coordination
The essence of any marketing campaign, as with any military one, is that all the actions must happen at the right time, and in the manner intended.

Attitudes
Most difficult of all is the process of changing attitudes.

Managing change
Perhaps the most important, but least well appreciated, aspect of 'inner marketing' is that it is a process of managing change; and the marketing department adopts the role (whether consciously or not) of 'change agent':

*   *adopting an (internal) customer perspective* – finding out what the 'internal customer' feels about the changes (where the customer here is the employee)
*   *investing in education* – stimulating change takes considerable, extended, effort
*   *planning for the change* – working out the complex relationships that will need to be addressed and modified
*   *using conviction marketing* – a change to the culture is the most powerful change that can be made, but this takes a considerable investment over a number of years

The last two objectives represent areas in which 'inner marketing' diverges most from conventional marketing; and where the techniques may often be closer to those of education – and, indeed, may revolve around significant amounts of retraining.
See also CULTURE, ORGANIZATIONAL; INNER MARKET; INNER MARKETING; INTERNAL MARKET; SERVICE QUALITY

inner model   *see* SYNTHESIS AND ASSIMILATION, OF MARKETING RESEARCH DATA

innovation   *see* DIFFUSION OF INNOVATION; GLOBALIZATION; NEW PRODUCT INNOVATION

innovation adoption model   This postulates a number of stages through which the targeted customer passes – awareness, interest and trial.

innovative imitation   Theodore Levitt (1983) points out that, despite the rhetoric, most so-called innovation in the field of product development is actually imitation:

by far the greatest flow of newness is not innovation at all. Rather it is imitation. A simple look around us will, I think, quickly show that imitation is not only more abundant than innovation, but actually a much more prevalent road to growth and profits. IBM got into computers as an imitator; Texas Instruments into transistors as an imitator: Holiday Inns into motels as an imitator . . . In fact, imitation is endemic. Innovation is scarce.

Peter Drucker (1985) also explains the advantages of this principle:

Like being 'Fustest with the Mostest', creative imitation is a strategy aimed at market or industry dominance. But it is much less risky. By the time the creative imitator moves, the market has been established and the new venture has been accepted. Indeed there is usually more demand for it than the original innovator can easily supply. The market segmentations are known or at least knowable. By then, too, market research can find out what customers buy, how they buy, what constitutes value for them, and so on. Most of the uncertainties that abound when the first innovator appears have been dispelled or can at least be analyzed and studied.

What they do not add is that the Japanese are perhaps the most successful exponents of this technique!
Kotler and Fahey (1982) report:

Succinctly stated, Japanese marketing revolves around the management of product market evolution. They manage not only the product life cycle of individual products, but the evolution of a complex of product lines and items. They carefully choose and sequence the markets they enter, the products they produce, and the marketing tactics they adopt.

An alternative approach, still based upon 'imitation', is to find (by market research) what are the major problems associated with existing products in a market, and then to develop a product which resolves these problems (or at least resolves those that are seen by consumers as having the highest priority). This approach will not work, however, against the majority of brand leaders, that have wisely already taken care to address their weaknesses – one reason why on-going 'maintenance' of the brand is so im-

portant for those in the fortunate position of owning a market leader.
See also GENERATING IDEAS

References: Drucker, Peter F. (1985) *Innovation and Entrepreneurship*. London: Heinemann.
    Kotler, Philip and Fahey, Liam (1982) The world's champion marketers. *The Japanese Journal of Business Strategy*, 3(1).
    Levitt, Theodore (1983) *The Marketing Imagination*. New York: The Free Press.

innovators   *see* DIFFUSION OF INNOVATION

in-process inventory   *see* MATERIALS REQUIREMENTS PLANNING (MRP)

input–output diagrams   *see* SYSTEMS APPROACHES

inseparability, services   Generally speaking, production and consumption of services are inseparable; the 'sale' occurs before both (but frequently only just before). This means that distribution usually has to be direct (it cannot be stocked by a distribution chain).

insertions   *see* MEDIA SELECTION; PRESS MEDIA

inserts, direct mail   There is an almost infinite variety of material that can be put into a mailing – the most frequently used item is a brochure. The most important rule appears to be, once more, to keep it simple, and in line with the message of the letter. If there are conflicting messages between the letter and the inserts, or between different inserts, this will just confuse the reader. If it needs two mailings to avoid this confusion, take consolation from the fact that the most effective mailing campaigns are those with a number of separate mailings. Like most advertising, the effect is cumulative, and it can take a number of mailings before the recipients become aware of the existence of the product or service. Over the years, a large number of devices (such as gifts, 'yes/no' stamps, samples, etc.) have been developed, and have (on the basis of testing) been found to be effective. This work is usually the province of a specialist mailing house.
See also PRECISION MARKETING

inspection visit   *see* SUPPLIER SELECTION

inspiration   *see* PRODUCT DEVELOPMENT

installations   *see* TERRITORY SALES PLAN

instalment plan   Payment for a purchase by regular (monthly) payments; similar to hire purchase.

instant prizes   *see* NON-PRICE PROMOTIONS

instinctive management   *see* COARSE MARKETING

institutional advertising   *see* CORPORATE PROMOTION VERESUS BRAND PROMOTION

in-store promotion   A promotion which is run, at the point of sale, in the retail outlet; for instance, with demonstrations, special sales personnel, etc.
See also NON-PRICE PROMOTIONS; SALES PROMOTION; SAMPLING

intaglio   Printing from a depressed surface.

intangibility   Pure services usually cannot be defined in terms of the physical dimensions that are so important to many tangible products, and the customer cannot see or feel them before purchase. This poses problems in terms of defining these services, and in particular of demonstrating their 'quality'. Rushton and Carson (1989) state that:

> The evidence . . . strongly supports the hypothesis that product intangibility does have a profound effect on the marketing of services. It also underlines the lack of guidance for service marketers in tackling problems, and capitalising on the opportunities, created by having a product which is predominantly intangible . . . The lack of knowledge and control is reflected in inadequate and sometimes inappropriate use of generalised tools of marketing such as conservative and often unsuitable pricing policies, and promotional methods and messages which are confused and which frequently focus on the fringe areas of the product package simply because they are tangible.

Indeed, the customer for many services has to buy them 'on trust'; since they cannot be inspected before use. This also means that service consumers are often 'loyal' to the service that they have found justifies their trust. The competitive suppliers' investment in overcoming that loyalty may be correspondingly higher than in product markets, where trial use is more easily obtainable. The result is often

that, as indicated in the above quotation, the few 'tangible' elements that are associated with the service become especially important. Examples are:

- people
- place
- promotion
- branding

Reference: Rushton, Angela M. and Carson, David J. (1989) The marketing of services: managing the managers. *European Journal of Marketing*, 23(8).

integrated channel   *see* CHANNEL STRUCTURE

integrated marketing   This is a philosophy that stresses the need to coordinate (integrate) all business functions, in order to best meet the shared goal of meeting customer needs. Most (non-marketing) managers see one important role of the marketing function as being to provide this form of coordination.
See also MARKETING DEFINITIONS; MARKETING STRATEGIES

integrity   *see* LEADERSHIP, OF SALES PERSONNEL; SELLING SERVICES

intellectual property   This was formerly referred to (and frequently still is), on a more limited basis, as 'copyright'; but it has now been extended to include other material, including patents and trademarks. It confers on the owner (typically the originator/author or publisher) the exclusive right to the material.
See also BRAND MONOPOLY

intelligence   *see* DATA, INFORMATION AND INTELLIGENCE

intelligence, commercial   *see* INTERNATIONAL MARKETING RESEARCH

intensive distribution   *see* CHANNEL MEMBERSHIP

intensive interviews   *see* INDIVIDUAL DEPTH INTERVIEWS

intent buyer strategies   *see* STRATEGIES FOR INTENT BUYERS

interaction, and the organizational purchase   One generally ignored aspect of the organizational

purchase is its interactive nature. This tends to be left out by most authors and practitioners; with the honourable exception of the International Marketing and Purchasing Group (IMP) – a pan-European group of researchers – who have investigated it in some detail. In practice, both sides contribute to the purchasing process, and it would be foolish to assume that the buyer has a purely passive role. Thus, the discussions and meetings – which may extend over a considerable period – are designed to achieve a 'negotiated' outcome that is satisfactory to both sides. Miller, Heiman and Tuleja (1989) hint at this when they say that both sides must 'win'. It is also at the heart of 'customer partnership' and 'relationship management'. The important aspect to note here is that the process is dominated by interaction – and cannot, therefore, be adequately described as a single-sided sales process.
See also CUSTOMERS; WIN–WIN; INDUSTRIAL PURCHASING

Reference: Miller, Robert B ., Heiman, Stephen E. and Tuleja, Tad (1989) *Strategic Selling*. London: Kogan Page.

interactive system of marketing　*see* PRECISION MARKETING

interdepartmental net　*see* POLITICAL CONTACTS

interdependence　*see* INTER-ORGANIZATIONAL RELATIONS

interdisciplinary forecast　*see* SCENARIOS

interest　*see* AIUAPR (AWARENESS, INTEREST, UNDERSTANDING, ATTITUDES, PURCHASE, REPEAT PURCHASE); ENHANCED AIUAPR MODEL; FACTORS OF PRODUCTION; LEADERSHIP, OF SALES PERSONNEL; THREE PILLARS OF THE PURCHASING PROCESS

interest, advertising　It is not sufficient for advertising to grab the reader's attention for a second or so, until it wanders again. In that brief time the message must interest that reader, and persuade him or her to 'read' on. The content of the message(s) must be meaningful and clearly relevant to the needs of the target audience. This is where marketing research can come into its own as the basis for effective advertising. In the first instance, the 'advertiser' needs to know exactly who the audience is. Then the advertiser has to understand what the audience's interests and needs are, which must be addressed, and what the exact benefits are (in the consumer's own

terms) which the product or service will provide. In short, the message must be in the language of the consumer and must make an offer that is of real interest to the specific audience. This may mean that the message is boring to all other audiences (including those who are commissioning and creating the advertisement), but that is not the point – it only has to be of interest to the specific target audience.

interested groups　*see* PROACTIVE PR

interest, in advertising models　*see* BUYING DECISION, ADVERTISING MODELS

interest rates　*see* MONETARY POLICY

interface between consumer and supplier　*see* MARKET POSITIONING AND SEGMENTATION

interface with the customer　*see* SALES TEAM MANAGEMENT

interference　*see* PLANNING PITFALLS

Interflora　*see* MESSAGE, ADVERTISING

interior design, service sector　*see* SERVICE-SECTOR LOGISTICS

intermediaries or end-users　In terms of the basic 'dimensions' on which marketing is often organized, many of the marketing processes use intermediaries, such as retailers, to convey the product or service to the end-user or consumer; and these intermediaries themselves represent a significant proportion of the whole service sector. These intermediaries, therefore, make very different demands on the product or service. According to Western 'capitalist' theory at least, they will be seeking profit, together with a match to their own marketing needs.
See also AGENTS OR DISTRIBUTORS; CHANNEL DECISIONS; CHANNELS, AS CUSTOMERS; DISTRIBUTION CHAIN; ORGANIZATIONAL PIGEON-HOLES

intermediaries, pricing　*see* PRICE AND THE DISTRIBUTION CHANNEL

intermediate closes　*see* CLOSING TECHNIQUES

intermediate good　One which is in the process of being manufactured, and is neither raw material nor finished goods. It may be part of work-in-progress.

internal audit   An audit, which may cover items other than financial accounts, carried out within an organization by its own staff.

internal capacity, and ' buy-in'   *see* MAKE OR BUY

internal customers of purchasing   The buying department has, above all, to appreciate the needs of the internal 'customers';those departments that will be the users of the bought-in products and services. Very few purchasing departments actually approach their role with this in mind. They assume, because the 'users' are internal, that they do not have the same rights as 'customers'. They will take – indeed, be forced to take – what they are given! Needless to say, this is an inefficient and unproductive viewpoint, no matter how prevalent it is. Instead, their 'customers' have every right to demand that their requirements are met – and 'internal marketing' can sometimes here resolve apparently intractable organizational problems. All of the techniques of marketing (with a very few exceptions) can, and should, be applied.
See also PURCHASING

internal factors   *see* SWOT ANALYSIS

internal market   Many of the marketing principles and techniques that are applied to the external customers of an organization can be just as effectively applied to each subsidiary's, or each department's, internal customers. In some parts of certain organizations this may in fact be formalized – as goods are transferred between separate parts of the organization, at a 'transfer price'. To all intents and purposes, with the possible exception of the pricing mechanism (which may have as much to do with optimizing tax positions as with market mechanisms!), this process can be viewed (and should be viewed) as a normal buyer/seller relationship. The fact that this is a captive market, resulting in a 'monopoly price', should not discourage the participants from employing marketing techniques. Less obvious, but just as practical, is the use of 'marketing' by service and administrative departments, to optimize their contribution to their 'customers' (the rest of the organization in general, and those parts of it that deal directly with them in particular). The lessons of the not-for-profit organizations in dealing with their clients offer a very useful parallel.
See also CHANNEL MEMBERS; CHANNEL STRUCTURE; DISTRIBUTION CHAIN; INNER MARKET

internal set-up   *see* SET-UP TIMES

internal sources of information   Most organizations have vast stores of data locked away on their computers. That data should be a major resource, available as an input to the planning of any marketing activity. It is not limited to sales data. It should also offer data on profit. It can also offer data on a wide variety of other issues, such as customer returns or product reject levels, which will allow an insight into some of the other dimensions of marketing. Regrettably, though, many of the key measures may not have been recorded. The data collected by the average system is driven by accounting needs. Even if the system is near perfect, it records only those transactions that result in the organization actually completing a sale. It will be a very unusual system if it records details of sales lost;for example, because the item wanted was out of stock or did not quite meet the specification required. This information may be available, typically to those handling the receipt of orders, but it is usually discarded as soon as it is obvious that a sale is not to be made – yet an analysis of such lost orders can be another invaluable input to marketing planning. The main internal sources (relevant to marketing needs) are performance analysis, sales reports, written reports and informal (oral) reports.
See also INFORMAL (ORAL) REPORTS; PERFORMANCE ANALYSIS; WRITTEN REPORTS

international accounting   *see* INTERNATIONAL PRICE DECISION

international *ad hoc* research   This largely follows the rules for domestic (national) research. The main difference is that the work will be conducted in another country. To handle this problem, there are a number of possible solutions, including the following.

Do-it-yourself
The conditions for conducting market research (the sampling framework, the regulatory requirements, the social environment, the availability of interviewers, etc.) vary considerably from country to country. In Isalmic countries, for instance, it may not be permitted to interview the housewife unless her husband is present! DIY is, thus, even less advisable than in domestic market research.

Use a local agency (in each of the foreign countries)
This follows the usual national practice, of appointing a research agency to carry out the field work;but,

in this case, the agency is in the foreign country. However, this approach does require a significant amount of (expensive) time visiting the market to brief the agency and supervise activities; always assuming that you can cope with the intricacies of local conditions (many of the factors – methodology, systems and, not least, language – possibly being alien).

Use a multinational agency
This is the easiest approach, as easy as using an agency in your own market (which is where the office you deal with will be located). The 'global' agency is, on the other hand, only as strong as its local links (which will probably be subcontractors in the smaller countries). This may cause problems for specialist investigations; for example, those in industrial markets, where the local subcontractor might not have the skills needed to handle such work.

Use a domestic agency (to coordinate foreign agencies)
This allows for a free choice of local agencies in the foreign markets, but it assumes that the domestic (UK, say) agency has a good grasp of the (foreign) local scene (comparable with that of the multinational agencies).

It is generally recommended that one of the last two alternatives is adopted – organizing research locally in the foreign market is beyond the capacity of most organizations.

Selecting an agency
Some sources of information (in the UK) on suitable agencies are as follows:

* the *Market Research Society Yearbook*
* the *International Directory of Market Research Organisations* (Market Research Society and BOTB, British Overseas Trade Board)
* *Market Research in Europe* (The European Society for Market Research, ESOMAR)

Funding of research
It is worth checking to see whether you can receive assistance in meeting the costs of such research. Governments, to encourage exporting, often give grants at least partially to cover the cost of such activities. In the UK, these are administered by the BOTB. Even so, the cost of international marketing research may be so prohibitive (and the accuracy so dubious) that many organizations do not undertake it to any significant degree but, instead, 'learn by

doing'; they test the 'temperature of the water' by exporting first on a relatively small scale.
See also EXPORT MARKET ELIMINATION; INTERNATIONAL MARKETING RESEARCH

International Business Machines (IBM)   *see* IBM

International Marketing and Purchasing Group (IMP)   *see* INTERACTION, AND THE ORGANIZATIONAL PURCHASE

international marketing pitfalls   When all the various country selection procedures have been completed and truly international marketing has been put in place, what can go wrong? Kamran Kashani's (1989) research highlighted five pitfalls:

* *'Insufficient research'* – nearly half the programmes included no formal research before start-up and most of the companies paid for this omission afterwards . . .
* *'Overstandardization'* – despite a need to supply products which have succeeded in home markets, he comments that 'When a local program is burdened with too many standards, local inventiveness and experimentation close to the market dry up . . .'
* *'Poor follow-up'* – poor post-launch involvement.
* *'Narrow vision'* – not recognizing local needs.
* *'Rigid implementation'* – standardized marketing is a means to reaching an end, never an end in itself.

See also MARKET ENTRY TACTICS

Reference: Kashani, Kamran (1989) Beware the pitfalls of global marketing. *Harvard Business Review*, September–October.

international marketing research   As with any new venture, the one very important stage in the approach to an overseas market should be to conduct market research. In many respects, this will follow the same paths as those of domestic market research; and any research overseas must follow just as rigorous an approach.

Desk research
As usual, you can undertake the research yourself, you can subcontract it to a specialist department in your own organization, or you can use an outside consultant.

Whatever the route, the first step is, as always, to search the existing 'literature'. This is where, in particular, the sources of data are very different and perhaps more limited than those for the larger home markets of many exporters.

Government sources
Most governments (including those of the UK and the USA) are anxious to promote exports, and invest considerable sums in research around the world, for the benefit of their exporters. Typically, they will maintain trade departments in each of the main embassies, collecting commercial intelligence – which is often more valuable nowadays than military intelligence! In the UK this information is usually provided to exporters via the BOTB (British Overseas Trade Board), but local chambers of commerce and the main banks may also be able to help. Publications by the UN (United Nations), the OECD (Organization for Economic Co-operation and Development) and the EC (European Commission) also provide valuable information. In addition, many foreign embassies maintain their own libraries, which are good sources of their national statistics. You must recognize, however, that the prime mission of such embassies is to support their own exporters, not you!

Libraries
Local, central, reference libraries may also hold many other reports. The following may be the most useful:

- OECD – *Economics Surveys, Statistics of Foreign Trade, Trade by Commodities, Economic Outlook*
- UN – *Yearbook of International Statistics, Yearbook of Industrial Statistics, Monthly Bulletin of Statistics*
- IMF (International Monetary Fund) – *International Financial Statistics*

In addition, there are a number of commercial publications, such as the following:

- Euromonitor – *Market Research Europe, International/European Marketing, Data and Statistics, Consumer Europe*
- EIU (Economist Intelligence Unit) – *Marketing in Europe*

If you have the funds, there are also a number of international agencies that will undertake the desk research for you (though even their coverage may be limited in some countries). Examples are:

- The Economist Intelligence Unit (London and Brussels)
- Stanford Research Institute (Menlo Park, California, London and Zurich)
- The Battelle Institute (Columbus, Ohio, Geneva and Frankfurt)
- Business International (New York and Geneva)

Finally, there is a wide range of trade directories, many of which are nationally based. The most widely available directories with the widest (albeit sometimes patchy) coverage are *Kompass* and Dun & Bradstreet.
See also EXPORT MARKET ELIMINATION

international marketing structure and multinationals   *see* TRANSNATIONALS/ MULTINATIONALS AND EXPORTERS

International Monetary Fund   *see* INTERNATIONAL MARKETING RESEARCH

international price decision   Some global organizations, such as IBM, might choose to maintain much the same prices worldwide (although typically these will, even so, be higher than those in the domestic market of the parent company) – always, of course, subject to the limitations imposed by varying currency exchange rates. Others, such as those in the pharmaceutical industry, may set prices by what each market will bear, leading to very different prices in each country. The problem with significant variations between country prices, particularly where the countries are close to each other, is that customers may indulge in 'cross-border shopping', to take advantage of the lower prices. Even worse, wholesalers may do so – and create a 'grey market' in the higher-priced country (thus destabilizing marketing operations in that country). The price that the parent company charges for the product that it ships into the country is called the 'transfer price'. This can be based upon actual, or notional, costs; IBM, for instance, is very careful to ensure that this reflects true costs. However, the price can occasionally be manipulated to avoid or minimize local taxes. In any case, Kenneth Simmonds (1985) believes that international management accounting practices are not sound enough to provide for accurate transfer prices.

On the other hand, some exporters have been known to set very low prices in some overseas markets; 'dumping' product, with the intention of undermining local suppliers, so that there will ultimately be less competition (and the prices can then be raised to a profitable level).

See also GLOBAL MARKETING

Reference: Simmonds, Kenneth (1985) Global strategy: achieving the geocentric ideal. *International Marketing Review*, Spring.

international product decision　Even if the 'entry decision' is made, a further decision to be taken is 'With what product?' Many global marketers appear to use the same product worldwide, a simple 'extension' of what is offered in the home market; for example, McDonalds and Coca Cola, along with IBM, offer almost identical products worldwide (although in the latter case the product range may vary from country to country; not least because of mandatory differences such as differing power supplies or differing legal requirements). On the other hand, many multinationals market very different products in diverse countries. Often, these are marketed as different brands. Sometimes, however, the brand name is the same but the formulation is different, adapted to meet local needs. General Foods (the manufacturer of Maxwell House), for instance, blends different coffees for the UK (where it is mainly taken with milk), for France (where they often take it black) and for Latin America (whose consumers like a taste of chicory). This may not just be a matter of taste or culture but of physical needs; the Japanese, being small (though growing fast!), demand smaller versions of almost everything – even of some consumer durables. Even if the product, or service, is the same in all markets, the promotional vehicles – and the promotional messages – may be very different. The cultural constraints may mean that exactly the same basic message has to be told in different ways to be meaningful to different national audiences. However, one advantage of entering international markets for the first time is that the products to be offered can be chosen in the full knowledge of which are winners and losers on the domestic scene. And the losers, which are often maintained as a sop to management ego, can be avoided – providing the possibility of a particularly strong product line (the Japanese have the great advantage that we only see their winners!).

See also GLOBAL MARKETING

international segmentation　A sophisticated approach is proposed by Kale and Sudharshan (1987).

This applies the powerful technique of segmentation across groups of countries as well as within them: 'By standardising across similar cross-national segments the advantages of both standardisation and the targeting of within country segments can be reaped. Thus, within-country heterogeneity and cross-country similarity form the basis of our analytical approach. This method, we argue, preserves consumer orientation, but at the same time reduces the total number of marketing mixes a firm has to offer.' This approach would appear, on the surface, to be eminently sensible; since within-country segmentation works well. The essence is that geography (here on an international scale) simply becomes an extra factor in the clustering processes. The problems of cross-country market research comparisons may, however, limit the number of markets in which this approach can be used. In any case, this degree of sophistication is rarely applied – although that may say more about the management systems involved than about any technical difficulties!

See also GLOBAL MARKETING; INTERNATIONAL PRODUCT DECISION

Reference: Kale, Sudhir and Sudharshan, D. (1987) A strategic approach to international segmentation. *International Marketing Review*, Summer.

international (strategic) alliances　*see* STRATEGIC (INTERNATIONAL) ALLIANCES

international trade　*see* COMPARATIVE ADVANTAGE, GLOBAL; MARKET ENTRY DECISION

Internet　As yet, the volume of goods and services sold over the Internet is relatively small; and, indeed, some of the initial operators have withdrawn. On the other hand, many retailers, including the out-of-town superstores, are running serious pilots.

It has also been suggested that the Internet (or the Web) will be extensively used as a source of information prior to making a purchase. As yet, this does not seem to be happening. The information to be found on the Web – if it can be found, since the search engines are less than efficient to meet this specific need – is of questionable authority. When it carries more authority, perhaps usage will increase.

inter-organizational relations　Selling has traditionally been seen as a confrontational activity; with the salesperson 'hierarchically' subservient to the buyer – the former trying to persuade the latter to buy something not wanted or needed. It is seen as a 'zero-sum game', in which each of the participants can gain only at the expense of the other. In recent years, however, it has been argued that the most productive relationship in such sales deals is based on a 'win–win' approach; in which it is expected that both sides will 'win' – will gain from the deal (albeit in different ways) – so that they start out with the intention of producing a mutually beneficial arrangement. An increasing number of organizations have, indeed, come to see the relationship as one of interdependence, the two sides adopting a 'peer-to-peer' relationship. The sales role here is sometimes described as 'relationship management'. As this type of relationship requires a higher level of personal support, from a more skilled sales professional (a 'relationship manager'), it will typically be limited to the five or ten most important customers.

See also COMPLEX SALE; DECISION-MAKERS AND INFLU-ENCERS; ORGANIZATIONAL BUYING SITUATIONS; SALES PROFESSIONAL; SELLING; TERRITORY MANAGEMENT; TERRITORY SALES PLAN

interrelated costs   *see* PRODUCT-LINE PRICING

interrelated demand   *see* PRODUCT-LINE PRICING

interruptions   *see* OBJECTION HANDLING

interviewing process, recruitment   *see* RECRUITMENT, OF SALES PERSONNEL

interviewing (survey research)   *see* PERSONAL INTERVIEWING

interviews and public relations   *see* PUBLIC RELATIONS

intimations of mortality   *see* COMPETITIVE SAW

intransient advertisement   An advertisement that the reader can keep, to refer to later; as opposed to television commercials, say, which are transient.

in transit   In the process of shipment to a customer.

intrapreneurship   *see* SKUNKWORKS

introductory stage, product life cycle   At this first stage of a product's life, the supplier can choose from a number of strategies; but in essence these range from 'penetration', where the supplier invests (typically in terms of promotion; but possibly by a low price) to gain the maximum share of a new market, through to 'skimming', where the maximum short-term profit is derived (typically by a high price, justified in terms of the uniqueness of the new product or service) from the 'innovation', before others cash in on the new market. The other main variable is the speed at which this happens, which may primarily be determined by the rate at which the supplier is willing (or able) to invest in order to create the new market. The ideal situation, for both penetration and skimming, is to develop the market as fast as possible, on the basis that this takes advantage of the 'lead time' before potential competitors can respond. On the other hand, where a market is going to be slow to develop, this may simply be preparing the way for later (better funded) suppliers to capitalize on the pioneer's investment (as Microsoft sometimes does to its smaller competitors). In general, though, the 'pioneer' retains the highest market share, even after competition becomes the order of the day. Robinson and Fornell (1985) show that such 'pioneers' usually hold double the share of later entrants, even over the longer term.

See also PROMOTIONAL MIX FACTORS

Reference: Robinson, William T. and Fornell, Claes (1985) Sources of market pioneer advantage in consumer goods industries. *Journal of Marketing Research*, August.

inventory control   For many, if not most, organizations, control of inventory is a crucial activity. If it is not available when the customer wants it, the sale is lost; and the customer, who is dissatisfied, takes the business elsewhere. If, on the other hand, too much inventory is held, the cost can be exorbitant; in most industries inventory holding costs (physical warehousing, financing, administration and deterioration) can easily exceed 30 per cent of the inventory value per annum. Methods of inventory control vary in sophistication, from the simplest of manual systems through to the most complex of computerized systems.

See also CARD SYSTEM INVENTORY CONTROL; COMPUTER INVENTORY CONTROL; ECONOMIC BATCH QUANTITY; KANBAN; MATERIALS REQUIREMENTS PLANNING (MRP); MATERIALS REQUIREMENTS PLANNING II (MRPII); OPTIMIZED PRODUCTION TECHNOLOGY (OPT); SET-UP TIMES; TWO-BIN INVENTORY CONTROL

investment   *see* INVESTMENT MULTIPLIER; STEPPED SAW

investment multiplier The most successful brands have very long lives. Thus, the 'rule of 123' simply states that the first brand in a market – the brand leader – will typically hold twice the share of the second brand and three times that of the third. This rule describes the normal state in stable markets (that is, in markets in which brand leadership positions do not change, even over the longer term). Thus a new product/service package entering the market (in this case, called a 'starter', in a more positive vein than the equivalent 'problem child' of the Boston Matrix) can be plotted (in terms of the investment being made in it) on two dimensions; that of the cumulative investment level itself, and that of time:

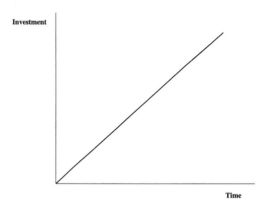

If, like the great majority, the product/service is unsuccessful (in this terminology called a 'loser' rather than a 'dog'), the investment is eventually cut off. If it is in a state of limbo in which it is not clear whether or not it will be a long-term success (although it may be one in the shorter term – the timescales involved are such that the true long-term potential may not be obvious for a decade or more), the investment will continue; until, most often, it plateaus when it is realized that it does not, after all, have major potential (this equivocal position is described as a 'runner' rather than a 'star').

Just a few products or services will reach long-term positions, at 1 or 2 or 3, but these will be the major cash generators that drive successful organizations (and are called 'winners', rather than the somewhat derogatory 'cash cows'). Thus, eventually, the investment levels – for a successful brand – are likely to reflect its profit performance. High investment will return high profits (once again, assuming success) and lower investment will return lower profits. Hence, the investment graph is also a good (albeit indirect) indicator of performance:

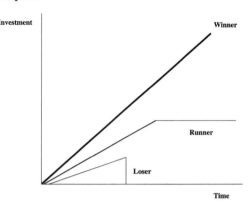

The difference in philosophy is most evident in the terminology – of 'runners' versus 'stars', and 'winners' versus 'cash cows'. 'Winners' are to be cared for, rather than being 'cash cows' to be milked; and 'runners' have to be carefully assessed, and not automatically presumed to be future 'stars'.

If you plot the historical performance of your current brands (allowing for them to plateau as investment is eventually matched by depreciation), it is likely that you will obtain a pattern such as the following:

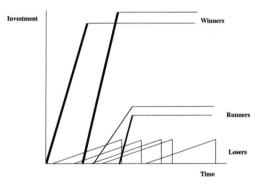

This can be simplified if we ignore the cumulative figures that build during the launch, and extend the plateau back to the launch point:

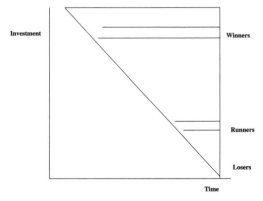

It should be obvious from this diagram that the normal pattern is one of an inverted pyramid. The higher-performance brands are also the longer-lived ones.

A more general approximation, or rule of thumb, can also be derived. This is the 'rule of history'. In this way, the history of a brand can be viewed as the best indicator of its future. If it has been a high performer, it will continue to be so. If it has been long-lived, it will have a long life in the future too.

The 'investment multiplier' incorporates this rule of thumb by simply mirroring in the future what has happened in the past:

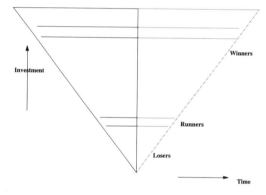

The 'multiplier' in this case is not that shown on the vertical axis, since it is assumed that – in one way or another – the performance (the profit out, say) is roughly proportional to the investment put in. It is, instead, the life of the brand. A successful high-investment brand multiplies its return by having a longer life, over which the annual returns accumulate.

Finally, we can apply the equivalent boxes to the Boston Matrix (with their new terminology):

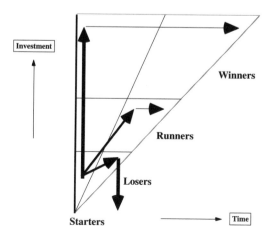

This diagram contains the important lesson of the Boston Matrix, that of mortality. Complacency, even when you have the brand leader, is ultimately rewarded by death (a message even more strongly conveyed by the competitive saw). More than this, though, it graphically illustrates the odds against long-term success, and the significant leverage to be gained if success can be achieved. Most importantly, it highlights the importance of maintaining those few winners; whereas the Boston Matrix, and much of marketing mythology, takes exactly the reverse view (and demands that you milk cash cows to death!).

See also ADVANTAGE MATRIX (BOSTON CONSULTING GROUP); BOSTON MATRIX; CORPORATE PLAN; CORPORATE STRATEGY AND MARKETING; GE (GENERAL ELECTRIC) MATRIX; MARKETING STRATEGIES; PRODUCT (OR SERVICE) STRATEGY; THREE CHOICE BOX

Reference: Mercer, David (1997) *New Marketing Practice.* London: Penguin.

invoice discounting   *see* FACTORING

invulnerability   *see* GROUPTHINK

inward mission   A formally arranged visit from a group of foreign businesspeople or buyers.
See also EXPORTING

irrational processes   *see* COARSE MARKETING

irrevocable acceptance   Acceptance that cannot be withdrawn.

Ishikawa diagram   The diagram invented by Kaoru Ishikawa, originally developed as an aid to quality control, that plots the causes of an effect as spurs, and sub-spurs, running off either side of a horizontal backbone, and leading to the effect that they cause to the right of this horizontal line. It gives a good visual summary of the causes (to check that they are comprehensive), as well as the relationships between them, and looks like a fishbone – hence the alternative name of 'fishbone diagram'.

ISIC   *see* STANDARD INDUSTRIAL CLASSIFICATION (SIC)

Islamic countries, alcoholic drinks   *see* CONVICTION MARKETING; EXPORT MARKET ELIMINATION; SOCIAL AND BUSINESS STRUCTURES, FILTERING UNSUITABLE MARKETS

island position An advertisement in a magazine or newspaper separated from other advertising; ideally, surrounded by editorial.

island site A stand at an exhibition that is separated from others, and so has a premium value.

isolation close *see* CLOSING TECHNIQUES

issue management *see* PROACTIVE PR

iterative planning *see* PLANNING PROCESS

Itoh, C. *see* MARKET ENTRY TACTICS

ITV companies *see* TELEVISION

J

Janis, Irving L.   *see* GROUPTHINK

Japan   *see* TRIAD POWER

Japanese approach to implementation   *see* MARKETING PLAN USE

Japanese approach to marketing research   *see* WALKABOUT

Japanese business   *see* SOCIAL AND BUSINESS STRUCTURES, FILTERING UNSUITABLE MARKETS

Japanese corporate strategies   *see* EMERGENT STRATEGY

Japanese decision-making   *see* RINGI

Japanese leapfrog   *see* CREATIVE IMITATION; LEAPFROG

Japanese retailers   *see* RETAIL ORGANIZATION; SOCIAL AND BUSINESS STRUCTURES, FILTERING UNSUITABLE MARKETS

Japanese trading houses   *see* MARKET ENTRY TACTICS

jargon   *see* LETTER, DIRECT MAIL

Jenkins, Box and   *see* TIME-SERIES ANALYSES

JICNARS   *see* AUDIENCE RESEARCH

jingle   The advertising jingle is a specially written short melody or song, which is intended to be remembered by the viewer.

JIT (Just In Time)   *see* JUST IN TIME (JIT)

job satisfaction, sales   *see* MOTIVATION, OF SALES PERSONNEL

Jobs, Steve, at Apple   *see* CONVICTION MARKETING TYPES

John Lewis Partnership   *see* COARSE MARKETING

Johnny Walker Scotch Whisky   *see* GLOBAL MARKETING

joint close   *see* CLOSING TECHNIQUES

joint demand   This occurs when the demand for two or more products (or services) is interdependent, normally because they are used together. The demand for razor blades may depend upon the number of razors in use; hence the reason why razors have sometimes been sold as 'loss leaders' – to increase demand for the associated blades.
See also INDUSTRIAL PURCHASING

Joint Industry Committee for National Readership Surveys   *see* AUDIENCE RESEARCH

joint marketing operation   *see* HORIZONTAL MARKETING

joint purchasing across plants   *see* ECONOMIES OF SCALE, GLOBAL

joint selling company   *see* LOCAL SALES ORGANIZATION

joint venture   This arrangement has much in common with licensing. Both usually involve a local organization that handles the marketing (and typically production too) in the foreign market. The difference with a joint venture is that the international partner has an equity holding in the local operation. The skills for setting up a local joint venture, and sharing the running with the local partner, are not those of conventional marketing (and are, perhaps, more related to those of diplomacy!). They are beyond the scope of this encyclopedia. They are also probably beyond the capability of many of the organizations that do seek to enter international markets this way!
See also HORIZONTAL MARKETING; MARKET ENTRY TACTICS; STRATEGIC (INTERNATIONAL) ALLIANCES; WIN–WIN

joke   *see* MESSAGE, ADVERTISING; SALESMAN STEREOTYPE

journalists and public relations   *see* PUBLIC RELATIONS

journey planning   *see* TERRITORY MANAGEMENT

judgement sample   *see* QUOTA SAMPLES

jump cut, images   *see* DISSOLVE

junk mail, direct mail   *see* DIRECT MAIL ADVANTAGES AND DISADVANTAGES; ELECTRONIC DIRECT MAIL; MAILING LIST

jury method forecasts   This is one of the 'formal' ways of applying 'scientific method' (or perhaps a gloss of respectability) to individual opinion in forecasting. In essence, a panel of experts (or corporate executives) is brought together in committee, to pool their individual forecasts. Then, having agreed (or at least discussed) their individual cases, a corporate forecast 'emerges' and is agreed. As the quality of the forecast depends upon the quality of the participants, the jury should comprise the best possible team of relevant experts – both from within the organization and from outside it. It is arguable that such a jury may dilute the expertise of the best forecasters on it, or – even worse – follow the ideas of the most persuasive (or those with the highest status) rather than the most knowledgeable. On the other hand, as with the judicial system, such juries do seem to be able to take commendably sensible decisions as to which really are the best forecasts, particularly where the members of the 'jury' also have to implement these forecasts. Such 'judgmental' approaches are, however, not necessarily as accurate as some of their proponents would suggest. A healthy scepticism as to the accuracy of forecasts, and an awareness of the related dangers posed by 'groupthink', might be seen as the main skills required! This does, however, highlight a major problem; which is that in general the uncertainty associated with future events is severely underestimated. Schnaars (1989) suggests that you 'Be conservative in your estimates of the potential for new products based on innovative technologies. Cut or damp any trend estimates with which you are provided . . . Be suspicious. Be especially suspicious of forecasts that are based on accelerating trends in growth.'

See also DELPHI TECHNIQUE; QUALITATIVE FORECASTING METHODS; SCENARIOS

References: Janis, Irving L. (1971) Groupthink. *Psychology Today*, November.

Schnaars, Steven P. (1989) *Megamistakes: Forecasting and the Myth of Rapid Technological Change*. New York: The Free Press.

justify   To adjust the separation of the letters and words on a line so that the end of the line is aligned exactly with the ends of the adjacent lines.

Just In Time (JIT)   A development in inventory holding, pioneered by Toyota in the 1950s, is JIT. In this approach, components are delivered, from the suppliers, direct to the production line just as they are needed (or at least only a few hours before). In this way, little or no stock need be held by the manufacturer. It is, accordingly, a very efficient method of dealing with inventory.

However, it does have a number of hidden disadvantages. Of these, the most important is the lack of flexibility. It demands 'flat scheduling', which means that the production runs must be forecast exactly several weeks in advance; since the comparable production runs by the suppliers will take place some time in advance of the final assembly, and their plans must allow for this. Changes in plan are not possible in the short term; although if the key components are produced in-house and flexible manufacturing (especially reduced set-up times) is employed, this disadvantage may be minimized. Equally, the much vaunted inventory savings by the manufacturer may sometimes come about simply because the suppliers are holding buffer stocks instead.

It should be noted, however, that – in Japan, at least – JIT is not a technique. It is an outcome of a very rich package of measures, that is based upon the use of the kanban (the card system that pulls the components through) and also includes techniques such as 'zero defects' (total quality management, TQM) and flexible manufacturing (probably with group technology and cellular manufacturing), as well as the by now traditional levels of workforce dedication (such as 'quality circles' and multifunctional workers) – all of which offer powerful advantages to any organization. It is the practical combination of these which offers the greatest reward when JIT is actually achieved!

One aspect of JIT that is often overlooked is the need to support it with sophisticated Management Information Systems (MIS). As Sangjin Yoo (1989) points out, 'there are some who [have] assumed that JIT . . . sometimes called Kanban [the Japanese name for the 'card' or docket that drives the system] can be implemented without the aid of a management information system.'

Ronald Ballou (1987) summarizes the position when he states that 'for the logistician, an important lesson is that by shortening lead times and making them more predictable and supplying operations in small quantities, quality is indirectly improved, and investment is lowered. This happens irrespective of whether the Kanban or MRP approach is used.'

A final comment is contained in a quote from a senior manager at Toyota: 'JIT is straightforward, indeed easy, when you get everything working correctly. Mind you, it took us several decades to achieve this!' This was delivered as a joke, but it contains a great deal of truth. It undoubtedly took Toyota many years – probably decades – to achieve the many benefits that they now gain from JIT.

See also ECONOMIC BATCH QUANTITY; INVENTORY CONTROL; KANBAN; LOGISTICS MANAGEMENT; MAKE OR BUY; MATERIALS REQUIREMENTS PLANNING (MRP); MATERIALS REQUIREMENTS PLANNING II (MRPII); OPTIMIZED PRODUCTION TECHNOLOGY (OPT); SET-UP TIMES

References: Ballou, Ronald H. (1987) *Basic Business Logistics* (2nd edn). Englewood Cliffs, NJ: Prentice-Hall.

Yoo, Sangjin (1989) An information system for Just-In-Time. *Long Range Planning*, 22

K

kaisen This is the Japanese philosophy of continuous improvement, which requires that an organization (and especially the people within it) should continually strive to improve performance in all details. It has been responsible for much of the success of the Japanese corporations. Once a target (typically one in an area such as quality or JIT) has been achieved, a more difficult one is immediately set. It is encapsulated in the 'zero' philosophies, especially zero defects.

See also JUST IN TIME (JIT); KANBAN; SET-UP TIMES; ZERO DEFECTS; ZERO DEFECTS VERSUS AQL

kanban This is a production system, developed by Taiichi Ohno at Toyota, in which two cards are used to pull the components through the various stages of production. One card is the move card, which is always issued by the workstation downstream (closest to the customer) – and, indeed, the process is simply started (in theory) by the customer's order being given to the final (assembly) workstation. The whole kanban system depends just as much on the containers in which the standard quantities of components are moved around. When a workstation has completed its work on one of these and it is empty, it is sent back to the previous workstation with a move card, which describes the product (and the quantity to be made) and both the workstation to make it and the one to receive it. The 'making' workstation then sends a new supply (drawn from its outgoing stock).

The second card only operates within a workstation, and follows much the same principle in instructing the operative(s) to make a container of parts to be put into the outgoing stock.

The process is governed by a very simple, but powerful, set of rules, which include the following:

- only standard, authorized containers may be used
- these containers must have a move or production card attached to them at all times
- only the user (downstream) workstation may issue the move kanban
- the operatives must produce exactly the amount specified on the production kanban

- they may only produce components when they have a production kanban

In theory, at least, it is both a simple and very powerful way of driving production. In practice, it requires much more sophistication. In particular, it typically requires balanced production with level (or flat) scheduling, in which there is a constant load on production with only small variations in mix – and certainly no surging (the significant variations of customer orders from period to period which are typical of most companies). It takes a considerable length of time to get this simple system working effectively. Toyota say that it took them years – even decades – to get it working properly.

See also INVENTORY CONTROL; JUST IN TIME (JIT); KAISEN; LOGISTICS MANAGEMENT; MATERIALS REQUIREMENTS PLANNING II (MRPII); OPTIMIZED PRODUCTION TECHNOLOGY (OPT); SUGGESTIONS SCHEMES; TWO-BIN INVENTORY CONTROL; ZERO DEFECTS

Keep It Simple, Stupid *see* KISS

Keep It Simple Stupid, advertising impact *see* KISS ADVERTISING

Kelloggs *see* GLOBAL MARKETING

Kelly grids *see* REPERTORY GRIDS

Kennedy, John F. *see* GROUPTHINK

kerbside conference The analysis of a sales call, made after the call, by a sales trainer who has accompanied the salesperson into the call.
See also SALES TRAINING

key account plan *see* ACCOUNT PLANNING

key accounts selection *see* TERRITORY SALES PLAN

key activity planner *see* MARKETING PLAN STRUCTURE

key code An address for the return of direct mail that indicates the source (typically of the journal in which the advertisement was placed).
See also DIRECT MAIL

keyed advertisement One that carries a coded 'reply to . . .' address, so that the advertiser will know which publication generated the response.
See also DIRECT MAIL

Keynesianism The macroeconomic theory based on the works of J. M. Keynes, the most widely quoted aspect of which holds that governments can influence the overall economic climate by means of their own investment in public works. Indeed, there is a 'multiplier' whereby such spending is multiplied in terms of its impact on the overall economy.
See also CROWDING OUT; MONETARISM; RATIONAL EXPECTATIONS THEORY

Reference: Keynes, J. M. (1936) *The General Theory of Employment, Interest and Money*. London: Macmillan.

key words *see* SYNECTICS®

kickback Illegal commission paid to a third party, such as a government official, who aids a sale.

kickers, mid-life *see* MID–LIFE KICKERS

kings *see* GLOBAL MARKETING

KISS *see* DESIGNING DEMONSTRATIONS; DIRECT MAIL OFFER

KISS advertising In terms of creating advertising messages, perhaps the best advice of all is KISS ('Keep It Simple, Stupid'). This is another way of saying that 'less is more', which applies in many fields. It is especially relevant, however, in the case of advertising (or any other form of promotion). The simpler the message is, the greater the impact it will make and the greater the attention it will receive.

This is best tracked (by marketing research) in terms of 'spontaneous awareness' of the advertising.
See also CREATING THE CORRECT MESSAGES; CREATIVE DEPARTMENT, ADVERTISING AGENCY

kit of parts *see* MATERIALS REQUIREMENTS PLANNING (MRP)

knitting, stick to the *see* NEW PRODUCT INNOVATION

knocking copy Advertising material that attacks a competitor.

know-how *see* LICENSING

Kompass *see* INTERNATIONAL MARKETING RESEARCH

Kondratieff wave Theoretical long (40 years +) cycles in the state of the economy, postulated by Nicholai D. Kondratieff.
See also DERIVED FORECASTS; MATHEMATICAL FORECASTING TECHNIQUES

Kroc, Ray, at McDonalds *see* CONVICTION MARKETING FACTORS

KSIM *see* CROSS–IMPACT MATRICES

Kuhn, Thomas *see* PARADIGM SHIFT, STRATEGY

L

labour *see* FACTORS OF PRODUCTION

labour of 'buy-in' *see* MAKE OR BUY

laddering, interviewing/questioning This is a particular questioning technique, used for example by skilled researchers. In this case, the question 'Why?' is repeated until the respondent cannot explain in any further depth. It is a powerful technique for finding the underlying motives. Unfortunately, in most normal discussions (as opposed to its use in research), it is a very aggressive technique and must accordingly be used with great care.
See also QUESTIONING; RAMBLING, INTERVIEWING/QUESTIONING

laggards *see* DIFFUSION OF INNOVATION

laissez-faire The view that the government should not interfere with the economy.

land *see* FACTORS OF PRODUCTION

landscape layout A layout (an advertisement, say), that is wider than it is high. The reverse of 'portrait'.

language and culture *see* ACCESSIBILITY, FILTERING UNSUITABLE FOREIGN MARKETS

large accounts *see* ACCOUNT PLANNING

Last In First Out *see* LIFO (LAST IN FIRST OUT)

Last In Last Out *see* FAULTS

latecomer *see* RISK VERSUS TIME, NEW PRODUCTS

lateral communications *see* ELECTRONIC MAIL

lateral thinking *see* SYNECTICS®

later majority *see* DIFFUSION OF INNOVATION

latin square Where the effects of experimental research are believed to differ on two dimensions, a combination/permutation of split runs needs to be implemented. For example, three studies (A, B and C) over two dimensions (place and time) would need a test comprising nine separate split runs in order for all of the possible combinations to be tested:

Time

		1	2	3
	1	A	B	C
Place	2	B	C	A
	3	C	A	B

See also EXPERIMENTAL RESEARCH

laws *see* REGULATORY CONSIDERATIONS, FILTERING UNSUITABLE MARKETS

laws governing advertising *see* GLOBAL MARKETING

laws of service *see* SERVICE QUALITY

laws of supply and demand *see* NEOCLASSICAL ECONOMICS

layout The arrangement of text and illustrations as part of the process of designing advertisements.
See also ADVERTISING PROCESSES; CREATING THE RIGHT MESSAGES; CREATIVE DEPARTMENT, ADVERTISING AGENCY

leader pricing *see* COMPETITIVE PRICING

leadership, of sales personnel The personal characteristics of the sales manager are probably the most important element in sales management. In particular, 'leadership' is all-important: there is probably more debate about what makes an effective 'leader' than almost any other aspect of management.

Suffice it to note that Strafford and Grant (1986) reflect this complexity when they note six key qualities needed:

* enthusiasm
* courage
* self-confidence
* integrity
* interest
* humour

It is likely that other commentators would each produce a rather different list. 'Charisma', 'ability to delegate' and 'communication ability' are often also quoted. The point to note, though, is how complex, and unpredictable, the mix is – and how important is the capability of the individual sales manager!
See also MOTIVATION, OF SALES PERSONNEL; PEOPLE (SALES) MANAGEMENT

Reference: Strafford, John and Grant, Colin (1986) *Effective Sales Management*. London: Heinemann.

leaders of opinion   *see* OPINION LEADERS; SOCIAL CLASS INFLUENCES, ON THE PURCHASE DECISION

leading   Creating space between words or lines in typesetting (originally in letterpress, where special lead type was used).

leading indicators   As part of the forecasting process, it may be possible to establish that certain factors are 'leading indicators' (sometimes called 'tied indicators'), in that they provide advance warning of future trends, advance warning which can be very useful. It may be, for example, that suppliers of pop records should study the birth-rate statistics, to see how their total teenage market may vary in future years. However, in such a competitive and fashion-conscious business, it is more likely that they will be preoccupied with more urgent matters. The exact relationship (especially, in this context, the time interval by which the variable lags behind the indicator) between the leading indicator(s) and the variable that is being forecast is typically determined by regression analysis. In the UK, there is a range of useful published statistics, which are widely used as indicators: The Financial Times Ordinary Share Index (movements of which may indicate the state of the general economy some 6 months ahead), New Housing Starts (perhaps 10 months ahead), Companies Net Acquisition of Financial Assets (that is, investment, possibly up to 12 months ahead) and –

most exotic of all, perhaps – Interest on Three Month Bank Bills (which is supposed to give an indication for 18 months ahead). One of the most useful – and most obvious in its workings – is the 13-month (ahead) leading indicator offered by the CBI survey of business confidence. IBM, for example, used this indicator (along with a parcel of other, more short-term, indicators) as the basis of its own macro-forecasts.
See also MACRO- AND MICRO-FORECASTS; QUANTITATIVE FORECASTING TECHNIQUES; TIME-SERIES ANALYSES

lead management   The process of managing the leads generated by prospecting by the sales force or, more typically, by promotional campaigns run in support of a sales force. It should offer the (systems) organization in which sales personnel are usually deficient; so that all leads are dealt with in a manner that is appropriate.
See also PROSPECT QUALIFICATION

lead time   This is an important element of customer service level. It relates to the time taken to meet an order (where the product is not delivered 'ex-stock'). This is called the 'lead time' (or sometimes the 'order cycle time'). Clearly, the shorter the lead time, the better the service is. On the other hand, it is frequently the case that it is the reliability of the lead time that is more important. A customer who has to arrange a number of other activities to mesh in with the delivery of the product will often prefer that the delivery date is certain, albeit at a later date, rather than its being uncertain at an earlier one (especially when the other elements of the customer's operation may be kept waiting – unproductively, and often very publicly – until the delivery actually occurs!). A subsidiary, but important, element is the length of time (the response time) that it takes a customer to find out what is actually happening to the order!
See also INTRODUCTORY STAGE, PRODUCT LIFE CYCLE; SERVICE LEVELS

lead time, manufacturing   *see* SET-UP TIMES

leakage   *see* SHRINKAGE

leapfrog   A more sophisticated version of creative imitation is not just to launch an imitation (although that may also be done to protect the immediate market position) but to put a very high level of resources into developing the next 'generation' of product based on the imitation – and to launch this before the competitor does so, thus 'leapfrogging' it. The Japanese have managed to turn this process of creative leapfrog almost into an art form, due to their mastery of time management in the field of product development. In part, this comes from the practices that they have built up in their manufacturing systems, which stress time (JIT, for example) as much as flexibility. What is not appreciated, however, is that these are not production techniques in the Western sense, but are an outcome of many years of training their workforce to apply such approaches. Despite those 'experts' who would promise instantaneously to provide you with these secrets, you would be wise to assume that they take decades (as they did at Toyota), rather than a matter of days, to become effective.

The communications that lie at the heart of these processes are often aided, in the case of product development, by siting the developers in the plant. This may reduce the productivity of the developers, at the early stages, by a notch or two, but it vastly improves the implementation stage – where (as we have seen earlier) the Japanese gain nearly all of their advantage.

In the area of product development, however, the Japanese use another technique – that of parallel development. Western organizations complete one stage of development before they start the next; because they believe, quite correctly, that otherwise development effort may be wasted (as each stage sets unexpected requirements for the next). The Japanese recognize this inefficiency, but believe that the benefit gained, which is a much faster overall development process (with overlap of stages still giving faster times, despite some of the work having to be redone), far outweighs the extra costs – since it gives them market leadership.

Existing market leaders may take this process a stage further, by having two development teams working in parallel. While one is implementing the last stages of the next generation, the other is working on the earlier stages of the next generation but one!

See also CREATIVE IMITATION; CUSTOMER BONUS; EXISTING PRODUCT CHANGES; FEATURE MODIFICATION; GAP ANALYSIS; GENERATING IDEAS; NEW PRODUCT CREATION; NEW PRODUCT INNOVATION; PRODUCT CHURNING, NEW PRODUCTS

learning curve   *see* CONCEPT TEST, NEW PRODUCTS

learning processes   *see* HOWARD AND SHETH MODEL, OF CONSUMER BEHAVIOUR

leasing   *see* OFF-BALANCE-SHEET FINANCING

legal expertise   *see* AGENTS OR DISTRIBUTORS; LICENSING

legal requirements   *see* INTERNATIONAL PRODUCT DECISION

legend   *see* CAPTION

legitimacy   *see* ENHANCED AIUAPR MODEL; PEER PYRAMID; THREE PILLARS OF THE PURCHASING PROCESS

less developed countries   *see* STANDARDIZATION VERSUS ADAPTATION

less is more, advertising impact   *see* KISS ADVERTISING

lessons of the life cycle   *see* LIFE CYCLE, LESSONS

letter, direct mail   It is, of course, quite possible to send out a mailing without any letter; and many, perhaps most, mailings (particularly those in consumer markets) simply comprise such unaccompanied 'flyers'. But most mailings sent out as part of overall campaigns in the industrial sales environment – even mass mailings – usually include a letter. In any case, the evidence suggests that enclosing a letter improves the response rate; and enclosing a personalized letter improves it significantly. Market research amongst personal computer buyers has shown that between 60 per cent and 80 per cent of them read a letter addressed to them by name (the range being due to the extent to which the letter looked as though it had been typed, at the top end, or obviously word-processed, at the lower end), whereas less than 40 per cent read one addressed to them by title, and only just over 20 per cent when it was addressed to the company. According to this evidence, personalization can improve the performance by a factor of four! On the other hand, the letter has to be at least as well written as any of the enclosures, since it is probably the first (and maybe the only) thing that will be read. As such, once more, the message that it contains must be well thought out – powerful and simple.

There is some controversy as to what is the best form of letter. Some would swear by short letters, enlivened by catchy headlines and full of highlighting and underlining. Others feel that this smacks of gimmickry, and prefer longer letters, which encapsulate the whole message on one page (or even on several pages, without any enclosed flyers). In the absence of firm evidence, you should choose the style that best matches the marketing objectives, the subject matter and your prospects. Clearly, a simple price promotion (still one of the most powerful ways of gaining attention) will benefit from the shorter, more punchy, style; whereas the more 'serious' nature of a technical brief on a sophisticated new product might be better suited to the longer format.

The letter is still, however, very much a key element of the promotion. Whatever its format, it should be written (preferably by a trained copywriter) in a style that is easy for the reader to understand; with the minimum of jargon, for example. It is not just another business letter. It should be laid out so that it is easy to read; with short paragraphs, indented if necessary, and with headings if it is a long letter – and with plenty of white space to break up the slabs of verbiage into easily digestible bites. Howard Dana Shaw (one of the most respected US authorities on writing mail order letters) has produced 'Six Checking Points for Writing That Gets People to Do Things':

1. Be Natural Instead of Literary [don't be pompous] . . .
2. Simplify Your Sentences [keep them short] . . .
3. Write in Pictures [make the prospect see what you want] . . .
4. Make Things Move [give it a sense of direction] . . .
5. Use Personal Pronouns [you are 'I' not 'the writer'] . . .
6. Don't Inflate [don't use too many superlatives] . . .

The one point that most commentators seem to agree on is that the areas at the top and bottom of the letter receive the most attention from the recipient. At the top, the best way to use this is to try to encapsulate the overall message in a punchy headline (in capitals and underlined, to grab attention); and then make the hottest offer immediately, in the first paragraph (instead of the bland courtesies with which most letters start). The best way to use the bottom area of attention is a 'P.S.' (a postscript). This is a particularly useful device for gaining attention, although most letter-writers would not think of using one. It seems to be just about the best read part of most letters.

See also PRECISION MARKETING

letterpress The original printing process which used (inked) raised type to produce the letters in the newspaper, say.
See also ADVERTISING; ADVERTISING AGENCY ELEMENTS

level of assembly *see* MATERIALS REQUIREMENTS PLANNING (MRP)

level of service *see* ADVERTISING BELIEVABILITY

level scheduling *see* KANBAN

levels of distribution *see* CHANNEL MEMBERS

leverage *see* GLOBAL MARKETING

Levis *see* GLOBALIZATION

libraries The widest ranging source of published data (on everything from details of ancient civilizations through to the latest stock-market prices) is usually a library; possibly one within the organization itself (universities simply could not exist without their libraries) but more usually a public library. You may be lucky enough, particularly if you are located in the centre of a large city, to have a local library that has miles of shelves full of books – some of which may meet your needs. Indeed, many libraries (even branch libraries) have a wide selection of non-fiction books that will provide background reading on most subjects, and should not be ignored as a source of data. The reference libraries that are usually part of the central library will hold even more. More importantly, though, these libraries can, and will, obtain books that are not on their shelves. They will typically have a catalogue (usually now on microfiche or computer) that will list the stock of all of their branches, from which the staff will be able to obtain books for you.

Furthermore, the library will also have access to national collections. In the UK, this is the British Library, the lending section of which is located at Boston Spa. As a result, if you can find sufficient information to specify the book (usually author, title, publisher and date of publication – although often just the author and title may suffice) it can usually be retrieved from this source. The even better news is that, even though (in the UK) this may cost the libraries involved somewhere around £10, the service may be free to users!

On the other hand, much of the published data is located in journals – often specialist periodicals. It is possible that a librarian who specializes in information retrieval (or simply in 'reader enquiries'), usually to be found at the central library, may be able to conduct a search for you. In any case, perhaps you will know the specific journal that you want. Again, it is quite possible that the journal (or a photocopy of the article) can be obtained for you from a national collection, such as the Library of Congress or the British Library.

Possibly, though, the best source may be one of the more specialized libraries, such as those run by trade associations.

If the book you want is not in the library's own catalogue, you may be able to find it in *Books in Print*, which lists all books currently in print in the USA (*British Books in Print* provides the same information for books in the UK). If all else fails, you can refer to a national bibliography; such as the British National Bibliography which, in its various yearbooks and cumulative indices, covers all of the books ever published in the UK. Be warned, however, that this may be no easy task; and it is perhaps better to persuade a friendly librarian to undertake it for you.

Finally, there are a number of abstracting services that give details of business articles published, together with a brief description of the contents. Probably the best known of these is ANBAR, which provides five separate services covering marketing, accounting/DP, personnel, work study and top management, and ABI-INFORM (which is available on CD-ROM).

See also DIRECTORIES; EXTERNAL DATA; INTERNATIONAL MARKETING RESEARCH

licensee know-how   *see* LICENSING

licensing   This may be a means of rapidly, and cost-effectively, entering a large number of markets (including with a service offering). It does not require the investment of resources that direct entry would demand. Coca Cola, for example, used to license local bottlers in some markets (including in the UK), although it has since switched to direct operations in the main markets. Pilkingtons licensed its float glass technology in some of the smaller, more difficult markets. Even Philip Morris licenses its global brands in markets where governments hold a monopoly of cigarette production. A range of different forms of licensing agreements and contracts (including those relating to franchising) is available, so this is an area in which specialist legal expertise is essential. The clear advantage is that it requires no knowledge of the local market, but only of the areas of expertise that the organization already possesses.

The disadvantage is that this approach may limit future development of the organization's position in the market. Indeed, it may not only limit future access to that market, but may also create competition in third markets – as the licensee gains experience and know-how (a technique that was used very successfully by some Japanese companies in the 1970s).

See also MARKET ENTRY TACTICS

lie detector   *see* PSYCHOGALVANOMETER

life cycle, criticisms   There has been remarkably little criticism of the life cycle concept, but that which has been published has been damning – in terms of the use of the theory as a practical aid to marketing management. Even so, the most influential criticism, from Dhalla and Yuspeh, was published in the *Harvard Business Review* as long ago as 1976. They summarized the position as follows:

> The PLC concept, as developed by its proponents, is fairly simple. Like human beings or animals, everything in the marketplace is presumed to be mortal. A brand is born, grows lustily, attains maturity, and then enters declining years, after which it is quietly buried . . . clearly, the PLC is a dependent variable which is determined by market actions; it is not an independent variable to which companies should adapt their marketing programs. Marketing management itself can alter the shape and duration of a brand's life cycle.

Trevor Watkins (1986) comments, 'There are obviously disagreements about the exact value of the PLC concept, in particular about the practical use of the technique. The predictive rather than the descriptive role of the technique must be open to question. The strategic value of the technique is difficult to assess from the evidence but the PLC concept must be treated with care.'

Enis et al. (1977) make much the same point: 'As usually graphed, the independent variable (time) is a proxy variable for the various marketing decisions. That is, the product's stage in the product life cycle depends primarily upon the marketing strategy for the product at a particular time . . .'

These views are ones to which my own research lends credence. The life cycle is useful as a description, but not as a predictor, and usually should be firmly under the control of the marketer!

In terms of the use of the PLC to provide practical aid to marketers, Lazer and Shaw (1986) state, for instance, that 'While it is possible to set forth general strategies for each stage of the PLC, such generalizations should be approached with caution. Like other marketing generalizations, there are exceptions. It is not always possible to apply insights gained from previously determined PLC sales patterns to forecast future product movements.' More directly, Yoram Wind (1982) says that 'these recommendations have usually been vague, nonoperational, not empirically supported, and conceptually questionable, since they imply that strategies can be developed with little concern for the product's profitability, market share position, and other management objectives and constraints.'

Thus, although the life cycle may – in the right context – be a useful theoretical device, there are frequently significant problems in trying to put it into practice; even if it exists. How, for example, do you determine just where you are in a life cycle, when real-life sales or usage curves do not follow the smooth path that the theory shows? How do you predict when turning points will be reached when, again, the picture is 'fuzzy' and you have to take decisions well in advance (without the theoretician's invaluable advantage of hindsight)?

The important point is that in many – if not most – markets, the product, brand or market life cycle is significantly longer than the planning cycle of the organizations involved. Even if the PLC exists for them, their plans will be based just upon that segment of the curve on which they currently reside (most probably in the 'mature' stage); and their view of that part of it will almost certainly be 'linear', rather than encompassing the whole range from growth to decline.

References: Dhalla, Nariman K. and Yuspeh, Sonia (1976) Forget the product life cycle concept. Harvard Business Review, January–February.

Enis, Ben M., Lagarce, Raymond and Prell, Arthur E. (1977) Extending the product life cycle. Business Horizons, June.

Lazer, William and Shaw, Eric H. (1986) The product life cycle. In Victor P. Buell (ed.), Handbook of Modern Marketing (2nd edn). New York: McGraw-Hill.

Watkins, Trevor (1986) The Economics of the Brand: a Marketing Analysis. New York: McGraw-Hill.

Wind, Yoram J. (1982) Product Policy: Concepts, Methods, and Strategy. Reading, MA: Addison-Wesley.

life cycle, lessons A good volume of literature has been created on the subject of product life cycles. Many marketers, like economists, seem obsessed with the scientific approach; particularly that offered by graphs. The product life cycle is a very clear example of such a graph, and one whose validity cannot be challenged – every product or service must, almost by definition, have a life cycle. It is launched, it grows and then it dies. As such, it offers a useful 'model' to keep at the back of your mind, when making your plans – whether you are marketing a product or service, or are in the non-profit sector. Indeed, if you are in the introductory or growth phases, or in that of decline, it perhaps should be at the front of your mind; for the predominant features of these phases may be those revolving around life and death. Between these two extremes, it is useful to have that vision of mortality in front of you; if for no other reason than to remind you that if you take no action, that decline, and then death, will come that much earlier.

Lazer and Shaw (1986) summarize the position when they say that 'Although the PLC is generally accepted as useful, it is not without its practical difficulties. The PLC can lead to the wrong marketing decisions, such as withdrawal from markets too soon. For if management is convinced the PLC is declining (when it is not) and acts as though it is, a self-fulfilling prophecy can occur.'

The most important aspect of market life cycles is, however, that to all practical intents and purposes they do often not exist! Undoubtedly, over very long periods (running into many decades), some markets may be seen to grow and die. But there are many markets that have existed (albeit with dramatic changes in the presentation of the products that they contain) for the best part of a century or more. Even those markets that have come and gone have often had lives which ran into decades – and which, therefore, can be discounted in terms of practical marketing plans that rarely look beyond three years ahead.

The market life cycle is, thus, a useful intimation of mortality; but is rarely of practical relevance – despite the great body of marketing theory that has been built upon it (from the Boston Matrix through to new product development).

The same comment applies almost as forcefully to product life cycles. In most markets, the majority of the major (dominant) brands have held their position for at least two decades. The exceptions appear to be the minority of markets in which there have been a number of brands with comparable shares, where an on-going battle for brand supremacy may have led to changes in the nominal leadership – but where, even then, the brands involved in this contest have largely remained the same (despite the introduction of numbers of new brands). There have, of course, been exceptions to this rule of continuity, especially in those (typically industrial) markets that are the province of many small suppliers – although the few dramatic changes have usually been instigated by managements that have succeeded (against the odds) in destroying the brand leader in their charge!

The dominant product life cycle, that of the brand leaders which almost monopolize many markets, is therefore one of continuity. Again, therefore, for all practical purposes there is no life cycle!

See also AGE INFLUENCES, ON THE PURCHASE DECISION; BUDGETS; INVESTMENT MULTIPLIER; PRODUCT LIFE CYCLE (PLC); PROMOTIONAL MIX FACTORS

Reference: Lazer, William and Shaw, Eric H. (1986) The product life cycle. In Victor P. Buell (ed.), *Handbook of Modern Marketing* (2nd edn). New York: McGraw-Hill.

life cycle pattern The conventional pattern of a life cycle is one of a gradual rise to a long plateau, before entering a slow decline. However, there are other patterns of life cycle that may be possible – and which, in view of their shorter timespans, may be of more practical significance.

life cycles and the marketing mix One of the favourite uses of life cycle theory is to predict what the marketing mix (the four Ps) should be at each stage. The lessons derived from this theory are rather more useful at the beginning of the cycle. At this stage, the clear priority must be to get the brand established. This generates three main activities:

- building distribution
- building awareness
- obtaining trial

life, of a product *see* PRODUCT LIFE

life-stage influences *see* AGE INFLUENCES, ON THE PURCHASE DECISION

lifestyle, and the (customer) decision-making process In deciding to buy a product or service, apart from the 'physical' experience of the product, the prospective purchaser may also demand that it conforms to their 'lifestyle'. Thus, some consumers may positively seek out tins of Heinz baked beans, because these match their 'emotional' need to be seen as caring parents. On the other hand, a few may deliberately buy the supermarket's own brand, just because they think that makes a statement about their opposition to advertising.

See also CONVICTION MARKETING; DECISION-MAKING PROCESS, BY CUSTOMERS

lifestyle changes *see* CREATIVE IMITATION; LEAPFROG

lifestyle groups *see* MARKETING RESEARCH, PRECISION MARKETING

lifestyle influences, on the purchase decision It used to be possible to predict buying patterns almost exclusively on the basis of class and age. Indeed, much of the marketing research industry still uses these factors as the main 'discriminators'; and the research of O'Brien and Ford (1988) would tend to support the continued use of these elements. In the past decade or so, however, increasing affluence in the West has resulted in a much greater freedom for the individual to choose his or her lifestyle. The resulting spending patterns may now vary quite considerably – even within the same age and class groups – and now reflect individual lifestyles. Philip Kotler (1991) defines a person's lifestyle as 'the person's pattern of living in the world as expressed in the person's activities, interests and opinions'. A number of lifestyle classifications have been proposed by researchers, including:

- AIO (Activities, Interests, Opinions)
- VALS (VAlue LifeStyles)

See also AIO (ACTIVITIES, INTERESTS, OPINIONS); CONVICTION MARKETING; CULTURES, INFLUENCES ON THE PURCHASE DECISION; DECISION-MAKING PROCESS, BY CUSTOMERS; REPEAT PURCHASING PROCESS; SOCIAL CLASS INFLUENCES, ON THE PURCHASE DECISION; VALS (VALUE LIFFSTYLES)

Reference: Kotler, Philip (1991) Englewood Cliffs, NJ: Prentice Hall.
O'Brien, Sarah and Ford, Rosemary (1988) Can we at last say goodbye to social class? *Journal of the Market Research Society*, 30(3), July.

LIFO (Last In First Out) The inventory control procedure whereby the newest stock is used first; and new stock is, for example, put at the front of the shelf.

See also FAULTS; FIFO (FIRST IN FIRST OUT); INVENTORY CONTROL

light users *see* USAGE AND LOYALTY

Likert scales A form of survey question in which respondents are asked to rate the product against, say, a range of statements on a verbal scale that runs

from agree strongly to disagree strongly (with five categories).
See also CLOSED QUESTIONS, ON QUESTIONNAIRES; QUESTIONNAIRE DESIGN

likes and dislikes   *see* MOTIVATION RESEARCH

limited resources   *see* COARSE MARKETING

limit price   The highest price that can be set by existing suppliers to a market before new suppliers are attracted into it.

limits of action   *see* MARKETING STRATEGIES

linear or non-linear models   *see* MODEL CATEGORIES

linear programming   *see* MEDIA BUYING, ADVERTISING AGENCY; TRANSPORT DECISIONS, LOGISTICS MANAGEMENT

line drawing   An illustration created only by lines, without the use of any halftone images.
See also ADVERTISING PROCESSES; CREATING THE CORRECT MESSAGES; CREATIVE DEPARTMENT, ADVERTISING AGENCY; HALFTONE

line managers   *see* MARKETING PLAN BENEFITS

line of best fit   *see* TECHNOLOGICAL FORECASTING

line pricing   *see* PRODUCT-LINE PRICING

line-rationalization   *see* PRODUCT (OR SERVICE) MIX

line-stretching   *see* PRODUCT (OR SERVICE) MIX

Linotype   The continuous cast (hot lead, often called hot metal) line of type that used to be used in (letterpress) production of newspapers. It could be compared with Monotype, where each letter was cast separately. Now optical typesetting is more frequently used.
See also BLOCKS; FLONG; LETTERPRESS

list broker   A supplier of direct mail lists.
See also DIRECT MAIL

list cleaning   The removal of incorrect names and addresses from mailing lists.
See also DIRECT MAIL

listening   Just as important a skill as questioning is listening. Many managers are too busy trying to put their own views across to hear what is being said in reply, and thus they miss much of the key data in such conversations. However, listening implies far more than hearing. It also involves the process of analysing what is heard, to understand it – to make sense of it in general, and then to put it into the 'intellectual framework' of the organizational activities that are being discussed. Listening is a very active pursuit, not a passive one – or the listener will soon become a sleeper. It is conventionally reckoned that a good sales professional (and any good questioner) should spend two-thirds of the time listening and only one-third talking – the reverse of the sales stereotype. This is probably the ideal ratio to aim for, although the particular ratio will vary with the specific conditions. What is important, though, is how you use that time. It is the quality of the listening (which has much to do with how you analyse what you hear) that is as important as the quantity – a factor that most sales training pundits overlook.
See also NOTE-TAKING; QUESTIONING; UNDERSTANDING

References: Mercer, David (1988) *Sales Professional*. London: Kogan Page.
   Mercer, David (1989) *High Level Selling*. Houston, TX: Gulf Publishing.

list, mailing   *see* MAILING LIST

List Of Values (LOV)   *see* VALS (VALUE LIFESTYLES)

list prices   These are the set prices, often listed in catalogues, on which discounts may be offered. If there are standard discounts, this may be referred to as 'administered pricing'.

lists, direct marketing   *see* PRECISION MARKETING

literacy   *see* SOCIAL AND BUSINESS STRUCTURES, FILTERING UNSUITABLE MARKETS

literal   A typographical error (by the typographer, or typist) that requires correction. It is often called a 'typo'.

literature search   *see* INTERNATIONAL MARKETING RESEARCH

litho The lithographic printing process, now used for most printing.
See also DIRECT MAIL

litho plates *see* BLOCKS

litigation *see* AGENTS OR DISTRIBUTORS

livery The special design used by an organization to identify itself to the outside world, on its letterheads, uniforms, vehicles, etc.
See also BRANDING; LOGO

living standards, filtering unsuitable markets
see EXPORT MARKET ELIMINATION

lobbying *see* PROACTIVE PR

local agencies, data In recent years, a considerable amount of data has been collected locally; by local authorities and enterprise agencies, for example. The local Chambers of Commerce (while rather variable in their own provision of such data) are often a good starting point for this local material.
See also NATIONAL AGENCIES, DATA

local neighbourhoods *see* MARKETING RESEARCH, PRECISION MARKETING

local press *see* TEST MARKET

local sales organization The largest, and most attractive, markets may well justify the establishment of a local sales operation (although often this occurs after the market is tested by using an agent for a period). A number of possibilities are open for such a sales organization:

- *Subsidiary/branch office*. This is the vehicle chosen by most truly international/multinational organizations.
- *Joint selling company*. A joint venture may be set up with a local partner or another supplier.
- *Purchase of an existing organization*. If sufficient resources are available, then the quickest route to widespread distribution may be to buy into an existing company, which is already in the market (either with a 100 per cent takeover, or a controlling interest – or even with a minority interest that guarantees co-operation).

See also MARKET ENTRY TACTICS

local shoppers *see* LOCATION, RETAIL

location filming Filming at a real location rather than in the studio.

location, retail The hub of retailing is normally still the high street, but this is by no means the whole story:

- *High street (or central shopping area)*. This is (or used to be) the province of the multiples, and the location with the highest property costs. The high rents are paid because location, above all, determines a retail outlet's turnover – hence the old retail adage that 'the three most important elements of retailing are location, location and location'. There are surveys that show, for every high street, where consumers shop. A multiple retailer will use these to determine where to place his outlet (and will be confronted by a property developer who will use the same surveys to value his property!). The pedestrian flows can be quite dramatically different on opposite sides of a street. Obtaining the best location (balancing pedestrian traffic against property cost) is a skill that retailers, justifiably, rate highly.
- *Neighbourhood stores*. There are still many thousands of corner shops and stores that are located on minor high streets, which are the almost exclusive province of the independents; and which offer convenience for local shoppers – often now also offering equally convenient hours (from 7 a.m. to 11 p.m. and through the weekends).
- *Out of town*. Sites away from the high street, but with good road links, have become the preferred location of the 'warehouse stores' (sometimes called 'sheds' by those in the industry) and the no-frills discount operations, particularly in the DIY field.
- *Superstores and malls*. Increasingly, however, such sites are also the chosen location for superstores (very large supermarkets of up to 80 000 sq. ft), which – in the UK at least – are rapidly taking share from the smaller, more conventional supermarkets. Hypermarkets (similar, but typically between 100 000 and 200 000 sq. ft, and carrying a range which might match that of a department store) are also based in similar locations – since the car has now become the main means of travel to such stores. The ultimate outcome of these developments is the regional 'shopping mall', in which a high street is effectively recreated (offer-

ing air-conditioned comfort) on a green fields site. In this way, advantage can be taken of good road access, low costs and the opportunity to start from scratch without the problems of the existing high streets.

See also CUSTOMER SERVICE CATEGORIES; RETAILING; RETAIL ORGANIZATION; RETAIL PRODUCT OR SERVICE CATEGORIES

locations of warehouses   *see* FACILITY DECISIONS, LOGISTICS MANAGEMENT

loco   The price quoted for goods that are located in a specific place, and for which the purchaser must pay all charges for loading and transport from there.

logical incrementalism   As described by Quinn (1980), an incremental approach to setting strategy has certain implications. Thus, the manager must be prepared to follow a number of stages that are quite different from those traditionally described for (annual) planning:

1. *Scanning.* Since the trigger for the incremental change in strategy is a change in the environment, this approach is very dependent upon sensing the signals which indicate such changes in the environment – and a rigorous approach to environmental analysis is needed.
2. *Information networks.* A consequent requirement is that managers build the widest possible networks (of human contacts not just computers) to obtain the input which will tell them what is happening in their environment and, more important, to help them sense when change is likely to be needed – the human neural network is a very good analogy for this.
3. *Generation of alternatives.* It might seem that incrementalism would imply instant decisions: 'shooting from the hip'. Yet a key requirement, observed by successful managers, is that they develop a range of alternative solutions which they then think through, often at length, with their colleagues before committing themselves to any one approach.
4. *Building credibility.* Having taken the personal decision, such managers then set about preparing the ground for the necessary changes. This may be started, by CEOs for instance, by making symbolic moves (by, say, a very public commitment to a new philosophy). It is often accompanied by moves to legitimize new viewpoints – for

example, by setting up workshops (or retreats) to talk through the issues; preferably off-site, so that they are not interrupted (but also so that they are symbolically divorced from the present work).
5. *Tactical moves.* Even then, the changes may first be introduced as (experimental) tactics rather than strategy – this is where incrementalism can be used to bypass opposition which might otherwise emerge against a formal announcement of the change in strategy.
6. *Political support.* These new moves will still, though, require the building of political coalitions if they are to be sustained; committees and task forces are favourite devices for developing such support. At the same time opposition will need to be neutralized.
7. *Creating commitment.* When the strategy is finally in place it is necessary to actively build commitment to it throughout the organization.

One of the less obvious implications of the above processes, which is supported by significant amounts of research data, is that making of strategy is a much more diffused process than most managers think. One aspect which is most often stressed in relation to logical incrementalism is that of timing – the decisions take place almost randomly throughout the year rather than tidily during the annual planning process.

A less obvious implication is that the process is not limited to senior management alone, as traditional theory would suggest. In this case, and in practice, the process is spread through a number of layers of management – with different degrees of involvement depending upon what particular incremental aspect of strategy is under review. This has major implications for managers throughout the organization, who before probably did not realize just how important their contribution was.

See also CORPORATE PLAN; CORPORATE STRATEGY AND MARKETING; EMERGENT STRATEGIES; MARKETING STRATEGIES

References: Quinn, J. B. (1980) *Strategies for Change: Logical Incrementalism. Richard D. Irwin.*

logistic curve   *see* DIFFUSION OF INNOVATION; LONGER-TERM COMPETITIVE SAW; TECHNOLOGICAL FORECASTING

logistics management   Logistics management is the term classically given to management of the whole process by which physical materials are taken through the various production stages and thence, by the distribution system, to the end-user. The 'distribution' processes are often seen as lying outside mainstream marketing. Typically, they are handled as an adjunct to the 'warehousing' processes of production; or, frequently, as part of the purchasing function. On the other hand, they are clearly at the heart of the marketing of many service industries (and particularly of retailing). Even in other markets, in view of their impact on customer service, this may also be short-sighted! The application of logistics management is most complex in the case of those products that incorporate many components and many levels of distribution. However, the principles involved may apply – albeit in simpler terms, since there are fewer 'components' of input – to the service industries. In these, too, all of the elements have to be brought together at the right time to be 'in stock' for the customer to purchase. In terms of physical products, this can be divided up into two parts; materials management and physical distribution management.

Almost all logistics decisions are major decisions, taken only infrequently (except in the retail sector), but of crucial importance to the future of any company. They need to reflect the marketing realities just as much as any other factors. The products that they 'produce' will need to be the right ones in the right place at the right time to meet customer needs. It is a function, therefore, which cannot be neglected with impunity, since these changes can lead to major shifts in competitive advantage. It is arguable, for instance, that the worldwide success of Japanese organizations would not have emerged without the dramatic improvements in sea-borne transport.

See also DATA PROCESSING, LOGISTICS; FACILITY DECISIONS, LOGISTICS MANAGEMENT; INVENTORY CONTROL; KANBAN; MATERIALS MANAGEMENT; MATERIALS REQUIREMENTS PLANNING II (MRPII); OPTIMIZED PRODUCTION TECHNOLOGY (OPT); PHYSICAL DISTRIBUTION MANAGEMENT; PRODUCTION DECISIONS, LOGISTICS MANAGEMENT; SET-UP TIMES; TRANSPORT DECISIONS, LOGISTICS MANAGEMENT

logo   Called, in full, a logotype, this is the design – either a symbol or letters – used by an organization to identify itself, and to distinguish itself from other organizations, on its packaging and in its advertising.

See also BRANDING; LIVERY

longer-term competitive saw   Traditionally, advertising and promotion have been treated as a cur-

rent cost; with an immediate, but short-term, effect. Although this view is probably justified in terms of most forms of sales promotion, it seriously distorts some important aspects of advertising and PR. A more useful view in this context is that advertising investment should, in effect, be treated as a fixed asset.

The adoption of such a long-term perspective has a number of important implications. The first of these revolves around the patterns of performance that might expected. Thus, the basic pattern is not that of the short-run supply and demand curves, but that of the 'longer-term competitive saw'. Indeed, it is a level saw. Its overall trend is relatively flat, but the teeth represent the impact of the individual campaigns; or even that of the individual insertion, or even of words within the single advertisement – it shares with fractals the ability to continue to display new detail at ever greater degrees of 'magnification':

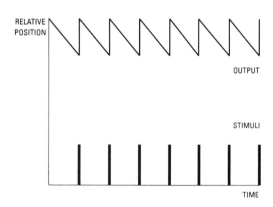

Following the implied principle of the fixed asset, this sawtooth maintenance pattern can be overlaid on a gradually declining trend in performance: this is notionally equivalent to depreciation in financial accounting. Thus, over time, there may be a slow drift away from the ideal position – as the customers' needs and wants change and/or competitive positioning improves. Your own response to this may take two forms. The first, and perhaps the most effective, is that of 'dynamic repositioning'. The need for change is regularly tracked and the brand's position readjusted – in much the same way that an autopilot's feedback mechanisms ensure that an airliner follows the correct flight path. The emphasis here is on the dynamic approach to (current) change – whereas most of marketing theory revolves around decisions based upon static (historic) positions.

If such dynamic repositioning is not possible, perhaps because the necessary product changes come in discrete steps, then periodic readjustments may be needed. This is where the concept of depreciation is especially valuable. Thus, it allows the build-up of reserves to cover the significant costs of such repositioning exercises:

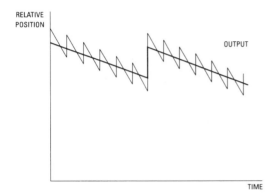

This long-term asset investment aspect of brand performance is largely ignored by traditional marketing theory.

The above pattern of responses assumes a complementary repositioning process, which builds upon existing strengths. However, this process cannot be held to be true of the new product launch, where the logistic curve may be most effectively used to represent the relatively slow build-up of brand position that results from even quite high levels of investment; because the key aspect is the level of investment needed. It is seen in two main dimensions. One is the amount of (financial) investment needed. To buy your way into a market is a very expensive process indeed. The main feature is the level of risk. On the other hand, most managements believe, quite incorrectly, that risk is reduced if the levels of investment are minimized – the reverse is true. Once you accept the basic level of risk, the more money you invest, the lower that risk will become. If you want to make a major impact on a market (one that will, for instance, put you into the most profitable 'rule of 123' slots), you must recognize that that the level of investment needed will be correspondingly high. In practice, where major markets are concerned, it is probably beyond the reach of all but the largest Japanese corporations.

The second dimension is time. Any new penetration of a market takes far longer than is expected. Rather than the one or two years that optimists expect, and the three or four years that pessimists allow for, the reality is a mean of eight years to break even – even for successful introductions!

See also ADVERTISING; COMPETITIVE SAW; MARKETING MIX; PROMOTIONAL LOZENGE; PROMOTIONAL MIX; RULE OF 123; SELLING; STEPPED SAW

Reference: David Mercer (1997) *New Marketing Practice.* London: Penguin.

long-term (advertising)   *see* LONGER-TERM COMPETITIVE SAW

long-term forecasts   The long-term, or strategic, forecast (which is usually a 'qualitative' forecast) typically covers a five-year period or longer. As a result, it is often seen as a luxury, which only the larger organizations can afford. In reality, though, it is probably the most important forecast of all – certainly in terms of setting the direction for the overall marketing plan:

- *Strategic direction.* The long-term forecast usually consolidates the long-term strategy. Having to quantify this strategy as a forecast, or a series of forecasts, helps to concentrate attention on those ideas which are practical and meaningful.
- *Resource planning.* The long-term planning period should be chosen to cover the period over which the long-term investments, in plant or research for example, will be completed.
- *Communication.* Not least, the strategic forecast tells everyone in the organization, workers just as much as management, where the organization intends to go. As a result, it is also one of the key bases for the organizational culture (as per Peters and Waterman, 1982), which is an essential, if still largely unrecognized, aspect of most organizations.

The longer-term forecasts are the least likely to be confused with 'budgets', and are perhaps less biased by the organization's view of its own activities. On the other hand, they are just as likely to be constrained by its parochial view of the future. This 'market myopia' may well preclude its forecasters from taking into account all of the factors involved. In particular, as described by Theodore Levitt (1969), they may focus only on a very small portion of their potential market – and not recognize the importance of changes taking place elsewhere.

See also MEDIUM-TERM FORECASTS; SHORT-TERM FORECASTS; SHORT- VERSUS LONG-TERM FORECASTS

References: Levitt, Theodore (1969) Marketing myopia. *Harvard Business Review*, July–August.

Peters, Thomas J. and Waterman, Robert H. (1982) *In Search of Excellence.* New York: Harper & Row.

long-term indicators   *see* MONITORING, PROGRESS

loose insert   A leaflet inserted loose inside a publication, and distributed with it.

Lord Leverhulme   *see* ADVERTISING

Lorenz curve   A graph used to demonstrate inequality in the distribution of income.

lose–lose   *see* WIN–WIN

loser brand   *see* INVESTMENT MULTIPLIER

losers   *see* FORECASTS OF SALES BUSINESS; TERRITORY SALES PLAN

loss leader pricing   *see* COMPETITIVE PRICING; PROMOTIONAL PRICING

lost business   *see* MONITORING, PROGRESS

LOV (List Of Values)   *see* VALS (VALUE LIFESTYLES)

low and high budgets   *see* FORECASTS INTO BUDGETS

low-budget, conservative strategy   *see* NEW PRODUCT INNOVATION

lower classes   *see* SOCIAL CLASS INFLUENCES, ON THE PURCHASE DECISION

lower-cost media   *see* SHARPENING THE CUTTING EDGE OF MEDIA

low-involvement product   One where the customer will spend little time making any purchase decision.

loyalty   *see* ADVERTISING; ENHANCED AIUAPR MODEL; MOTIVATION, OF SALES PERSONNEL; PEER PYRAMID; PROMOTIONAL PRICING; THREE PILLARS OF THE PURCHASING PROCESS; USAGE AND LOYALTY

loyalty programmes   These are used as a long-term marketing tactic to secure the brand loyalty of a company's most profitable customers. Typically, they are sales promotion programmes that provide an incentive to complete a number (often a relatively large number) of purchases. Thus, Diners Club has used a points system, related to purchases over time, that can be used by the customer to claim free gifts. The most recent, and most important, examples are those offered by the supermarket loyalty cards – which typically offer only a 1 per cent discount, but which have proved very successful.
See also SALES PROMOTION

lozenge, promotional   *see* PROMOTIONAL LOZENGE

Lux soap   *see* GLOBAL MARKETING

luxury good   Defined in economics as one for which demand will rise more than proportionately as income rises.

3m   *see* NEW PRODUCT INNOVATION

macho image   *see* CONVICTION MARKETING TYPES

macro- and micro-forecasts   Forecasts can be categorized by the breadth of the factors that they encompass:

Macro-forecasts
This form of forecasting looks at the 'aggregates', at total markets; and even at total national economies. It attempts to predict what large-scale forces are at work, which will result in 'macro' changes in the market environment. This borders on, and sometimes overlaps, the area of macroeconomic forecasts which so preoccupy governments of all persuasions – and which has led to the emergence of very sophisticated and complex econometric models. Some companies have the resources, and the need, to undertake these forecasts of whole markets; indeed, sometimes of whole economies. The most important input to these models may be the various 'leading indicators' (the key statistics derived from the economy, such as movements in share prices and the number of house starts, which are supposed to indicate what may happen in the future). When taken to these limits, however, this type of forecasting is both very elaborate and exceedingly expensive – and, accordingly, is rarely undertaken!

Micro-forecasts
At the other end of the spectrum, micro-forecasting builds on predictions of individual (or group) customer behaviour; to accumulate overall forecasts for, typically, sales of particular products or services. These forecasts are classically based upon projections of observed historical trends. But before we examine such techniques we need to examine one problem of such historical projections. The first graph below may be seen as a typical sales graph, covering two or three years (which is the historical period that many organizations look at when they come to produce forecasts), with the minor fluctuations smoothed out. But it is possible that behind this two- to three-year curve there lies a four-

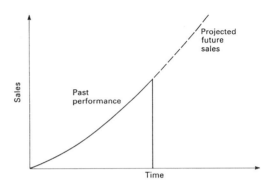

year 'trade cycle'; as indeed, until very recently, there has been. The long-term sales chart may thus look as follows:

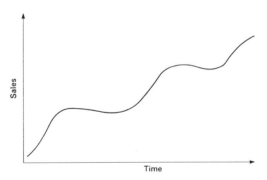

If this is the pattern, but the sales projections are made on the 'traditional' basis of two years' historical data, then the following picture will emerge:

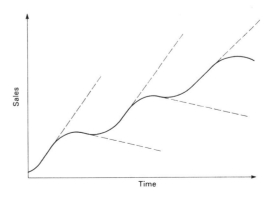

This is known as the 'fishbone effect', and clearly can produce significant mismatches of organizational resource to opportunities – expecting plenty when famine is about to set in, and conserving to allow for famine just when plenty is about to return. On the other hand, if the product life cycle is taken into account – where a downturn may not follow from a temporary hiccup in the economy, but may represent the onset of the decline phase for the product – the results of such forecasting may even be counterproductive! Having issued this caveat, however, estimates based on past sales are very widely used, and (in the absence of the more sophisticated forecasting tools) can justifiably be used as the main indicators in many situations. They must, however, be checked as far as possible against predictions derived from other sources – and, always, treated as predictions of an uncertain future.

See also LONG–TERM FORECASTS; MEDIUM–TERM FORECASTS; SHORT–TERM FORECASTS; SHORT– VERSUS LONG–TERM FORECASTS; USAGE GAP

macroeconomics   The theory that studies the economy as a whole; as compared to microeconomics, which describes that relating to the individual elements within the economy.

See also KEYNESIANISM; MICROECONOMICS; MONETARISM; RATIONAL EXPECTATIONS THEORY

magazines   *see* DELIVERY SYSTEMS, PRECISION MARKETING; PRESS MEDIA

magazines sampling   *see* SAMPLING

magic of copywriter   *see* ATTITUDES, ADVERTISING

mail, electronic   *see* ELECTRONIC MAIL

mailer   Printed material, such as a mailing piece (leaflet), specially produced for mailing.

See also DIRECT MAIL; EPOS AND EFTPOS, PRECISION MARKETING

mail houses   *see* IN-HOUSE DATA, PRECISION MARKETING

mailing list   The first question to ask, in organizing a mailing, is whom you wish to mail. The answer will probably come most frequently, and most successfully, from your own database (of customers and prospects). On the other hand, even though you have a great many names on your files, it may still be worthwhile being selective, choosing just those who

will be susceptible to the subject of the mailing. This saves on cost, but it also protects the investment in the database; by not exposing recipients to mounds of irrelevant 'junk mail' like those that they already receive from most other organizations. You may, however, not have a suitable list of prospects on your database. In these circumstances there may be a specialist mailing house which does have such a list (often compiled from customer and prospect lists bought from other suppliers such as yourself!). Mailing houses have lists that cover a wide range of subjects, from hospital doctors through to purchasers of wigs! They will usually sell the list for a one-time use (they will normally not relinquish control of it, since it represents their 'capital'), providing labels (or sometimes computer-readable material for your own use) or, most often, the complete mailing service. In the UK the best list of such mailing houses is probably that contained in the *Direct Mail Databook*. The most important question to ask in buying such a list is how accurate it is. The sources of many lists may be suspect (they are frequently derived from subscribers to magazines, for example, or respondents to free offers – who may not be the ideal prospects), but then they may be the only way you can get to anyone in the target audience! They may also be out of date (12 per cent of the UK population changes address every year) and may need 'cleaning' (containing, for example, duplicate entries or the wrong contacts within organizations). Usually the only satisfactory way of finding out how useful they are is to run a test mailing, but that represents an investment of money and, in particular, time – but then, once again, it may be the only way in which you can reach this group of prospects at an economic rate.

See also DATABASE, INVESTING IN YOUR OWN; DIRECT MAIL ADVERTISING; PRECISION MARKETING

mail message   *see* DIRECT MAIL OFFER

mail order   *see* CHANNEL DECISIONS; PRECISION (DIRECT) MARKETING, RETAIL

mail response   *see* COUPON RESPONSE

mail surveys   Based on questionnaires sent, and returned by mail, this is the cheapest solution to survey research. Hence, large overall samples can be used, allowing investigation of small market groups – especially in industrial markets – still within acceptable statistical levels. However, in many respects, it is the least satisfactory solution. The questions that can be asked are necessarily simpler and the questionnaire shorter; and it must be particularly well de-signed – to keep the respondent interested and moti-vated to reply. More fundamentally, the response rates are often so low that their statistical validity may be questioned, since it is arguable that the ma-jority, the non-respondents, might behave differ-ently from those who have responded. On the other hand, it should be noted that non-response for other forms of survey (especially those using quota sam-ples) may also be high – but this is not recorded! Apart from making the material easy to complete and explaining the reason why the research is being con-ducted (in order to justify the time taken), this prob-lem may be addressed in two main ways. The first is to increase the response rate by offering some form of reward (typically a 'free gift') in return for the completed questionnaire. The second is to follow up (typically by telephone) a subsample of those not completing the questionnaire, to see if they are dif-ferent from those replying; and if they are not differ-ent, the assumption is made (perhaps somewhat questionably) that those res-ponding are representa-tive of the sample as a whole. All mail 'interviews' are, of necessity, of the 'self-completion' kind. This technique can also be used very successfully in con-junction with normal face-to-face interviews. The respondent is left with a questionnaire to complete and then return to the market research agency (usually by post). MRB, for example, use this tech-nique successfully on its Target Group Index (TGI), where the respondents are asked to complete literally thousands of questions, on a questionnaire which is nearly 100 pages long; and do so very willingly and accurately (although it has to be noted that this is because the questionnaire is very well designed, and tested, and the 'fieldwork' particularly well controlled).

See also DATA COLLECTION

maintenance   *see* ORGANIZATIONAL PURCHASING

major accounts   *see* PEOPLE (SALES) MANAGEMENT

majority, early   *see* DIFFUSION OF INNOVATION

make-good   The publisher repeats, without fee, an insertion that was subject to error.

make or buy   It used to be an accepted fact of business life that an organization should add as much value to its product or service as possible. This 'added value' was a good measure of what the organi-zation had to offer. This almost inevitably led to an

emphasis on manufacturing (or on 'producing' in the more general sense – of services, for example) 'in-house'. Only those items that required special exper-tise, which the organization did not possess, or were standard 'off-the-shelf' items, were bought in. In recent years, the trend – an important one – has been to reverse this philosophy; and to buy out all those items which can be purchased elsewhere. Only those items that cannot be bought elsewhere, and hence represent the special expertise of the organization, should (according to this new philosophy) be manu-factured in-house. More realistically applied, the new approach compares the 'cost' (and preferably of all the factors – not just direct cost) of producing in-house with that of buying-in, and places the business wherever it will be most efficiently handled. Heinritz et al. (1986) suggest that the following factors should be taken into account in this decision:

- *Quality*. It may be that the quality produced by the outside supplier is higher than that which could be produced in-house: this should be true if a supplier specializes in this element of the prod-uct or service. On the other hand, control over quality becomes less direct when given to an outside supplier (particularly when the quality of bought-in items is the responsibility of purchas-ing rather than manufacturing).
- *Capacity*. The need for outside supply may be forced by the lack of internal capacity. On the other hand, the organization will need to be con-vinced that external supplies can be guaranteed; and will not be 'cornered' by competitors when industry-wide demand increases. This factor, for instance, has been particularly significant in the computer industry; and is one reason why IBM manufactures so many of its key components in-house – and 'multiple sources' most of the others.
- *Labour*. The impact on the organization's own staff (who are 'stakeholders' too) may be critical.
- *Scheduling*. The degree of control (as well as the proximity) of in-house production allows a much easier response to crises. Conversely, the use of outside suppliers demands tighter control of sup-plier deliveries (as is the case with JIT) and more progress chasing – or higher inventories. How-ever, the development of this degree of discipline may have many indirect benefits in an organiza-tion that is less efficient than it might be!
- *Skill*. Again, the supplier may offer greater skills. On the other hand, any organization would be foolish to contract-out operations that are the key to its own competitive advantage (as it would

train others, potential future competitors, in these skills); although IBM did just this with its PC – and subsequently paid the price!

- *Cost.* Only when all the other factors have been satisfied does cost come into play (the reverse of what happens in most of such decisions). Unfortunately, in practice, it is not easy to compare costs on a like-for-like basis. Outside prices may be easy to determine, although it may not be clear how long these prices will hold for. They may be 'special offers' to win the business, or they may simply be lower due to inexperience of the difficulties, in either of which cases future prices will be higher – perhaps much higher! Internal costs, however, are often more a matter of arbitrary allocation (since they will usually contain large amounts of overhead) than accounting facts.

The make-or-buy decision is, therefore, a complex one. As a result, it is often taken on the basis of principle (or dogma) rather than clear facts!
See also LOGISTICS MANAGEMENT

Reference: Heinritz, S. F., Farrell, P. V. and Hall, C. L. (1986) *Purchasing: Principles and Applications.* Englewood Cliffs, NJ: Prentice Hall.

Make Your Mark With Parker   *see* GLOBAL MARKETING

making the strange familiar   *see* SYNECTICS®

mall   A collection of stores, called a shopping mall in the USA, sharing a common covered area.

malpractice   *see* PLANNING PITFALLS

management accounting   *see* MARKETING AUDIT

management by objectives   This important aspect of the planning process (usually referred to as MBO) was formalized in the 1960s and 1970s. It was reasoned that each manager should be clear as to exactly what were his or her responsibilities; in terms of specific objectives that he or she was required to achieve. Peter Drucker (1977) spells out the approach: 'Each manager from the "big boss" down to the production supervisor or the chief clerk, needs clearly spelled out objectives. These objectives should lay out what performance each managerial person's own unit is supposed to produce . . . the objectives of all managers should spell out their contribution to the attainment of company goals in all areas of the business.' Since the 1970s there has been

less talk of MBO; possibly because the concept has now been absorbed as part of normal management practice, or possibly because the problems of managing in more turbulent times demanded more complex approaches – MBO requires that the manager's job be defined exactly (which is much more difficult if the future is uncertain). Even so, the principles of MBO still have a place; in terms, in particular, of ensuring that – as far as possible – each element contributed to the overall plan is measurable, and is the responsibility of one individual manager. The emphasis is now perhaps on 'self-control'. As Peter Drucker also says, 'Self-control means stronger motivation; a desire to do the best rather than just enough to get by. It means higher performance goals and broader vision.'
See also PLANNING PROCESS; STRATEGIC BUSINESS UNIT (SBU)

Reference: Drucker, Peter F. (1977) *People and Performance: the Best of Drucker on Management.* London: Heinemann.

Management Information Systems (MIS)   *see* JUST IN TIME (JIT); MARKETING INTELLIGENCE SYSTEMS (MIS)

management, retail   *see* RETAIL MANAGEMENT

management (sales) activities   *see* SALES PROFESSIONAL

managing change   *see* MARKETING MYOPIA

managing change, inner market   *see* INNER MARKETING CAMPAIGN

managing channels   *see* CHANNEL DECISIONS; MONITORING AND MANAGING CHANNELS

managing in turbulent times   *see* STRATEGIC BUSINESS UNIT (SBU)

managing stability, not change   *see* MARKETING MYOPIA

managing strategy is mostly managing stability   *see* MARKETING MYOPIA

mandatory   Required by law.

manifest   A list of goods in a shipment, especially that going by sea or air.

manpower   *see* HUMAN FACTORS, NEW PRODUCTS

manpower plan, sales The most important decision for any sales manager to make (and then justify to the board) is how many sales personnel are needed. This is a complex decision. It can be based on a number of different approaches:

Resources needed to exploit the potential
This is the mirror image of the 'calls available annually' calculation. The amount of sales time needed to support the projected number of customers and prospects is calculated. This may be by rule of thumb, based on experience; allowing for the fact that customers should, against most salespersons' natural inclinations, be budgeted for a greater amount of support than prospects – and large accounts considerably more. Alternatively, it may be based on the resources needed to support the specific accounts (although this is rare, except where account planning is implemented). The resulting total sales time is then divided by the sales time available per person, to give the number of salespeople needed. There are a number of alternative models (based on market penetration or sales response factors, for instance) that attempt to provide more accurate estimates.

Marginal analysis
This calculation, suggested by Walter Semlow (1959), follows the same principles as marginal costing. Extra salespeople are added to the payroll until the profit generated by the 'marginal' salesperson exactly matches the cost of this person. In view of the difficulties of determining what the cost of an individual salesperson is, let alone what their profit might be, this is, needless to say, little used in practice – no matter how attractive it is in theory! Indeed, few sales forces are ever allowed to recruit to the levels deemed necessary by such calculations. This may not necessarily be a bad thing, depending on the scale of the under-resourcing. It is better – in terms of morale and management control – to have a sales force that is overworked, by a small margin, than one that has too little potential for its members to work towards. Sales personnel work best when they have too much work, as they can then afford to concentrate on the 20 per cent of customers and prospects who will produce the (80 per cent) most profitable business (without the distractions of having to chase marginal business).

Resources needed to meet target
This is the most popular technique amongst the few organizations that actually produce a sales manpower plan. It may follow the above calculations, but it is more likely to be based upon experience: How many salespeople, in our experience, will we need to meet next year's targets? An extension to this process involves 'negotiations' (for example, as a division justifying its sales plan to the group headquarters) for extra sales personnel in return for increased targets.

Affordable method
Following the same principles as those for the overall promotional budget, the organization decides (usually on the basis of historical precedent) how much it can 'afford' (after all the other costs, and the planned profit, have been deducted from revenue).

Percentage of revenue
Or sales can be allocated a budget based on an (often arbitrary) percentage of the planned revenue. IBM, for instance, uses a variation on this approach, as an incentive for its sales management to increase their targets (since that is the only way in which they will be able to afford extra sales personnel!).

Negotiated levels
This last remark leads into what is, by default, the most widely used technique for making changes to the numbers in the sales force. The sales manager negotiates with the board (or sells his 'package' to them – usually on the basis of emotional rather than rational arguments) to increase the numbers of sales personnel. It must have happened somewhere, but I have yet to hear of a sales manager who proposed a reduction in size of the overall sales force!

Business as usual
Most likely of all is that the sales manager does not mention the subject, since no change is proposed (and it does not occur to anyone involved to consider that this too needs justification!). There is a fixed pattern of territories, and sales personnel are simply replaced as and when they leave. The only exception is those territories that have moved so far out of line that they have to be split, or (even more rarely) that they have to be combined. The main force for manpower planning is therefore that of 'inertia'.

See also CALLS AVAILABLE ANNUALLY; SELLING; TERRITORY MANAGEMENT

Reference: Semlow, Walter (1959) How many salespeople do you need? *Harvard Business Review*, May–June.

manufacturer brand One belonging to a manufacturer as opposed to, say, a retailer.
See also BRANDING

manufacturing flexibility *see* FLEXIBLE MANUFACTURING

manufacturing forecast   *see* FORECASTS INTO BUDGETS

manufacturing improvements   *see* EXISTING PRODUCT CHANGES

map of consumer needs   *see* MARKET POSITIONING AND SEGMENTATION

mapping, multidimensional   *see* MARKET GAP ANALYSIS

Map Present Position (Current)   *see* POTSA PLANNING

maps, multidimensional   *see* MULTIDIMENSIONAL MAPS

Map Targets (Targets)   *see* POTSA PLANNING

Marathon brand   *see* STANDARDIZATION VERSUS ADAPTATION

marginal analysis, sales manpower budget   *see* MANPOWER PLAN, SALES

marginal costing, new products   A key concept, which is widely used in marketing and particularly for new 'products', is that of marginal costing. This says that, when considering future plans, any additional (and hence 'marginal') business should only bear the variable costs incurred. The existing overhead costs, which are normally allocated (by a variety of possible methods, but typically by 'absorption costing') to the products or services, are not included in this case; since it is reasoned that they will be unchanged by the new activity. The aim is to maximize net profit; to reach the 'optimal' point at which the additional (marginal) costs of the products, services or activities added are exactly matched by the marginal revenues that they generate. Sensible marketers will, however, draw the line somewhat below this point, recognizing that costs are frequently underestimated. Marginal costing can thus prove to be a particularly valuable accounting technique, which favours growing marketing organizations. This should not, however, be allowed to hide the fact that the overheads do eventually have to be picked up by someone. If all the new brands bear no overheads, and the old brands eventually die (perhaps hastened to their grave by the high overheads that they have to

bear!), the marginal profit (conventionally called the 'net contribution') will look excellent – but the organization itself, with no cover for the overheads, may be making a loss!

See also ADVERTISING BUDGETS; COST-PLUS PRICING; MANPOWER PLAN, SALES; PRODUCT DEVELOPMENT PROCESS

marginal utility   *see* PRICES, CUSTOMER NEEDS

market attractiveness   *see* GE (GENERAL ELECTRIC) MATRIX; THREE CHOICE BOX

market-based pricing   This form of pricing is classically what marketing theory would require. It is sometimes called 'perceived value pricing', because the price to be charged is deemed to be a match to the value that the customer perceives the product or service has to offer. Clearly, it is near ideal, because it is likely to be optimal in terms of obtaining the maximum premium on the commodity price – and very few suppliers price too high, with the great majority pricing too low. This is also the ideal price in that it matches the 'position' of the product in the customer's perceptions. The price is an element, particularly in the luxury goods markets (where a low price may positively damage image), of the overall 'description' of the product, and one which is seen as reflecting its quality. There are many examples of new luxury products that have done badly until the price has been increased, in line with the quality expected. Godley (1975) gives a sensible list of the factors that may come into play in what he calls 'market value pricing':

1.   Value to the customer (this will vary according to the customer).
2.   Alternative buying possibilities open to him; prices, values and performances (as soon as a product has any special features, or unique elements, this factor is difficult to appraise).
3.   Product differentials: Is the product really different and in what way? Product differences that exist for a manufacturer may be non-existent to the customer.
4.   The selling company's impact and reputation.
5.   The buyer's attention to price as a factor.

The problem is, of course, determining just what the perceived value is – or, more basically, finding out what price consumers will be willing to pay. Even in the mass consumer markets, where extensive research is undertaken, establishing optimal prices is difficult. It is not suitable to ask market research respondents how much they would be willing to pay, because such research has almost invariably given wildly optimistic results. The typical answers to this research problem usually involve some form of simulation of the buying situation; for example, offering the product for purchase as part of the research – as part of conventional interviewing or by running a series of 'mini-test-markets' (in test towns or even supermarkets) with different prices. Even then, it is very difficult to standardize the results, and to be sure that other factors are not involved.

See also COMPETITION PRICING; COST–PLUS PRICING; PRICING POLICIES, PRACTICAL

Reference: Godley, C. G. A. (1975) Overall marketing management. In E. F. L. Brech (ed.), *The Principles and Practice of Management*. London: Longman.

market boundaries Consumers – of both products and services – can be grouped on the basis of a number of factors. Their position against these factors, which may be different for each market, 'maps' the true boundaries of that market. The market is defined by the consumers' view of it – and in their 'language'. The car manufacturers may see the market as being in small cars with fuel-injected engines and harder suspensions, but the (male) consumers may well see cars as a way of demonstrating their virility, and it is the latter view that counts. If a 'beach buggy' offers a better image of virility – as it once did in California – that is where the market will be. On the other hand, producers, especially those without marketing expertise, tend to have much more 'physical' ideas of where markets lie. They want to be able to go and 'touch' them; and often feel somewhat uncomfortable when trying to deal with what they see as an ephemeral 'lifestyle'. Despite all the very sound marketing theory, therefore, the practical definitions of markets tend to revolve around the following factors:

- *Product or service category*. This approach defines the market boundaries by what is bought, as defined in the 'physical' terms of the producer. Thus, the service is seen as a certain number of seats on an airliner flying between London and Miami, and not a device for providing the holidays that its passengers are dreaming of. To reverse Leo McGinneva's example, so often quoted by marketing theorists, the product is the 2 mm drill, not the 2 mm hole that the end-user wants to make!
- *Geography*. This approach defines the market

boundaries by where the product or service is sold or delivered – London or Scotland, say – and as such is a clearly understood concept.
- *Customer groupings*. Most producers recognize obvious groupings of customers – teenagers versus senior citizens, for instance. In the industrial markets, for example, suppliers of medical diagnostics recognize that hospitals have different needs to those of corporate health centres.
- *Intangibles*. The only intangible that is widely recognized, and then only as differentiating commercial markets, is price; though even then many, if not most, marketers would treat price as if it was fully tangible. Thus there is sometimes seen to be a 'cheap' market, often described rather patronizingly as 'down market', which also carries some class connotations – as opposed to a 'quality' market.

See also CUSTOMERS; MARKETS; PROSPECTS; USERS

market building role *see* ENHANCED AIUAPR MODEL; PEER PYRAMID; THREE PILLARS OF THE PURCHASING PROCESS

market capitalization *see* CUSTOMER FRANCHISE

market clearing *see* EQUILIBRIUM PRICE; SUPPLY AND DEMAND

market data *see* MARKETING AUDIT

market discipline There has been much political debate about the 'discipline of the market'. This is, however, a concept from economics rather than from marketing. In any case, there are almost as many views of how markets work as there are economists! In the political sphere, over recent years, the 'market' has assumed increasing importance as the symbol – and purportedly much of the substance – of capitalism. This was especially evident in the discussions (in both West and East) that surrounded the introduction to the Eastern bloc countries, at the beginning of the 1980s, of 'perestroika' – a process in which even the communist governments exhorted their managers to 'accept the disciplines of the market'. The 'market' described was, however, that of the economists. 'Market discipline', in their eyes, revolves around a model based almost exclusively on prices (and the related demand) – as the sole vehicle for 'communicating' the wishes of the market. Thus, the market's ultimate sanction, which was not available in a fully planned ('command') economy, is to

buy or not to buy. On the other hand, the 'market' as described by marketers is much more complex – and the attributes of the 'extended' product are frequently much more important than price alone.
See also MACROECONOMICS MICROECONOMICS

market elimination, exporting   *see* EXPORT MARKET ELIMINATION

market entry decision   Once the screening process has reduced the number of potential countries down to a relatively small number, these can be categorized (and prioritized) by the techniques (of new market and portfolio management, for example) that you would use in judging any move into a new market. You should recognize, however, that such a move should be considered (because of its requirement for new resources and skills – and because of the greater degree of uncertainty) as a diversification; even though the products or services involved may be the mainline ones from the home market. Divessification, as described by the Ansoff Matrix, should be the subject of much more serious consideration. At the end of this process of prioritization, you should have divided your potential overseas markets into a number of categories, each requiring different courses of action. Three of these categories may, for example, be as follows:

- markets not to be exploited
- markets to be covered by agents or distributors
- markets for major development

Depending upon the strategies adopted (based on the portfolio planning, say), some of these latter, major markets will be scheduled for development at some time in the future, but others will require immediate attention.
See also EXPORTING

market entry tactics   Having decided to enter a specific market, that entry may be made via a number of routes, in addition to *licensing*, *joint ventures* and *local sales organization*. A simple categorization is as follows.

Domestic-based (direct) export sales
In this case, all activity will be handled by an office located in the organization's home headquarters, although the documentation and shipping are often subcontracted to a third party. This will, necessarily, be a limited operation; handling unsolicited orders from overseas, and selling to foreign government

buying offices (often by bidding against tenders) or those of other foreign buying groups (retail chains, for example). This approach can, very occasionally (where the exporter has special expertise or can offer a very low price), generate high volumes with low overheads (as the Taiwanese personal computer component suppliers have shown). This approach is unlikely to work for a service.

Indirect export sales
In this case, the whole overseas operation is subcontracted to an export/import house; which takes over all responsibility for export and distribution of the product (or, much less likely, the service) overseas. An alternative might be to let another organization, which is well established in overseas markets but which wishes to spread its overheads, handle export sales – this is sometimes called 'piggy-back marketing' or 'mother henning'. For many years, the largest Japanese organizations were the giant trading houses (the 'Sogo Shosha', including C. Itoh – the largest – Mitsui and Mitsubishi), which handled the export sales of many Japanese corporations (which were often very large in their own right). Again, this is a route unlikely to be used for services.

Co-operative distribution
Sometimes suppliers, for example those in commodity (typically agricultural) markets, join together to export as a group. Occasionally, an export consortium (an essentially short-term grouping) may be formed to tender for a specific bid (usually for a large-scale, turnkey, contract). One device that the Japanese, and their later imitators, have very successfully used to break into markets has been to supply 'own' ('private') brands to distributors. Thus, for example, Fujitsu has supplied mainframe computers to Amdahl and Siemens, just as Taiwanese suppliers of consumer electronics and personal computers have provided supplies for a wide range of retailers – all for 'badging' by the local distributors. This gains 'technical' experience of the market, by riding on the known brands of existing companies. If the position in the market is to be consolidated (and not to be left at the whim of the distributor who owns the local brand), there remains the transfer to full-scale marketing, with the organization's own brand(s). This is a transfer that some of the Japanese corporations, at least, have managed with great success – but it is definitely not guaranteed (and takes a deal of courage, in risking the 'own brand' business which has already been built up).
See also JOINT VENTURE; LICENSING; LOCAL SALES ORGANIZATION

market evolution *see* INNOVATIVE IMITATION

market extension (strategy) This involves finding new uses for the existing product or service, thereby taking it into entirely new markets; such as Apple did in persuading customers to use its PCs for desktop publishing. Alternatively, it may be achieved by moving into other countries: in this context, most export operations can be viewed as 'market extensions'.
See also ANSOFF MATRIX; PRODUCT (OR SERVICE) STRATEGY

market failure A theoretical (economic) imperfection in the price system that prevents an efficient allocation of resources.
See also NEOCLASSICAL ECONOMICS; PRICE FACTORS

market forecasting *see* DERIVED FORECASTS

market franchise *see* DIFFUSION OF INNOVATION

market gap analysis This approach to the search for new products looks for gaps in the market that the company could profitably address, regardless of where its current products stand (in a variation on 'product positioning', and using multidimensional 'mapping'). In essence, this takes the 'product gap' of traditional gap analysis to its logical conclusion. In such traditional gap analysis, on the other hand, only gaps in the existing product range are looked for. Many marketers would, indeed, question the worth of this traditional gap analysis. Instead, they would immediately start 'proactively' to pursue a search for a competitive advantage, say!
See also COMPETITIVE GAP; DISTRIBUTION GAP; EXISTING PRODUCT CHANGES; GAP ANALYSIS; PRODUCT (OR SERVICE) GAP; USAGE GAP

market growth rate *see* BOSTON MATRIX

marketing audit The first step in the marketing planning process is that of conducting the market audit. Ideally, at the time of producing the marketing plan, this should only involve bringing together the source material that has already been collected, throughout the year, as part of the normal work of the marketing department. Kotler et al. (1977) define it, rather at length, as follows: 'A marketing audit is a comprehensive, systematic, independent and periodic examination of a company's – or business unit's – marketing environment, objectives, strategies, and activities with a view to determining problem areas and opportunities and recommending a plan of action to improve the company's marketing performance.'

While some organizations have successfully employed external consultants to conduct such audits, generally speaking they are best undertaken by the management who 'own' the marketing process. This is partly because they are the best people to understand the subtleties of the information revealed (always assuming that they have managed to cast aside their preconceptions and prejudices). Even more important, though, the audit is the best possible learning process for these managers, introducing them to the factors that are most important to their management of marketing. Finally, and most important of all, it ensures that those who will have to implement the results of the planning process understand, and are committed to, the assumptions that lie behind it. Indeed, this material will have been best organized as a 'facts book' or 'facts library'. As such, it will have been organized so that facts pertaining to any issue can be easily and rapidly extracted. As part of this process, a degree of analysis may well have already begun, as key elements are highlighted.

The emphasis at this stage is on obtaining a complete and accurate picture. In a single organization, however, it is likely that only a few aspects will be sufficiently important to have any significant impact on the marketing plan – but all of them may need to be reviewed to determine just which are the few important ones. In this context, some factors related to the customer, which should be included in the material collected for the audit, may be as follows:

• Who are the customers?
• What are their key characteristics?
• What differentiates them from other members of the population?
• What are their needs and wants?
• What do they expect the 'product' to do?
• What are their special requirements and perceptions?
• What do they think of the organization and its products or services?
• What are their attitudes?
• What are their buying intentions?

A 'traditional' (albeit 'product-based') format for a 'brand reference book' (or, indeed, a 'marketing facts book') is suggested by Godley (1975):

1. *Financial data* – Facts for this section will come from management accounting, costing and finance sections.
2. *Product data* – From production, research and development.
3. *Sales and distribution data* – Sales, packaging, distribution sections.
4. *Advertising, sales promotion, merchandising data* – Information from these departments.
5. *Market data and miscellany* – From market research, who would in most cases act as a source for this information.

His sources of data, however, assume the resources of a very large organization. In most organizations they would be obtained from a much smaller set of people (and many of them would be generated by the marketing manager alone).

It is apparent that a marketing audit can be a complex process, but the aim is simple; it is only to identify those existing (external and internal) factors that will have a significant impact on the future plans of the company. It is clear that the basic material to be inputted into the marketing audit should be comprehensive. Accordingly, the best approach is to accumulate this material continuously, as and when it becomes available as part of normal work; since this avoids the otherwise heavy workload involved in collecting it as part of the regular, typically annual, planning process itself – when time is usually at a premium. Even so, the first task of this 'annual' process should be to check that the material held in the current 'facts book' or 'facts files' actually is comprehensive and accurate – and can form a sound basis for the marketing audit itself.

The structure of the 'facts book' will be designed to match the specific needs of the organization, but one simple format – suggested by Malcolm McDonald (1984) – may be applicable in many cases. This splits the material into three groups:

1. *Review of the marketing environment* – a study of the organization's markets, customers, competitors and the overall economic, political, cultural and technical environment; covering developing trends, as well as the current situation.
2. *Review of the detailed marketing activity* – a study of the company's marketing mix; in terms of the 4 Ps – product, price, promotion and place.
3. *Review of the marketing system* – a study of the marketing organization, marketing research systems and the current marketing objectives and strategies.

The last section is one that is too frequently ignored. The marketing system itself needs to be regularly questioned, for the validity of the whole marketing plan is reliant upon the accuracy of the input from this system – and 'garbage in garbage out' applies with a vengeance.

To these, Kotler et al. (1977) add two further (more 'bureaucratic', but nevertheless important) audits:

• *Marketing productivity audit* – to see where marketing costs could be reduced.
• *Marketing function audit* – to identify weaknesses.

See also MARKETING PLANNING, ANALYSIS; MARKETING PLAN STRUCTURE; PLANNING PROCESS; POTSA PLANNING; SWOT ANALYSIS

References: Godley, C. G. A. (1975) Market research. In E. F. L. Brech (ed.), *Principles and Practice of Management*. London: Longman.
    Kotler, Philip, Gregor, William T. and Rodgers, William H., III (1977) The marketing audit comes of age. *Sloan Management Review*.
    McDonald, Malcolm H. B. (1984) *Marketing Plans*. London: Heinemann.

marketing budget   *see* BUDGETS

marketing concept   *see* ORGANIZATIONAL (MARKETING) ORIENTATIONS

marketing costs   *see* MARKETING AUDIT

marketing decision support systems   *see* MARKETING INTELLIGENCE SYSTEMS (MIS)

marketing definitions   The classic Western definition, summarized by Philip Kotler (1976), is 'Marketing is human activity directed at satisfying needs and wants through exchange processes.'

It is a complex issue, however – as are many such apparently simple topics in marketing. Even Kotler, who is one of the acknowledged leaders of marketing theory, found the subject increasingly complex; for by the sixth edition of the book (1988) his definition had been elaborated to 'Marketing is a social and managerial process by which individuals and groups obtain what they need and want through creating and exchanging products and value with others.'

In the UK, a very similar definition is given by the Chartered Institute of Marketing: 'Marketing is the management process responsible for identifying, anticipating and satisfying customer requirements profitably.'

Marketing theory, like much of other business theory, is far from an exact science. Peter Bennett

(1988), for instance, suggests that 'A societal marketing orientation adds an additional consideration to the marketing concept: the impact of a firm's activities on society.'

The key element of all marketing is that, unlike almost all other business activities, it is outward-looking; it is firmly centred on the customer. This is sometimes – rather perversely, given the perspective of the management involved – described as the 'outside-in' view. It is described particularly well in these terms by Gareth Morgan (1988), who requires that the managers involved should adopt the perspective of looking (with the customer's-eye view) from the outside, inwards towards the organization itself. The concepts (if not all of the details) may be applied to almost all types of organization, even to those not-for-profit organizations that have traditionally seen themselves as set apart from normal commercial processes. The needs and wants of the 'customer' (or 'client') should almost always be paramount. The difference and the difficulty, for such organizations, is to decide who are their customers (clients) – and what their needs and wants are.

Peter Drucker (1964) stated the position even more comprehensively: 'Every business can be defined as serving either customers or markets or end-users.'

See also MARKETING DEFINITIONS, EUROPEAN; MARKETING DEFINITIONS, JAPANESE; MARKETING DEFINITIONS, PHILOSOPHY OF BUSINESS VERSUS A BUSINESS FUNCTION

References: Bennett, Peter D. (1988) *Marketing.* New York: McGraw-Hill.
    Drucker, Peter F. (1964) *Managing for Results.* London: Heinemann.
    Kotler, P. (1976) *Marketing Management* (3rd edn). Englewood Cliffs, NJ: Prentice-Hall.
    Kotler, P. (1988) *Marketing Management* (6th edn). Englewood Cliffs, NJ: Prentice-Hall.
    Morgan, Gareth (1988) *Riding the Waves of Change.* San Francisco: Jossey-Bass.

marketing definitions, European   Most definitions of marketing fail to emphasize the long-term aspect of marketing; that of building long-term relationships (or even partnerships) with customers. Christian Grönroos (1990), however, summarized recent European developments in his definition: 'Marketing is to establish, maintain and enhance long-term customer relationships at a profit, so that the objectives of the parties involved are met. This is done by mutual exchange and fulfilment of promises.'

Reference: Grönroos, Christian (1990) Marketing redefined. *Management Decision*, 28(8).

marketing definitions, Japanese   Kenichi Ohmae (1982) says, of Japanese business strategy in general, 'What business strategy is about – what distinguishes it from all other kinds of business planning – is, in a word, competitive advantage. Without competitors there would be no need for strategy, for the sole purpose of strategic planning is to enable the company to gain, as efficiently as possible, a sustainable edge over its competitors.' To some Western ears, this is a very aggressive interpretation (even if it does chime with the widely accepted views of Michael Porter), and it does not directly mention the 'customer' at all. But, even here, 'competition' implies that the customer is king; since he, and he alone, can decide the winner of the competition. However, this is probably an overstatement. Kotler and Fahey (1982) make the important observation that 'Japanese marketing strategy, strangely enough, is not based on the discovery of new and fresh marketing principles. Japan's secret is that they thoroughly understand and apply the existing textbook principles. The Japanese came to the United States to study marketing and went home understanding its principles better than most US companies did.'

References: Kotler, Philip and Fahey, Liam (1982) The world's champion marketers. *The Japanese Journal of Business Strategy*, 3(1).
    Ohmae, K. (1982) *The Mind of the Strategist.* New York: McGraw-Hill.
    Porter, Michael E. (1980) *Competitive Strategy.* New York: The Free Press.

marketing definitions, philosophy of business versus a business function   Michael Baker (1985) points out one frequent source of confusion, when he states that 'marketing is both a philosophy of business and a business function . . . a state of mind concerning the optimum approach to business, and the activities whereby such ideas are translated into practice . . .'. He also widens coverage of the activities (though not the viewpoint) even further when he suggests that:

. . . real marketing has four essential features:
1.   Start with the customer.
2.   A long-run perspective.
3.   Full use of all the company's resources.
4.   Innovation.

His is a particularly wide-ranging specification, covering activities to which other disciplines (corporate strategy in particular) would also lay claim.

Reference: Baker, Michael J. (1985) *Marketing Strategy and Management.* London: Macmillan.

marketing dimensions   *see* ORGANIZATIONAL
PIGEON-HOLES

marketing environment   *see* CONTINGENCY
PLAN; MARKETING AUDIT

marketing expense to sales ratio   *see*
MONITORING, PROGRESS

Marketing Intelligence Systems (MIS)   In recent years, and in particular since the widening availability of computerized databases, the whole process
of collecting and distributing marketing information
has become systematized. The system that handles
these processes in a controlled and coordinated fashion has come to be called the 'Marketing Intelligence
System' or 'Marketing Information System' (MIS) –
which is slightly confusing, since the more widely
implemented Management Information Systems (of
which the marketing element is just a part) also go by
the acronym 'MIS'! However, such a system can be
very simple – and is often most effectively used in
these simplest of forms. In this context, it is just the
systematic collection and organization of the 'data'
that are relevant to the needs of the marketer.

Philip Kotler (1988) defines a Marketing Information System somewhat elaborately (but comprehensively) thus:

> A marketing information system is a continuing
> and interacting structure of people, equipment
> and procedures to gather, sort, analyze, evaluate,
> and distribute pertinent, timely, and accurate in-
> formation for use by marketing decision makers to
> improve their marketing planning, implementa-
> tion, and control.

Much of this information is already held in most
organizations. On the other hand, without an organized Marketing Intelligence System it is often only to
be found in a fragmented and uncoordinated form. It
is thus claimed, by supporters of MIS approaches,
that adopting a systems approach to information requirements – which does not have to be computer-
based – can provide managements with banks of data
that are oriented to their particular information
needs.

The value of marketing information is having the
right information available (to generate the right intelligence – to solve a marketing problem) at the right
time. Even so, it is all too easy to be over-ambitious.
It is important to be able to control, and hence use,
the monster that you may be creating; particularly
if you choose the computer route, where the main

danger may be that you become a servant of the
computer rather than the other way around.

In particular, this may potentially pose the problem of 'information overload'. There will be so much
information, most of it redundant (and definitely not
pertinent), that it will effectively be useless as a management tool. If it cannot be used, more information
is not necessarily a boon.

There are a number of possible answers to this
potential torrent of data:

- ABC analysis
- variance analysis
- *ad hoc* database enquiries and reports

Perhaps the most important new use of MIS data on
the large scale is in 'precision marketing', where the
resulting knowledge of small groups of customers (or
even of individuals) is used to target promotional
efforts very accurately. As the systems become more
sophisticated they are being referred to as 'Marketing Decision Support Systems', which are more
versatile, interacting with users (and offering 'what
if . . .' questions).

See also ABC ANALYSIS; *AD HOC* DATABASE ENQUIRIES
AND REPORTS; PRECISION MARKETING; VARIANCE
ANALYSIS

Reference: Kotler, P. (1988) *Marketing Management* (6th
edn). Englewood Cliffs, NJ: Prentice-Hall.

Marketing Management (book by Philip
Kotler)   Historically, this is probably the most influential book in the field of marketing, first published in 1967. It influenced a whole generation
of marketers. The book is firmly rooted in the approach of the 1970s, but is none the worse for that –
especially where the techniques it describes are
now returning to favour. Philip Kotler has also
written another, more general, marketing textbook,
Principles of Marketing.

References: Kotler, Philip (1967) *Marketing Management*.
Englewood Cliffs, NJ: Prentice-Hall.
   Kotler, Philip *Principles of Marketing*. Englewood Cliffs,
NJ: Prentice-Hall.

marketing mix   This is the term given to the
overall 'bundle' of marketing activities applied to a
given product or service. It comprises a number of
elements, which are usually considered separately.
The first is the product, or service, itself. This is
ultimately what the customer will decide on, and will
then determine whether it matches his or her needs.
As far as possible, therefore, the marketer must

match the 'product' to those needs. This may be accomplished by radically changing the product, or just changing its features or its packaging; or even by describing it in a different way. It is a complex process. But the whole aim of marketing is to match those customers' needs.

The second aspect is the delivery system. The producer must get the product or service to the customer, and even before that he or she must get the message of the product to the prospective purchaser or client.

There are a number of ways in which these separate aspects may be described, or categorized. Many business schools use the framework of the four Ps (as proposed by E. Jerome McCarthy, 1981) to group marketing activities.

See also INTERNATIONAL PRODUCT DECISION; LIFE CYCLES AND THE MARKETING MIX; MARKETING AUDIT; PROMOTIONAL LOZENGE; 3 Ps; 4 Ps; PUBLIC RELATIONS; TEST MARKET

Reference: McCarthy, E. Jerome (1981) *Basic Marketing: a Managerial Approach.* Boston, MA: Richard D. Irwin.

marketing mix and promotion All promotion must be seen in the context of the whole marketing mix. Promotion is just one of the four Ps. Price and place may be just as important, and certainly make their own impacts on any promotion. A high-price product sold through specialist outlets will demand a very different form of promotion to that of a cut-price brand sold through supermarkets. In addition, the most important element of the marketing mix must almost always be the product or service itself. Despite the popular misconceptions, it is a hard fact of advertising life that consumers will not buy – at least not more than once – a product or service that does not meet their needs, no matter how persuasive the promotion. At the same time, the form of the promotion itself, the message and even the medium, may be largely determined by the specification of that product or service. Thus, by defining the product, you largely define the whole marketing mix. In this way, then, all of the elements of the marketing mix (all four Ps) contribute to the overall promotion of a product or service or company; and the 'input' into promotion may come from areas even further afield.

See also ADVERTISING; SELLING

marketing models *see* MODELS

marketing myopia Theodore Levitt (1969), in his very influential article, stated that:

The viewpoint that an industry is a customer-satisfying process, not a goods-producing process, is vital for all businessmen to understand. An industry begins with the customer and his needs, not with a patent, a raw material, or a selling skill. Given the customer's needs the industry develops backwards, first concerning itself with the physical delivery of customer satisfactions. Then it moves back further to creating the things by which these satisfactions are in part achieved. How these materials are created is a matter of indifference to the customer, hence the particular form of manufacturing, processing, or what-have-you cannot be considered as a vital aspect of the marketing.

His reason for this emphasis, supported by considerable anecdotal evidence in the rest of the article, was that most organizations defined their business perspectives (now often referred to as 'corporate missions') too narrowly; typically on the basis of the technological processes that they employed (but, at best, upon internal factors). His view, which was enthusiastically seized upon by the more adventurous organizations, was that the link with the consumer – the 'customer franchise' – was the most important element. The corporate vision must, therefore, be defined in terms of the customer's needs and wants.

The adoption of a wider perspective helped many organizations better to appreciate how they could develop; and to avoid the problems that had, for instance, beset those locked into the business of supplying electric streetcars! Some organizations, however, took the process very literally. It is arguable, indeed, that this viewpoint (compounded by the Boston Consulting Group's work on 'portfolio management') led to the rapid increase in mergers and acquisitions at the beginning of the 1970s. Indeed, it is worth noting that such merger and acquisition activities must be considered as viable alternatives to traditional marketing developments.

On the other hand, Levitt himself recognized the danger of the possible over-reactions in his later book (1983), where he added the comment, 'Marketing Myopia was not intended as analysis or even prescription; it was intended as manifesto. It did not pretend to take a balanced position. . . . My scheme, however, tied marketing more closely to the inner orbit of business policy.' The last sentence is perhaps the best comment on the true importance of his contribution.

See also VISION, CORPORATE

Reference: Levitt, Theodore (1969) Marketing myopia. *Harvard Business Review*, July–August.

Levitt, Theodore (1983) *The Marketing Imagination.* New York: The Free Press.

marketing objectives   These state where the company intends to be at some time in the future. James Quinn (1980) succinctly defines objectives in general as follows: 'Goals (or objectives) state what is to be achieved and when results are to be accomplished, but they do not state how the results are to be achieved.' They typically relate to what products will be where in what markets (and must be realistically based on customer behaviour in those markets). They are essentially about the match between those products and markets. Objectives for pricing, distribution, advertising and so on are at a lower level, and should not be confused with marketing objectives. They are part of the marketing strategy needed to achieve marketing objectives. To be most effective, objectives should be capable of measurement, and therefore quantifiable.

It is conventionally assumed that marketing objectives will be designed to maximize volume or profit (or to optimize the utilization of resources in the non-profit sector), by creating demand or rejuvenating existing demand, say; although the various sub-objectives may indicate many different routes to achieving such optimization. However, as Kotler suggested (in the third edition of his book), there may be a number of other objectives, such as synchromarketing, demarketing or counter-marketing.

See also ADVERTISING PROCESSES; CORPORATE OBJECTIVES; COUNTER-MARKETING; DEMARKETING; MARKETING PLAN STRUCTURE; MARKETING STRATEGIES; MONITORING, PROGRESS; PLANNING PROCESS; POTSA PLANNING; SYNCHROMARKETING

References: Kotler, P. (1976) *Marketing Management* (3rd edn). Englewood Cliffs, NJ: Prentice-Hall.

Quinn, James Brian (1980) *Strategies for Change: Logical Incrementalism.* Boston, MA: Richard D. Irwin.

marketing plan   *see* PLANNING PROCESS

marketing plan benefits   The need for planning is now almost universally accepted by managers, even though it is not so widely implemented in practice. The use of such plans has a number of benefits, just some of which may be:

- *Consistency*. The individual action plans will then be consistent with the overall corporate plan; and with the other departmental/functional plans that should be put in place elsewhere in the organization. They should also be consistent with those of previous years, minimizing the risk of management 'fire-fighting'.
- *Responsibility*. Those who have responsibility for implementing the individual parts of the marketing plan will know what their responsibilities are – and can have their performance monitored.
- *Communication*. All of those involved in implementing the plans will also know what the overall objectives are, together with the assumptions that lie behind them, and what the context is for each of the detailed activities.
- *Commitment*. Assuming that the plans have been agreed with all those involved in their implementation, as well as with those who will provide the resources, the plans should stimulate a group commitment to their implementation.

See also PLANNING PROCESS

marketing planning, analysis   The analysis of material inputted into the planning process from the marketing audit will, no doubt, require significant effort. In the first instance it is a matter of selection – of sorting the wheat from the chaff. What is important, what will need to be taken into account in the marketing plan that will eventually emerge from the overall process, will be different for each product or service in each situation. One of the most important skills to be learned in marketing is that of being able to concentrate on just what *is* important. In addition, all of the usual analytical techniques can be applied; and should be applied where relevant. It is important to say not just what happened but why! The marketing planning process encompasses all of the marketing skills. A number of these may, however, be particularly relevant at this stage:

- *Positioning*. The starting point of the marketing plan must be the consumer. It is a matter of definition that his or her needs should drive the whole marketing process. The techniques of positioning and segmentation therefore usually offer the best starting point for what has to be achieved by the whole planning process.
- *Portfolio planning*. In addition, the coordinated planning of the individual products and services can contribute towards the balanced portfolio.
- *80:20 rule*. To achieve the maximum impact, the marketing plan must be clear and concise – and simple. It needs to concentrate on the 20 per cent

of products or services, and on the 20 per cent of customers, that will account for 80 per cent of the volume and 80 per cent of the 'profit'.

- *Four Ps.* The four Ps can result in sometimes attention being diverted from the customer; but the framework that they offer can be very useful in building the action plans.

See also MARKETING AUDIT; MARKETING OBJECTIVES; MONITORING, PROGRESS; PLANNING PROCESS; POTSA PLANNING

marketing plans and programmes Having decided your marketing strategies, you will need to convert these into detailed plans and programmes. Although these detailed plans may cover each of the four Ps, the focus will vary, depending upon your organization's specific strategies. A product-oriented company will focus its plans for the four Ps around each of its products. A market- or geography-oriented company will concentrate on each market or geographical area. Each will base its plans upon the detailed needs of its customers, and on the strategies chosen to satisfy these needs. The most important element is, indeed, that of the detailed plans, which spell out exactly what programmes and individual activities will take place over the period of the plan (usually over the next year). Without these specified – and preferably quantified – activities, the plan cannot be monitored (even in terms of success in meeting its objectives), and is just so much wishful thinking, so much hot air. It is these programmes and activities that will then constitute the 'marketing' of the organization over the period. As a result, these detailed marketing programmes are the most important, practical outcome of the whole planning process. These plans should therefore be:

- *Clear.* They should be an unambiguous statement of exactly what is to be done.
- *Quantified.* The predicted outcome of each activity should be, as far as possible, quantified; so that its performance can be monitored.
- *Focused.* The temptation to allow activities to proliferate beyond the numbers that can realistically be controlled should be avoided. The 80:20 rule applies in this context too. Bonoma and Crittenden (1988), reporting the results of their research into marketing implementation, noted that 'The number of marketing programs in a firm, compared to relevant competitors, will be inversely related to the quality of marketing practices observed.'

- *Realistic.* They should be achievable.
- *Agreed.* Those who are to implement them should be committed to them, and should agree that they are achievable.

The resulting plans should become a working document that will guide the campaigns taking place throughout the organization over the period of the plan. If the marketing plan is to work, every exception to it (throughout the year) must be incorporated; and the lessons learned, from why the deviation was justified, to be incorporated in the next year's plan. It is at this stage that all the various elements of the plan – from objectives to strategies to detailed plans – are finally brought together.

See also CORPORATE OBJECTIVES; MARKETING STRATEGIES; PLANNING PROCESS; POTSA PLANNING

Reference: Bonoma, Thomas V. and Crittenden, Victoria L. (1988) Managing marketing implementation. *Sloan Management Review*, Winter.

marketing plan structure The marketing plan itself should be formalized as a written document; but, in practice, too few companies take this stage seriously enough. The shape that this document takes will depend upon the exact requirements of the business. It might, however, contain the following sections:

(a) *Executive summary* – a short summary of the proposed plan, partly to provide the perspective for the rest and partly as a quick reference.

(b) *Marketing audit summary* – a brief summary of the very detailed marketing audit that will have taken place. This should not be a large section. If it is necessary for management to understand the complexities of the information uncovered in the audit, this should be accomplished in a previous, separate, document.

(c) *Audit (SWOT) analysis* – this must also be brief, and should concentrate on the few critical issues that are addressed by the strategies and plans that come later in the document.

(d) *Marketing objectives* – in as much detail as is needed.

(e) *Marketing strategy* – again in as much detail as is necessary to convey this most important element of the plan.

(f) *Action programmes* – the plans themselves, stating 'what will be done', 'who will do it', 'when it will be done' and 'how much it will cost'.

Malcolm McDonald (1984) suggests a rather more specific layout (to be prepared for each Strategic

Business Unit, or SBU), with rather more emphasis on the analytical elements, which the simple approach recommended above assumes will have already have been largely covered by preceding documents:

1. Mission Statement
2. Summary of Performance [to date, including reasons for good or bad performance]
3. Summary of Financial Projections [for three years]
4. Market Overview
5. SWOT Analyses of Major Projects/Markets
6. Portfolio Summary [a summary of SWOTs]
7. Assumptions
8. Setting Objectives
9. Financial Projections for Three Years [in detail]

More importantly, he deliberately separates this three-year strategic marketing plan (sometimes just called the 'strategy') from the one-year operating plan (often what is called the 'marketing plan' itself), which is derived from the strategic plan (but only after this has been approved).

His suggested format for this one-year plan includes the following:

1. Summary of Strategic Plan – Overall Objectives [in numerical terms] and Overall Strategies
2. Resulting Annual 'Strategies' – Sub-Objectives [relating to specific products, markets, segments or customers] and Strategies [the means by which these will be achieved] Actions/Tactics
3. Summary of Marketing Activities and Costs
4. Contingency Plans
5. Operating Results and Financial Ratios
6. Key Activity Planner

It can be seen from this list that the short-term (one-year) plan should concentrate on very specific and quantifiable actions. Indeed, he provides a very useful set of 'forms' that can be filled in to create most of this plan.

See also CORPORATE OBJECTIVES; MARKETING PLAN; MARKETING PLANS AND PROGRAMMES; MARKETING STRATEGIES; PLANNING PROCESS; POTSA PLANNING

Reference: McDonald, Malcolm H. B. (1984) *Marketing Plans*. London: Heinemann.

marketing plan use   A formal, written marketing plan is essential; in that it provides an unambiguous reference point for activities throughout the planning period. Perhaps the most important benefit of these plans is, however, the planning process itself. This typically offers a unique opportunity, a forum, for 'information-rich' and productively focused discussions between the various managers involved. The plan, together with the associated discussions, then provides an agreed context for their subsequent management activities – even for those not described in the plan itself. Igor Ansoff (1984) contrasts the Western and Japanese approaches to implementation, showing how the latter (albeit spending more effort on the planning stages – but, even then, not taking any longer in elapsed time, by running this work in parallel) can reduce the implementation stages dramatically:

The Western model:

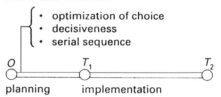

{
• optimization of choice
• decisiveness
• serial sequence

O T_1 T_2

planning   implementation

Results: • quick decisions
     • long action cycle
     • resistance to planning
     • implementation delays/frustrations

The Japanese model:

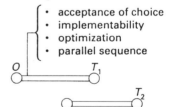

{
• acceptance of choice
• implementability
• optimization
• parallel sequence

O T_1 T_2

Results • longer decisions
     • shorter action cycle
     • co-operative planning ('ringo')
     • supportive implementation

See also CORPORATE OBJECTIVES; MARKETING PLANS AND PROGRAMMES; MARKETING STRATEGIES; PLANNING PROCESS; POTSA PLANNING

Reference: Ansoff, H. Igor (1984) *Implanting Strategic Management*. Englewood Cliffs, NJ: Prentice-Hall.

marketing process *see* MARKETING PLANNING, ANALYSIS

marketing research The most generally recognized aspect of marketing (or market) research is that conducted on consumers/customers (usually on a sample, and by professional interviewers). The stereotype is the market research interviewer standing on the street corner, approaching passers-by, or walking the streets, clipboard in hand, calling from door to door. In fact, far more research is now undertaken by mail surveys, and even then this probably represents only a very small part of the data available to any organization. However, it is particularly important data (since it often provides the only true 'listening' part of the dialogue with the consumer). In the main, it is a process undertaken by consumer goods companies. Despite lower levels of usage in some fields, marketing research should be seen to be just as important for all organizations (since, for all of them, it often represents the only available, and reliable, 'contact' with the consumer or end-user). It is particularly important, indeed, for not-for-profit organizations; since their 'cultural' problems, in coming to terms with client needs, mean that the best possible research is needed to counteract these inherent tendencies.

See also ACCURACY, OF MARKETING RESEARCH RESULTS; ANALYSIS OF MARKETING RESEARCH DATA; CONSULTANCIES, AND MARKETING RESEARCH; CUSTOM RESEARCH; EXPERIMENTAL RESEARCH; EXTERNAL DATA; GROUP RESEARCH; INDIVIDUAL DEPTH INTERVIEWS; INDUSTRIAL MARKETING RESEARCH; INTERNATIONAL MARKETING RESEARCH; MARKETING RESEARCH STAGES; MARKETING STRATEGIES; MOTIVATION RESEARCH; OBSERVATION, RESEARCH; OMNIBUS SURVEYS; PANEL RESEARCH; QUALITATIVE RESEARCH; REPERTORY GRID; RESEARCH DIAMOND; RESEARCH PLANNING RETAIL AUDITS; SERVICES AND MARKETING RESEARCH; SUBCONTRACTORS, MARKETING RESEARCH; SUPPLIERS OF MARKETING RESEARCH; SURVEY RESEARCH

marketing research costs Over recent decades, much of the market research industry has almost become a commodity market. Price has been all. Clients have placed business with agencies (and agencies with their subcontractors) almost entirely on the basis of the lowest price tendered, with little regard to the quality of the work (on the, often incorrect, assumption that quality was guaranteed and was the same for all of the proposals). The standard of such 'commodity-based' work has, therefore, declined, both in quality (of the controllable factors of the research) and in creativity (this is one of the reasons why the techniques have not advanced significantly over the period). The wise 'buyer' of marketing research needs, therefore, to be aware of what quality (and creative) aspects he or she wants to see guaranteed in the 'product' that is being bought.

See also APPOINTING A MARKETING RESEARCH AGENCY; MARKETING RESEARCH; SAMPLING; SURVEY RESEARCH

marketing research objectives Defining the objectives is the most important stage of almost all market research, and the one at which the research is most likely to be misdirected. Only the client can know what he or she wants the research to investigate; although an expert from the market research organization is usually involved before the research itself takes place – to translate the client's ideas into a framework that will be most suitable for that research. Indeed, the sooner a market research expert is involved, the better. Without his or her expertise, it is all too easy to unwittingly introduce bias that will skew the final results. The objectives need to be clear and clearly stated (so that the researcher understands them). They need to be unambiguous. On the other hand, they should not prejudge the issue. Most market research fails because it is merely asked to confirm the existing theories of the commissioning organization. This can result in errors of commission (the questions can be slanted to produce the answers that the organization expects or wants). A good market research agency should, however, detect such bias and remove it. More difficult to deal with are the errors of omission (key questions that are never asked), and this is a problem that few market research organizations would be in a position to detect. Market research is usually expensive in terms of the resources deployed by the commissioning organization and its market research agencies. It can be much more expensive (even if savings have been made on the research itself) if the results are wrong, and stimulate actions that are correspondingly wrong! Therefore, this initial stage of defining the objectives should never be skimped.

See also MARKETING RESEARCH; MARKETING RESEARCH STAGES

marketing research, precision marketing Over recent years, there has been a growing awareness that the broad averages typically used in marketing hide considerable variations in terms of specific groups. At one level, this has been explored by very large surveys (such as TGI, Target Group Index, run by MRB, who interview 24 000 people each year), which are statistically significant in terms of the smaller groups and allow, for example, the complementary relationships between different brands (as well as their relation to quite specific lifestyle groups) to be investigated. At another level, the geographical dimension has been developed by organizations (such as ACORN and PIMS in the UK) that have categorized local neighbourhoods, so that suppliers can target specific groups with greater accuracy. As John Whitehead (1990) describes, 'Neighbourhood classifications have spawned a whole portfolio of techniques that are able to dissect markets in great detail. Geodemographics is used primarily to analyse customer addresses and market research data; to target door-to-door advertising; and in the use of census and other demographic data to describe and model markets locally.' He goes on, though, to describe the most recent developments which (in the UK) link this data with lifestyle data: for instance, 'CCN Marketing, linking up with National Shoppers Survey, has launched Persona, a "behaviourgraphic classification", defining electoral roll households by categories such as "Bon Viveurs" and "Wildlife Trustees", which relate to consumers' priorities and lifestyles.'

See also PRECISION MARKETING

Reference: Whitehead, John (1990) Paying attention to detail. *Marketing*, 22 February.

marketing research stages   The six stages that are most generally followed in setting up and conducting programmes of marketing research are:

* defining the objectives
* planning the research
* collecting the data
* analysing the results
* interpreting the findings
* reporting the findings

See also ANALYSIS OF MARKETING RESEARCH DATA; DATA COLLECTION; MARKETING RESEARCH; MARKETING RESEARCH OBJECTIVES; REPORTING RESEARCH FINDINGS; RESEARCH PLANNING

marketing research subcontractors   *see* SUBCONTRACTORS, MARKETING RESEARCH

marketing services manager   *see* ADVERTISING MANAGER

marketing skills   *see* PEOPLE (SALES) MANAGEMENT

marketing strategies   There are numerous definitions (and as many misdefinitions) of what strategy is, but James Quinn (1980) gives a succinct general definition: 'A strategy is a pattern or plan that integrates an organization's major goals, policies and action sequences into a cohesive whole.' He goes on to explain his view of the role of 'policies', with which strategy is most often confused: 'Policies are rules or guidelines that express the limits within which action should occur.' Even then, his co-editor in another handbook, Henry Mintzberg (1988), adds 'Human nature is such that we tend to insist on a definition for every concept. But perhaps we fool ourselves, pretending that concepts such as strategy can be reduced to a single definition. . . . Let us, therefore, propose five formal definitions of strategy – as plan, ploy, pattern, position and perspective . . .'. Simplifying somewhat, therefore, marketing strategies can be seen as the means, or 'game plan', by which marketing objectives will be achieved and, in the framework we have chosen to use, are generally concerned with the four Ps. Examples are:

* *Product* – developing new products, repositioning or relaunching existing ones, scrapping old ones; adding new features and benefits; balancing product portfolios; changing the design or packaging.
* *Price* – setting the price to skim or to penetrate; pricing for different market segments; deciding how to meet competitive pricing.
* *Promotion* – specifying the advertising platform and media; deciding the public relations brief; organizing the sales force to cover new products or services or markets.
* *Place* – choosing the channels; deciding levels of customer service.

These strategies describe, in principle, the 'how'; how the objectives will be achieved. The four Ps are a useful framework for deciding how the company's resources will be manipulated (strategically) to achieve the objectives. It should be noted, however, that they are not the only framework and may divert attention from the real issues (if they are followed too rigorously). The focus of the strategies must be the objectives to be achieved – not the process of planning itself. Only if it fits the needs of these objectives should you choose to use, as we have done here, the four Ps framework.

The strategy statement can take the form of a purely verbal description of the strategic options that have been chosen. Alternatively, and perhaps more positively, it might include a structured list of the major options chosen, such as:

- target market
- target segment
- position(s)
- product(s)
- price(s)
- channel(s)
- promotion – selling, advertising, sales promotion and PR
- marketing research

One aspect of strategy that is often overlooked is that of timing. It is often critical to determine exactly when is the best time for each element of the strategy to be implemented. Taking the right action at the wrong time can sometimes be almost as bad as taking the wrong action at the right time. Timing is, therefore, an essential part of any plan; and should normally appear as a schedule of planned activities.

Having completed this crucial stage of the planning process, you will need to re-check the feasibility of your objectives and strategies in terms of the market share, sales, costs, profits, etc. that these demand in practice. As in the rest of the marketing discipline, you will need to employ judgement, experience, market research or anything else that helps you to look at your conclusions from all possible angles.

James Quinn, more pragmatically, sees strategy emerging 'incrementally':

Strategy deals with the unknowable, not the uncertain. It involves forces of such great number, strength, and combinatory powers that one cannot predict events in a probabilistic sense. Hence logic dictates that one proceed flexibly and experimentally from broad concepts towards specific commitments, making the latter concrete as late as possible in order to narrow the bands of uncertainty and to benefit from the best available information. This is the process of 'logical incrementalism'.

See also BUDGETS; CORPORATE OBJECTIVES; GE (GENERAL ELECTRIC) MATRIX; MARKETING OBJECTIVES; MARKETING PLANS AND PROGRAMMES; MARKETING PLAN STRUCTURE; MARKETING TRIAD; PLANNING PROCESS; POTSA PLANNING; THREE CHOICE BOX; VISION, CORPORATE

References: Argenti, John (1974) *Systematic Corporate Planning.* London: Thomas Nelson.

Mintzberg, Henry (1988) Opening up the definition of strategy. In James Brian Quinn, Henry Mintzberg and Robert M. James (eds), *The Strategy Process: Concepts, Contexts and Cases.* Englewood Cliffs, NJ: Prentice-Hall.

Quinn, James Brian (1978) Strategies for change: logical incrementalism. *Sloan Management Review*, Fall.

Quinn, James Brian (1980) *Strategies for Change: Logical Incrementalism.* New York: Richard D. Irwin.

marketing support   *see* SALES PROFESSIONAL

marketing system   *see* MARKETING AUDIT

marketing triad   This graphical concept (not to be confused with Kenichi Ohmae's 'Triad' of global markets) is intended to bring together the main relationships in marketing:

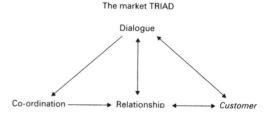

The market TRIAD

- *Dialogue* – to establish what the customer needs are, and to negotiate suitable solutions to them.
- *Relationship* – investment in the effective external exchanges necessary to optimize these solutions, in practice, to the mutual benefit of both sides.
- *Coordination* – management of internal operational resources across the whole organization in order to deliver this relationship.

See also CORPORATE PLAN; CORPORATE STRATEGY AND MARKETING; MARKETING DEFINITIONS; MARKETING STRATEGIES; PRODUCT (OR SERVICE) STRATEGY

market, internal   *see* INTERNAL MARKET

market leader knows best   *see* DEDICATED FOLLOWERS

market leader pricing   *see* COMPETITIVE PRICING; PRICE COMPETITION

market leaders   *see* MONITORING, PROGRESS

market life cycle   What is little appreciated is that the life cycle of the market, overall, may be different to that of a product within it:

- *Introductory stage*. This is, by definition, the same as that for the first 'generic' brand(s). The form that this takes will be decided by whether the initial supplier(s) decides upon a policy of 'skimming' or 'penetration'.
- *Growth stage*. This is frequently the stage at which further brands enter the market, in competition with the pioneer brands; although this does not necessarily result in price competition – since the market growth is usually enough to satisfy the ambitions of all of the managements involved.
- *Maturity*. This is the stage at which most markets are to be found. Their characters will, however, change as the various brand owners decide to differentiate their products and create segments or niches. It is, thus, the processes of segmentation and positioning/differentiation that dominate this stage, which in turn dominates the whole life cycle. These are processes that are rarely described in the literature of life cycles, which tends to look at the more interesting beginnings and endings (even though these are peripheral to most real-life marketing).
- *Saturation*. Despite those theorists who would insist that this is an inevitable stage of almost all life cycles, in real life this is not necessarily a stage that affects all markets. It should, indeed, be viewed more as a feature of competitive activity, which is independent of the life cycle. It simply reflects the fact that, for whatever reason (and there may be a number of these), there is more capacity than demand. This is, in fact, more likely to occur during the growth phase, when the vendors are unsure of the projected demand, than at maturity when they will have a sound knowledge of it. At maturity the stability is most likely to be destroyed by a (usually foolish) brand owner who wants to buy share.
- *Decline*. This stage often results in a reduction in the number of brands, perhaps back to just the single 'generic' brand, as the distributors limit the range of products that they are willing to stock. Once again, therefore, it closely parallels the pattern of the single brand.

market needs   *see* EMERGENT STRATEGY; VISION, CORPORATE

market opportunities   *see* BUDGETS

market orientation   *see* SELLING VERSUS MARKETING

market penetration   The most frequently used product strategy is to take the existing product (or service) in the existing market and try to obtain improved 'penetration' (or, more accurately, an increased share) of that market. There are two ways in which this can be achieved:

- increasing sales to existing customers
- finding new customers in the same market

In general, the former means persuading users to use more. This may be achieved by motivating them to use it on more occasions, perhaps by replacing an indirect competitor – for example, inducing a household to eat beans on toast an extra time each week, instead of fish fingers. It may, on the other hand, simply be to use the product more often without any need to take business from competitors; as Unilever used Timotei to promote the more regular shampooing of hair. Possibly, it may be to use more each time; promotions offering '30 per cent more free' may have, as one objective, the intention of persuading customers to get into the habit of using more – two spoonfuls of baked beans on their slice of toast rather than one.

The second category almost invariably relates to taking business directly from competitors, increasing both penetration and market share.

As such 'penetration' is the main objective of much of marketing, almost any of the four Ps can be brought into play. Product performance may be improved, price may be reduced, distribution may be extended, promotion may be increased, or the marketing mix as a whole may be restructured. All of these – singly or in combination – could be used to improve 'penetration'.

market portfolio management   *see* MARKET ENTRY DECISION

market positioning and segmentation   The interface between the consumer and the supplier is the 'market'. The 'position' chosen in that market, by the supplier, for the product or service – against the 'map' of consumer needs – defines all of the marketing actions thereafter. As such – and whether decided formally or by default – it lies at the heart of marketing. The initial stage, though, may be to 'segment' the market itself; to choose a smaller part, or segment, of that market, on which to concentrate the organization's resources – to gain control over the competitive position. However, the segment has to be viable; and sophisticated marketing research is needed to optimize the 'segmentation', against the most important needs and wants of consumers, as seen by them. Positioning/targeting then places the product or service in the optimal position mapped against the competitors, on the 'dimensions' that are most critical to users.

See also MARKETS; POSITIONING; SEGMENTATION

market potential   *see* USAGE GAP

market price   The (theoretical) price of a good set in an open market.
See also PRICE FACTORS

market research   *see* AUDIENCE RESEARCH; MARKETING AUDIT; MARKETING RESEARCH; MONITORING, PROGRESS; SELLING

market research agency selection   *see* AGENCY CHOICE

market research, cross-country   *see* INTERNATIONAL PRODUCT DECISION

Market Research Society   *see* INTERNATIONAL *AD HOC* RESEARCH

markets   To a producer or service provider, the most practical feature of a market is that it is 'where' the product or service is sold or delivered – and where the profits are generated. In earlier days, it actually was a physical location – the market square or hall – where the producer set up stall. Now it is just a name, which covers a wide range of systems and activities that connect the end-user to the producer. It is most obviously evidenced by the 'high-street' shopping areas in towns and cities. On the other hand, it can be defined in terms of the product or service (where the 'market' describes all the buyers and sellers, at the time, for that product or service) and this is the framework favoured by many economists – the automobile market, the money market, etc. It can also be defined geographically (Germany, the European Union, etc.) or even demographically (the teenage market, pensioners, etc.). The key for a marketer, however, should be that the market is always defined in terms of the customer. Philip Kotler (1988) sees buyers (actual and potential) as constituting the market, whereas sellers constitute the industry, and he defines it as follows: 'A

market consists of all the potential customers sharing a particular need or want who might be willing and able to engage in exchange to satisfy that need or want.' The market is, thus, the group of customers. However, it is, in many practical ways, still defined in the short term by the suppliers. They say, in effect, what is to be supplied to whom, and hence where the initial boundaries are to be set. After all, the consumer cannot make his or her wishes known if there is no suitable product on offer; and this lack of short-term feedback became a major long-term problem for the planned economies of Eastern Europe – hence one of the reasons for the enthusiasm for 'perestroika'. In the long run it is the customers, however, who will decide what the market really is, through their buying patterns. They set the boundaries, and by their purchases choose what products or services will remain in the market. The inevitable outcome is that to understand the market, the producer must understand the customer. This is why market research is so important – it provides the cornerstone for effective marketing. The more the supplier can know of the customer, the more that can be known of the market, and the greater the degree of control which may be exerted. The basis of sound marketing practice is the ability to identify with the customer or client, to be able to adopt the consumer's viewpoint.

See also CUSTOMERS; MARKET BOUNDARIES; NOT-FOR-PROFIT ORGANIZATIONS AND THE MARKET; POSITIONING; PROSPECTS; SEGMENTATION; USERS

Reference: Kotler, P. (1988) *Marketing Management* (6th edn). Englewood Cliffs, NJ: Prentice-Hall.

market segments   *see* SEGMENTS OF MARKETS

market share   *see* BRAND (OR MARKET) SHARE; MARKETING OBJECTIVES; MARKETING STRATEGIES; MONITORING, PROGRESS

market size   *see* USAGE GAP

market socialism   A socialist economy in which, however, most of the microeconomic issues are left to market forces.

market splitting   *see* PRICE CHALLENGE REACTIONS

market test   *see* TEST MARKET

market usage   *see* USAGE GAP

market value pricing   *see* MARKET-BASED PRICING

market versus product life cycle   In the literature, and amongst practitioners, there is considerable
confusion between the life cycle for the product
and that for the market; and frequently the two are
used interchangeably. In some, typically new, markets this confusion is understandable, since the
pattern of growth of the market follows that of the
main brands, until maturity of the market is reached
– and in some markets even the subsequent decline
phases parallel each other (as the products in the
market are superseded by those in the new market).
Even in well-established markets, the emergence of
major new products often creates new segments, the
life cycle of which parallels that of the new entrants.
Even so, the two must be separated: many of the
features that are described in the literature (especially those of price competition) supposedly relate
to the stage of development of the market as a whole
– but some, such as salesforce activity, relate to the
product. In addition, while the product life cycle is of
most direct significance to the supplier, the market
life cycle is likely to be much more important for
the other participants in the marketing process,
especially the retailers.

Markov switching model   *see* BRAND-SWITCHING
MODEL ('MARKOV')

Marks & Spencer   *see* CORPORATE PROMOTION
VERSUS BRAND PROMOTION

Marlboro cigarette brand   *see* CONVICTION
MARKETING; CONVICTION MARKETING FACTORS;
CONVICTION MARKETING TYPES; GLOBALIZATION;
GLOBAL MARKETING

married print   A print of a film in which the
visual and sound track elements (which are kept
separate until the final edit) are married together on
one film.

Mars   *see* STANDARDIZATION VERSUS ADAPTATION

mask   This is used to cover up the parts of a photograph that are not wanted.

Maslow's Hierarchy of Needs   Perhaps the most
widely quoted approach to psychological influences
on the purchase decision is that of Abraham Maslow
(1954), who developed a hierarchy of 'needs', ranging from the most essential, immediate physical
needs to the most luxuriously inessential:

- self-actualization needs (self-development and
  realization)
- esteem needs (self-esteem, recognition, status)
- social needs (sense of belonging, love)
- safety needs (security, protection)
- physiological needs (hunger, thirst)

These were developed in the context of the individual's employment, but they can also be seen to apply to
the other aspects of the individual's developing lifestyle.

Maslow's contention was that the individual addresses the most urgent needs first, starting with the
physiological. But as each is satisfied, and the lower
level physical needs are (at least in terms of modern
affluence) soon satiated, the attention switches to the
next higher level; resulting ultimately in achievement of the level of 'self-actualization'. It is argued
that marketers are increasingly required to address
their attentions to the two highest levels; and, even
in the near future, almost exclusively to those of
'self-actualization'.

See also CULTURES, INFLUENCES ON THE PURCHASE
DECISION; DECISION-MAKING PROCESS, BY CUSTOMERS;
PSYCHOLOGICAL INFLUENCES, ON THE PURCHASE DECI-
SION; REPEAT PURCHASING PROCESS; SOCIAL CLASS IN-
FLUENCES, ON THE PURCHASE DECISION

Reference: Maslow, Abraham (1954) *Motivation and
Personality.* New York: Harper & Row.

mass mailings   *see* DIRECT MAIL ADVERTISING

mass marketing   *see* SEGMENTATION APPROACHES;
SERVICE CULTURES

mass media   *see* OPINION LEADERS; TELEVISION

master schedule   *see* MATERIALS REQUIREMENTS
PLANNING (MRP)

master/servant relationship   *see* SUPPLIERS

masthead   *see* FUDGE

matched test markets   *see* TEST MARKET

match (for not-for-profit organizations)   In
the non-profit context, the measure most frequently
suggested as a replacement for 'profit' appears to be
'match'. Thus, the not-for-profit organization seeks,
or should seek (if it is not overwhelmed by its bureaucracy), to best match use of its resources to the
needs of its customers or clients. In this context,

marketing is a means of optimizing this 'match'; of most productively matching the resources available to provide what the users need, and want – exactly as in any commercial operation (with the degree of 'match' reflecting the efficiency of this process just as directly, but in somewhat less measurable terms, as profit does). In this way, marketing to optimize for 'match' can have just as important a place in not-for-profit organizations.

See also NOT-FOR-PROFIT ORGANIZATIONS

match with existing range(s), product screening 'New products' will be easier to sell if they complement the existing 'product' ranges. Then, it will be possible to build on existing distribution patterns, and perhaps even to capitalize upon existing awareness and favourable consumer attitudes. The 'new products' may possibly be able to help sell more of the existing ones, because they make the range more comprehensive. They may also obtain a bigger display ('facings') at point of sale, up to the point beyond which the retailer will not stock additional packs. A secondary option is that the new products may address the market segments that the existing range is targeted upon. Although this may still gain some of the benefits (especially 'facings'), it is less attractive, since it may result in 'cannibalism'.

See also NEW PRODUCT SCREENING, PRODUCT FACTORS

material costs *see* COMPARATIVE ADVANTAGE, GLOBAL

materials management This element of logistics management controls movement through the production processes. It takes raw material or components/sub-assemblies that are held in stock and schedules them through the various processes (typically involving assembly, but also forming and machining) until the final assembly is put into the finished goods warehouse. During each of these stages, and in particular between them – awaiting the completion of the 'parts kit' that is needed to start the next stage – is 'work in progress'.

See also LOGISTICS MANAGEMENT

materials procurement *see* QUALITY SPECIFICATION

Materials Requirements Planning (MRP) The most sophisticated computerized inventory control systems are those that track all of the components, possibly running into hundreds, that come

together to make a technologically sophisticated product, where the demand of these components is 'dependent'; that is, the decision to make one 'assembly', say, automatically generates a demand for a range of components, each in different volumes. The starting point for such systems is usually a 'Bill of Material Processor' (BOMP) package, which is a tree-structured database that records which components go into each sub-assembly – which in turn go into ever larger assemblies that make up the final product. Materials Requirements Planning also allows for the time taken at each level of assembly, thus offsetting the orders for each 'kit' of parts. The advantage of MRP, in theory, is that work can be accurately scheduled, so that there is no waiting between stages. Most other systems have large stocks of in-process inventory, which wait between the various stages until the kits of parts (and the machine and manpower resources) are available for the next stage. This increases inventory and also results in long, and unpredictable, lead times.

See also INVENTORY CONTROL; JUST IN TIME (JIT); KANBAN; LOGISTICS MANAGEMENT; OPTIMIZED PRODUCTION TECHNOLOGY (OPT)

Materials Requirements Planning II (MRPII) This a (computer software) production scheduling package that plans production, issues the paperwork for this, monitors progress and coordinates activities.

See also INVENTORY CONTROL; JUST IN TIME (JIT); KANBAN; LOGISTICS MANAGEMENT; OPTIMIZED PRODUCTION TECHNOLOGY (OPT)

materials supply, new products The availability of raw materials or components, or subcontract services, may be critical for a new product. Producers increasingly depend on outside suppliers for the greater part of the final product or service that they are assembling. If suppliers are scarce, or erratic, they will pose major problems.

See also NEW PRODUCT SCREENING, ORGANIZATIONAL FACTORS

mathematical analysis *see* ANALYSIS OF MARKETING RESEARCH DATA

mathematical forecasting techniques There are a number of mathematical techniques (some of great complexity) that apparently give a more scientific basis for forecasting than 'manual' methods. But, in essence, most of these allow for four components in any such forecast:

• *Trend.* The ongoing growth (or decline) of the product or service (determined by fitting a straight, or occasionally a curved, line to the historical sales data). The marketing culture almost demands an upward trend!

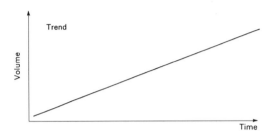

• *Cycle.* Any wavelike movement over the years, reflecting, for example, general business trends – such as the four-year cycle which was once supposed to be a feature of the national economy.

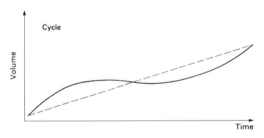

The problem, in this case, is identifying which (if any) is the true cycle, and not just an artefact. More difficult still is to determine whether the cycle will be repeated again in future. Thus, for example, the four-year trade cycle became much less evident during the 1980s (indeed, the 'boom' stretched to cover almost the whole decade and, arguably, this means that this approach may no longer be useful as an element in forecasting 'models'). The decades long Kondratieff cycles, which are often discussed in economic theory, are more difficult to observe (if they are present at all), and are consequently more controversial.

• *Season.* Many products or services are seasonal, and this pattern is overlaid on the others. If the product is seasonal, this seasonality may be one of the most important factors in the forecast. If it is highly seasonal, such as the toy business with its Christmas peak, it may swamp every other factor.

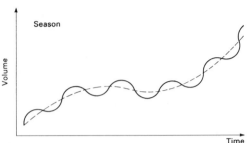

• *Erratic events.* Almost every sales graph shows the effects of erratic events, such as industrial disputes, though some (such as planned promotional campaigns) may be predictable to a certain extent. By definition, erratic events are not fully susceptible to prediction; but any prediction should be aware of them – and allow for the possibility of the deviations which may result.

See also QUALITATIVE FORECASTING METHODS; QUANTITATIVE FORECASTING TECHNIQUES; SALES TREND FORECASTING

mathematical models   *see* MODELS

matrices   The most frequently used (2 × 2) matrices are intended simply to convey a useful visual representation of the four categories to be obtained by splitting two groups of variables (or characteristics/dimensions) each into two further categories – giving four possible permutations. The resulting 'pigeon-hole' matrix just shows these four resulting combinations.

matrices, cross-impact   *see* CROSS-IMPACT MATRICES

matrix   *see* FLONG

3 × 3 matrix   *see* GE (GENERAL ELECTRIC) MATRIX; THREE CHOICE BOX

matrix management   *see* PRODUCT/BRAND MANAGEMENT

Matsushita   *see* VISION, CORPORATE

maturity stage, product life cycle   According to PLC theory, no market can grow forever; and eventually all the significant potential uses will have been developed. The sales curve will flatten and the market or product will have reached maturity. In practice, the majority of products or services currently in the market place are at this stage, and much of the theory and practice of marketing revolves around this 'steady state', where PLC theory has little to contribute. Sales may continue to grow, albeit more slowly. Suppliers may attempt to stimulate sales by expanding their ranges, or by more clearly differentiating them from their competitors. There may be an emphasis, in the face of the 'stagnation' of the market, on building groups of loyal users and attracting those from competitors, with price competition playing its part in this. At the beginning of this phase profits are likely to be at their maximum, but these then fall as the competition increases and prices fall. Some of the minor brands may drop out in the face of the competition, but it is not unheard of for new brands to enter.

maximizing brand/product share *see* PENETRATION PRICING

maximizing current revenue *see* PENETRATION PRICING

maximizing profit *see* CORPORATE OBJECTIVES

maximum attainable average usage *see* USAGE GAP

Maxwell House *see* INTERNATIONAL PRODUCT DECISION

MBO (management by objectives) *see* STRATEGIC BUSINESS UNIT (SBU)

McCann Erickson *see* CLIENT/AGENCY RELATIONSHIP; ECONOMIES OF SCALE, GLOBAL

McCluhan, Marshall *see* ENCODING

McDonalds *see* CONVICTION MARKETING FACTORS; CONVICTION MARKETING TYPES; GLOBALIZATION; GLOBAL MARKETING; INTERNATIONAL PRODUCT DECISION; TRANSNATIONALS/MULTINATIONALS AND EXPORTERS

McDonalds clown advertising, Japan *see* ACCESSIBILITY, FILTERING UNSUITABLE FOREIGN MARKETS

McDonalds Hamburger University *see* CONVICTION MARKETING FACTORS

McDonalds promotions *see* SALES PROMOTION ADVANTAGES AND DISADVANTAGES

McDonalds Q. S. C. & V. *see* CONVICTION MARKETING

McKinsey, consultants *see* CONSULTANTS

means–end relationships *see* NOT-FOR-PROFIT ORGANIZATIONS, OBJECTIVES

measured responses, direct mail *see* RESPONSE RATES, MAILING

measurement activities *see* MONITORING, PROGRESS

mechanical data The technical specifications, in particular size, needed to produce a block for a publication.
See also BLOCKS

media *see* ADVERTISING AGENCY ELEMENTS; DELIVERY SYSTEMS, PRECISION MARKETING; MARKETING STRATEGIES; OPINION LEADERS

media authority *see* PRESS MEDIA

media brief *see* MEDIA BUYING, ADVERTISING AGENCY

media buyer *see* ADVERTISING PLAN; MEDIA BUYING, ADVERTISING AGENCY; PRESS MEDIA; TELEVISION

media buying, advertising agency An important element of the traditional agency is the department which buys the space, or time, in the media which best meets the client's marketing objectives. This follows a number of stages:

Brief
The first and most important step is the client's brief. In this case the need is for the media buyers to understand exactly who the advertising is supposed to reach. This will primarily be specified, in the media buyer's terms, as a profile of who is to be included in the target audience. This used to be based mainly on the relatively crude measures of age and class. The measures have now been expanded by a range of more sophisticated tools, which allow a more sophisticated audience profile to be met. In addition to specifying the coverage, however, the client may also wish to indicate the spread of OTS

(Opportunities To See) desired; good coverage may still be ineffective if most of the audience see the commercial, say, only once whereas a minority see it (wastefully) many times (as can happen with a schedule comprising very cheap off-peak slots). Again, the onus is on the client to say exactly what is expected to be achieved.

Media schedule

Based on this profile, and taking into account any restrictions imposed by the likely creative treatment, the media buyer will construct the optimum schedule of publications and/or television/radio to provide the best match and to deliver the message most economically. A careful selection of media can reduce the per capita costs quite significantly. In the case of more specialist campaigns, such as those in the trade press, specialist media buyers will have the advantage. Here the profiles (both from the client and from the media) are likely to be inexact, and scheduling becomes much more of an art than a science.

John Wilmshurst lists the stages of media selection as:

1. Select those publications that are likely to reach as many of the target audience as possible.
2. Establish the cost of reaching these readers (often on a 'cost per thousand readers' basis).
3. Arrive at the best publications in terms of the maximum number of readers within the target audience at the lowest cost per thousand.
4. Consider whether any supporting publications are needed (for example, the 'best buy' publication may only reach 65 per cent of the target audience; to use a second would reach a further 24 per cent).

He adds, reasonably, that other considerations (such as the need for colour or demonstration) may override these careful calculations. The final schedule is, once more, approved by the client, since it can, and often does, represent the major element of the marketing budget.

Media buying

This stage is the province of the expert media buyer alone, to negotiate the best deals; to achieve the lowest possible costs (usually expressed in terms of 'cost per thousand' viewers or readers in the target audience). Although the core of any schedule will probably be based upon a number of peak-time spots, the overall costs are typically reduced by shopping around for suitable bargains in off-peak time – seeing which slots are going cheap, taking advantage of last-minute bargains and pressurizing the media owners into offering more favourable packages. Few agreed media schedules are ever implemented exactly; they are normally modified 'in flight', to allow for the last-minute bargains and, hopefully, to achieve better than forecast costs. This is an area where, in particular, the client must have confidence in the abilities of the chosen agency.

Research

When the campaign is ended the client, through the agency, should establish exactly what has been achieved. The research in this case is relatively routine, for all the various forms of media have their own research organizations, and the output from these – especially those relating to television (which is most variable in terms of its specific audiences) – should be an accurate measure of who was exposed to the advertisement. This research report is the acid test of an agency media buying department and, as such, is essential reading for any client.

See also ADVERTISING; ADVERTISING AGENCY ELEMENTS; MARKETING RESEARCH

media buying agency   *see* SPECIALIST AGENCIES

media contact, and public relations   *see* PUBLIC RELATIONS

media impact   One element in the media selection equation is impact. The reader or viewer does not react to all advertisements (even conveying the same message) equally. In part this may be the creative treatment, but it is also a function of the media:

*   *Size*. A full-page advertisement or a two-minute commercial may be more expensive than the average advertising cost (and increase the cost per thousand) but it may also have significantly greater impact.
*   *Position*. An insertion facing the contents page at the front of a Sunday colour supplement will be more effective than one buried in the mass of advertisements at the end. A commercial run during a prestige programme will have more impact than one during an early evening soap.
*   *Medium*. The medium itself may contribute to the impact. This may relate to the specific product – a luxury food product may have more relevant impact in an upmarket women's magazine

than in the national press. But the medium may also carry some inherent impact. Thus, it has long been a saying in agencies that 'we carefully evaluate the best, most cost effective, media plan and then choose television anyway!' For those campaigns which can afford it, television normally has the highest impact.

See also ADVERTISING; MARKETING RESEARCH; MEDIA SELECTION

media inserts, sampling *see* SAMPLING

media planners *see* MEDIA SELECTION

media selection In theory, at least, media selection should be the process of choosing the most cost-effective media to achieve the necessary coverage, and number of exposures, amongst the target audience. Thus, at least in theory, media are selected on the basis of cost, combined with performance. Performance is typically measured on two dimensions:

Coverage (sometimes called 'reach')
To maximize overall awareness, the maximum number of the target audience should be reached by the advertising. There is a limit, however, for the last few per cent of the general population are always difficult (and accordingly very expensive) to reach since they do not read the main media used by advertisers. Indeed, cumulative coverage typically follows an exponential pattern. Reaching 90 per cent can cost double what it costs to reach 70 per cent, and reaching 95 per cent can double the cost yet again. The coverage decision is, in practice, a balance between the desired coverage and the cost of achieving this. A large budget will achieve high coverage. A smaller budget will limit the ambitions of the advertiser.

Frequency
Even with high coverage, however, it is not sufficient for a member of the target audience to have just one OTS (Opportunity To See) the advertisement. It is generally reckoned that around five OTS are needed before any reasonable degree of impact is achieved; and significantly more may be needed to build the attitudes which lead to brand switching. To achieve five OTS, even across a coverage of only 70 per cent of the overall audience, may require 20 or 30 peak-time transmissions of a commercial or a significant number of insertions of press advertisements in the national media. A related point is that, as these

figures suggest, most consumers do not get as bored with advertising campaigns as many advertisers think; they simply do not see the commercials that frequently (where the brand manager, say, looks out for every one and has already seen them many times before their first transmission – and is, justifiably, bored with the whole thing). The message is that the life of advertising campaigns can often be extended far beyond the relatively short time usually expected of them. Indeed, as indicated above, the research shows that advertisements need to obtain a significant number of exposures to consumers before they even register! As David Ogilvy (1983) recommends, 'If you are lucky enough to write a good advertisement, repeat it until it stops selling. Scores of good advertisements have been discarded before they lost their potency.'

The more sophisticated media planners will also look at the spread of frequencies. Ideally all the audience should receive the average number of OTS (since those who receive less are insufficiently motivated, and the extra advertising is wasted on those who receive more). Needless to say, it is impossible to achieve this ideal. As with coverage, the pattern will be weighted towards a smaller number of heavy viewers, for example, who will receive significantly more OTS and away from the last few per cent who are difficult to get at. The good media buyer will, however, manage the resulting spread of frequencies so that it is weighted close to the average, with as few as possible of the audience away from it.

Frequency is also complicated by the fact that it is a function of time. A pattern of 12 OTS across a year may be scarcely noticed, where 12 OTS in a week will be very evident to most viewers (though it will leave the brand uncovered for the other 51 weeks of the year!). This is often the rationale for advertising in 'bursts' or 'waves' (sometimes described as 'pulsing'), whereby expenditure is concentrated into a number of intense periods of advertising, which are noticed, but with these bursts spread throughout the year – so that brands do not remain uncovered for long periods.

In the end, it is the media buyers who deliver the goods – by negotiating special deals with the media owners and buying the best parcels of 'slots' to achieve the best cost (normally measured in cost per thousand – per thousand viewers, per thousand household 'impressions' or per thousand impressions on the target audience). The growth of the very large, international, advertising agencies has been in part justified by their increased buying power over the media owners.

See also ADVERTISING; BUYING DECISION, ADVERTISING MODELS; CONVICTION MARKETING

Reference: Ogilvy, David (1983) *Ogilvy on Advertising.* London: Pan Books.

media types   The main types are:

- press
- television
- posters
- radio
- cinema

In terms of overall advertising expenditures, media advertising is dominated by press and television, which are of comparable size (by value of 'sales'). Posters and radio follow some way behind, with cinema now representing a very specialist medium.

The Henley Centre for Forecasting neatly summarizes the positionings of the various media:

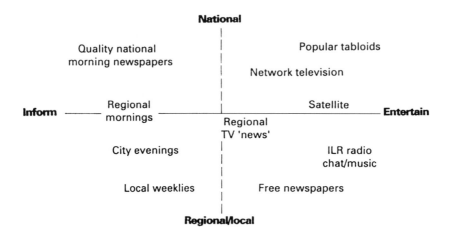

See also ADVERTISING; BUYING DECISION, ADVERTISING MODELS; CINEMA; CONVICTION MARKETING; POSTERS; PRESS MEDIA; RADIO; TELEVISION

media weight   *see* PRESS MEDIA

medium   *see* PROMOTIONAL MIX FACTORS; TELEVISION

medium is the message   *see* ENCODING

medium-term forecasts   The classical image of forecasting revolves around those hectic few weeks in the year when the planning processes, usually driven by the budgets, demand the input of the annual forecasts – the medium-term forecasts. Much 'quantitative' forecasting is concerned with this type of forecast.
See also LONG–TERM FORECASTS; SHORT–TERM FORECASTS; SHORT– VERSUS LONG–TERM FORECASTS

meetings   *see* SEMINARS

meetings, planning   *see* MARKETING PLAN USE

membership groups   *see* PEER PRESSURE INFLUENCES, ON THE PURCHASE DECISION

membership lists   *see* DATA AVAILABILITY, PRECISION MARKETING

membership of channels   *see* CHANNEL DECISIONS

memory lapse   *see* REMINDER ADVERTISING

merchandising data   *see* MARKETING AUDIT

merchandising, retail   *see* RETAIL 'PRODUCT' DECISIONS

merchandising, wholesalers   *see* WHOLESALERS AND DISTRIBUTORS

merchantable   A legal term indicating that the product is of good enough quality to be sold.

merge-purge   Combining two or more mailing lists (and cleaning the output of duplicates).

mergers and acquisitions   *see* TAKEOVER BIDS

message, advertising   The main message in an advertising campaign will usually be based on the specific benefit which the advertiser has identified as the main advantage that the product offers over its competitors. This may not be the main benefit which the buyer will receive from the product, for that may also offered by all the competitors; though it is the foolish advertiser who does not check that the consumer really is aware that all products are identical in offering the main benefit. The advertiser will aim to find a USP (a Unique Selling Proposition) – an important benefit which is unique to the product or service. This USP may be based on 'physical' (or intangible) features associated with the product, ranging from what it actually does through to the quality of the support services. Most advertising follows this route, and it is particularly easy to target, communicate and monitor messages of this type. David Ogilvy (1983) recommends 'Wherever you can, make the product itself the hero of your advertising. If you think the product is too dull, I have news for you: there are no dull products, only dull writers. I never assign a product to a writer unless I know he is personally interested in it.' He was also much quoted as advising fellow admen, even more memorably, that 'the consumer is not a moron: she is your wife'. On the other hand, the message may occasionally be based upon a psychological appeal. It may, somewhat dangerously (in more ways than one), be based on fear; which often has to be a hidden feature of much of financial services advertising, as well as that for condoms! It may be based on guilt (educational toys perhaps?). It may be based on positive emotions such as love, selling boxes of chocolates or Interflora; this is the emotion which usually features, in one guise or another, in those advertisements which are sometimes expanded into 'minisoaps' – either in the family context or the more direct personal drama. It may be, frequently, based upon humour. If this is successful, the viewer or reader shares the joke and develops positive attitudes towards the product. Unfortunately, if the joke is not shared – and humour is a notoriously difficult artform – it may be just as likely to alienate! Finally the message may be communicated by association. This may be directly by association with a specific (well-known) personality, such as Pepsi Cola's use of Michael Jackson – who was not even shown drinking the product! Sometimes it may be just in terms of the voice-over – for example, Victor Borge's distinctive voice was used for the earlier Heineken commercials.

But it may also be by association with a situation – as, for example, with the family in the Oxo soap operas, or the sexually stimulating atmosphere which used to pervade the vermouth advertisements before this approach was banned. David Ogilvy adds the important footnote that 'When faced with selling "parity" products [that is, products that are the same as their competitors, as many are], all you can hope to do is explain their virtues more persuasively than your competitors, and to differentiate them by the style of your advertising. This is the "added value" which advertising contributes . . .'. But, as the *Economist* magazine reported, 'Creative advertising is as difficult to produce as it is to describe. Aldous Huxley, who worked in advertising, reckoned it was easier to write ten passable sonnets than one effective advertisement.'

See also ADVERTISING; BUYING DECISION, ADVERTISING MODELS; DIRECT MAIL OFFER; PROMOTIONAL MIX FACTORS; UNDERSTANDING, ADVERTISING

References: Micklethwaite, John (1990) The advertising industry. *The Economist*, 9 June.
    Ogilvy, David (1983) *Ogilvy on Advertising*. London: Pan Books.

message consistency   One factor which is often ignored by marketers, and in particular by agencies, is the need for successive campaigns to be consistent with their predecessors. Too often, campaigns are seen in isolation, with just the current 'task' to carry out. In reality, in most cases they will be building upon what has gone before, and to achieve the maximum effect they must be consistent with these previous messages (or at least allow for the inherent 'investment' in consumer image built up by these messages). All too frequently, the new campaign ignores past history and has to fight to overcome this unnoticed legacy of the past, as well as its current opposition. The first recourse in creating new advertising should be to the 'guard book' (the historical record of all past advertising, kept by every wise marketer and agency), to see exactly what has gone before.

See also ADVERTISING; BUYING DECISION, ADVERTISING MODELS

message creation   *see* CREATING THE CORRECT MESSAGES

message distortion   *see* ENCODING

message, in advertising models   *see* BUYING DECISION, ADVERTISING MODELS

message selection   The advertising messages to be used in a campaign, which will usually have been created by the advertising agency's creative department, need to be evaluated so that the most effective of these may be chosen for use. The experts recommend that an effective advertisement concentrates on just one central selling proposition. Complicating advertisements by adding further messages will generally dilute the main message, as well as the overall impact. The most effective method of selection is that of 'pre-testing' the advertisement on a sample of the target audience. This is a specialized form of marketing research, which is usually the province of specialized research agencies. An audience is typically shown a new commercial (sometimes in 'storyboard' form – though this is a very difficult approach to use) and questioned to determine its impact (before as well as after seeing it, to detect shifts in opinion).
See also ADVERTISING; BUYING DECISION, ADVERTISING MODELS

metamarketing   The theory of all forms of marketing across all sectors.

me-too products   *see* NEW PRODUCT INNOVATION

micro- and macro-forecasts   *see* MACRO- AND MICRO-FORECASTS

microeconomics   The theory relating to the individual elements (including those which relate to individuals or organizations) within the economy – as compared with macroeconomics, which studies the whole economy.
See also EQUILIBRIUM PRICE; MACROECONOMICS; TRANSACTION COST ECONOMICS

middlemen/agents   By far the most widely used approach to distribution (in terms of the number of exporters using it, if not in terms of the volumes shipped) is to use agents or distributors. This offers a relatively low initial cost and risk, and bypasses many of the barriers which countries erect against the direct entry of foreign companies. On the other hand, open-ended agency agreements may also exclude the exporter when, later, direct operations might be more productive.
See also CHANNEL STRUCTURE; MARKET ENTRY TACTICS

mid-life kickers   Most products or services are in the mid-range of their lives, in maturity or satura-

tion. Much of marketing is therefore concerned with profitably extending that phase. Few marketers with brands in this phase see their actions in terms of the product life cycle; they usually see them in terms of responding to their current competitive pressures. Even so, the effect is much the same and this model adds another useful perspective to following the performance of such brands. The effect of mid-life kickers is to extend the life cycle, countering the drop in sales and continuing the progress of the sales curve upwards. 'New product development', in comparison, starts the next product life cycle. 'Diversification' may be a variation on this process, moving into a completely new market with a new product range – either developed in-house or obtained by a purchase or takeover.
See also INVESTMENT MULTIPLIER; PRODUCT LIFE CYCLE (PLC)

milking   *see* BUDGETS; DECLINE STRATEGIES

Miller Brewing Company of Milwaukee   *see* CONVICTION MARKETING TYPES

mini-cultures   *see* GLOBALIZATION

minimizing costs   *see* CORPORATE OBJECTIVES

ministerial briefing   *see* POLITICAL CONTACTS

minor brands, pricing   An exception to strictures about price competition relates to minor brands in markets which are dominated by major brands. Minor brands will typically make the biggest offer (usually a price reduction) per unit (which represents the greatest impact they can make), whereas the response of the leaders is to promote (most economically) across the whole market (usually by advertising). This situation rarely leads to damaging price wars.
See also COMPETITION PRICING; COST-PLUS PRICING; PRICE INCREASES; PRICING POLICIES, PRACTICAL; PRICING STRATEGY

minority interest   *see* LOCAL SALES ORGANIZATION

minor point close   *see* CLOSING TECHNIQUES

minstrel   *see* SALES CALL OPENING

MIS   *see* JUST IN TIME (JIT); MARKETING INTELLIGENCE SYSTEMS (MIS)

misinterpretation *see* PARADIGM SHIFT, STRATEGY

mismatch of interests, consultants *see* CONSULTANTS

mission Behind the corporate objectives, which offer the main context for the marketing plan, lies the 'corporate mission', which in turn provides the context for the corporate objectives. This 'corporate mission' can be thought of as a definition of what the organization is and what it does: 'Our business is . . .'. This definition should not be too narrow, or it will constrict the organization's development. On the other hand, it should not be too wide or it will become meaningless. Abell (1980) suggests that the definition should cover three dimensions:

- customer groups to be served
- customer needs to be served
- technologies to be utilized

Malcolm McDonald (1989) states that the 'mission statement' should be the first item in a marketing plan. He goes further when he suggests that it should contain a brief statement about four points:

1. *Role or contribution of the unit* – is it, for instance, a line or staff function?
2. *Definition of business* – a combination of the (external) points listed above.
3. *Distinctive competence* – the (internal) factors which give you competitive advantage.
4. *Indications for future direction* – the areas you might consider moving into.

See also CORPORATE OBJECTIVES; MARKETING MYOPIA; MARKETING PLAN STRUCTURE

References: Abell, D. (1980) *Defining the Business: The Starting Point of Strategic Planning.* Englewood Cliffs, NJ: Prentice-Hall.
McDonald, Malcolm H. B. (1989) *Marketing Plans* (2nd edn). London: Heinemann.

missionaries *see* CONVICTION MARKETING

mission flow diagram *see* TREE STRUCTURES, FORECASTING

Mitsubishi *see* MARKET ENTRY TACTICS

mixed economies The dominant form of economic organization, in which the market is allowed to regulate prices but governments intervene to cope with instability and market failures.
See also LAISSEZ-FAIRE; MACROECONOMICS; MARKET FAILURE; MARKET SOCIALISM

mixing, images *see* DISSOLVE

mix, marketing *see* MARKETING MIX AND PROMOTION

mix test *see* TEST MARKET

mock-up A non-working model of a new product, typically to show to potential buyers.

model categories As seems to be the case for most elements of business theory, there are a number of dimensions which may be used to categorize the various approaches to (theoretical) models:

Individual or global
Models can approach their subjects from two extremes. 'Micro' models start with the individual ('atomic') component, typically the individual in society – and, in the context of this book, the individual customer or client. All the features of the model (e.g. market shares) are thereafter developed by the aggregation of that individual's actions. At the other extreme, 'macro' models (such as the national econometric models) aim to describe the complete environment – the whole of society or, in our case, the market.

Static or dynamic
Because they are so much easier to explain, most simple models are static. They typically describe very limited situations, usually at one point in time.

Descriptive/predictive or normative
Lilien and Kotler (1983) split models into those which are 'descriptive' – describing the situation as it is, to aid understanding of the processes involved (this form of 'model' building is, for example, an integral aspect of the multidimensional 'mapping' which is often central to the major 'positioning' exercises) – and 'predictive' – those which can be used to predict what will happen in the future (the time-series- or multiple regression analyses used for forecasting fall into this category). They also distinguish between such models and the purely normative ones often used (albeit frequently unconsciously) for decision-making. These latter are typically based on 'values', or even 'beliefs', rather than being strictly rational and 'scientifically' thought out.

Linear or non-linear

Most models in marketing, and in business theory generally, are assumed to be 'linear'; that is, the graph of the relationship (sales versus advertising, say) can be represented by a straight line. Even the most complex of computer analyses, such as multiple regression analysis, often may assume that, although the picture is complicated by the number of factors involved, each individual relationship is a simple linear one. But this is often simply an approximation (one which is sometimes brought closer to reality by using logarithmic relationships – resulting in curved rather than straight lines). It is as well to recognize the existence of such approximations, since the results of the elaborate computer analyses may not always be as accurate as the immense computing power involved in their generation might seem to imply! On the other hand, there are many situations (particularly those which relate to 'catastrophe theory') where the assumption of simple linear relationships may be very misleading.

Strong or weak relationship

Lilien and Kotler (1983) distinguish between decisions which are taken on subjects that have considerable significance for the decision-makers (where, for example, there is 'high involvement' with the product and there are significant differences between it and its competitors) – here the decision-making process may be complex (and involve learning) – and, at the other extreme, those where the matter is relatively insignificant (low involvement and no significant brand differences, say) – and here decision-making may initially be almost random (and thereafter show considerable inertia). The former is the stuff of classical marketing theory. The latter is less often discussed – but probably applies to at least as many products and services. The 'inertia' is due to the fact that the consumer cannot, or will not, devote time to searching out and testing alternatives for these borderline decisions, but develops a 'spurious loyalty' to the brand that is already known. Weak influences are therefore much less predictable. Starting from a random choice, they will most likely tend to reflect existing brand shares and perpetuate these, giving a degree of inertia to the market as well as to the individual decision.

See also MODELS

Reference: Lilien, Gary L. and Kotler, Philip (1983) *Marketing Decision Making.* New York: Harper & Row.

modelling   *see* SPREADSHEETS, AND FORECASTING

models   Throughout this dictionary you will find references to 'models'. In this context a 'model' is anything which claims to describe the relationships between the factors involved.

Schoner and Uhl (1975) explain 'three basic purposes of building a model. One is to predict the future. . . . Such models are descriptive . . . they become fixed, in a given prediction. . . . A second purpose in building a model is explanation of some phenomenon. Explanatory models may also be termed "theories". A third purpose in model building is problem solving.' This last category is the one to which most marketing models belong.

In its most mathematically 'rigorous', and perhaps most recognizable, form it usually comprises one or more equations. Thus, $z = x + y$ is a model (predicting what will happen to z when x or y changes). In the largest econometric models it may contain several hundred such equations, many of which are interrelated.

Some of the statistical models – especially those which are used to bring together the results of multiple regression analyses – are, on the other hand, content to treat the model as a 'black box'. They make no attempt to explain what processes lie within, but simply offer a prediction as to what 'outputs' might be expected from any given set of 'inputs'.

These mathematical constructs are obviously 'formal' models, but some verbal (descriptive) models can be just as formally recorded. There are many of these in marketing theory, from the simple 'AIDA' (Attention, Interest, Desire, Action), which is supposed to describe the individual processes involved in face-to-face selling, through to the Boston Matrix, which describes how product portfolios should be handled by large organizations. Most models, however, use even less definitive words – and are very informal. Indeed, in most decision-making the models behind the decisions are hidden, as are the assumptions inherent in these. Those taking the decisions do not even consider that they might need to re-evaluate these assumptions.

As Lunn et al. state, 'It cannot be emphasised too strongly that even the most unsympathetic critics of formal models in practice base their management decisions upon implicit models, which may well be totally misleading'. They go on to suggest, in the specific context of market modelling, that 'a particularly important function of a modelling exercise is to make explicit the implicit assumptions held about market structure by both marketing men and researchers, thereby enabling these assumptions to be criticized, tested and developed'. This principle also holds true of all the other areas where decision-making is endemic.

The main use of models, consciously or not, is to predict the future. The user of a model, in basing his or her decision upon it (and upon the assumptions inherent in it), is assuming that the outcomes predicted by the model will occur.

If the model is explicit, and its features are debated amongst those involved, a number of other benefits may accrue:

- *Understanding*. It may improve understanding of the processes, particularly where it brings together the separate ideas of a number of contributors.
- *Communication*. Indeed, perhaps the most important element of explicit models is that they allow the participants to communicate their ideas (and assumptions) to each other.
- *Limitations*. Making the model explicit can highlight its inadequacies and, in particular, gaps in its coverage.

See also HOWARD AND SHETH MODEL, OF CONSUMER BEHAVIOUR; MODEL CATEGORIES; WEBSTER AND WIND MODEL, OF ORGANIZATIONAL BEHAVIOUR

References: Lunn, Tony, Blamires, Chris and Seaman, David (1986) Market modelling. In Robert Worcester and John Downham (eds), *Consumer Market Research Handbook*. Maidenhead: McGraw-Hill.
  Schoner, Bertram and Uhl, Kenneth P. (1975) *Marketing Research: Information Systems and Decision Making*. New York: John Wiley.

models of consumer behaviour   *see* HOWARD AND SHETH MODEL, OF CONSUMER BEHAVIOUR

modems   *see* COMPUTER-MEDIATED COMMUNICATIONS (CMC)

modification, product (or service)   *see* PRODUCT (OR SERVICE) MODIFICATION

modified rebuy   *see* BUYGRID ANALYSIS; ORGANIZATIONAL BUYING SITUATIONS

modular stand systems   *see* EXHIBITIONS

mom and pop stores   *see* RETAIL ORGANIZATION

monadic testing   Product testing where the respondent is only given only one product to test rather than the two or more – which are tested against each other – more usually offered.

monetarism   As developed by Milton Friedman, this school of thought, which replaced Keynesianism as the most influential school, holds that changes in money supply are the major cause of macroeconomic fluctuations.
See also GLOBALIZATION; KEYNESIANISM; NEOCLASSICAL ECONOMICS; RATIONAL EXPECTATIONS THEORY

Reference: Friedman, Milton and Heller, Walter (1969) *Monetary vs. Fiscal Policy*. Norton.

monetary policy   The control of a government, or a central bank, over money supply, interest rates and credit. The instruments it uses are typically the interest rate and open-market operations (in which it sells or buys back government stock). Along with fiscal policy, it is one of the main tools used to control the economy.
See also FISCAL POLICY; GLOBALIZATION; NEOCLASSICAL ECONOMICS

money available   *see* PROMOTIONAL MIX FACTORS

money markets   *see* PRICE FACTORS

money off   *see* PROMOTIONAL PRICING; PROMOTION OBJECTIVES

monitoring and managing channels   In much the same way that an organization's own sales and distribution activities need to be monitored and managed, so will those of the distribution chain. In practice, of course, many organizations use a mixture of different channels; in particular they may complement a direct sales force, who call on the larger accounts, with agents covering the smaller customers and prospects.
See also CHANNEL DECISIONS; CHANNEL MEMBERSHIP; CHANNEL MOTIVATION

monitoring forecasts   Many organizations track their performance against their predictions (represented by budgets or targets), but very few invest significant effort in monitoring actual results against forecast (and hence tracking how the underlying factors are changing). But as Spyros Makridakis states, 'Monitoring is an essential aspect of any forecasting situation. . . . The role of monitoring, either implicitly or explicitly, is to identify the occurrence of non-random changes from existing patterns or relationships.'
See also FORECASTING TECHNIQUES

Reference: Makridakis, Spyros and Wheelwright, Steven C. (1989) *Forecasting Methods for Management* (5th edn). Chichester: John Wiley.

monitoring performance   *see* BUDGETS

monitoring, progress The final stage of the marketing planning process is to establish targets (or standards) against which progress can be monitored. Accordingly, it is important to put both quantities and timescales into the marketing objectives (e.g. to capture 20 per cent by value of the market within 2 years) and the corresponding strategies. Changes in the environment mean that the forecasts often have to be changed. Along with these, the related plans may also need changing. Continuous monitoring of performance against predetermined targets represents a most important aspect of this. But, perhaps even more important, is the enforced discipline of a regular formal review. In many cases the best (most realistic) planning cycle will revolve around a quarterly review. Best of all, at least in terms of the quantifiable aspects of the plans if not the wealth of background detail, is probably a quarterly rolling review – planning one full year ahead each new quarter. This does, of course, absorb more planning resource; but it also ensures that the plans embody the latest information – and, with attention focused on them so regularly, forces both the plans and their implementation to be realistic. Plans only have validity if they are actually used to control the progress of a company; their success lies in their implementation, not in the writing.
See also CORPORATE OBJECTIVES; MARKETING PLANS AND PROGRAMMES; MARKETING PLAN STRUCTURE; MARKETING STRATEGIES; PLANNING PROCESS

monocultural   *see* STANDARDIZATION VERSUS ADAPTATION

monopolies   *see* BRAND MONOPOLY; PRICE FACTORS; PRICE REGULATION; PRICING, PRODUCT POSITIONING

monopsony A market where there is just one buyer – the reverse of a monopoly, where there is just one seller.

Monotype A typesetting machine that casts and sets each letter separately.
See also LINOTYPE

monument to diseased ego   *see* VISION, CORPORATE

morphological analysis This method of idea generation was developed by Fritz Zwicky as a more rigorous form of attribute listing. It requires that the 'problem' be broken down into 'variables' or parts which can be treated independently, and then works through all possible relationships between all the variables or parts involved. For each of the combinations, of which there may be many, a 'new product' is postulated. Inevitably, most of these will not be viable, but perhaps a few will.
See also ATTRIBUTE LISTING

mortality   *see* COMPETITIVE SAW; INVESTMENT MULTIPLIER

MOSAIC   *see* RESIDENTIAL NEIGHBOURHOODS

most favoured nation clause The agreement between two countries that they will give each other the best terms of trade. In practice, this is usually the same as almost everyone else – despite the grand title.
See also EXPORTING

mother henning   *see* MARKET ENTRY TACTICS

motivation; of channels   *see* CHANNEL, MOTIVATION

motivation, of sales personnel Alfred Tack puts the problem boldly: 'Even the above average salesman rarely works at more than sixty per cent of his capacity. There are the days he stays at home . . .' The problem is very different to that of 'managing' teams of other employees, for a number of reasons:

- *Lack of contact.* It is almost inevitably the case that sales personnel rarely see their own management. They spend most of their time (as they should do!) 'on the road', visiting customers. As a result, though, the sales manager may only occasionally see his subordinates on an individual basis – as opposed to the regular (and essential) sales meetings, which force them to attend *en masse*. This means that the limited management time spent individually with sales professionals must be used very productively. It also means that such time acquires a heightened, more dramatic aspect – which is often unrecognized by the manager (although keenly felt by the subordinate) and thereby hinders normal communications.
- *Complexity of role.* The sales professional's job is complex. It covers as many separate functions as almost any other in the organization (up to and including that of the chief executive). Furthermore, it is constantly shifting to embrace

new knowledge, new skills and new directions, as the needs of each customer, and often of each situation, make different demands. It is difficult, therefore, for a 'remote' sales manager to fully comprehend exactly what is needed at any given moment.

- *Entrepreneurship*. Sales professionals have in effect to be managers of their own small businesses; indeed, it is often necessary to describe their roles in such a context. As such, they have many of the characteristics of small business owners – especially those of independence. This poses one of the most difficult, if potentially most productive, challenges for many sales managements.

These challenges are answered (or perhaps, more accurately, evaded) by the traditional tools of sales force motivation, which concentrate almost exclusively on the single task of motivating sales personnel to achieve their narrow short-term targets. Examples are as follows.

Compensation
Much has been written about compensation plans for sales personnel. It is assumed, with some justification, that at least part of a sales professional's income should be 'performance related' – usually as 'commission on sales'. This requires a number of decisions by sales managements, including:

- *Proportion of commission*. How much of a sales professional's income should be commission and how much salary? Many commission schemes aim for a ratio of 1:1 (though, interestingly, the salary half in those sales forces which can afford to attract the best personnel often matches the total salary in other equivalent occupations!). Many sales forces, though often the more marginal ones, only offer commission. On paper this is very cost effective (you only pay for what you get), but it is not obvious that this attracts high quality personnel – or outstanding results! Relatively few organizations pay on a salary only basis.
- *Structure of commission*. Many schemes offer a straight percentage of sales revenue; which has the great advantage of being easy to administer and very obvious to the sales personnel. Other schemes relate similar incentives to performance against target; which allows for a degree of direction, in terms for example of weighting important products or markets (or types of business). Many also have varying rates, with for example 'accel-erators' to award performance above target; or special rates for the products or markets which management wants to concentrate upon.
- *Targets*. Commission schemes cannot be divorced from the targets which are set. Many organizations offer, at least on paper, very high 'on target' earnings to attract sales personnel, but these targets are so unrealistic as to be achievable by only the very exceptional, and the very lucky, few. This fools nobody for very long! IBM, on the other hand, deliberately sets its targets so that 80 per cent of its sales personnel are 'winners', and are motivated as such. (Most sales forces, on a similar basis, save money by ensuring that they have more than 50 per cent of 'losers' – who are also motivated as such!)

Sales promotions
Many organizations use short-term incentive schemes to motivate, and to direct, their sales personnel. Examples are:

- *Competitions* – for given periods (to revive flagging sales in order to meet mid-year targets, for example) or on specific products (to back launches or drives for wider distribution etc.).
- *Gifts* – coupons, or actual products, are offered in return for achieving certain targets (such as running a number of demonstrations or sales drives).
- *Holidays* – as prizes for achieving targets, IBM's most effective incentive was the HPC (the 'Hundred Percent Club') – a three-day event, held in a foreign holiday resort, for sales personnel achieving all their annual targets.

This last example, though, illustrates one very powerful incentive which is often, indeed usually, neglected: self-esteem.

Self-esteem
The main motivator for many of the best sales professionals is their own self-image. They are highly motivated to succeed, and that desire to succeed is often what drives them on. IBM thus mainly used its HPC (mentioned above) to tap this source of motivation. The incentive was not really the holiday (which was worth only £1000) but the honour of achieving it; and, conversely, the embarrassment of failing to achieve it. In the USA it is quite literally described as a 'recognition event' because that is what it is all about – receiving the recognition of your peers! Alfred Tack puts the point simply and positively:

'Because it breeds loyalty, job satisfaction motivates salesmen to ride those moments of depression which occur throughout the lives of most men in the field'.
See also PEOPLE (SALES) MANAGEMENT

Reference: Tack, Alfred (1983) *How to Succeed as a Sales Manager.* London: The Windmill Press.

motivation research   Much of marketing research revolves around the measurement of consumers' actions: how much they buy of a product or service, what brand(s) they buy, when they buy it, what they do with it, etc. But a significant amount of research goes much further to discover why they take these actions; not in rational terms, but in the context of their underlying, hidden motivations (which may be very different – crucially so for the marketer who is planning to influence them – from their stated, rational explanations). This research tries to understand their motives – why certain 'attitudes' (likes and dislikes) lead to specific buying behaviour. Because this is less 'tangible', it is an area of much debate and, indeed, controversy. The complexity is evidenced by Schoner and Uhl's (1975) theoretical definition: 'An attitude is composed of a predisposition to respond favourably or unfavourably to some object or symbol, the beliefs (cognitions) held concerning this object or symbol and the emotional feelings (affect) surrounding this object or symbol'. Rather less obscurely, though still in terms of theory rather than practice, they go on to explain this definition: 'an attitude is defined to possess three components: an action or behaviour tendency, a set of beliefs and a set of feelings'. Whatever theoretical view is taken, though, the outcome is that (at least in theory) marketing research can only measure them indirectly; in essence, therefore, it can only measure properties derived from these hidden attitudes. Even so, the market researchers in the field have learned to detect underlying behaviour patterns which can be used to explain why consumers take certain actions – and, in particular, why they buy a brand. Thus, the 'attitudes' (here used in its popular sense rather than its theoretical one) of consumers to brands – their likes and dislikes about specific aspects, intangible and 'irrational' as well as tangible and 'rational' – may be measured. They can be expected to indicate buying behaviour, and, indeed, can practically be used so to do. Similarly, consumers' 'attitudes' to wider aspects of their environment (sometimes grouped as 'lifestyles', for instance) may also say something about their possible buying behaviour.
See also HALO EFFECT; MARKETING RESEARCH

Reference: Schoner, Bertram and Uhl, Kenneth P. (1975) *Marketing Research: Information Systems and Decision Making.* New York: John Wiley.

motivator   *see* PSYCHOLOGICAL INFLUENCES, ON THE PURCHASE DECISION

motivator, sales performance   *see* CONTROL, OF SALES PERSONNEL

move kanban   *see* KANBAN

moving annual total (MAT)   This is a graphical technique for recording sales data (and for subsequently assisting the production of annual forecasts) which smoothes out short-term fluctuations (especially seasonality) by moving forward the accumulated total for the preceding 12 months. Thus, each new month's figures are added to the previous (MAT) total and the comparable figures from a year ago are deducted. The forecast is once more obtained by extending the trend line, this time 'smoothed' by the incorporation of the whole year's data.
See also QUANTITATIVE FORECASTING TECHNIQUES

MPs   *see* POLITICAL CONTACTS

MRB   *see* MARKETING RESEARCH, PRECISION MARKETING

MRP (Materials Requirements Planning)   *see* MATERIALS REQUIREMENTS PLANNING (MRP)

MRPII   *see* MATERIALS REQUIREMENTS PLANNING II (MRPII)

MSP   *see* DELIVERY SYSTEMS, PRECISION MARKETING

multibrand promotions   *see* NON-PRICE PROMOTIONS

multibrands   In a market that is fragmented amongst a number of brands a supplier can choose to deliberately launch totally new brands (multiple brands, or multibrands) in apparent competition with its own existing strong brand (and often with identical product characteristics) simply to soak up some of the share of the market which will in any case go to minor brands. The rationale is that having 3 out of 12 brands in such a market will give a greater overall share than having 1 out of 10 (even if much of the share of these new brands is taken from the existing one). In its most extreme manifestation, a supplier pioneering a new market which it believes will be particularly attractive may choose to immediately launch a second brand, in competition with its first. This is in order to pre-empt others entering the market, as the evidence suggests that brands that enter early into most markets end up with significantly larger shares than later entrants. In any case, as Roberts and McDonald point out, 'Individual brand names naturally allow greater flexibility by permitting a variety of different products, of differing quality, to be sold without confusing the consumer's perception of what business the company is in or diluting higher quality products'. Procter & Gambol is a leading exponent of this philosophy (running as many as ten detergent brands in the US market!), though in recent years it has been cutting back on the numbers of such competing brands. This allows it to have brands which can address very specific market segments. It also increases the total number of 'facings' it receives on supermarket shelves! Sara Lee, on the other hand, used the philosophy to keep the very different parts of its business separate: Sara Lee (cakes) from Kiwi (polishes) from L'Eggs (pantyhose/tights). In the hotel business, Marriott uses the name Fairfield Inns for its budget chain (and Ramada uses Rodeway for its own cheaper hotels).

Cannibalism

A particular problem of a 'multibrand' approach, but one that can also occur with other modes of operation, is that of 'cannibalism'. The new brand, or product, takes business away from an established one which the organization also owns. This may be acceptable (indeed, is to be expected) if it carves a greater share from external competitors – so that there is a net gain overall. Alternatively, it may be the price the organization is willing to pay for shifting its position in the market, the new product being one stage in this process. But the cost may sometimes, unexpectedly, reach an unacceptable level – in terms of the attrition of existing profitable business.
See also BRAND EXTENSION; BRANDING POLICIES

Reference: Roberts, C. J. and McDonald, Gael M. (1989) Alternative naming strategies: family versus individual brand names. *Management Decision*, 26(6).

multidimensional mapping *see* MARKET GAP ANALYSIS

multidimensional maps   There are alternative graphical approaches – for the 'static' product posi-

tioning map – to the two-dimensional ones normally used. For example, to try and produce just one diagram which contains all the information which would otherwise be contained in the various dimensions (needing three, four or more maps), a computerized (plotting) compression technique is used. As most often used, this initially plots the brands, say, against the two dimensions shown to be most significant (exactly as in the two-dimensional maps). On this it then overlays 'vectors' (from the origin) showing the other, less important dimensions. The direction of these vectors is calculated so that the relative displacement of the brands from each of them reflects its position against them on the original two-dimensional map. It is claimed that this type representation offers a useful shorthand, which is easier for managers to digest. On the other hand, if the manager is capable of digesting the contents of the three or four separate two-dimensional plots (and most are), then the basic approach should offer a better, inherently more understandable picture, for the relation to the vectors on the compressed picture is often some what less than obvious!
See also PRODUCT (OR SERVICE) POSITIONING; SEGMENTATION

multidimensional scaling   This gives somewhat similar results to cluster analysis. It is a less well known approach, but its supporters would claim that its graphical presentation (usually in two or three dimensions) gives a better feel for the relationships between the variables.
See also ANALYSIS OF MARKETING RESEARCH DATA

multifunctional workers   *see* JUST IN TIME (JIT)

multinational accounting   *see* COMPARATIVE ADVANTAGE, GLOBAL

multinationals   *see* EXPORTING; GLOBALIZATION; GLOBAL MARKETING; INTERNATIONAL PRODUCT DECISION; MARKET ENTRY DECISION; STRATEGIC (INTERNATIONAL) ALLIANCES; TRANSNATIONALS/ MULTINATIONALS AND EXPORTERS

multiple choice, on questionnaires   *see* CLOSED QUESTIONS, ON QUESTIONNAIRES

multiple discriminant analysis   An analytical method used to predict behaviour, classifying people into groups discrete from other (known) variables.

See also ANALYSIS OF MARKETING RESEARCH DATA

multiple outlets   *see* RETAIL ORGANIZATION

multiple regression analysis   This mathematical analysis (typically used on survey research data) is one form of a number of 'multivariate' analyses using complex and sophisticated statistical (computerized) methods which attempt to determine the structure of relationships where there are more than two factors involved. It is concerned with establishing what the contribution of each of these factors, the 'independent variables' (e.g. price and advertising), is to the overall results or 'dependent variables' (e.g. sales or customer attitudes).

In 'simple regression' a linear relationship of the form $y = a + bx$ (i.e. a straight line) is assumed, where a and b are constants (to be found). The relationship between x and y is thus, indeed, simple. It does not even require a computer to calculate the values of a and b for any given model – but such simple relationships are rare. Usually a number of factors are involved, so these become 'multiple regression analyses'. Computer programs are then used to determine statistically, from the historical data and the changes in the various factors, the likelihood of each of the factors having an impact on the main variables. The parameters of the 'model' and the overall probabilities of each outcome can then be determined. It may not be very scientific and its accuracy can be questioned, but just plotting the various points measured (typically historical sales versus time) on a graph can often allow for a simple visual estimation of some of these 'constants'. These rough estimations may contain much of the information which the more sophisticated computer analyses achieve – and, being much simpler, are a useful precursor to such 'sophisticated' analyses. (They can even stand by themselves, if suitably qualified, in the absence of the more sophisticated techniques.)

See also ANALYSIS OF MARKETING RESEARCH DATA; QUANTITATIVE FORECASTING TECHNIQUES; TIME–SERIES ANALYSES

multiplier   *see* KEYNESIANISM

multistage sample   *see* STRATIFIED SAMPLE

multivariate analysis   *see* ANALYSIS OF MARKETING RESEARCH DATA; FACTOR ANALYSIS; MULTIPLE REGRESSION ANALYSIS

Murphy's Law   The statement, reportedly put forward by a US physicist of the same name, that if anything can go wrong it will go wrong.

mutual benefit (win–win) bargaining   *see* SUPPLIERS

mutual confidence   *see* SUPPLIERS

mutually beneficial arrangement   *see* INTER-ORGANIZATIONAL RELATIONS

mutual trust and PR   *see* PUBLIC RELATIONS

myopia, marketing   *see* CONVICTION MARKETING AND MYOPIA; MARKETING MYOPIA

myths   *see* CULTURE, ORGANIZATIONAL; SALES CALL

N

name dropping *see* REFERENCES

narrowcasting Reaching, for example by cable or satellite, a small – possibly narrowly defined – audience for television or radio; as compared with broadcasting, which is received by the whole population.
See also MEDIA IMPACT; MEDIA SELECTION; MEDIA TYPES

national agencies, data Government departments are major providers of data – often to support specific 'initiatives', but still useful for other purposes. Perhaps the most useful source of basic information in the UK, for example, is the Central Statistical Office, and its most useful report is probably *Annual Abstract of Statistics*. This and the *Guide to Official Statistics* (which is the main guide to what government statistics are available) are worth buying (for your organization, not yourself, if it does not already have them). These statistics typically summarize the mass of data generated by, or submitted to, government departments. More detailed information can come from the Census of Population (which is, however, compiled only once every 10 years – so that it can be very out of date), as well as the more specialized Census of Production (which covers manufacturing industry) and Census of Distribution (covering wholesalers and retailers), which may also suffer from being out of date.
See also EXTERNAL DATA; LIBRARIES; LOCAL AGENCIES, DATA

national brands *see* GLOBAL MARKETING

national cultures *see* GLOBALIZATION

nationalization *see* MARKET ENTRY DECISION

national marketing *see* TRANSNATIONALS/ MULTINATIONALS AND EXPORTERS; TRIAD POWER

national media *see* MEDIA SELECTION; PRESS MEDIA; PUBLIC RELATIONS

National Shoppers Survey *see* MARKETING RESEARCH, PRECISION MARKETING

natural consumer groupings *see* SEGMENTATION

natural resources *see* FACTORS OF PRODUCTION

NCR sales operation *see* TERRITORY MANAGEMENT

necessary good A term in economics defined as those goods whose demand rises proportionately more slowly than a rise in income.

needs *see* MASLOW'S HIERARCHY OF NEEDS

needs of customers *see* ACCOUNT PLANNING; MARKETING PLANS AND PROGRAMMES

negative option programmes These are club programmes, such as book or record clubs, which are in regular (typically monthly) contact with their members to offer them the 'month's choice', which their members may accept or refuse (according to the rules of the club). They represent the most complex (and expensive) of direct mail activities.

negotiation *see* STRATEGIC (INTERNATIONAL) ALLIANCES

negotiation, price *see* PRICE NEGOTIATION

negotiation procedures *see* SOCIAL AND BUSINESS STRUCTURES, FILTERING UNSUITABLE MARKETS

negotiation, purchasing *see* PRODUCT OR SERVICE, TO BE PURCHASED

negotiation, sales manpower budget *see* MANPOWER PLAN, SALES

neighbourhood classifications *see* MARKETING RESEARCH, PRECISION MARKETING; RESIDENTIAL NEIGHBOURHOODS

neighbourhood stores   *see* LOCATION, RETAIL

neoclassical economics   The traditional micro-economic theory, based on the nineteenth-century work of W. Stanley Jevons, Carl Menger and Leon Walras, which countered the bias in classical economics by developing the laws of supply and demand.
See also PRICE FACTORS; PRICES, CUSTOMER NEEDS; SUPPLY AND DEMAND

Nestlé   *see* LOCAL SALES ORGANIZATION

net contribution   *see* MONITORING, PROGRESS

net cover   *see* COVERAGE

net profit   *see* MONITORING, PROGRESS

network approach to long-term forecasting   *see* BAYESIAN DECISION THEORY; TREE STRUCTURES, FORECASTING

network building   *see* LOGICAL INCREMENTALISM

networking   *see* EMERGENT STRATEGY

'never out' list, retail   *see* RETAIL 'PRODUCT' DECISIONS

new account   *see* ENHANCED AIUAPR MODEL; THREE PILLARS OF THE PURCHASING PROCESS

new classical economics   The economic theory, developed from the 1970s onwards, based on the concept of rational expectations.
See also RATIONAL EXPECTATIONS THEORY

new customers   *see* SELLING

new ideas   *see* GENERATING IDEAS

newly married couples   *see* AGE INFLUENCES, ON THE PURCHASE DECISION

new product creation   In the 1960s and 1970s, when marketing was a relatively young profession, it was often claimed that the best new products were bound to be those which were specifically created to meet the needs of the marketplace. This was clearly spelled out by Professor Corey of the Harvard Business School: 'the form of a product is a variable, not

a given, in developing market strategy. Products are developed and planned to serve markets.'

Ideally such products originated with the market researcher discovering unsatisfied wants. It is still held to be true that new product ideas, once they have emerged, should be rigorously tested against the needs of the market – before the organization's full resources are committed. To that extent, the beliefs of the earlier years are still important now.

Marketing practice has, however, since shown that the really creative ideas can rarely be turned on like a tap to meet the market researcher's specifications. They come, instead, from every direction, sometimes emerging from the unlikeliest of places. They may come from technical developments in the laboratories (the Sony Walkman was, according to one of a number of stories about the product, created by an engineer for his own fun!), they may come from the sales force, or they may come from practice in other countries or other industries. The secret of finding new products is not, it turns out, to be able to specify them but simply to be able to recognize them!

This means, then, that the managers of new products must be constantly scanning the sources available to them, particularly the literature, to find these new ideas. The need is therefore for an open mind (the Sony Walkman was eventually shown to Akio Morita, Sony's chairman, who had the very good sense to back its commercial development).

The NIH (Not Invented Here) syndrome is the worst enemy of new product development. Surprisingly, the intensely inward-looking elements of the IBM culture meant that its laboratories sometimes positively shunned ideas from outside – even from other parts of IBM!

Peter Doyle makes the very sensible point that 'Perhaps the most common means of building an outstanding brand is being first into a market'. He adds a very important footnote, however: 'This does not mean being technologically first, but rather being first in the mind of the consumer. IBM, Kleenex, Casio and McDonalds did not invent their respective products, but they were first to build major brands out of them and bring them into the mass market.'
See also ANSOFF MATRIX; COMPETITIVE GAP; CREATIVE IMITATION; CUSTOMER BONUS; DISTRIBUTION GAP; EXISTING PRODUCT CHANGES; FEATURE MODIFICATION; GAP ANALYSIS; GENERATING IDEAS; IMAGE MODIFICATION; LEAPFROG; MARKET GAP ANALYSIS; NEW PRODUCT NEEDS; PRODUCT (OR SERVICE) GAP; QUALITY MODIFICATION; STYLE MODIFICATION; USAGE GAP

References: Corey, E. Raymond (1976) *Industrial Marketing, Cases and Concepts* Englewood Cliffs, NJ: Prentice-Hall.

Doyle, Peter (1989) Building successful brands: the strategic options. *Journal of Marketing Management*, 5(1).

new product failures *see* CONCEPT TEST, NEW PRODUCTS

new product innovation Dramatically innovative new 'products' have had major impacts in a number of markets. Their influence in these markets has been vastly greater than that of the evolving products or services – 'supernovas' outshining the 'stars'. What is more, they follow few of the rules of conventional marketing. Even market research is of little use in the basic decisions (though it is still of considerable use in helping to determine the exact details of the launch). The main requirement is for faith in the new development. The most successful organizations try to create the sort of environment in which such creativity is nurtured. They also foster the attitude of mind which will quickly recognize the merits of such outstanding innovations.

As a result of the lack of conventional marketing input to these important new developments, a number of practitioners, as well as some academics, have recently tended to downplay the importance of conventional marketing. That is a mistake. With the distorting benefit of hindsight, we tend to notice the few major developments. We do not see the many hundreds of failures – which were just as sincerely believed in by their creators (and which not infrequently destroyed the hopes of those creators!). We are also blind to the many thousands of products and services which continue to evolve slowly.

The great bulk of marketing revolves around the 'steady state' of mature markets and mature products. In this context most new products are incremental. The supplier who neglects these more mundane processes in the hope that something spectacular will emerge is gambling with the future of the organization; a gamble which may be won, but which will more likely be lost – there are many more stars than supernovas.

Booz, Allen & Hamilton's 1981 research measured the proportions as follows:

New to the world products (entirely new markets)	10%
New product lines (new products in existing markets)	20%
Additions to existing lines	26%
Improvements in/revisions to existing products	26%
Repositioning (existing products in new segments/markets)	7%
Cost reductions (similar performance at lower cost)	11%

Innovation is important (indeed, essential) to the future of most organizations. It must, though, be kept in context. Peters and Waterman's (1982) well-known exhortation still offers sound advice: 'Stick to the knitting . . .While there were a few exceptions, the odds for excellent performance seem strongly to favour those companies that stay reasonably close to the businesses they know.' 'Focus', as it is now more fashionably known, is a sound policy. More important, perhaps, is a keen awareness that the future usually also depends on the existing products – albeit so (incrementally) changed over time that they would be unrecognizable to today's customers!

In this context it is worth noting that Robert Cooper (1985) found, in 140 companies in Canada, five new product strategy scenarios:

- '*Technologically driven strategy* (26.2 per cent of firms)'. A strategy based on technological sophistication, but lacking marketing orientation and product fit/focus. New products ended up in unattractive, low synergy markets; with 'Moderate results: high impact on firm, but low success rate . . .'
- '*Balanced, focused strategy* (15.6 per cent of firms)'. This winning strategy featured a balance between technological sophistication, orientation and innovativeness, and a strong marketing orientation. The programme was highly focused, and new products were targeted at very attractive markets. 'By far the strongest performance . . .'
- '*Technologically deficient strategy* (15.6 per cent of firms)'. A 'non-strategy': weak technology, with low technological synergy, yet involving new markets and new market needs. 'Very poor results . . .'
- '*Low budget, conservative strategy* (23.8 per cent of firms)'. A low level of R&D spending, involving 'me-too' products, but with a 'stay-close-to-home' approach – high technological synergy and high product fit/focus. A safe, efficient but undramatic programme. 'Moderate results: good success rate and profitability, but low impact . . .'
- '*High budget, diverse strategy* (18.9 per cent of firms)'. A high level of R&D spending, but poorly targeted; (highly competitive) markets new to the firm; no programme focus. 'Very poor results . . .'

The ideal approach, as Robert Cooper identifies, is that well-planned one which nicely balances all these factors (which is, in its own way, the strategy towards which many marketing textbooks build). On the other hand, the authors do seem to dismiss too glibly the 'conservative approach'. This may not have the 'impact' (glamour?) of the other, but if you do not yet know the well-planned, balanced route, better stay where you are until you can find it!

Above all, it should be remembered that, despite the glamour of the new product process, it is the plodding (steadily regenerated) 'cash cow' which continues to dominate even the 'development' process in most markets!

See also ANSOFF MATRIX; COMPETITIVE GAP; CREATIVE IMITATION; CUSTOMER BONUS; DISTRIBUTION GAP; EXISTING PRODUCT CHANGES; GAP ANALYSIS; LEAPFROG; MARKET GAP ANALYSIS; NEW PRODUCT NEEDS; PRODUCT (OR SERVICE) GAP; USAGE GAP

References: Booz, Allen & Hamilton Inc. (1981) New Products Management for the 1980s.
Cooper, Robert E. (1985) Overall corporate strategies for new product programs. Industrial Marketing, 14.
Peters, Thomas J. and Waterman, Robert H., Jr (1982) In Search of Excellence. New York: Harper & Row.

new product launches   see ADVERTISING; PROMOTIONAL PRICING

new product needs   Donald Cowell (1988) offers a pragmatic list of reasons for developing new 'products' (in his case the list refers to 'services', but much the same list could be applied to physical products):

Obsolescence – service organisations cannot continue to rely on their existing range of services for their success. Sooner or later they become obsolete . . . Change is a way of life for the innovative service organisation.
Competition – new services are required to maintain present sales success and customer loyalty . . .
Spare capacity – new services may be introduced to use up spare capacity . . .
Seasonal effects – new services may be introduced to even out these fluctuations.
Risk reduction – new services may be introduced to balance an existing sales portfolio.
New opportunities . . .

Only the last category is conventionally seen to be the target of new product development – but the reality often is that the other categories (typically involving incremental change upon existing products or services) represent the greater part of 'new product development' in its widest sense, and certainly of new 'business opportunities' in the average organization.

See also ANSOFF MATRIX; COMPETITIVE GAP; DISTRIBUTION GAP; GAP ANALYSIS; MARKET GAP ANALYSIS; PRODUCT (OR SERVICE) GAP; USAGE GAP

Reference: Cowell, Donald W. (1988) New service development. Journal of Marketing Management, 3(3).

new products   see BUDGETS; DIFFUSION OF INNOVATION

new product screening, organizational factors   The first consideration in deciding on a new product will be how it 'meshes' with the existing activities undertaken by the organization. The context for this examination should be that of the formal 'corporate strategy' – the statement of where the organization has decided it is going. If the change is in conflict with the strategy, then it will need to be abandoned, or the whole corporate strategy should be reviewed.

Some of the 'internal', corporate factors which may, therefore, need to be taken into account in the further investigations will be:

- production capabilities
- financial performance
- investment potential
- human factors
- materials supply
- cannibalism
- time

See also CANNIBALISM, NEW PRODUCTS; HUMAN FACTORS, NEW PRODUCTS; MATERIALS SUPPLY, NEW PRODUCTS; PRODUCTION CAPABILITIES, NEW PRODUCTS; STRATEGIC SCREENING, NEW PRODUCTS; TIME, NEW PRODUCTS

new product screening, product factors   In the process of screening for new products, the process will have to take into account how the new product might work alongside the existing marketing operations, in terms of:

- match with existing range(s)
- price and quality
- distribution patterns
- seasonality

See also DISTRIBUTION PATTERNS, PRODUCT SCREENING; MATCH WITH EXISTING RANGE(S), PRODUCT SCREENING; NEW PRODUCT SCREENING, ORGANIZATIONAL FACTORS; PRICE AND QUALITY, PRODUCT SCREENING; SEASONALITY, PRODUCT SCREENING; STRATEGIC SCREENING, NEW PRODUCTS

new products, growth stage In the case of mass consumer goods, following a successful introduction, distribution will be extended to all the outlets available. In other sectors the sales force will canvass the remaining, smaller prospects. The main task, though, will be to develop customer or consumer sales. The advertising, possibly using relatively long commercials with more emphasis on features and image, will be formulated to explain the product and create a favourable attitude so that the consumer is persuaded to switch buying patterns from the existing brands. Sales personnel will follow-up their leads to start closing significant amounts of business. Money-off coupons, and similar promotional devices, may be used to extend the trial period.

new 'products', pricing *see* PRICING NEW 'PRODUCTS'

new products, sampling *see* SAMPLING

new product strategy *see* NEW PRODUCT INNOVATION

news conferences and public relations *see* PUBLIC RELATIONS

news items and public relations *see* PUBLIC RELATIONS

newsletters *see* CORPORATE PUBLIC RELATIONS

news media, data The most prevalent, but unrecognized, source of external data for all managers (and the one which covers, or 'scans', the widest perspective) is that of the news media (especially the morning newspaper, and the television news and current affairs programmes). The amount of information these provide is probably vastly greater than that received from any other source, even though their coverage is also much wider. The choice of news media, in particular of newspapers, taken thus becomes important. The 'broadsheet' papers are likely to be of more value than the 'tabloids'. Ideally, a number of newspapers should be read to judge the bias each almost inevitably imparts to even the sim-

plest news item. The reader of *The Times* might be well advised to sometimes read *The Guardian*. A positive approach to 'news' in general, essentially that of an enquiring mind, is also necessary. Ideally, there should be some commitment to 'scanning', but an enquiring mind is the next best thing! Reading relevant business journals (such as the *Economist*, *Business Week*, *Fortune*) is also informative, as well as often entertaining.
See also EXTERNAL DATA; LIBRARIES; PUBLIC RELATIONS

newspapers *see* PRESS MEDIA

new suppliers *see* ORGANIZATIONAL BUYING SITUATIONS

new task buying *see* BUYGRID ANALYSIS; ORGANIZATIONAL BUYING SITUATIONS

new technologies *see* CREATIVE IMITATION; LEAPFROG; TRIAD POWER

next matter Advertisements placed in a newspaper or magazine next to reading (editorial) matter. *See also* MEDIA IMPACT; MEDIA SELECTION; MEDIA TYPES

next to reading (editorial) matter *see* NEXT MATTER

niceties, social *see* SALES CALL OPENING

niche A specialized, and indeed extreme, version of segmentation is that of creating 'niches'. It is practised especially by some organizations in the retail sector. In this form the 'niche' (the segment) chosen is barely viable for one 'supplier'. The organization then sets out to capture this segment (and possibly to expand it), confident in the knowledge that no competitor will subsequently be able to (profitably) follow. However, as Sock Shop, for instance, discovered, competitors based in other segments may still be able to draw sales from the niche market – and in the process reduce the viability of the niche operation itself!
See also DECLINE STRATEGIES; GLOBAL MARKETING; PRICING, PRODUCT POSITIONING; PRODUCT (OR SERVICE) POSITIONING; SEGMENTATION; SKIMMING, PRICING

Nicosia model A model, based on a computer flowchart technique, of consumer behaviour.
See also MODELS

noise   *see* ENCODING

nominal group technique (NPT)   A (group) creative technique, sometimes described (in a slightly different version) as 'brainwriting', which requires participants to add ideas (anonymously) to those already written on one of a number of different cards (or pieces of paper) before passing to others to add their own ideas.
See also NEW PRODUCT CREATION

non-core businesses   *see* PLANNING PITFALLS

non-executive director   A member of the board – often an outside director who is not employed directly – who is involved in taking strategic decisions but not in the day-to-day operations of the company.
See also CONSULTANTS

non-financial measures   *see* MONITORING, PROGRESS

non-linear models   *see* MODEL CATEGORIES

non-price competition/factors   Competition between organizations in the market which does not involve price competition, but is conducted by other means – usually by promotional (advertising) spending.
See also ADVERTISING; COMPETITION PRICING

non-price promotions   There are a number of forms of promotion which aim to offer 'added value' but which are not directly 'price' related:

Competitions
In this case the purchaser receives the right of one or more entries in a competition. If the main prize is very large (and it is the size of the top prize which reportedly determines the interest of the consumer) this can be a very attention-getting form of promotion (and can add interest to a product or service – especially when there is little else to say about it!). It can be very easy and cheap to mount, and has a guaranteed fixed maximum cost. Overall, though, it has a lower level of interest for the consumer, with a low 'redemption' rate, and is now often just used as a means of gaining extra in-store impact.

Personality promotions
In earlier days, in particular, teams of 'sales promoters' toured the country (sometimes dressed in the most outlandish of costumes – such as hens!), offering incentives ('instant prizes', for example) to potential customers. More recently, this has been largely superseded by 'in-store promotions', staffed by the same personnel (who are, in any case, usually part-time staff employed by specialist agencies). The process can be expensive, and difficult to control – though it may occasionally generate some of the benefits of face-to-face selling.

Free gifts and mail-ins
These give the customer an additional offer (a 'giveaway' either 'on-pack', at point of sale or by mailing in). They can be expensive to run (if the 'free offer' is not so cheap as to damage the image; free plastic daffodils and glasses have almost become clichés). They can be used to establish repeat purchase if a number of coupons (and hence packs) have to be collected. The administration, though, can be complex; and additional sales may just come from heavy users buying forward. Once again, a database can be created if 'mailing in' is the vehicle chosen. A special form of the 'give-away' is one where the container itself is 'reusable' (for instance, a shelf-storage jar containing an instant coffee brand). This can be cheap to run (where the cost of the normal container can be offset against it), but it will require special production facilities, and may be counter-productive if customers do not want the reusable container (and, more important, do not want to pay for the extra cost it incurs). Such free gifts are not, though, restricted to FMCG products: the Royal Bank of Scotland, for example, has offered free legal help and surveys to those taking out a mortgage.

'Self-liquidating' offers
In this case the offer is not free, but, rather, the customer makes some payment for it (as a result of which some writers call it a 'premium' offer). Like a competition, it can add interest (and create readership for advertisements), and the impression is usually given that the supplier is subsidizing the offer, so that the customer will obtain a good deal on the item. In practice, as is evidenced by the 'self-liquidating' name, the intention is usually to cover the cost within the amount paid by the customer – offering, in effect, the customer only the benefit of the supplier's buying power (or the special deal which has been negotiated). It is, on the other hand, now seen as having low consumer interest (according to Schultz and Robinson (1982) 'It's estimated that less than 10% of the population have ever sent away for a self-liquidating premium . . . redemption of self-liquidating premiums is usually less than 1% of the media circulation where it is offered') and is only used in those marginal situations where such marginal

impact is worthwhile, though there would appear to be few of these! It can also have significant hidden costs, since it is difficult to administer and forecasting stock levels is a very problematic experience.

Multibrand promotions
This is a variant where a number of brands, typically from one supplier, share a single promotion in order to maximize impact for given costs. It can also be used, though, to recruit new users to these other brands. It will, however, only work well if all these brands are in widespread distribution and there is some logic to the link.
See also PRECISION MARKETING

Reference: Schultz, Don E. and Robinson, William A. (1982) *Sales Promotion Essentials*. New York: Crain Books.

non-profit customer types   One complication in the case of not-for-profit organizations is that there may be several types of 'customer'. There are the 'clients' for the service, as well as those who 'decide' who the 'clients' will be (for example, sponsors of open business school students) and the 'donors' of the funds to provide that service. Each of these groups will have a different set of needs and will need to be marketed to separately. As a result there may be multiple objectives, and, in particular, activities may be subject to public scrutiny.

In the RNLI (the Royal National Lifeboat Institution), for example, the main 'clients' may be sailors and seafarers (and, more specifically, seafarers in trouble!), while the 'donors' are those members of the general public who succumb to the pressures of its collectors. In addition, the government, as an arbiter of standards (and possibly a provider of some funds), can also be seen as a 'customer'. The RNLI has to balance all these separate groups of 'wants and needs' if it is to provide the correct level of service, and obtain the funds to cover its costs and investments. To manage this balance, it needs all the skills involved in marketing. At one end of the process, it certainly needs to appreciate its external environment, be it through market research or through its local support groups. At the other end, it has to 'promote' itself to its 'donors', to persuade them to part with their money – which can require considerable persuasion by its army of face-to-face salesmen (its collectors), where the 'donor' receives no tangible product in return!
See also NOT–FOR–PROFIT ORGANIZATIONS

non-profit 'new products'   With many of the commercial pressures removed, and probably with no competitive challenges in sight, it might be asked why should the sophisticated new product process apply, for example, to the public sector. The answer is that most of the elements, if not all, are just as applicable in the context of making sure that the 'product' is the best possible match to the clients' needs – and the most productive use of resources. After a 10 year development period, the Royal Air Force's 'Lightning' fighter flew. It was a magnificent achievement, and a great favourite with the crowds at air shows. It flew at twice the speed of sound and reached its operational height of 60 000 feet in a matter of minutes. The only problem was that by then the 'enemy' bombers were operating at only a few hundred feet above the ground – at which height the Lightning was hopelessly inefficient, and could only handle contact for a few seconds. This illustrates the general point that an on-going evaluation of any product development process is essential if the producer is to avoid some very expensive mistakes.
See also PRODUCT DEVELOPMENT PROCESS

non-response   *see* RANDOM SAMPLES

non-runners   *see* EXPORT MARKET ELIMINATION

non-tariff barriers   *see* REGULATORY CONSIDERATIONS, FILTERING UNSUITABLE MARKETS

non-users   *see* USAGE AND LOYALTY

normal curve   A statistically 'normal' (bell-shaped) frequency curve, defined in terms of the standard deviation. The latter is a measure of the spread of the results – derived from the square root of the average of the sum of the squares of the individual deviations from average (hence it may be referred to as the root mean square deviation). Where a normal curve applies, just under 70 per cent of results fall within one standard deviation of the mean, 95 per cent within two and 99 per cent within three; and these same figures may be applied as probabilities that the result will fall into these same ranges. Normal curves are used, for example, in statistical quality control based on taking samples of batches.
See also ZERO DEFECTS

normative or descriptive/predictive models   *see* MODEL CATEGORIES

North/South divide   *see* MARKET ENTRY DECISION

notes   *see* PRESENTATION STYLE

note-taking   It is usual to take notes during a sales call (though less conventional in a normal conversation between managers!), but only after asking permission. There is, however, a peculiar reluctance on the part of some sales professionals to take notes. Perhaps they believe that their prospects will object. In practice, many sales prospects expect it, and will not feel that the sales professional is taking them seriously enough if they do not record the words for posterity.

See also QUESTIONING; UNDERSTANDING

not-for-profit organizations   Perhaps the area where there is the most difficulty in coming to terms with marketing, not least in the acceptance of the basic concepts, is that of not-for-profit organizations. Possibly the main reason for this is that most marketing theory, having been developed by commercial organizations, is described in terms of improving profit performance. This use of profit as the main measure of marketing effectiveness allows for a practical, and very measurable, approach in these commercial organizations, but it obviously poses major problems for those organizations which cannot measure their performance in such terms.

One resulting problem, therefore, may be that some not-for-profit organizations simply do not recognize the requirement to meet their customers' needs. Keith Blois (1987), for instance, reports that 'There are a significant number of non-profit organisations which basically hold the view that they know what is best for their consumers. As a consequence of this, they are instinctively ill at ease with marketing for it appears to make the consumer dominant.'

On the other hand, as Philip Kotler (1979) points out:

> Administrators and businessmen who have a stake in the third sector are beginning to recognize the contributions that marketing thinking can make. Marketing will lead to a better understanding of the needs of different client segments; to a more careful shaping and launching of new services; to a pruning of weak services; to more flexible pricing approaches; and to higher levels of client satisfaction.

See also MATCH (FOR NOT-FOR-PROFIT ORGANIZATIONS); SERVICE CULTURES

References: Blois, Keith J. (1987) Managing for non-profit organizations. In Michael J. Baker (ed.), *The Marketing Book*. London: Heinemann.

Kotler, Philip (1979) Strategies for introducing marketing into nonprofit organizations. *Journal of Marketing*, 43.

not-for-profit organizations, and marketing research   *see* SERVICES AND MARKETING RESEARCH

not-for-profit organizations and the market   The market concept is clearly just as applicable to services as to the products around which the theory normally revolves. But the term 'market' can even represent a powerful concept in the 'non-profit' sectors. Although the word 'market' itself might sound strange, emerging from the mouths of civil servants say, the idea of defining the 'set' of 'customers' who are the focus of their activities is a powerful one. It helps concentrate their attention (externally) on the needs they are meant to be addressing, rather than (internally) on the problems of the bureaucratic processes. It helps put service before red-tape! Every not-for-profit organization has clients, or 'customers' in the conventional marketing terminology. They may have just a few very powerful clients, as the International Monetary Fund does, or they may deal with millions of individuals, as the Department of Social Security does. But defining exactly who these clients are, in relation to the activities of the organization itself, is just as important an exercise as for a commercial organization. It helps decide what the organization should be doing to most effectively deliver the services or products it is charged with producing. This 'market', albeit not usually complicated by the same competitive overtones as its commercial equivalents, is ultimately just as powerful a force on a not-for-profit organization.

See also MARKETS; SEGMENTATION

not-for-profit organizations, objectives   In the case of not-for-profit organizations, objectives may be even less clear than for those in the private sector. Keith Blois (1987) suggests five main reasons for the differences from 'commercial' organizations:

1. *'Ambiguous goals'* – more actors and groups of actors (including those external to the organization, such as its members or providers of funds) are involved.
2. *'Lack of agreement in means–end relationships'* – even where there is consensus on the goal, there may be disagreement on how to get there.
3. *'Environmental turbulence'* – not-for-profit organizations seem to be more exposed to turbulence than commercial ones.

4. '*Unmeasurable outputs*' – unfortunately, by definition, not-for-profit organizations do have the classically convenient simplicity of 'bottom-line profit' (and such organizations often have a poor idea of what their key outputs are – and do not measure them accurately).

5. '*The effects of management intervention are unknown*' – the lack of precision caused by factors 1–4 is problem enough, but the 'culture' seems to add further barriers to managing these organizations.

Even so, Kotler and Andreasen (1987) suggest some possible objectives for such organizations:

- '*Surplus maximisation*' – equivalent to profit maximization.
- '*Revenue maximisation*' – as for profit-making organizations.
- '*Usage maximisation*' – maximizing the numbers of users and their usage.
- '*Usage targeting*' – matching the capacity available.
- '*Full cost recovery*' – breaking even.
- '*Partial cost recovery*' – minimizing the subsidy.
- '*Budget maximisation*' – maximizing what is offered.
- '*Producer satisfaction maximisation*' – satisfying the wants of staff.

See also CORPORATE OBJECTIVES

References: Blois, Keith J. (1987) Managing for non-profit organizations. In Michael J. Baker (ed.), *The Marketing Book*. London: Heinemann.

Kotler, Philip and Andreasen, Alan R. (1987) *Strategic Marketing for Nonprofit Organizations*. Englewood Cliffs, NJ: Prentice-Hall.

noting score   The percentage of readers noticing a particular advertisement in a newspaper or magazine.
See also ADVERTISING RESEARCH

notional costs   *see* INTERNATIONAL PRICE DECISION

NPT   *see* NOMINAL GROUP TECHNIQUE

null hypothesis   The basic hypothesis (proposition) against which significance testing is undertaken, so called because it is often expressed in null or negative terms. Despite the academic language, the test is often as simple as 'most customers buy this product'.
See also ANALYSIS OF MARKETING RESEARCH DATA

number of exposures   *see* MEDIA SELECTION

numbers game   *see* CALL TARGETS; CONTROL, OF SALES PERSONNEL; DIRECT MAIL ADVERTISING; PROSPECT QUALIFICATION; RECRUITMENT, OF SALES PERSONNEL; RISK, OF NEW PRODUCTS; SAFETY IN NUMBERS; SALES CALL CLOSE

numbers on questionnaires   *see* CLOSED QUESTIONS, ON QUESTIONNAIRES

numerical data   *see* MARKETING PLAN STRUCTURE

numerical differences   It is often easier to convey details of numeric results better by looking at the differences between them (relative values, say, rather than absolute ones). Best of all, if you can, is to look for deviations from targets or budgets.
See also RESEARCH REPORTS, USAGE

objection handling It seems almost as if many sales training writers, having spent most of the first half of their books on features/benefits, fill the second half with 'handling objections'. They, and many sales professionals, appear to be obsessed with objections. This is a topic which is included here because it gives an insight into the psyche (and the problems) of many sales personnel. On the other hand, you should be clear that the topic has no relevance to management discussions – and it would be counter-productive to think of any of these communications in terms of 'objection handling'. In fairness it should be pointed out that much of sales training originated in the field of selling to retail outlets, where the one-call sell (and then perhaps only a 15 minute call) was a matter of sheer survival. In these specific circumstances effective objection handling is important; there is no time for the niceties, or the sale is lost. But most professional selling is now a rather different game, often extending over several calls, and certainly using calls in a much more complex manner.

The views which follow would be considered idiosyncratic by many sales trainers who make a proportion of their comfortable living by teaching such objection handling techniques! I would agree, though, with Alan Williams (1983) – perhaps predictably, as he was once an IBM sales professional – when he says that:

It is unfortunate that the term 'sales objection' has somehow crept into the selling vocabulary without being identified as the negative expression it really is, responsible for much self-inflicted, irrational anxiety for many salesmen. There is seldom such a thing as a sales objection! . . . It should be welcomed as a clear indication of the buyer's interest and involvement! . . . The sales objection should always be seen for what it really is – a plea for more information.

Tom Hopkins (1982) makes a similar comment: 'Objections are the rungs of the ladder to sales success . . . you'll learn to love objections – because they announce buying intention and point the way to closing the sale'.

Most of the 'objections' that sales professionals fight are nothing more than innocent questions. Most buyers, once the sales professional has established a good rapport with them, have no reason to try to score points. Buyers are interested in what they are buying, and will ask many questions, more than a few of them difficult and complex. But that is good, because it shows that they are still interested. As Miller et al. (1985) point out, 'Serving the customer's best interest is ultimately the best way of serving your own'. In this scenario, an 'objection' is deliberately recognized as a 'question' so that it can be redirected in the form 'How can we solve this; so that you (the prospect) can still obtain the best solution?' The buyer has just as much incentive to work for the best solution.

Although I disagree with many of the pundits on the basic attitude to adopt, there are a few ground rules for making the handling of 'objections' an easier process, where I would be in agreement with most sales trainers. Alfred Tack, once more, best sums up the most important of these:

1. Don't interrupt.
2. When it is dealt with do not return to it later.
3. It is sometimes wise to repeat it to ensure understanding.
4. Use the apparent-agreement technique: 'I can understand your thinking at this stage . . .' (but only showing understanding, not agreement – simply to relax the buyer).

There are many 'proprietary' techniques for handling objections and they still represent much of the sales training industry's output. If you want to read about these then pick up almost any popular sales book; it is likely that as much as a third of it will cover this topic.
See also SALES CALL

References: Hopkins, Tom (1982) *How to Master the Art of Selling*. London: Champion Press.
Miller, Robert B., Heiman, Stephen E. and Tuleja, Tad (1985) *Strategic Selling*. New York: William Morrow.
Williams, Alan (1983) *All About Selling*. Maidenhead: McGraw-Hill.

objections close   *see* CLOSING TECHNIQUES

objective and task, advertising budget   *see* ADVERTISING BUDGETS

objectives   *see* MARKETING OBJECTIVES; MARKETING PLAN STRUCTURE; MARKETING STRATEGIES; MONITORING, PROGRESS; STRATEGIC BUSINESS UNIT (SBU)

objectives, advertising   *see* ADVERTISING PLAN

objectives, corporate   *see* CORPORATE OBJECTIVES

objectives for not-for-profit organizations   *see* NOT-FOR-PROFIT ORGANIZATIONS, OBJECTIVES

objectives, marketing research   *see* MARKETING RESEARCH OBJECTIVES

objectives of promotions   *see* PROMOTION OBJECTIVES

objective trees   Objectives are usually described consecutively, without any clear relationship between them. A useful technique is to write them in the form of a hierarchy – a tree structure where sub-objectives are clearly related to overarching ones:

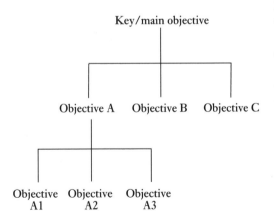

Key/main objective

Objective A   Objective B   Objective C

Objective   Objective   Objective
   A1   A2   A3

In practice it may prove more difficult to assign objectives to such a hierarchy, but it should not be impossible – and it often provides a very illuminating insight into the relationship between them, especially their underlying conflicts.
See also CORPORATE OBJECTIVES; MARKETING OBJECTIVES

objectivity, consultants   *see* CONSULTANTS

observation, research   This approach to marketing research is based upon watching participants as they undertake some activity, simply to see what happens. Traffic census data, for example, is often based on just counting the number of cars travelling along a particular road, or turning right or whatever. Similarly, the pattern of customer flow in a supermarket is best determined by simply watching it (albeit using sophisticated video recording and computer analysis to make the data more meaningful).
See also MARKETING RESEARCH; MARKETING RESEARCH STAGES

obsolescence   *see* NEW PRODUCT NEEDS

obsolescence, advertising   *see* ADVERTISING OBSOLESCENCE

obtaining trial   In mass consumer markets the launch of new products, or variations on existing ones, is the stage at which door-to-door deliveries of samples, or money-off coupons, in selected areas will be used to try to achieve an early trial of the new product. Here persuading potential users to take the risk of such a trial is one of the main barriers to entry into markets. In industrial markets, or those of capital goods, the 'free trial' is often used as the equivalent – even extending to the free test drive of a new car.

occasions (when used)   *see* SEGMENTATION

occupational influences, on the purchase decision   The occupation of the individual, or the head of the household, can sometimes significantly affect his or her way of life. This may be less important now than when there was the great split between manual ('blue-collar') and clerical ('white-collar') jobs. Even so, a manager in a 'high-tech' industry may still have a different set of values to those of a worker on a production line in a declining industry; and different again to those of a university academic in the public sector.
See also DECISION-MAKING PROCESS, BY CUSTOMERS; REPEAT PURCHASING PROCESS; SOCIAL CLASS INFLUENCES, ON THE PURCHASE DECISION

odd–even pricing   Pricing a product in an odd number, just below the next rounded number ($4.99 rather than $5.00, say), to make it seem cheaper.

OECD *see* DERIVED FORECASTS; EXPORT MARKET ELIMINATION; INTERNATIONAL MARKETING RESEARCH

off-balance-sheet financing This is the payment for the use of an asset by hiring it or leasing it over the longer term, so that it offers a method of financing assets and does not appear on the balance sheet (and hence improves its reported return on capital).

offer *see* NON-PRICE PROMOTIONS

offer, direct mail *see* DIRECT MAIL OFFER

offering *see* 4 Ps

offering, retail *see* RETAIL 'PRODUCT' DECISIONS

off-peak The transmission times when low audiences are to be expected.

off-peak pricing *see* PRICES, CUSTOMER NEEDS

off-peak slot *see* MEDIA BUYING, ADVERTISING AGENCY

off-price label A label showing a reduced price on a product.
See also PROMOTIONAL PRICING

offset deals *see* COUNTERTRADING

off-the-page buying Buying of items advertised for direct sale in newspapers and magazines.
See also MEDIA IMPACT; MEDIA SELECTION; MEDIA TYPES

off-the-shelf items *see* MAKE OR BUY

Ohno, Taiichi *see* KANBAN

omnibus surveys These are very similar to *ad hoc* surveys, except that 'space' on the questionnaire is 'sub-let' to different researchers, who provide, in effect, their own 'mini-survey'. Such omnibus surveys are often run (covering 2000 respondents per week, say) on the back of on-going research, for example political or opinion polls (such as MORI or NOP in the UK). The cost benefits can be significant if fieldwork forms the major element of the market research costs. Such surveys may also provide a faster turnaround of results, particularly if the survey is conducted by telephone. The 'questionnaire' will,

however, need to be short, its questions cannot be complex and the context may be unpredictable (where the questions asked by the other researchers are not controllable). Such surveys can also be used to locate individuals belonging to minority groups, so that they can be followed up by conventional *ad hoc* surveys.
See also CONSULTANCIES, AND MARKETING RESEARCH; CUSTOM RESEARCH; MARKETING RESEARCH; PANEL RESEARCH; RETAIL AUDITS

one-level distribution *see* CHANNEL MEMBERS

one-stop shopping A shopping centre which contains the whole range of stores and services needed to meet shoppers' needs.

one-stop solution, advertising *see* SPECIALIST AGENCIES

on-line booking systems *see* BOOKING SYSTEM

on-order items *see* COMPUTER INVENTORY CONTROL

on-pack *see* NON-PRICE PROMOTIONS; PROMOTIONAL PRICING; PROMOTION OBJECTIVES

on-site (plant visit) evaluation *see* SUPPLIER EVALUATION

on-target earnings *see* OTE

open auction *see* PRICE, PURCHASE

open brief *see* AGENCY BRIEFING

open dating Printing a sell-by date on the product which is understandable to the customer.

opening, sales call *see* SALES CALL OPENING

open-market operations *see* MONETARY POLICY

open pricing Co-operation by companies to obtain conformity in pricing. It may be seen as price fixing (by the sellers) or ringing (by the buyers) – and may be illegal in some countries.
See also COMPETITIVE PRICING; PRICING STRATEGY; PRISONER'S DILEMMA

open questions The most important, and productive, questions are the 'open' ones which cannot

be answered by a simple 'yes' or 'no', or by just a few words. They allow the person being questioned to expand on the subject, to 'ramble on'. They also seem to be the most difficult to ask – perhaps because they are not so obviously leading directly to the answer that is wanted, or maybe because the questioner feels less in control. But they are the key to unlocking the tongue of the person facing you. If the conversation proceeds with very short replies (and particularly just 'yes' or 'no'), it is likely that you are not using enough open questions, and may be missing the real needs. The more open the question the better. The most powerful question is quite simply 'Why?', often closely followed by 'How?'
See also LADDERING, INTERVIEWING/QUESTIONING; QUESTIONING; RAMBLING, INTERVIEWING/QUESTIONING; SILENCE, INTERVIEWING/QUESTIONING

open questions, on questionnaires These questions, as part of a marketing research questionnaire, allow the respondent to answer in his or her own words. Although the question is fixed, there is no preconceived set of expected answers. This means, however, that to be statistically useful the answers later have to be 'coded' into groups which make some sort of sense. This imposes extra costs, and requires that the person coding the results understands what the cryptic comments from the respondent really mean.

These open questions may take the simple form of words such as 'Why did you buy Brand A?'

Where there are barriers (in particular, psychological barriers, but also language or social barriers) they may, however, be overcome by a variety of devices (sometimes called 'projective techniques') such as:

* *Sentence completion* – 'When I chose Brand A, the most important thought on my mind was ... (complete the sentence)'
* *Thematic apperception tests (TAT)* – where the respondent is shown an ambiguous picture or cartoon, related to the topic, and is asked to make up a sentence (or even a short story) about what is happening.

Other projective techniques which may be used are word association (so beloved of psychiatrists), picture drawing or 'the friendly Martian' (where the question is asked in terms of how someone else might see the situation).
See also QUESTIONNAIRE DESIGN

open to buy *see* CHANNEL MOTIVATION

operating plan *see* MARKETING PLANNING, ANALYSIS; MARKETING PLAN STRUCTURE

operational research *see* SYSTEMS APPROACHES

opinion leaders It is often argued that, in the case of a new product, the effect of promotion may occur in two stages. The promotion itself (usually advertising) persuades the more adventurous opinion leaders in the population to try the product or service. These opinion leaders then carry the message to those who are less exposed to it (in the mass markets this often means those who may be less exposed to the mass media). As Gatignon and Robertson (1985) describe it:

> The extant two-step model depicts mass media reading opinion leaders who, in turn, influence a set of followers. This information-giving flow may, in fact, be valid for some percentage of personal influence transactions. However, other flows are possible, including information seeking and information sharing ... Most personal influence is transmitted within a network of peers who possess similar demographic characteristics ... The probability of such influence is high simply because people are most likely to interact with similar others.

This is not the same as the 'trickle-down' theory, much favoured in certain parts of the social sciences, which assumes that patterns of consumption are led by the upper classes and then 'trickle down' to the lower classes. 'Opinion leaders', rather, influence members of their own class – horizontally, in terms of class groupings. Whichever of these approaches is adopted, however, it is clear that the impact of media advertising may be much more complex than many of its practitioners allow for.
See also ADVERTISING; ADVERTISING OBSOLESCENCE; BUYING DECISION, ADVERTISING MODELS; ENHANCED AIUAPR MODEL; PEER PYRAMID; SOCIAL CLASS INFLUENCES, ON THE PURCHASE DECISION; THREE PILLARS OF THE PURCHASING PROCESS

Reference: Gatignon, Hubert and Robertson, Thomas S (1985) A propositional inventory for new diffusion research. *Journal of Consumer Research*, 11.

opinion research *see* PROACTIVE PR

Opinion Survey, IBM *see* INNER MARKETING

opportunism   *see* TRANSACTION COST ECONOMICS

opportunities   *see* ANSOFF MATRIX; MARKETING AUDIT; NEW PRODUCT NEEDS; SWOT ANALYSIS

Opportunities To See (OTS)   *see* ADVERTISING PLAN; BUDGETS; ENCODING; MEDIA SELECTION; SHARPENING THE CUTTING EDGE OF MEDIA

opportunity cost   The (alternative) opportunities lost by not deploying resources to the most beneficial (profitable) alternatives available.

OPT   *see* OPTIMIZED PRODUCTION TECHNOLOGY (OPT)

optical typesetting   *see* LINOTYPE; PHOTOCOMPOSITION

optimal impact   *see* SHARPENING THE CUTTING EDGE OF MEDIA

optimal prices   *see* MARKET-BASED PRICING

optimization   *see* CORPORATE OBJECTIVES; MARKETING OBJECTIVES

optimization, direct mail   *see* DIRECT MAIL ADVANTAGES AND DISADVANTAGES

Optimized Production Technology (OPT)   A proprietary computerized production scheduling system developed by Eli Goldratt (1986) which is based on optimizing performance measures, rather than traditional financial measures. One of the three main scheduling approaches – the others being MRPII and the kanban system (often referred to as JIT) – it focuses on throughput rather than capacity utilization (unlike MRPII – which typically optimizes plant utilization). In particular it concentrates on the bottleneck(s) which limit throughput (its basic philosophy is that an hour lost at a bottleneck is an hour lost overall). It schedules around these, typically aggregating the largest possible batches (to reduce the proportion of the set-up time) at bottlenecks. Using variable sizes of batch, it schedules both backwards from the bottleneck (to keep it supplied) and forwards (to optimize the lead time).
See also INVENTORY CONTROL; JUST IN TIME (JIT); KANBAN; LOGISTICS MANAGEMENT; MATERIALS REQUIREMENTS PLANNING (MRP); MATERIALS REQUIREMENTS PLANNING II (MRPII); SET-UP TIMES

Reference: Goldratt, E. M. and Fox, R E (1986) *The Race*. Croton on Hudson: North River Press.

optimum cost point   *see* FLEXIBLE MANUFACTURING

option   A contract to buy (or sell) a commodity or a security (or foreign exchange) at some time in the future.

options forecast   *see* SCENARIOS

options list   *see* MARKETING STRATEGIES

order   *see* SALES CALL CLOSE

order cost overhead   *see* PRODUCTION DECISIONS, LOGISTICS MANAGEMENT

order cycle time   *see* LEAD TIME

order form close   *see* CLOSING TECHNIQUES

order frequency   *see* PRODUCTION DECISIONS, LOGISTICS MANAGEMENT

order lead time   *see* MONITORING, PROGRESS

order point   *see* PRODUCTION DECISIONS, LOGISTICS MANAGEMENT

order processing   The starting point of logistical management systems is usually the 'order'. In commercial organizations this is the agreement, by the customer (either the end-user or an organization in the distribution chain, such as the retailer), to buy. In not-for-profit organizations it may be the decision to initiate an action (to provide money to a benefit claimant or book an operation for a patient, for example). It is not necessarily a single document or piece of paper, for the transaction may involve a range of activities – and the document(s) may be required to detail the specific product (including a host of features to be specified), its price and terms of payment, its delivery details, etc. Most formally, however, it is the 'purchase order' – generated by the buying department – which also carries details of all the contractual buying elements (which are typically then ignored by all involved, until such time as they find themselves involved in litigation!). As the item details, on the other hand, do form the basis of most of the subsequent transactions, they must all be entered correctly; most errors originate at this point. It also has to be processed rapidly, and the product or service delivered when the customer wants it – which is usually as soon as possible! In many cases it is most important that the item is delivered on time, even if that agreed time is later than the customer would ideally like. If it is not delivered on time, even if the agreed date was a very ambitious target, this will almost certainly result in a dissatisfied customer, who may well have made extensive arrangements on the basis of delivery at that time – a holiday delivered a day or two late is usually not acceptable! What is not often commented upon, but is an essential aspect of the work (on the other side of the fence) of purchasing departments and, indeed, of production control departments which plan and monitor the progress of internal orders (on production), is 'progress chasing'. Making certain that the 'components' of a 'product' are available at the right time in the right place often takes a considerable amount of effort – and is accordingly a critical, if often undervalued, function.

organizational advertising   *see* CORPORATE PROMOTION VERSUS BRAND PROMOTION

organizational behaviour   *see* WEBSTER AND WIND MODEL, OF ORGANIZATIONAL BEHAVIOUR

organizational buying situations   Some writers, such as Robinson et al. (1967), identify different buying situations:

- *Straight rebuy.* Repeat purchase of an existing product or service which has given satisfactory performance, where no new information is needed for the buying decision. The 'sitting tenant' – the existing supplier – is usually difficult to displace in such situations. Webster and Wind postulated a 'source-loyalty' model, which maintained that buyers favour existing (known risk) suppliers as much of their buying is routine.
- *Modified rebuy.* The buyer may be dissatisfied with the existing product or service (because it is not performing to specification, or because the supplier is providing unsatisfactory support), and in this case the buying decision has to be re-evaluated when buying is contemplated. This is the occasion when new suppliers are most likely to make changes to existing purchasing patterns. It does imply, however, that in many markets it is the existing supplier who loses the business – by incompetence or inattention – and not the new one who wins it!
- *New task buying.* In this situation there is no previous history, so the buyer has to start from scratch, all suppliers beginning with the same chance.

See also COMPLEX SALE; DECISION-MAKERS AND INFLUENCERS; SALES PROFESSIONAL; SELLING; TERRITORY MANAGEMENT; TERRITORY SALES PLAN

Reference: Robinson, P. J., Faris, C. W. and Wind, Y. (1967) *Industrial Buying and Creative Marketing.* New York: Allyn & Bacon.

organizational culture   *see* CULTURE, ORGANIZATIONAL; PARTNERSHIP TRIANGLE

organizational design   *see* CONTINGENCY PLAN

organizational factors, new product screening   *see* NEW PRODUCT SCREENING, ORGANIZATIONAL FACTORS

organizational (marketing) differences   Much has been made about the differences in the marketing environment between different types of organization. The evidence shows, however, that most of the different categories of organization have more marketing theory and practice in common than it might seem. Indeed, most marketing activities are widely applicable. Even 'pricing', which should surely have little relevance for non-commercial organizations, turns out to have many lessons for them. Fern and Brown (1984) conducted a very thorough search of the literature to determine what various authors have held to be the key differences between two supposedly very different groups (individual consumers and industrial buyers). They record that there are at least 27 different, 'expert' views of what separates the groups! The conclusion they come to (albeit controversial) is that the differences within the groups (between, for example, consumers buying convenience foods and those buying a car) are more important than those between the groups (between, say, a consumer buying a packet of cornflakes and a manager ordering a replacement stock of stationery). They believe, perhaps uncontroversially, that those items requiring major decisions demand a different level of buyer decision-making to the routine ones. They then make the claim, more controversial but one which I would at least partially support, that the difference between the industrial buyer making a routine decision and a householder making a similar level of decision is not necessarily greater than the difference between either of these routine decisions and major decisions taken in a more complex way. Others might disagree with the conclusion that there is much similarity between major household decisions, no matter how complex the interactions between family members, and those taken by groups in

organizations. The message is simply that there is probably more theory in common than is often allowed for, even if the names are changed!
See also ORGANIZATIONAL PIGEON-HOLES

Reference: Fern, Edward F. and Brown, James R. (1984) The industrial/consumer marketing dichotomy: a case of insufficient justification. *Journal of Marketing*, 48, Spring.

organizational (marketing) orientations Different organizations may adopt very different approaches to how they market their products and services. Philip Kotler describes a range of approaches:

The production concept – the production concept holds that consumers will favour those products that are widely available and low in cost. Managers of production-oriented organisations concentrate on achieving high production efficiency and wide distribution coverage . . .
The product concept – the product concept holds that consumers will favour those products that offer the most quality, performance, and features. Managers in these product-oriented organisations focus their energy on making good products and improving them over time . . .
The selling concept – the selling concept holds that consumers, if left alone, will ordinarily not buy enough of the organisation's products. The organisation must therefore undertake an aggressive selling and promotion effort . . .
The marketing concept – the marketing concept holds that the key to achieving organisational goals consists in determining the needs and wants of target markets and delivering the desired satisfactions more effectively and efficiently than competitors . . .

As usual, Kotler's contribution is helpful in resolving the confusion which surrounds much of the discussion. It shows a spectrum (rather than a simple dichotomy) from the 'production concept' (and perhaps to a lesser extent the 'product concept'), which is totally inward looking – with a supplier focusing very narrowly on the efficiency of his production processes – through to the full-blown 'marketing concept', which is firmly based on customer needs. But it also shows that the selling concept is not necessarily product based, and may be much closer to 'pure' marketing than is often allowed for.

Reference: Kotler, P. (1988) *Marketing Management* (6th edn). Englewood Cliffs, NJ: Prentice-Hall.

organizational perimeter   *see* INNER MARKET

organizational pigeon-holes   The categories, or pigeon-holes, of 'marketing organization' can be derived from a number of bases, some of which are meaningful in more general terms. In this way, a multidimensional matrix can be built to suit almost any aspect of marketing you are investigating.

The main dimensions, which have the widest application across the breadth of marketing activities, are:

*   product or service
*   individual consumer or corporate customer
*   profit or non-profit
*   capital goods or consumables
*   intermediaries or end-users

There are other dimensions which may be particularly important to specific sectors; for example, whether or not the sector is largely controlled by government intervention or legislation, as is the ethical pharmaceuticals industry. It should also be apparent that a five-dimensional matrix is needed to handle all five main dimensions. This will have in excess of 30 categories or pigeon-holes, ranging from the least prepossessing corner grocer, who is the for-profit intermediary that provides very consumable products to individual end-users, through to the Department of Trade and Industry, which is a not-for-profit organization using a wide range of intermediaries itself to provide a service to wide sectors of industry.
See also CAPITAL GOODS OR CONSUMABLES; CONSUMER OR CORPORATE CUSTOMER; INTERMEDIARIES OR END-USERS; PRODUCT OR SERVICE; PROFIT OR NON–PROFIT

organizational purchasing   *see* DECISION-MAKERS AND INFLUENCERS; INDUSTRIAL PRODUCT CATEGORIES; INTERACTION, AND THE ORGANIZATIONAL PURCHASE

organizational relations   *see* INTER-ORGANIZATIONAL RELATIONS

Organization for Economic Co-operation and Development   *see* DERIVED FORECASTS; EXPORT MARKET ELIMINATION; INTERNATIONAL MARKETING RESEARCH

original goods   An economic term describing goods which have no economic value until the factors of production are applied to them.
See also FACTORS OF PRODUCTION

OTE   On-target earnings, the income a salesperson will make if they reach 100 per cent of their target.
See also SALES (MARKETING) MANAGEMENT

OTS   *see* OPPORTUNITIES TO SEE (OTS)

outers   *see* PACKAGING

outgoing stock   *see* KANBAN

outlets   *see* CHANNEL MEMBERSHIP

out of town   *see* LOCATION, RETAIL

out-seller   A prospective supplier competing for an organization's business who is not an existing supplier to that organization and is thus at a disadvantage.
See also PROSPECT QUALIFICATION; PROSPECTS

outside director   *see* NON-EXECUTIVE DIRECTOR

outsourcing   Purchasing goods (for instance, components) and services (such as catering) from outside suppliers rather than using internal sources.

overarching idea   *see* CONVICTION MARKETING

overhead projected 'foils' (transparencies/acetates)   *see* PRESENTATION MEDIA

overheads   *see* BREAK-EVEN ANALYSIS, NEW PRODUCTS; MARGINAL COSTING, NEW PRODUCTS

overheads, sales personnel   *see* TERRITORY PLANS

overkill   *see* BUDGETS

overlay   Transparent sheet put over artwork with instructions on it on how to make the 'plates'.
See also ADVERTISING PROCESSES; CREATIVE DEPARTMENT, ADVERTISING AGENCY

overseas markets   *see* TRANSNATIONALS/MULTINATIONALS AND EXPORTERS

overspecifying   *see* SPECIFICATION

overstandardization   *see* INTERNATIONAL MARKETING PITFALLS

overstock pressures   *see* TRADE DISCOUNTS

overstressed systems   *see* CATASTROPHE THEORY

own brands   *see* OWN BRANDS AND GENERICS

own brands and generics   With the emergence of strong retailers there has also emerged the 'own brand', the retailer's own branded product (or service). Where the retailer has a particularly strong identity (such as Marks & Spencer in clothing and Sainsbury in food) this 'own brand' may be able to compete against even the strongest brand leaders – and may dominate those markets which are not otherwise strongly branded. There was a fear that such 'own brands' might displace all other brands (as they have done in Marks & Spencer outlets), but the evidence is that (at least in supermarkets and 'department' stores such as Boots) consumers generally expect to see brands other than those of the retailer making up over 50 per cent (and preferably over 60 per cent) of the goods on display. Indeed, even the strongest own brands in the UK (Sainsbury, Marks & Spencer and Boots) rarely achieve better than third place in the overall market. So the strongest independent brands (such as Kelloggs and Heinz), which have maintained their marketing investments, should continue to flourish. More than 50 per cent of UK FMCG brand leaders have held their position for more than 20 years – though it is arguable that those which have switched their budgets to 'buy space' in the retailers may be more exposed. Leslie DeChernatony's (1989) research with consumers led to the conclusion that 'Branded products were recognized as an entity distinct from own labels and generics. Years of branding by major manufacturers have set brands on a pedestal away from own labels and generics. Branded manufacturers need not think that because of retail pressure they no longer have an asset in their brands.'

Generics
Possibly as an outgrowth of consumerism, 'generics' (that is, effectively unbranded goods) emerged. These made a positive virtue of saving the cost of almost all marketing activities, emphasizing the lack of advertising and, especially, the plain packaging (which was, however, often simply a vehicle for a different kind of image!). It would appear, though, that the penetration of such generic products peaked in the early 1980s. Most consumers still seem to be looking for the qualities that the conventional brand provides. As Harris and Strong (1985) comment, 'for

generics to continue to attract the consumer, they will need to be positioned by the retailer as a sensible value alternative and backed by the retailer's guarantee of acceptable and consistent quality . . .'.

See also BRAND EXTENSION; BRANDING; BRANDING POLICIES; MARKET ENTRY TACTICS; MULTIBRANDS; RETAIL 'PRODUCT' DECISIONS

References: DeChernatony, Leslie (1989) Marketers' and consumers' concurring perceptions of market structure. *European Journal of Marketing*, 23(1).
  Harris, Brian F. and Strong, Robert A. (1985) Marketing strategies in the age of generics. *Journal of Marketing*, Fall.

ownership of local companies   *see* REGULATORY CONSIDERATIONS, FILTERING UNSUITABLE MARKETS

ownership, services   The purchaser of a 'good' has that 'product' in his or her ownership, to use as he or she pleases, in perpetuity. The purchaser of a service, on the other hand, only receives the direct benefit at the time it is taking place (though the indirect benefits, of a haircut say, may last longer). Comparison is, therefore, more dependent on the memory of previous transactions. It also means that, according to Grönroos (1980), there is a need for marketing activities throughout the whole purchase process – or customers may be lost at a number of the stages.

See also SERVICE CATEGORIES; SERVICES, FEATURES

Reference: Grönroos, C. (1980) Designing a long range strategy for services. *Long Range Planning*, April.

own summary, of research reports   Only after you have analysed the detailed results of a research project can you determine (and put down on paper) the key results in terms of what affects your own work. It is a long process, but if the research is worthwhile then the effort you give to it should match its importance – and, hopefully, your subsequent decisions will be correspondingly better informed.

See also RESEARCH REPORTS, USAGE

Oxo   *see* AWARENESS, ADVERTISING; MESSAGE, ADVERTISING

ozalid   A high quality, black and white, copy of artwork or print in general, used as a final check on the content.

See also ADVERTISING; ADVERTISING AGENCY ELEMENTS

P

packaging In its most basic sense packaging is simply necessary to deliver a product to the consumer in sound condition. This requirement may demand, say, a bottle for a shampoo, or a box with moulded shock-absorbing padding to protect delicate electronic goods. The requirement here is purely technical; the container has to be designed to be most efficient at containing and protecting the product. This requirement most obviously predominates in the fibre-board 'shipping outers' or 'cases' which are used to protect the product or to hold numbers of packs during delivery to retailers. Even here, though, the 'case' is increasingly being used as a vehicle for advertising, just in case a customer sees it and may be swayed by the message printed on it.

This leads on to the most obvious aspect of modern packaging: its promotional role. In recent years, particularly as 'self-service' has become a predominant feature in most distribution chains, the packaging of a product has become a major element of the promotion of that product. It is often the supplier's only opportunity, at the point of sale, to present the benefits of the product to the potential consumer who has picked it up to judge its potential value. Packaging requirements therefore include:

- product 'description'
- product image
- product value
- shelf display

It should be noted that some packaging represents an important element of the physical product itself. Thus, it delivers pharmaceuticals in tamper-proof and child-proof containers for dispensing exact quantities – occasionally with built-in applicators, such as inhalers. Built-in handles allow 'giant economy' packs to be carried, albeit with difficulty. It also delivers the aerosol spray of a hair product or deodorant, and, again, it adds the stripe to toothpaste!

Pack design has now become a science as well as an art, and can be the subject of as much testing (via market research) as the product itself. There are now a number of specialist design consultancies which make a particularly good living out of this one activity – with a host of very satisfied clients who have come to appreciate just how important a part of the overall product is the humble pack.

pack forecasting *see* DERIVED FORECASTS

pack size reduction *see* PRICE INCREASES

page rate The price for a whole-page advertisement in a newspaper or magazine. It may vary depending upon the position: the run of paper (anywhere, at the discretion of the publisher), the facing matter (opposite editorial), etc.
See also MEDIA IMPACT; MEDIA SELECTION; MEDIA TYPES

page traffic The percentage of the readers of a publication who see a particular page.
See also MEDIA IMPACT; MEDIA SELECTION; MEDIA TYPES

pagination The numbering of pages in a publication.

pain level, customers *see* COMPLAINTS

paired comparison A marketing research technique where consumers are asked to choose between pairs of competing products (or other stimuli) in order that, over a large number of such individual tests, an overall brand preference may be determined.
See also EXPERIMENTAL RESEARCH; MARKETING RESEARCH

panel research One approach to accurately measuring consumer behaviour (that is, their actions – not opinions) is by panel. At its best this may approach the accuracy of retail audits (with the added, complementary, advantage that it is categorized in terms of consumer profiles). The two main approaches are as follows.

Home audit
In this form of marketing research, the member of a permanent (sample) panel of consumers is required

to save used wrappers in a special receptacle (and hence the name sometimes used of 'dustbin audit'). Once a week, say, an auditor checks the contents of this, as well as checking stocks of products in the house and asking the householder a short list of questions. This technique is particularly successful in terms of the recruitment of respondents and the low subsequent attrition rate of these, and, accordingly, provides relatively accurate results.

Diary method

In this form of marketing research, the householder, say, records the required information in a diary which is collected by the interviewer or (less successfully, but more cheaply) returned by mail.

These methods have, over long periods, been shown to provide accurate share data. Most important, and in contrast to *ad hoc* surveys, these panels can show trend data (and, again, have been shown to do so accurately). They can also show repeat purchasing and brand switching information, which is almost impossible to obtain with other methods.

See also CUSTOM RESEARCH; MARKETING RESEARCH; MONITORING, PROGRESS; OMNIBUS SURVEYS; RETAIL AUDITS

panning   Moving the movie camera slowly across the scene.

pantry check   *see* PANEL RESEARCH

paradigm shift, strategy   The ultimate emergent strategy – the corporate strategy which is based on trends emerging in the external environment of the organization – is the paradigm shift. In this case the emergent effects are so powerful that they force a complete shift in perspective by the organization. It is forced to rethink its complete strategic position from this new viewpoint. It is most obvious in the field of science (indeed, the term 'paradigm shift' was coined by Thomas Kuhn to describe the dramatic changes which take place in science when a new set of theories – the new paradigm – supersedes the old set).

The important implication of this theory is that a paradigm shift is a discontinuous process (rather like catastrophe theory). There is no gentle move from one viewpoint to the other which takes place over a lengthy period; instead there is a near-instantaneous, almost violent, shift.

The reason for this is the investment (in terms of management commitment) in the previous paradigm. Because it is too 'painful' to abandon their

cherished viewpoint, managers may adopt a number of devices to deny or minimize the existence of the changes:

* *Blindness* – most basic of all, they simply will not see them, or will persuade themselves that they do not apply to their own position (thus the British motorcycle industry in the 1960s and 1970s convinced itself that the Japanese were only making small bikes, which was a different market and no threat to themselves!).
* *Misinterpretation* – the signals may be forced to fit the existing paradigm.
* *Opposition* – if the signals are too obvious to ignore, then the management may fight them by a number of means. These may include calling on the basic philosophies of the organization (the new paradigm is a 'heresy'), developing highly political defences within the organization against them and/or partially assimilating those elements which can be accepted by the existing paradigm.

The above tools may represent stages which take place before the new paradigm overpowers the old. Assuming its overthrow is inevitable, these delays in recognition may be very damaging and are often fatal.

Unfreezing an organization which is caught in such a trap is not an easy task. It may involve political moves to encourage dissent, particularly by more junior managers, but it often requires a very strong lead from the CEO – and often the appointment of an outsider (and a charismatic one) to provide this new lead.

See also CORPORATE PLAN; CORPORATE STRATEGY AND MARKETING; CREATIVE IMITATION; EMERGENT STRATEGY; LEAPFROG; LOGICAL INCREMENTALISM

parallel development   *see* EMERGENT STRATEGY; FLEXIBLE DEVELOPMENT; INNOVATIVE IMITATION; LEAPFROG

parallel running   *see* RISK VERSUS TIME, NEW PRODUCTS

parcels   *see* TRANSPORT DECISIONS, LOGISTICS MANAGEMENT

parcels of slots   *see* MEDIA SELECTION

Pareto, 80:20, effect   At the end of the nineteenth century, Pareto noted that the bulk of the wealth of Italy was in the hands of 10 per cent of the population. This principle has since been adopted by management in general, and enshrined as a very valuable 'rule of thumb' – the '80:20 rule' – which can be applied to a wide range of situations. Thus, in a marketing context, there may be, and usually are, heavy and light users. Both are customers, but the heavy users are that much more important to the producer. The Pareto rule says that the top 20 per cent of customers, the heavy users, will buy 80 per cent of the product. Conversely, the bottom 80 per cent, the light users, will only account for 20 per cent of the total sales. Despite its seeming over-simplification, the principle applies to many markets – mass consumer as well as industrial. It applies to groupings of customers: in the industrial sales field the top 20 per cent of customers will account for 80 per cent of sales. It also applies to groupings of products, where there is an extended product list: the best-selling 20 per cent of products will often take 80 per cent of the volume or value of overall sales. It needs to be recognized, though, that it is only a rule-of-thumb; the exact figures may be different in given situations (70:30 or 90:10, say), but they are frequently approximately right. The importance of the principle is that it highlights the need for most producers to concentrate their efforts (often against their natural inclinations) on the most important customers and products.

See also BOOST CORE COMPETENCES; DISCARD PERIPH-ERALS; SUPPORT SUCCESS FORGET FAILURE (SSFF)

Parker Pen Company   *see* GLOBAL MARKETING

Parkinson's Law   One of a number of modern sayings put forward by this writer, of which the most popular is 'work expands to fill the time available'.

partial cost recovery   *see* NOT-FOR-PROFIT ORGANIZATIONS, OBJECTIVES

participative leadership   *see* GLOBALIZATION

partner evaluation   *see* STRATEGIC (INTERNATIONAL) ALLIANCES

partnership   *see* INTERACTION, AND THE ORGANIZATIONAL PURCHASE; WIN–WIN

partnership, pricing   *see* COST-PLUS PRICING

partnership sourcing   Sourcing on an exclusive basis from a single supplier over the long term, and admitting them, as 'partners', to the organization's inner workings.

partnerships, retail   *see* RETAIL ORGANIZATION

partnership triangle   The most important aspect of handling the complex sale is understanding how a partnership may be built – of which the important aspect is finding out how the customer's organization can, in effect, be fused with your own. Shared elements of identity or values, shared group membership or simply shared business interests are often what makes such partnerships work, with the emphasis on 'shared'. It is important to recognize these synergistic components, which often revolve around intangible elements (such as the organizational cultures or even – with more volatility – personal relationships between the key participants).

It is also important to adopt the right perspective, the right frame of mind. 'Partnership' best describes this approach, which should be adopted from the very start of any business relationship. It is best illustrated by the partnership triangle:

This diagram usefully emphasizes several of the key elements in such a partnership:

- *Three-way involvement.* The customer is formally involved with the organization as a whole, and the relationship with that corporate body – typically enshrined in the formal relationship with the sales professional who is the formal contact – is clearly important, especially in terms of mutual trust. But the customer's contacts overall are mainly informal ones, with the sales professional but also with a range of staff throughout the vendor's organization. It is often these 'staff' relationships which are most important to, and have the most impact upon, that customer. This is an aspect of the relationship which is often forgotten.
- *Internal stress.* In turn, the tension between these formal (organizational) and informal (staff) relationships often leads to tension within the

vendor organization – which may be communicated to the customer, with distinctly unwanted results.

• *Power lies at the base*. It is no accident that in the diagram the most direct relationships, and the heaviest weighted ones, are at the bottom of the pyramid (triangle), between the equals who interact on various issues from both sides. It is they, not the senior management, who will ultimately make the partnership work or fail.

See also BALANCING UNDER THE INFLUENCE; COMPLEX SALE; INTERACTION, AND THE ORGANIZATIONAL PURCHASE

parts kit   *see* MATERIALS REQUIREMENTS PLANNING (MRP)

part-time agents   *see* AGENT (PERSONAL) SELLING

party selling   The agent (personal) selling approach was extended, most notably by Tupperware, to encompass a situation where the social environment (a 'party') was the key to the sale. This ('party plan') principle has been taken up by sellers of costume jewellery and 'erotic' lingerie, amongst others. These techniques can be considered 'precision marketing' in that they involve a very direct approach to the customer and often a very knowledgeable one, in terms of understanding customer needs, because of the very direct (friendly) relationship between the seller and the buyer. On the other hand, since the organization employing the seller has not (as yet) obtained access to this knowledge (but depends upon the informal relationship being handled by its 'agents'), it encounters some problems in terms of applying the other techniques of precision marketing. These direct selling methods are, though, relatively under-used – considering how well they have worked for those who have become expert in their use.
See also AGENT (PERSONAL) SELLING; PRECISION MARKETING

pass level   *see* ZERO DEFECTS VERSUS AQL

pass-on readership   Readership by people other than the buyers; the reason why readership figures are often higher than circulation figures.
See also AUDIENCE RESEARCH

paste-up   Putting the illustrations and text, literally pasting them, onto the artwork.

patch, sales   *see* TERRITORY MANAGEMENT

patents   *see* BRAND MONOPOLY; INTELLECTUAL PROPERTY; PRODUCT TEST

pattern, advertising   *see* BUDGETS

pattern book   A book showing available designs.

pattern of diffusion   *see* DIFFUSION OF INNOVATION

payback pricing   *see* SKIMMING, PRICING

pay-offs   *see* BAYESIAN DECISION THEORY

PDM (physical distribution management)
see PHYSICAL DISTRIBUTION MANAGEMENT

peak pricing   *see* SELECTIVE PRICING

peak time   The television (or radio) time for which the highest rate is charged. This is usually during the middle of the evening.

peak-time spots   *see* MEDIA BUYING, ADVERTISING AGENCY

Pearl curve   *see* TECHNOLOGICAL FORECASTING

Peat Marwick Mitchell & Co., consultants
see CONSULTANTS

pedestrian flows   *see* LOCATION, RETAIL

peer group   *see* ENHANCED AIUAPR MODEL; PEER PYRAMID; THREE PILLARS OF THE PURCHASING PROCESS

peer pressure   *see* CONTROL, OF SALES PERSONNEL

peer pressure influences, on the purchase decision   This is the pressure for conformity to the values shared by the individuals with whom (typically as a group) the purchaser associates (his or her peers). Thus, within cultures and subcultures there is a powerful force at work requiring members to conform to the overall values of the group, to their 'reference group'. These are sometimes referred to as 'membership groups', when the individual formally is a member (for example, of a political party or trade union), though individuals may also have 'aspiration groups' (social cliques, say, such as 'yuppies') to which they would like to belong. They may also recognize 'dissociative groups' with which they would not wish to associate (thus drinkers may go to great lengths to avoid being associated with 'lager louts'). This peer pressure can sometimes be used to great effect by marketers, for if they can sway the few 'opinion leaders' in the reference group, they can capture the whole group. Even those customers who are not obviously involved in an active 'subculture' are influenced in their buying decisions and consumer behaviour by the members of the less obvious groups to which they belong or aspire. These 'peer' groups exert an influence in that individual customers try to emulate the behaviour patterns of their peers. For example, teenagers are greatly influenced by peer group pressure and might also follow the dress and manner of a pop group, or families might purchase home computers and video recorders once their neighbours have acquired these products.

See also CULTURES, INFLUENCES ON THE PURCHASE DECISION; FAMILY INFLUENCES, ON THE PURCHASE DECISION; OPINION LEADERS

Peer Pyramid Whilst the AIUAPR-based models (including the Three Pillars of Purchasing) may be especially useful in providing a framework which most effectively handles new consumers' progress over time, it does not really do justice to the interaction of the individual consumer with the whole community rather than just the direct peer group, and the 'inertia' which this, combined with the wealth of (personal and community) experience built up over time, may lead to.

The model which best demonstrates this aspect is that of the 'Peer Pyramid':

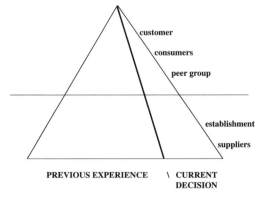

PREVIOUS EXPERIENCE \ CURRENT DECISION

The pyramid deliberately represents the customer as being at the apex of a layered set of influences. Not least amongst these are the consumers – the family for consumer goods and services, and the users in an

organization. Their views are frequently decisive – perhaps, over the longer term, even more so than those of the direct customer. But beyond them, and beyond the peer group which is so influential in the 'Pillars' model, are the whole range of 'establishment' forces which regulate what may happen, as do a range of government bodies, or which control the processes of communication, as do the various media. These in turn may be influenced by the vendor, who typically enjoys a position as a respected member of that establishment.

Even so, and despite the advantages of modern marketing, the vendor – at the bottom of the pyramid – often seems very remote from the customer (even, sometimes, when face-to-face selling is involved).

The vertical/diagonal split in the diagram is normally even more important. The large part to the left represents the great body of past experience that the customer, along with all those involved in the various layers of the pyramid, has already built up before coming to the current decision. This may indeed be at the forefront of the customer's mind, but need not necessarily outweigh that body of previous experience (despite the fervent hopes of the vendor – and the lack of reference to such past experience by most marketing theory).

Vendors need to recognize the investment which is needed to overcome the inertia which comes from this accumulated history.

See also AIUAPR (AWARENESS, INTEREST, UNDERSTANDING, ATTITUDES, PURCHASE, REPEAT PURCHASE) MODEL; CALL STRUCTURE; DECISION-MAKING PROCESS, BY CUSTOMERS; ENHANCED AIUAPR MODEL; MODELS; REPEAT PURCHASING PROCESS; THREE PILLARS OF THE PURCHASING PROCESS

pegged prices Prices that are held, in the hope of recruiting new customers, when prices (and costs) rise elsewhere.

penetration This is the proportion (per cent) of individuals in the market who are users of the specific (brand) product or service, as determined by the numbers who claim in response to market research – such as the TGI (Target Group Index) surveys of MRB – to be users. In the non-profit sector it can often be used as effectively, for example as a measure of the number of clients receiving help as a proportion of the total population who might need the service. The measure of 'penetration', though, does not allow for the rate of usage or purchase by different individuals. The most commonly used measure, therefore, is market share or brand share.

See also BRAND (OR MARKET) SHARE; CUSTOMERS; INTRODUCTORY STAGE, PRODUCT LIFE CYCLE; MARKETING STRATEGIES; MARKET PENETRATION; MARKETS; OPINION LEADERS; PRICING, PRODUCT LIFE CYCLE; PROMOTIONAL PRICING; USERS

penetration pricing   In this pricing policy, usually for new products, the price is set deliberately low, with a number of objectives in mind. The initial low price might make it less attractive for would-be competitors to imitate innovations, particularly where the technology is expensive. It encourages more customers to buy the product soon after its introduction – which hastens the growth of demand and earlier economies of scale. The main value of this policy is that it helps seize a relatively large market share and increases turnover whilst (on the basis of economies of scale) reducing unit costs, so that the price domination can be maintained and extended. It has been the very successful policy behind the move of Japanese corporations into a number of existing markets – including video recorders and single lens reflex cameras. Its major disadvantage lies in losing the opportunity for higher profit margins.

Under this broad category, however, there are a number of more specific policies:

• *Maximizing brand/product share.* This is the most usual theoretical justification given, and there is some evidence that the brands with the highest share in a number of markets indeed are the most profitable (because of the economies of scale mentioned above). Again, this is the philosophy which drives many of the leading Japanese brands. This justification is sometimes made in terms of maximizing sales growth – particularly in new markets, where competitive activity is less evident.

• *Maximizing current revenue.* More often, particularly with existing products in sales-oriented organizations, the pressure from senior management is to maximize sales. The assumption is that higher sales automatically lead to higher profits – though in practice most products are more sensitive, in terms of profit, to price than to volume.

• *Survival.* For some organizations, such as those with high overheads or overcapacity, maximizing revenue by price cutting may be seen as the only way to survive their problems. This is the philosophy of despair.

See also PRICING NEW 'PRODUCTS'; SKIMMING, PRICING

people (sales) management   The most obvious, and crucial, role of any sales manager (and particularly of field sales management – those, often junior, managers in the field whose exclusive job it is to manage the teams of sales personnel) is the 'people management' of the sales professionals. The same applies almost as forcefully to the managers of service and support personnel (including the very large numbers in the service industries). Strafford and Grant (1986) give a typical list of the qualities a successful sales manager must have:

(a)   Want to be a manager.
(b)   Have the ability to lead and motivate others.
(c)   Be a good organizer and planner.
(d)   Be capable of control and administration.
(e)   Fully understand the implications of finance.
(f)   Have the skills to recruit, train, motivate and develop those who will form part of the team.
(g)   Accept the fact (and use it accordingly) that the computer is here to stay!

Apart from the rather idiosyncratic emphasis on the last item, this list is fairly typical of what many writers on sales management also recommend. In common with those others, it is significant, paradoxically, for a lack of any direct reference to marketing skills. On the other hand, it is even more significant (I believe justifiably) for its emphasis on people management, which (to a lesser, but mainly greater, extent) accounts for five out of the six main categories. It is important to note just how important people management, and the manager's own motivation, are to this part of the overall marketing function. Despite the above (very sensible) advice, most sales managers are still recruited for their sales rather than management ability. John Fenton makes the point rather more forcefully: 'At least half the sales managers . . . are still salesmen at heart; thinking like salesmen: still trying to be "one of the boys" rather than leaders of men. They gained promotion because they were the best salesmen in the company, and able to get on well with the people around them.' Allen, on the other hand, put the traditional view when he said 'The sales manager has to be a good salesman, and since it is usual practice to promote the "best" salesman to be sales manager, this is generally so . . . he will also be responsible for the company's major accounts'. This entry cannot offer a definitive treatise on people management. There are many other excellent books which cover that subject. It is necessary in this context, though, to highlight the separate tasks which characterize the management of sales teams, and make the whole especially difficult:

- recruitment
- motivation
- control
- training

See also COMPLEX SALE; CONTROL, OF SALES PERSONNEL; RECRUITMENT, OF SALES PERSONNEL; SALES PROFESSIONAL; SALES TEAM MANAGEMENT; SALES TRAINING; SELLING; TERRITORY MANAGEMENT

Reference: Allen, P. (1973) *Sales and Sales Management.* MacDonald & Evans.
    Fenton, J. (1979) *The A–Z of Sales Management.* Heinemann.
    Strafford, John and Grant, Colin (1986) *Effective Sales Management.* London: Heinemann.

people, services In the service industries there almost needs to be an extra 'P' added to the 4 Ps – for People. They are often the most tangible evidence of quality, from the face-to-face salesman selling financial services in the customer's home to the counter-clerk in the travel agency. These people often become, by default, the service as seen by the prospective customers. In many fields the service is the people; and in the others the people are often the critical element in its successful delivery. In the hotel and catering trades it is people who make the difference between the good and the bad, and yet, paradoxically, they are traditionally grossly underpaid!
See also 3 Ps

Pepsi Cola *see* MESSAGE, ADVERTISING

per capita costs *see* MEDIA BUYING, ADVERTISING AGENCY

perceived risk pricing One price factor (which sometimes leads to the constrained choice model) is that of 'perceived risk'. As Cyert and March (1963) explain, 'The perceived risk model emphasises the buyer's uncertainty as he evaluates alternative courses of action . . . buyers are motivated by a desire to reduce the amount of perceived risk in the buying situation to some acceptable level, which is not necessarily zero'. Something approaching this view surely led to the famous motto 'Nobody ever got fired for buying IBM'!
See also PRICE FACTORS; PRICING, PRODUCT POSITIONING

Reference: Cyert, Richard M. and March, James G. (1963) *A Behavioural Theory of the Firm.* Englewood Cliffs, NJ: Prentice-Hall.

perceived value pricing *see* MARKET–BASED PRICING; PRICE AND NOT–FOR–PROFIT ORGANIZATIONS; PRICES, CUSTOMER NEEDS

percentage availability *see* SERVICE LEVELS

percentage distribution *see* MARKETING OBJECTIVES

percentage of revenue/sales *see* BUDGETS

percentage of sales, advertising budget *see* ADVERTISING BUDGETS

perception *see* ADVERTISING BELIEVABILITY; SERVICE QUALITY

perceptual mapping *see* SEGMENTATION; SEGMENTATION METHODS

perceptual processes *see* HOWARD AND SHETH MODEL, OF CONSUMER BEHAVIOUR

per diem The rate per day employed, charged by a member of a profession.

perestroika *see* GLOBALIZATION

perfect binding A form of binding, for books, by which sections are glued onto a spine to give a flat back.

perfect markets *see* PRICE FACTORS

performance analysis In most organizations the key data on performance are likely to be available already on their computer databases. This is because the paperwork, typically deriving from order processing and invoicing, is now usually handled by computer. This should provide accurate sales data, split by product and by region. It should also provide this in a timely manner. In this electronic age it should even be possible to obtain this information on a terminal (usually now the manager's own personal computer), up to the very minute. It should be recognized, however, that such accounting systems are driven by accounting requirements, and in particular by accounting periods; they will therefore often reflect an unbalanced picture until the month-end procedures have been completed. Thus, despite the 'hype' about having up-to-the-minute data instantly available through the terminal on your desk, it is still usually most realistic to examine figures based on whole months. In the case of not-for-profit organizations it is just as important to keep track of the clients (recipients, donors, patients, customers, etc.), as well as the transactions related to them. If the computer systems have been designed to cope with the level of detail needed, performance figures should be available down to individual customers or clients.

The most important elements of marketing performance, which are normally tracked, are:

- *Sales analysis*. Most organizations track their sales results or, in not-for-profit organizations for example, the number of clients. The more sophisticated track them in terms of sales variance (the deviation from the target figures), which allows a more immediate picture of deviations to become evident. 'Microanalysis', which is a nicely pseudo-scientific term for the normal management process of investigating detailed problems, then investigates the individual elements (individual products, sales territories, customers, etc.) which are failing to meet targets.
- *Market share analysis*. Relatively few organizations track their market share. In some circumstances this may well be a much more important measure. Sales may still be increasing, in an expanding market, whilst share is actually decreasing – boding ill for future sales when the market eventually starts to drop. Where such market share is tracked, there may be a number of aspects which will be followed: overall market share; segment share – that of the specific, targeted segment; relative share – in relation to the market leaders; and expense analysis. The key ratio to watch in this area is usually the 'marketing expense to sales ratio', though this may be broken down into other elements (advertising to sales, sales administration to sales, etc.).
- *Financial analysis*. The 'bottom line' of marketing activities should, at least in theory, be the net profit (for all except not-for-profit organizations, where the comparable emphasis may be on remaining within budgeted costs). There are a number of separate performance figures and key ratios which need to be tracked. The main ones will usually be: gross contribution; gross profit; net contribution; net profit; return on investment; and profit on sales. There can be considerable benefit in comparing these figures with those achieved by other organizations (especially those

in the same industry), using, for instance, the figures which can be obtained (in the UK) from the Centre for Interfirm Comparison. The most sophisticated use of this approach, however, is typically by those making use of PIMS (Profit Impact of Marketing Strategy), initiated by the General Electric Company and then developed by Harvard Business School, but now run by the Strategic Planning Institute. This covers nearly 3000 Strategic Business Units (SBUs) across North America and Europe.

The above performance analyses concentrate on the quantitative measures which are directly related to short-term performance. But there are a number of indirect measures, essentially tracking customer attitudes, which can also indicate the organization's performance in terms of its longer-term marketing strengths and may accordingly be even more important indicators. Some useful measures are:

- *Market research* – including customer panels (which are used to track changes over time).
- *Lost business* – the orders which were lost because, for example, the stock was not available or the product did not meet the customer's exact requirements
- *Customer complaints* – how many customers complain about the products or services or the organization itself, and about what. Tom Peters (1987) supports the point:

Our fixation with financial measures leads us to downplay or ignore less tangible nonfinancial measures, such as product quality, customer satisfaction, order leadtime, factory flexibility, the time it takes to launch a new product, and the accumulation of skills by labor over time. Yet these are increasingly the real drivers of corporate success over the middle to long term . . .

See also ABC ANALYSIS; CORPORATE OBJECTIVES; INFORMAL (ORAL) REPORTS; MARKETING PLANS AND PROGRAMMES; MARKETING STRATEGIES; MONITORING, PROGRESS; PLANNING PROCESS; VARIANCE ANALYSIS; WRITTEN REPORTS

Reference: Peters, Tom (1987) *Thriving on Chaos*. New York: Alfred A. Knopf Inc.

performance goals   *see* STRATEGIC BUSINESS UNIT (SBU)

period actuals   A forecast may simply continue the trends observable in previous periods. This may be achieved either by calculating the average percentage increase or by drawing the best possible straight line through the historical figures when plotted on a graph. If the rate of change is high, it is preferable to use a logarithmic graph, on which constant percentage increases show up as a straight line – whereas they would result in a curve on a normal graph.

See also QUANTITATIVE FORECASTING TECHNIQUES

period of plan   *see* MARKETING PLANS AND PROGRAMMES

perishability, service prices   *see* SERVICE PRICES; SERVICE-SECTOR LOGISTICS

perishability, services   Most services are produced and consumed at the same point, and are totally perishable. The service may be available over time, but if the 'time-slot' is not available, or is not sold, the lost revenue can never be recouped (whereas a product held in stock can always be sold later). Surprisingly, then, 'stock' control becomes even more important for a service provider.

permanent income hypothesis   The hypothesis, developed by Milton Friedman, that individuals base their current expenditure on the total income they expect to receive over their whole lifetime.

persona   *see* CONVICTION MARKETING FACTORS; MARKETING RESEARCH, PRECISION MARKETING

personal (agent) selling   *see* AGENT (PERSONAL) SELLING

personal delivery of service   *see* SELLING SERVICES

personal interviewing   This is the traditional (face-to-face) approach to marketing research and is still the most versatile. The interviewer is in full control of the interview and can take account of the body language as well as the words. It is the most expensive approach, however, and is dependent on the reliability of the interviewer – and on his or her skill, in the case of some of the more sophisticated techniques. This means that the quality of the supervision provided by the field research agency is critical; which may be a problem with so many organizations now placing emphasis on cost-cutting. There are also horror stories of interviewers making up interviews to avoid going out on cold and rainy

days. Fortunately these stories are few in number, and the reputable agencies (even if they are relatively fewer in number than one might wish!) do exert the necessary control over their personnel – usually by having a field manager conduct follow-ups of a subsample.

See also DATA COLLECTION

personality of brand   *see* CONVICTION MARKETING FACTORS

personality promotions   Use of teams of merchandisers in fancy dress who give away, in the street, product-related prizes.

See also NON-PRICE PROMOTIONS; SALES PROMOTION

personalization   *see* BRANCH MARKETING; DIRECT MAIL ADVANTAGES AND DISADVANTAGES; LETTER, DIRECT MAIL; PRECISION (DIRECT) MARKETING, RETAIL

personalized reply form   *see* REPLY-PAID CARDS

personal presentations   The main instrument you will use in presentations – the real focus for most of the time – will be yourself. There are several aspects of personal presentation that need attention:

Physical projection
A presentation usually requires a larger than life performance; indeed, at times it may get close to a stage performance. The gestures, for example pointing to the visuals (and, if you need to use one, do make certain you have a pointer that will reach), do need to be slightly theatrical. Most of the texts on presentation comment, at length, that you should remove annoying personal habits. It goes without saying that if you do suffer from a particularly distracting habit it will not impress your audience. But most personal habits are only noticed if the presentation is not succeeding in conveying content matter that the audience finds interesting.

Vocal projection
This too needs to somewhat larger than life. You will have to speak louder than normal – and always towards the audience (if you talk with your back to them they certainly will not be able to hear). Always, when you present in a strange environment, get your colleagues to check that you can be clearly heard in all parts of the room.

Humour, anecdotes and references
It is often thought that it is wise to open a speech with a joke, to break the ice. It is possible, and I have

heard some marvellous speakers who have got away with it; but for every one who succeeds I would estimate there are a hundred who fail. Being a successful comedian is a very rare talent. Using an anecdote is, however, a much safer ploy – particularly if it is from your own (or your organization's) background. A particularly safe topic to use, and one that you generally cannot make too much use of, is 'references'. In a presentation they both lighten the material and personalize it.

Mistakes

The greatest fear of many inexperienced presenters is that they might make a mistake. They should not worry. As long as you do not allow your terror to destroy your presentation, mistakes are useful for breaking down the barriers between you and the audience. Audiences like to find out that presenters are only human after all; it brings the presenter down to their own level. This should, in any case, be the aim of the presenter. It actually makes audiences more sympathetic towards you; perfection is always seen as a very cold virtue.

Confidence

With time and experience you will relax and enjoy yourself, and give an even better performance. In any case it is said that all the greatest actors suffer from nerves before each performance; and they believe that this is almost necessary, since it means that they are taking their work, and the audience, seriously. Once in front of the audience the actor's adrenalin takes over.

Rehearsals

If the content is what will convince the audience, rehearsal is what will ensure that this content is communicated and that it does convince. To a large extent you cannot rehearse too much. In the first instance rehearsals will help reveal whether the messages are correct, are powerful and can be communicated. It is only when you put them to a trial audience that you can really judge their effectiveness. The overall content should not need to change dramatically, but the detail of how this content is communicated, by the various specific messages in the presentation, may change significantly. Rehearsing also allows you to learn the material. Whichever 'notes' you use, you must rehearse until you are word perfect. If you rehearse time and time again, until you absorb the material almost by osmosis, you will not be exposed to the vicissitudes of drying up or being thrown off course by unexpected events.
See also PRESENTATIONS

personal recommendation, promotion   *see* SECONDARY SOURCES OF COMMUNICATION

personal selling   *see* SELLING

personal services sector   *see* CUSTOMER SERVICE CATEGORIES

personnel management   *see* MANPOWER PLAN, SALES; RECRUITMENT, OF SALES PERSONNEL

perspective   *see* MARKETING MYOPIA; MARKETING STRATEGIES

persuading   *see* ADVERTISING

Philip Morris   *see* LICENSING

Phillips curve   A graph of inflation against unemployment, derived from statistics by the economist W. H. Phillips. It was disproved by Milton Friedman in the 1970s, and this – incidentally – led in part to the emergence of monetarism as an influential force in economic theory.
See also MONETARISM

phone mail   *see* ELECTRONIC DIRECT MAIL

photocomposition   Optical typesetting which produces on photographic film what monotype produced in metal.
See also LINOTYPE

photographers   *see* ADVERTISING PROCESSES; CREATIVE DEPARTMENT, ADVERTISING AGENCY

photosetting   *see* BLOCKS

physical distribution management   In addition to external distribution chains, the producer may also have an internal distribution chain, with the central warehouse supplying regional depots.

The objectives of 'physical distribution' are simply, and rather modestly, defined by Peter Attwood (1971) as: 'to provide a service to the marketing and production functions by holding and delivering products efficiently and economically'. He goes on to describe the main elements as:

• *Warehousing* – physically holding the units of inventory (either of finished goods or work in progress).

- *Delivery* – transporting the products to the end-users.

In line with these objectives, there are five key decision areas for logistics management as it relates to the movement of materials and product. They are:

- Production decisions
- Transport decisions
- Facility decisions
- Inventory decisions
- Communication decisions

These are, arguably, more the province of corporate strategy than of pure marketing, but most of them hinge very closely on marketing factors.
See also FACILITY DECISIONS, LOGISTICS MANAGEMENT; LOGISTICS MANAGEMENT; PRODUCTION DECISIONS, LOGISTICS MANAGEMENT; TRANSPORT DECISIONS, LOGISTICS MANAGEMENT

Reference: Attwood, Peter R. (1971) *Planning a Distribution System*. Aldershot: Gower Press.

physiocrats Eighteenth-century French economists who are credited with laying the foundations for Adam Smith's work.

physiological needs *see* MASLOW'S HIERARCHY OF NEEDS

picking list Document, usually now produced by computer, which lists, for the benefit of warehouse staff, where all the items on a customer's order may be found and picked.

picture drawing *see* OPEN QUESTIONS, ON QUESTIONNAIRES

piggy-back *see* SAMPLING

piggy-back freight Carriage of trucks on rail.

piggy-back marketing *see* MARKET ENTRY TACTICS

pilferage *see* SHRINKAGE

Pilkingtons *see* LICENSING

Pillars Purchasing Process Model *see* PEER PYRAMID; THREE PILLARS OF THE PURCHASING PROCESS

pilot installations *see* TEST MARKET

PIMS *see* PROFIT IMPACT OF MARKETING STRATEGIES (PIMS)

pioneer *see* INTRODUCTORY STAGE, PRODUCT LIFE CYCLE; RISK VERSUS TIME, NEW PRODUCTS

pirate copy An illegal copy of a product which is protected by intellectual property.

pitch A talk by a salesperson intended to persuade the listener to buy.
See also SALES CALL

place *see* MARKETING STRATEGIES

place, in banks *see* BANKS

place, retail *see* RETAIL 'PRODUCT' DECISIONS

place, services Where there are local centres for delivering a service (branches of banks or travel agents, for example), the premises themselves become a means of demonstrating the quality of that service. In this computer age, even the equipment used has to be of the latest technology, to reinforce the image.

place, wholesalers *see* WHOLESALERS AND DISTRIBUTORS

plain cover In a plain envelope, without any indication of whom it is from.

plan, account *see* ACCOUNT PLANNING

plan, advertising *see* ADVERTISING PLAN

plan assumptions *see* ASSUMPTIONS, MARKETING PLAN

plan, contingency *see* CONTINGENCY PLAN

plan, corporate *see* CORPORATE PLAN

plan, manpower *see* MANPOWER PLAN, SALES

plan, marketing *see* MARKETING PLAN BENEFITS

planned activities *see* BUDGETS

planned orders *see* MATERIALS REQUIREMENTS PLANNING (MRP)

planning forum   *see* MARKETING PLAN USE

planning gap   *see* GAP ANALYSIS

planning loop   *see* FLEXIBLE MANUFACTURING

planning meetings   *see* MARKETING PLAN USE

planning period   *see* MARKETING PLAN USE

planning pitfalls   The strategic planning process, in general, is subject to a wide range of problems; indeed, it is arguable that it is more prone to 'malpractice' than almost any other activity. In the most complex environment of all, that of the large corporation, Goold and Campbell (1987) developed:

a list of 12 common pitfalls – problems that frequently distort the strategic decision-making process, but which they believe could be avoided with good management practice:

1. '*Habits of mind*' – the tendency for managers to fall into habits of mind, i.e. to adopt tunnel vision with respect to their strategies ... The most effective way ... is to introduce fresh views and opinions continuously. The use of outside consultants, secondment of managers to training courses that challenge conventional thinking, special project responsibilities that cut across established organizational structure, a willingness to recruit new blood at senior levels from outside the company ...
2. '*Barons*' – managers have a natural tendency to fight their corners, to argue for growth and priority for their own areas of responsibility ... To avoid baronial problems a number of companies ... now make a clear distinction between main board corporate roles and divisional line management ...
3. '*Interference*' – at its worst, corporate influence over business unit strategies can be seen as little more than counter-productive interference ... To avoid this pitfall, there must be free flow of information about each business to the centre, and the centre must devote as much time as is needed to assimilate and discuss this information ...
4. '*Exercise in cleverness*' – to fall into an adversarial mode, in which corporate and business levels try to score points off each other ... with destructive criticism and nit-

picking over disputed details taking precedence over search for strategies that will succeed for the company ... In companies where the views of the centre are well respected ... an adversarial atmosphere is less likely to be found.
5. '*Bureaucracy*' – at its worst in organizations with many different review levels ... Bureaucracy can be reduced if planning and control processes are flexible and selective, and focus on key issues instead of simply generating quantities of unused paperwork ...
6. '*Non-core*' – non-core businesses are less well understood by corporate management ... Our belief is that once a business has been identified as non-core, an early exit benefits both the business and the corporate parent.
7. '*Hockey sticks*' – long-term plans make projections that fail to materialize and, more importantly, were never likely to ... Lack of realism is closely linked to the control process. If over-optimistic forecasts are rewarded, they will be made.
8. '*Lip service*' – the competent business manager does not take long to discover the central objectives that really count in his company ... strategic goals soon became a matter for lip service only ... A conflict between strategy and controls can and should be avoided ...
9. '*Control games*' – where control objectives become ends in themselves, there is a danger that gamesmanship to meet defined targets will actually impair the long-term health of the business ... Both consistency over time and coherence across the whole range of controls can prevent the exercise of control degenerating into such game playing ...
10. '*Moving the goalposts*' – the particular problem of shifting objectives ... The way to avoid this pitfall is through constancy and consistency in corporate objectives ...
11. '*Yes, Chairman*' – it can be argued that efforts to please the boss are inevitable in any hierarchy ... The preferences of the CEO, and the sort of behaviour he is seen to reward, have much to do with the openness of debate ...
12. '*Strategy and inaction*' – the need to sell the strategy within the organization is overlooked, or left to take care of itself at lower levels ... Communications and consensus building need to be an integral part of the strategic decision-

making process, not left as an unmanaged after-thought.

This is a long list, but those who have had experience of corporate planning in large organizations will recognize that it demonstrates a convincing ring of truth – and many more managers will acknowledge that these phenomena occur in planning processes in their own organization at almost all levels! The important point is to check that their impact on your marketing planning processes is minimized.

See also CORPORATE OBJECTIVES; MARKETING PLANS AND PROGRAMMES; MARKETING STRATEGIES; PLANNING PROCESS

Reference: Goold, Michael and Campbell, Andrew (1987) *Strategies and Styles: The Role of the Centre in Managing Diversified Corporations.* Oxford: Basil Blackwell.

planning process In most organizations 'strategic planning' is an annual process. It typically covers just the year ahead. Occasionally, a few organizations may look at a practical plan which stretches three or more years ahead (though, even then, not beyond five years – that is the domain of very few organizations, such as the oil multinationals). To be most effective, the plan has to be formalized, and this usually means in written form – as the formal 'marketing plan'. This is a process which traditionally follows a number of distinct steps, as described by Malcolm McDonald (1989):

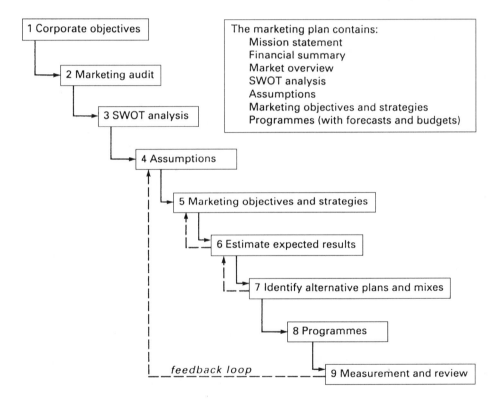

The essence of the process is that it moves from the general to the specific, from the overall objectives of the organization down to the individual action plan for a part of one marketing programme. It is also an iterative process, so that the draft output of each stage is checked to see what impact it has on the earlier stages – and is amended accordingly. As Philip Kotler (1988) states, there are three main approaches, in terms of involvement of the organization as a whole:

- *Top down planning.* Here top management set both the goals and the plans for lower level management. Based upon, or at least having parallels with, military organization, it raises the 'Theory X' criticism that the troops have 'but to do and die'!
- *Bottom up planning.* In this 'Theory Y'-based approach the various units (divisions, groups and departments) of the organization create their own goals and plans, which are then approved (or not)

by higher management. It can lead to more creative approaches, but can also pose problems for coordination. The most important element, if a successful strategy is to emerge, is the iteration and reiteration.

- *Goals down–plans up planning.* This is the most common version (at least amongst the minority of organizations which invest in such sophisticated planning processes). The top management set the goals, but the various units create their own plans to meet these goals. These plans are then typically approved as part of the annual planning and budgetary process.

See also MARKETING AUDIT; MARKETING OBJECTIVES; MARKETING PLAN BENEFITS; MARKETING PLANNING, ANALYSIS; MARKETING PLAN STRUCTURE; MARKETING PLAN USE; MONITORING, PROGRESS; PLANNING PITFALLS; POTSA PLANNING

References: Kotler, P. (1988) *Marketing Management* (6th edn). Englewood Cliffs, NJ: Prentice-Hall.
McDonald, Malcolm H. B. (1989) *Marketing Plans* (2nd edn). London: Heinemann.

planning resource   *see* MONITORING, PROGRESS

planning, strategic   *see* PLANNING PROCESS

plan, product   *see* PRODUCT PLAN

plan structure   *see* MARKETING PLAN STRUCTURE

plant visit evaluation   *see* SUPPLIER EVALUATION

plan use   *see* MARKETING PLAN USE

plates, printing   *see* BLOCKS

platform   The copy platform, or main theme of the advertisement.
See also ADVERTISING PROCESSES; CREATING THE CORRECT MESSAGES; CREATIVE DEPARTMENT, ADVERTISING AGENCY

PLC (product life cycle)   *see* PRODUCT LIFE CYCLE (PLC)

plug   To promote, by PR and other means, a new product.
See also PUBLIC RELATIONS; SALES PROMOTION

point of no return   *see* CATASTROPHE THEORY

point of sale   *see* NON-PRICE PROMOTIONS PROMOTIONAL LOZENGE; PROMOTION OBJECTIVES

poison pill   A tactic used by companies fighting takeovers which ensures that, if the takeover succeeds, something will happen which dramatically reduces the value of the company. A similar defence is that of porcupine provisions.

police   *see* BALANCING UNDER THE INFLUENCE; COMPLEX SALE; SAFETY IN NUMBERS

policies   *see* MARKETING STRATEGIES

political contacts   There are various levels of political contact which may be cultivated by the corporate PR group of an organization. At the lowest level there are the senior civil servants, who are very influential (but who are just as conscious of their need to be seen to be impartial – so contacts must be very ethically, discreetly and professionally handled). Then there are the many interested politicians (where, paradoxically – despite their potential power – they are subject to fewer restrictions). Highest of all are the ministers who directly decide policy; they are, needless to say, the most important contacts – and are, not surprisingly, accessible to only a few organizations.

The highest level contacts have to be built up over time. In the political sphere they are usually made by senior management during the course of their 'moving in the right circles'. This frequently means attending suitable conferences and political events. They may also be made, rather more questionably, by suitable intermediaries (as close familiarity with such political leaders may at times become a very saleable commodity!). They may also be stimulated by such devices as sponsorship – particularly of the arts. Most directly they may be 'earned' by the power and status of the organization itself. Few politicians (even the most senior) can afford not to listen to the most powerful organizations. 'Clout' is what counts here, and such meetings can almost be demanded (albeit very discreetly, if the organization wishes to continue to wield its power) when matters directly affecting the organization are known to be in discussion at such high levels. In any case, it is perfectly reasonable to seek (and even 'demand') access to an MP who represents a constituency where the organization has a branch (and workers who need to be represented!); for large organizations this can add up to a large number of MPs.

At the lower levels it is possible, and indeed desirable, to arrange regular events of suitable interest (usually of a serious business nature and not obviously pure entertainment) which junior politicians and civil servants will wish to attend, though politicians may (with some justification) be increasingly sceptical of such lobbying. Indeed, as Charles Miller (1990) points out, they receive an enormous number of invitations and will have to think that the event is really worth giving up their valuable time for before they will attend. It is, though, a long process.

How to handle such contacts

Assuming that the right to a contact has been earned (by 'clout' or by hard PR work), the arrangements for setting up a 'meeting' with a minister (which are similar to those for lower level contacts, but more formal) might be:

1. The rule is that a minister will usually have only two or three days 'free' over the next four months or so.
2. He or she will usually only be prepared to meet the most senior executive (the CEO/chairman or, if the organization is very powerful, the deputy chairman).
3. One of these dates will then be agreed with the minister's private office. If the chief executive has another engagement on that day he or she will simply have to postpone it!
4. Before the meeting, members of the minister's staff will expect to be fully briefed by the organization (usually by the corporate PR group). This briefing will be in considerable depth, and can last for several hours. In turn, the chief executive will also need to be briefed. Such meeting time is precious (to both sides), so both need be very well briefed indeed if they are not to waste the opportunity (which the minister will probably take as an insult!).
5. After all this preliminary work, the meetings themselves are intense (typically lasting just 35–45 minutes) and are not social events. Properly used, though, they are invaluable opportunities to influence the course of events – ministers respect input from outside organizations (and, in their insulated environment, depend upon it for a feel as to what the 'real world' is like!).

Charles Miller (1990) stresses the importance of civil servants in the UK, explaining what ministers are constrained by:

Knowledge is Power – Ministers rely on their officials to provide them with the information they need to make decisions . . .

Ministers are overburdened – their diaries can easily be filled with appointments by their officials unless they are careful . . .

The interdepartmental net – if Ministers reject the advice of their officials, the latter will often enlist the support of other Departments connected with the issue . . .

Access to departmental papers is limited – Ministers are by convention unable to see the papers of previous administrations and are therefore at a disadvantage compared to their officials . . .

Civil servants, though, have a rather different approach to lobbying – one which is much more related to the slow building up of trust. They would, in any case, usually prefer to deal with representative bodies (such as trade associations – with which they will probably have established links) rather than individual lobbyists, and, indeed, may resent the whole lobbying process! They will be very intelligent, especially at the most senior levels, but they will not be experts on the subject (since, at senior level, they are regularly moved between departments) and will therefore be nervous of any pressure based upon expertise – hence the emphasis on building 'trust' over the longer term.

See also CORPORATE PUBLIC RELATIONS; PROACTIVE PR; PUBLIC RELATIONS

Reference: Miller, Charles (1990) *Lobbying: Understanding and Influencing the Corridors of Power* (2nd edn). Oxford: Basil Blackwell.

political developments   *see* MARKET ENTRY DECISION

population (samples)   *see* SAMPLES

population size, filtering unsuitable markets
see EXPORT MARKET ELIMINATION

porcupine provisions   *see* POISON PILL

portfolio, creative   *see* AGENCY BRIEFING

portfolio pricing   If, as is likely, the organization has a portfolio of products, it can follow different pricing policies on each, balancing them against each other so that the overall impact is optimized. In any case, such pricing may be forced upon it. A 'problem child' may fail to become a 'star'; and if it is not to be immediately discontinued, its price will probably need to be raised so that it can be 'milked' to retrieve some profit from the situation. Looking at the portfolio in more general terms, it may even be possible to run two or more very similar brands with different pricing policies. Thus one can be in the mainstream of the market and at a reasonably high price, as is Unilever's Persil detergent, whereas another is quite specifically targeted at a lower price to cover those consumers who are particularly price conscious, as Unilever's 'Square Deal' Surf very obviously was for a number of years – though it may be significant, in terms of the true effectiveness of pure price competition even in this most competitive of markets, that this brand is no longer promoted on a price basis! The portfolio approach is a powerful one, not least because it can 'underwrite' any attempts to set a high price policy by differentiation, thereby balancing the risk of such experiments against the security offered by the brand(s) remaining in the lower price position. Such a higher price policy often succeeds, not infrequently against the expectations of most of those involved! The portfolio approach, however, is only available to those who have the financial resources, and the position in the market, to make it worthwhile.

See also PRICE FACTORS

portfolios, of products   *see* PRODUCT PORTFOLIO

portrait (layout)   *see* LANDSCAPE LAYOUT

position   *see* MARKET POSITIONING AND SEGMENTATION; MARKETING AUDIT; MARKETING STRATEGIES

position drift   In most markets customer requirements change over time, perhaps due to social factors or fashion or – perhaps more likely – to technological changes in the market. These changes may be relatively slow for long-established brands or very rapid for some fashion products. It is imperative, therefore, that you develop your existing products in line with these changing requirements. This is just as true for long-established brands as new ones – though, because the changes are slow, there is a danger that these new requirements will be overlooked. If you do not develop existing brands in a regular and rigorous manner, you may find yourself the victim of 'position drift'.

Thus, the positioning map which is the key element behind product/service policies shows only a static picture. Over time, 'position drift' can significantly change the picture. This may come about for three main reasons:

1. *Consumer drift*. As consumer tastes change, the segment (cluster) which contains them will shift its position. Its centre of gravity will move – and its size may change as consumers switch to other, perhaps newer, segments. The position of your brand relative to the ideal position, within this cluster, will reflect this drift.
2. *Competitor drift*. Alternatively, your competitors may shift their positions – so that your own relative position, your competitive advantage, may become less than optimal. This may pose a particular problem if you are trying to target several segments with just one brand.
3. *Ego drift*. Perhaps the most prevalent drift of all, however, occurs where 'brand managers' (or their advertising agencies) gratuitously reposition their own brand in a less optimal location. This is usually justified on the basis that consumers are bored with the existing messages and an exciting new approach is needed. The real reason is that members of the management team, frequently persuaded by an agency creative team itching to make their own distinctive mark, are themselves bored.

The biggest problem is that drift, of any of these types, usually occurs so slowly that it is not noticed by the brand manager – in the timescales that he or she works to the changes are imperceptible. It is for this reason that brand positioning maps must be updated regularly and the changes plotted as accurately as possible – so that the trajectory of any drift may be determined and corrected.

See also POSITIONING; SEGMENTATION

positioning   *see* LONGER-TERM COMPETITIVE SAW; MARKETING PLANNING, ANALYSIS; PRODUCT (OR SERVICE) GAP; PRODUCT (OR SERVICE) POSITIONING

positioning over time   If positioning research is carried out regularly over time, the map can also show these positions are changing – hopefully in line with the strategy. An example of an organization failing to track such market changes over time is that of the Cadillac Division of General Motors. Even when it finally revamped its range in 1985, its slimmed down versions actually seemed to move away from where the core of its market was, thereby offering Ford's Lincoln-Mercury Division, which continued to produce larger cars, a major competitive advantage. Tracking changes in position is thus a very powerful tool of marketing.

See also PRODUCT (OR SERVICE) POSITIONING; SEGMENTATION

positioning, price   *see* COMPARATIVE ADVANTAGE, GLOBAL; MARKET-BASED PRICING

positioning, product   *see* MARKET GAP ANALYSIS

positioning (strategy) map   *see* POTSA PLANNING

positioning/targeting   *see* MARKET POSITIONING AND SEGMENTATION

positive and negative aspects   *see* SWOT ANALYSIS

positive delegation   *see* EMERGENT STRATEGY

positive philosophy of 'do nothing'   Many organizations by default 'do nothing'. They simply do not recognize the need for change, or they are afraid of what it involves. These organizations have, justifiably, been criticized for this – and not a few of them have later paid a high price for their neglect. There is therefore a commendable incentive for management to 'do something'. This is truly commendable where a sound course of action is obvious. This approach, though, becomes a problem in its own right when no obvious solution is immediately to hand. The pressure to 'do something' quickly turns into pressure to 'do anything'. Managements accordingly tend to grasp at very short-term fixes, while they try to find the right long-term one. The problem is not that these fixes are inherently damaging to the organization, but that their very existence tends to predetermine (incrementally, if not logically) the long-term solution chosen.

Under some circumstances, if you are brave enough, the best solution is literally to 'do nothing'. This is often best, for the following reasons:

1. If you do not know what to do, then doing nothing will force those closer to the problem (the staff on the ground) to take the necessary actions instead. They are, in any case, the people most likely to develop the best short-term fixes – and to implement them.
2. The long-term solution can then be investigated without any need to take account of these fixes – there is no obligation to incorporate them incrementally in any final solution. More important, the final solution can be implemented without

any arguments about how it interfaces with these fixes.

It is a very brave philosophy, which demands a management which is confident of its own position, but it can remove many of the short-term pressures which lead to panic – and thence to disaster.

See also CORPORATE PLAN; CORPORATE STRATEGY AND MARKETING; MARKETING DEFINITIONS; MARKETING STRATEGIES; PRODUCT (OR SERVICE) STRATEGY; 4 Ps

possibles   *see* FORECASTS OF SALES BUSINESS

postal surveys   *see* MAIL SURVEYS

posters   This is something of a specialist medium, which is generally used in support of campaigns using other media. On the other hand, some advertisers, particularly those in brewing and tobacco, have successfully made significant use of the medium; though, to achieve this, they have developed the requisite expertise to make efficient use of its peculiarities. Main roadside posters are described in terms of how the poster is physically posted onto them (pasted on, one sheet at a time, by a bill-poster) – as 16 sheet (the main, $10' \times 6'8''$ size in vertical format) or 48 sheet ($10' \times 20'$, in horizontal/landscape format). Those smaller ones, seen in pedestrian areas, are typically 4 sheet ($5' \times 3'4''$). The best sites are typically reserved for long-term clients – mainly the brewers and tobacco companies (and hence one reason for their success in use of the medium) – so new users may find this a relatively unattractive medium.

See also MEDIA TYPES

Post-It Notes   *see* NEW PRODUCT INNOVATION

post-Keynesianism   The economic theory, based on modified Keynesian theories and new theories (such as efficiency-wage theory and implicit contract theory), which is intended to restore Keynesianism as the dominant economic force – as yet with little practical success.

See also KEYNESIANISM

post-paid reply card   *see* REPLY-PAID CARDS

post-purchase behaviour   *see* REPEAT PURCHASING PROCESS

postscript   *see* LETTER, DIRECT MAIL

post-testing   *see* COPY TESTING

potential consumers   *see* ENQUIRY PROCESSING; PROSPECTS; USAGE GAP

potential markets   *see* EXPORT MARKET ELIMINATION

potential penetration level   *see* DIFFUSION OF INNOVATION

POTSA planning   This approach to marketing planning is a simple one, since it assumes that most of the work has already been undertaken across the whole year rather than concentrated into the few weeks of the annual planning process. It is therefore a genuine review of what has been happening and what needs to be changed to improve performance in the future.

There are just five simple steps, which closely follow the more conventional marketing planning processes (with the conventional steps shown in the brackets below).

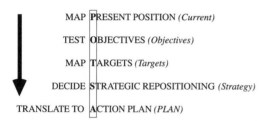

MAP PRESENT POSITION *(Current)*

TEST OBJECTIVES *(Objectives)*

MAP TARGETS *(Targets)*

DECIDE STRATEGIC REPOSITIONING *(Strategy)*

TRANSLATE TO ACTION PLAN *(PLAN)*

If you need a mnemonic to help remember these stages, then the initial letters (of the 'second' words) highlighted above spell out POTSA, which is the name given to this approach.

Map present position (Current)
The starting point must be a definitive statement, ideally a formal 'map' of some kind, of where your product/service packages(s) currently is in terms of the market(s). This is arguably the most important step of all, and the one where most organizations fail. This must be condensed into just one page (of no more than 500 words and, in any case, preferably shown in terms of diagrams/maps, or at least in measured numeric terms). If you feel that there must be some explanatory expansion, this should be put into an appendix – but be ruthless in limiting yourself to one page here.

Assumptions
An especially important outcome of the analysis of the current position, one which justifies a separate

subsection (but of just half a page – no more than 250 words in addition to the rest of the current section), is the key assumptions about the future. It is essential to spell these out.

Test objectives (Objectives)
The organization will have existing marketing objectives, by design or by default. These will state where the organization intends to be in the future and when it intends to be there.

Map targets (Targets)
The relatively general long-term objectives need to be quantified as a series of targets, and given timescales as well as numeric projections. Even intangible objectives, such as those relating to image, should be quantified in terms of measurable marketing research results. The importance of setting measurable targets, so that progress may be monitored (and changes made to the plans to allow for any divergence), is such that this justifies a separate main section – though only one page (no more than 500 words – but further explanations may be included in an appendix).

Map
As this is the key stage of the development of strategy, a further page should be dedicated to four (two-dimensional) maps of the eight most important parameters, each map showing the current position (along with that of the customers' ideal and that of key competitors), the targeted future positions and the planned path to these. This should primarily be used to summarize the whole plan – but should in the process be used as a further check on the validity of the proposed moves. Full-sized maps (along with further dimensions if needed) should be relegated to an appendix.

Decide strategic repositioning (Strategy)
This step, documented again on just one page (no more than 500 words), should simply explain which marketing strategy is to be adopted to move the organization over the longer term from its present position to its targeted ones. These strategies describe, in principle, the 'how' – how the objectives will be achieved.

Having completed this crucial stage of the planning process, you will need to recheck the feasibility of your objectives and strategies in terms of the market share, sales, costs, profits, etc. which these demand in practice. As in the rest of the marketing discipline, you will need to employ judgement, experience, market research and anything else which helps you to look at your conclusions from all possible angles.

Translate to action plan (Plan)
Finally, the shorter-term (more certain) elements of the strategies need to be translated into the necessary actions (and related timescales). Again, this should not take more than one page – though this time in the form of a table which describes the key activities in terms of the most relevant parameters (but at least their prioritization levels and resource requirements should be listed, along with their quantified targets and times). Ideally, the plan should also contain space for the entry of actual results versus these.
See also ASSUMPTIONS, MARKETING PLAN; CORPORATE OBJECTIVES; MARKETING AUDIT; MARKETING OBJECTIVES; MARKETING PLANS AND PROGRAMMES; MARKETING PLAN STRUCTURE; MARKETING PLAN USE; MARKETING STRATEGIES; PLANNING PROCESS

power   *see* MARKET PENETRATION

powerful idea   *see* CONVICTION MARKETING FACTORS

PR   *see* CORPORATE PUBLIC RELATIONS; MARKETING STRATEGIES; PROMOTIONAL LOZENGE; PUBLIC RELATIONS

practical pricing policies   *see* PRICING POLICIES, PRACTICAL

practical value chains   A more practical approach to value chains is to split the activities of the organization into those characteristic groupings which are natural to its specific operations – rather than the theoretical nine categories described by Michael Porter (1985). In this approach his upper set of cross-organization activities should be ignored, since it may tend to confuse managers trying to use the approach.

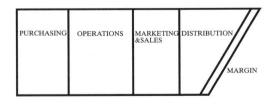

As can be seen from the diagram above, the visual presentation is also made more meaningful if the size

of each segment of the value chain reflects its importance (on whatever basis you decide is most useful, e.g. volume, added value, sensitivity).

Reference: Porter, Michael (1985) *Competitive Advantage: Creating and Sustaining Superior Performance.* New York: The Free Press.

practice of marketing   *see* COARSE MARKETING

PR agencies   *see* PUBLIC RELATIONS AGENCIES

precipitous failure   *see* CATASTROPHE THEORY

precision (direct) marketing, retail   Direct marketing is a general promotional vehicle, but it also offers a 'retail' dimension.

Mail order
The most obvious manifestations of direct marketing in this context are the large, lavishly illustrated catalogues that are mailed by organizations such as Littlewoods and Grattan in the UK and previously, and most famously, by Sears Roebuck in the USA (though this operation has now been closed). These offer a range of goods which matches that of a department store (and, indeed, the majority of the catalogue operations are owned by department store operators). The advantage to the supplier is reduced cost, where there are no expensive high street locations to maintain. The advantage to the consumer is convenience – the archetypal mail-order operation, Sears Roebuck in the USA, made a large part of its fortune supplying the needs of remote farming communities. There are, though, many other, more specialized catalogue sales operations, offering goods ranging from seeds to exotic lingerie. There are also many small businesses which sell single products by mail order, through the small ads in newspapers (or, on a larger scale, occasionally via television). Perhaps most successful of all, however, have been organizations (such as Reader's Digest, as well as the other 'subscription sellers' and the book/record clubs) which have specialized in tightly defined markets.

Direct mail
Some mail order houses use direct mail, based on lists of individuals which match their product or service profile, as an alternative to media advertising.

Teleselling
Some mail order houses use telesales personnel to contact the people on their lists. The QVC television channel in the USA (and now in Europe) is dedicated to telesales and has been a dramatic success.

Electronic shopping

The visionaries promise us that in the future we will be able to order almost everything via our computer terminals. As yet, the volume of goods and services sold in this way is relatively small. On the other hand, many retailers, including the out-of-town superstores, are running serious pilots – so they at least still think this is the future. Most notably, one or two Web-based bookstores have revolutionized that area of retailing, showing the way for others.

Direct selling

Door-to-door selling has a long history, but it was revitalized by the arrival of Avon and (in a revised form) Tupperware.

The great advantage of any such direct contact (be it by mail or face-to-face) is that (to a varying degree) it shares the precision of all 'personal selling'. The vendor can have a precise relationship (based upon exact information, from historical records as well as the current transaction, of the customer's needs and wants) with each individual. This is the basis of 'precision marketing'. With the availability of cheap computing power and data capture, it is growing rapidly and (in a variety of forms – not necessarily directly related to those which already exist) is set to be one of the more important elements of promotion over the next decades. It shares many of the features of face-to-face selling, albeit to a greatly reduced extent. It offers precise targeting, accompanied by a degree of immediacy and personalization (though it will be a computer 'talking' to the recipient). It also allows the supplier some ability to concentrate resources; the 'cost per thousand' may be high but the wastage is very low (ideally all the recipients should be potential purchasers – and, as the experience of the database grows, this ideal can be approached). The greatest benefit of all comes when there is continuity. The supplier runs a 'continuity program' (such as a 'club'), extending the customer contact beyond the initial transaction. In the process the relationship (which can be seen here as an investment in future sales) is developed and more is learnt about that customer – so that future marketing may be even more precise. Edward Nash (1986) indicates the potential benefits arising from this process, in the specific context of 'subscription selling': 'As a general rule, 50 to 60 percent of first-year subscribers will renew for a second term; 70 to 90 percent of renewed subscribers will then renew again for a subsequent term – on to infinity'.

See also RETAILING

Reference: Nash, Edward (1986) *Direct Marketing: Strategy, Planning, Execution* (2nd edn). Maidenhead: McGraw-Hill.

precision marketing   The explosion of data over the past decades has only recently been harnessed in the most direct way – that of marketing directly to individual customers or small groups of customers. Martin Baier (1983) describes one aspect of this: 'Direct marketing, with its historical roots in direct mail (an advertising medium) and mail order (a selling method), has evolved as an aspect of the total marketing concept. . . . It is characterised by measurability and accountability as well as reliance on lists and data.' He goes on to offer the definition 'Direct marketing is an interactive system of marketing which uses one or more advertising media to effect a measurable response and/or transaction at any location'.

Another form of 'direct marketing' has traditionally been the approach employed by the salesperson in the industrial (complex sale) markets. He or she often spends considerable time face-to-face with the customer, tailoring the sale to that individual's specific needs. The key to success in both the fields described above is detailed information about individual customers.

See also DATA AVAILABILITY, PRECISION MARKETING; DATA MANIPULATION, PRECISION MARKETING

Reference: Baier, Martin (1983) *The Elements of Direct Marketing*. New York: McGraw-Hill.

pre-close   *see* CLOSING TECHNIQUES; DEMONSTRATIONS

predatory pricing   Pricing, usually by the market leader, at such a low level that it forces other firms out of the market, thus creating a quasi-monopoly, when prices can be raised again to higher levels.

prediction   *see* FORECASTS INTO BUDGETS

predictive or normative models   *see* MODEL CATEGORIES; MODELS

pre-emptive defence   *see* DEFENCE STRATEGIES; DEFENDING MARKET SHARE

preference in advertising models   *see* BUYING DECISION, ADVERTISING MODELS

preferred clientele   *see* STRATEGIES FOR INTENT BUYERS

presentation content   Despite what many of the
more flamboyant practitioners might aspire to, it is
inevitably the content that is the driving force of a
professional presentation. If you haven't got the content don't make the presentation. If you have got the
content make certain that you communicate it. The
following sections make some suggestions as to how
this communication might be achieved.

Overall content
Where inexperienced sales professionals concentrate
on the mechanics of a presentation, more experienced presenters recognize that most of the time
spent in preparing a presentation needs to be directed at establishing the correct overall content.
The average IBM sales professional's presentation
sometimes lacked in bravura, but was carried by the
superb content. On the other hand, brilliant style can
rarely carry poor content; at least, not for the dura-
tion of a sales campaign. Within IBM it is a rule of
thumb that largely new material requires a ratio of
between five and ten times as long in the preparation
as in the presentation; and totally new material a ratio
of up to 20:1. Thus, a 45 minute presentation could
take up to 15 hours of concentrated work (probably
spread over at least 3 days) – and would take at least
5 hours to rework for a different audience. The ratio
for distance teaching (such as that carried out by the
Open University) is, for comparison, something in
excess of 200:1!

Level
Having chosen the key messages to be conveyed, the
next exercise is to pitch the presentation at the correct level for the audience. The categorization that is
normally most important is that of 'level' within the
organization. Within the IBM customer set, for
example, the most notable split was between the
technical management (and staff) and the board
members. The former were very interested in the
technical details, whereas the latter were mainly concerned with the overall impact on the business, particularly in terms of profit. To get the level right you
have to see the world with the eyes of the audience;
you have to understand just what is important to
them, what interests them, and from what perspective they would want to see it. There will probably be
quite distinct differences of interest between the
main categories – the users, technical advisers,
buyers and board members. Getting the level right is
the first acid test of any presentation, a test that the
audience themselves will have made within the first
few minutes.

Verbal content
This highlights the fact, common to all sales situations, that you should use the right 'language'.

Visual content
It is inevitable that in a presentation what an audience
will remember most clearly is what it sees rather than
what it hears. As a result, the organization of the
visual messages is crucial if they are to do the selling
job you want. This is perhaps the most difficult new
skill of all (and the most important to learn) for sales
professionals (or managers) whose previous experience has been almost totally verbal. The mistakes
made by the inexperienced tend to fall at either end of
the spectrum. The classic mistake is to show too
much information – for example, projecting a trans-
parency/acetate of a fully typed sheet of A4 paper
that contains perhaps 1000 words. There is no way
that any audience can quickly absorb such visual
complexity. The result is that they spend the next
two or three minutes desperately trying to read it, and
in the process ignore every word the sales professional is uttering. The next mistake is usually made
by those sales professionals who have recognized the
folly of overcomplexity but who react against this
with oversimplicity. The resulting transparency/
acetate typically contains just a few very general
words, which tend towards 'motherhood'. These certainly do not interfere with the verbal material – but
neither do they significantly add to it, which misses
the benefit of the very powerful visual stimulus. The
ideal lies somewhere between these extremes. Visuals
do need to be kept simple, with perhaps no more than
five items of information on each, but they also need

to be informative. The words, or visuals, have to be very carefully chosen to most powerfully encapsulate the messages you want to put across. There is some argument as to how many transparencies/acetates you can present (before you once more confuse the audience by presenting too much information) – but a rule of thumb says that you should think twice before using more that 10–15 transparencies/acetates (or flipcharts) in a 45 minute presentation. You can, though, usually present more slides, since they will typically contain less information each. Even so, if you use more than 80 slides (the contents of a Kodak carousel) in a 45 minute show you will probably make the audience's heads ache.

Pruning
Once you have the content, and are happy with it, get out your pruning shears and set to work with a certain degree of savagery. It really hurts to cut out material which has taken hours of sweat and tears to create, but which turns out on inspection not to be central to your theme. It is a necessary sacrifice if you want to produce the most powerful argument.

Material quality
Quality is important chiefly because it shows your audience that you are taking them seriously. Amateurish, crude visuals will not hide good content, but they will distract from the message – and will counter any message of quality that you will probably wish to convey. One aspect of quality that is important is consistency of style. Using the same typeface across all the visuals, with a standard layout, is all that is required to achieve this.
See also PRESENTATIONS

presentation media   Having decided on the overall structure of the presentation and the audience that is to receive it, the next choice is the medium that is to be used. There are a range of options, of which the main ones are as follows.

Overhead projected transparencies/acetates ('foils')
The medium used in most presentations is that of A4 (US Quarto)-size transparencies/acetates shown by means of an overhead projector. These have become the standard because they are probably the easiest medium of all to use, and certainly the easiest to prepare. The capital cost of the overhead projector and screen is affordable by most companies; indeed, most companies of a size able to afford a sales force (or a marketing department) already have at least one. They are easy to prepare because of their size, which is the same as the normal A4 or US Quarto

(letter size) sheet of paper. Thus, all the techniques (such as typing and photocopying) that can be applied to a normal sheet of paper are available for use on transparencies/acetates.

Recently, it has become possible to put a computer display panel on top of an overhead projector – so allowing you to present 'slides' prepared, and held, in your computer. There are a range of software packages which support this approach, of which Microsoft's *Powerpoint* is probably the most widely used.

Flipcharts
Occasionally you may have no alternative to using flipcharts as your prime medium. For example, you can carry a full-size portable flipchart stand (with a presentation already set up) in the back of your car and be ready to present in about 30 seconds – less than a tenth of the time it would take to set up any other form of presentation. The problem with this medium is that of achieving the correct quality of visual material. It demands considerable practice, and not a little effort in preparation, to produce tidy, readable flipcharts. These days it is more normal to use flipcharts to back up an overhead transparency/acetate presentation.

Slides
Most professionally produced company presentations – the sort that are produced centrally – are made available on slides, simply because this is the best (and cheapest) way of copying them. Their drawback is that they need a special environment, and their inflexibility means that they tend to dictate the style of the presentation.
See also PRESENTATIONS

presentation, personal   *see* PERSONAL PRESENTATIONS

presentations   Unlike a call, a successful presentation cannot normally be seen in isolation; it is usually part of an overall campaign – whether a sales campaign or a management campaign to achieve a specific end. Typically it will be part of the close of that campaign. The objectives of the presentation will therefore be inextricably intertwined with those of the overall campaign. It also means that the presentation will not usually introduce new material, but will bring together the previously (informally) agreed material for final, formal, approval. These objectives must be kept simple, for the complexity that can be handled in a call (with diversions resulting from questioning being followed by clarification in the form of a restatement of the perspective) is simply not possible in a presentation. It is possible (and, indeed, desirable) to encourage questions during a presentation, but these are qualitatively different to those used in a call. The various stages which go into planning a presentation may include:

- *Structure.* If you can arrange for the format of the presentation to match your own style, then you have a major advantage. In this way a presentation can be productively used to act as a showcase for your 'sales skills'. Some ideas to bear in mind are:
- *Tell them what.* The traditional, almost infamous, IBM approach was to split a presentation into three parts. In the first you told the audience what they were about to be told. In the second you told them. In third you told them what you had told them. In other words, the presentation always started with a clear and concise introduction, which explained what the audience was about to be told. The main body of the material came next. Finally, it was concluded by a clear and concise summary of all the key points which had just been presented in detail.
- *'KISS'.* In the case of presentations, KISS (Keep It Simple, Stupid) can be a particularly productive concept. There is inevitably much less interaction in a presentation – and hence less opportunity to explore more complex arguments. As a result it is essential to keep the concepts as simple as possible; whilst still encapsulating what has been agreed in the previous meetings. Accordingly these should be perhaps limited to no more than half a dozen concepts, or arguments, at a time.
- *Ask for the 'order'.* It should be obvious, to everyone involved, that in making the presentation you are looking for an 'order', or at least (in terms of a management presentation) to agreement for some course of action. It is just as obvious to the 'prospects' (the board, for example) as it is to you – they too will be giving up their valuable time, presumably because they too expect to do business. The one simple objective – that of obtaining agreement for the intended course of action – automatically provides the framework for the whole presentation, and allows you subsequently to check progress in the context of what really matters: are you progressing towards that agreement?

See also SALES CALL; SEMINARS

presentation style   Style is an individual matter; it is what works for you as an individual – what you, and your audience, are comfortable with. Having made that disclaimer, it has to be admitted that there is limited flexibility in a presentation, and hence less room for developing an idiosyncratic style. In general, there are a number of main categories of style:

Formal or informal
There is a tendency for inexperienced presenters to make presentations very formal affairs. This is understandable where they are new to the techniques, and want to keep the complexities under control by the use of a controlled, formal structure. The 'formal' style takes the term 'presentation' almost literally and involves mainly one-way communication – from the presenter to the audience. My own preference, where it is possible, is for a more informal style, with significantly more feedback from the audience – and ideally with interactive involvement of that audience. The success of a presentation can often be directly proportional to the degree to which the key participants are actively involved.

Room layout
The traditional 'formal' layout is 'theatre' style, with the audience in rows of chairs facing the presenter (who is sometimes even on a raised stage). This allows the audience the best possible view of the proceedings. Sometimes it is supplemented by providing tables (still in rows) to make it easier for the audience to make notes. These tables create a physical barrier, but this is no greater than the psychological barrier that is created by the formal separation of the presenter from the audience in any theatre-style meeting. The layout that I personally prefer, if the group is small enough, is 'conference' style – seated around a table (or, for larger meetings, around a horseshoe of tables). This confers the ambience of a 'discussion' meeting, anticipating such discussion and providing the best psychological environment for interaction.

Sitting or standing
It may come as a surprise to some that you can give a presentation sitting down. This style enjoyed quite a vogue at IBM, and is still the normal style for many internal meetings there; for, with the overhead projector alongside your seat (and your pointing on it rather than to the screen), you can comfortably remain seated, remaining integrated with the group. It is an effective style for very informal presentations and can be much less nerve-racking for an inexperienced presenter. Most presenters, of course, do it

standing up! This is the traditional style, and it does have the advantage of making certain that the presenter is the clear focus of the meeting. It also integrates him or her with the visuals, if not with the audience.

Notes

The use of a verbatim script is widespread; it is the staple diet of most political speeches. By itself it is relatively foolproof – just so long as you do not lose your place or mislay a page. On the other hand, the opposite extreme (of having no notes at all) is fraught with as many dangers, and it is well nigh impossible (at least for the great majority of sales professionals) to give a good presentation that is genuinely *ad hoc* (that is, without any previous consideration of what is to be said). The happy mean lies somewhere between these extremes. The conventional wisdom holds that presenters should use brief notes – essentially subject headings. It is normally recommended that these are put on cards (usually 5″ by 3″, so that they can be conveniently held in the palm of the hand). Some people just write down a simple list of the topics to be covered. Others go to great lengths, adding symbols and colour coding, and verbatim quotes where these are particularly important. Once again it is up to you to decide just what suits your style; only experience will tell you just how little you can get away with.

See also PRESENTATIONS

press advertisement   *see* ADVERTISING PROCESSES; CREATIVE DEPARTMENT, ADVERTISING AGENCY

press advertisement coupons   *see* PROMOTIONAL PRICING

press advertisement testing   *see* ADVERTISING RESEARCH

press advertising effectiveness   *see* COUPON RESPONSE

press and public relations   *see* PROACTIVE PR; PUBLIC RELATIONS

press media   Spending in this medium is dominated by the national and regional newspapers, with the latter taking almost all the classified advertising revenue. The magazine and trade/technical journal markets are about the same size as each other, but less than half the size of the newspaper sectors.

National newspapers

These are traditionally categorized, from the media buyer's viewpoint, on the basis of class, even though this is of declining importance to many advertisers. It is more difficult, however, to segment readerships by age categories. The medium is obviously best matched to national advertisers who are happy with black and white advertisements (which can still carry quite detailed messages), though limited-quality run-of-the-paper colour is now available, and high-quality colour is available in some supplements. National newspapers in general, and the quality press in particular, are supposed to carry more 'weight' with their readers (since they are deliberately read, not treated just as 'background'), so that an advertisement placed in one (especially a Sunday paper) is taken more seriously than a comparable one in a regional newspaper – though it may be more transitory (since it is not kept for reference, as some local weeklies may be).

Regional newspapers

These may be dailies, which look and perform much like the nationals, or weeklies, which are rather more specialized – and are often supposed to carry less 'weight' (but may be kept longer, for reference) – though they dominate the market for classified advertising. Indeed, there is usually much more advertising competing for the reader's attention, and the weekly newspaper is fast becoming the province of the 'free-sheets'. These are typically delivered free to all homes in a given area, obtaining all their revenue from the very high proportion of advertising which they carry, and accordingly have the least 'weight' of all. Advertisements in newspapers, referred to as 'insertions', are usually specified as so many centimetres across so many columns. In these days of metrication, a multiple of 3 cm is used as the standard measure instead of the previously traditional inch! Thus, a '30 cm double' would be an advertisement which is 30 cm long, down the page, and across two columns of type (note that the width of columns varies from paper to paper – an important consideration when you are having the printing 'blocks' made). Alternatively the space may be a full page, or a half or quarter. In addition the position is also often specified – so that, for example, an advertiser of a unit trust will probably pay extra to make certain the insertion is next to the financial pages.

Magazines

These offer a more selective audience (which is more 'involved', with the editorial at least) and are traditionally categorized into general interest, special

interest and trade/technical. The advertiser will therefore be able to select those magazines which match the specific profile demanded by the advertising strategy. The audience is usually concentrated, comprising only those with that specialist interest. The magazines' weight, or 'authority', is correspondingly high, and they may be kept for a considerable time for use as reference – as well as passed to other readers (so that 'readership' figures may be much higher than 'circulation' figures). They can offer excellent colour – but, again, the clutter of many competing advertisements may give the advertiser's message less impact. In the trade and professional fields there are now a significant number of 'controlled circulation' magazines. These are like the 'free press' in that they are delivered free to the recipients, but, at least in theory, those recipients should have been carefully screened to ensure that they are of value to the advertisers – and the circulation can, if properly controlled, represent a wide cross-section of the buyers, and influencers, in the advertiser's target audience. As with newspapers, the insertions are normally placed as full page, half page, etc. The rates for positioning are, however, usually more varied, with premiums paid for facing editorial matter (rather than buried in a mass of other advertisements) and, of course, for colour.
See also MEDIA TYPES

pressure groups   *see* DEFENSIVE (CORPORATE) PR

prestige   *see* CONVICTION MARKETING FACTORS

prestige advertising   *see* CORPORATE PROMOTION VERSUS BRAND PROMOTION

pre-testing advertisements   *see* COPY TESTING; MESSAGE SELECTION

pre-testing sales promotions   *see* SALES PROMOTIONAL PLANS AND RESEARCH

price   Probably the single most important decision in marketing is that of price. This is partly because price may have an impact on sales volumes. If the price is too high and the market is competitive, sales may be correspondingly reduced. Indeed, many economists would see price as the main determinant of sales volume. On the other hand, many of the more sophisticated marketers have found ways to reduce the impact of price. Thus, in practice the main reason for the importance of price is that it is one of the three main variables which determines the

profit. Hence, the profit per unit is equal to the price less the total cost of producing that unit. Put at its simplest:

Profit = Price – Cost

The third factor is the volume of sales, since the organization's net profit is equal to the number of 'units' sold multiplied by the net profit obtained on each of those units. At this level the mathematics are very simple, but also very important!

The higher the price can be raised (assuming that unit costs and sales volume do not change), the greater the profit the organization makes. Many of the most powerful marketing techniques have therefore been designed to maximize the price which can be achieved. In practice, the calculation of profit is much more complicated than this simple explanation allows for. The long-term problems caused for the large Australian corporations by that country's relatively loose accounting definitions were evidenced by the massive insolvencies which resulted when reality caught up with theory. Even so, the basic principle still holds – even if it is not necessarily easy to implement!
See also MARKETING MIX; MARKETING STRATEGIES 4 Ps

price and not-for-profit organizations   Price is an element of the marketing mix which seems, at least at first inspection, largely irrelevant to not-for-profit organizations. Even so, there are a number of such organizations which (whilst having charitable status and, accordingly, not being allowed to make a profit) still charge for their services. It is frequently the case that in these organizations the term 'surplus' is interchangeable with 'profit', and they behave exactly the same as profit-making organizations – although the terminology for their 'pricing' may have more variety.

There remain, however, a large number of organizations (typically in the government sector) where no money changes hands. There simply is no price. Allocation of the service to the consumer is by other means, such as need (determined by a doctor, for example) or queuing (such as in hospital waiting lists). Many aspects of pricing are therefore not fully applicable. On the other hand, some of the principles can still be applied if 'price' is replaced by the 'perceived value' of the consumer. Thus, the consumer still puts a value (often a high value) on the service, and this can be dealt with much as 'price' itself. Certainly, if the service providers are to best match their consumers' needs they should have a good appreciation of the value the consumers put on the service. The government's difficulty with the 'value' to put on the various services offered by the National Health Service – because the services are not charged for – is just one possible example, in the government sector, of the problems caused by the lack of a 'price' or 'perceived value' to its 'customers'. On the other hand, hospital consultants, who have a large degree of control over the disposition of resources (and as a result, over the queues) in the NHS, could (and perhaps should) take into account the patients' 'perceived value' of the various treatments rather than just their own view of the medical needs. In the light of this, it might, for example, be found that increasing the proportion of resources devoted to minor surgery (rather than that dealing with life-threatening ailments) would increase the overall 'satisfaction' of the patients as a whole. Without asking the patients (which is a central concept of marketing) which choice they would make, at least in terms of 'perceived value', it is difficult to see how their total 'satisfaction' could be maximized. In terms of the 'life cycle', for example, the perceived value of the 'product' may vary with its 'age' – a social service may be seen as more valuable when newly launched (perhaps because it will be tapping a backlog of clients with the most need) than it will be late in its life cycle, when alternatives will probably have been developed. A portfolio of offerings may also be used to present the community as a whole with the best possible perceived value, balancing those little-used services which (whilst they may have a high value for each of the individuals involved) may be seen as marginal by the community against those meeting mass demands – and hence probably seen as being of high value. Segmentation, or positioning, in particular is an especially valuable technique for ensuring that the 'perceived value' offered to groups is maximized.

The position in 'social marketing' is, inevitably, more complex. As Kotler and Andreasen (1987) point out, there may be other 'costs' that some of these 'consumers' might be asked to pay, including:

Sacrifices of old ideas, values or views of the world . . .
Sacrifices of old patterns of behaviour . . .
Sacrifices of time and energy . . .

See also PRICE; SERVICE PRICES

Reference: Kotler, Philip and Andreasen, Alan (1987) *Strategic Marketing for Nonprofit Organizations* (3rd edn). Englewood Cliffs, NJ: Prentice-Hall.

price and quality, product screening   With a new product or service, there has to be at least a rough comparability with the existing products or services in terms of consumer perceptions of what price (and quality) range the organization lies in. This is particularly so when introducing a cheaper product into a high-quality range. The buyers of the existing range may see this as reflecting a reduction in quality of their normal products, and this may have a disastrous effect overall. It may not even help the new product, for consumers in general may assume that, in line with the price, quality has been abandoned. At the other extreme, adding a higher priced product to a cheap range will probably not be a successful strategy either, for the obvious reason that it is out of line with the overall strategy and is unlikely to meet the needs of the existing customers who are, presumably, interested in price.

price and the distribution channel   In many situations the producer cannot determine the final price to the end-user or consumer. The intermediaries in the distribution channel will apply their own pricing strategies, which may be totally unrelated to those of the producer (and may be, and often are, opposed to these). Thus they may even choose to absorb any price increases which the producer imposes. On the other hand, they may equally keep a price decrease which the producer has introduced (to improve penetration of the product, say) for themselves, to increase their own profit – again meaning that the consumer sees no difference.
See also PRICE FACTORS

price categories   *see* SELECTIVE PRICING

price challenge reactions   Faced with a price reduction by a competitor, there are a number of choices open. The first reaction should always be to carefully consider the situation (and metaphorically count to ten before indulging in righteous retaliation!). Has the competitor decided upon a long-term price reduction, or is this just a short-term promotion? If it is the latter then the reaction should be purely that relating to short-term promotional activity (and the optimum response is often to simply ignore the challenge). All too often price wars have been started because simple promotional activities have been misunderstood as major strategic changes. If, on the other hand, it emerges that this is a long-term move, then there are a number of possible reactions:

- *Reduce price.* The most obvious, and most popular, reaction is to match the competitor's move. This maintains the status quo (but reduces profits pro rata!). If this route is to be chosen it is as well to make the move rapidly and obviously – not least to send signals to the competitor of your intention to fight (in the hope that the competitive management will get the message and retreat – though these messages are all too often misinterpreted!).
- *Maintain price.* Another reaction is to hope that the competitor has made a mistake; though, if the competitor's action does make inroads into your share, this can rapidly lead to a loss of confidence as well as of volume.
- *React with other measures.* Reducing price is not the only weapon. Other tactics, such as improved quality or increased promotion (to improve the quality image perhaps), may be used – often to great effect.
- *Split the market.* A particularly effective tactic (most notably used by Heublein, the owner of the Smirnoff brand of vodka) is to combine a move to increase the 'quality' of the main brand at the same time as launching a 'fighting brand' to undermine (by price cutting even further) the price position of the competitor.
- *Avoide price wars.* The best advice is to avoid price wars. This advice may not always be taken, however, if the benefits seem attractive (as, unfortunately, they will to the competitors as well).

See also COMPETITION PRICING; COST-PLUS PRICING; PRICE COMPETITION; PRICE INCREASES; PRICING POLICIES, PRACTICAL; PRICING STRATEGY; PRISONER'S DILEMMA

price competition Price competition is usually seen to be the most savage and destructive form of commercial warfare. It is particularly destructive because at one end of the chain it destroys the profit of the suppliers (and with it the capacity to invest in the future of the market) and at the other it as often destroys the belief of consumers in the quality of the offering (and, thus, in their expectations of development of the market). Some of the possible reasons for indulging in the very risky pursuit of price competition are as follows.

- *Volume sales.* Not all price reductions are destructive. Some result in such increases in the volume of purchases that absolute profit is increased despite the relative reductions in price (and econo-

mies of scale may mean that even the relative profit per unit increases) and the whole market expands rapidly. Matsushita's decision to reduce the price of VCRs (video cassette recorders) was responsible for making this product available to the mass market. The key to making a success of price competition is to ensure that this reflects a genuine cost advantage. Economies of scale, and hence the justification of lower prices to increase volumes, is one aspect. Another is that your own cost structure must offer advantages over those of the competitors. When these factors apply in your favour, price competition can be very advantageous, in exactly the same way that any other 'product' advantage would be. Unfortunately, most price competition occurs between companies with very similar cost structures and thus frequently leads to a debilitating price war.

- *Market leadership targeting.* In an 'open' market, with a number of similar-sized brands (or a new market which has not yet stabilized), a brand owner may decide to make an investment to achieve market leadership (a 'penetration' policy in new markets), and price is often the main weapon – particularly where there is a belief (often no more than an unjustified hope) that this may also lead to falling costs per unit.
- *Excess capacity.* Perhaps the most dangerous move is where price is reduced to use up excess capacity, and hence to absorb more overheads. Unfortunately, this often takes place when there is spare capacity in the market as a whole, so competitors are faced with similar problems – and will respond similarly.
- *Falling brand share.* Defence of share often involves a more aggressive price position, and hence it may be wise to watch how rapidly share is being taken from competitors by non-price means (since too rapid an erosion may stimulate a savage price war).

On the other hand, the dangers of initiating a price war include:

- *Low quality image.* Consumers partly judge the quality of brands by price. A low price may be equated to low quality (and, in a price war, may actually represent just that, as the opponents shave quality in order to fund the cost cutting).
- *Temporary advantage.* A price advantage is often only held in the short term, and consumers will be rapidly attracted to an even lower one (which you can be sure will eventually appear).

Temporary price advantage only buys temporary customer loyalty!

- *Investment potential.* Above all, price reductions should be seen as an investment to generate greater sales (for, if they do not, they can only result in reduced profits). It is wise, under these circumstances, to work out which company has the deepest pockets and so can invest in such a war of attrition the longest. History tends to show that it is often the initiator of the war who is the first victim of it! In the airline industry both Laker and People's Express fell into these traps – though, as always, other factors were also involved.

See also COMPETITION PRICING; COST-PLUS PRICING; PRICE CHALLENGE REACTIONS; PRICE INCREASES; PRICING POLICIES, PRACTICAL; PRICING, PRODUCT LIFE CYCLE; PRICING STRATEGY; PRISONER'S DILEMMA

price discrimination   This describes the situation where different prices are charged to different customers for the same products or services.

price elasticity of demand   The degree to which demand is sensitive to price is called 'price elasticity of demand'. This is often shortened to 'elasticity of demand', though strictly this is incorrect, since economists recognize that demand may also depend on other factors (such as income). Begg et al. (1987) give the classical definition: 'The price elasticity of demand is the percentage change in the quantity of a good demanded divided by the corresponding percentage change in its price', or:

Price Elasticity of Demand
    = (% Change of Demand)/(% Change of Price)

This simply recognizes that some products or services are more sensitive to price than others. In the commodities market, for example, the demand for your product will be very dependent upon the price you ask; and if you foolishly set the price above that which prevails in the market, you will be very unlikely indeed to sell anything – for the buyers well know that they can buy exactly the same goods elsewhere at lower prices. The demand, or even sometimes the price itself, here is said to be 'elastic'; though purists would once more object, for the reasons mentioned earlier.

At the other end of the spectrum there are those products where demand is very insensitive in terms of price. This, again offending the purists, is often called 'inelastic demand'.

See also COMPETITIVE PRICING; PRICE FACTORS; SUPPLY AND DEMAND

Reference: Begg, David, Fischer, Stanley and Dornbusch, Rudiger (1987) *Economics* (2nd edn). McGraw-Hill.

price equilibrium   *see* EQUILIBRIUM PRICE

price factors   Neoclassical economic theory assumes 'perfect markets', in which all consumers and suppliers come equipped with perfect knowledge of all the prices available for products (commodities) which are identical to each other. In addition, the market always 'clears'; that is, all the demand is exactly matched by supply and vice versa. This may be true of a few money markets and the pure commodity markets, though even in these cases other factors are often also at work. It clearly is not true of most markets in which marketers are plying their trade. Indeed, it is almost impossible, by definition, for a marketer to have any effect in a 'perfect market'. In economics this unwelcome intrusion of real life is the subject of extensions to the basic theory, to cover 'monopolies and imperfect competition', for example. These extensions are generally rather esoteric – and the one general conclusion about them is that they cannot explain all the facts! Despite the claims of their supporters, they typically only describe certain limited cases; and there is no general agreement on 'models' which have universal applicability.

Even so, an understanding of the basic theories of supply and demand does offer the marketer a useful insight into some of the key factors which may affect the prices they are able to obtain. In particular, the concept of 'elasticity of demand' is one which is widely discussed, and it does have a major role to play in pricing decisions. In some markets, such as the car market – where there is a long sales history available and the behaviour of the participants has been reasonably consistent and rational – it may even be possible to use 'regression analysis' (described under that heading elsewhere) to establish what the curves of supply and demand actually are. As always, though, this is historical, and future behaviour may not be so consistent.

Several factors can influence 'elasticity of demand', and thus affect price. The main factors can be grouped into those which are almost totally under the control of the organization and those which are out of its control, or can only be partially controlled:

- *organization factors* – life cycle, portfolio, product line pricing, segmentation and position, branding

- *customer factors* – demand, benefits, value
- *market factors* – competition, environment, life cycle, portfolio, product line pricing, segmentation and position, branding

See also COMPETITION, PRICING; PRICE ELASTICITY OF DEMAND; SUPPLY AND DEMAND

price gap   *see* COMPETITIVE GAP

price increases   The normal reason for price increases is inflation, which these days appears to be inevitable. The resulting increase in cost has to be passed on if profits are not to be adversely affected. Fortunately, the widespread expectation of inflation usually means that price increases can be imposed without too many problems. Price increases are also often expected (at least by economic theorists) when there is 'excess demand'. On the other hand, when costs rise but price increases cannot be easily imposed, the solution may be to reduce the specification, or to produce smaller packs – as the confectionery manufacturers often do. Alternatively it may be possible to remove some elements from the support.

John Winkler (1987) gives a six-part practical guide to making price increases:

- *'Put the prices up when everyone else does'* – do not hold back for the sake of competitive edge, as you will have to increase eventually and the action will be more noticeable then.
- *'Not too much at any one time'* – incremental increases (around the level of inflation) are less noticeable.
- *'Not too often'* – the buyer will react against too frequent change.
- *'Move something down when you move something up'* – even if it is only the price of a minor product.
- *'Look after your key accounts'* – the 80:20 rule says that it is the reactions of these which are most important.
- *'Provide sound – and true – explanations'* – customers, after all, understand that prices sometimes have to increase when cost increases justify it.

See also COMPETITION PRICING; COST-PLUS PRICING; PRICE COMPETITION; PRICING POLICIES, PRACTICAL; PRICING STRATEGY; PRISONER'S DILEMMA

Reference: Winkler, John (1987) Pricing. In Michael J. Baker (ed.), *The Marketing Book*. London: Heinemann.

price lining   *see* RANGE PRICING

price maintenance   *see* PRICE CHALLENGE REACTIONS

price-minimizing model   *see* EQUILIBRIUM PRICE

price negotiation   The most difficult area of pricing seems to be that where the price results from a process of negotiation, typically as part of face-to-face sales activities. There are probably three main reasons for the greatest difficulty arising in this area:

- *Each is believed to be a unique situation.* The buyer and, more important, the seller (the salesperson) believe that each such negotiation starts afresh, without any established ground rules – no matter what the seller's policies might be.
- *Negotiation takes place under immediate pressure.* The price is set not by the leisurely processes of the office bureaucracy, but under the severe pressures of 'real-time' negotiations with the customer – where the salesperson has to think on his or her feet at the same time as keeping all the other sales issues under control.
- *The negotiator is less well prepared and motivated.* The negotiator is typically the salesperson, who is not well versed in the factors which should influence any pricing decision. More important, he or she is normally motivated, partly by the whole ethos of selling and partly (often largely) by actual monetary incentives, to close the sale rather than obtain the highest price – most sales managements look first at the volume figures and only belatedly (if ever) at those for profit, and motivate their sales forces in line with this philosophy.

It is not a great exaggeration to state that many, if not most, sales personnel (at all levels) go into a price negotiation believing that they are in an inherently weak position and, indeed, are bound to lose. Many sales courses on 'negotiation' are largely designed to convince those attending them that this is not true – but that, as is surely true, the participants should be in control of their sales situations at all stages, including that of price negotiation.

In general, then, most sellers put themselves in a weak bargaining position. As a result many, if not most, prices arrived at in such bargaining are lower than they need be. Michael Porter (1980) succinctly sums up the factors which offer the seller a strong position over the buyers (and, by inference, also the reverse). Thus, sellers are in a strong position when:

- *Buyers each buy small quantities relative to the total sales of the sellers* – the seller can afford to lose the business of individual buyers.
- *Buyers lack suitable alternative sources* – the seller has a quasi-monopoly.
- *Buyers face high 'switching costs'* – the buyer would have significant costs and problems associated with switching to a new supplier.
- *The cost of the item is a small part of the buyer's costs* – the buyer has more pressing problems.
- *The cost of the product failing would be high* – the buyer needs to play for safety, and cannot afford to cut corners.
- *Cost savings resulting from use of the product are significant* – the product more than pays for itself.
- *Buyers have high-quality images* – they cannot afford to buy 'cheap' inputs.
- *Buyers want customer-designed products* – the seller again has the potential of a quasi-monopoly.
- *Buyers' organizations are highly profitable* – the buyer is not primarily motivated by cost savings.
- *The buyer is poorly informed* – lack of information always undermines a negotiating position.

Large buyers are not necessarily the most price conscious – though they will happily accept the gift of low prices which many sales personnel, who assume that price is always a function of quantity, hand to them.

The main necessity is to recognize when, as is most often the case, price is not the most important factor in a sale!

This last comment is probably the most important, even in the more general context. Most sellers in a negotiating position forget all that has happened previously and precipitously assume that price has become the only important factor. In reality, it is a minor factor in most sales processes. Buyers often find negotiating as irksome as sellers, and are just as glad to put such painful exercises behind them!

See also COMPETITION PRICING; COST-PLUS PRICING; DISCOUNTS; PRICE, PURCHASE; PRICING POLICIES, PRACTICAL

Reference: Porter, Michael E. (1980) *Competitive Strategy.* New York: The Free Press.

price-off   *see* PROMOTIONAL PRICING

price of services   *see* SERVICE PRICES

price positioning   In addition to a determination of where the 'market' price lies, a further decision needs to be taken – where the brand price is to be positioned in relation to this:

Quality pricing
Some organizations make a conscious decision to deliberately price above the market average. This price is intended to demonstrate the quality, or even the luxury, of the product or service. Rolls Royce is the oft-quoted example, but Hilton Hotels, Sony and many of the cosmetic/perfume houses follow the same policy. James Myers (1986) nicely demonstrates this in terms of the related demand curve:

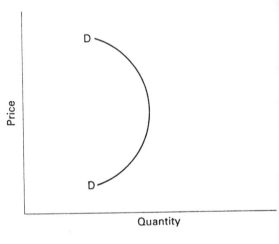

Although the initial reductions in price will (as normal) result in increased sales, beyond a critical point any further reduction in price in this situation will lead to a reduction in sales (as the curve bends back upon itself). For this reason it is arguable that the problems encountered by the Cadillac division of General Motors at the beginning of the 1990s were actually exacerbated by the price cuts which were made to try and restore its competitive position!

Cut pricing
The organizations with the most obvious price positioning are those deliberately choosing to price below the market, since such cut-prices are often the main element of the marketing mix for these organizations. BIC ballpoint pens, Amstrad computers and the Virgin airline have all been exponents of this approach.

Alfred Oxenfeldt (1979) makes the important point that 'Most firms can command a premium from some customers. They might want to deal with only those customers; on the other hand their numbers might be so few as to preclude that possibility. Price setters will usually err badly if they base their price demands on the evaluations of the average or typical customer.'

Whatever the choice, albeit often by default (in line with the market), pricing must be seen as a key element of the overall marketing mix – and of the positioning of the product or service (and not simply as a purely financial element).

See also COMPARATIVE ADVANTAGE, GLOBAL; COMPETITION PRICING; COST-PLUS PRICING; MARKET-BASED PRICING; PRICING POLICIES, PRACTICAL

References: Myers, James (1986) *Marketing.* Maidenhead: McGraw-Hill.
Oxenfeldt, Alfred R. (1979) The differential method of pricing. *European Journal of Marketing,* 13(4).

price premium   *see* COMPETITIVE PRICING; MARKET-BASED PRICING

price, purchase   The one aspect around which most purchasing is supposed to revolve is price. Clearly, price negotiation is important, but it is by no means all! Yet it is often the main focus of buyers (and is too frequently their only focus!). But, it is just one of several components, such as quality, and even then it is the final, overall cost of the organization's output which really matters. Thus, obtaining the lowest price may often represent a false economy if the operation of the whole organization depends upon this ingredient. It is true that over-specification can result in unnecessary costs. But it also true that shaving the specification (even if this is not the overt intention) to minimize costs can significantly increase the risk of failure of the overall operation – at a disastrous cost! The buyer had therefore better be aware of the overall implications and not just the price.

As Michael Porter (1985) says, 'In some instances a firm may lower total cost by spending more on purchased inputs. Minimizing the unit cost of purchased inputs is not necessarily appropriate.' He does, though, go on to say that 'it is still clearly desirable to seek the best possible unit cost for purchased inputs after choosing the appropriate type and quality of inputs'.

This price may be obtained by a number of processes.

Bidding
The classical approach, beloved of the commodity markets and the economists (as well as government

departments, when operating overtly), is the tender. The prospective suppliers bid against each other in open auction (or, often even more viciously, by 'sealed bid') to obtain the business. Less obviously, this may also be the process involved when supplier representatives are, over a period of time, 'allowed' (and actively encouraged) to compete against each other in terms of price. In these circumstances, clearly, the business will not be given to the highest bidder. On the other hand, the quote from the lowest bidder may sometimes be seen as questionable (possibly just because it is the lowest – and especially if it is much lower than the others)! Whatever the outcome, it is a very aggressive process which is definitely not conducive to building 'supplier relationships' and it concentrates almost exclusively on price – which may not be the most important factor.

Negotiation
The other end of the spectrum is represented by the approach (employed by buyers from organizations, such as Marks & Spencer, who are committed to the 'supplier partnership') where a 'reasonable' price is negotiated. It is claimed that 'negotiated bids' in general come closer to the correct prices; and it is probable that the majority of major purchases now involve this type of procedure.

The 'reasonable price' is typically based on three elements:

*   *Cost.* It would definitely be unreasonable to expect a supplier to sell below cost price, though some buyers still do just this!
*   *Profit.* The supplier is expected to make a reasonable (sometimes mutually agreed) level of profit.
*   *Competition.* Ultimately, however, the context for such prices is still what competitors might offer.

The last element is needed because 'cost-plus' contracts have landed many government departments, in particular, in massive cost overruns, for the supplier's profit increases, in this case, in line with cost, so the supplier has every incentive (no doubt earnestly justified) to raise costs!

Competitive pricing
In this very common situation prices are quoted by suppliers (not specifically as 'bids' – though some of the features are similar). If price competition is known to be 'keen' then prices may drop (and the process approaches 'bidding'); in any case, a whole range of discounts will also be available to the buyer. 'Questionable' low-pricing may also appear in this

context because, for instance, new suppliers want to 'buy' their way onto the 'approval list' – those fortunate suppliers who are considered for any business to be placed. This may, despite its apparent benefits, cause problems when prices subsequently rise – if the buyer has not allowed for this in advance. A new division in IBM, for example, achieved very competitive prices from its new suppliers, and accordingly offered the new machines it was making at equally competitive rates. When, subsequently, these IBM suppliers were forced to raise their prices steeply to economic levels, IBM found that (due to its legal and ethical constraints) it could not do the same; and the division's management, very embarrassingly, found the operation running at a loss for a period of time!

Reference: Porter, Michael E. (1985) *Competitive Advantage: Creating and Sustaining Superior Performance*. New York: The Free Press.

price–quality relationship   *see* PRICES, CUSTOMER NEEDS

price regulation   In some circumstances, such as those enjoyed by the power and water utilities, the organization holds a near-absolute monopoly and can set its own prices. Paradoxically, there is evidence that such monopolists often choose to set lower prices, to expand the market and preserve their monopoly position (at least from the threat of regulation). Indeed, regulation, including self-regulation, is a factor which has significant impact on the pricing policies employed by many organizations; and perhaps also, down the line, in those other organizations whose demand derives from these.
See also PRICE FACTORS

price, retail   *see* RETAIL 'PRODUCT' DECISIONS

prices, customer needs   The major determinant of prices will be what the consumer is prepared to pay, which is in turn related to a number of other factors:

Customer demand
Following from economic theory, and assuming a steady supply – as is often the case – variations in customer demand should result in changes in price. This is most obvious in the commodity markets, such as that of oil – where consumers reduced their demand for oil to such an extent following the massive 1973 price rises that there was eventually a glut and prices were forced down again. It is also evident in other markets, such as that of housing, which have alternating periods of boom or bust, often seasonally related. Holiday markets are closely tied to the seasons (few would want to lie on a Spanish beach in January) and in particular to the school holidays. Demand is thus highest in summer, when the schoolchildren are on holiday, and the prices reflect this. In the 'off-peak' periods – the spring or autumn, when the weather is often as good but there are no school holidays – prices are lower, reflecting the lesser demand and the competition between operators trying to fill their spare capacity. This whole process is regularized by price lists which are related to calendar periods. The railways operate a similar approach, but on a daily basis – with the 'rush-hour' prices high, but bargains at 'off-peak' times. In the nonprofit sector such surges in demand may be controlled, at least to some extent, by allowing queues to lengthen (as happens for 'cosmetic' surgery in the NHS).

Customer benefits
The products and services offered by competitors are often not identical – to some extent they will be differentiated. Each will offer a specific bundle of benefits. It is this bundle of benefits which the consumer wants, and which is traded off against price. The more important, or desirable, the benefits, the more the consumer will be prepared to pay. Thus, there is the basic 'commodity price' which would be paid for any product of an identical type, assuming that there was perfect competition. Beyond this there is the 'premium price' which consumers will pay for the additional benefits they believe the specific brand will give them. This emphasizes, yet again, the importance of the producer or service provider understanding which are the most important benefits in the eyes of the consumer, since these are the very ones which will justify a premium price.

Customer value ('perceived value')
These benefits are conceptualized as the 'value' the customer sees in the product and, in theory, there should be a balance between this and the price asked. This 'perceived value' can then be matched against the price on offer, to see whether the purchase is worth making. This theory recognizes that different buyers, or groups of buyers, may have different motivations. The Volvo buyer was renowned as placing a higher value on personal safety than did the buyer of a Porsche; and it is likely that the latter considered that its value as a status symbol was not to be ignored, in comparison with that of a similarly specified Japanese car, for example. In this 'model'

the rational consumer is seen to weigh up all the benefits and determine what they are worth. This idea also lies behind the economists' theories of supply and demand. It is assumed that each 'consumption bundle', which may be made up of a number of different goods, offers the consumer a specific value of 'utility' which is, in essence, what it is worth – its usefulness – to that consumer. Different combinations of goods may offer the consumer the same amount of 'utility', so that a line can be drawn on a graph linking these points of equal utility. This is called an 'indifference curve' since, as the consumer is believed to be indifferent between any of these choices, they are all equally attractive. 'An indifference curve shows all the consumption bundles which yield the same utility to the consumer'. This is an interesting concept, but utility is very difficult to define – let alone measure – and few workable indifference curves have been produced. It is not normally a viable basis for pricing. Paradoxically, price itself is often seen as a measure of quality. The higher the price, the higher the quality is presumed to be! As Erickson and Johansson's (1985) research showed, 'The price–quality relationship appears to be operating in a reciprocal manner. Higher priced cars are perceived to possess (unwarranted) high quality. High quality cars are likewise perceived to be higher priced than they actually are.'

See also PRICE FACTORS

References: Begg, David, Fischer, Stanley and Dornbusch, Rudiger (1987) *Economics* (2nd edn). McGraw-Hill.
   Erickson, Gary M. and Johannson, Johny K. (1985) The role of price in multi-attribute product evaluations. *Journal of Consumer Research*, 12.

price wars   *see* PRICE CHALLENGE REACTIONS

Price Waterhouse, consultants   *see* CONSULTANTS

pricing and geography   *see* GEOGRAPHICAL PRICING

pricing, competition   *see* COMPETITION PRICING

pricing, customary   *see* CUSTOMARY PRICING

pricing environment   The wider environment can also have an impact. Whether the economy is booming or in recession may have a direct impact on what consumers can afford to spend, though this effect seems to have been very selective, mainly hitting those supplying capital goods to industry whilst consumer sales, to those still in work, continued to rise! There are also, despite the government's suggestions to the contrary, all the various aspects of legislation which constrain freedom to move prices. At least, there is often the veiled threat of interest from the Office of Fair Trading hanging over those who are especially effective in managing their price competition! The possibility of such regulatory intervention should never be discounted.

See also PRICE FACTORS

pricing new 'products'   The time when an organization is most free to determine the price of its products or services is when they are launched. Once the price has been set, so has a precedent. In the case of any future changes the consumers will not have only the competitive prices as a comparison, but will also have the previous prices as a very direct reference point! This makes it very difficult to make substantial changes to the prices of existing products or services. Consumer reactions may be severe if they think they are being taken advantage of. The moral is to set the price right in the first place.

The new product may be entering an existing market. If this is the case then price will be just one of the positioning variables. On this basis, the price will be carefully calculated to position the brand exactly where it will make the most impact – and profit. At a less sophisticated level, perhaps, the producer of a new brand will decide which of the existing price ranges, cheap or expensive, the product or service should address. A supplier entering a mass consumer market can simply go to the local supermarket, or specialty store, and see what prices are already accepted. In industrial markets it may be much more difficult to obtain competitive prices, even where published price lists are available, since these are often only the starting point for negotiations which result in heavy discount.

In the case of a totally new product or service, the pricing exercise will be that much more difficult, for there are no precedents to indicate how the consumer might behave, and this is an area where market research is notoriously inaccurate. In the end it will have to be a judgement decision as to what 'perceived value' the consumer will put on the offering.

Within these limits, however, there are two main approaches possible for a new product, and to a lesser extent for an existing one:

- skimming
- penetration

The circumstances generally favouring the skimming and penetration policies are summarized below:

Skimming	Penetration
prices are likely to be inelastic	prices are likely to be elastic
the product or service is new and unique	competitors are likely to enter the market quickly
there are distinct segments	there are no distinct segments
quality is important	products will be undifferentiated
competitive costs are unknown	economies of scale apply

See also PENETRATION PRICING; PRICE FACTORS; SKIM-MING, PRICING

pricing policies, practical   Very little of the pricing theory which has been reported has any great value in practical pricing. Prices are often set by one of a number of pragmatic 'rules of thumb':

- cost-plus pricing
- target pricing
- historical pricing
- range pricing
- competitive pricing
- market-based pricing
- selective pricing

Godley (1975) makes the practical observation that there are two extremes, between which the price should lie:

1. A price above which the product will not sell.
2. A price below which no extra sales can be made.

See also COMPETITIVE PRICING; COST-PLUS PRICING; HISTORICAL PRICING; MARKET-BASED PRICING; RANGE PRICING; SELECTIVE PRICING; TARGET PRICING

Reference: Godley, C. G. A. (1975) Overall marketing management. In E. F. L. Brech (ed.), The Principles and Practice of Management. London: Longman.

pricing policy   see PRICING STRATEGY

pricing, portfolio   see PORTFOLIO PRICING

pricing, product life cycle   In theory, at least, the stage of the life cycle through which the 'product' is currently passing may have an impact on prices. At the 'introduction' it may be set high to capitalize on its uniqueness ('skimming') – as the first video casette recorders were. This high price may be carried through to 'maturity' or later, taking 'skimming' to its logical conclusion – as a 'niche player', such as Bang and Olufsen, might do. More probably, the price will be reduced to maximize 'penetration'. It is only at the end of 'maturity', when the market moves into 'saturation', that, according to this theory, price competition should break out in earnest. Even then, as products go into decline, prices should rise again as they are 'milked':

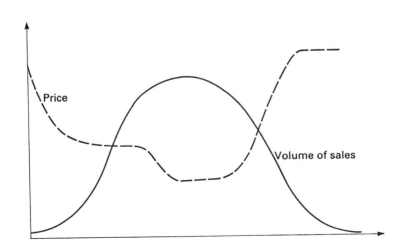

Thus, the main problems theoretically only occur in 'saturation'. In practice, other factors may predominate at various stages of the life cycle. For example, price may be 'managed' to remain high throughout the whole of the maturity phase, or it may be deliberately reduced to increase share in a market which is mature but which still offers an attractive investment. The theory also requires that, to be under the control of the organization, the 'product' has a life cycle which is separate from that of the overall market; and this only happens if the organization develops a segment, or 'niche', of its own. Overall, then, the PLC is usually not a particularly useful guide to pricing policy.
See also PRICE FACTORS

pricing, product positioning The 'classical' techniques for obtaining higher prices are those of positioning and segmentation. By creating a distinct segment which the brand can dominate, the producer hopes that the price can be controlled. Indeed, unlike some of the more theoretical approaches, experience shows that this can often be achieved in practice. If price competition is severe, the first action should be to see if segmentation can offer a degree of protection.
See also BRAND 'MONOPOLY' PRICING; PRICE FACTORS

pricing projects *see* PROJECT PRICING

pricing, promotional *see* PROMOTIONAL PRICING

pricing, selective *see* SELECTIVE PRICING

pricing strategy Whatever the rationale behind the final pricing decisions, be it the most elegant of economic theory (as the Conservative government often stated it had applied to the share prices being asked for the companies it privatized) or the most pragmatic of competitive reactions (as the government decisions largely were in practice!), it is necessary to consolidate this as a pricing strategy. This is needed, in the first instance, to ensure that what is being implemented matches what the participants in the decision actually thought they were agreeing to – too often there are major misunderstandings in management decision-making which are only revealed when the damage has been done. Formalizing decisions, such as those on pricing, in writing should remove the possibility of such misunderstandings – though it does not always do so! It is also needed to ensure that the individual prices are carefully man-

aged, and that there is a balance across the whole portfolio. The key to this process is the formalization – almost inevitably in writing, and often as part of the marketing plan.
See also COMPETITION PRICING; COST-PLUS PRICING; PRICE CHALLENGE REACTIONS; PRICE COMPETITION; PRICE INCREASES; PRICING POLICIES, PRACTICAL; PRISONER'S DILEMMA

primary sources of communication *see* SECONDARY SOURCES OF COMMUNICATION

prime time The periods (on television and radio) which attract large audiences.

printing blocks *see* PRESS MEDIA

print run The number of copies ordered to be printed by the customer.

priorities *see* BUDGETS

Prisoner's Dilemma This is a theory from the social sciences which is useful in the context of price competition. The basic, imaginary, dilemma (a 'philosophical problem' known for many years, and even described by Herodotus, but given this name and description by Alfred Turner) has two prisoners accused of a crime. If one confesses and the other does not, the one confessing will be released immediately and the other gaoled for ten years. If neither confesses, each will only be held for a few months. On the other hand, if both confess they will each receive a sentence of five years. The problem, for the prisoners, is that they are not allowed to communicate with each other. The calculation is that self-interest will be best served for each by confessing, no matter what the other does. But, of course, this is a less satisfactory solution for them than if they both held out! Fortunately, the position in the case of price competition (whilst sharing some of the features of this dilemma, especially if the participants react without thinking) is somewhat more favourable. The 'prisoners' are not held incommunicado. They can exchange 'signals', which indicate their intentions. Under these circumstances, the best outcome can be achieved, and often is.
See also COMPETITION PRICING; COST-PLUS PRICING; PRICE COMPETITION; PRICE INCREASES; PRICING POLICIES, PRACTICAL; PRICING STRATEGY

private brand *see* MARKET ENTRY TACTICS; OWN BRANDS AND GENERICS

proactive PR   Relatively few organizations use PR to influence 'external' activities, such as those in the political arena, to their advantage. Those that do, however, may gain considerable advantage. In view of the investment required, on the other hand, this may be the province of the larger organizations. It also requires special personnel, with expert skills and knowledge, and will usually (even in the case of larger companies) demand the employment of an outside agency; for example, one that specializes in 'lobbying' politicians. The scale of resource required can be substantial. There are a wide range of audiences to be contacted in this proactive role, including:

- the general public ('public opinion' is very influential)
- the press (the 'power of the press' is legendary)
- the financial community (which wields considerable power of its own, not least over the future funding of the organization)
- the government (usually the prime target for such 'proactive' lobbying)

However, other influential bodies (such as trade unions, religious groups, international bodies) should not be ignored.

In many of these fields it will be the top management who have, and build upon, the most important contacts; but the corporate PR function should co-ordinate and support (indeed 'nourish') these. It should be assumed, incidentally, that lobbying is best handled in-house (or by agencies employed directly). Roger Haywood (1984) reports that 'much of the lobbying undertaken by some trade associations . . . is extremely rudimentary; it may make them feel good, but will have very little influence on the shape of legislation. Too often, the case is being presented far too late and without enough authority or substantial evidence.' Some trade associations (particularly those of the professions and farming) are powerful lobbyists, but rather more are not. In any case, the lobbying (and power struggles) within trade associations to capture their 'votes' for 'interested groups' often means that individual members may find their interests not represented at all (and sometimes opposed!).

Issue management
The first task of corporate PR is to determine what 'issues', relevant to the future of the organization, are likely to emerge over the next few years. 'Scanning' the environment (of which issue management is a specialized element) is not an easy task. It can, in this case, be more directly based upon opinion research – though this may be expensive (particularly where it has to be carried out worldwide, since issues vary from country to country). Alternatively, it can be obtained by buying syndicated reports from specialist consultancies (such as the Henley Centre for Forecasting or Stanford Research Institute). It is recommended, however, that no more than 10–20 issues are 'managed' at any one time; more than this will simply cause confusion and spread effort too thinly. More rigorous methods for forcing these issues to emerge may be used, but the most generally reported view is that they emerge by 'osmosis' – based on discussions, over time, by the experts involved. Once the issues have 'emerged', it is important to try and understand them, and, in particular, to obtain political input on their perceived importance. It is also important to start 'lobbying' (possibly on an international scale) as soon as possible. At the highest level, multinational organizations will lobby at a very senior level indeed. BP, for instance, lobbied the 1989/1990 GATT round directly since it had doubts that individual governments would lobby as effectively on its behalf!

Preparatory work
Another aspect of proactive corporate PR may be working, perhaps over a number of years, to prepare the ground for future developments. At least one multinational puts a PR/lobby team into a country anything up to two years in advance of a major move (an acquisition, a new plant, etc.) so that, when that move takes place, the politicians have been primed (and potential opponents identified, and hopefully neutralized) – and ideally legislation put in place to support the move. The PR team then works alongside the corporate negotiators as the move is implemented, to smooth the way.

Instruments to be used – planning
Having decided what issues (or 'preparatory' work) are to be addressed, the next move is to decide what 'instruments' (the range of PR resources: press contacts, events, publications, etc.) are to be used – and what priorities are to be assigned between them. Again, a detailed plan is essential, not least to coordinate the 'contacts' undertaken by the various managers involved, and this needs to be tracked and reported upon. One corporate PR group issues a new plan every quarter, covering the six months ahead. This details all contacts being made – so that each senior manager understands what the other members of management are doing! An annual operating plan

is also required, especially where the budget can run into millions of dollars per annum for the larger multinationals!

See also CORPORATE PUBLIC RELATIONS; POLITICAL CONTACTS; PUBLIC RELATIONS

Reference: Haywood, Roger (1984) *All About PR: What to Say and When to Say It.* Maidenhead: McGraw-Hill.

proactive strategy *see* EMERGENT STRATEGY

probabilities, forecasting *see* BAYESIAN DECISION THEORY

probability *see* RISK ANALYSIS

probability distribution *see* NORMAL CURVE

probability of closing *see* TERRITORY SALES PLAN

probables *see* FORECASTS OF SALES BUSINESS

problem child Often called a 'question mark', in the popular application of the Boston Matrix a 'problem child' is a product in the quadrant with low market share but high market growth rate. It is a product, typically a recently launched one, which has not yet built its market share. As it does not yet have the share to deliver reasonable profits, it will almost certainly be a net user of cash; possibly substantially so – such 'problem children' are often where most of the cash flow generated by the 'cash cows' transfers to – but the organization hopes this will be a good investment, as the market is attractive and the 'problem child' could eventually become a winner as one of its future 'cash cows'. The organization will need to very carefully monitor the progress of its 'problem children', and review their futures – especially if they were once 'stars' which have now fallen back to this quadrant and thus have a problematical, indeed dubious, future which could well lead to discontinuation before they can bleed away too much of the organization's profits.
See also BOSTON MATRIX

problem recognition, repeat purchasing The buying process starts with the buyer's recognition of a need. That recognition may be internally generated, or externally influenced by environmental factors in general or by suppliers' promotional stimuli in particular. As a general rule there is not much that the individual marketer can do about the buyer's internal processes, except to recognize them. On the

other hand there may be a great deal that can be done even in terms of external environmental influences on the buyer: from recognizing them and allowing for them or preferably capitalizing on them, to acting to steer those environmental influences in the directions most favourable to the supplier's own needs.
See also DECISION-MAKING PROCESS, BY CUSTOMERS; PURCHASE DECISION, MATCHING; REPEAT PURCHASING PROCESS

problem-solving models *see* MODELS

Procter & Gamble *see* ECONOMIES OF SCALE, GLOBAL; GLOBAL MARKETING

procurement *see* PURCHASING

producers *see* CREATIVE DEPARTMENT, ADVERTISING AGENCY

producer satisfaction maximization *see* NOT-FOR-PROFIT ORGANIZATIONS, OBJECTIVES

product *see* MARKETING STRATEGIES

product as hero *see* MESSAGE, ADVERTISING

product audit The starting point, at least for existing products or services, is to decide exactly what it is you have. As Peter Drucker (1964) said, 'The best way to come to grips with one's business knowledge is to look at the things the business has done well, and the things it apparently does poorly. This is particularly revealing if other apparently well-managed and competent businesses have had the opposite experience'.

This may seem obvious, but it is not necessarily so. Even the 'physical' features of the 'brand' may need reviewing, and a separate section included in the 'facts book' for those managers (possibly including the brand manager) who have become so used to seeing the brand around – doing the things it has always done – that they have forgotten what other features it may have.

Thus, the first need is to revisit the product or service, and remind yourself of exactly what it is capable of.
See also BENEFIT ANALYSIS

Reference: Drucker, Peter F. (1964) *Managing for Results.* London: Heinemann.

product/brand management Many large organizations take the product focus very seriously, even though they are market rather than product oriented. In large organizations with a plethora of products there is often a failure to understand the needs of the individual product (and its market). It may simply become lost in the bureaucratic demands of functional specializations. By the time a request for more stock, for an urgent sales promotion, say, has passed up the sales chain of command and down that of production, with diversions into accounts to authorize the necessary expenditure, the customers will probably have changed to another brand!

The conventional functional (marketing based) structure may be:

Managing Director

Production Director

Financial Director

Marketing Director

Marketing Manager

Marketing Services

Sales Manager

One way, though, to achieve a tighter focus on the individual brands is to structure marketing by product, creating product or brand managers:

Managing Director

Production Director

Financial Director

Marketing Director

Marketing Manager

Marketing Services

Sales Manager

(or Group Product Manager)

Product Managers

This is usually a form of 'matrix management', since the product management structure (depicted as running horizontally) is superimposed on the traditional functional structure (running vertically).

Theodore Levitt says:

> Putting somebody in charge of a *product* that's bought and used essentially in the same way by a large segment of the total *market* (as is the case, say, of packaged detergents sold through retail channels) or in charge of a specific market (as in the case, say, of isopropanol sold directly to manufacturers or indirectly via distributors) so clearly focuses attention, responsibility and effort that clear competitive advantage generally goes to the firms so organised.

Amongst brand managers themselves, the favourite definition used to be that such a brand manager was 'to the brand what the managing director was to the whole company'. More cynically it was also reckoned that a brand manager carried all the responsibility, but none of the authority! Brand managers typically have no staff, and hence little direct control over most of what happens in the organization. Their authority is that exercised on behalf of the marketing director or managing director – often only by means of their charm and charisma. Wolf and Smith (1986) report that the position has moderated in recent years: 'Although product managers remain enthusiastic champions of their products, their role is now more of making recommendations than making decisions. The product manager may control marketing research, special promotions and minor decisions involving advertising, but major decisions are more likely to be made at higher levels.'

On the other hand, the success of brand management may simply derive from its ability to cross, and even break down, interdepartmental barriers. Tom Peters makes the point that 'It is imperative today that managers and nonmanagers be induced to cross "uncrossable" boundaries as a matter of course, day after day. Standing on the formality of a written job description (as an excuse for inaction, or the reason you have to "check up – and up and up – the line") is a guaranteed strategy for disaster.'

Recently, another approach has been developed: that of category management. Though it shares many of the properties, the focus – set by the increasing power of retailers – is on the overall 'category' the retailer has on the shelf. The relationship with the retailer may be so strong, indeed, that the 'management' also covers competitor products.

Another new approach is to use teams – 'cross-disciplinary teams' – instead of individual brand managers.

Reference: Levitt, T. (1983) *The Marketing Imagination.* New York: Free Press.

Wolf, Jack and Smith, Wendell R. (1986) Market needs and market changes. In Victor P. Buell (ed.), *Handbook of Modern Marketing* (2nd edn). New York: McGraw-Hill.

product categories, retail *see* RETAIL PRODUCT OR SERVICE CATEGORIES

product champion Often the most important ingredient of all for ultimate success is a 'champion' – a manager who is so committed to the strategy that he or she will fight for it, often beyond any reasonable call of duty. The pressures applied by such a champion, may result in a decision going against the odds and, more important, being more effectively implemented than an equivalent one emerging from an anonymous consensus.

This is most often described in terms of the 'product champion' – the manager who pushes for his or her pet product. The positive aspect is that many, if not most, of the great product breakthroughs (and strategic breakthroughs) can be traced back to one individual champion.

One outcome therefore, is to find such a product champion. It is usually possible to find someone in the organization who has a strong interest (for reasons of self-advancement, if no other) who can be persuaded to take on the role. A more important corollary is that you should never neglect an existing product champion unless he or she poses impossible problems. Such enthusiasm is rare, and is a valuable commodity which no organization can afford to throw away.

See also CONVICTION MARKETING; NEW PRODUCT INNOVATION; PRODUCT/BRAND MANAGEMENT

product changes *see* EXISTING PRODUCT CHANGES

product churning, new products The carefully controlled approach to the introduction of new products has generally been successful in the West, where there may be heavy penalties, to brand/corporate image in particular, in backing failures. In Japan, though, the reverse is often true. Rather than screening out potential failures, many new products may be launched (as many as 1000 new soft drinks a year, for example). This process, called 'product churning', apparently works well in Japan because their corporations develop new products in one-half to one-third of the time, and at a quarter to one-tenth of the cost, of their Western counterparts! Investment in expensive screening processes may even be, under these circumstances, counter-productive. In addi-

tion, the Japanese public has been persuaded to accept, indeed to want, new developments at this breakneck pace (almost regardless of their true worth).

See also CREATIVE IMITATION; CUSTOMER BONUS; LEAP-FROG; PRODUCT DEVELOPMENT PROCESS

product description, packaging The pack must convey to the potential consumer not just what the product is, but also what it does in terms of the benefits it offers – the promotional message. This may be conveyed by the words, but for the most impact it is usually the graphics and overall design which are chosen to deliver the main, initial messages. The potential buyer is expected to read these messages in a few brief seconds, and probably at a distance of three feet or more. It may also relate to how the pack itself works; so for Signal toothpaste the package is used to deliver the stripe in the toothpaste, which is linked to the particular benefit of the product, and perfumes are offered in elegant glass atomizers – ready to deliver their precious contents.

product development Having a viable concept is one thing, having a developed product is another. Between the two may lie a number of years and millions of dollars of research expenditure. Such development should ideally be driven by product parameters which have been determined by earlier market research (and, in particular, by the outcome of the concept tests). The reality, though, is that product development is often more of a creative art than a scientific certainty, and what emerges may only be the best possible approximation to what is needed. Indeed, the majority of new products are probably developed (based on creative inspiration) before any market research is undertaken, and the subsequent market research is only carried out to test their viability (and probably to 'justify' their launch). This diversity may be ideal for giant multinationals such as IBM, but could pose problems for smaller organizations – where 'focus' is normally suggested as the best policy! On the other hand, the most important change to the product development process over recent years, led by the Japanese, has been speed. As Ralph Gomory (1989) explains, 'One cannot overestimate the importance of getting through each turn of the [development] cycle more quickly than a competitor. It takes only a few turns for the company with the shortest cycle time to build up a commanding lead.' As has been widely reported, the Japanese corporations have succeeded in reducing this development time by a factor of two or three –

and their development costs by a factor of between four and ten! They have reportedly achieved this on the back of a highly trained workforce, a willingness to build from off-the-shelf components and very close relationships with their suppliers, as well as by approaches such as joint development teams and parallel development. Whatever the reasons, this competitive advantage poses a major challenge to their Western counterparts. It is worth noting, however, that organizations in the service sector frequently do not have the equivalent of new product development departments. This may be understandable in view of the less tangible and more transitory nature of their 'products'. It may, however, also represent an inherent weakness in their marketing armoury, leaving them very exposed to the developments being explored by their increasingly sophisticated competitors, who are learning all the lessons of conventional marketing.

See also ANSOFF MATRIX; PRODUCT DEVELOPMENT PROCESS; PRODUCT (OR SERVICE) STRATEGY

Reference: Gomory, Ralph E. (1989) From the 'ladder of science' to the product development cycle. *Harvard Business Review*, November–December.

product development process The complete development process can be conveniently split into a number of stages:

*   scanning
*   idea generation
*   strategic screen
*   concept test
*   'product' development
*   'product' testing
*   test market
*   launch

Idea generation, often based on some form of scanning of what is happening in other fields, initiates the process. Much of the subsequent process comprises steps which are designed to minimize the risk which is inherent in any new product launch. The importance of 'formalizing' the process is evidenced by Booz, Allen & Hamilton's (1981) comment that 'According to our survey results, companies that have successfully launched new products are more likely to have had a formal new product process in place for a longer period of time'.

See also CONCEPT TEST, NEW PRODUCTS; GENERATING IDEAS; PRODUCT DEVELOPMENT; PRODUCT TEST; SCANNING, AND MIS; STRATEGIC SCREENING, NEW PRODUCTS; TEST MARKET

Reference: Booz, Allen & Hamilton Inc. (1981) *New Products Management for the 1980s.*

product differentiation *see* DIFFERENTIATION AND BRANDING; PRODUCT (OR SERVICE) POSITIONING

product elimination The process of orderly withdrawal of a product or service from a market, such that it does not impact the image of the organization or harm any of the other products it might have in that market.

See also DECLINE STRATEGIES

product features *see* BENEFIT ANALYSIS; DIFFERENTIATION AND BRANDING

product iceberg One of the first rules of product strategy is that you must recognize all the hidden elements of the product/service package. Like an iceberg, 90 per cent of what matters in any such package is hidden from view.

See also PRODUCT PACKAGE

product image, packaging The pack must at least match the required image, so that the boxes for expensive chocolates look expensive in themselves – so much so that one almost hates the waste of throwing the packaging away. This reaches its extremes in cosmetics, and in particular for perfumes, where it is often the package itself which becomes the product – conveying the image which is the essence of the product.

product innovation *see* NEW PRODUCT INNOVATION

production batch *see* PRODUCTION DECISIONS, LOGISTICS MANAGEMENT

production   capabilities,   new   products Whether a new product or service can actually be produced will depend upon what is available within the organization. Are the requisite technical skills already present? A weighing machine manufacturer may have to acquire a complete team of electronic and computer engineers before moving from mechanical to electronic scales. Is there existing, suitable plant capacity? Plants tend to be expanded in fairly large increments. Adding extra demand onto equipment which is already being run close to full capacity may either place impossible demands on production or lead to a disproportionately large investment. The existing plant may in any case be unsuitable or simply located in the wrong place. The limitations on services might at first sight appear to be less serious, though expansion of local branch premises, if needed, may not be a trivial matter. But the constraints imposed by the availability of human resources, especially those involving specialist skills, may prove to be as severe.

See also NEW PRODUCT SCREENING, ORGANIZATIONAL FACTORS

production capacity *see* PRODUCTION DECISIONS, LOGISTICS MANAGEMENT

production card *see* KANBAN

production decisions, logistics management
In the context of logistics, management concerns such issues as the quantity in each production batch and the lead time required for production. Production of a good can be continuous, as it is in an oil refinery or on a car assembly line. In these cases the whole production process has to be matched to demand. Very expensive mistakes can be made if the capacity installed turns out to be greater than demand and this results in frequent shutdowns. More generally, production is 'batched'. Certainly most stock is transferred to depots in batches – usually now in the form of a container load, or as a number of pallets.

This 'order' on production can be generated by 'order point', in which the stock is constantly monitored. As soon as it falls below a predetermined level it is reordered – usually as a 'standard reorder quantity'. It may, on the other hand, be handled by 'cyclical ordering', where the stock is reviewed periodically. Every week, say, the level is checked and an order placed (this time often of variable size) to top up the stock to the desired level. Because it is much easier to handle by mechanized systems (these days computerized ones), the former is probably the most prevalent in larger organizations. The size of the 'production order', and the frequency with which the order is placed, may thus be a matter for calculation on two separate fronts. The first of these is that of the economies of scale. There is a certain cost overhead involved in placing every order, so the number of orders placed should ideally be minimized. At the same time, there is also an on-going cost involved in holding stock, thus the amount of stock should also be minimized. Needless to say, these two factors are in opposition.

The lead time is the time taken from placing an order on the plant, say, until it is received in the warehouse or depot. Stock has therefore to be available at the time of reorder, to cover demand for that (lead-time) period. But, in addition, a buffer stock is needed to cover variations in demand which may also occur. Depending upon the known pattern of demand, the optimal size of this buffer stock can be calculated statistically.

See also DATA PROCESSING, LOGISTICS; FACILITY DECISIONS, LOGISTICS MANAGEMENT; INVENTORY CONTROL; LOGISTICS MANAGEMENT; TRANSPORT DECISIONS, LOGISTICS MANAGEMENT

production kanban *see* KANBAN

production-line balancing This is the process of scheduling a balanced load to each workstation on a production or assembly line so that it will work efficiently.

See also JUST IN TIME (JIT); KANBAN; MATERIALS REQUIREMENTS PLANNING II (MRPII); OPTIMIZED PRODUCTION TECHNOLOGY (OPT); SET-UP TIMES

production order point *see* PRODUCTION DECISIONS, LOGISTICS MANAGEMENT

production scheduling package *see* MATERIALS REQUIREMENTS PLANNING II (MRPII)

productivity audit *see* MARKETING AUDIT

product liability The legal liability for defective products (including that for death or injury) which rests on organizations which market them.

product life In general, the one aspect of life cycle theory which is little discussed, but is vital to the brands involved, is that of the total life. The theoretical graph is rarely shown with any figures on it. In practice the life of products, and of markets, can vary dramatically. Producers will use 'mid-life kickers' to extend the life of a product or service, though no doubt the theoreticians would argue that this is a distortion of the underlying life cycle. But life cycles, of whatever type, do cover a wide range – from the few days of a fad, a pop record, say, to the many years of the Boeing 747 airliner, which, in its basic form, has survived very much unchanged for several decades. Even in markets that are very similar the length of the cycle can vary significantly. The formulation of baked beans has barely changed in generations, but much of the snacks market has now become almost a fad market, changing every few months.

Indeed, continuity rather than life cycle is the practical norm in most markets.

product life cycle (PLC) The 'life cycle' is a very important element of marketing theory. It has been reported and discussed, at length, by many theorists. It is incorporated as a basic assumption in many other theories, including the Boston Matrix and those relating to new product introduction. Not least, it is now accepted as a basic fact of life by many managers, and fuels the drive for change in as many markets. You should be aware, though, that its supposed universal applicability is largely a myth, albeit an important one, which you will need to appreciate (and to understand its impacts on theory) before you can dismiss it! It nevertheless has some applicability in terms of new products (which are based upon 'technical change').

The 'intuitive appeal', based on the analogy of natural (human) lives, is still a very important aspect of the product life cycle. The concept of the 'product' life cycle (PLC) thus suggests that any product or service moves through identifiable stages, each of which is related to the passage of time (as the product or service grows older) and each of which has different characteristics:

- introduction
- growth
- maturity
- saturation
- decline

With each stage is an associated profit level. It is likely that this will be negative at the beginning, when there is investment in the introductory stage. Hopefully, however, it will be positive (more than recouping the investment) by the maturity stage.
See also COMPETITIVE SAW; INVESTMENT MULTIPLIER; MARKET LIFE CYCLE

product-line pricing A variation in the pricing process may be caused because the pricing of one product or service has an impact upon others supplied by the organization. There may be, for example:

- *Interrelated demand.* The price of one product may affect the demand for another. They may be complementary (for example, the computer and the software which runs on it), so that an increase in one part of the 'package' results in demand for both falling. They could, however, be alterna-

tives; Procter & Gambol have a range of detergents, and increasing the price of one may switch demand to another.

- *Interrelated costs.* Sometimes the products use the same facilities (the same car assembly line may produce a range of models) or may be derivations of the same process (so that petrol and heating oil are different 'fractions' of crude oil, and one cannot be produced without the other). Changing sales volumes, in these circumstances, can obviously have knock-on effects on other costs. Even calculating costs can be almost impossible; the oil industry sets the costs of the fractions on the basis of the 'spot prices' currently obtained in Rotterdam – arguing that, even though they cannot know what is its cost, they can say what it is worth!

Pricing strategies under these circumstances can be complex and are usually a matter of judgement (though there are large 'linear programs' which can be run on computers, to tell you the optimum solution – always assuming you know the effect of each individual price change!).
See also PRICE FACTORS

product line, retail *see* RETAIL 'PRODUCT' DECISIONS

product map *see* POTSA PLANNING

product/market attractiveness *see* GE (GENERAL ELECTRIC) MATRIX; THREE CHOICE BOX

product orientation *see* SELLING VERSUS MARKETING

product-oriented company *see* MARKETING PLANS AND PROGRAMMES

product or service Much of marketing is still based on a framework which derives from the concepts applying most directly to the sale of physical products; more specifically, to consumer goods. There are good reasons why this is the case, and for why most business schools, for example, still follow this approach. One is that describing what happens to physical, tangible products (which students can see and touch) is rather easier than applying the same descriptions to the intangible. Perhaps the most important reason, however, is that all their students will have had some contact with such products (which can be found in any supermarket), and will appreciate their main characteristics, albeit as consumers rather than as marketers.

This approach can, however, sometimes be disconcerting to those who work in the service sector (and, in particular, to those who work in not-for-profit organizations). Theodore Levitt (1981) suggests that 'instead of talking of "goods" and of "services", it is better to talk of "tangibles" and "intangibles"; but the issue is much the same'. Many of the concepts of marketing, as well as many of the specific techniques, will work equally well whether directed at products or at services, though the words sometimes used to describe them may be different. In particular, developing a marketing strategy is much the same for products and services in that it involves selecting target markets and formulating a marketing mix.

As Levitt's paper suggests, marketing a physical product, indeed, is often more concerned with intangible aspects (frequently the 'product service' elements of the total package) than with its physical properties. Charles Revson made the famous comment regarding the business of Revlon Inc.: 'In the factory we make cosmetics. In the store we sell hope.' Arguably, service industry marketing merely approaches the problems from the opposite end of the same spectrum. As Philip Kotler (1988) says, 'Whereas product marketers are challenged to add abstract ideas, service marketers are challenged to put physical evidence on their abstract offers'.

In the marketing of 'services', adaptations and adjustments to the basic theory may be required, and the marketing mix may have to be revised. In particular, 'people' resources may have to be incorporated more since they are often an essential part of the offering itself and the consistent quality of the 'product' is thus much more difficult to control.

The 4 Ps (Product, Price, Place, Promotion) is often chosen as the framework for exploring the marketing factors, including the 'product' itself. It is worth reiterating that this is purely a convenient framework for gathering together the theoretical arguments, not the only possible approach – and, indeed, a different balance might better suit many products or services (particularly those in the non-profit sector).

Whatever the framework, the most important contribution to the overall marketing mix will almost certainly be the product or service itself. A good product might sell even if the promotion is mediocre. A bad product will rarely obtain repeat sales no matter how brilliant the promotion is. Unilever developed a toothpaste dispenser which was able to add stripes to the paste coming out of the neck of the tube. In the USA they emphasized this feature with the copy 'Looks like fun, cleans like crazy'. It was a smash hit, as it seemed that almost everyone bought a tube – to take it apart and see how it worked. However, repeat sales were dismal, because the 'fun' only justified one purchase. In the UK, however, the company sold it on the basis that the stripe contained the fluoride and was an essential part of the product. It is still going strong! Despite the feelings of some advertising agencies, and the echoes in popular myth, a good product or service is the essential prerequisite to a successful marketing campaign; most other elements are secondary.

See also SERVICE CULTURES

References: Kotler, P. (1988) *Marketing Management* (6th edn). Englewood Cliffs, NJ: Prentice-Hall.

Levitt, Theodore (1981) Marketing intangible products and product intangibles. *Harvard Business Review*, May–June.

product (or service)/brand management *see* PRODUCT/BRAND MANAGEMENT

product or service categories In terms of the basic 'dimensions' on which marketing is often organized, the most basic is often thought to relate to the 'product' itself. Is it a tangible product, such as a refrigerator, which is manufactured in a factory by the supplier? Is it an intangible service, such as hairdressing, where the customer has no tangible product to take away in a carrier bag?

In practice there are difficulties in allocating organizations even on this apparently simple dimension. Some products, such as personal computers, have a great deal of 'service' attached to them; the total 'package' of these is sometimes described as the 'extended product'. On the other hand, there are services which are very dependent upon physical products – in the hairdressing mentioned above, the hair care treatments used are very important, and are clearly physical.

There are differences in the way that organizations might market a product, which will often be promoted on the basis of its physical features, as opposed to a service, where promotion may be more associated with the quality of the organization providing it. In general, however, the basics of marketing are shared by both sorts of organization (albeit some of the names used to describe the activities are, confusingly, different).

Even within the overall categorization marketers often presume that there are significant differences between the various product or service types. In the general category of consumer goods, for example, there may be:

- *FMCG (Fast Moving Consumer Goods)*. Sometimes called 'consumables', these are the archetypal 'marketed' goods (that is, those goods heavily advertised to build awareness, trial and preference) such as groceries.
- *Durables*. These are sometimes further subdivided into 'white goods' (refrigerators and cookers, for example) and 'brown goods' (such as furniture, as well as 'electrical' and now 'electronic'). As the 'capital' goods of the personal sector, these require more personal selling and support.

See also ORGANIZATIONAL PIGEON-HOLES

product or service constraints   *see* EXPORTING

product or service decisions The focus of suppliers' activities is the product or service that is offered. While all other aspects of marketing, the remainder of the 4 Ps, have their part to play, it is the product or service itself that ultimately matters. That is what will determine whether the customer is satisfied. By defining the product/service offer (which, in its extended form, will involve most of the 4 Ps), the supplier defines almost all of the marketing mix.

This area evidences the strongest, most influential, theories of marketing. The Ansoff Matrix, covering degrees of diversification, is one example. The most important and pervasive, however, is the product life cycle (PLC). A significant amount of other marketing theory relates to the PLC and hence the theory behind this is crucial, if often fundamentally flawed in terms of practical applicability. The other main element of theory is the Boston Matrix, which is also very influential – albeit also potentially flawed in practical use. This is based, in part, upon the assumption of 'economies of scale' (or 'learning effects').

product (or service) development (strategy) In the context of product strategy, this involves a relatively major modification of the product or service (which will continue to be sold through the same distribution channels to the same general markets), such as quality, style, performance or variety. In the example of the car market, the provision of high-performance versions of existing cars (by engine

modifications and, just as important, making the superficial styling look more 'racy') can be used to extend the ranges to cover additional customers. Similarly, adding sausages to tinned baked beans will possibly cause some existing users to increase their usage but may also attract new users. To be most effective, such developments should extend the 'product' into a new segment, or to a new competitive position in relation to the clusters of consumers.

product (or service) gap This represents that part of the market from which the individual organization is excluded because of product or service characteristics. This may have come about because the market has been segmented and the organization does not have offerings in some segments, or it may be because the positioning of its offering effectively excludes it from certain groups of potential consumers because there are competitive offerings much better placed in relation to these groups. This segmentation may well be the result of deliberate policy. Segmentation and positioning are very powerful marketing techniques, but the trade-off, to be set against the improved focus, is that some parts of the market may effectively be put beyond reach. On the other hand, it may frequently be by default – the organization has not thought about its positioning, and has simply let its offerings 'drift' to where they now are. This is probably the main 'gap' where the organization can have a productive input. This is just as true if the product is a tin of baked beans or a benefit being offered by government to a disadvantaged group.

See also COMPETITIVE GAP; DISTRIBUTION GAP; GAP ANALYSIS; MARKET GAP ANALYSIS; USAGE GAP

product (or service) mix In classical marketing terms 'the product mix' is balanced across two most important dimensions:

- *Width*. This is the number of different (independent and distinct) 'product' lines carried, and is a measure of the number of different markets addressed. Thus, Unilever has a very wide range of product types (covering Birds Eye Frozen Foods as well as Persil Detergent) but Coca Cola for many years had a very narrow one (based on just the one product).
- *Depth*. This refers to the total number of products carried, across all the product lines, and thus relates to the market segments addressed. These may be very simply defined segments – for exam-

ple, where a range of pack sizes (from 'trial size' to 'jumbo economy') can address the differing value needs of consumers. Alternatively, they may be carefully targeted brands, such as Unilever uses in the detergent market, precisely aimed at different segments of a very large market.

The balance of the product mix also concerns the volumes achieved by the different lines. What may appear to be a wide and deep portfolio may be an illusion if just one product within it produces 90 per cent of the total sales. The same is true, and is more frequently found, in relation to profit. A sound product portfolio, product mix, will show a balanced profit contribution from a number of lines (though, as predicted by the Pareto 80 : 20 rule, it will be likely even then that a minority of products will contribute most of the profit).

The other major overall 'product' decision will therefore be on portfolio size – 'product line' width and depth. How many items are to be carried, and in what markets and segments?

In theory there should be an optimum number. If too few lines are carried then sales opportunities will be missed. By adding a variation on an existing line – a different pack size, for example – additional sales will be created; and the additional revenue created will be greater than the additional costs, so that these extra sales will generate extra profit. On the other hand, there is a tendency for product lines to grow in size (as new items are, justifiably, added but old items are, unjustifiably, not removed to make way for the new) to the point at which some products in the list will actually make a loss.

There are, therefore, two types of product mix decision to be taken in this context:

- *Line-stretching*. Additional items need to be added to tap potentially profitable extra business.
- *Line-rationalization*. Items need to be removed, to reduce costs and improve profitability.

product (or service) modification   A great deal is written about new products where the assumption is that these are totally new. In practice most 'new' products are modified existing ones. How many times have you seen a television commercial that tells you 'NEW BRAND X now has added Y'? Such changes are incremental, often barely even that, and follow somewhat different rules to genuine new products. Typical modifications may include:

- feature modification
- quality modification
- style modification
- image modification

See also ANSOFF MATRIX; COMPETITIVE GAP; DISTRIBU-
TION GAP; EXISTING PRODUCT CHANGES; FEATURE
MODIFICATION; GAP ANALYSIS; IMAGE MODIFICATION;
MARKET GAP ANALYSIS; NEW PRODUCT NEEDS; PRODUCT
(OR SERVICE) GAP; QUALITY MODIFICATION; STYLE
MODIFICATION; USAGE GAP

product (or service) positioning   There can be some confusion between 'segmentation' and 'positioning'; indeed, the two processes often overlap. The key difference is that the former applies to the market, to the customers (or occasionally 'products') who are clustered into the 'natural' segments which occur in that market. The latter relates to the product or service, and to what the supplier can do with these 'products' to best 'position' them against these segments. A further complication is that 'positioning' can sometimes be divorced from 'segmentation' in that the supplier can choose dimensions on which to position the brand that are not derived from research but are of his or her own choosing. Indeed, such positioning can be applied (to differentiate a brand, for instance) even when segmentation is not found to be viable! Conventionally, product positioning maps (sometimes described as 'product space') are drawn with their axes dividing the map into four quadrants. This is because most of the parameters upon which they are based typically range from 'high' to 'low' or from '+' to '−' (with the 'average' (mean) or zero position in the centre, where these axes cross). The value of each product's (or service's) sales (or 'uptake'), as well as the value of each cluster of consumers, is conventionally represented by the area of the related circle. It is, of course, possible (at least in theory) to use promotion to move the consumer ideal closer to the brand rather than the other way around. This technique is much favoured by 'conviction marketers' – though usually by 'gut feel' rather than with the benefit of these sophisticated maps. Equally, the launch of a really innovative new product (such as the compact disc audio player) may change the dimensions of the whole market. Such approaches, whilst very effective indeed when they succeed, are, however, very difficult to achieve – and rarely do succeed in practice! The one key point to remember, though, is that the dimensions of these product positioning maps must be those that are important to the consumer, not just those that the supplier favours.

Finding out exactly what these dimensions are (and the product positions against them) is the task of sophisticated marketing research. Such knowledge can be worth a great deal of money to the supplier, who can use it to optimally position the brand to become most attractive to the market segment(s) on which it is targeted. It can be almost as valuable to a public service provider, who can then very productively position an offering so that it best meets the real needs of the maximum number of recipients. *See also* MULTIDIMENSIONAL MAPS; POSITIONING OVER TIME; SEGMENTATION; SEGMENTATION APPROACHES; SEGMENTATION METHODS; SEGMENTS OF MARKETS; TARGET MARKETING

product (or service) strategy The 'product' strategy, the route you choose by which to reach your long-term product objectives, will need to be developed specifically for each product or service. In general, there are said to be four basic product strategies for growth in volume and profit (which is what shareholders conventionally demand):

• market penetration
• product development
• market extension
• diversification

These were originally, and best, described by Igor Ansoff (1957), and were subsequently developed as the well-known Ansoff Matrix.
See also ANSOFF MATRIX

Reference: Ansoff, Igor (1957) Strategies for diversification. *Harvard Business Review*, September–October.

product or service, to be purchased The 'tangible' centre of purchasing is the item to be bought; just as, in marketing, it is the item to be sold! The 'buyer' thus must understand that 'product', just as well as the marketer understands his or her 'brand'. This may be an awesome responsibility, where the 'product' can be a very complex entity. On the other hand, in the larger organizations, where the range of purchases to be made is widest, it is usually split between a number of buyers. In addition, the 80:20 rule is just as applicable here. It may accordingly be necessary to distinguish, in this context, between minor purchases (the routine purchasing of office supplies, for instance) and major purchases (key components and capital equipment). Generally speaking, the current theory and practice of purchasing revolves around the former, 'minor', category. Buyers are encouraged to 'decouple' themselves

from any knowledge of the 'product' (which is seen to be a problem only for the 'specifiers') and to concentrate on the processes of purchasing, notably handling the paperwork and negotiating (sight unseen?) the price! This is, by mirror-image analogy, very similar to the position of many sales personnel, who are still allowed by sales trainers to ignore product knowledge. The 'purchasing profession', therefore, tends (to varying degrees) to ignore the 'major' purchases – the ones where what is bought has a significant impact on the operations of the organization and on the achievement of its objectives. These are the purchases, however, which are most susceptible to the application of marketing techniques. In this setting, the 'professional buyer' needs to understand the 'product' requirements in much the same way as his opposite number, the 'product manager'. The needs of the internal users also should be investigated and balanced against the external resources (of the suppliers) on offer. This will involve the buyer in knowing, in some depth, about a number of topics:

• *Specification.* What exactly is the 'product' required to do, and what standards should it meet?
• *Quality.* How rigorously must these 'standards' be met?
• *Delivery and support.* How and when is it wanted, and what support is essential?
• *Price.* What are the pricing constraints?

These all relate to the 4 Ps (only 'Promotion' is missing). But, as with marketing, before any of these elements can be addressed, the buyer must consider, and understand, the 'customers' needs' (in this case both the internal customers and the external suppliers).
See also PURCHASING

product package The product (or service) as perceived by the customer, and hence in reality (rather than in the supplier's more blinkered perspective), is a much more complex construct than is normally allowed for. Indeed, the most important specification of that product or service is that contained in its 'positioning' in 'product space'.

For example, baked beans are often described as if they were just the beans – in a sauce. In practice, even the 'unbranded' products are supplied in packaging, the design of which may well contribute as much to the consumer's appreciation of the character of the product as the physical contents. For branded products, such as Heinz Baked Beans, the physical product itself is submerged under layers of image, not to say emotional involvement built up from childhood, which the decades of advertising and promotion have wrapped around the brand. Even with industrial goods, such as computers, it is often the intangibles which are most important. This overall combination of product, packaging and service is often referred to as the 'extended product'.

Confusion may sometimes be caused by taking too unsophisticated a view of superficial answers by consumers. As Gardner and Levy point out:

> the reasons people usually give for using a product are inclined to be either strongly rationalized or related to the product's most obvious purposes ... When such goals as these are taken at their face value, and considered to be the end of the matter, they lead up many blind alleys. The belief that people are fretting over these minute differences ... results, sometimes, in a shrill focus on product merits beyond all proportion and sensible differentiation.

This is the reason that the more sophisticated research techniques (such as 'repertory grids') have been developed to explore the consumer's hidden motivations.

Even within the organization itself, what makes up the 'product' is more complex than is usually allowed for. Michael Porter (1985), for instance, adopts a view – at one ('price-conscious') end of the spectrum – based on competitive strengths, one that is largely performance/cost based: 'A firm gains competitive advantage by performing these strategically important activities more cheaply or better than its competitors'. He encapsulates these elements of the 'product' in what he calls a 'value chain', which describes the logistic flow through the organization (together with its related support).

References: Gardner, B. and Levy, S. (1955). The product and the brand, *Harvard Business Review*, March–April.

Porter, Michael E. (1985) *Competitive Advantage: Creating and Sustaining Superior Performance*. New York: The Free Press.

product plan   Having decided upon the 'position' of the brand (which in real life represents a variety of decisions covering a rich mix of attributes – tangible and intangible), as well as the 'product' and portfolio combinations, the 'product plan' should be prepared. This should document the strategy and proposed implementation deriving from these ideas. It is a variation (containing rather fewer elements) of the marketing plan. It is important to note, however, that the product plan should be formulated at an earlier stage and incorporated in the overall marketing plan later – as all the separate elements of that overall plan (promotion and pricing plans as well) are usually best developed separately, before being finally combined.

product portfolio   Most organizations have more than one product or service, and many operate in several markets. In the context of the product life cycle, this brings the advantage that the various products, the 'product portfolio', can be managed so that they are not all at the same phase in the life cycle; indeed, ideally, so that they are evenly spread throughout it. This allows for the most efficient use of resources. Thus, the sales force will have only one introduction to handle at a time, and will probably have recovered from the follow-on effort of the growth phase before it must deal with the next introduction. The marketing department, and its outside agencies, will also have the load on its scarce people resources spread more evenly. Most important of all, though, the cash flow will be reasonably even. Experiencing substantial peaks and troughs in cash flow can be very inefficient. It usually means that extra funds will have to be raised on the money markets at the times of high investment – which is expensive both in terms of the interest payments and of diversion of significant amounts of senior management's time to set up the loans. In any case, shareholders (and employees) do not appreciate varying profit (and work) levels. They would usually much prefer an even stream, even if they do want it to gradually grow. An organization looking for growth can introduce new products or services which it hopes will be bigger sellers than those which they succeed. Perhaps an easier, and more likely, route is to introduce more products or services, of equal size, than are being lost, thus increasing the size of the portfolio, and with it the volume of sales. On the other hand, if this expansion is undertaken too rapidly many of these brands – at the beginning of their life cycles – will be hungrily demanding investment; and even the earliest of them will be unlikely to generate profits fast enough to support the numbers of later launches. So, the producer will have to find a source of funds until his investments pay off.

See also GLOBAL MARKETING; MARKETING STRATEGIES

product replacement   One form of 'new product launch' which is little discussed, but is probably the most prevalent – and hence most important – of all, is that of replacement of one product by a new (usually 'improved') one. The risk levels may be much reduced, since there is an existing user base to underwrite sales (as long as the new product does not alienate them – as New Coca Cola did in the USA and New Persil did in the UK). Such an introduction will be complicated by the fact that, at least for some time, there will be two forms of the product in the pipeline – the old and the new. Some firms may opt for a straight cut-over: one day the old product will be coming off the production line, the next the new. Most will favour parallel running for a period of time, even if only because this is forced upon them by their distribution chains. This ensures that the new really does, eventually, replace the old (if this does not happen, the old will not be discontinued – which would have saved Coca Cola from a great deal of embarrassment), and it may also reveal that both can run together (as Coke and Coke Classic subsequently did).

See also PRODUCT DEVELOPMENT PROCESS; RISK, OF NEW PRODUCTS; RISK VERSUS TIME, NEW PRODUCTS

product screening   *see* NEW PRODUCT SCREENING, ORGANIZATIONAL FACTORS; STRATEGIC SCREENING, NEW PRODUCTS

product/service offer   *see* PRODUCT OR SERVICE DECISIONS

product space   *see* SEGMENTATION METHODS

products versus benefits   It is a basic, and oft-quoted, tenet of the sales profession that:

> Customers don't buy products . . .
> . . . they seek to acquire benefits.

Behind this statement lies a basic principle of successful marketing: when people purchase products they are not motivated in the first instance by the physical attributes of the product, but by the benefits that those attributes offer.

An indication as to what actually (tangible and intangible) makes up a product can be found by looking closely at the difference between what customers buy and what they actually want. Taking an example, one which is a favourite of many marketers, when customers buy a 2 mm drill what they really want is a 2 mm hole!

The drill itself is only a means to an end. The lesson for the drill vendor is that his business is providing a means of making holes in materials, not that of manufacturing drills. If he fails to understand

this, he is in grave danger of losing his business when a better means of making holes is invented. This phenomenon, of being locked into the product rather than the market, has led to the demise of many businesses. In 1960 Theodore Levitt memorably described the problem as 'marketing myopia'.

Reference: Levitt, Theodore (1960) Marketing myopia. *Harvard Business Review*, July–August.

product territories   *see* TERRITORY MANAGEMENT

product test   During the product development process, with luck, a workable new product or service will be delivered by the product development 'labs'. There still remains, however, the investment to be made in the launch itself. To reduce the risk, a further round of testing is normally undertaken. This takes the new product or service and tests it on potential consumers, in much the same way as the concept should have been tested earlier. The testing may, however, be more detailed, since the output of this research can be used to modify the 'product' itself to best match the consumers' needs. This filter must be taken seriously, and must be comprehensive; products which are not accepted by consumers, and cannot be made acceptable, must be discarded. Even though considerable sums may have been spent on development, they will pale into insignificance against the losses which might be incurred at later stages. Ideally, however, this testing process should not be limited to determining the outcome of a single purchase. Products, in order to recoup their development and launch costs (and only then to make a profit), usually have to benefit from repeat purchasing over an extended period. Philip Kotler (1988) states that the researcher, in this context, needs to estimate four variables – 'trial', 'first repeat', 'adoption' and 'purchase frequency' – in order to be certain that the product will have a life after the first purchase. The technique suggested, to establish this information, is 'sales-wave' research, whereby the respondents (those testing the new product) are offered a choice between the product or its competitors (at reduced prices to provide an incentive to purchase a further time, using their own money). This may be repeated up to five times, to check the repeat-purchase pattern. 'Simulated store technique' attempts to achieve a similar end, by exposing the 'testers' to the 'promotional material' on test (amidst other material) and allowing them subsequently to select products from a 'store', again asking them to demonstrate, by 'spending their money', the likely purchase (trial) rate. They can also be reinterviewed later to obtain a measure of their repurchase intention over time.

On the other hand, the most usual form of 'product testing' still remains that of the single test of acceptability (almost inevitably in comparison with the alternatives, including the existing product and its competitors). It has to be recognized, however, that this may not, as indicated above, be a good measure of longer-term performance. Coca Cola, in introducing New Coke, reportedly conducted some 200 000 taste tests before settling on its new formula – which was then rejected in the marketplace by many consumers and the old Coke Classic had to be reinstated. Jeffrey Pope (1986), however, makes the very valid point that 'It is usually difficult, if not impossible, to simulate or pre-test a service'. Making a prototype of a service is often not a practical proposition and, in any case, side-by-side comparisons with competitive services are typically not feasible (and certainly not as 'blind tests').

See also PRODUCT DEVELOPMENT PROCESS

References: Kotler, Philip (1988) *Marketing Management* (6th edn). Englewood Cliffs, NJ: Prentice-Hall.

Pope, Jeffrey (1986) Marketing research for service industries. In Victor P. Buell (ed.), *Handbook of Modern Marketing* (2nd edn). New York: McGraw-Hill.

product value, packaging   The pack is often designed to make its contents look more than they really are. Those apparently 'artistic' designs – for example, those which feature 'cut-outs' for use as handles – are frequently chosen to give a bigger outline without using extra product; and in the hole for the 'handle' the supplier is selling 'air'. Some cosmetic packs even have false bottoms so that the contents may occupy less than one-third of the total volume.

product variety   *see* VARIETY

professional-indemnity insurance   A specialized form of third-party insurance which covers members of the professions against any claims of professional negligence.

professionals of the specialism   *see* SELLING SERVICES

profile of target audience   *see* MEDIA BUYING, ADVERTISING AGENCY

PROFILES   *see* RESIDENTIAL NEIGHBOURHOODS

profit-and-loss statement   Also called the 'income statement'. It shows sales or revenue (income) earned during the time period being reported upon (usually one year) and all the costs charged (again in that time period) against them. The difference is the profit or loss.

profit forecast   *see* BUDGETS; FORECASTS INTO BUDGETS

Profit Impact of Marketing Strategies (PIMS)   This is a US database, which has now run for several decades, covering 3000 businesses with a wide range of standard data on each (including environment, strategy, performance, competition as well as internal data). It is used for comparison and benchmarking.

See also BRANCH MARKETING; MARKETING RESEARCH, PRECISION MARKETING; MONITORING, PROGRESS

profit maximization   *see* CORPORATE OBJECTIVES; NOT-FOR-PROFIT ORGANIZATIONS, OBJECTIVES

profit maximization, price   *see* EQUILIBRIUM PRICE

profit or non-profit   In terms of the basic 'dimensions' on which marketing is often organized, one of the divisions which causes the most soul searching is that between profit-making organizations – the companies which typically leap to mind when marketing is mentioned – and the not-for-profit sectors, such as the National Health Service or voluntary organizations. The former are easy to deal with. They are, at least in theory if often not in practice, driven by the sole motive of making a profit, and good marketing is an excellent way of increasing the bottom-line (profit) figures.

On the other hand, employees of the not-for-profit sectors, typically those in government departments or charities, frequently have difficulty in seeing how marketing (which is too often associated in the public mind with hard-selling advertisements for FMCG, such as baked beans) is appropriate to their own organization. It is necessary, though, to point out that all organizations (even the most self-contained of monasteries) necessarily have links with the outside world, and such links are the stuff of marketing. The government department which wishes to influence motorists not to drink and drive will use market research to find out what are the motivations of those who do, and what is the most effective means of influencing them. It then uses the mass media to convey those messages – in the process often becoming one of the largest advertisers. But even the smallest charity has to decide who are its clients, and what are their needs, before communicating with them.

Philip Kotler and Alan Andreasen (1987) suggest a further five 'questions' which help to define the exact environment not-for-profit organizations are operating in:

Is the organization donative in whole or in part? [if so, they may be subject to tighter regulation, or restrictions set by sponsors, in terms of marketing activities – and may have to 'market' to sponsors/ donors as well as users]
Is the organization's performance likely to be subject to public scrutiny? [this may limit the marketing options even further]
Is marketing seen as undesirable from the standpoint of some or all members of the organization or its major sponsors or reviewers? [this may be because marketing is seen as 'a waste of the public's money' or 'intrusive' or 'manipulative' – these are criticisms to which answers can usually be found, but it has to be recognized that such opposition can be a major factor in limiting marketing campaigns]
Is the organization largely staffed by volunteers? [this adds a further group, volunteers, to the marketer's audience]
Is performance judged largely by nonmarketing measures? [if these 'measures' are extremely intangible, that is to say unmeasurable, as they sometimes are, this may seriously limit any attempt to measure the benefits arising from the market]

They summarize the position as follows: 'Although nonprofit organizations seek to influence exchanges of money for goods and services just like for-profit organizations, what makes them unique is their concentration on exchanges involving non-monetary costs on the one hand and social and psychological perspectives and modified techniques'.

On the other hand, perhaps not-for-profit organizations are not as unaware of marketing as some might believe. Thus, for instance, Laura Cousins (1990) found in the UK that 62 per cent of not-for-profit organizations she surveyed claimed to produce a written annual marketing plan, which was no less than that (57 per cent) of for-profit firms!
See also ORGANIZATIONAL PIGEON-HOLES

References: Cousins, Laura (1990) Marketing planning in the public and non-profit sectors. *European Journal of Marketing*, 24(7).

Kotler, Philip and Andreasen, Alan R. (1987) *Strategic Marketing for Nonprofit Organizations*. Englewood Cliffs, NJ: Prentice-Hall.

progressives The set of separate proofs taken from each of the colour-separated plates in four-colour printing.

progressive taxes These are taxes which take proportionately more from the wealthier members of society. A regressive tax does the opposite.

progress monitoring *see* MONITORING, PROGRESS

progress payment An agreed instalment of the overall payment made to a contractor when a specified part of the work has been completed.

prohibition *see* REGULATORY CONSIDERATIONS, FILTERING UNSUITABLE MARKETS

projection media *see* PRESENTATION MEDIA

projective techniques *see* OPEN QUESTIONS, ON QUESTIONNAIRES

project management Perhaps the most important skill in handling customers, as part of a complex sale, is that of project management. The customer sales 'business' tends to run as a series of projects. Clearly, each sales campaign can be thought of as a separate project, and managed as such. But, when an order is won, this is followed by possibly the most complex project of all – the installation – and this probably requires the highest management skills of all. In addition there are other smaller projects, such as training or extending the use of the product or service into new areas, that can also benefit from project management skills.
See also ACCOUNT PLANNING; PROPOSALS

project pricing The most vicious form of negotiation is often that associated with long negotiations, for large capital projects, say. By the time the 'tender' is awarded the sellers may have invested many thousands of dollars, perhaps many millions, in the tendering process itself, preparing all the specifications and designs for their submissions. The 'life or death' decision, of whether their tender will succeed, is all that stands between the project team and disaster (both in terms of the costs that have already been incurred and, just as importantly, in terms of their own egos). It is not surprising that, as a result, such teams try to shave their prices as low as possible –

as do all the other competitors! Such industries often have an abysmal profit record. Possibly the only solution is to get out of them; or to develop the sort of sales strengths which IBM used in such situations.

See also PRICE NEGOTIATION

project risk *see* MARKET ENTRY DECISION

promotion *see* COMPETITIVE GAP; MARKETING STRATEGIES; SALES PROMOTION; PUSH VERSUS PULL PROMOTION

promotion/advertising ratios *see* ADVERTISING

promotional budget *see* BUDGETS

promotional choice *see* PROMOTIONAL MIX

promotional discount *see* PROMOTIONAL PRICING; TRADE DISCOUNTS

promotional lozenge There is a range of alternative (and often complementary) promotional delivery vehicles available. As a very direct approach, there is face-to-face sales. There is the more indirect one, when it is too expensive to confront the customer personally, of advertising, or the even more indirect one of public relations (PR). Finally, there is the very immediate one of sales (point of sale) promotion – which, if the reports are to be believed, now accounts for the largest part of the spend on promotion as a whole. To put these in a more memorable context than just the rather amorphous 'marketing mix' (even though that does convey exactly what is involved), the 'promotional lozenge' may be used as a visual aid. It is shaped like a diamond, but is called a lozenge because (unlike the research diamond) it does not have any clear cutting edges. It is generally much less well defined and softer at its extremes, and there is definitely a quality of trial and error involved – suck the lozenge and see!

This lozenge is not as arbitrary as it may seem. It actually is organized along two dimensions. The vertical one is the move from direct (sales) to indirect (advertising) contact with the customer.

Perhaps less obvious, but in many respects more important, is the horizontal dimension. This shows the flow over time, from the start with the establishment of a general interest via PR through investment in image building with advertising and much of the selling process, to the very immediate impact of sales promotional devices at the point of sale. It also demonstrates the gradation from the long-term investment in PR and advertising/sales to the very short-term effect of promotion.

The demands posed by your product/service package determine the actual shape of the lozenge – another reason for choosing a soft, malleable lozenge rather than a hard diamond. For instance, if you need the face-to-face (sales) contact to explain a complex package, and the price of this is sufficiently high to cover the high costs this implies, then the lozenge becomes almost an inverted triangle:

The advertising element is almost missing, though even in the almost pure sales environment there will remain some element of indirect contact – often in the form of direct mail – to generate prospects for the face-to-face contact. The 'point of sale' here is a time (not a place), and the promotional element is usually only seen in the form of discounting the price.

See also ADVERTISING; MARKETING MIX; PROMOTIONAL MIX; SELLING

promotional message *see* PROMOTIONAL MIX FACTORS

promotional mix A major decision to be taken before 'talking' to the customer is what 'promotional mix' to use. Much as there are separate elements to the overall marketing mix, there are different 'media' which may be used to reach the customer. Choosing which of these to use is a key decision, because – depending upon the individual product and the customer set – different 'media' (in this context, simply ways of delivering the promotional message to the customer) may have different degrees of effectiveness. Typically, the major decision is on what medium to concentrate the main message(s). Often the campaign may revolve around just one medium, be it television commercials or personal selling. Even so, subsidiary decisions will be what other media to use and the balance between these, so that the optimal effect on the customer may be achieved. There are a wide variety of specific techniques which may be used to communicate with customers.

See also ADVERTISING; SELLING

promotional mix factors   The ideal promotional mix will be specific to an individual product or service, and to the marketing objectives which have been set for it. In deciding that optimal mix, however, there are a number of general factors which may need to be taken into account:

- *Budget available.* The prime practical determinant of the promotion mix, and one that is often ignored by theory, is usually the amount of money available. If you do not have a budget running well into six or even seven figures, you need not consider television – the cost of just making a single commercial, without transmitting it, can now reach six figures by itself! If your budget does not run into five figures, you had better start taking the small ads seriously! The size of the budget will also determine how important it is that the media schedule, for example, achieves the best cost per thousand and hence is cost effective. Such cost effectiveness is the ideal target for all campaigns, but if sufficient funds are available then it may be possible to justify setting this aside to take account of other factors, such as impact.
- *Promotional message.* The message which has been chosen will also largely determine the medium to be used. A demonstration of the product will demand either face-to-face selling of some form or television (or cinema). A coupon response will only work in the press or by direct mail (or door-to-door).
- *Complexity of product or service.* Sometimes the product or service will determine the medium. If, as often happens in industrial and capital goods markets, the product is complex or requires significant amounts of service support, then face-to-face selling may be the only route open.
- *Market size and location.* Where the target audience is located will be a determinant of the medium chosen. If the audience covers a large part of the population, and the budget can afford it, television will usually be the best choice. If it is very specialist, but spread throughout the whole population, then the relevant specialist press or even direct mail may be most suitable.
- *Distribution.* Often it is obtaining distribution, in particular through retailers, which is the key to success. The promotional mix chosen may therefore be as much designed to sway the buyers in the distribution chain as the end-users. Thus, television will often be used to impress those buyers with the producer's degree of commitment, but sometimes the press will be selected to allow for linked promotions with the main retailers.
- *Life cycle.* The stage of the life cycle may be critical. If the product or service is in the introductory stage, building awareness will be the main aim; if it is in the growth stage, the (different) requirement is to persuade potential consumers to switch their buying patterns.
- *Competition.* Finally, any marketer needs to take account of what his competitors are doing. If the main competitor starts a high-spending television campaign and you have a low-spending press campaign, then you will have to take some serious decisions. Do you also move into television, and probably increase costs to the extent that your profits will be hit – though you may often find that the increased sales more than cover the costs if the product has been under-advertised? Or do you stay where you are, and possibly have to accept a reduced market share?

See also PROMOTIONAL MIX

promotional plans   *see* SALES PROMOTIONAL PLANS AND RESEARCH

promotional pricing   One of the most frequently used sales promotional techniques is that of offering, in one form or another, promotional discounts. These can be grouped into a number of main categories:

Price reductions
The simple 'money-off' ('10p off') promotion is the most direct and hence may have the most immediate impact on sales levels. As it is shown on the 'pack' it is also difficult for any retailer to avoid passing this on to the consumer; though, even then, the retailer may choose to offset it against any existing price reduction. But it is also the most expensive, as to be

effective it usually needs to represent 15–20 per cent off the regular retail price, and this comes straight out of the profit margin! It may also prove difficult to restore the price to its original level at the end of the promotion if consumers, and in particular retailers, decide to stockpile in order to hold off their purchases until the next promotion (indeed, Schultz and Robinson (1982) report that 'more than 25% of all retail customers are considered regular "price-off" buyers'). It may also do considerable damage to the image of quality products or services, especially where the price-off 'burst' or 'flag' may visually dominate the label. In the case of sales to retailers, a wide range of promotional discounts may be available, though these may also be tied to specific objectives, such as special displays, rather than just to sales. Even financial services providers may use this tool. Thus, the Abbey National bank in the UK offered 1.5 per cent off its loan rates to new borrowers.

Free goods
A variation is the offer of 10 per cent more of the product for the same price. This has a number of advantages. It often costs the supplier significantly less than a 10 per cent cut in the price. It forces the customer to buy more than usual and, hopefully, to use more – possibly setting new usage patterns. It possibly has less impact on the established price. It will, though, usually require a special pack (and accompanying changes, and disruption, to production lines). It can also set a precedent which is difficult to ignore. At the end of the 1980s it was reported that, in this way, '13.5% extra free' had almost become the standard offering on 440 ml cans of lager in the UK. In the case of sales to retailers, a form of this may be run as a 'bonus' ('12 as 11', for instance, with a case of 12 units charged at the price of 11), but it has to be recognized that this is in effect a straight price cut (and one which the retailer may not even feel obliged to pass on to the consumer!).

Banded offers
Banded offers are two or more products sold together, almost invariably at a lower price (though one product may be offered as a 'premium') and physically joined (hence 'banded' – often just by adhesive tape). This promotion is typically meant to offer greater 'value', but it normally poses problems in terms of requiring changes to the production lines – often with considerable reductions in productivity.

Vouchers or coupons
Where the aim is to extend the penetration (or trial) of the product or service to new customers (particu-larly in the case of a 'new product launch'), coupons are often used. They are most effectively delivered door-to-door, where they achieve high redemption rates. Schultz and Robinson report that 'About 60 per cent of homes that receive direct mail coupons actually use them', though they also report that the redemption levels for individual coupons are around 10 per cent. In the USA it is claimed that 80 per cent of these are now delivered via FSIs (free-standing inserts; books full of coupons, delivered door-to-door). They may also be incorporated in press advertisements – which are cheaper to run but have a considerably lower redemption rate (Schultz and Robinson, again, report between 2 and 3 per cent). Depending upon the generosity of the offer, this is supposed to tempt consumers away from their existing brands to try the new one. It can be a very effective type of promotion (if coupon redemption levels are high enough) and may be more cost effective than sampling; and it clearly has only limited impact on the prices paid by existing customers. Depending upon how the coupons are delivered, this approach can be targeted/controlled (though coupons in the press are largely uncontrolled – causing redemption problems – and they may be very unpopular with retailers). Coupons can also be used to 'load' existing customers (for instance, as a defensive move where a competitive threat, a new brand say, is experienced). They can also be used to introduce the existing users to new (usually larger) pack sizes and range extensions. 'Stamps', which have risen and fallen in popularity, are a special form of this type of promotion. They are intended, in particular, to buy very-long-term loyalty (typically to retailers) or for use on a staple item of purchase (such as cigarette coupons). They can, though, be expensive and very complex to administer – particularly where they lose their 'competitive edge' and are taken for granted.

Cash refund
In this case the customer can obtain a cash refund (from the retailer or by mail), usually on the basis of a 'voucher' which is attached to, or is part of, the pack. This is a way of offering a controlled price reduction (the retailer cannot just absorb the offer as extra profit). It can also create a database of customers, if handled by mail – though there is little indication that this is ever done! On the other hand, the redemption procedures may be complex (and unwelcome to the trade). It can also be expensive; sometimes (when 'trial' is being sought) the refund may even be as much as the whole purchase price, though the redemption rates reported (of about

1–2 per cent for offers in newspapers and only around 4 per cent in-pack or on-pack) indicate that many purchasers never redeem the offers – so actual costs may be significantly reduced. A variation on this approach is that of giving the amount on the voucher to a charity rather than the purchaser – thus, at the same time, enhancing the 'community' image of the supplier and offering useful public relations opportunities.

Money off next purchase

A somewhat similar coupon offer, this time on the label of the product itself, may be used to extend buying patterns and build customer loyalty. For instance, the UK jewellery chain offered a £50 voucher for every £150 spent – though (typically for a promotion) the indications were that this was possibly used to boost short-term sales and reduce stock levels (with some of the costs of this deferred) rather than to build loyalty!

Loss-leader pricing

In the case of the service and distribution industries, a product or service may actually be priced below cost in order to attract customers into the branch, in the hope that while they are there they will buy other products or services which are profitable.

Cheap credit

Where credit is offered, lower price or even free credit may be used instead of a simple price reduction. This may be cheaper to the vendor who has access to cheaper lines of credit (though the cost of bad debts must also be covered). It may be particularly attractive to the more naive consumer who sees it as a way of getting something now and paying for it later. It may also be a means of introducing the consumer to the use of the supplier's credit facilities, and hence locking that consumer into the supplier.

Special events

Certain parts of the retail trade offer 'special', usually seasonal, events to encourage buying during traditionally low turnover periods (as a result, these seasonal sales may now have made these periods of high turnover, but at a very low margin!).

See also PRECISION MARKETING

Reference: Schultz, Don E. and Robinson, William A. (1982) *Sales Promotion Essentials*. Crain Books.

promotional programme testing *see* TEST MARKET

promotional research *see* SALES PROMOTIONAL PLANS AND RESEARCH

promotion in not-for-profit organizations It should be easy to see that service providers in general have the same promotional needs as manufacturers of physical products, though the detailed messages may be very different. There may, however, be some questions from those working in not-for-profit organizations who can see no requirement to 'sell' or promote their 'products' or organizations. The UK National Health Service, for example, does not need to advertise for customers – though its private sector competitors do! One thing is clear, though: such organizations still have to communicate with their 'customers'. They need to let their consumers know that the organization exists, what it offers and how they can use it, hence the plethora of 'promotional' booklets the DSS offers to the unemployed in the UK. The requirements imposed by these 'communications' are often indistinguishable from conventional service industry promotions. Indeed, government 'information' campaigns (such as those to combat cigarette smoking and drug addiction) often dominate the mass media.

See also ADVERTISING; SELLING

promotion objectives In line with its essentially short-term objectives, a promotion may have a number of limited objectives:

- *Trial purchase.* Some promotions are expressly planned to induce trial purchases, the classic example being 'money-off coupons' distributed house-to-house (or in the press), or even samples of the product, at the time of the launch (again delivered door-to-door or 'banded' as a free gift on a related product).
- *Extra volume.* Other promotions are designed to stimulate the user's decision at point of sale; on-pack price-cuts are the obvious example (or occasionally 'money-back' against future redemption of a coupon on the current pack – to even more directly stimulate repurchase). It may often be found that a cheaper alternative is to offer more of the product ('free 20% extra') for the same price.
- *Repeat business.* Yet others are meant to build repeat business; for example, the 'money off next purchase coupons' mentioned above.
- *Point of sale.* Perhaps the greatest number, though, are intended only to have an indirect effect – to provide additional interest (to

differentiate the product) for an advertising campaign (for example, free gifts, such as glasses with petrol) or to obtain better display at point of sale (for example, a competition, with the prize of a 'holiday in Hawaii', jointly run with a retailer), where it is the extra shelf space that sells the product rather than the promotion itself.

It should be added that sales promotion and advertising (or, indeed, any of the other forms of promotion) are not mutually exclusive. In practice, they are complementary, and the most effective, well-balanced campaign will often include a mix of several types of promotion (in particular, of advertising and sales promotion, which tend to go hand-in-hand).
See also PRECISION MARKETING

promotion of services   Despite the fact that services follow much the same pattern of promotion as products, there may be some differences:

- *Personal selling and employees.* Services are usually produced and consumed at the same time, and frequently this is also the time of the sale itself. This means that the sale is often made personally by the staff who are providing the service. In this way many, perhaps the majority, of the staff in effect become sales personnel; and, equally, 'advertising' may have to target them as much as the external customers.
- *Word of mouth.* Because of the problems of demonstrating quality and value, and the provider's need to build up trust, word of mouth recommendation by loyal customers may be correspondingly more important – particularly for those services, such as personal services, which are based upon local branches with relatively small catchment areas.
- *Tangibility.* The promotional campaign needs to make tangible the intangible, possibly by the use of symbols, such as Lloyds Bank's 'black horse' or Legal & General's 'multi-coloured umbrella'.
- *Consistency.* As 'trust' can easily be destroyed by a single bad experience, it is important that the service, and its promotion, maintains consistency. It must continue to offer, and deliver, what was promised to the customer.

See also ADVERTISING; SELLING

prompt card   *see* ADVERTISING RESEARCH

prompted awareness   *see* ADVERTISING RESEARCH

prompter   *see* AUTOCUE

proofs   *see* ADVERTISING PROCESSES

propagandist model   *see* CONVICTION MARKETING

property costs   *see* LOCATION, RETAIL; RETAIL MANAGEMENT

prophecy, self-fulfilling   *see* LIFE CYCLE, LESSONS

proposals   Proposals often form a major element of the complex sales process. The skills needed for producing these proposals are close to those needed for project management, and (in particular) relate to those of 'surveying' (where a good survey is almost a prerequisite of a proposal). But the first question the sales professional (or the manager) has to ask is 'Does this sale (or proposed management action) need a proposal?' Often the answer will be 'no'! Proposals are time- and resource-consuming. Much better that the agreements are confirmed with a short letter (or memo), and the time saved used for more prospecting to build the prospect base (or getting on with the project). Occasionally, however, it will be necessary to produce a full proposal, particularly for a competitive sale (or, in management, where approval for an internal project will be difficult to obtain). A well-prepared and -presented proposal is very impressive; and if the 'competitors' have not produced one (or have produced one to a very poor standard), it may well give a competitive edge. It is also a very useful record of all the 'agreements'.

The content will be a direct reflection of the 'sales campaign'. If that sales campaign has a sound structure, as it should, the proposal too is likely to have a sound structure. The one rule, however, is that all the main material in a proposal should have been previously agreed with the prospect (or, in the case of managers, with the others involved in the project). None of the material should come as a surprise. One favourite format is:

1. Summary
2. 'Prospect' (or senior management) requirements (in summary)
3. Summary background (including a review of the problems to be solved)
4. Proposed solutions (in summary)
5. General benefits
6. Financial justification and costs
7. Appendices:

(A) Detailed background (survey results)
(B) Detailed solutions (including flowcharts)
(C) 'Product' (or concept) descriptions
(D) References (descriptions of similar systems with customers, or – for internal proposals – use of similar approaches by other organizations)

This is, however, just one of many possible structures. As always, you yourself must choose one that suits – that suits your 'prospects' (those to whom you, as a manager, say, wish to sell your ideas), the material you are using and, above all, your own needs.
See also ACCOUNT PLANNING; CALL TARGETS

prospect database   *see* TERRITORY SALES PLAN

prospect generation   *see* REPLY–PAID CARDS

prospective suppliers   *see* SUPPLIER SELECTION

prospect qualification   'Qualification' is a central feature of prospect management, and accordingly of the questioning process, though it is little stressed by sales trainers and even less by the average sales manager! Too many sales professionals ask the question 'What business might there be?', but not the question 'Is there business realistically available?' or the even more difficult question 'Will this business be worthwhile?'. Miller et al.'s (1985) view is that: 'The reason that up to 35 percent of the prospective business in most people's Sales Funnels [their analogy for the "numbers game"] at any given time is poor is that these sales representatives lack a dynamic, field-tested, process for analysing their customers needs'. 'Qualification' was one of the keys to IBM's sales success. As a company it always had too few sales professionals, so that they were overloaded with work and, in particular, with prospects. The only way they could function at all was by very rigorously sorting out the most productive prospects and ruthlessly discarding the less productive ones. As Tom Hopkins (1982) says (of most sales professionals, who do not qualify):

Their problem is that they try to close the wrong people too often and too hard. In other words, they don't fail to close, they fail to qualify . . . Champions know better. They know that qualification is the key to high production . . . The primary difference is that your sales are 500 per cent

greater with qualified leads than they are with the non-qualified type.

See also PROPOSALS; SALES CALL; SELLING; TELESALES

References: Hopkins, Tom (1982) *How to Master the Art of Selling*. London: Champion Press.
    Miller, Robert B., Heiman, Stephen E. and Tuleja, Tad (1985) *Strategic Selling*. New York: William Morrow.

prospects   The term 'prospects' is most often used in face-to-face selling, 'potential customers' often being used to describe an equivalent group of people in mass markets, but the meaning is the same: those individuals in the market who are not the organization's customers. The boundaries are, however, not quite so clear. Are lapsed customers to be included? Is everyone in the market a prospect, or should only those who are likely to buy the particular brand be included? The concept of 'prospects' may sometimes be just as applicable in the public sector. The government undertakes extensive advertising campaigns because as few as 50 per cent of those entitled to family benefits actually claim them. The government, here, wants to give money to more people; to convert prospects into customers! Once more the boundaries need defining for each situation.
See also CALL TARGETS; MARKETS; SELLING; TELESALES; TERRITORY MANAGEMENT; TERRITORY SALES PLAN; USERS

prospects A or B   *see* TERRITORY SALES PLAN

prospect sets   *see* TERRITORY SALES PLAN

protocol   *see* POLITICAL CONTACTS

prototype of a service   *see* PRODUCT TEST

providers of funds   *see* NOT–FOR–PROFIT ORGANIZATIONS, OBJECTIVES

PR plans and budgets   PR is very cost effective. In addition the amount which can be spent on it is usually relatively low in comparison with the other promotional spends, and is self-limiting (there are just so many events you can arrange, and just so many journalists you can entertain). Thus, there is a good argument for saying that, in setting promotional budgets, PR should come at the head of the queue. Only when you have obtained the maximum you can achieve from PR should you allocate the remaining funds to other promotional activities. Since you get what you pay for, it is thus also better to pay more for high-calibre personnel than waste the rest of the PR budget. You can use any of the methods normally deployed in calculating promotional budgets, but Roger Haywood (1984) states that 'Experience shows anything less than 15 per cent of the total promotional budget being spent on PR will not achieve anything substantial; with smaller budgets or more specialized markets the minimum proportion will rise. For example, an industrial marketing company will probably need to spend upwards of 30 per cent on the PR area.' It may be difficult to overspend on PR, but even so it is very easy to lose control of PR costs (PR agencies do like to indulge in very expensive entertaining!), so they must be agreed in advance and controlled as closely as any other part of the overall promotional budget. To be most effective, PR needs to be a continuous activity, with carefully planned events and activities scattered throughout the year – to maintain press interest – or alternatively concentrated at the times of the year when they can be most effective. This means that PR has to be planned just as carefully as any other marketing activity. The audiences have to be defined, and the messages constructed and delivered just when and where they will have the most impact. This should be spelled out in the PR plan.

See also PUBLIC RELATIONS

Reference: Haywood, Roger (1984) *All About PR: What to Say and When to Say It*. Maidenhead: McGraw-Hill.

PR, proactive   *see* PROACTIVE PR

P.S.   *see* LETTER, DIRECT MAIL

3 Ps   Real life may be (and often is) more complex than the much quoted 4 Ps allow for. The oversimplicity of the 4 Ps approach is most obvious in the services sector. Booms and Bitner (1981) therefore suggest the addition of a further 3 Ps (to make 7 Ps in total):

- people
- process
- physical evidence

People
This clearly is an important difference – probably the most important – across most of the service sector. It is often people who are the service itself.

Process
How the service is delivered to the consumer is frequently an important part of the service. In particu-

lar, the quality controls which are built in are typically the only guarantee that the service will consistently meet the standards that the consumer demands. This is a wider requirement than that demanded of the 'place' element of the product marketing mix.

Physical evidence
This could, with some justification, be considered to be part of the 'product package'. On the other hand, it is so important in the case of services, adding the tangible (the design of the retail outlet and its electronic facilities, say) to the essentially intangible (even money being, these days, largely unseen), that it is argued that it should be considered separately by service providers.

See also MARKETING MIX; 4 Ps

Reference: Booms, B. H. and Bitner, M. J. (1981) Marketing strategies and organisation structures for service firms. In J. Donnelly and W. R. George (eds), *Marketing of Services*.

4 Ps   In terms of the marketing mix, many business schools use the framework of the 4 Ps (as proposed by E. Jerome McCarthy) to conveniently (and perhaps arbitrarily) group these activities into related areas:

- product
- price
- place
- promotion

The first two are, in effect, the product-related elements. Perhaps influenced by economics, price is split off as an element worthy of separate consideration; though this may, in many cases, overemphasize its importance.

The other two are parts of the delivery system; 'place' (a very clumsy term, but easily remembered), which is about delivering the physical product or service, and 'promotion', which is about delivering the 'sales message'.

Criticism
It should be recognized that the 4 Ps offer just one, albeit frequently used, way of approaching marketing; providing a succinct summary of the main splits in the marketing mix. Some pundits may argue for less, as did Albert Trey, who proposed just two factors – the 'offering' (product, price, etc.) and 'methods and tools' (distribution, promotion, etc.). Other writers argue for the need to subdivide these categories further; for example, differentiating

between 'sales' and 'advertising' as forms of 'promotion'.

To give one example, in the days before the simplification offered by the 4 Ps became popular, Godley identified ten major factors in the marketing mix:

- market research
- the products
- the presentation, packaging and image
- the policy for pricing
- the policy for discounting and trade terms
- the selling policy and method
- the sales organization and operations
- after-sales service, technical aid and complaints service
- the channels and method of distribution
- the advertising and promotional policies, PR

This probably goes too far towards the opposite extreme, but it does illustrate the possible complexity that is often hidden behind the deceptively simple mask of the 4 Ps.

Perhaps the most significant criticism of the 4 Ps approach, which you should be aware of, is that it unconsciously emphasizes the inside-out view (looking from the company outwards), whereas the essence of marketing should be the outside-in approach (looking from the customer's viewpoint), which is about delivering benefits.

See also CORPORATE PLAN; MARKETING AUDIT; MARKETING MIX; MARKETING MIX AND PROMOTION; MARKETING PLANS AND PROGRAMMES; MARKETING STRATEGIES; PRODUCT OR SERVICE DECISIONS; 3 PS; SWOT ANALYSIS

Reference: McCarthy, E. Jerome (1981) *Basic Marketing: a Managerial Approach.* Boston, MA: Richard D. Irwin.

7 Ps   *see* 3 PS

pseudo-product testing   A method of pack testing whereby the respondents are given the same product in different packs to test their reactions to these.

See also MARKETING RESEARCH; PACKAGING; PRODUCT TEST

psychogalvanometer   A device which is sometimes used as a 'lie detector', but is occasionally used in advertising research to test consumers' reactions (to advertisements, for instance) by measuring, electrically, the amount they perspire.

See also ADVERTISING RESEARCH

psychographic   *see* SEGMENTATION

psychological influences, on the purchase decision   A number of 'psychological' factors are proposed as influences on the purchase decision, from the widely reported teachings of Freud through to Herzberg's discussion of 'dissatisfiers' (product characteristics which would veto its purchase for a given customer – called, in the context of employment, 'hygiene factors') and 'satisfiers' ('motivators' which would persuade the customer to choose that brand).

In the context of marketing, however, perhaps the most widely quoted approach is that of Abraham Maslow (1954), who developed a hierarchy of 'needs', ranging from the most essential, immediate physical needs to the most luxuriously inessential.

See also CULTURES, INFLUENCES ON THE PURCHASE DECISION; DECISION-MAKING PROCESS, BY CUSTOMERS; MASLOW'S HIERARCHY OF NEEDS; REPEAT PURCHASING PROCESS; SOCIAL CLASS INFLUENCES, ON THE PURCHASE DECISION

Reference: Maslow, Abraham (1954) *Motivation and Personality.* New York: Harper & Row.

psychological pricing   *see* RANGE PRICING

publications, precision marketing   It is now possible for those publications reaching the bulk of their readers by mail to produce tailored versions of the publication, depending upon what even relatively small groups of consumers may want. Rapp and Collins, for instance, describe how *Farm Journal* uses computer-collated binding to send out a minimum of 2000 different versions (and a maximum of 8896 versions) to its 825 000 readers. Advertisers of that journal are similarly matched to readers, based on computerized subscriber profiles. One of the biggest users of direct mail is Reader's Digest. Its subscriptions in 1990 made up 90 per cent of its circulation (worth $624 million). As yet, it does not produce tailored versions; but it is significant that the largest part of its business is books and home entertainment (worth $1.22 billion in 1990) – capitalizing on its vast databases (holding details of close on 100 million households).

See also COMPUTER-MEDIATED COMMUNICATIONS (CMC); PRECISION MARKETING

public opinion   *see* PROACTIVE PR

public relations The most important 'influence-able' (albeit to a very limited extent) element of secondary sources of communication is that of press relations. It can be a very effective (and very inexpensive) part of the marketing strategy but is one that many companies neglect. Although there is a limit to the amount that can be productively spent on PR, up to that point it is often the case that (pound for pound) the money spent can be many times more productive than that spent on other types of promotion (including advertising). This is just as true of a small company (which may find such PR the most effective vehicle for promoting its products, as it simply cannot afford large budgets) as for a large one. Again, though, it really needs the specialist expertise of a PR agency. PR is often a particularly valuable promotional device for services, since the 'authority' offered by independent recommendations in editorial matter can add vital credibility to an intangible service. PR is a particularly easy promotional device for not-for-profit organizations to use; the Open University, for example, has little need to advertise, whereas it is a very legitimate topic for considerable editorial comment. It is claimed that Anita Roddick built her Body Shop retail empire without a single advertisement – but with superb PR! There are a wide range of vehicles available to PR (a good practitioner of PR will use any opportunity to hand to further the cause of the client). Some of the main ones are as follows.

Media contact

One of the most important tasks of the PR professional is to maintain contact with the key journalists in the relevant media (usually national press, journals, radio and television). This is a two-way process. The PR professional learns about, and can contribute to, features which will be appearing in the media, while, in the other direction, the journalists become more receptive to news stories from the PR professional. It is, indeed, an 'investment' process. The relationship with the media (and especially with individual journalists) has to be cultivated until a mutual trust has been earned. When working properly, this is not a process of exploitation – by either side – but of mutual respect. It is significant that a US survey (carried out by Sheila Tate, press secretary to Mrs Nancy Reagan – as reported by Roger Haywood) revealed that more than 90 per cent of journalists rated 'candor' as the key quality they required in an executive responsible for public relations, and the same percentage said they were more likely to deal with PR people they knew personally.

News stories

The backbone of PR is the news item – either genuine or 'manufactured' – which shows the client product or service in a good light (and, most important, is interesting and entertaining enough to be run by the news media). Such stories are best placed by personal contact. For more general distribution (to the local press, for example) carefully written press packs (with suitable black and white photographic enlargements) also demand the attention of an expert. The most important aspect of any story, though, is that it should be 'newsworthy'. There are some parts of the press (particularly the local press) which accept less newsworthy stories (as long as they are relevant, and that usually means a local connection), but in general you get the coverage the story is worth! Consequently you need professional (journalistic) experience to recognize just what is a newsworthy story (which may not be what the amateur would expect) and then to be able to present it in a way that interests a (very cynical) press corps. PR handbooks tend to stress that you must have good writing skills to deliver such stories, but that is only the starting point. PR is like any other form of marketing: you must know the customers (here the journalists) and provide (and sell) the right 'product' (the story they want). The personal touch, such as personal delivery, helps. Surprisingly, perhaps, the same US survey quoted above showed that most press releases were read by journalists (who were even happy to be reminded, by telephone, of press events). Journalists need sources for their stories, just so long as they are worthwhile. This is tempered by a UK survey which showed that press releases achieved only a 22 per cent rating as a 'source of information most useful to your work as an editor' compared with 86 per cent for articles in other newspapers (and, rather strangely perhaps, 81 per cent for 'your own journalists'!).

Media events

One device often used is a media event – the launch of a new product, for example – which is an excuse for inviting journalists to a free lunch and exposure to the accompanying PR messages. Unfortunately, despite journalists' reputation for being able to smell a free drink from more than a block away, this rarely works as a device unless the groundwork has already been done and the personal contacts with the media well and truly established. Once again the material which will get the coverage is that which deserves it; which has been presented, and explained, in a way that attracts the attention of journalists. The US survey showed, though, that two-thirds of journalists believed that news conferences were abused as a communications technique. On the other hand, discreet use of bona-fide executives from the organization may pay better dividends. The UK survey mentioned above rated interviews with 'company officials' at 58 per cent, compared with 19 per cent for 'company public and/or press relations officers' and a mere 14 per cent for 'public relations agencies' (and, surprisingly perhaps, only 22 per cent for trade or industry associations!).

Press office

It is just as important that you are able to react to press enquiries. A continuously manned press office, which can handle any level of question from journalists and is almost effusively enthusiastic to help, is essential if PR is to be taken seriously. Again, professionalism is essential. Not least is the ability to find answers quickly, to meet deadlines – by which almost all journalists are driven. It is well worthwhile ensuring that all senior executives who come into contact with the media are trained in handling such interviews (not least in avoiding giving 'hostages to fortune'!). It is also a sound investment to have suitable executives professionally trained in the techniques of handling radio and television interviews, since it requires some skill (which few 'amateurs' possess) to make the most of these – but beware, poor training will result in very stilted techniques (which will just mean that the interview will end on the cutting room floor – unless the director wants to show your organization in a particularly bad light!).

See also CORPORATE PUBLIC RELATIONS; DEFENSIVE (CORPORATE) PR; ENHANCED AIUAPR MODEL; PROACTIVE PR; PROMOTIONAL LOZENGE; PUBLIC RELATIONS AGENCIES; THREE PILLARS OF THE PURCHASING PROCESS

Reference: Haywood, R. (1984) *All About PR: What to Say and When to Say it*. McGraw-Hill.

public relations agencies   All PR activities require the attention of expert professionals – usually in the form of a PR agency. Even if the press contacts have been made it is usually difficult to persuade journalists to come to you. Indeed, as journalists have now been dispersed all round London, it is no longer an option to arrange an event, for example, on the borders of Fleet Street itself in the hope that journalists might walk the 50 yards to it. It requires real expertise to make such PR work. Choosing a PR agency follows much the same rules as for choosing an advertising agency. It is, arguably, even more im-

portant that you meet the personnel who will be working on your account since they will become your representatives to the media. You should also ask for recommendations, so that you can see if their ideas are likely to be in line with your own, rather than a full proposal (since the latter would require too great an investment – PR agencies are usually much smaller, and less well resourced, than advertising agencies). Finally, check out (with some journalists, for instance) how good their target audience think they are! Choose the agency with the proven ability! It may be as well to use such an agency to provide the professional staff organization, which should be their forte, as a basis for developing the use of your own executives as the front-line troops.

See also PUBLIC RELATIONS

puff   An insubstantial claim made for a product.

pull   *see* FINAL PROOF

pull system   *see* KANBAN

pulsing   *see* MEDIA SELECTION

purchase decision, matching   Philip Kotler (1988) describes one model of the consumer's decision-making process in terms of matching his or her chosen attributes to the products or services which possess these. The process, as seen by him, is thus one in which the consumer first decides exactly which attributes are important. At the same time, he or she builds a picture in terms of these attributes of each of the brands. These lists are then matched against those of the 'competing' brands, taking account somehow of the varying importance of the attributes and the various degrees of match or mismatch to them. These 'attributes' are not, though, just the physical features beloved of suppliers. They include price, of course, but also a wide range of attitudinal factors. A related approach is often used by marketers involved in 'brand positioning' exercises – where the brand is carefully 'positioned' in the various 'dimensions' which are important to the consumer. This approach determines what would be the position of the consumer's 'ideal' brand if it were available. The theory is that the consumer will search for this ideal and choose the brand which most closely matches it.

See also DECISION-MAKING PROCESS, BY CUSTOMERS; REPEAT PURCHASING PROCESS

Reference: Kotler, Philip (1988) *Marketing Management* (6th edn). Englewood Cliffs, NJ: Prentice-Hall.

purchase process   *see* DECISION-MAKING PROCESS,
BY CUSTOMERS

purchasing   The purchasing function probably
has more to learn from marketing than from any
other group of management. After all, buying is – in
most important respects – the mirror image of selling! As Kotler and Levy stated in 1973:

> Buyer marketing is a valid procedure to improve
> the buyer's position. Just as sellers use various
> marketing techniques to attract buyers, buyers
> can resort to various marketing techniques to
> gain a response from sellers. Just as sellers
> study buyer behaviour, buyers may study seller
> behaviour. Marketing is a tool available to both
> parties in the transaction. Marketing scholars
> have too long looked at the marketing process
> from the seller's point of view. With the increased
> consumerist and social concerns of our time,
> it is fitting that marketers again concern
> themselves with the buyer's side of the marketing
> equation.

Indeed, it is fair to say that purchasing is still generally seen as the 'poor relation' of the management
disciplines and, as such, is grossly under-resourced.
This is despite the fact that bought-in elements often
(indeed, usually) account for more than half the total
cost of products, and sometimes of services too.
Thus, inefficient or ineffective purchasing can easily
lose far more than the best possible management can
'add value' in the remaining processes under their
control!

Michael Porter (1985) also comments:

> *Ignoring Procurement.* Many firms work diligently
> to reduce labour costs but pay scant attention to
> purchased inputs. They tend to view purchasing
> as a secondary staff function and devote few man-
> agement resources to it . . . Linkages between
> purchased inputs and the costs of other value
> [chain] activities go unrecognised. Modest
> changes in purchasing practices could yield major
> cost benefits for many firms.

Unfortunately this 'second class citizen' view is also
reflected in many textbooks about purchasing. The
purchasing activities described by these tend to revolve around routine, mechanistic, administrative
activities. Paperwork and administration are essential
parts of marketing too, but they are now rarely seen
as the most important aspects of the discipline

(though they often were in the days of its youth!).
Regrettably, them – and the regulatory bureaucracy
which accompanies they – are still too often seen as
the central function of purchasing!

The 'purchasing function' represents a critical aspect of management in most organizations. Its theory
and perspective, however, are derived from marketing. This is partly because the marketing discipline
has much to offer purchasing (in many respects they
should be mirror images of each other), but also
because as yet purchasing appears to be remarkably
thin on academic content. The main elements to be
considered in purchasing are:

- product or service
- internal customers
- suppliers
- specification

See also INTERNAL CUSTOMERS OF PURCHASING; PROD-
UCT OR SERVICE, TO BE PURCHASED; SPECIFICATION;
SUPPLIERS

References: Kotler, Philip and Levy, Sidney J. (1973)
Buying is marketing too. *Journal of Marketing,* 37.
   Porter, Michael E. (1985) *Competitive Advantage: Creat-
ing and Sustaining Superior Performance.* New York: The
Free Press.

purpose   *see* CORPORATE OBJECTIVES

push versus pull promotion   If a supplier uses
any form of distribution chain, as most of those in the
mass consumer markets in fact do, he or she is faced
with two extremes in terms of promotion:

- *Push.* In this case the supplier directs the bulk of
  the promotional effort at selling the 'product'
  into the channel (into the various organizations
  which make up the chain of distribution) in order
  to persuade the members of that channel to
  'push' the product forward until it reaches the
  final consumer. It thus tends to revolve around
  sales promotion and is sometimes referred to as
  'below the line' (derived from the days when advertising agencies managed all promotional activity – and the items on the accounts which did not
  relate to advertising were put below the line
  which divided off the agency's main activity on
  the expenditure reports). This is a technique
  particularly favoured by organizations without

strong brands which are involved in price competition.

- *Pull.* Here the supplier focuses the promotional effort (typically advertising) on the consumer, in the belief that he or she will be motivated to 'pull' the product through the channel (for example, by demanding it from retailers). It is (due to its association with advertising) sometimes referred to as 'above the line'. This is the technique usually favoured by the owners of strong, differentiated brands (such as Procter & Gambol or Nestlé).

In practice, most suppliers choose a route somewhere between these two extremes, blending both elements to obtain the optimum (balanced) effect. The art of marketing is achieving the optimum blend of the overall marketing mix.

See also ADVERTISING; SELLING

Q

Q.S.C. & V. **(Quality, Service, Cleanliness & Value)** *see* CONVICTION MARKETING TYPES; SERVICE QUALITY

qualification of prospects *see* PROSPECT QUALIFICATION

qualitative forecasting methods These methods lead to a description of what will happen using words but with, as far as possible, an indication of the scale of the impact that the events will have (in some cases this may include significant amounts of statistics – but the context will be different to that of the more normal, numeric/quantitative forecasts based on trends). There are a range of sources for such forecasts:

- sales force forecasts
- customer contact
- jury method
- technological forecasting
- Delphi technique
- scenarios
- tree structures
- networks
- morphological analysis
- Bayesian decision theory

See also BAYESIAN DECISION THEORY; CUSTOMER CONTACT FORECASTS; DELPHI TECHNIQUE; DERIVED FORECASTS; FORECASTING TECHNIQUES; JURY METHOD FORECASTS; LONG-TERM FORECASTS; MACRO- AND MICRO-FORECASTS; MEDIUM-TERM FORECASTS; MORPHOLOGICAL ANALYSIS; QUANTITATIVE FORECASTING TECHNIQUES; SALES FORCE (QUALITATIVE) FORECASTS; SCENARIOS; SHORT-TERM FORECASTS; SHORT- VERSUS LONG-TERM FORECASTS; TECHNOLOGICAL FORECASTING; TREE STRUCTURES, FORECASTING

qualitative research This covers all research which does not produce rigorously validated numeric output. Peter Sampson (1986) identifies four main categories:

- individual depth interviews
- repertory grid

- semi-structured interviews
- group research.

See also GROUP RESEARCH; INDIVIDUAL DEPTH INTERVIEWS; MARKETING RESEARCH; REPERTORY GRIDS

Reference: Sampson, Peter (1986) Qualitative research and motivation research. In Robert Worcester and John Downham (eds), *Consumer Market Research Handbook* (3rd edn). Maidenhead: McGraw-Hill.

qualitative screen, new products *see* STRATEGIC SCREENING, NEW PRODUCTS

quality In recent years there has been much discussion about 'quality'. It has become a key philosophy, of management consultants if not management, that 'quality' is important! Tom Peters (1987), for instance, reports:

> My unequivocal findings are: (1) customers – individual or industrial, high tech or low, science-trained or untrained – will pay a lot for better and especially best quality; moreover, (2) firms that provide that quality will thrive; (3) workers in all parts of the organization will become energized by the opportunity to provide a top-quality product or service; and (4) no product has a safe quality lead, since new entrants are constantly redefining, for the customer, what's possible.

In these discussions quality is usually represented by improved standards (and by less defects against those standards) – closer tolerances in production, for example, or better (higher specification) materials. But it can also include additional features. The definition of 'quality' is, indeed, almost totally variable. As a result, it is usually related to 'cost' – to the inputs rather than the outputs, since these are easier to define! The greater the cost elements included, the higher the presumed quality; and, conversely and rather easier to observe, the lower the sums spent on the 'product' (that is, the greater the cost-cutting), the lower the quality.

As you might expect in a marketing dictionary, I would suggest that, at least in this context, quality is defined by meeting the customer's needs and wants. By definition, good marketing results in high quality. The other, self-imposed, judgements as to what is 'quality' are irrelevant. It is the quality the customer wants, and this is inseparable from the total package demanded, which determines true quality.

John Besford (1987) makes the same point:

> quality as a perception is how the customer reacts to a product at first sight and his or her further reactions after using that product. Reactions will depend upon whether the product meets their aspirations and expectations. Does it perform efficiently? Is it pleasing to own and use? Is it easy to clean and maintain? These qualities communicate the image of a company to the end-user. The end product reflects a company's attitude to product development and its view of its customers, the intention being to achieve customer satisfaction. Quality is synonymous with customer satisfaction.

See also CONVICTION MARKETING FACTORS; CUSTOMER SATISFACTION SURVEY; ZERO DEFECTS VERSUS AQL

References: Besford, John (1987) Designing a quality product. *Journal of Marketing Management*, 3(2).
Peters, Tom (1987) *Thriving on Chaos.* New York: Alfred A. Knopf Inc.

quality circles   An important element of achieving zero defects has been the involvement of the whole workforce. At Toyota, for example, this starts with a 'creative ideas and suggestions' box, to be found in many locations throughout the factories. In 1986 the total number of suggestions was reported to be 2.65 million – an average of 48 per employee – of which no less than 96 per cent were accepted by management! Beyond that, though, the employees of Toyota form 'quality circles', small groups of about six people 'in which they discuss and assist each other in carrying out improvements in quality, cost, safety and so forth. Spontaneity and autonomy are particular features of these activities.' In 1987 there were '6,650 Circles active in the company as a whole, and a total of 25,000 of their proposals were implemented'.

Reference: Toyota Motor Corporation (1988) *Production at Toyota – Our Basic Philosophy.* Tokyo: Toyota Motor Corporation.

quality circles, idea generation   The primary purpose of quality circles is not to generate new product ideas; it is to talk through the current 'production' problems that the group of 'workers' are experiencing. In that context, such circles are an excellent way of bringing expertise (often otherwise untapped) to bear on these problems. They are also highly motivational for the participants. On the other hand, quality circles can often prove to be useful sources of the all-important incremental improvements to products or services. Revolutionary changes are few and far between. Quality circles may thus turn out to be a rich source of such incremental ideas.
See also GENERATING IDEAS; JUST IN TIME (JIT)

quality control department   *see* BALANCING UNDER THE INFLUENCE; COMPLEX SALE; ZERO DEFECTS VERSUS AQL

quality control, statistical   *see* NORMAL CURVE

quality management   *see* TOTAL QUALITY MANAGEMENT (TQM)

quality modification   As consumers grow more discriminating, many suppliers (often led by their Japanese competitors) have gradually increased the quality of the basic product. This 'product change' may be difficult to convey to consumers, particularly if the product already has a bad image (who wants to admit that their product was, even previously, of a lower quality?). It can, though, be very powerful if successful – as the Jaguar Car Company demonstrated with its quality improvement programme in the 1980s, and as shown by similar advances the Rover Group made in the same industry in the late 1980s and early 1990s.
See also PRODUCT (OR SERVICE) MODIFICATION

quality–price relationship   *see* PRICES, CUSTOMER NEEDS

quality pricing   *see* PRICE POSITIONING

Quality, Service, Cleanliness & Value   *see* Q.S.C. & V. (QUALITY, SERVICE, CLEANLINESS & VALUE)

quality specification   There is much talk of quality, and of 'total quality management'. Quality, though, is often 'in the eye of the user'. Thus, it is important for the buyer to understand exactly what his or her users mean by 'quality' in each situation. Above all, the buyer (and his or her 'materials procurement' department) is the one individual who is able to, and is given the responsibility to, monitor

quality levels on incoming goods. It is an unfortunate fact of life that the quality delivered by many suppliers does tend to slip over time. It is the buyer's responsibility to ensure that this is detected and rectified, so that quality levels are guaranteed.
See also PURCHASING; SPECIFICATION; TOTAL QUALITY MANAGEMENT (TQM); VALUE ANALYSIS

quantitative forecasting techniques The most important of these are:

- period actuals and percentage changes
- moving annual total
- cumulative totals
- Z charts
- exponential smoothing
- time-series analyses
- multiple regression analysis
- leading indicators

See also CUMULATIVE TOTALS; EXPONENTIAL SMOOTHING; LEADING INDICATORS; MOVING ANNUAL TOTAL (MAT); MULTIPLE REGRESSION ANALYSIS; PERIOD ACTUALS; TIME-SERIES ANALYSES; Z CHARTS

quantitative techniques In general, most quantitative techniques revolve around time-series analysis of the historical statistics, recorded in previous periods. They treat the 'systems' involved as a 'black box'. As such, at best they can only be as reliable as those statistics, and hence are best applied to in-house statistics such as sales figures – where the accuracy (and likely limitation) is better understood. 'Explanatory models', on the other hand, try to understand how these 'systems' work, so the effect of future changes can also be predicted. They are consequently more powerful, but significantly more difficult to build.
See also MATHEMATICAL FORECASTING TECHNIQUES; QUALITATIVE FORECASTING METHODS; QUANTITATIVE FORECASTING TECHNIQUES; SALES TREND FORECASTING

quantity discount *see* TRADE DISCOUNTS

quantum leap development Always assuming that the owners of the market leaders which you must inevitably challenge are not totally incompetent (though there have been some surprising losses of leadership which must be attributed to gross incompetence on the part of the losing managers), your new development must represent a quantum leap in 'product characteristics' if it is to succeed. Results show that almost all genuinely new brand leaders have depended on such dramatic changes. These are most obvious in terms of physical (technological) changes, but they can just as easily be based on dramatic changes in taste or image.
See also CREATIVE IMITATION; CUSTOMER BONUS; EXISTING PRODUCT CHANGES; FEATURE MODIFICATION; GAP ANALYSIS; GENERATING IDEAS; LEAPFROG; NEW PRODUCT CREATION; NEW PRODUCT INNOVATION; PRODUCT CHURNING, NEW PRODUCTS

quarterly review *see* ADVERTISING BUDGETS; FORECASTING DYNAMICS; MONITORING, PROGRESS

quartiles The division of results (data) into four parts, each with an equal number of results – usually on the basis of decreasing numerical values.

quasi-retailing Outlets selling services rather than products.

questioning Most people are not very effective at questioning. They ask very specific questions ('closed' questions) which tend to narrow discussion and, in particular, tend to confine the discussion to the areas set by the questioner's personal preferences or prejudices. Much more useful are those ('open') questions which allow the person being questioned to adopt a wider view. These questions (of which the simplest – Why? How? What? – are the most powerful) encourage the speaker to say what he or she considers is most important about the topic. (Examples are: What did you do? Why did you choose that equipment?) The listener can then gain the most benefit from the speaker's knowledge and expertise. Later in the conversation the 'directive' and then 'closed' questions can be used to steer the conversation to the topics of greatest interest to the listener. Thus, it is important to understand that there are different types of questions:

- open questions
- reflective questions
- directive questions
- closed questions
- agreement

See also AGREEMENT, INTERVIEWING/QUESTIONING; CLOSED QUESTIONS; DIRECTIVE QUESTIONS; LISTENING; NOTE-TAKING; OPEN QUESTIONS; REFLECTIVE QUESTIONS; SALES CALL; UNDERSTANDING

question mark *see* PROBLEM CHILD

questionnaire design The questions are the key to survey research. They must therefore be developed very carefully and skilfully. In the first instance they must be comprehensive. If a key question is not asked it will not be answered. Secondly, they will need to be in a language the respondent understands, so that the answers will be clear and unambiguous. Many words used by researchers and their clients, even those used in their daily language, may be strange to the respondents they are testing, particularly where the respondents are less well educated. Even such a word as 'incentive', in seemingly widespread use, is only fully understood by about half the population in the UK! In addition, if the form of questioning is too complex (or, on the other hand, too vague) it, too, may elicit confused answers. Finally, they should not be leading questions, leading to the answer preconceived by the researcher (or the client). The most basic fault of much research is that, as a result of bad design, it plays back the answers that the researcher expects (or even wants) to hear. The questions must be neutral, to encourage the respondent to reply truthfully.

To ensure that the questions asked are valid and meaningful, it is sound practice to pilot the questionnaire on a number of respondents, so that potential problems can be debugged before the cost of a full survey is incurred.

Morton-Williams (1986) identifies six functions a questionnaire has to fulfil:

(a) maintaining the respondent's co-operation and involvement;
(b) communicating to the respondent;
(c) helping the respondent to work out his answers;
(d) avoiding bias;
(e) making the interviewer's task easier;
(d) providing a basis for data processing.

The 'communications' elements of questionnaire design she identifies are all too easily forgotten by researchers – and confusion, as much as bias, is a (largely unrecognized) problem in much research work. It is worth remembering at all times that marketing is about a dialogue – and that means communications both ways. Clarity in the questionnaire (and in the ideas behind it) is amply rewarded by clarity in the results.

The questions to be asked may be of two main types: open questions and closed questions.
See also CLOSED QUESTIONS, ON QUESTIONNAIRES; MARKETING RESEARCH; OPEN QUESTIONS, ON QUESTIONNAIRES; SURVEY RESEARCH

Reference: Morton-Williams, J. (1986) Questionnaire design. In Robert Worcester and John Downham (eds), *Consumer Market Research Handbook* (3rd edn). Maidenhead: McGraw-Hill.

queue   In the specific context of queues associated with provision of a service, David Maister (1988) lists a number of 'proportions':

1. Unoccupied time feels longer than occupied time . . .
2. Preprocess waits feel longer than in-process waits . . .
3. Anxiety makes waits seem longer . . .
4. Uncertain waits are longer then known, finite waits . . .
5. Unexplained waits are longer than explained waits . . .
6. Unfair waits are longer than equitable waits . . .
7. The more valuable the service the longer the customer will wait . . .
8. Solo waits feel longer than group waits . . .

They are all reasonably well known principles, indeed almost obvious, yet how often have you recognized a management that has taken notice of them? Even the classically quoted recommendation, of putting a mirror by the doors to elevators so that people can spend time attending to their appearance and do not notice the delays in elevator service, seems to be honoured by the practice of putting mirrors *inside* elevators where they do not serve this purpose; but, then, the elevator manufacturers, who know of this research, can influence the design of the inside of the elevator but not that of the lobby outside!
See also SERVICE LEVELS

Reference: Maister, David H. (1988) The psychology of waiting lines. In *Managing Services: Marketing, Operations and Human Resources*. Englewood Cliffs, NJ: Prentice-Hall.

quick kill   The negotiating strategy of making the final offer first.
See also SALES CALL CLOSE

quota samples   This approach to sampling aims to achieve (as part of the process of survey research), at least in theory, an effect similar to stratified random samples, by asking the interviewers to recruit respondents to match an agreed quota of subsamples. This is supposed to guarantee that the overall sample is an approximately representative cross-section of the 'population' as a whole. The interviewer, by means of knocking on doors or standing in a busy street, is required, for example, to select certain numbers of respondents to match specified age and social categories. This clearly may be subject to 'skew', selecting only the more accessible – those who make a habit of visiting their local high street, for example – and excluding the more elusive members of the population. Though this 'non-response' has been reported to often exceed 50 per cent (and may at times approach the levels experienced, and criticized, in mail surveys), it is not recorded, and is almost always ignored. It is also difficult to apply rigorous statistical tests to the data; which does not, of course, stop exponents of this approach from applying them – and (with some restrictions), it has to be admitted, obtaining a reasonable estimate of the probabilities involved! Quota sampling is significantly cheaper than using random samples, so it is the approach most frequently chosen for commercial research. It has to be said that, despite its apparent theoretical shortcomings, it often works well, and has done so, with documented results, for several decades. As its quality does, however, depend very directly upon the quality of the interviewer, and in particular on the quality of supervision, it is the approach most likely to suffer from the shaving of quality to achieve cost savings. At the worst level, badly controlled, it may all too easily degenerate into 'convenience sampling' – which is a polite phrase for interviewing whoever comes easiest to hand, and is not a genuine form of sampling by any standard!

'Judgement samples' are a form of convenience sample whereby the researcher chooses the participants as 'typical of the population', with significant risk of bias. 'Snowball samples' ask the initial contact to suggest others for interview.

See also CLUSTER SAMPLING; DATA COLLECTION; RANDOM SAMPLES; SAMPLES; STRATIFIED SAMPLE; SURVEY RESEARCH

quotations   *see* SALES CALL CLOSE

R

rack jobbers *see* WHOLESALERS AND DISTRIBUTORS

radical innovation This arises from major discontinuities in technical development, where incremental development (bit by bit) is more common. Radical innovation can result in major changes in competitive positions.

radio The use of this has increased greatly in recent years, with the granting of many more licenses. It typically generates specific audiences at different times of the day, for example, adults at breakfast, housewives thereafter, with motorists in the rush hours. It can be a very cost-effective way of reaching these audiences (especially as production costs, too, can be much cheaper) – though the types of message conveyed will be limited by the lack of any visual elements and may have a 'lightweight' image.
See also MEDIA TYPES

ragged Printed text which is not justified.
See also JUSTIFY

rambling, interviewing/questioning One of the less stressful approaches to questioning is 'rambling'. Eden et al. (1983) report that:

> Probably the most obvious method for getting to know about the view a person has of the problem is to give him the time and space to 'ramble' around his subject. This can be an enormous strain on the listener, for it is difficult to concentrate and difficult not to interrupt. The client will wander down several alleys that seem to bear little relationship to the problem as it was labelled at the start. Nevertheless by concentrating on collecting impressions of the more general parts of the client's 'world-taken-for-granted' it will be possible to see something of what he sees and to describe something about the spectacles through which he makes sense of people and events. In the same way as interrogation methods often depend upon allowing the prisoner to ramble so that they inevitably give away 'too-much' of themselves, it seems possible that if the helper simply gives a client time

and space then he will manage to communicate much of his problem.

See also LADDERING, INTERVIEWING/QUESTIONING; QUESTIONING; SILENCE, INTERVIEWING/QUESTIONING

Reference: Eden, Colin, Jones, Sue and Sims, David (1983) *Messing About in Problems*. Oxford: Pergamon.

Rand Corporation *see* DELPHI TECHNIQUE; FUTURISM; SYSTEMS APPROACHES

random route samples A form of sampling, sometimes called 'random location', in which the interviewer is given a (stratified) random starting point and then has to follow a random route for subsequent (defined) interviews.
See also RANDOM SAMPLES; SAMPLES; SURVEY RESEARCH

random samples The classically correct method of (marketing research) sampling is to select a sample at random. A list of the total 'population' to be sampled is chosen. Usually, for consumer research, it is the electoral register, though this is not necessarily comprehensive since it excludes those who have chosen not to register. There is also the problem of those who have moved since the last time it was compiled – a group with special characteristics, the loss of which may skew (that is, bias) the resulting sample. This list is then used as the basis of selecting the sample, most rigorously by using tables of random numbers, but most simply by selecting every nth name (when it may be called a 'systematic sample'). A reasonable degree of accuracy may be achieved with samples as small as a few hundred. Occasionally, much larger overall samples (up to 30000 on the UK National Readership Survey, for example) are used in order that smaller subsamples may also be accurately observed; thus, in the case of TGI (MRB's Target Group Index), for instance, the need to follow the detailed performance of 5000 brands justifies the overall sample of 45000 respondents per year. The great advantage of random samples is that they are statistically predictable. Apart from any questions over how comprehensive the original lists

are, they cannot be skewed. Even then, results from poorly controlled research may be biased by poor sampling. This may be by inadequate coverage – due to incomplete lists of the overall population. It is more usually due to 'non-response', where a high proportion of those approached do not respond; and it has to be assumed that their responses would have been different to those who did – so that particular groups of respondents are over-represented. Whatever the circumstances, however, the statistics, particularly those related to the degree of confidence which can be placed on the results (on the sampling variability or inherent errors), are easily applied. The major disadvantage of random samples is that they are usually more expensive (and, in any case, the necessary lists may not be available). Accordingly they may be less frequently used for commercial work (except that based upon mail questionnaires) than other types of samples, but they do usually offer a greater degree of guaranteed quality.
See also CLUSTER SAMPLING; DATA COLLECTION; QUOTA SAMPLES; SAMPLES

range pricing   The pricing for a given product may be decided by the range within which it fits. There may thus appear to be an inevitable logic, derived from the rest of the range. A 10 oz pack, for example, is expected to have a price somewhere close to the median of the 6 oz and 14 oz packs. A premium price on a member of a cut-price range would pose questions; and, at the other extreme, a cut-price entry into a luxury range might do severe damage to the quality image of that range. A more specific example of range pricing comes from retailing, where it is often called 'price lining'. In this case there are a limited number of predetermined price points, and all items in a given price category are be given a specific price, say $9.99. This also illustrates the 'psychological' aspect of choosing certain price points – on the basis that customers will read $9.99 as $9 rather than the $10 it much more nearly is!
See also COST–PLUS PRICING; PRICING POLICIES, PRACTICAL

range, retail   *see* RETAIL 'PRODUCT' DECISIONS

ranked data   In this case the data on, say, differences between products is only obtained in terms of their rankings – which comes first, second, etc. – rather than as numeric measurements of their position on a scale.

See also ANALYSIS OF MARKETING RESEARCH DATA

Rank Xerox   *see* JOINT VENTURE

rate card   The price list issued by television (and radio) stations, as well as publishers, showing the prices of the various advertisement offerings available.
See also MEDIA BUYING, ADVERTISING AGENCY; MEDIA SELECTION; MEDIA TYPES; TELEVISION

rating scales   Used in questionnaires, these allow respondents to indicate the level of their response by making an entry against a numbered scale (or one based on a series of categories).
See also CLOSED QUESTIONS, ON QUESTIONNAIRES; LIKERT SCALES

rational decision-making   *see* CORPORATE OBJECTIVES

rational expectations theory   This theory, embraced by many monetarists but led by Robert Lucas and Thomas Sargent and developed into a highly sophisticated set of mathematical analyses by other economists (such as David Begg), is in general based on the assumptions that the markets clear quickly and that individuals are rational (as are their expectations) and well informed (rather than constrained by the 'bounded rationality' expected by transaction cost economics). The result is that they adjust to the predictable effects of changes in government policy in such a way that these policy changes (fiscal and monetary) are ineffective.
See also KEYNESIANISM; MONETARISM; TRANSACTION COST ECONOMICS

Reference: Begg, D., Fischer, S. and Dornbusch, R. (1987) *Economics* (2nd edn). McGraw-Hill.

rationality, bounded   *see* CORPORATE OBJECTIVES

rationing scarce resources   *see* SELLING

raw material   *see* MATERIALS MANAGEMENT

reach   *see* MEDIA SELECTION

reactions to price challenges   *see* PRICE CHALLENGE REACTIONS

readership   *see* AUDIENCE RESEARCH; PRESS MEDIA; USERS

Reagan, Nancy and public relations   *see*
PUBLIC RELATIONS

realistic marketing   The basic philosophies of
'realistic marketing' are defined as:

(a) *pragmatism* – above all, any theory claiming
    adherence to these philosophies must offer valu-
    able, practical support for the marketing practi-
    tioner;
(b) *subservience* – but it must clearly limit itself to
    being just an aid to the manager's own marketing
    (decision-making), never a replacement for it;
(c) *common sense* – and it must be explained in terms
    which mean that it can be fully understood by,
    and supported by, all those implementing it;
(d) *individuality* – it should normally be seen only
    as providing support for the specific elements
    of marketing currently under consideration,
    and should not be derived from irrelevant
    generalizations;
(e) *optionality* – and it ideally should signal that it is
    only one of a number of options, one of the
    alternative approaches to the specific topic;
(f) *incrementalism* – an especially important point is
    that its action should usually be capable of (and
    usually be seen to be) operating incrementally
    upon the factors involved;
(g) *iteration* – and this action should generally
    be repeatable until an optimal outcome is
    reached;
(h) *resourceability* – but it must take account of the
    reality of the resources – human and technical as
    well as financial – available to the organization;
(i) *integrability* – indeed it should, as far as possible,
    make clear what role it also plays, if any, in
    coordinating the operational resources across the
    organization as a whole;
(j) *investment* – the time dimension, which means
    that marketing decisions must be viewed as
    investment decisions affecting the long term as
    well as the short term, must be allowed for;
(k) *zero-level* – finally, in summary of a number of
    the above factors, any theory, such as it is,
    should be directly relevant to the situation in
    hand.

real-life marketing   *see* COARSE MARKETING

reassurance   *see* COGNITIVE DISSONANCE

rebuy   *see* ORGANIZATIONAL BUYING SITUATIONS

recall tests   *see* ADVERTISING RESEARCH

recency   The term used in direct mail to indicate
how recently people on a direct mail list last made a
purchase.
See also DIRECT MAIL

reciprocal trading   Organizations buying and
selling to each other, switching roles dependent upon
whether they are the buyer or the seller. This typically happens between different members of a group
of companies. If it is between independent organizations they may make a contra-deal, whereby they
exchange the goods or services (without payment or
with only partial payment taking place).

recommendation, services   *see* PROMOTION OF
SERVICES

record clubs   *see* PRECISION (DIRECT) MARKETING,
RETAIL

recording and organizing informal data   Even
before the advent of the Filofax, managers used to
carry notebooks in which to write notes on their
various meetings and conversations. This is an excellent habit, and forms the basis of the process needed
to convert these conversations into a form which is
then retrievable. Ideally, such rough notes should
then be converted into formal (if brief) reports which
then go into the main filing system; indeed, this is the
basis of the formal 'call reporting' systems used by
many sales forces.
See also NOTE-TAKING; QUESTIONING

recruiters   *see* RECRUITMENT, OF SALES PERSONNEL

recruitment of consumers   *see* ENHANCED
AIUAPR MODEL; PEER PYRAMID; THREE PILLARS
OF THE PURCHASING PROCESS

recruitment, of sales personnel   Recruitment is
a particularly difficult process where sales personnel
are concerned. Their quality is all important in the
sales process. There are relatively few good sales
professionals but considerably more mediocre ones,
many of whom hamper their performance even more
by an unnecessary (and often enthusiastic) commitment to the stereotype. The success of a sales team is
therefore often almost entirely dependent upon the
number of such high-quality sales personnel who can
be recruited. The recruitment process is thus probably the single most important task for sales management, and yet it is often the most neglected 'chore'.
The first requirement for successful recruitment is

that it must be taken seriously, and it must be given the resources, including the sales management time, it deserves. In simpler, more generally applicable terms, recruitment can be broken down into a number of stages:

Generation of 'prospects'
As with any sales programme, this is a numbers game in which the first task is to stimulate the maximum numbers of applicants (of the right quality). It demands the usual marketing skills (especially where it may require a 'national' campaign – compared with the strictly local requirements of most job recruitment). The task may be undertaken, at one end of the spectrum, by discreet contact with the sales manager's own list of sales professionals he or she believes would be suitable (or a similar approach by a headhunter, or an agency which has a range of prospective movers on its books), or at the other extreme, by an advertising campaign (typically run by one of the agencies which specialize in this field). Whichever approach is used, it is a marketing campaign, and should be run and controlled as such.

Creation of shortlist
Having obtained the list of 'prospects', the task is to sort out the sheep from the goats. The key to success at this stage is to have a sound, comprehensive application form which gives all the (relevant) information needed to judge candidates. Screening the application forms is a matter of judgement, but it is a process which should not be hurried. It can often best be finalized by a meeting of the 'selection committee' – since the interplay of interpretations of what is written on the forms frequently adds further insight (and prepares the committee for the interviewing process).

Final selection
The most difficult element, and the one which is most often skimped, is that of interviewing the candidates. This is all too often limited to a badly prepared half-hour of chat – which is a poor investment (for both parties) in employment which may cost the organization some tens of thousands of pounds before any mistake is recognized! There are many excellent books (and courses) on interviewing, and the purchase of one of the more reputable ones is probably a very worthwhile investment for any manager.

Having made the final selection, the rule must be to rigorously check up on references – preferably by phone, since referees are unlikely to say anything adverse in a letter but might, by the tone of their voice, for example, be rather more forthcoming in a conversation. You should remember that it is not unheard of, particularly in a profession as 'theatrical' as that of selling, for qualifications (in terms of work experience) to be more fictional than fact!

Persuasion
The one aspect which is forgotten by most recruiters is that it is also a sales process. The candidate will be buying the organization just as much as a customer, and for him or her it is a very important decision. The whole recruitment process should therefore have as a high priority selling the organization and the job. Saul Gellermann goes further, to suggest 'The only way to capture rare birds is to hunt for them continuously. Continuous recruiting may be costly but it costs less than constant high turnover.'
See also PEOPLE (SALES) MANAGEMENT

redemption procedures   *see* NON-PRICE PROMOTIONS; PROMOTIONAL PRICING

redemption rate   *see* PROMOTIONAL PRICING

reducing price   *see* PRICE CHALLENGE REACTIONS

reel fed   Printing (for example, in web offset litho, where the 'web' is what carries the continuous paper between the various stages) from continuous paper on a reel; not sheet fed (each sheet separately). Reel fed is cheaper, but demands long runs.
See also LITHO

reference customers   *see* REPEAT PURCHASING PROCESS

reference group   *see* PEER PRESSURE INFLUENCES, ON THE PURCHASE DECISION

reference libraries   *see* INTERNATIONAL MARKETING RESEARCH

references   A 'reference' is the use of information about an existing customer as part of a sales call (or as part of an overall campaign). Correctly used, sound 'references' can swing the whole sale. More than any other factor, they can show prospects that the specific offering is the safe solution – and that is probably the prime (if undeclared) objective of most buyers. But, despite their importance, the evidence is that remarkably few sales professionals ever use references (unless specifically asked for them). Some use of references will be prompted by specific queries, to which the easiest, and most effective, answer is to describe exactly how someone else has already dealt with the problem. Some references will be quite deliberately introduced to add authority to specific claims. Just a few will be deliberately introduced as an integral part of the sales campaign, where it is expected, and encouraged, that the prospect should actually contact these references for reassurance. The prospect may be satisfied with the mention of a reference, or he or she may accept (as both John Fenton (1984) and Tom Hopkins (1982) separately suggest) the evidence of a testimonial letter from the reference customer. But, if the reference forms an integral part of the sales campaign, the experienced sales professional will probably want to use the opportunity more positively, and take him or her to visit the reference account.

See also SALES CALL

References: Fenton, John (1984) *How to Sell Against Competition*. London: Heinemann.

Hopkins, Tom (1982) *How to Master the Art of Selling*. London: Champion Press.

reference sell close   *see* CLOSING TECHNIQUES

reference support   *see* ENHANCED AIUAPR MODEL; PEER PYRAMID; THREE PILLARS OF THE PURCHASING PROCESS

reference visits   *see* SUPPLIER SELECTION

reflective questions   This is sometimes split out as a separate category of open questions. These are questions, typically open questions, which are used to develop or clarify what has been discovered by the initial questions, for example, 'Why is that important to you?' They are designed to reflect on what has been said and give it some consideration or further thought.

See also QUESTIONING

refunds   *see* PROMOTIONAL PRICING

regression analyses   *see* MULTIPLE REGRESSION ANALYSIS

regressive tax   *see* PROGRESSIVE TAXES

regular users   *see* USAGE AND LOYALTY

regulations   *see* PRICE REGULATION; REGULATORY CONSIDERATIONS, FILTERING UNSUITABLE MARKETS

regulatory considerations, filtering unsuitable markets   There are a number of countries which have regulations or laws which can constrain the marketing of certain products or the activities of certain organizations (particularly foreign companies). The main areas of concern will probably be:

• *Prohibition*. Certain categories of product may be legally barred, for example, alcoholic drinks in Saudi Arabia or some Israeli products in a number of arabic countries. Less obvious are bans such as that which the US government imposes on high technology equipment being shipped to some Third World countries, especially those from the old Communist bloc, and which can apply even to products which contain only small elements of US technology (and even then perhaps made under licence).

• *Foreign ownership*. In order to protect emerging local industries, a number of countries impose restrictions on the 'ownership' of local companies. This may mean that it becomes impossible to establish a local branch, or the conditions which would be imposed are unacceptable.

• *Currency restrictions*. Because of their fragile economies, some countries have controls on the 'export' of currency, sometimes to the total exclusion of commercial money transactions. This may make it impossible to extract any profit from the country, or even to receive payment for a product shipped into the country – unless a complex web of barters (local goods taken in exchange) is set up.

• *Tariffs*. By far the most common (official) trade barriers are those enforced by tariffs. For a variety of reasons (for example, to protect newly developing industries, to control its balance of payments, or just in retaliation to someone else's tariff!) a country will require 'tariffs' (extra duties payable on certain categories of imported goods), so that imports will be at a cost disadvantage (and hence a price disadvantage – typically of between 5 per cent and 30 per cent, but sometimes more than 100 per cent) against local goods.

• *Non-tariff barriers*. Non-tariff barriers are much less obvious, though that which the French government erected by requiring Japanese video cassette recorders to be imported via Poitier was highly publicized! Less publicized are those where the government enacts special local standards (as did France and Germany, for example, before the EC harmonization of standards) which require imported products to have expensive changes made to them. Even more difficult to detect are 'structural' barriers, such as the very complicated distribution systems which effectively exclude most foreign products.

See also EXPORT MARKET ELIMINATION

reject rate   *see* ZERO DEFECTS; ZERO DEFECTS VERSUS AQL

related variables   *see* FACTOR ANALYSIS

relationship diagrams   *see* SYSTEMS APPROACHES

relationship (marketing) management   This replaces the traditional short-term transactional focus with longer-term relationships with customers; the emphasis is therefore on the timescale of the decisions. As Theodore Levitt (1983) says:

> The relationship between a seller and a buyer seldom ends when the sale is made. In a great and increasing proportion of transactions, the relationship actually intensifies subsequent to the sale. This becomes the critical factor in the buyer's choice of the seller the next time around . . .The sale merely consummates the courtship. Then the marriage begins. How good the marriage is depends on how well the relationship is managed by the seller.

Regular contact is essential to maintain rapport, to maintain the partnership. It is also very productive in terms of growing the account. Rodgers and Shock (1986) say:

> Successful salespeople understand the importance of long term customer connections. The size of their paycheck is determined to a large extent by their ability to develop sound, lasting relationships with enough customers. For the best of them, it's easy enough. They are respectful and thoughtful and go out of their way to be helpful.

The emphasis that IBM places on this aspect is demonstrated by the example of account-planning, also as described by Rodgers and Shock (1986):

> What IBM calls account-planning sessions are conducted annually. Here, both line and customer-support people spend from three days to a week reviewing the entire status of an account. With a major customer like Citibank or General Motors, as many as fifty IBM people could be involved. In the case of a small account, the session might include a handful of IBMers . . .The customer has a well documented action plan that covers the upcoming year as well as years to come.

Tom Peters (1987) suggests that a simple calculation will reveal the importance of long-term relationships and provide the incentive to nourish them: 'estimate the ten-year or lifelong value of a customer, based upon the size and frequency of a good customer's average transaction. Then multiply that number by two to take into account the word-of-mouth factor . . .'. The investment in a satisfied customer may not show on the balance sheet, but it contributes handsomely to the bottom-line profit!

See also ACCOUNT PLANNING; COMPLEX SALE; CUSTOMER FRANCHISE; INTERACTION, AND THE ORGANIZATIONAL PURCHASE; INTER-ORGANIZATIONAL RELATIONS; MARKETING TRIAD; ORGANIZATIONAL BUYING SITUATIONS; SALES CALL; SALES PROFESSIONAL; SELLING; SUPPLIERS; TERRITORY MANAGEMENT; WIN–WIN

References: Levitt, Theodore (1983) After the sale is over. *Harvard Business Review*, September–October.
Peters, Tom (1987) *Thriving on Chaos*. New York: Alfred A. Knopf Inc.
Rodgers, Buck with Shock, Robert L. (1986) *The IBM Way*. New York: Harper & Row.

relative market share   *see* BOSTON MATRIX

relaunching existing products   *see* MARKETING STRATEGIES

relevance, of research reports   Before you even look at the first page of a (marketing) research report, you should ask yourself whether the subject is relevant to your specific needs. The producers of such reports, proud of their achievements (occasionally with justification), often give them the widest possible circulation – possibly wider than they really justify. It is thus incumbent upon you, as the recipient, to decide whether you can afford the time to study it; and you should be clear that giving it all your attention may, for a complex document, take a significant amount of time. Only you can decide whether such an expenditure of time would be justified. Fortunately, the relevance can usually be deduced from a quick skim through the summary, coupled with an understanding of where the report has come from and why it was produced.

See also RESEARCH REPORTS, USAGE

relevance, segment viability   The basis for segmentation must be relevant to the important characteristics of the product or service; it must be 'actionable'. The type of pet owned, if any, will be highly relevant in the pet food market, but will rarely be so in the car market. The above may seem an obvious statement, but much marketing work is still undertaken (mistakenly) on the basis of overall population characteristics rather than those directly relating to the specific product or service, and checks for relevance are not always made. Thus, for example, in many markets the tacit segmentation has been in terms of social class. Yet the major manufacturers' segmentation of the car market, as one example, no longer follows these lines.
See also SEGMENT VIABILITY

relevance tree   *see* TREE STRUCTURES, FORECASTING

reliability, of lead time   *see* LEAD TIME

reliability, of research reports   Perhaps the most important question to ask about research presented to you, but the one which is least often asked, is 'How reliable are the results reported?'. What weight can be put on them and on the judgement of the researchers and, probably even more important, on the 'experts' who are likely to be recommending some form of action to be taken on the basis of the findings. The reliability may sometimes be 'guaranteed' by personal knowledge, though be aware that personal reliability in a social context does not necessarily underwrite technical reliability in a business context (and, indeed, usually tends to blinker those involved to even the most dubious shortcomings of the material!). A more rigorous approach would, however, be to examine the methodology (the questionnaire and sample design, say) since this is likely to give the best indication of the 'quality' of the work.
See also RESEARCH REPORTS, USAGE

religious barriers   *see* SOCIAL AND BUSINESS STRUCTURES, FILTERING UNSUITABLE MARKETS

religious organizations   *see* CONVICTION MARKETING

reminder advertising   Accounting for a significant proportion of advertising, this offers a regular reminder to those consumers who have had a memory lapse (when they break off their regular purchasing of a brand through forgetfulness).

See also ADVERTISING; MESSAGE CONSISTENCY; REPEAT PURCHASING PROCESS

rent   *see* FACTORS OF PRODUCTION

rental services   *see* CHANNEL DECISIONS

reorder quantity   *see* COMPUTER INVENTORY CONTROL; PRODUCTION DECISIONS, LOGISTICS MANAGEMENT

repeat purchasing process   In the case of those products which are purchased frequently, and repeatedly, the simplest model breaks the process of customer decision-making down into just three stages:

- awareness
- trial
- repeat purchase

This is a very simple model, and can be applied fairly generally. Its lessons are that you cannot obtain repeat purchasing without going through the stages of building awareness and then obtaining trial use, which has to be successful. It is a pattern which applies to all repeat purchase products and services – industrial goods just as much as baked beans.

Although this simple theory is typically concerned with, and limited to, repeat purchases, it is rarely taken any further – to look at the series of transactions which such repeat purchasing implies. The consumer's growing experience over a number of such transactions is often the determining factor in the later – and future – purchases. All the succeeding transactions are thus interdependent, and the overall decision-making process may accordingly be as complex as that in any industrial buying process.

Philip Kotler (1988) favours a slightly more complex model, with five stages. It places more emphasis on the earlier stages and less on the 'new product' aspects:

- problem recognition
- information search
- alternatives evaluation
- purchase decision
- post-purchase behaviour

This assumes that the purchaser is rational, and is following a rational decision-making process – an assumption which may not be justified in practice. However, it does give some insight into how the marketer may exert influence at each of these broad stages.

See also AIUAPR (AWARENESS, INTEREST, UNDER-
STANDING, ATTITUDES, PURCHASE, REPEAT PURCHASE)
MODEL; CAPITAL GOODS, REFERENCE SEEKING; DECI-
SION-MAKING PROCESS, BY CUSTOMERS; ENHANCED
AIUAPR MODEL; ORGANIZATIONAL BUYING SITUA-
TIONS; PEER PYRAMID; PRODUCT TEST; PROMOTION
OBJECTIVES; PURCHASE DECISION, MATCHING; THREE
PILLARS OF THE PURCHASING PROCESS

Reference: Kotler, Philip (1988) *Marketing Management*
(6th edn). Englewood Cliffs, NJ: Prentice-Hall

repertory grids Sometimes called 'Kelly' grids,
the aim of this technique of marketing research
is to discover what the key dimensions of the
respondent's attitudes towards the matter in hand
are (usually a product or brand – typically as part
of a positioning exercise). By removing interviewer
(and questionnaire-designer) bias whilst allowing
the respondent to give free rein to his or her own
ideas (and, indeed, 'forcing' this process), it can
give a very clear picture of what really motivates
respondents.

In this individual interview, each respondent is
presented with a list of 'stimuli' (which may be, for
example, lists of products or brands or statements).
These stimuli (around 15–20 being the recommended number) are normally presented in simple
word form, though other stimuli, such as photographs or packs, may also be used.

Three of the stimuli ('triads'– chosen at random)
from the list are presented to the respondent at a
time. The respondent is asked to choose the two
most alike (called, rather strangely, the 'emergent
pole'!). He or she is then asked to say why these two
are similar but are different to the third. The remaining stimuli on the list are then sorted equally between
these two 'poles'. The process is repeated with three
further stimuli, again selected at random, and the
respondent is asked to give another way in which the
selected pair are the same but different to the third.
The whole process continues until the respondent
cannot find a further new reason for the similarity/
difference (which typically occurs after ten or so
triads, depending upon the complexity of the subject
being studied).

A number of such interviews (10–50) are conducted and the output analysed – usually these days
by computer – to see which factors can be clustered.
This stage of the process (as well as the interview
itself) requires considerable skill if the information is
to have any worth.

The selected dimensions are then used as the basis
for more conventional (quantitative) research. Often,

as mentioned earlier, this is part of a positioning
exercise. Also as stated above, its great virtue is that
it forces the market researcher to investigate dimensions which are meaningful to the consumer rather
than to the supplier. It is arguable that this offers
such a benefit that it should be seen as an almost
obligatory part of any extensive research process –
but, in reality, this type of technique is used relatively rarely.

See also MARKETING RESEARCH; QUALITATIVE RESEARCH

replicability of test markets *see* TEST MARKET

reply-paid cards A reply-paid card (or a Freepost card – the effect is the same) improves the
chances of generating a response. As reported by
Riso (1979):

> The cheapest way to get inquiries for a product
> service is the post-paid reply card. An offer to
> send some helpful booklet, or to send some article
> of use, to a list of prospects has been known to
> produce as high as 37 percent replies at a cost of
> less than 54 cents each. Returns of five percent to
> ten percent on reply paid cards of this kind are
> common.

Better results (by a factor of three or four) can be
obtained if the reply-paid card is personalized (in
other words, the prospect's name and address are
already filled in on the card, in addition to personal-
izing the covering letter). The best results of all are
generated by sending a personalized reply form,
together with a ready-stamped envelope (using a
normal first class stamp – not a reply-paid cover).
The better returns these generate may be because
they are seen as being more personal and more committed, but this approach increases costs dramatically as all the stamps have to be paid for, even the 90
per cent that are not returned.

See also CALL TARGETS; DIRECT MAIL OFFER; PRECISION
MARKETING; RESPONSE RATES, MAILING

Reference: Riso, Ovid (ed.) (1979) *The Dartnell Sales Promotion Handbook*. New York: The Dartnell Corporation.

reporting research findings The final stage of
marketing (survey) research is to disseminate the
results to all who need to know them. This process
may require more effort, and be more important,
than the simple clerical task it superficially seems to
be. For one thing, it requires some understanding of
to whom the results may be useful; indeed, important results may have relevance to managers
throughout the organization.

Equally important, the 'language' of the report may need to be 'translated' for these different audiences. Very few of these managers will understand the terminology of market research (or, rather more important, its limitations). The results will therefore have to be conveyed in terms which are meaningful to them.

This does, however, pose some problems. It is inevitably a process of simplification, and may accordingly result in the loss of some meaning (and some of that which remains will be subtly changed). The favourite approach (at least in presentation to top management) seems to be that the dry statistics (which have probably already been considerably simplified) are illustrated by verbatim quotes from individual respondents. William Wells describes the advantage (in the context of focus groups, but the comments apply more widely): 'Instead of mysterious symbols and dull tables, there are direct quotations in which believable people give their views at length and in their own words. For many clients this is the texture of the world.' The particular, and very real, danger here is that the senior management, being thus confronted (and unversed in market research skills), will remember those comments with the most impact (particularly the ones that reinforce their existing prejudices) rather than the boring statistics!

Ideally, the results presented to each audience should be tailored to their particular needs. There is no need, for example, to inflict the detailed results of readership (no matter how important these are to marketing management) on a development team whose only interest is in what the customers want to say about the product!

The presentation of research results is quintessentially a communication process and, indeed, a sales process – the recipients of the information will usually need to be persuaded to make use of it. This will in part be by the mandatory (and hopefully well-written) report. On the other hand, perhaps the best approach (and one favoured by many marketing research agencies – in presenting the results to their clients) is a formal face-to-face (usually group) presentation. This seems to offer the best forum for communication (partly because it adds a human face to the dry data, but mainly because it allows the audience to interrupt and ask questions).

See also ANALYSIS OF MARKETING RESEARCH DATA; MARKETING RESEARCH; MARKETING RESEARCH STAGES

References: Wells, W. (1974) Group interviwing, *Handbook of Marketing Research*, ed. Rebot Ferber. McGraw-Hill.

reports   *see* WRITTEN REPORTS

repositioning   *see* ADVERTISING OBSOLESCENCE; LONGER–TERM COMPETITIVE SAW; MARKETING STRATEGIES

repro pulls   High-quality proofs of typesetting for paste-up as part of the production of finished artwork. *See also* CREATIVE DEPARTMENT, ADVERTISING AGENCY

reputation monopoly   *see* BRAND MONOPOLY

reputation of the vendor   *see* REPEAT PURCHASING PROCESS

research, audience   *see* AUDIENCE RESEARCH

research diamond   Research projects have a characteristic shape, in terms of their use of resources over time:

THE RESEARCH DIAMOND

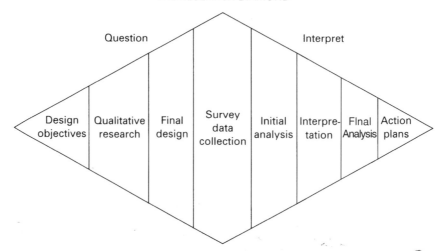

In broad terms the horizontal dimension indicates the passing of time as the project progresses, and the vertical one the number of people involved at each stage:

- *Hidden time.* The main message which emerges from the horizontal progression is that the more obvious elements where you might expect time to be taken, especially those involved in the complex and relatively lengthy process of data collection, typically only represent a minor part of the overall process. If the research is to be fully productive then the periods at the beginning, when it is designed, and at the end, when it is used as the basis for action plans, must be allowed to progress at their own pace. Rushed research is too often wasted research. Sometimes you do need answers very fast, but you must then recognize that the questions should be very simple.
- *Bulge in the middle.* It is in the middle of the diamond where the main manpower resources are eaten up (and the major costs incurred). But this is usually a matter of relatively menial legwork. Getting the first, design stage right can often reduce this bulge to a more manageable size. Thus, time spent earlier on design can often save money, and not infrequently time as well, since the later stages will have been better planned.
- *The cutting edges.* The diagram is well named the 'research diamond' since its most important features (albeit the least well recognized) are the cutting edges at the beginning and end. The most important input into research is the design objectives. If at the beginning you have only a fuzzy idea about what you want out of it, you will get a fuzzy set of results at the end. By far the most important cutting edge, however, is that at the end: the action which is generated as a result. Indeed, the focus on that action must begin with the objectives. If the research has no planned actions depending upon it, you must question why it is being done. But, above all, you must act on what you eventually find.

See also PROMOTIONAL LOZENGE

research planning The design of marketing research is a complex and sophisticated process, and demands the skills of specialist staff. It is at this stage that the initiative passes to the research agency – though the more sophisticated client will still want to remain involved. Do-it-yourself research is usually a recipe for disaster, unless the requisite skills are available in-house. Clearly the amount of design will vary, depending upon what data are required. A simple question of customer brand awareness may need virtually no design – just a single question tacked onto an omnibus survey. On the other hand, a major new piece of attitude research may require many important decisions to be made. Ideally it will also incorporate a number of different approaches to the subject, so that the results can be compared – to establish some indication of their likely accuracy. Thus, the best research may employ not just one method but a set of methods; though it has to be admitted that few organizations ever approach this ideal in their (cost-justified) research work.

See also MARKETING RESEARCH; MARKETING RESEARCH STAGES

research reports, usage Many managers find themselves on the receiving end of research reports, often those derived from marketing research. Almost as many managers, on the other hand, are poorly trained in the skills needed to make sense of such reports. As a result, they tend to read the related conclusions uncritically, accepting (or sometimes rejecting) them at their face value, usually on the basis of what they think of the researcher presenting them or whether the results confirm their own prejudices. What, then, should you do? To a certain extent the answer to this question must depend upon the specific circumstances: what is contained in the report, and what you will want from it. Even so, there are a number of initial guidelines you might wish to bear in mind:

- relevance
- reliability
- accuracy
- bias
- scope

It is only at this stage that you should start to read the main body of the report. The reason for this circuitous approach is that without it the writer of the report probably has gained your uncritical attention, and the opportunity to manipulate your judgement, as soon as you start to read his or her introduction. A good writer can permanently warp your judgement long before you get to any of the details listed above!

The subsequent stages are:

- report summary
- detailed results
- own summary

See also ACCURACY, OF RESEARCH REPORTS; ANALYSIS OF MARKETING RESEARCH DATA; BIAS, OF RESEARCH REPORTS; MARKETING RESEARCH; MARKETING RESEARCH STAGES; RELEVANCE, OF RESEARCH REPORTS; RELIABILITY, OF RESEARCH REPORTS; SCOPE, OF RESEARCH REPORTS

research techniques   *see* BEFORE-AND-AFTER RESEARCH; DIFFERENCE (EXPERIMENTAL RESEARCH); LATIN SQUARE; SPLIT RUNS

resellers   *see* CHANNEL MEMBERSHIP

reserve army of the unemployed   A term used in Marxist economics to describe the fact that there are always unemployed labourers looking for work, and this can be used to force wages down.

reserve price   Minimum price acceptable to the seller, usually at auctions.

reshoot   *see* RUSH

residential neighbourhoods   Closely targeted 'geographical' segments have been offered by 'MOSAIC' and 'PROFILES' systems, in the UK. The most widely used, though, is 'A Classification Of Residential Neighbourhoods (ACORN)'. Based on the range of census data available (including obvious categories such as occupation, household size and composition – together with some unexpected ones, such as mode of travel to work and household facilities), cluster analysis was used to derive 36 categories of neighbourhood types. These were subsequently further reduced to a simpler set of 11 types. These 11 types are now used to map, geographically, where certain types of people are likely to live in the UK:

	% of UK population
A Modern family housing for manual workers	9.6
B Modern family housing, higher incomes	7.4
C Older housing of intermediate status	10.4
D Very-poor-quality older terraced housing	9.2
E Rural areas	5.8
F Urban local authority housing	20.6
G Housing with most overcrowding	2.9
H Low-income areas with immigrants	4.2
I Student and high-status non-family areas	4.3
J Traditional high-status suburbia	19.1
K Areas of elderly people	6.4

Each of these categories can be subdivided, so that the marketer can target a mailing or door-to-door delivery exactly where it will be most productive. It has perhaps been most effectively used by market researchers wanting to select very specific samples (for mini-test markets, for example), and the retail trade (for optimizing the siting of retail outlets).

See also DOOR-TO-DOOR; GEOGRAPHICAL INFLUENCES, ON THE PURCHASE DECISION; SAMPLING; SOCIAL CLASS INFLUENCES, ON THE PURCHASE DECISION; TEST MARKET

resource planning   *see* LONG-TERM FORECASTS

respondent (informant)   *see* SURVEY RESEARCH

response, coupon   *see* COUPON RESPONSE

response rate   *see* LETTER, DIRECT MAIL; TELESALES

response rates, mailing   The great advantage of direct mail advertising is that every aspect of promotion can be tested simply by measuring the resulting response rates – sometimes referred to in the trade as 'back-end performance'. All that is required is that the reply-paid card (or the response coupon in advertisements, if these are used to supplement the campaign) can be identified to the specific element of the campaign under test. Indeed, Pierre Passavant (1984) states that 'The objective of the direct marketer is to get a response . . .'. The most useful, and most frequently used, technique is to include 'Department xxxx' (where xxxx is the number of the test) in the address; this is sometimes called the 'key number'. In this way, every element of direct mail promotion may be optimized. The mailing list can be categorized and the letter (and other promotional material) designed to have the greatest impact (as measured by response). This is a technique honed to a fine edge by large-scale users, such as Reader's Digest. Every part of the mailing, every bit of the complex package of incentives (with so many competitions and special offers that it is almost impossible to find out what the mailing is really about!) will have been tested, and selected precisely because it is the most effective in terms of generating measured responses. This testing is often carried out using 'split runs', in which some of the (randomly selected) customers receive one version of the mailing and other customers receive the one with which it is to be compared. In this way, the effectiveness of two (or more) approaches may be directly compared. An alternative would be to compare them on sequential mailings, but in that case other factors might complicate the picture. The trap into which such organizations may fall is that this incremental approach to testing direct mail may gradually concentrate on an ever smaller group of the population who are particularly susceptible to these direct mail techniques, in the process neglecting the much larger part of the population which is less susceptible (and, indeed, research shows that the majority of the population actually object to such – competition/incentive-based – approaches).

See also PRECISION MARKETING

Reference: Passavant, Pierre A. (1984) Direct marketing strategy. In Edward L. Nash (ed.), *The Direct Marketing Handbook*. Maidenhead: McGraw-Hill.

response time   *see* LEAD TIME

response to the brand   *see* USAGE AND LOYALTY

retail audits   These are designed to provide data on sales of products through retail outlets. As provided, for example, by A. C. Nielsen, retail audits are one of the most sophisticated of market research operations in terms of logistics. The concept, though, is simple. An 'auditor' regularly visits each retail outlet on the panel (which has been recruited randomly). The auditor carries out a physical stock check on the lines being surveyed. The change in stock from the previous visit (combined with the other stock movements, receipt of stock, etc., which are obtained from the store's records) gives the 'consumer sales'. These days the data from the major multiples may be input direct from their own (EPOS) computer records, but it is processed (again for 'panel' stores) in exactly the same way. Such retail audits are generally believed to offer the best results in terms of accuracy of the volumes of consumer sales and, in particular, of the value of such sales (where, for example, the memories of respondents in doorstep surveys are not a reliable source of price data). These data are the main basis for brand share calculations, as well as for the all-important figures of prices and distribution levels (and also the level of retailers' stocks, which is often very important where 'pipeline filling' in response to promotions is a feature). This information is, needless to say, invaluable to any FMCG company wishing to control its sales though retail outlets.

See also CONSULTANCIES, AND MARKETING RESEARCH; CUSTOM RESEARCH; MARKETING RESEARCH; OMNIBUS SURVEYS; PANEL RESEARCH

retail cycle   *see* WHEEL OF RETAILING

retailing   In one form or another, retailing represents a large part of the service sector and covers a wide variety of activities. Philip Kotler (1988) defines it very broadly: 'Retailing includes all the activities involved in selling goods or services directly to final consumers for their personal, non-business use'. In recent decades, moreover, the power of some retailers has grown dramatically. Robert Grant (1987) states the position as:

> A major feature of the 'retailing revolution' in the UK of the past two decades has been the replacement of the manufacturer's dominance of distribution channels by that of the retail chains. This shift in power is apparent at three levels. In terms of structural change it is seen in the changing relative size ... In terms of control, retailers have increasingly assumed control over a range of functions traditionally performed by manufacturers ... In terms of performance, the shift of power is reflected in the growth of profitability ...

Retailers can be categorized by a number of dimensions. The most obvious of these are:

- retail product or service categories
- customer service categories
- retail organization
- location, retail

See also BANKS; BRANCH MARKETING; CUSTOMER SERVICE CATEGORIES; LOCATION, RETAIL; PRECISION (DIRECT) MARKETING, RETAIL; RETAIL MANAGEMENT; RETAIL ORGANIZATION; RETAIL 'PRODUCT' DECISIONS; RETAIL PRODUCT OR SERVICE CATEGORIES; VOLUNTEERS; WHEEL OF RETAILING; WHOLESALERS AND DISTRIBUTORS

References: Grant, Robert (1987) Manufacturer–retailer relations: the shifting balance of power. In Gerry Johnson (ed.), *Business Strategy and Retailing*. New York: John Wiley.
    Kotler, Philip (1988) *Marketing Management* (6th edn). Englewood Cliffs, NJ: Prentice-Hall.

retailing wheel   *see* WHEEL OF RETAILING

retail management   Who takes the 'marketing' decisions in a 'retail' organization is rather different to the position in a product marketing organization. In the latter most, or all, of the equivalent decisions would be taken in the marketing department and ultimately coordinated by the marketing manager or director. In a retailer they tend to be split between a number of functions:

- *Estates (or property department)*. The all-important initial decisions, about location and design, tend to be the responsibility of the estates (or equivalent) department.
- *Store management*. What happens within each store tends to be delegated to the store manager, who may, in any case, be running a major enterprise in his or her own right – a superstore can have a turnover of tens of millions of pounds per year, and some 'department' stores can run into hundreds of millions! This store management will, typically, report into a regional structure and thence into the main 'line management' structure at head office.
- *Buyers*. What is stocked in the stores will, on the other hand, usually be the sole responsibility of the buyers. They, and they alone (and usually without a great deal of contact with even store management, let alone marketing!), will decide what lines are to be sold (and often at what price and when). Unlike the purchasing departments of most organizations (which are, elsewhere, often the poor relations of the rest of management), in many retail organizations the buyers are very high-powered indeed.
- *Support services*. Areas such as EPOS (the very important, emerging, area of Electronic Point Of Sale) may, though, be the responsibility of specialist head office departments.

It is clear, from this list of split responsibilities, that coordination of marketing policy in retailers may be a much more complex problem than, for example, it is in FMCG (Fast Moving Consumer Goods). It is interesting to note, however, that many of the more successful retailers are now addressing this problem and moving to the leading edge of sophisticated marketing, where, because of the closer contact with consumers, they have major advantages over many other marketers.

See also CUSTOMER SERVICE CATEGORIES; LOCATION, RETAIL; RETAILING; RETAIL ORGANIZATION; RETAIL 'PRODUCT' DECISIONS; RETAIL PRODUCT OR SERVICE CATEGORIES

retail organization   A retail outlet may be owned by one person or, at the other end of the scale, by a large multinational. The specific forms of organization may include the following.

Partnerships

By law most of the suppliers of professional services, such as solicitors and accountants, have to be partnerships. Apart from a few exceptions (the international firms of accountants, for example), this means that, generally speaking, the retail forms of these organizations are small, typically with only a handful of partners involved, trading out of offices above the shops on the high street.

Independents

Most retail outlets used to be independent ('mom and pop') stores. In Japan this is still the case, to the chagrin of Western suppliers, who find it a barrier to entry. Even in the West, though the proportion of independents has been greatly reduced over recent years, there are still many thousands of such retailers and, if the personal services sector is included, the retail sector accounts for the largest number of small businesses.

Multiples

The high street is now dominated by the branches, the 'multiple' outlets, of large corporate chains – from the supermarkets through to estate agents. These represent a very specialized form of business enterprise in which the focus is on branch management – from EPOS (Electronic Point Of Sale, which increasingly provides the raw data for remote control) through to branch accounting (which uses specialized accounting techniques to monitor the performance of each branch). Their 'economies of scale' (bulk buying and spreading their overheads across branches) give them a major advantage over their smaller competitors; indeed, some would argue that the number of branches (or at least their coverage) is a major determinant of their success.

Co-operatives

Amongst 'multiples' there are, of course, the 'pure' co-operatives – co-operative societies, now often trading under brand names. But there are also voluntary groups which tend to be sponsored by wholesalers. The overall organizational structure may be very different but within the individual outlet most of these effectively trade as independents.

Franchises

An increasing number of retail outlets are run by franchisees who personally own the outlet, but the 'format' for the franchise (how it is run, its products or services, its technical and management expertise, and its promotion) is the responsibility of the franchisor. The franchisor owns the 'format' and typically receives a commission on sales (or a margin on supplies). Examples, such as McDonalds, do not look any different to any other multiple; it is only the ownership (which is supposed to provide incentives to the manager/owner of the branch) which is different.

A slightly different form of franchise is that, such as the one employed by Benetton, which is a very powerful form of (formal) vertical integration, where even production is subcontracted (almost on a 'reverse franchise' basis) to several hundred small businesses. In this case, a supplier uses the franchise to obtain tightly controlled outlets (something in excess of 2000 for Benetton) for the products it produces. The car, brewery and petroleum industries employ similar strategies.

See also CUSTOMER SERVICE CATEGORIES; LOCATION, RETAIL; RETAILING; RETAIL PRODUCT OR SERVICE CATEGORIES

retail 'product' decisions The retailer has to produce a 'product' strategy in exactly the same way that other marketers must do. The parameters tend, however, to be rather different. The main ones are likely to be:

- *Target market.* The first decision is the same as for any marketer. It is about which market (defined in terms of the customers and their needs) to address and the position within that market to be aimed for.
- *Offering.* The next part of the strategy, and perhaps the most important one (for all the other decisions should result from it), is exactly what the offering is to be. What is it that the retailer will be offering the customers? In addition to the basic service, is it convenience, low cost, atmosphere or what? An increasing element, over recent decades, has been the growth of 'own brands'. This has been partly to directly improve profit margins, but also to improve image.
- *Place.* This may be, in many respects, the most important long-term decision since, in terms of the investment in bricks and mortar, it is difficult to justify changes to, say, a superstore in less than 7–10 years. The issues such as location and store design are therefore critical decisions for a retailer – and will have to be lived with for many years!
- *Range.* As usual, the number of items in the range (the 'assortment' to be stocked) must be decided, in terms of width (the number of product lines) and depth (number of brands per line). Within this overall range, however, there will be a small proportion of 'key items' or 'bestsellers', and (in line with the 80:20 rule) these will probably need to be handled rather differently. For example, they may be included on a 'never out' list – a list of items where very high safety stocks are held, so that customers are never disappointed.
- *Price.* Another decision about what is to be stocked is the pricing policy. This is partly in terms of whether low-, medium- or high-priced products are to be stocked, but it is also about the position to be taken on cut-pricing (perhaps an unwise decision, in respect of image if not also profit, for a store, such as Harrods, depending upon premium-price brands – though, of course, the Harrods sale is world-famous!).
- *Promotion.* How items are to be promoted is, as with any product or service, a critical decision. It is, moreover, an increasingly important one as retailers move to the leading edge of marketing and start to compete by means of the most sophisticated of marketing techniques.
- *Merchandising.* Traditionally, though, the main vehicle for promotion has been 'merchandising' – the use of in-house techniques for presenting (promoting) the lines the store wishes to push. This has conventionally been seen as separate from marketing, and usually as more important than it! The store layout, where the 'products' are located, how they are presented, how they are featured, the signage, etc. are all major promotional decisions – which are normally taken by merchandisers (and usually without reference to the marketers!).
- *Store services.* Finally, the level of support in the store has to be decided. A critical customer requirement for supermarkets is that they are delayed for as short a time as possible at the checkouts – hence the increasing use of computer-based checkout equipment, and in particular bar code scanners. In-store assistance is another decision; do the assistants in a fashion store merely offer a 'cash and wrap' service or do they offer 'consultancy' advice?

All of these decisions, and many more, will need to be taken in combination, for they will interact with each other in what is a very complex 'package' of benefits to be offered to the consumer.

See also CUSTOMER SERVICE CATEGORIES; LOCATION, RETAIL RETAILING; RETAIL ORGANIZATION; RETAIL PRODUCT OR SERVICE CATEGORIES

retail product or service categories   Consumers themselves will most obviously categorize retail outlets by what they find in them:

- *Specialty outlets.* Much of the typical high street is filled with outlets handling just one type of merchandise. Many of these, such as estate agents, are the sole providers of the 'commodity' involved. Some are the major providers, such as shoe and fashion shops. A few, such as greengrocers and butchers, duplicate what can now be more readily found elsewhere. In marketing terms, such stores will typically have a narrow product line. In fashion, for example, outlets now aim not just at women, but at women in a relatively narrow age range (say, 25–40 years) with a particular viewpoint. Within that narrow product line, however, these outlets will usually have a 'deep' assortment of products, offering a wider range, and greater expertise, than their more generalized rivals. They will also tend to offer a greater degree of personal service, as butchers do; though, recognizing the challenge, supermarkets increasingly also offer such personal service in these specialized areas.
- *Supermarkets.* In the last few decades these have become the source of most consumers' general needs, with just four groups in the UK (Sainsbury, Tesco, Asda and Kwik Save) accounting for more than half of sales across a wide range of repeat purchase goods, not just food. They have increased in floor area and product range; a typical store now occupies 20 000 sq. ft and offers up to 10 000 product lines, sometimes including fashion and furniture alongside the food. The increasing number of 'superstores' (typically based in 'out of town' locations) will double these levels, with an average, say, of 40 000 sq. ft and 20 000 lines. They are also the epitome of self-service, with even the checkout operators now relegated to feeding the computerized bar code scanners.
- *Department stores.* These used to be the 'flagships' of the retail sector, with separate departments covering a very wide range of products. They have in recent years suffered from the competition offered by supermarkets at one end of the spectrum and by specialty stores (particularly those in fashion) at the other. On the other hand,

the sector also now includes, at least in terms of the consumers' perception, some of the more diversified and successful of the specialty stores – such as Boots, Marks & Spencer and British Home Stores in the UK.
- *Discount outlets.* These specialize in high turnover at low cost – 'stack it high, sell it cheap' – on the basis of their '30 days' credit, often obtaining much of their corporate funds from their suppliers (since they 'turn' their stock more rapidly than 30 days). They usually specialize in one field.

A further split is that of high inventory turnover versus high margin (some fashion outlets, for example). This split, though, is now less important in all except very specialized, luxury outlets.
See also CUSTOMER SERVICE CATEGORIES; LOCATION, RETAIL; RETAILING; RETAIL ORGANIZATION

returns to scale   *see* ECONOMIES OF SCALE

reusable container   *see* NON-PRICE PROMOTIONS

revenue maximization   *see* BUDGETS; CORPORATE OBJECTIVES; NOT-FOR-PROFIT ORGANIZATIONS, OBJECTIVES

reverse takeover   *see* TAKEOVER BIDS

review, quarterly   *see* MONITORING, PROGRESS

rhetoric   *see* CONVICTION MARKETING

ringi   The wider involvement of managers and staff in decision-making, across the organization, is formalized in Japanese corporations. Thus, this Japanese 'ringi' system requires that any significant decision is formally agreed upon by all those involved. This takes the form of signing a ringi – a document detailing the decision. All those affected by the decision have to agree that they support the decision, by adding their signature to the ringi, before the decision can receive approval.

A somewhat similar process may be seen in some Western organizations where approval of ('sign-off' by) key departments must be obtained before certain types of decision are approved. The important differences in Japan are that all significant decisions are handled in this way, and that all the managers (at least) affected have to sign the ringi. Thus, whereas in the West the sign-off process might involve five or six signatures at most, in Japan it will typically require 50 or more signatures.

This may seem an unduly lengthy process, and indeed it does usually take longer than in the West – though, having been through the process many times, obtaining the signatures of many of the managers more peripherally involved becomes almost a formality (albeit an important one).

The gain is in commitment. Whereas Western decisions are the start of building the necessary commitment to deliver the effective implementation, the Japanese have already covered this stage. As a result their implementation phase is usually much shorter than in the West and, because the implementation phase is normally far longer than the decision-making one, in terms of the overall process they make significant gains in time. Perhaps even more important, it forces them to gain active commitment from all involved, whereas the Western equivalent may just demand grudging commitment – with all the implications for effective implementation that implies.

See also CORPORATE PLAN; EMERGENT STRATEGY; LOGICAL INCREMENTALISM; MARKETING STRATEGIES

risk   *see* ANSOFF MATRIX

risk analysis   The variability of future prospects now tends to be handled, at least in the most sophisticated corporate planning departments, by the use of scenarios which describe the alternatives. Another approach, which was much favoured in earlier decades, is 'risk analysis'. This breaks down each element of the proposed plan (costs and revenues for a new product, or just for the ongoing business) into its component parts – and then assigns a probability to each of these actually happening in the way predicted. This probability may be derived (most frequently) from the judgement of the management involved or from known statistics (as it may be in the most complex applications, such as the forecasting of risk associated with nuclear power stations). These 'risks' are then added together (often cumulatively, and sometimes geometrically – which can very rapidly escalate the risks, and losses, expected!) to give the overall figure for the product or plan (or for the competing alternatives), most usually in the form of the expected 'profit' (that is, the aggregation of the separate profits multiplied by the probability of each occurring) but sometimes in terms of the overall risk of failure (sometimes of catastrophic failure!). 'Risk management' can then be applied to minimize the potential exposures which are discovered. Perhaps the most frequently used version of this is now 'country risk analysis'.

See also PRODUCT DEVELOPMENT PROCESS; RISK, OF NEW PRODUCTS; RISK VERSUS TIME, NEW PRODUCTS

risk-averse strategies   *see* BAYESIAN DECISION THEORY

risk, country   *see* COUNTRY RISK

risk index, international   *see* BERI (BUSINESS ENVIRONMENT RISK INDEX)

risk of doing business   *see* MARKET ENTRY DECISION

risk of event occurring   *see* CONTINGENCY PLAN

risk, of new products   It has to be recognized that the development and launch of almost any new product or service carries a considerable element of risk. Indeed, in view of the on-going dominance of the existing brands, it has to be questioned whether the risk involved in most major launches is justifiable. Booz, Allen & Hamilton (1982) reported (in a survey of 700 consumer and industrial companies) an average new product success rate (after launch) of 65 per cent, though they noted that only 10 per cent of these were totally new products and only 20 per cent new product lines. These two highest risk categories also dominated the 'most successful' new product list (accounting for 60 per cent of this). New product development is therefore something of a numbers game: a large number of ideas have to be created and developed for even one to emerge (something between the seven reported in the latest survey and the nearly 60 of an earlier one!). There is safety in numbers, which gives an advantage to the larger organizations.

See also PRODUCT DEVELOPMENT PROCESS; RISK VERSUS TIME, NEW PRODUCTS

Reference: Booz, Allen & Hamilton Inc. (1982) *New Products Management for the 1980s.*

risk reduction   *see* NEW PRODUCT NEEDS

risk versus time, new products   Most of the stages of new product testing are designed to reduce risk, to ensure that the product or service will be a success. All of them, though, take time. In some markets – those in the fashion businesses, for example – such time is a luxury which is not available. The biggest risk here is not having the 'product' available at the right time and ahead of the competitors. These markets consequently obtain less benefits from the more sophisticated new product processes, and so typically do not make use of them. When to enter a market with a new product should, in any case, be a conscious decision. In relation to competitors, there are two main alternatives:

- *Pioneer*. Being first into a market carries considerable risks. On the other hand, the first brand is likely to gain a major, leading and on-going share of that market in the long term. Pioneering is often the province of smaller organizations, on a small scale, since their investment can be that much less than that of the majors (who have positions and images to maintain!).
- *Latecomer*. This offers the reverse strategy. The risk is minimized, since the pioneer has already demonstrated the viability of the market. On the other hand, the related rewards, of being the market leader, may also be missed. The solution to this, as, for instance, was practised by Microsoft, may be to move into a market immediately it is proven and then to invest heavily to wrest leadership from the pioneer before it becomes impregnable. This is not a cheap solution, since all the development work (on a range of products) has to be undertaken anyway and the battle for the command of the new market may be very expensive. Even then it may not succeed, as IBM found when Compaq consolidated its position in the portable PC market (and went on to successfully assault the desktop PC market as well).

To a certain extent this debate has now been overtaken by events. Japanese corporations have led the way to reducing development times to as little as one-third of their previous levels in some industries, such as television, and have even managed to halve it in the very mature industry of car production. To quote George Stalk (1988) of the Boston Consulting Group: 'The effects of this time-based advantage are devastating; quite simply, American companies are losing leadership of technology and innovation . . . Unless US companies reduce their product development and introduction cycles from 36–48 months to 12–18 months, Japanese manufacturers will easily out-innovate and outperform them.'

Accordingly, the choice of whether to pioneer or to follow no longer exists in a number of industries. The only way for an organization to even survive may be to shorten development times below those of its competitors.

The great advantage of product replacement is that the investment is minimized. This is both in terms of technology (where the new product is likely to use the production technology, and associated risk investment, already in place) and marketing (where the investment in position has already been made).
See also PRODUCT DEVELOPMENT PROCESS

Reference: Stalk, George, Jr (1988) Time – the next source of competitive advantage. *Harvard Business Review*, July–August.

r.m.s. deviation   *see* NORMAL CURVE

robust strategies   For all but the most sophisticated of organizations it is advisable to conduct a separate investigation of the long-term strategies needed to exploit future opportunities at one extreme and to survive major threats at the other, for these robust strategies need not necessarily be the same as the conventional (short-term) strategy. Indeed, the two sets of strategies should have very different objectives. 'Robust' (long-term) strategies are, above all, about survival in the longer term, ensuring that all the potential threats are covered. 'Corporate' (short-term) strategies, on the other hand, are quintessentially about optimizing current performance:

	Corporate strategies	Robust strategies
Objective	optimizing performance	ensuring survival
Characteristics	short-term, single-focus effectiveness	long-term, divergent-coverage
Outcome	commitment	understanding

Thus, corporate strategy requires that you find the single short-term strategy which will deliver the optimal (internal) performance most effectively and to which members of the organization can commit themselves. The classical example demands the single objective of producing the highest bottom-line profit for the current year.

Robust strategies, on the other hand, require that multiple, and often divergent, objectives are met in order to exploit the potential emerging from changes in the (external) environment and especially to guard against the whole range of threats which might endanger survival in the longer term, with the aim of understanding what these might be.
See also CORPORATE STRATEGY; GENERIC ROBUST STRATEGIES; MARKETING STRATEGIES

Roddick, Anita and PR   *see* PUBLIC RELATIONS

ROI maximization   *see* CORPORATE OBJECTIVES

role playing   A variation on the use of experts' opinion in long-term forecasting is that of 'role playing' (sometimes, in specialized situations – such as government strategy exercises – referred to as 'games' or 'simulation'). The experts involved in this play the main 'actors' involved, attempting to deduce how they might react in equivalent real-life situations. As Scott Armstrong (1987) comments, 'From a theoretical viewpoint, role-playing offers advantages over opinions for predicting the outcomes in conflict situations. It facilitates a realistic examination of the interaction among the parties. This is expected to not only improve accuracy, but also to provide a better understanding of the dynamics which, in turn, might lead to the development of new strategies.' This is, though, an expensive approach, and accordingly is little used.
See also QUALITATIVE FORECASTING METHODS

Reference: Armstrong, J. Scott (1987) Forecasting methods for conflict situations. In George Wright and Peter Ayrton (eds), *Judgmental Forecasting*. New York: John Wiley.

rolling forecasts   *see* FORECASTING DYNAMICS

root mean square deviation   *see* NORMAL CURVE

rough   *see* SCAMP

rough commercial   *see* CONCEPT TEST, NEW PRODUCTS

roughs   *see* ADVERTISING PROCESSES; CREATIVE DEPARTMENT, ADVERTISING AGENCY

rounding of figures   This is an arithmetical process aimed at reducing the size (the written length) of numbers. Thus, many figures are presented to the nearest six digits, or even six decimal places, when the accuracy may be to the nearest 1 per cent – if you are lucky! It is possible that the perpetrator is deliberately trying to convey a false sense of accuracy. More likely, he or she just did not think! The main problem is that, regardless of the accuracy, most people cannot handle these numbers. In mid-1987 the population of the UK was, at some point, 55 355 759, but a figure of this complexity is meaningless to most audiences. People cannot easily handle more than two significant figures, so the statement that there were 55 million inhabitants will be easier for them to remember and will lose little in the translation, and a figure of 60

million will be even more memorable. It is worthwhile, therefore, shortening numbers to just one or two significant figures – in terms of percentages it is even recommended that you round them to the nearest 5 per cent! This will give you, or your audience, a more immediate grasp without losing a great deal of the information content. This is why, incidentally, items are often priced at $19.95. Buyers are supposed to read this as $19 (not $20), or perhaps even as approxim-ately $10+ – and the evidence, of the amount of store pricing using this approach, suggests that it works!
See also RESEARCH REPORTS, USAGE

routine buying   *see* ORGANIZATIONAL BUYING SITUATIONS

routine purchasing   *see* PRODUCT OR SERVICE, TO BE PURCHASED

routing   *see* TRANSPORT DECISIONS, LOGISTICS MANAGEMENT

routing rules   Cyert and March (1963) describe two bureaucratic rules which often work against an orderly process of information flow within an organization:

Routing rules
> Routing rules specify who will communicate to whom about what. The most obvious, best known, and one of the most important of such rules is the 'through–channels' rule, where the organization requires that certain kinds of information be only handled through channels . . . For many purposes the standard organization chart is viewed as a rule for communication.

Filtering rules
> Information is condensed and summarized as it goes through the organization and some information never reaches some parts . . . it is clear that biases introduced in the filtering rules are real. Sales departments have consistent biases with respect to sales estimates; accounting departments filter cost data differently from other departments . . . in the long run the organization learns to provide counter biases for each bias.

Reference: Cyert, Richard M. and March, James G. (1963) *A Behavioural Theory of the Firm*. Englewood Cliffs, NJ: Prentice-Hall.

Royal Dutch/Shell petroleum　*see*
STANDARDIZATION VERSUS ADAPTATION

123 rule　*see* RULE OF 123

80:20 rule　*see* MARKETING PLANS AND
PROGRAMMES; MARKETING PLAN USE; PARETO, 80:20,
EFFECT; USAGE AND LOYALTY

rule-based product or service strategies
Product strategy is most often described as if for just
one product, so that all the activities explained,
requiring any significant investment of resources
(from initial segmentation onwards), are applied to
just that one product. In many organizations,
especially industrial goods companies and retailers,
there may instead be many products (perhaps tens of
thousands in the case of a superstore operator). In
these situations it is clearly not possible to devote
the same level of management attention to each
individual item.

Under these circumstances it may be advisable,
therefore, to introduce a 'rule-based' process. Making the 'rules' (which determine what happens to
each of the lines; for instance, whether it should be
promoted, whether it should be stocked generally or
only in certain locations, or – most critical of all –
whether it should be deleted from the range) is a very
difficult and time-consuming process. However,
once these rules are available, they can be rapidly
applied to the whole range (even if it has thousands
of elements) – although each 'decision' should still be
manually supervised, to catch the inevitable oddball
situations which break every rule!

The most sophisticated 'rule-based' systems use
'artificial intelligence', driven by computers. As they
need the (very scarce and expensive) resources of
'knowledge engineers', they are, as yet, rarely used.

A less sophisticated, but still very effective,
approach is to use simple 'indices'. Each line is given
an 'index value', calculated from a number of individual components (which are the subjects of the
'rules'). These components will usually tend to incorporate substantial elements of sales and profits

levels (though they may equally include growth rates
and market potential). But they may also cover relations with other members of the range and importance to customers.

The outcome should be a well-balanced range and
(a not negligible benefit) a much better understanding of what is really important in terms of the organization's products or services.

Formal use of rule-based systems is not very
common, but use of informal 'rules of thumb' is
widespread (and probably represents the main form
of decision-making in a wide range of organizations)!

rule of 123　*see* INVESTMENT MULTIPLIER

rule of history　*see* INVESTMENT MULTIPLIER

rules of thumb　Rules of thumb are a valuable
form of 'theory', because they offer practical help
which is immediately of use whilst highlighting their
limitations. The classic such rule is the 80:20 rule.

runner brand　*see* INVESTMENT MULTIPLIER

running parallel　*see* RISK VERSUS TIME, NEW
PRODUCTS

run of paper　A press advertisement whose position is determined by the publisher; it can be anywhere in the newspaper or magazine.

run-on　The extra copies printed after the original
order has been completed, but while the work is still
on the machine. These will usually be at a cheaper
price, since the printer does not have to set up the
machinery.

rush　Film rush, the first print after filming, to
check whether the material just shot meets the
requirements – otherwise a reshoot may be needed.

rush-hour pricing　*see* PRICES, CUSTOMER NEEDS;
SELECTIVE PRICING

S

Saatchi & Saatchi *see* ECONOMIES OF SCALE, GLOBAL; GLOBALIZATION

safety in numbers A simple principle which holds generally, but is especially applicable to complex sales. It is a basic fact of marketing life that the amount of business which can be generated is proportional to the number of prospects which can be recruited ('the numbers game'). 'Safety in numbers' is a rather more specific principle. It says that, in a given sales situation, the more people you can recruit to your side from the group who will decide or influence (or police) the purchase decision, the higher become your chances of winning that decision (and the safer your position).

This is true in a consumer goods situation where there are a number of consumers of a product or service who make their wishes known to the purchaser – the more of these consumers who vote for your product, the greater the chance of its being bought. It is especially true of the complex sale where, by definition, there are a number of powerful inputs to the decision-making process. 'Safety in numbers' simply says that the more of these who are recruited to your side in advance of the decision, the safer are your chances of winning.

There is one very important caveat to this simple philosophy, and that is the need to recognize that the decision is not dependent upon a majority vote among equals. For one thing, the voters will have different weights attached to their votes. The direct users (consumers) will often have more influence than the supposed senior decision-maker.

Most important, however, is the existence of veto power in general (not just in the special case of the 'police'). Even the vote of the most junior member of the decision-making group could, if he or she feels strongly enough about the issue, outweigh all the votes of the others (giving him or her in effect a veto). Unless the rest of the group feel almost as strongly about your offering they will be tempted to switch to a less controversial decision – and there will usually be a number of other offerings almost as good (in their eyes) as yours. It is rare indeed that a supplier has a virtual monopoly that can overcome such resistance.

It is an onerous chore, but the answer is that all the bases must be covered; all members of the group must be canvassed for their support – and for information as to whether there are any unseen vetoes in the offing (which often demands some very sensitive detective work). If a possible veto is unearthed, then the person involved should either be converted to the majority view or isolated so that their (veto) power is taken away from them.
See also BALANCING UNDER THE INFLUENCE

safety needs *see* MASLOW'S HIERARCHY OF NEEDS

safety stocks, retail *see* RETAIL 'PRODUCT' DECISIONS

Saint James model A model once popular in marketing research, which stated that consumers will buy the brand which comes closest to their requirements in terms of a 'city-block' model (that is, one which relates a brand's distance from the ideal on a number of scales and then combines them to calculate the 'overall' distance).
See also BUYING DECISION, ADVERTISING MODELS; MARKETING RESEARCH; MODELS

sale, complex *see* COMPLEX SALE

sales call The sales call is at the heart of the whole process of selling. It is what happens in the individual sales call which determines whether the product or service is sold or not. It is also the key element of the 'management of the customer interface', or management of the relationship with the customer (and, before this, the prospect who may ultimately become the customer). Sales professionals recognize this fact, as do their management, and it dominates their lives – with a great deal of mythology surrounding its processes. Perhaps the greatest myth, though, is that the sale has to be made in one call. Thus, the sales trainer's call runs the gamut from first introduction to signing the order in just 30 minutes or so! The reality is that for most sales professionals a number of months, and a complete programme of calls (supported by demonstrations, reference visits, etc.), may elapse between these two points. Although the handling of the 'call' (the selling call to a customer or prospect) may represent a 'skill' you will not specifically need, it also encapsulates many of the communications skills which managers need to sell their ideas. The sales call simply formalizes and dramatizes them, but you should be aware that they are just as relevant, though not normally recognized, in many management negotiations (or even in informal discussions).

See also COMPLEX SALE; ORGANIZATIONAL BUYING SITUATIONS; RELATIONSHIP (MARKETING) MANAGEMENT; SALES PROFESSIONAL; SELLING; TERRITORY MANAGEMENT; TERRITORY SALES PLAN; WIN–WIN

sales call close   The 'close' is, at the same time, the simplest and the most difficult of 'sales techniques', for the manager just as much as for the sales professional. It is the simplest because all the work should have already been done. It should almost be a formality, with the sales professional only having to ask for the order – which, if the groundwork has been correctly completed, the prospect will quite naturally give; after all, he is there as much to buy as the sales professional is to sell. It is a natural part of any sales (or buying) campaign. Indeed, it is the only essential part of such a campaign. Only if the sales professionals have not put in all the necessary work to win the orders will the closes be difficult. Having said that, a 'close' will not always be successful; indeed, the odds of the numbers game say that most sales professionals will be unsuccessful more often than then they will be successful. In the part of IBM where its sales professionals were expected to bring in as much business from new prospects as from existing customers, they rarely lost customers; the sales professional earned his keep here by maximizing the size of the order. But in the case of prospects, where they faced severe competition, even they were lucky to win perhaps 30 per cent of the business. For every one close where they were successful there were at least two others where they were unsuccessful. But even if they did not expect to win every sale (as many pundits imply you should), they always closed. If you are going to lose the business it is still better that you should know, so that you can redeploy your resources and concentrate on winning the next time. If winning really is difficult, closing should not be.

The difficulty for many sales professionals is introduced by the psychology of the situation. Sales personnel are naturally results oriented, and only one result counts: winning the order. The effort (involving perhaps months of work) is all to be decided on a single word: 'yes' or 'no'. It is much easier in the environment where the investment of effort has just been two or three minutes – for example, selling to retailers – and the next 'sale' is also only two to three minutes away (whereas for a sales professional trying to make a sale of capital goods it may be as many months before his next prospect closes). For the sales professional his whole reputation rests on the one word – at least until his next close. It is often said that a sales professional's reputation is only as good as his last order. Memories can be very short in the sales game. The result is that most sales professionals approach the close with trepidation, and many with something akin to panic. As Alfred Tack (1975) says, 'The average salesman so rarely asks for a decision. This is due to timidity or fear . . . Every buyer knows why salesmen are employed. Yet possibly as many as 30 per cent of all orders are lost because salesmen will not ask the direct question, "May I have the order?"'

The normal close, therefore, is one not described by any of the pundits, it is the 'default close'. The prospect (rather than the sales professional) eventually gives the order to the sales professional. If Tack is to be believed, and my own experience (both as a sales manager and, particularly, as a buyer) supports his evidence, it is normally the prospect who closes; and it is he who is therefore totally in control during the critical phase of finalizing the order. It should be a natural process. As Tack says, every buyer is well aware that the sales professional is going to ask for the order (though the above evidence suggests that the buyers are somewhat optimistic in this view!). The buyer will not have been entertaining the sales professional for so long purely as a social duty; the buyer, just as much as the seller, is dependent on the order being placed. Yet sales professionals still fudge the issue. At its most ludicrous extreme, many sales professionals prefer to ask for an order in a letter rather than face-to-face. As Alfred Tack, once more, says, 'Many salesmen, asked to submit quotations, lose orders because they substitute the GPO [Post Office – Mail] for themselves'.

See also SALES CALL

Reference: Tack, Alfred (1975) *How to Succeed in Selling.* New York: Tadworth, World's Work.

sales call opening   In some respects, the opening is the most critical part of any call – though not necessarily of the typical management discussion, which usually has a more relaxed start. The first few minutes of the sales call set the tone for all that follows. The impact of those first few moments has been most extensively documented in the context of job interviews, where it is reported that the decision is usually made within the first three or four minutes, the remaining time just being used to justify that decision. The sales call is not as clear cut as this, but those first few minutes are still critical. For most sales professionals the opening is also the most difficult part of the call. It seems to be expected of sales professionals (at least by themselves) that they should start every call with a bouquet of social niceties. They talk about the weather, about sport, about television, about almost anything but business. On the other hand, Alfred Tack (1975) refers to these introductory niceties as the 'chat gap', and he stresses that the best sales professionals aim to minimize this unproductive gap. IBM sometimes characterized the opening as 'earning the right'. Indeed, there is often no real need for anything but the briefest of social niceties (though the social conventions must still be followed). The one thing that any sales professionals and their prospects are certain to have in common is not golf or a love of television soap-operas – it is business. The one justification for being there, and hopefully not wasting the prospect's time, is again his business. So the sooner they both get down to business, the better for all concerned!

Reference: Tack, Alfred (1975) *How to Succeed in Selling.* New York: Tadworth, World's Work.

sales campaign   *see* COMPLEX SALE; DEMONSTRATIONS; PRESENTATIONS; PROJECT MANAGEMENT; PROPOSALS

sales force (qualitative) forecasts   Sales forecasts normally tend to be viewed as quantitative, since they typically result from forecast sales figures which are obtained from each salesperson (which may, in turn, be derived from customers' forecasts). They are then aggregated to give the total forecast. In reality, despite their apparent numerical accuracy, they fundamentally incorporate the qualitative judgement of each salesperson. Producing such composite forecasts, where sales personnel are typically either unduly optimistic or unduly pessimistic, is a skill or art which few sales managers possess. It can usually only be gained by long experience of the group dynamics within a specific sales force. A particular problem with this technique is that it is often used (by IBM, for instance) in conjunction with commission systems, where the sales professional, in submitting his or her 'forecast', is very aware that this will also be used as the basis for the

following year's targets (and hence that sales professional's income!). The process becomes, therefore, not one of forecasting but one of negotiating targets. This is a poor basis for 'unbiased' forecasts. However, it does have the (perhaps dubious) advantage that the resulting 'budget' (or target) is likely to be achieved, since the sales professional responsible for its implementation is already committed to its achievement! A more sophisticated, and time-consuming, version of this is to survey (but again probably using the sales force) all customers to record their buying intentions for the coming year.
See also QUALITATIVE FORECASTING METHODS

sales forecast   *see* FORECASTS INTO BUDGETS; TERRITORY SALES PLAN

sales funnel   *see* CONTROL, OF SALES PERSONNEL; PROSPECT QUALIFICATION

sales leads   *see* DIRECT MAIL ADVERTISING

sales manpower budget   *see* MANPOWER PLAN, SALES

sales manpower plan   *see* MANPOWER PLAN, SALES

salesman stereotype   One factor, above all others, overshadows most aspects of selling, and it is a totally artificial one. It is, though, essential to describe it, for it often largely determines the nature of the buyer–seller relationship. This factor is the 'stereotype' of the 'salesman' as the slick untrustworthy huckster, most notably characterized by Arthur Miller in the form of his salesman, Willy Loman – a characterization which was keenly felt by a whole generation of sales people. Even IBM's Buck Rodgers, for example, felt constrained to say 'Today's salesperson has to be a lot more to the customer than a genial back-slapping, joke-telling Willy Loman, who drops in each season to entertain and show his wares'. Unfortunately, the stereotype is all pervasive. For the rest of society the 'salesman' is to be despised, to be feared or even to be pitied. Miller, Heiman and Tuleja tell the story: 'when we asked a senior vice-president if "sales" was considered a dirty word by his people. "Oh, no" he assured us "Everybody is really on board with the importance of selling. But" he went on without batting an eye "we call it marketing."' This problem, of the poor opinion society holds of the sales 'profession', is beyond the scope of this entry. But what is important is that many members of the sales profession themselves hold very similar views! The relationship, in this all pervasive scenario, is seen as aggressively competitive; a 'zero-sum game' where the sales professional can only win by the customer losing. It is an environment in which the only contribution the sales professional has to make is the skilled use of techniques of deception. There are, of course, many exceptions to this stereotype, in terms of both individuals and whole sales forces. In its heyday IBM's mainframe sales force, for example, based on an almost academic pursuit of excellence (and training at a level which was effectively postgraduate), conducted near-perfect marketing, passing any definition of good marketing with flying colours. The enviable success of this sales force at that time, though, may be directly linked to this level of professionalism. Its subsequent fall from grace may be as closely related to its abandonment of many of these principles! In any case, it is as yet a fact of life that few other sales forces follow this excellent model. The stereotype is still the model for most organiza-

tions. It is well worth checking exactly what the situation in your own organization is.

See also COMPLEX SALE; ORGANIZATIONAL BUYING SITUATIONS; SALES PROFESSIONAL; SELLING; TERRITORY MANAGEMENT; WIN–WIN

References: Miller, Robert B., Heiman, Stephen E. and Tuleja, Tad (1985) *Strategic Selling.* New York: William Morrow.

Rodgers, Buck with Shock, Robert L. (1986) *The IBM Way.* New York: Harper & Row.

sales (marketing) management In many organizations, perhaps most, the 'sales manager' is responsible for all marketing activities. Even in those where there is a parallel marketing structure, he or she is usually responsible for a range of marketing activities beyond those of simply managing the sales force. In this context, therefore, the sales management role often requires an appreciation of the range of techniques. The complexity of the wider role is particularly well illustrated by the factors below, described by Lyonski and Johnson (1983):

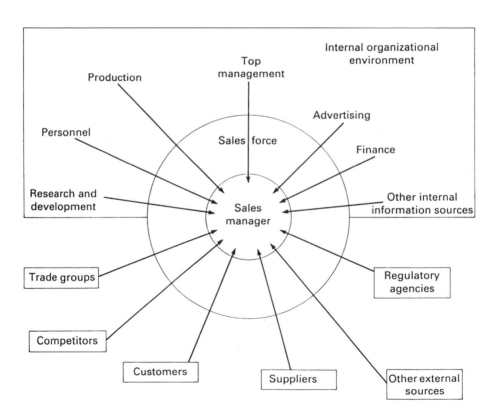

It is important to realize, however, just how important this 'marketing' aspect is in the sales man-

ager's role. What is more, it is one which is all too frequently neglected when the sales manager is under pressure to achieve results in the short term!

See also COMPLEX SALE; SALES PROFESSIONAL; SALES TEAM MANAGEMENT; SELLING; TERRITORY MANAGEMENT

Reference: Lyonski, Steven J. and Johnson, Eugene M. (1983) The sales manager as a boundary spanner: a role theory analysis. *Journal of Personal Selling and Sales Management*, November.

salesmen 'tricks'   *see* SALES TRAINING

sales organizer   A presentation kit (sales aid), in which the material (typically brochures) they want to use is organized, used by sales personnel when making a call. Sometimes this is called a portfolio.
See also SALES CALL

sales patch   *see* TERRITORY MANAGEMENT

sales pitch   *see* PITCH

sales plan   *see* ACCOUNT PLANNING

sales professional   The basic building block of all sales operations is the individual sales professional. His or her actions will build up to produce the overall sales impact. Individual sales activities are conventionally not treated as management activities, but they are as much 'tools' of marketing as any of the other techniques. Accordingly, you should appreciate what they imply; and thus what lies behind one of the most important operations of almost all commercial organizations (and, probably under a different name, such as 'client services', of many not-for-profit organizations as well).
See also CALLS AVAILABLE ANNUALLY; INDIVIDUAL MANAGEMENT OF SALES; MANPOWER PLAN, SALES; SALESMAN STEREOTYPE; SALES TRAINING; SELLING; TERRITORY MANAGEMENT; TERRITORY SALES PLAN

sales promotion   Using the British terminology, sales promotion is normally an adjunct to personal selling or advertising; usually of products, but some techniques can also be applied to services. Kenneth Runyon (1984) succinctly defines its key characteristics as:

1.   A relatively short-term activity.
2.   Directed towards sales force, distribution channels, or consumers, or some combination of these groups.

3.   Used in order to stimulate some specific action.

It covers a wide range of possibilities, as demonstrated by the list on the next page, developed by Malcolm McDonald (1984) – to which 'sponsorship' (typically of events, such as sports meetings), which a growing number of companies are using to get in front of the public, should be added.

Unlike most other forms of promotion (such as advertising, which can be considered, at least in part, to have a cumulative effect over the longer term – and hence can be considered as partly an investment), sales promotions are almost always developed to have a direct, and immediate, effect. As a result the extra sales should be directly linked to the sales promotion. Each such sales promotion can, and should, be set specific performance objectives (usually additional sales – but possibly greater display at point of sale, though this too should lead to greater sales). The performance should be monitored to ensure that these objectives are attained, and as a basis for judging the usefulness of such promotions in similar future situations. The exception to this rule of measurement of results may be those many promotions which are run solely as an 'incentive' for the retailer to give additional (temporary) support to the brand.
See also MARKETING STRATEGIES; PRECISION MARKETING; PROMOTIONAL LOZENGE; SALES PROMOTION ADVANTAGES AND DISADVANTAGES

References: McDonald, Malcolm H. B. (1984) *Marketing Plans: How to Prepare Them, How to Use Them*. London: Heinemann.
   Runyon, Kenneth E. (1984) *Advertising* (2nd edn). New York: Charles E. Merrill Publishing.

sales promotion advantages and disadvantages
The essence of sales promotion is that it is intended as a very-short-term influence on 'sales'. It typically has an insignificant effect long term, but may be used as a powerful additional factor added to the competitive balance and sales promotion; in the short term, to sway sales in the supplier's favour and to bring forward sales, or even to generate extra sales.

Advantages
• *Sales increase.* The main benefit, therefore, must usually be the short-term increase in sales.
• *Defined target audience.* They can be, if required, targeted on specific groups (especially selected retailers and their customers).

Type of promotion

Target market	Money		Goods		Services	
	Direct	Indirect	Direct	Indirect	Direct	Indirect
Consumer	Price reduction	Coupons Vouchers Money equivalent Competitions	Free goods Premium offers (e.g. 13 for 12) Free gifts Trade-in offers	Stamps Coupons Vouchers Money equivalent Competitions	Guarantees Group participation events Special exhibitions and displays	Co-operative advertising Stamps, coupons Vouchers for services Event admission Competitions
Trade	Dealer loaders Loyalty schemes Incentives Full-range buying	Extended credit Delayed invoicing Sale or return Coupons Vouchers Money equivalent	Free gifts Trial offers Trade-in offers	Coupons Vouchers Money equivalent Competitions	Guarantees Group participation events Free services Risk reduction schemes Training Special exhibitions, displays Demonstrations Reciprocal trading schemes	Stamps, coupons Vouchers for services Competitions
Salesforce	Bonus Commission	Coupons Vouchers Points systems Money equivalent	Free gifts	Coupons Vouchers Points systems Money equivalent	Free services Group participation events	Coupons Vouchers Points systems for services Event admission

- *Defined role.* They can also be targeted to achieve specific objectives: to increase repeat purchase, to recruit specific competitors' customers, etc.
- *Indirect roles.* They can also be used to achieve other objectives; for instance, to widen distribution or 'shelf facings' (by offering extra benefits to specific retailers, say).

Disadvantages
- *Short term.* Almost all their effect is immediate. There is rarely any lasting increase in sales.
- *Hidden costs.* Many of the costs, not least the management/sales force time and effort, do not appear in the direct costs.
- *Confusion.* They can conflict with the main brand messages and confuse the customer as to what the image really is. It is believed, for instance, that Burger King's promotional activities, in its war with McDonalds at the end of the 1970s, may have actually had an unfavourable influence on consumers' brand perceptions!
- *Price-cutting.* Perhaps the worst disadvantage, which applies to many types of promotion, is that they in effect offer a price cut; this persuades users to expect a lower price in future – as well as, at the same time, potentially damaging any element of 'quality' in the image.

Perhaps its greatest disadvantage, though, may be its lack of effectiveness. Abraham and Lodish (1990) report that 'only 16% of the trade promotion events we studied were profitable, based on incremental sales of brands distributed through retailer warehouses. For many promotions the cost of selling an incremental dollar of sales was greater than one dollar.' They go on to record that, despite this, 'promotions have become so popular that they now account for more than 65% of typical marketing budgets'.
See also PRECISION MARKETING

Reference: Abraham, Magid M. and Lodish, Leonard M. (1990) Getting the most out of advertising and promotion. *Harvard Business Review*, May–June.

sales promotional plans and research In exactly the same way as for advertising, the objectives for each sales promotion should be carefully defined; and its subsequent performance monitored – perhaps by sales, or sometimes by research (though the very specific nature of many promotions means that lessons learned may not be generally applicable). Sales promotions can also be pre-tested, on the smaller scale (often in just one store/residential neighbourhood), to check that they will work. The message, which is not understood by many of those organizations which are the perplexed users of promotional techniques, is that market research is just as applicable to (and just as beneficial for) promotion as it is to the product or service itself.
See also SALES PROMOTION

sales reports *see* WRITTEN REPORTS

sales results *see* MONITORING, PROGRESS

sales skills courses There are almost as many sales training courses as there are sales training books; one spawns the other. If you wanted, you could probably attend a new one every day, and you could learn how to negotiate (the buzzword for discounting!), how to close that sale and how to make a million – all in less than a week. The problem is that the great majority of such courses are delivered by presenters who appear to be rather more interested in making a million themselves than in helping you make one. It is significant that the opinion amongst many sales trainers (with a few honourable exceptions) seems to be that they can teach a sales professional all he needs to know for the rest of his or her 'professional' life (in what should be one of the most skilled occupations) in just three days; and then can teach all the skills of sales management in a further three days. This probably says more about the naivety of these sales trainers than the lack of skills needed by sales personnel. IBM took more than a year, with training which was at the postgraduate level, to produce its own sales professionals – and the difference was obvious in their performance! Miller et al. (1985) comment: 'Many sales-training systems actually encourage manipulation and deceit, by teaching salesmen "tricks" and "techniques" for getting the order in spite of what the customer really wants'. There are some good training courses, but they are in the minority; and it is difficult to find them amongst all the colourful claims made in the brochures. The best approach is to ask for independent advice, such as that in the UK from the Chartered Institute of Marketing, which also runs its own courses as part of a programme leading to a professional qualification. In any case, as Alfred Tack (1983) simply says, 'There is no substitute for experience'.
See also PEOPLE (SALES) MANAGEMENT

References: Miller, Robert B., Heiman, Stephen E. and Tuleja, Tad (1985) *Strategic Selling.* New York: William Morrow.

Tack, Alfred (1983) *How to Succeed as a Sales Manager.* London: The Windmill Press.

sales team management   In many respects sales management has been a neglected part of management, certainly in terms of the teachings of business schools and management textbooks. Yet the role of sales manager – managing the totality of the interface with the customer – is probably the most critical of all, in terms of ultimate success for the organization. Alfred Tack says 'Surely, there is no other executive requiring the all-round knowledge of the competent sales manager or sales director. The accountant, or even the financial director, need possess no understanding of salesmanship, direct mail or advertising – but the sales manager must have an appreciation of finance, budgetary control and cash flow.'

See also COMPLEX SALE; SALES PROFESSIONAL; SELLING; TERRITORY MANAGEMENT

Reference: Tack, Alfred (1983) *How to Succeed as a Sales Manager.* London: The Windmill Press.

sales territories   *see* TERRITORY PLANS

sales trainers   *see* ACCOUNT PLANNING; PROSPECT QUALIFICATION; SALES CALL; SALES TRAINING

sales training   The most important training, in the context of this entry, is that which impinges on the sales professional's primary skills, on the 'techniques' of selling. But these must be put in perspective. They are only a part of the training of a sales professional, even if they usually represent the whole income of most sales trainers – which fact may explain their preoccupation with them (to the exclusion of other, equally important, matters). Specific 'sales training' typically represented only about a quarter of IBM's 'sales' training programmes, with the other three-quarters given over to knowledge training in the products, technical and business areas – but (where these were seen as the key elements of sales training) still under the supervision of, and largely taught by, the sales training staff. There was no distinction between these elements; all was sales training, with the aim of producing the well-rounded sales professional – which aim was demonstrably achieved, since the IBM sales force had the reputation of being the best in the world (as also had its sales trainers). Unlike almost all other sales training programmes, even the specific sales training in IBM was not wedded to techniques. It was deliberately designed to allow each individual sales professional to develop his or her own unique, 'well-rounded' style. The core of the IBM sales training programme was a series of 'dummy calls'. The principle was simple: it was to simulate real calls (in every respect possible) – for the trainees to learn by experience. Each trainee made perhaps 20–30 calls each, and saw another 100 or so made by his or her fellows. These trainees learnt their skills by experience. The most widely used internal training, though, is 'field training', typically given by the sales professional's own manager accompanying him or her 'on the job'.

See also PEOPLE (SALES) MANAGEMENT; SALES SKILLS COURSES

sales trend forecasting   This is the 'scientific' approach favoured by most managements, since it is seen to project forward the historical trends they have already observed. Thus, if sales have increased by 15 per cent for each of the previous three years, the assumption will be that they will also increase by 15 per cent in the coming year (or 20 per cent if the management feel optimistic!). The 'fishbone effect', as just one example, may sometimes invalidate these confident assumptions. The simplest form of forecasting, and that most often undertaken, is that handled 'manually', or at least by using the now omnipresent electronic pocket calculator or even the personal computer – the processes are still simple 'mechanized' analogues of the manual processes. These forecasts project the trends shown by (recent) historical sales figures. Despite its apparent factual basis, this is still best viewed as a variation on pure judgement. Clearly, these 'naive' manual techniques do not seem to have the power of some of the more sophisticated mathematical techniques. On the other hand, they have great strengths. Not least is the fact that the element of judgement is (or at least should be) recognized, giving a greater awareness of their limitations. The more sophisticated techniques have almost as many assumptions built into them, but (because these 'value judgements' are not immediately obvious) they tend to be seen (incorrectly) as having inherently greater accuracy. Indeed, the greatest strength of all of the simplest techniques is that the users of the forecasts, just as much as the forecasters, understand how they are derived, and can accordingly make the best use of them – in full knowledge of their inherent limitations.

See also MATHEMATICAL FORECASTING TECHNIQUES; QUALITATIVE FORECASTING METHODS; QUANTITATIVE FORECASTING TECHNIQUES

sales variance   *see* MONITORING, PROGRESS

same size An instruction (commonly abbreviated to SS) to a printer to work to the same size as the original.

sample (batch) control *see* NORMAL CURVE

sample case A case in which are contained, typically in the form of a display, the samples the salesperson will need in a sales call.
See also SALES CALL

sample, free *see* DIRECT MAIL ADVERTISING

sample inspection *see* ZERO DEFECTS VERSUS AQL

sample, multistage *see* STRATIFIED SAMPLE

samples In marketing research the basic principle of sampling (derived from statistical theory) is that you can obtain a representative picture of a whole 'population' (the term used by theorists to describe the total group of people, or objects, being investigated) by looking at a small 'sample' (usually, in this context, of only a few hundred – which in this way may give an accurate picture of an overall population of millions). This applies to testing grain sold by the farmer just as much as it does, here, to market research. It is, needless to say, a very cost-effective way of obtaining information. Samples are a somewhat academic subject. They are, however, important in terms of understanding the accuracy (in terms of just how representative of the overall population they may be) of the results which emerge; and (as they represent a large part of the costs involved) they offer a good indication of the quality of the work being carried out. The overall theory is summarized by Michael Baker:

> Sampling is based on two fundamental principles of statistical theory which are usually termed 'The Law of Statistical Regularity' and 'The Law of Inertia of Large Numbers'. The first law holds that any group of objects taken from a larger group of such objects will tend to possess the same characteristics as the larger group. The second law holds that large groups are more stable than smaller groups owing to the compensating effect of deviation in opposite directions.

To guarantee a known 'accuracy', the respondents to any respectable market research should, at least in theory, be chosen to offer a statistically valid sample,

so that valid statistical analyses may be undertaken. There are a number of ways such a sample may be chosen. The two main approaches are random samples and quota samples.
See also DATA COLLECTION; QUOTA SAMPLES; RANDOM SAMPLES; SAMPLING STATISTICS

Reference: Baker, Michael J. (1985) *Marketing: An Introductory Text* (4th edn). Macmillan.

sampling This is generally the most powerful form of promotion for 'new products' (always presuming that the 'product' is demonstrably better than its competitors) where the immediate aim is to obtain 'trial' by users – and a free sample offers just this. It is normally used as one of the very early elements in a 'new product' launch. Interestingly, though, Schultz and Robinson say 'Sampling seems to work best for new products when it is preceded by four to six weeks of advertising. That generates interest which the sample then converts into trial.' For example, to follow the launch of Radion detergent, Target Group (on behalf of its client, Lever Brothers) delivered 200 g trial packs of this product to ten million households in the UK. It is a very expensive promotional device; often less cost effective than any of the other forms of promotion. But it is the most effective, direct and immediate way of obtaining consumer trial. Retailers also recognize its power to pull in customers, and it may accordingly also help to achieve distribution. It is often, indeed, combined with a money-off voucher, to ensure that a successful trial is rapidly followed by a purchase. Thus, the Radion sample mentioned above also carried a '20p off' coupon.

Sampling is better than coupons at obtaining trial, though some of this advantage is clawed back where coupons have a higher conversion rate (from trial to users).

There are a variety of methods of getting such samples to the prospective users:

- *Door-to-door.* This is the most direct form of delivery, and can be closely targeted (using residential neighbourhoods, ACORN, say). It offers a very high rate of trial, but is very expensive and requires a great deal of administrative/management time and effort.
- *Other delivery methods.* Samples can also be sent by direct mail or given away with media (inserts in women's magazines, for instance), though both of these approaches are limited in the range of sample types they can handle. They can also be handed out in-store or at events.

- *'Piggy-back' sampling.* A special form of sampling is to offer the free 'sample' (usually a small pack of it) banded to another product. This benefits the other product, since it represents a free offer, as well obtaining trial for the product being sampled. It is expensive, however; the sample packs typically have to be larger than normal samples (to make them look worthwhile), and to this must be added the cost of the special production runs for the other product.
- *Trial size.* The product can, of course, be sold in a special size designed for trial.

See also PRECISION MARKETING

Reference: Schultz, Don E. and Robinson, William A. (1982) *Sales Promotion Essentials.* New York: Crain Books.

sampling frame   This is a technical term used to describe the population from which a (survey research) sample is drawn.
See also DATA COLLECTION; SAMPLES

sampling, industrial markets   All forms of (survey research) sampling are most difficult to apply in industrial goods markets. At one extreme so few customers, in total, may be involved that a typical survey will cover them all (and a survey with a 100 per cent coverage of the population is a 'census'). At the other, there may be many thousands of ill-defined, and difficult to reach, potential customers and end-users; here the sampling universe is almost impossible to specify, and response rates are so low (where the mail questionnaire is the usual vehicle) as to prompt doubts as to the validity of the results.
See also DATA COLLECTION; SURVEY RESEARCH

sampling new users   *see* DOOR-TO-DOOR

sampling statistics   It is assumed, based on statistical theory, that the results of sample surveys (more specifically those using random samples) will follow a 'normal' curve ('normal' here being used in a particular, statistical sense to describe a symmetrical bell-shape curve). Under these circumstances, the statistical chance of deviation from the mean (the central part of the curve – which can loosely be thought of as the average) is given by the 'standard error'. This, statistically, means that 68% of any results would lie within one 'standard error' of the mean, and 95% within two standard errors.

The equation giving the standard error is:

standard error (SE) = $\sqrt{(p(100 - p)/n)}$

where p is the percentage of the population having the 'attribute' being measured and n is the sample size.

Thus, for example, if 1000 households are included in the sample and we find that 10% of them record the behaviour we are measuring, then (assuming the sample is truly random) we can calculate that:

SE = $\sqrt{(10(100 - 10)/1000)}$ = 0.3%

This would enable us to say that we were 68% 'confident' that the result lies between 9.7 and 10.3%; and 95% confident that it was between 9.4 and 10.6%. If, on the other hand, the sample was just 400, then the range within which we could be 95% confident would need to be much wider (between 7 and 13% – as the standard error would be 1.5%). It is clear, therefore, why sample sizes often approach 1000 respondents.

What is less obvious is that the absolute level of error is higher at around 50%. For example, again with a sample size of 400, a result of 50% could be (at the 95% confidence level) anywhere between 45 and 55%:

SE = $\sqrt{(50(100 - 50)/400)}$ = 2.5%

In other words, the less clear the respondents' decision (50:50 is the worst split) the less the accuracy! It also means that, as the standard error applies to each result, in the above case one could not say (at the 95% confidence level) that a 55% brand share, for example, was actually greater than one of 45% so recorded! As much of the interest in market research revolves around such marginal differences, this is yet another argument for using larger sample sizes (of, say, around 1000), since the accuracy quadruples as the sample size doubles.

This is an important statistical equation (in terms of understanding how the accuracy of market research may be judged). What must not be ignored, however, is that much of market research is not based on random samples and, accordingly, such statistical measures of accuracy cannot be applied!

These days, in any case, they are normally calculated as part of computer analysis packages; and here the necessary 'skill' is knowing which is the best expert to use – and how much reliance can be placed on his or her judgement!
See also DATA COLLECTION; SAMPLES

sandwich board   A poster carried by an individual (parading around a shopping centre, say), usually as two boards (slung one at the back and one in front) sandwiching the individual between them.

sans serif   The simple, plain form of type which has no serifs (the cross strokes at the end of the main part of the character).

SAS   A mainframe (marketing research) computer analysis software package.
See also ANALYSIS OF MARKETING RESEARCH DATA

satellite   *see* NARROWCASTING

satellite television   *see* TELEVISION

satisfaction   *see* ADVERTISING BELIEVABILITY; SERVICE QUALITY

satisfaction, customer   *see* CUSTOMER SATISFACTION; WIN–WIN

satisfaction level   *see* CUSTOMER SATISFACTION

satisfaction, pricing   *see* PRICE AND NOT-FOR-PROFIT ORGANIZATIONS

satisfaction survey   *see* CUSTOMER SATISFACTION; CUSTOMER SATISFACTION SURVEY

satisficing   *see* CORPORATE OBJECTIVES

satisfiers   *see* PSYCHOLOGICAL INFLUENCES, ON THE PURCHASE DECISION

saturation   *see* PRICING, PRODUCT LIFE CYCLE; PRODUCT LIFE CYCLE (PLC)

saturation coverage   A (costly) campaign with a very high level of advertising.

saturation stage, product life cycle   According to PLC theory, sometimes the point is reached where there are so many competitors in the market, which is no longer growing, that price wars break out. The product has reached the saturation stage. Because this stage shares many of the characteristics of the preceding ('maturity') stage, it is frequently included in it, so that the model is reduced to just four stages.

Saudi Arabia   *see* REGULATORY CONSIDERATIONS, FILTERING UNSUITABLE MARKETS

sawtooth maintenance pattern *see* LONGER-TERM COMPETITIVE SAW

SBA (Strategic Business Area)   *see* STRATEGIC BUSINESS UNIT (SBU)

SBU   *see* STRATEGIC BUSINESS UNIT (SBU)

scale, economies of   *see* ECONOMIES OF SCALE

scamp   A rough layout of an advertisement; often quite simply called a rough.
See also CREATING THE CORRECT MESSAGES; CREATIVE DEPARTMENT, ADVERTISING AGENCY

scanner   A machine which scans the artwork to electronically separate out the four colours used in colour printing.
See also FOUR-COLOUR PRINT

scanning, and MIS   Much of market intelligence in general, and of marketing research in particular, is gathered in response to specific stimuli. The information is needed for the development of a new product, or a new marketing campaign. Such information is valuable, but it is necessarily partial (focusing on one set of questions at one point in time). Much more powerful is a continuous approach (which, in any case, should automatically happen with internally generated data). This is often described as 'scanning', or sometimes as 'environmental scanning' (or 'environmental analysis') when it covers all the external factors not just those in the marketing environment. An 'observer' in the organization (usually the marketing manager or, preferably, the whole marketing department) 'scans', or watches, what is happening in the outside world. The most direct input normally comes from trade journals and general business publications, so subscriptions to these periodicals represent a very sound (indeed, essential) marketing investment. On the other hand, the most important indirect input comes from the 'mass media' (television as well as newspapers and magazines), which give up-to-date information on how society as whole (and specific markets in particular) is developing – in the context of the related news stories. A basic requirement for any 'scanner', therefore, is an interest (perhaps an almost obsessive one) in news of any description.
See also MARKETING INTELLIGENCE SYSTEMS (MIS); TEAM SCANNING

scenarios   This is a particularly important method of combining the input from various forecasting techniques, especially the jury and Delphi methods, to give an integrated view – which essentially spells out the 'future history' of the organization.

Regrettably, it is relatively little used, since it requires some significant effort (and may be seen by the uninitiated as complex), but the fleshing out of the bare-bones forecasts, and their integration into a whole scenario, means that on the one hand it is easier to detect incompatibilities between the various forecasts, and on the other that it allows extrapolation of these individual forecasts to cover all the activities of the organization. It can offer a very lifelike picture, though this is a danger. It must always be remembered that it is a work of fiction – albeit, hopefully, a very well informed one.

Abt et al. identified three main methods for generating the main contents of such scenarios (in addition to the details generated by the other forecasting methods):

- *Consensus* – very similar to Delphi, in which a panel of experts interact to choose the variables. In its totality, this approach decreases the bias which may occur in Delphi work, but limits what is considered and the interactions may be obscure.
- *Synopsis* – develops independent scenarios for each 'discipline' and then integrates them. This approach improves the 'interdisciplinary' consistency, but can run into difficulty in resolving the relations between some of them.
- *'Cross impact'* – use of matrices. This leads to internal consistency, but is still very subjective.

To be most useful (in terms of highlighting the options open to the organization), several (alternative) scenarios should be produced to illustrate the range of futures which might come about (depending upon how the key factors turn out).

Using this technique of forecasting, therefore, it is necessary to provide at least two contrasting scenarios (for each 'domain' being investigated; be it local or global, short or long term). In the 1970s, for example, Shell's Group Planning Department produced six long-term scenarios. When, later, they had developed greater expertise and a better understanding of the technique, they reduced the number to just two 'archetypal' scenarios, and the number of pages of description from several hundred to 30.

Scenario writing is a very broad concept; almost the only common factor is that of producing a 'story' which encompasses a range of future options (and in the process helps the organization using the technique to better understand what might happen in that future).

See also QUALITATIVE FORECASTING METHODS; RISK ANALYSIS; SENSITIVITY ANALYSIS, NEW PRODUCTS

Reference: Abt, C. C., Foster, R. N. and Rea, R. H. (1973) A scenario generating methodology, *A Guide to Practical Technological Forecasting*, ed. James Bright and Milton E. F. Schoemann. Englewood Cliffs, NJ: Prentice-Hall.

schedule, media   *see* MEDIA BUYING, ADVERTISING AGENCY

scientific analogies   *see* SYNECTICS®

scientific breakthroughs   *see* CREATIVE IMITATION; LEAPFROG

scope, of research reports   Before studying on the main body of a research report, the final question is what range of extra information might it provide (often researchers only report the results that interest them – whereas you may be able to ask further questions of the material about topics which interest you!). This 'scope' can be found most easily by looking at the questionnaire to determine exactly what questions were asked (the results of which will be held on a database somewhere, even if they are not reported upon, and can thus be subsequently analysed in whatever form you wish).
See also RESEARCH REPORTS, USAGE

screen   The pattern placed over a photograph or illustration to break it up so that a half-tone is produced; and the ink does not run or smudge when printing relatively large areas of solid colour.
See also BLOCKS

screening   *see* STRATEGIC SCREENING, NEW PRODUCTS

script, telesales   *see* TELESALES

S curves (discontinuities)   *see* DIFFUSION OF INNOVATION; TECHNOLOGICAL FORECASTING

sealed bid   *see* PRICE, PURCHASE

seasonality, product screening   The ideal organizational trading pattern is an even one, with no seasonality, so that resources may be most efficiently utilized without the unproductive problems posed by having to meet peaks and troughs of sales. A new product or service will, therefore, ideally not be seasonal; or, even better, it will be one which complements existing seasonal patterns – making its peak sales when the others are in a trough, and vice versa. It was reportedly for this reason that, many years ago, Walls decided to complement its range of ice creams, with its summer peaks, by starting a sausage business, with its peaks in winter.

See also NEW PRODUCT SCREENING, PRODUCT FACTORS

secondary sources of communication Face-to-face selling, advertising and sales promotion can all be described as the primary sources of communication, since they are under direct control and you pay for them. But there are also secondary sources of communication, which are not under direct control and for which no payment is made. These include word of mouth, editorial comment, personal recommendation and the like. Although these secondary sources are not under immediate control, they may still be influenced by promotional activities. In turn, because of their supposed 'impartial' nature, they may carry considerable weight with consumers (possibly even more so than direct, primary, sources!).

See also PUBLIC RELATIONS

secret police   *see* BALANCING UNDER THE INFLUENCE

see-safe   Arrangement whereby a supplier will credit unsold goods at the end of the period.

segmentation   'Segmentation' in one sense is a strategy used by vendors to concentrate, and thus optimize, the use of their resources within an overall market. In another sense, it is also that group of techniques which are used by these vendors for segmenting the market, splitting it into smaller parts which they can target separately.

One possible focus for a producer setting about the process of 'segmentation', deciding what useful segments there are in the market which can be addressed separately, is that of consumer behaviour; though an alternative focus for segmentation may be the product or service itself – but this follows much the same rules, from a different perspective. In the context of the consumer, the main influences on that consumer provide one set of starting points. In this context, these are often grouped as follows:

- *geographic* – region, urban or rural, etc.
- *demographic* – age, sex, marital status, etc.
- *socio-economic* – income, social class, occupation, etc.
- *psychological* – attitudes, lifestyle, culture, etc.

Philip Kotler (1988) distinguishes between two major approaches:

- *Consumer (inherent) characteristics* – geographic, demographic, psychographic
- *Consumer (product-related) responses* – occasions (when used), benefits, usage (inc. heavy or light), attitudes (inc. loyalty)

The first of these categories reflects 'who buys'; the second is generally based on 'what is bought'. If the emphasis is on the supplier's viewpoint, which it often is, this section can be expanded to include elements of the 4 Ps:

- price
- distribution channels
- physical characteristics of product or service
- packaging

These often provide the practical 'segmentation' patterns chosen by suppliers or forced on them by circumstance. Such suppliers should realize, however, that these patterns are probably unrelated to the consumers' own perceptions. The customer may genuinely believe, like a supplier, that a disinfectant bought in a plastic bottle from a supermarket belongs to a different segment of the market than one in a glass bottle bought from a pharmacy. On the other hand, the consumer may actually be making the choice on totally different grounds – that it offers especially gentle protection for the baby in the family, say. It behoves a supplier to know what the true reasons are, not least because the promotional message often determines what the product is in the eyes of the consumer.

The characteristics that are important to a specific market may, however, be much more closely defined than these generalities allow for. The aim of much market research is to identify what are the exact characteristics that are the most important delineators of buying behaviour. That is, on what does the user base his or her buying decisions (consciously or subconsciously)? It is then these specific characteristics (as diverse as the mundane flavour of a pipe tobacco or the exotic sexual fears of 'impotence' from a burst tyre) which are the most powerful tools for segmentation.

In practice, the picture may be much more complex, with the truly meaningful segments based on intangible benefits which only the consumer sees or on natural consumer groupings which emerge from much more deep-seated social processes. In some consumer markets it may need the use of significant amounts of research, using 'factor analysis' and 'cluster analysis' techniques, just to start to identify what the key segments are.

These 'intangibles' are, of course, the characteristics most often used for segmentation of consumer markets (services as well as products). Those used in industrial markets may be more directly related to the product or service characteristics (for example, powerful single-use cleaners rather than general cleaners), or at least to product usage characteristics (cleaners to be used on floors rather than on upholstery), but also to 'customer set' characteristics (cleaners to be used in workshops in heavy industry rather than in operating theatres in hospitals).

In one approach, designed to reduce this confusion and demonstrate the validity of the segments eventually chosen, the Henley Centre for Forecasting has used cross-elasticities of demand as a measure of the separation of segments. If a reduction in price of one group of products has no effect on the demand for another group of products, it is reasoned that the two ranges of products lie in two independent segments.

See also CROSS-ELASTICITY OF DEMAND; MARKETING PLANNING, ANALYSIS; MARKET POSITIONING AND SEGMENTATION; PRODUCT (OR SERVICE) GAP; SEGMENTATION BY BENEFIT; SEGMENTATION BY CONSUMPTION PROFILE; SEGMENTATION METHODS; SEGMENTS OF MARKETS; SEGMENT VIABILITY;

Reference: Kotler, P. (1988) *Marketing Management* (6th edn). Englewood Cliffs, NJ: Prentice-Hall.

segmentation approaches   There may be a wide range of detailed actions which are suggested by the outcome of a segmentation analysis. In overall terms, though, there are five main strategies which may be adopted:

Single segment
The simplest response to segmentation is to concentrate on one segment, and position the product firmly within that segment. This is often the case where limited funds are available. For example, this is the approach adopted in the UK by Camp (liquid) coffee. It is sometimes described as 'niche' marketing (when the segment is a minor segment of the overall market). This is a very effective form of marketing, especially for the smaller organization, since it concentrates resources into a very sharply focused campaign. It is, perhaps, more risky – since there may be a greater likelihood of the 'niche' disappearing than of the whole market being subject to catastrophic change. On the other hand, it is considerably less risky than spreading resources too thinly across a number of

segments. At the other extreme, however, there was a move in the 1980s to 'head-on positioning' – challenging the main competitor on exactly the same terms.

Customized marketing
In recent years two trends have combined to allow for ever-narrower segments of niches:

- *Increasing variety demanded.* Consumers have come to demand more variety from their suppliers, so that their 'exact' needs are catered for, rather than accepting a more uniform product (even if this means that a higher price has to be paid).
- *Flexible manufacturing methods.* With the aid of microprocessor technology (either in the product or in production processes), and led by the Japanese, organizations have found that they can deliver a much greater variety of products without reducing productivity to any significant extent.

The outcome has been that even some 'mass marketers' can now provide (at least to a degree) individually customized products. The 'segment', in this case, can become almost the individual.

With the addition of the techniques of 'precision marketing', the supplier is now able to talk to, and deliver a product specifically designed for, an individual (or at least to much smaller groups of consumers than previously).

Multiple segments
The more complex response to segmentation is to address several major segments with one brand, or to launch several brands each targeted against different segments. This latter is the approach chosen, for example, by Nestlé, which has brands to meet the segments of 'ground coffee' (the freeze-dried Gold Blend), 'continental' (Blend 37) and 'decaffeinated', as well as having a main brand (Nescafé) which, in line with the former strategy, bridges a number of segments. This technique may also be adopted by an organization which is intending, ultimately, to achieve full coverage but is approaching this invasion of the market segment by segment – probably in order to reduce the demands on its limited resources, but possibly also to limit competitive responses (until, hopefully, it is too late for the competitors to erect viable entry barriers).

Cross segment
Some – probably most – suppliers resolutely ignore the segments and pattern their marketing on other

factors. This is almost invariably the case in the more bureaucratic responses of the public sector – which are based on the demands of the 'delivery systems' rather than on the needs of the clients. But, in the commercial field, this often represents a successful strategy. For example, a company may specialize in a particular type of product which covers a number of segments and has a band of devoted supporters who recognize the specialized expertise embodied. This is a particularly prevalent, and successful, strategy in the industrial area. A more sophisticated approach would be based upon deliberately targeting across segments which have similar characteristics (such as similar production technology).

Full coverage
In this case, often described as mass marketing and limited to those organizations which can afford the strategy, the intent is to address the whole market. Full coverage can come in two forms:

1. *Undifferentiated.* A few organizations attempt, sometimes successfully, to address a whole market (including its segments) with a single product or non-segmented range. This coverage may be totally undifferentiated.
2. *Differentiated.* Alternatively, it may be to an ex-tent differentiated where the organization covers the market with a range of products or services (under the one brand) which are more or less individually targeted at segments. The most so-phisticated approach would match the pattern to the stage of development of the market. In a new market, typically being developed by one supplier, just one brand is launched to cover the whole market. As the market develops, and competitors enter (usually targeting specific seg-ments in order to obtain a foothold), the major supplier may move to pre-empt this competitive segmentation by launching its own new brands targeted at the most vulnerable segments. On the other hand, a competitor seeking to enter a market may initially target a particularly vulner-able segment and then use this as a base from which to grow incrementally by taking in more segments.

See also PRODUCT (OR SERVICE) POSITIONING; SEGMENTATION

segmentation by benefit   Using general factors as the basis for segmentation has its limitations. It is much more productive to relate segmentation to the specific characteristics of the market for the product or service. Different customers, or groups of cus-tomers, look for different combinations of benefits, and it is these groupings of benefits which then define the segments. It is these differences which the producers can use to target their brands, or the public service providers their offerings – to position them in that segment where they most clearly meet the needs of the consumers. As Russell Haley (1968) explains:

> The belief underlying this segmentation strategy is that the benefits which people are seeking in consuming a given product are the basic reasons for the existence of true market segments. Experi-ence with this approach has shown that benefits sought by consumers determine their behaviour much more accurately than do demographic char-acteristics or volume of consumption.

He further explains:

> Each segment is identified by the benefits it is seeking. However, it is the total configuration of benefits which differentiates one segment from another, rather than the fact that one segment is seeking one particular benefit and another a quite different benefit. Individual benefits are likely to have appeal for several segments . . . most people would like as many benefits as possible. However, the relative importance they attach to individual benefits can differ importantly and, accordingly, can be used as an effective lever in segmenting markets.

See also SEGMENTATION; SEGMENTS OF MARKETS; SEG-MENT VIABILITY

Reference: Haley, Russell I. (1968) Benefit segmentation: a decision oriented research tool. *Journal of Marketing*, 32.

segmentation by consumption profile   A number of research agencies have recently started to characterize consumer segments in terms of the buy-ing choices of the consumers in them. Thus, they are characterized by their purchases of a range of key products and, in particular, by a range of print media read and television programmes watched. The data for this may be provided in some depth by MRB's TGI survey, or in less depth (but still adequate) by less wide-ranging surveys. Key products may, for example, be items such as chilled versus tinned or frozen ready-prepared meals, or wine versus lager or beer. Whatever the set of products chosen, the profile as described in terms of the bundle of brands purchased is supposed to be more meaningful to marketers than the relatively esoteric categories offered by lifestyles. There is no reason why such segmentation cannot be used, as long as the products chosen as the variables do significantly differentiate in terms of the brand(s) being investigated.

See also SEGMENTATION; SEGMENTS OF MARKETS; SEGMENT VIABILITY

segmentation methods Practical segmentation needs to be based on characteristics or dimensions that are significant to the consumer rather than the supplier. On the other hand, most organizations choose to characterize their products or services by the parameters which they see as important (parameters which are usually related to the production or service itself, or to its delivery systems, rather than to the consumer). Hence, by default, they often unknowingly impose a segmentation or positioning policy – and one which may be counter-productive.

In order to achieve a genuine consumer-based segmentation, Richard Johnson (1971) suggests that three 'technical' problems need to be addressed:

1. To construct a product space, a geometric representation of consumers' perceptions of products or brands in a category.
2. To obtain a density distribution by positioning consumers' ideal points in the same space.
3. To construct a model which predicts preferences of groups of consumers towards new or modified products.

The basis for almost all effective segmentation must be sound market research. The characteristics which are to form the basis of the segmentation (or positioning) must be determined, and this demands that all the related characteristics are measured (including customer attitudes and their perceptions of product attributes as well as their 'demographic' characteristics and usage patterns). Thus, in practice, segmentation is so very clearly bound up with sophisticated market research programmes that it often almost becomes one element of this aspect of marketing activity (though it should never be forgotten that segmentation, even in this context, requires a very conscious and strategic – targeting – decision of just which segments are to be addressed).

To discover, and use, these 'natural segments' requires a number of steps. The main stages of segmentation are as follows.

Background investigation
As with most market research, the first stage of that relating to segmentation is to undertake the desk research which will (within the limits of such secondary data) best inform the researcher, and the marketer, as to what the most productive segments are likely to be. This is an essential stage, and one which will lead to the 'hypotheses' to be tested, but it must not be the only one used to define the segments. At each stage, the marketer must be prepared to abandon any preconceptions or prejudices in the light of actual data about the customer's view of such segments.

Qualitative research
It is vital that all the characteristics which are important to the consumer are measured, and that these are described in terms that are meaningful to him or her. The 'language' which is used by these consumers should be first investigated in the group discussions which are frequently used to pilot major research projects – best conducted by psychologists who are trained to recognize the important nuances of such conversations. Other techniques can also be used, though. One particularly effective one is that of 'repertory grids' or 'Kelly grids'. It is this research that discovers the 'dimensions' which are important to the consumer (and which are described in their language), from which the later strategies will be developed.

Quantitative research
Quantitative research in the case of segmentation frequently uses 'semantic differentials' based upon the dimensions, the key descriptive words, revealed by the qualitative research. The research will usually try to measure attitudes to the brand (and its competitors). This work may also, perhaps, extend to the consumer's 'ideal brand'. The validity of such 'idealizations' is often questioned, though, since they are artificial conceptualizations which are not easy for the consumer to understand and the results can be ambiguous. In practice, though, the concept (of the ideal) usually appears to work well – especially when the questions are carefully phrased and are specific (and are 'mapped' on the specific dimensions involved in the positioning exercise).

Analysis
This is the critical stage of segmentation. It is now almost invariably dependent upon the use of considerable computing power, since this is needed to undertake the complex analyses on the large number of variables involved. Usually some form of 'factor

analysis' is used to separate out those variables (the stimuli; such as product features/benefits or psychographic dimensions) that are highly correlated and hence are almost interchangeable in the consumer's eyes. These variables, though, are often seen as unrelated by the suppliers, and the news that they are related is thus often very enlightening. Only when this factor analysis is complete can 'cluster analysis' be used to create a specified number of maximally different clusters, or segments, of consumers. The number of such clusters specified is that which can reasonably be handled in marketing terms (but which still adequately describes the significantly different segments in the market). Each of these clusters of consumers is then homogeneous within itself, but as different from other clusters as possible. The typical outcome will be a set of prioritized position maps, preferably limited to the 6–8 most important dimensions – which is usually all that the average marketer can handle!

Implementation
The clusters found during the analysis stage of segmentation (typically no more than half a dozen in number, where more than this would probably fragment rather than segment the average market) need to be described in terms of the key characteristics which differentiate them. Then, and only then, can the supplier's products (and the competitors') be mapped onto these dimensions and the product 'positioning' exercise begun – so that the target segments are optimally addressed.

As with any general deciding his military strategy, the marketer must then pore over the 'maps' produced during the segmentation process to decide exactly what his or her battle plans should be, taking into account the resources available as well as the competition and consumer positioning on the 'map'. Which will be the target groups? Which will be the chosen segments? Where will the products or services be repositioned (if this is needed) to compete most effectively and/or to be most attractive to consumers? Which segment to choose is probably the most important decision any marketer has to make. From it most other decisions will emerge naturally.

This is a time- and resource-consuming process, but the benefits to be derived far more than outweigh this. Tony Lunn (1986) reports, for example, that (based on a major unpublished review of market structure projects from several European subsidiaries of a multinational corporation) 'In all cases examined in the review, marketing men volunteered the information that the benefits more than justified the time and expenditure involved. In some cases the findings were held to have contributed to substantial gains in market share, in others to arresting decline in share in the light of fierce competition'.

See also SEGMENTATION; SEGMENTATION BY BENEFIT; SEGMENTATION BY CONSUMPTION PROFILE; SEGMENTS OF MARKETS; SEGMENT VIABILITY

References: Johnson, Richard M. (1971) Market segmentation: a strategic management tool. *Journal of Marketing Research*, VIII.

Lunn, Tony (1986) Segmenting and constructing markets. In Robert Worcester and John Downham (eds), *Consumer Market Research Handbook* (3rd edn). Maidenhead: McGraw-Hill.

segmentation of suppliers   *see* SUPPLIERS

segment pricing   *see* PRICING, PRODUCT POSITIONING

segments of markets   For marketing purposes, it is often possible to break the larger markets into smaller segments. If we were following the process of defining markets in consumer terms precisely, this might not be possible. A market which is tightly defined in consumer terms, so that it only includes a homogeneous group of customers with exactly the same needs and wants, cannot be divided into smaller groups (which are meaningful in marketing terms). But producers tend to define markets quite broadly, in terms of the physical characteristics which are important to themselves. The result is that these larger markets often contain groups of customers with quite different needs and wants. Each of these represents a different 'segment', with different characteristics in terms of consumers. This process is called 'segmentation', or sometimes 'target marketing' – because the supplier carefully targets a specific group of customers. Although it is classically described in terms of products, the concept of segmentation can be just as applicable to services.

segment viability   There is a pure, customer-oriented marketing reason behind segmentation; segments are thus only useful to marketers if they are (commercially) viable. By designing products or services which are narrowly targeted on the needs of one specific segment, whose consumers are all looking for very much the same thing, it may be possible to offer them the best match to their needs. In practice, however, producers usually target segments rather than the overall market because this allows them to concentrate their resources on a limited group of consumers, so that the brand can be made to dominate that segment – and gain the benefits of segment leader, albeit on a smaller scale than if it were the overall market leader. In the public sector, greater efficiency, or effectiveness, may be the justification for such concentration, but in the commercial world, the ultimate objective in applying these concentrated resources is, of course, to make a profit. For this to happen, the segment has to be viable; it has to be worthwhile, in terms of revenue generated against the costs involved.

To be viable, a segment has generally to meet a number of broad criteria:

* size
* identity
* relevance
* access

All of these criteria are equally applicable to the segmentation available in the non-profit sector. Here, too, it needs to be determined if the segments are worthwhile; and the criteria used for concentration of the resources are very similar to those relating to the maximization of profit in the commercial organization.

If all these criteria are met, though, segmentation is a very effective marketing device. It can allow even the smaller organizations to obtain leading positions in their respective segments – often then described as 'niche' marketing – and gain some of the control this offers. The most productive bases for segmentation are those which relate to the consumers' own groupings in the market, not to the artificially imposed producers' segments.

See also ACCESS, SEGMENT VIABILITY; IDENTITY, SEGMENT VIABILITY; RELEVANCE, SEGMENT VIABILITY; SEGMENTATION; SEGMENTATION METHODS; SEGMENTS OF MARKETS; SIZE, SEGMENT VIABILITY

selection, of a marketing research agency   In order to make your selection, the proposals requested from short-listed agencies should be very carefully scrutinized, for they represent what you will get for your budget! The main factors which need to be taken into account in your judgement may be:

* *Methodology*. This is probably the main area where even the relatively uninitiated client can ask some searching questions, to determine the quality of the proposal. The essence of this scrutiny is to determine how 'rigorous' a control the agencies will have over the results. The main

contributing factors are likely to be basic technique, and sample design and recruitment.

* *Basic technique*. Will the study produce broadly qualitative results (by focus groups or small samples, for example) or detailed quantitative findings (by rigorously controlled, interviewer-conducted, questionnaire-based surveys on large samples of respondents)? In recent years much research has switched to the qualitative end of the spectrum, apparently to produce cost savings; but it is not clear that clients realize the very real limitations which apply to the results of such work.

* *Sample design and recruitment*. This is the area where agencies probably incur most costs (and are most likely to shave the quality to bring their price down!). The cheapest solution is an uncontrolled quota sample. The most expensive (but most predictable, in terms of quality) is a rigorously selected random sample. In view of the questionable quality of some market research, it is probably advisable to err on the side of caution; and, accordingly, on the side of random samples. There are, however, techniques (such as 'cluster sampling') which, properly handled, can reduce these costs – with only a marginal diminution of quality. Indeed, just as important is how recruitment of the respondents will be controlled: what leeway is the interviewer given, and what supervision underwrites the end results? Will the proposed sampling techniques actually be viable in the field? Again, the tighter the control, the more expensive it will be for the agency – but the more accurate, and useful, the information is likely to be to you.

* *Questionnaire*. At this stage only the outline is likely to be presented, though even this should indicate (at least to expert eyes) how rigorous the work will be. It is not unreasonable, however, to ask to see examples of previous questionnaires on similar surveys (though, of course, the agency may wish to protect client confidentiality – and occasionally their own incompetence!). The design of the questionnaire (Is it clear, remembering that relatively untrained interviewers will have to follow it? Is it unambiguous and unbiased? Who will design it?, etc.) often gives a very good indication of the quality of the work which can be expected. Indeed, when you are purchasing existing surveys, the first requirement should be to see the questionnaire before looking at any of the results, since this will give the best indication of the reliance which can be placed on

the findings (as well as showing what further analyses may be obtained). On the other hand, the best check on the quality of any questionnaire will be a pilot, to see what results may in fact be obtained (and what errors have been included in the draft questionnaire); so a good measure of particularly high quality can be what piloting is to be done.

- *Quality control.* How will interviewers be recruited? What instructions will be issued to them? How is the fieldwork to be monitored? How are the field force of interviewers to be supervised? It is normal practice for supervisors, in addition to regularly accompanying interviewers on their calls, to call back on 10 per cent of all calls made, to check the accuracy of the recorded responses – and to check that the calls have actually been made! This 'call-back' may sometimes be carried out by postal checks, less expensively but also less rigorously than face-to-face. What normalization (with regard to balancing the figures to allow for sample deviations) will be employed, and what accuracy can be attained? What statistics can be checked against previously measured data, to cross-check the results? It is sound practice that all questionnaires should be 'check-edited' by the agency to ensure that the answers have been correctly entered and, in the process, to obtain some measure of the interviewer quality.
- *Analysis.* How sophisticated are the analysis techniques to be used (the more complex the computer analyses to be employed, the higher the cost to the agency)?
- *Administration.* This is less a measure of the quality of the operation and more an indication of the 'internal overhead' which will need to be expended working with the agency.
- *People.* Who will be the prime contact, and can they communicate in your language (results are only useful if they are communicated, and many market researchers seem to speak a foreign tongue)?
- *Timing.* When will the results be available, and how reliable is that date?
- *Reports.* What analyses will be undertaken and what market research reports compiled, and what verbal analysis will accompany them?
- *Costs and terms.* Exactly what will the costs include, and what are the terms of doing business?
- *Background.* The 'history' of the agency will also give some measure of what can be expected.

See also APPOINTING A MARKETING RESEARCH AGENCY; MARKETING RESEARCH; SUBCONTRACTORS, MARKETING RESEARCH; SURVEY RESEARCH

selective distribution   *see* CHANNEL MEMBERSHIP

selective pricing   Some suppliers apply different prices for the same product or service:

- *Category pricing.* The supplier aims to cover the range of price categories (possibly all the way from cheap to expensive) with a 'range' of 'brands' based on the same 'product' (repackaged, and possibly with some minor features changed). This was particularly obvious when Unilever in the UK marketed Square Deal Surf as the price leader at the same time as it had Persil as the 'quality' (and market) leader. An extension of this principle is 'image pricing', where a supplier uses the same product (but usually with very different packaging) to meet very different (quality) 'images'. This is particularly evident in the cosmetics industry.

There are some forms of selective pricing, particularly prevalent in the service industries, where the supplier is in direct contact with the customer:

- *Customer group pricing.* The ability of various groups to pay prices may be met by having different categories of prices; for example, entrance fees and fares are often lower for students and senior citizens.
- *Peak pricing.* A variant is that the price is matched to the demand: high prices are demanded at peak times (the 'rush hours' for transport or the evening performances for theatres) but lower prices are charged at 'off-peak' times (to redistribute the resource demands – by offering incentives to those who can make use of the services off-peak).
- *Service level pricing.* The level of service chosen may determine the price. At its simplest, the buyer may pay for immediate availability rather than having to queue (or may pay more for the guarantee of a seat, by patronizing the first-class section of a train). This may be extended to levels of 'delivery': the product may be immediately available, gift wrapped, in an expensive store, or it may arrive some weeks later by post from a cheap mail house. There may also be levels of 'quality' in delivery; for instance, seats in different parts of a theatre may have differing levels of

access to the performance (and are priced accordingly!) even though the basic 'product' may be identical.

See also COMPETITION PRICING; COST–PLUS PRICING; PRICING POLICIES, PRACTICAL

self-actualization needs *see* MASLOW'S HIERARCHY OF NEEDS

self-censorship *see* GROUPTHINK

self-completion questionnaires Questionnaires, typically quite long, usually as part of a mail survey (but sometimes placed by an interviewer) which the respondent completes – unsupervised – and then returns by post.
See also MAIL SURVEYS; QUESTIONNAIRE DESIGN; SURVEY RESEARCH

self-fulfilling prophecy *see* LIFE CYCLE, LESSONS

self-liquidating offers *see* NON–PRICE PROMOTIONS

self-mailer *see* REPLY–PAID CARDS

self-service *see* CUSTOMER SERVICE CATEGORIES; RETAIL PRODUCT OR SERVICE CATEGORIES

selling This is potentially the ideal form of promotion, assuming that the sales force lives up to its promise – which, unfortunately, is not always the case. Face-to-face contact offers promotion which is:

- interactive
- responsive
- flexible

but, as it requires a salesperson to talk to every customer, it is inherently:

- expensive

If the value of the individual sale is high enough, and the customers may be contacted economically, personal selling will usually be the chosen approach.

Indeed, in most organizations more money is spent on personal selling than on advertising and sales promotions combined. This is in acknowledgement of its effectiveness. Many organizations are, accordingly, prepared to spend a high a proportion of their communications budget on personal selling. It

also indicates just how expensive personal selling is. On the other hand, use of the sales force is qualitatively different to almost all other aspects of marketing. It is much more dependent upon relationships between individuals; between sales personnel and customers; and between sales management and their sales personnel. It is generally the management of these human relationships, rather than the logistics, which is most important. Philip Kotler identifies a number of separate activities which may require sales-force attention:

- *prospecting* – finding new customers
- *communicating* – informing customers about the organization and its products or services
- *selling* – the 'classic' responsibility of the sales professional
- *servicing* – supporting customers, a major ongoing activity in most organizations – particularly where most business comes from existing customers
- *information gathering* – sales professionals are the main source of 'market research' information for most organizations
- *allocating* – not infrequently these same personnel have to switch from selling to rationing scarce resources – without offending too many long-term customers!

See also CALLS AVAILABLE ANNUALLY; COMPLEX SALE; MANPOWER PLAN, SALES; MARKETING STRATEGIES; ORGANIZATIONAL BUYING SITUATIONS; PROMOTIONAL LOZENGE; RELATIONSHIP (MARKETING) MANAGEMENT; SALESMAN STEREOTYPE; SALES PROFESSIONAL; TERRITORY MANAGEMENT; TERRITORY SALES PLAN; WIN–WIN

Reference: Kotler, P. (1991) *Marketing Management* (7th edn). Prentice-Hall.

selling proposition *see* MESSAGE SELECTION

selling services Face-to-face selling tends, in practice, to be more prevalent in the service industries. This is, in large part, because many such services are also 'delivered' in a personal form, with some service providers using 'professionals of the specialism' rather than salespersons. It is also because personal contact may be seen as necessary to establish the 'credentials' – the integrity – of the service provider where the service itself is an intangible quantity. In these situations the sales professionals, and the way they personally handle the sale, may be seen by the customers as the best measure of the service being offered; the method of promotion may become, by default, the 'product' (the medium will be the message!). Because of the involvement of so many personnel in face-to-face contact during the delivery of such a service, the 'sales' role may become diffused. All personnel providing the service are, in one way or another, 'salespersons'. This means that 'sales training' (often described, in this context, as 'customer service training') has to be provided on a much wider front, throughout the organization; and hence the emphasis on 'customer care' programmes in the retailing and financial services sectors. This is also true of not-for-profit organizations; for example, a doctor's 'bedside' manner represents an important 'sales' activity (and, by improving the consumers perception of the 'service', may actually improve the 'medicine').

See also ADVERTISING; SELLING

selling versus marketing 'Selling' has long suffered from a dubious image. It is, indeed, true that dubious selling practices may occasionally result in a sale – if the customer is particularly gullible – but it is arguable that, even then, only good marketing (which encompasses a far wider range of skills, with an almost diametrically opposed motivation) will lead him or her to buy again from the same company. Organizations seldom profit from single purchases made by first-time customers. Normally, they rely on repeat business to generate the profit they need. Thus, much of the selling effort of the well-organized marketing function will be directed towards keeping the number of dissatisfied customers down. In such organizations, feedback information from the market will alert the company to the main reasons why customers do not buy again – leading, if necessary, to an improvement or modification of the product or service. Effective selling is not about half-truths or overrated claims, because these practices are almost always counter-productive in the longer term. This highlights the 'contest' between marketing (often described as 'market orientation') and selling (sometimes described as 'product orientation'), which has been a source of some controversy since the 1950s. Much of the criticism of 'selling' (used here in its pejorative sense) is still valid, since there are many poor salesmen and almost as many poor sales managers. But it is also true to say that the good sales managers and salesmen, particularly those involved in industrial selling (who are now often called 'sales professionals'), have long recognized and supported the basic tenets of sound marketing.

On the other hand, the word 'marketing' is often used as an 'honorary' title, adopted by those who are in reality engaged exclusively in pure selling activities. For a number of years the term 'marketing executive' was, for example, applied to salespeople in general. Even as early as 1964 Peter Drucker observed that 'Not everything that goes by that name deserves it. But a gravedigger remains a gravedigger even when called a "mortician" – only the cost of the burial goes up. Many a sales manager has been renamed "marketing vice-president" – and all that happened was that costs and salaries went up.'

Bower and Garda (1986) suggest seven common elements which distinguish marketing based companies:

1. The use of market share, rather than volume, as the primary measure of marketing success (although if they ignore the cost of acquiring share, profits will be unsatisfactory).
2. The understanding and use of market-segmentation principles.
3. The process for monitoring customer needs, usage, and trends, as well as competitive activity – that is, market research.
4. A structure or process for coordinating all non-marketing functions toward the achievement of marketing goals.
5. A set of specific marketing goals and targets.
6. A corporate style and culture where marketing plays a key role.
7. A market-based business concept that provides unique value to the customer.

The key point, though, is that (put very simply, in the classical context) 'selling' is inward looking, persuading the customer to take what you have got (your product, hence a 'product orientation' which often accompanies such an approach). It also implies that product development is detached from the marketplace. Only when the product is ready is there a search for a market, for customers to persuade. On the other hand, 'marketing' is outward looking, trying to match the real requirements of the customer (or 'market', hence a 'market orientation'). The company looks for market opportunities and creates product solutions in response.

In practice, a mix of both the approaches is often used. It is a very poor salesman who does not, albeit instinctively rather than as a matter of theory, use sound marketing principles when he questions a customer to find out what he wants. Equally, it is the fortunate marketer who can produce the new product to exactly match the discovered gap in the market; most new products initially emerge from non-marketing processes and are only then opportunistically matched to markets.

References: Bower, Martin and Garda, Robert A. (1986) The role of marketing in management. In Victor P. Buell (ed.), *Handbook of Modern Marketing* (2nd edn). New York: McGraw-Hill.
 Drucker, Peter (1964) *Managing for Results*. London: Heinemann.

semantic differentials, on questionnaires *see* CLOSED QUESTIONS, ON QUESTIONNAIRES

seminars The one activity that brings together all the sales activities is the seminar. This represents the pinnacle of the sales professional's art. He or she is likely to be involved in presentations and demonstrations, and will coordinate the expert speakers. As a result, seminars demand a wide range of sales skills if they are to run well. On the other hand, they are a very powerful sales device. Market research undertaken on personal computer buyers, for example, showed that 70 per cent of them found an invitation to a seminar an acceptable approach from a sales professional; which was more than double that for any other sales activity (for example, only just over 30 per cent would have found acceptable a direct approach, asking for an appointment, from a sales professional). If the seminar content is targeted correctly, prospects expect to learn something from the event, and in the company of others feel less threatened by sales pressures. Having captured your audience, it is also a very positive way of introducing your company's products, and showing your own – and your company's – expertise. Seminars can be so effective, as an introductory device, that it is sometimes possible to take 'cold' prospects from their first contact through to a close in such a seminar.

There are two important aspects to a seminar:

- *Programme.* A half day is perhaps the most productive length for seminars. Beyond this, many participants may begin to lose concentration; however, many successful seminars do last a full day. The half–day format fairly naturally breaks down into four three-quarter-hour sessions (though many organizers choose to run only two sessions, of one and a half hours each), running from 9.30 a.m. to 1.00 p.m., or from 1.30 p.m. to 5.00 p.m.
- *Coffee and lunch breaks.* Logistically it is necessary to have these. They do not, however, have to be very elaborate. The only rule to make is that they should normally be in the form of buffets, so that

everyone can circulate (and, of course, these are much easier to provide).

See also DEMONSTRATIONS; DIRECT MAIL ADVERTISING; PROMOTIONAL MIX; SELLING; TELESALES

semiotics The study of signs and symbols and their use (especially in languages). In the context of marketing it is particularly important in advertising research.
See also ADVERTISING RESEARCH

semi-solus An advertisement appearing on the same page as another, but not touching it.
See also MEDIA BUYING, ADVERTISING AGENCY

semi-structured interviews *see* INDIVIDUAL DEPTH INTERVIEWS

sensitivity analysis, new products One the most powerful uses of a personal computer spreadsheet facility is as a measure of 'sensitivity' – as a test (for example) of the viability of proposed new products. In this test, each of the main variables is, say, altered by 10 per cent and the resulting change in profit noted. Typically, a 10 per cent change in price will result in a considerably greater than 10 per cent change in net profit; and a 10 per cent change in volume will also have a disproportionate effect. The value of this technique is to determine to which factors net profit is the most sensitive, so that the manager can focus on these variables – and, usually not least, perhaps think twice before embarking on a low-price strategy. The one critical requirement of such a financial analysis is that it must be honest; indeed, where most new product managers are justifiably enthusiastic about their new 'products', it should probably aim to be on the pessimistic side. This means that the forecast sales volume in particular should be realistic, and that all the costs should be included. Ideally, worst-case scenarios should also be prepared – even if these do not have as wide a distribution!
See also NEW PRODUCT CREATION; POTSA PLANNING; PRODUCT DEVELOPMENT PROCESS; STRATEGIC SCREENING, NEW PRODUCTS

sentence completion *see* OPEN QUESTIONS, ON QUESTIONNAIRES

serendipity *see* MARKET PENETRATION

series discount A discount given by a publisher in return for booking a number of insertions in a publication.

See also MEDIA BUYING, ADVERTISING AGENCY

serif   *see* SANS SERIF

service categories   'Service' is a very general classification, which covers a spectrum of activities ranging from services which support products to pure services which stand by themselves:

* services related to a physical product
* services which have a product attached
* pure services

Within these overall categories there are other dimensions which may also be used to categorize services:

* people based
* equipment based

and

* personal services
* business services

A further dimension which can be applied to services is that of time – when the service is supplied:

* *Before the sale.* Some products (such as fitted kitchens) require a substantial investment of service support before the sale can be made. Thus, for example, designs may need to be prepared, technical advice proffered or quotations submitted (and, on the larger scale, tenders drawn up).
* *At the time of the sale.* This usually represents the service that the distribution chain offers, and the added value this represents. It may be related to the physical product – stockholding so that the product is immediately available, for example. On the other hand, it may, once more, relate to technical advice.
* *After the sale.* This is the element relating to after-sales support, which is traditionally seen as the main element of (product) service support.

See also CUSTOMER SERVICE CATEGORIES

service categories, retail   *see* RETAIL PRODUCT OR SERVICE CATEGORIES

service cultures   In recent years some of the organizations which come within the service sector have been at the forefront of marketing – even ahead of the leaders in other sectors. In general, though, it has to be recognized that much of management in the service sector has been antipathetic towards marketing. There have been a number of alternative reasons proposed for this:

Lack of tangibility
The very intangible nature of services makes them less immediately responsive to unsophisticated marketing techniques. There is no 'packaging' on which to emblazon marketing slogans, and often nothing to demonstrate on television or even to thrust under the nose of the customer in a face-to-face sale. It requires, therefore, a quantum leap in marketing sophistication to apply many of the techniques.

As Theodore Levitt (1981) says, 'The most im portant thing to know about intangible products is that the customers usually don't know what they're getting until they don't get it. Only then do they become aware of what they bargained for; only on dissatisfaction do they dwell. Satisfaction is, as it should be, mute. Its existence is affirmed only by its absence.'

Lack of 'mass' marketing
Many service suppliers have a structure based upon a network of relatively small local branches, which are almost autonomous in their face-to-face contact with their customers. The compelling arguments for 'mass marketing' which have driven the consumer packaged goods sector have, in this way, been diluted. There is apparently less need for marketing communications; and rarely is any central marketing group strong enough to develop them.

Lack of direct competition
Some of the organizations, such as the high street banks, have not seen their role as having 'customers', but have at times behaved almost as if they themselves were the customers (as if those people visiting banks, for instance, had to sell themselves before the bank would accept their business!). Such organizations have often been in the fortunate position where the supply of their offering was swamped by considerably more demand than could be met, so that their role was to ration this scarce supply.

Some organizations, enjoy a monopoly, still often enforced by law, since any other solution would be hopelessly inefficient.

Finally, many of them are 'non-profit' and – in the absence of profit – do not see their role in terms of competition with any other provider.

Professional status

Other groups of service providers have long been organized into professions, for instance, lawyers, accountants and dentists. Their 'profession' therefore is the predominant force, the focus of their 'business' thinking; and, due to its monopoly power, it often effectively removes direct competition in the conventional sense – and with it marketing (indeed, a number of professions have enacted rules which specifically bar their members from almost every form of marketing activity!).

In addition, as a justification for their monopoly power (and as a protection from any pressure to weaken this position) these professions impose 'ethical' constraints; which, once more, act against marketing in the traditional sense.

Lack of management

For a combination of the above reasons, many organizations in the service sector have not stressed the importance of management. Indeed, many of them have de-emphasized it – focusing instead on 'professionalism'. Often, though, in the context of management, this may be seen as just another word for amateurishness! It has only been in relatively recent years that the 'science' of management has been seen to apply to the service sector in general. The result has been less emphasis on the development of management skills and, in particular, those of marketing.

The above reasons are, though, mainly related to self-imposed limitations. They do not relate to any genuine problems inherent in marketing itself.
See also SERVICE CATEGORIES

Reference: Levitt, Theodore (1981) Marketing intangible products and product intangibles. *Harvard Business Review*, May–June.

service decisions   *see* PRODUCT OR SERVICE DECISIONS

service encounter   *see* SERVICE QUALITY

service levels   Perhaps the most important aspect of customer or client service, in terms of delivery of a product or service, is that it should be available when and where the customer wants it. If it is not so available, an immediate sale may well be lost. More important, long-term sales may also have been lost if the customer is forced to change to another brand and then decides to stay with that brand. The percentage availability is described as the service level. It might seem that the simple answer would be to achieve 100 per cent availability. The problem is that the cost of achieving these service levels rises very steeply as it approaches 100 per cent, as the diagram below – by Thomas and Donaldson (1989) – shows:

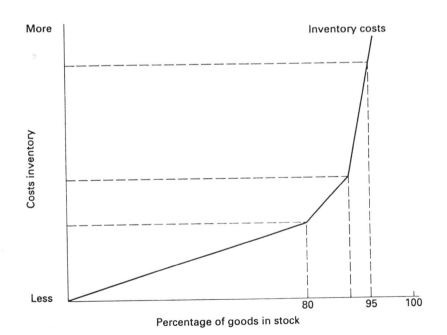

There is a very clear trade-off here between customer service (level) and cost. Fortunately, the indications are that, in terms of demand generated, customers are not significantly affected by minor variations if there are generally high levels of availability.

See also FAULTS; LEAD TIME; QUEUE; SERVICE QUALITY

Reference: Thomas, Michael J. and Donaldson, W. G. (1989) Customer service/customer care. In Michael J. Thomas (ed.), *Marketing Handbook*. Aldershot: Gower Press.

service modification   *see* PRODUCT (OR SERVICE) MODIFICATION

service package   *see* DIFFERENTIATION AND BRANDING; PRODUCT PACKAGE

service prices   Most pricing theory talks in terms of products, but that for services adds the potential complication that some service providers tend to have different terms for price: admission, tuition, cover charge, interest, fee, etc. The result is exactly the same, however. The consumer has to pay a price, and the mechanisms for fixing that price are much the same, though there may be some marginal differences – for example:

- *Negotiation.* In view of the variability of the service being offered, there may be more scope for individual negotiation.
- *Discounts.* Due to the 'perishability' of the service, there may be incentives to use it at unpopular times (off-peak train fares, matinee prices for theatres, etc.).
- *Quality.* Higher pricing, to demonstrate quality (which is usually much more intangible in a service), may be more prevalent.

See also PRICE AND NOT-FOR-PROFIT ORGANIZATIONS; PRICES, CUSTOMER NEEDS

service providers   *see* SELLING SERVICES

service quality   In the industrial goods sector, in particular, 'customer service' may be especially important – and complex. For example, it was often stated (not least by the company itself) that IBM's outstanding success as a marketing company was almost entirely due to its commitment to 'customer service'. This was one of the 'philosophies' which was the mainspring of that company's culture, and was applied just as rigorously to all parts of the organization – not just to the sales functions. Everyone (whether they are accounts clerks or shop-floor workers) was equally exhorted to provide excellent customer service.

In the service sector (particularly in the area of personal services), customer service is often, by definition, the 'product' itself. The 'quality' of the customer service represents the quality of the 'product' the customer is buying. Indeed, in many service sectors the customer has to buy the service 'on trust', since it cannot be inspected before use. Monitoring such customer service, and maintaining standards, may, however, be particularly difficult for some service providers, especially where there is a high content of personal service (for example, in hotels and catering in the private sector and in hospitals in the public sector). In these sectors there may be large numbers of workers who engage in contact with the customers. These workers are typically low-paid (paradoxically so, where their 'service' is the 'product' itself), and staff turnover may be high (so that most may be relatively, or totally, untrained). Providing an adequate, let alone a good, customer service under these conditions may require a great deal of creative management!

David Maister (1988) formulates two 'Laws of Service'. The first of these is expressed by the formula:

Satisfaction equals perception minus expectation. If you expect a certain level of service and perceive the service received to be higher, you will be a satisfied customer. If you perceive this same level where you had expected a higher one, you will be disappointed and therefore a dissatisfied customer. The point is that what is perceived and what is expected are psychological phenomena – not reality [and it is the relative level of service – related to expectations – which is important, not the absolute one].

Second Law of Service: It is hard to play 'catch-up ball'. There is a halo effect created by early stages of any service encounter . . . the largest payoff may well occur in the earliest stages of the service encounter [a problem early in the provision of the service sours the whole process!].

The importance of very high standards of customer service is evidenced here by two examples. The marketing philosophy of McDonalds, the world's largest food service organization, is encapsulated in its motto 'Q.S.C. & V.' (Quality, Service, Cleanliness & Value). The standards, enforced somewhat quixotically (but memorably) on its franchisees and managers at the 'Hamburger University' in Elk Grove Village (Illinois), require that the customer receive a 'good tasting' hamburger in no more than five minutes, from a friendly host or hostess in a spotlessly clean restaurant. The second example, Disneyland, also insists on spotless cleanliness, and on the customer being 'the Guest'. It is salutary to observe how few of the competitors in either of these fields manage the simple task of keeping their premises clean, let alone being able to think of their customers as 'guests'; the terms used in the fairground trade (with which Disney competes, albeit at a very different level) usually see the customer as some form of victim ('pigeon', 'mark', 'punter', etc.) – to be fleeced before the fair moves on!

See also SERVICE LEVELS

Reference: Maister, David H. (1988) The psychology of waiting lines. *In Managing Services: Marketing, Operations and Human Resources.* Englewood Cliffs, NJ: Prentice-Hall.

services and marketing research In theory services should be just as susceptible to almost all the marketing research techniques. In practice, the 'intangibility' of services makes most marketing research more difficult to conduct. The answers are less certain, because it is more difficult to frame the questions precisely; and the service is often intimately bound up with who delivers it – which makes generalizations (beloved of marketing researchers) less meaningful. In addition, the difficulty in establishing a permanent differentiation (in the absence of patenting, for instance) makes the level of investment tougher to justify.

Donald Cowell (1988) comments that:

The fuzziness and ambiguity of the service concept: the difficulty the customer may have in articulating what benefits are sought from a service . . . and what elements the service should consist of provide a 'researchability' problem for the market researcher. A particular problem is to identify, weight and rank the separate elements, tangible and intangible, that make up a service offer . . . This can mean that in order to determine what a service entity is to a market, a marketer must spend more time and effort on initial marketing research than in product marketing as a

tight service specification may be difficult to produce . . .

He adds the balancing advantage, though, that:

Some of the differences between services and products in fact offer advantages to the marketing researcher. First the researcher has the opportunity to evaluate services before the sale, after the sale and during the sale (i.e. during the performance of the service) . . . some services are consumed as they are being produced. The performer can thus obtain feedback while the service is being produced and make appropriate adjustments where these are required by the customer . . . Second, direct customer involvement with many services does allow the user to give a direct specification of what service is required to the seller or performer.

In practice, marketing research is often most neglected by not-for-profit organizations (with honourable exceptions – such as Mass Observation). Kotler and Andreasen (1987) observe:

Most nonprofit organizations carry out much less marketing research than they should. This is because they have accepted certain myths. They assume that marketing research should only be used for major decisions, that it involves big surveys, that it takes a long time, that it is always expensive, that it requires sophisticated researchers, and, when it is finished, that it is usually not read or used. But research using a diversity of techniques, many at low cost, can be extremely valuable to a wide range of decisions.

See also MARKETING RESEARCH

References: Cowell, Donald W. (1988) New service development. *Journal of Marketing Management,* 3(3).
    Kotler, Philip and Andreasen, Alan R. (1987) *Strategic Marketing for Nonprofit Organizations* (3rd edn). Englewood Cliffs, NJ: Prentice-Hall.

service-sector logistics Three key decision areas in traditional logistics management ('facility', 'inventory' and 'communications') clearly relate to service industries and, arguably, are even more important here than in manufacturing. Where a service has to be available 'locally', as is often the case, there may need to be a significant number of 'facilities'. The location of these facilities, where they may need to be very accessible to clients, may be critical. The facilities themselves may form a major element of what the customer sees, and hence of the 'promotion'; so the bricks and mortar, the architecture and interior design, may offer the most immediate 'proof' of the quality of the service.

It may seem that there would be no place for 'inventory decisions' in the context of an intangible service. But, in practice, the equivalent decisions are critical, and much more difficult to make. The reason is that the 'product' is totally 'perishable'. If it is not used when it is available it must be wasted; it cannot be put into stock until a customer wants it. If an airliner takes off with empty seats, or a hairdresser has no customers for several hours, the lost revenue can never be recovered. This means that the forecasting of demand is that much more important. The 'capacity' – the service – has to be available to clients exactly when and where it is needed.

This also means that 'communications decisions' become that much more important. The communications flow is increasingly central to delivery of, or at least control of the delivery of, the service. In the case of the financial services industry it (the computerized communications system) has become the service itself; the 'product' – the customer's insurance or investment – usually only exists as electronic 'paperwork' inside computers! It is for this reason that in recent years the service sector has been by far the biggest customer of the computer industry.

On the other hand, the two other traditional decision areas in logistics, 'production' and 'transport', relate most clearly to physical products, and cannot be readily extrapolated to service markets (the choice of which taxi should deliver the management consultant to his client cannot be considered to be a major 'transport decision'!).

See also DATA PROCESSING, LOGISTICS; FACILITY DECISIONS, LOGISTICS MANAGEMENT; INVENTORY CONTROL; LOGISTICS MANAGEMENT; PRODUCTION DECISIONS, LOGISTICS MANAGEMENT; SERVQUAL; TRANSPORT DECISIONS, LOGISTICS MANAGEMENT

services, features There are some distinctions which may apply to services (as opposed to products):

* intangibility
* inseparability
* variability
* perishability

See also INSEPARABILITY, SERVICES; INTANGIBILITY; PERISHABILITY, SERVICES; VARIABILITY, SERVICES

services related to a physical product The more complex products, such as computers, demand sophisticated support services. In the case of a computer, for example, these may include the provision of highly skilled engineers to maintain it, provision and tailoring of software to run on it, and the education of the people who are to use it. In cases such as these service elements are ultimately as important (and as costly) as the physical product itself; though, typically, customers still continue to think in terms of the physical product as being the dominant element.

services which have a product attached Some services (which are clearly seen by consumers as services) revolve around products. The home security service is based upon physical intruder alarms and smoke detectors, for example, but many householders will be happy to pay for a consultant to design and fit these, and will expect a large part of the cost to be accounted for by the 'people' cost (design and fitting) associated with the service. It is often argued that services such as those offered by holiday tour operators also have physical elements firmly attached, in that the capital items – the aircraft carrying the holidaymakers to their destination and the hotels they stay in – represent elements that the consumer may judge as they would physical products.
See also SERVICES, FEATURES

servqual This is Parasuraman's approach to measuring service quality via a questionnaire based on five major dimensions (tangibles, reliability, responsiveness, assurance and empathy) with 22 pairs of Likert-type scales.
See also SERVICE, QUALITY

set-up cost *see* ECONOMIC BATCH QUANTITY

set-up times Possibly the most important aspect of flexible manufacturing is the reduction of set-up times – the times when production has to be stopped (between batches of different products) so that different parts (dies, jigs, etc.) can fitted to the production line. Reduction in set-up times not only reduces costs but also allows for a much lower economic batch quantity – with consequent reductions in lead time and flexibility of operations overall. The most important development was made by S. Shingo (1987), who in 1969 was working on productivity improvements on a 1000 ton press at Toyota. He realized that there were two sorts of set-up: internal set-up, which could only be achieved when the production was stopped; and external set-up, which could be carried out before the line needed to be stopped. Using this approach on the 1000 ton press, (internal) set-up times, when it was unproductive, were reduced from four hours to a matter of minutes. *See also* INVENTORY CONTROL; JUST IN TIME (JIT); KAISEN; LOGISTICS MANAGEMENT

Reference: Shingo, S. (1987) *Key Strategies for Plant Improvement.* Cambridge, MA: Productivity Press.

seven Ps   *see* 3 Ps

seven S's   *see* CULTURE, ORGANIZATIONAL

shareholder communications   *see* CORPORATE PROMOTION VERSUS BRAND PROMOTION; CORPORATE PUBLIC RELATIONS

shareholders   *see* STAKEHOLDERS

shark watcher   A consultant who specializes in giving companies early warnings of any potential takeovers.

sharpening the cutting edge of media   In evaluating the possible impact of media, perhaps the most useful chart is a combination of OTS (Opportunities To See) and coverage, since this best demonstrates whether or not you are delivering your message to your chosen target audience with the optimal impact.

The ideal performance is represented here by a sharp-edged peak which closely matches coverage of your target audience to the optimal level of OTS. The reality is often closer to a broader, diffuse curve, where large proportions of the coverage receive inappropriate levels of OTS (either too low, which means that they are unlikely to recognize the message, or too high, where much of the exposure is wasted). Usually the best that can be hoped for is a more cost-effective curve, which is broader than the ideal but which takes advantage of the lower cost media and special deals to pull down the average cost per thousand whilst still using a core schedule which is quite tightly targeted. *See also* ADVERTISING; ADVERTISING BUDGETS; COVERAGE; MEDIA IMPACT

shaving the specification   *see* PRICE, PURCHASE

sheds   *see* LOCATION, RETAIL

sheet, display size   *see* POSTERS

sheet fed   *see* REEL FED

shelf display, packaging   The pack may be designed to make the most of the shelf space available – which may even mean making the pack as compact as possible, so that more may be stacked on the shelf. 'Stackability', so that the shelf can take several layers of product, is another possible pack feature. These are all promotion-based design decisions. It should never be forgotten, though, that the formal pack description, typically on the label, must conform to any legislated standards for the product category, particularly in terms of the contents list.

shelf items   *see* MAKE OR BUY

shelf life   The length of time a product may be safely stored by the retailer on the shelves (or in the stockroom).

shelf space   *see* PROMOTION OBJECTIVES

shelf talker   Promotional material attached to shelves in self-service stores.

shell scheme   Standard design exhibition stand (booth) usually provided by an exhibition organizer. *See also* EXHIBITIONS

shifting loyals   *see* USAGE AND LOYALTY

shipping and forwarding agent   A company which handles the transport of goods (and the related paperwork), especially those being exported or imported. *See also* EXPORTING

shipping outers   *see* PACKAGING

shoebox money, advertising   *see* ADVERTISING BUDGETS

shoe shops   *see* RETAIL PRODUCT OR SERVICE CATEGORIES

shoot   *see* RUSH

shopper typologies   This is a classification which identifies: convenience shoppers, leisure shoppers, price-conscious shoppers and store-loyal consumers.

shopping mall   *see* LOCATION, RETAIL; MALL

short-listing, a marketing research agency
The initial short-list (in the selection of a marketing research agency) can be drawn up from an existing, reliable list of agencies, such as *The Market Research Society Yearbook* in the UK. On the other hand, it may be based on practical experience (or news items in the marketing press) or on the experience of your contacts. The short-list can be as long as you like, but the normal procedure is to select three.
See also APPOINTING A MARKETING RESEARCH AGENCY

short-term forecasts   Most organizations need to know what is going to happen in the near future. They need these predictions for a number of reasons, including:

• *Capacity loading.* The classical use of short-term forecasting is that of scheduling production capacity; or, more often, deciding which of the alternative configurations that capacity is to be assigned over the next period – be it a week or a month. The input to this short-term forecasting may come from the sales force; its forecasts for the near future should represent a very confident measure of what will happen. On the other hand, the input may be from the marketing department, who may provide short-term forecasts based on, for example, recognized seasonal trends or short-term promotional activities.
• *Information transmission.* One element of short-term forecasts has little to do with predicting unknown quantities; instead, it is simply the formal process of transferring known information from one part of the organization to another. Thus, the order processing department produces 'forecasts', which are actually the totals for the orders already received and being processed, for the production scheduling system.
• *Control.* Forecasts, especially short-term ones, are frequently used as a key element of control. Thus, what the sales force is predicting will happen over the near future gives advance warning of problems that will need to be rectified, and hence are an early indicator for control purposes.

See also LONG-TERM FORECASTS; MEDIUM–TERM FORE-CASTS; SHORT- VERSUS LONG-TERM FORECASTS

short- versus long-term forecasts   There are different types of forecast to meet different needs. One of the main differences is the timespan the forecast covers:

• *Short term (tactical)* – monthly and quarterly, for example, as input to the normal business planning and control processes.
• *Medium term (annual plan)* – annually, say, as the main input to the budget planning processes.
• *Long term (strategic)* – typically for five years, as the basis for the organization's strategies.

See also LONG-TERM FORECASTS; MEDIUM–TERM FORE-CASTS; SHORT-TERM FORECASTS

shoulder time   Advertising time next to peak time.
See also PEAK TIME

shower approach to world trade   *see* STANDARDIZATION VERSUS ADAPTATION

showings   The display material on show (in-store) recorded as a part of retail audits.
See also RETAIL AUDITS

showthrough   Heavy print on the reverse of a sheet showing through to the front.

shrinkage   Sometimes called leakage, the euphemism for theft (or pilferage) by employees, especially from within stores.

shrink-wrap   Instead of being put in cardboard outers, products are often wrapped for shipment in polythene (or some similar plastic film) which is then shrunk by hot air to hold them tightly.
See also PACKAGING

SIC   *see* STANDARD INDUSTRIAL CLASSIFICATION (SIC)

sidehead   A subhead (subheading, under the main headline), which is placed to the left or right of the text.

sigmoid curve   *see* DIFFUSION OF INNOVATION

signage, retail   *see* RETAIL 'PRODUCT' DECISIONS

significance testing   Testing analyses (statistically) to see how significant (in statistical terms) the results may be. Such testing typically assumes (in the case of marketing research) that a random sample has been used. As this is rarely the case, the use of significance must be careful and well informed.
See also ANALYSIS OF MARKETING RESEARCH DATA

significative inputs   *see* HOWARD AND SHETH MODEL, OF CONSUMER BEHAVIOUR

sign-off   *see* RINGI

silence, interviewing/questioning   Even if people do ask the correct open questions, they often undermine the progress by stopping the prospect in mid-flow. The natural accompaniment to an open question is silence. John Fenton (1984) summed it up succinctly in his book, when he said: 'Whenever you ask a question . . . SHUT UP. After 6–7 seconds of silence REPEAT QUESTION. Silence is very effective. Don't let him off the hook because you are embarrassed by the silence.' Silence is probably one of the most under-used of questioning techniques. It is, though, a surprisingly aggressive technique, and you should not make it too obvious – it is best just to look very thoughtful. It requires a great deal of courage to use, particularly for a sales professional, who is supposed to be all mouth! But it is effective. The person you are questioning will eventually feel obliged to talk, and usually what he or she then says is especially enlightening (since he or she too will have had time to consider).
See also OPEN QUESTIONS; QUESTIONING

Reference: Fenton, John (1984) *How to Sell Against Competition.* London: Heinemann.

silent salesperson   A term used to describe point-of-sale display material.

silk screen   A relatively low-quality printing method in which the ink is forced by a squeegee through a fine-mesh screen, on which the design is placed, onto the paper or other material; often used for display material.
See also LETTERPRESS; LITHO

simplicity   *see* CONVICTION MARKETING FACTORS

simplicity, in advertising messages   *see* ENCODING

simulated real calls   *see* SALES TRAINING

simulation   *see* ROLE PLAYING

simultaneous introduction   *see* STANDARDIZATION VERSUS ADAPTATION

single supplier   *see* SUPPLIER SELECTION

sitting tenant   *see* ORGANIZATIONAL BUYING SITUATIONS

size, segment viability   The first question to be asked before targeting a particular segment is simply whether it is substantial enough to justify attention: will there be enough volume generated to provide an adequate profit? As segmentation is a process largely under the control of the producer (at least in the short term), it is usually possible to find ever smaller segments, which could be targeted separately. Ultimately, each consumer could be considered to be a separate segment, with different needs to be met; though in practice this 'ideal' can usually only be justified in the capital goods markets, such as that for mainframe computers, where the individual order may be large enough to warrant this treatment. In general, it is best to choose the smallest number of segments, and hence the largest average size (including the one you are targeting), which still allows the resources to be concentrated and head-on competition with the market leaders avoided. In part, however, the viable size will be defined in terms of the cost structures of the producer. The car market is heavily segmented, with Ford, for example, targeting a wide range of separate segments, but even the smallest of these (sharing the same assembly line as others) must be worth some tens of thousands of cars a year (simply to earn its place on that assembly line). But Aston Martin, with its custom hand-building, can very effectively target a segment which is worth just a few hundred cars a year.
See also SEGMENT VIABILITY

sketches   *see* ADVERTISING PROCESSES; CREATIVE DEPARTMENT, ADVERTISING AGENCY

skewed samples   *see* RANDOM SAMPLES

skimming, pricing   One pricing approach is to set the initial price high, to 'skim' as much profit as possible – even in the early stages of the 'product life cycle'. This is an option that is open to all products or services, and one which can apply throughout the life of the 'product' – assuming that the producer adopts a policy of limited competition, such as 'niche' marketing. It is particularly applicable to new products which, at least for a time, have a monopoly of the market because its competitors have not yet emerged. This is a pattern often seen in the introduction of new technology – video recorders and single lens reflex cameras, for example. The initial price is kept high, to make the maximum profit from the initially limited demand (and the probably equally limited supplies). It is then reduced, possibly in stages to gradually expand demand, until it reaches a competitive level just before the competitors enter the market. This is a fine judgement, though; and it is interesting to note that in the case of the video recorders and cameras it was the latecomers, with competitive prices, which actually swept the board!

The rationale behind the 'skimming' policy (sometimes called 'rapid payback') is normally quite simply that of maximizing profit. But there may occasionally be another motive – that of maximizing the image of 'quality'. In this case the policy of high pricing, to demonstrate quality, would continue throughout the life of the product or service. As indicated above, the danger of a skimming policy is that a high price encourages other manufacturers to enter the market because they see that sales revenue can quickly cover the expense of developing a rival product. Even if your prices are not exorbitant, you may still need, therefore, to plan for a steady reduction in price as competitors appear and you recover some of your launch costs. Such a price reduction will normally be helped by the unit-cost reduction that should occur as total output grows – 'economies of scale'.

See also INTRODUCTORY STAGE, PRODUCT LIFE CYCLE; MARKETING STRATEGIES; PENETRATION PRICING; PRICES, CUSTOMER NEEDS; PRICING NEW 'PRODUCTS'; PRICING, PRODUCT LIFE CYCLE

skip scheduling   Advertising in every other issue of a magazine.
See also MEDIA IMPACT; MEDIA SELECTION

skunkworks   This is a term used to describe development teams working outside the normal structures of the organization. James Quinn (1985) suggests that 'Highly innovative enterprises often use a skunkworks approach, which allows small teams of engineers, technicians, designers, and model makers to develop a product without intervening organizational barriers'. Tony Morden (1989) explains part of the reason for their success: 'Such unofficial cash flow is sometimes described as bootlegging. Skunks and bootleggers are often successful innovators precisely because they are so resource constrained. They have to get the basics right first time. They have to keep their work simple and to the point.' He also goes

on to describe the related but more formalized approach, much in vogue during the 1980s – 'intrapreneurship' – in which the organization deliberately sets up separate business units (small, but – critically – autonomous) in order to simulate the entrepreneurial activities of small businesses. At the level of the individual, Thomas Bonoma's (1986) research found that 'under conditions of marketplace change, success depended heavily on the presence of marketing subversives in a company. Subversive managers undermined their organization's structures to implement new marketing practices. By improving on their traditional skills – interacting, resource allocating, monitoring, and organising – they often took big risks to introduce unconventional practices . . .'
See also GENERATING IDEAS

References: Bonoma, Thomas V. (1986) Marketing subversives. *Harvard Business Review*, November–December.
  Morden, Tony (1989) Innovation: people and implementation. *Management Decision*, 27(3).
  Quinn, James Brian (1985) Managing innovation: controlled chaos. *Harvard Business Review*, May–June.

sleeper   A product which sells poorly initially and then takes off.

sleeper, mailing   *see* DIRECT MAIL ADVERTISING

slides   *see* PRESENTATION MEDIA

slogan   A memorable catchphrase used in promotion of a product or service.
See also ADVERTISING PROCESSES; CREATING THE CORRECT MESSAGES; CREATIVE DEPARTMENT, ADVERTISING AGENCY

slots   *see* MEDIA SELECTION

slots, service industry   *see* COMPUTER INVENTORY CONTROL

small firms   In terms of the basic 'dimensions' on which marketing is often organized, it is arguable that small firms are just as susceptible to marketing solutions as are large ones. The difference is that they usually do not have the resources or expertise to exploit marketing in its most sophisticated forms; and, in any case, would be unlikely to have anything other than a limited impact on their environment. As Carson and Cromie (1989) say:

small firms have a 'distinctive marketing style'. There is little or no adherence to formal structures and frameworks. Because of their limited resources the marketing activity of small firms is inevitably restricted in its scope and activity. This manifests itself in marketing which is simplistic, haphazard, often responsive and reactive to competitor activity . . . it is also product oriented . . . and oriented around price . . . the marketing style can be described as an 'involved' one which relies heavily on intuitive ideas and decisions and probably most importantly on common-sense.

On the other hand, 'common sense' is a very valuable commodity in marketing; and proprietors in such small businesses are usually much closer to their customers than many of the marketing managers in larger organizations, and thus can, and should, enter into a dialogue to apply that common sense to producing a product or service offering which exactly meets the needs of their customers. This would represent excellent marketing practice.

See also ORGANIZATIONAL PIGEON-HOLES

Reference: Carson, David and Cromie, Stanley (1989) Marketing planning in small enterprises: a model and some empirical evidence. *Journal of Marketing Management*, 5(1).

smoothed forecasts   *see* MOVING ANNUAL TOTAL (MAT)

snowball samples   *see* QUOTA SAMPLES

snowball technique   A technique for clustering ideas emerging from creative thinking sessions which requires members of a group to sort them (after they have been written on index cards) into groups by taping them to a wall.

See also NEW PRODUCT CREATION

social and business structures, filtering unsuitable markets   Culture can play a decisive role in deciding whether a product is to be accepted in a given market. The special problems of Islamic countries are one example, but there are many other cultural barriers – often also related to religious matters, as anyone selling contraceptives to Roman Catholic countries will testify! Business cultures, too, have their idiosyncrasies. In certain countries, for example, it is a way of life for 'access' to be 'purchased'; in US and UK eyes this may be seen as bribery, but locally it is often seen simply as part of the normal costs of trading. Equally, in certain countries the

structure of business may be very informal, so that it takes an amount of accumulated expertise to understand exactly what the deal which you just struck actually means! In other countries still, the negotiation procedures are alien, ranging from the haggling of the bazaar (which is meant to be an entertainment in itself for both participants) to the sophisticated nuances of Japanese business (most of which are lost on Western businessmen attempting to take part). In the other direction, however, when the large Japanese retailers – such as Sogo, Isetan and Daimaru – opened department stores in Hong Kong they ensured that they were upmarket Chinese stores (albeit with a Japanese brand image). On a more factual level, the state of development of the society can be, at least in part, gauged by the development of specific social structures, such as the degree (in percentage terms) of literacy and the employment levels – as well as the employment by sector (service versus manufacturing versus primary agriculture, for example). In any case, the level of education may become a deciding factor in the use of any product which requires a degree of skill, or even the following of written instructions!

See also EXPORT MARKET ELIMINATION

social class influences, on the purchase decision   The traditional, 'pigeon-holing', mainstay of much of the advertising industry has been that of social class, which – though it revolves around the occupation (usually of the head of the household) – is based on more than just income groups alone.

In earlier years the stereotypes were that the lower classes, the working classes, read the *Sun* newspaper, bought convenience foods and voted Labour. The upper classes read *The Times*, ate in restaurants and voted Conservative.

It was also assumed that the 'upper classes' were the first to try new products, and that these then 'trickled down' (the name of the theory) to the lower classes. Historically there may have been some justification for this. The refrigerator, the washing machine, the car and the telephone were all adopted first by the higher social classes. Recently, however, as affluence has become more widespread the process has become much less clear, and it is now argued that the new 'opinion leaders' come from within the same social class.

This approach has been reported to be of decreasing value in recent decades. Whereas, some four decades ago when these groupings were first widely used, the numbers in each of the main categories (C, D and E) were reasonably well balanced, today the C group in total (though now usually split to give C1 and C2) forms such a large sector that it dominates the whole classification system, and may offer that much less in terms of usable concentration of marketing effort. In addition, as described above, increased affluence has meant that consumers have developed tastes which are based on other aspects of their lifestyles, and class-related behaviour appears to have decreased significantly in terms of purchasing patterns!

It may, on the other hand, be too early to write it off as a predictor of behaviour. The 1988 research in the UK by O'Brien and Ford showed that, across all subgroups, 'Social Class' had a slight edge over 'Lifestage' (and a significant one over 'Lifestyle') in terms of discriminating between maximum and minimum penetrations of the range of 20 typical consumer items. Certainly, it may be a significant factor in some sectors. Thus, for instance, more than half of Sainsbury's supermarket customers are ABC1 whereas, on the other hand, over 40 per cent of those of its cut-price competitor (Kwik Save) are in the DE groups!

See also CLASS GROUPINGS; DECISION-MAKING PROCESS, BY CUSTOMERS; LIFESTYLE, AND THE (CUSTOMER) DECISION-MAKING PROCESS; OCCUPATIONAL INFLUENCES, ON THE PURCHASE DECISION; REPEAT PURCHASING PROCESS

Reference: O'Brien, Sarah and Ford, Rosemary (1988) Can we at last say goodbye to social class? *Journal of the Market Research Society*, 30(3).

social inputs   *see* HOWARD AND SHETH MODEL, OF CONSUMER BEHAVIOUR

social marketing   Some marketing, almost always originating in the non-profit sector, is quite deliberately targeted at changing the behaviour of its target audience, without selling any accompanying product or service. Examples have been the various attempts to stop cigarette-smoking or to increase the amount of charitable giving. Kotler and Andreasen (1987) define it thus: 'Social behavior marketing is the design, implementation and control of programs designed to ultimately influence individual behavior in ways that the marketer believes are in the individual's or society's interests'.

Reference: Kotler, Philip and Andreasen, Alan R. (1987) *Strategic Marketing for Nonprofit Organizations* (3rd edn). Englewood Cliffs, NJ: Prentice-Hall.

social marketing, pricing   *see* PRICE AND NOT-FOR-PROFIT ORGANIZATIONS

sociocultural change   *see* SWOT ANALYSIS

Sogo Shosha   *see* MARKET ENTRY TACTICS

solicitors   *see* RETAIL ORGANIZATION

solitary survivor   *see* AGE INFLUENCES, ON THE PURCHASE DECISION

solus advertisement   An advertisement which is not placed close to those for any competitive products.
See also MEDIA IMPACT; MEDIA SELECTION

Sony   *see* GLOBALIZATION

sound track   The optical strip alongside a movie film on which is recorded the sound.

source-loyalty model   *see* ORGANIZATIONAL BUYING SITUATIONS

space, media   *see* MEDIA BUYING, ADVERTISING AGENCY

spare capacity   *see* NEW PRODUCT NEEDS

special agent   An agent who is authorized to act only for a special purpose.
See also DISTRIBUTION CHAIN

special-interest magazines   *see* PRESS MEDIA

specialist agencies   Recent years have seen the growth of more specialist agencies. These usually take on just one of the functions which a traditional agency would cover. Typically they handle just the creative work (where they are often called 'hot shop' agencies) or just the media buying. The advertiser then buys their services 'à la carte', choosing what is considered to be the best specialist creative agency, to meet the specific needs of the product or service, and then the best media buying agency, to cover the media under consideration. Although these agencies still only cover a minority of the total business, they are growing in importance. At an even more specialist level are the agencies which specialize in handling industrial advertising and those dealing with recruitment or classified advertising – all areas where specialist expertise can be applied. At the other extreme, the largest agencies (such as Saatchi & Saatchi and

WPP) have carried out acquisition programmes worldwide, so they are now truly multinational, and also cover a wide range of consultancy services as well as advertising. This is often justified (particularly by Saatchi & Saatchi) as the 'globalization' of advertising – the idea being that the same creative message can be promoted in all markets worldwide. The validity of this assertion has been widely challenged, but the 'economies of scale' which such large agency multinationals can achieve (primarily by placing even heavier pressure on the media owners) may justify their size – and balance the inherent overheads incurred in running such large bureaucracies. The global agency does offer a 'one-stop' solution for the global corporation.

See also ADVERTISING; ADVERTISING AGENCY ELEMENTS; MARKETING RESEARCH

specialist magazines   *see* DELIVERY SYSTEMS, PRECISION MARKETEING

speciality sales   Another term for sales professionals selling (with specialized knowledge) face-to-face, typically to industrial users.

See also SALES PROFESSIONAL

specialized businesses   As represented by one quadrant in the Advantage Matrix (from the Boston Consulting Group), these businesses gain benefits from both economies of scale and differentiation (often characterized by experience effects in their own, differentiated, segment), examples being branded foods and cosmetics. The main strategies are focus and segment leadership.

specialty stores   *see* RETAIL PRODUCT OR SERVICE CATEGORIES

specification   According to many purchasing textbooks, this is the easy part of the purchasing process: you simply pass the buck to the using department! The 'buyer' (with no special expertise in specifying to match the varying needs of differing suppliers – and allowed no contact with those suppliers) will be able to generate the exact specification needed, though Heinritz et al. (1986) do issue the warning:

> The engineer tends to specify very wide margins of quality, safety and performance, whereas the purchasing manager tends to narrow such margins and work to minimum requirements. The engineer, by temperament and training, seeks the ideal material or design or equipment, frequently with insufficient regard for cost. The purchasing manager seeks materials and equipment adequate for the intended purpose, at the lowest ultimate cost . . .

Regretfully (as indicated by the quotation) the traditional approach can all too often lead to the most inefficient buying of all. Either the specifier does not understand the process, so that the specification is inadequate (leading to very expensive modifications later in the process), or he or she plays safe ('overspecifying', to allow for the inevitable downgrading by the purchasing department – and inevitably meaning that the 'product' costs are inflated by inessential elements!). Ideally, the buyer should know sufficient of both sides to be able to mediate the communications and bring the 'combatants' together. In this context, much of the specification becomes a matter of negotiation, building on the strengths of the supplier to meet the needs of the user. The buyer should be the best person to catalyse and control this process. Some of the factors which need to be taken into account in the specification are:

- quality
- delivery/support
- price

See also DELIVERY AND SUPPORT SPECIFICATION; PURCHASING; QUALITY SPECIFICATION; PRICE NEGOTIATION

Reference: Heinritz, Stuart F., Farrell, Paul V. and Smith, Clifton L. (1986) *Purchasing: Principles and Applications* (7th edn). Englewood Cliffs, NJ: Prentice-Hall.

spinarama   Poster made up of three-sided slats, in a venetian blind effect, which rotate to give a constantly changing poster.

See also POSTERS

spinner   Revolving stand on which goods are displayed in-store.

split runs   In this approach to experimental research, different stimuli are simultaneously applied to separate (but statistically equivalent) groups, and the results compared across these.

See also EXPERIMENTAL RESEARCH

sponsorship   This is a very specialized form of promotion. It can be very expensive indeed (whether it is in the field of arts or sport or whatever). It requires careful justification, though too often it is based upon the private interests of the members of the board rather than any logical business case! It can, however, be very productive for those organizations (such as tobacco companies) which have limited access to the media or have more complex objectives (such as arranging events for meeting customers which can be very conveniently linked, say, to sponsorship of the arts). It equally requires specialist help, and very careful planning and control – it is all too easy for excessive enthusiasm (not least on the part of the chief executive officer) to cause budgets to evaporate! Such sponsorship can be quite discreet or highly public.

See also POLITICAL CONTACTS; SALES PROMOTION

spontaneous answer   *see* QUESTIONNAIRE DESIGN

spontaneous awareness   *see* ADVERTISING RESEARCH; KISS ADVERTISING

spread of frequencies   *see* MEDIA SELECTION

spread of Opportunities To See   *see* MEDIA BUYING, ADVERTISING AGENCY

spreadsheets, and forecasting   Almost all managers now have access to a personal computer, even if they do not have one dedicated to their own use. Such PCs have a wide variety of uses in marketing; not least when, used as a terminal, they give access to the organization's databases. In the context of forecasting and planning, however, probably the most useful tool they provide (apart from specific statistical forecasting packages – which usually require a significant degree of statistical knowledge to use) is the now ubiquitous 'spreadsheet'. Despite its apparent simplicity, even this is often misused by managers, being seen merely as a more sophisticated form of calculator which at the same time incorporates, somehow or other, the 'magic of computing'. In the present context, though, it has a number of powerful contributions to make:

'Mechanizing' routine budgets
The whole planning cycle is bedevilled by the grind of cranking out large numbers of routine figures. Many, if not most, of these are derived from other figures (and ultimately lead back to a relatively few indirect variables entered into the 'model'). Once these linkages are entered onto a spreadsheet it be-

comes a much easier matter to produce the required figures. This is an obvious use for PCs and one that managers have, understandably, latched on to. There are, however, dangers even in this seemingly straightforward approach. Not least is that it locks into the 'model' all the existing assumptions about the relationships. It is, in any case, unlikely that managers will think to challenge these assumptions (and to investigate whether matters have changed either in the marketplace or in the workings of the organization), even when they are forced to recalculate them manually. In the case of the spreadsheet, where these assumptions are effectively hidden, it is almost inevitable that they will not be re-examined! There are two solutions to this dilemma:

1. *Clear structure.* The spreadsheet should be designed (and explained, by being 'self documented') in such a way that the linkages (and hence the assumptions) are obvious and are easy to change.
2. *Process of challenge.* As a routine part of the budgetary process, some of the time saved by the use of the spreadsheet should be used routinely to challenge the assumptions to ensure that they are still valid. This is no mere bureaucratic procedure, since much of marketing judgement is about setting these assumptions; and from them are derived the ensuing strategies and plans.

'What if?'
Perhaps the most important use of spreadsheets is to ask the question 'What if?' The ease with which the calculations can be repeated, with different assumptions, means that the marketing manager (or, indeed, any manager) can try out all the different alternatives. Entering the values relating to different assumptions and obtaining a print-out of the resulting performance levels may take little more than a minute! This iterative process can be used to fine tune, or optimize, the key parameters. The most important aspect, however, is that it should enable managers to consider all the alternatives; and they, and you, would be foolish to ignore the opportunity this affords. It should be remembered, though, that the spreadsheet is usually a very crude model of real life. It is too easy to get so involved in the process of 'fine tuning' the inputs that gross inaccuracies in the assumptions are forgotten; the 'model' will then start to obscure the reality – and may even become more real to the modeller (until real losses put him or her out of business!).

Modelling

As indicated above, spreadsheets can be used to build crude models. For example, a model of the seasonal, trend and cyclic components of sales figures (as well as the impact of promotions) can be created from 'eyeballing' the graphs of historical sales and 'fine tuning' the resulting model parameters until the results obtained from it most closely fit the historical results. This process may be time consuming and may lack the elegance of the more sophisticated techniques, but it may also produce results which are almost as good as them (and are better understood by the user). Aficionados of Excel, and these include not a few managers, will, of course, enjoy developing ever more refined models.

See also FORECASTING TECHNIQUES; QUANTITATIVE FORECASTING TECHNIQUES

SPSS The best-known statistical package, which offers a wide range of statistical analyses for use in (market) research. Other, similar packages include MINITAB and SAS.

SRI *see* PROACTIVE PR

SS *see* SAME SIZE

SSFF *see* SUPPORT SUCCESS FORGET FAILURE (SSFF)

stackability *see* SHELF DISPLAY, PACKAGING

stack it high, sell it cheap *see* RETAIL PRODUCT OR SERVICE CATEGORIES

staff, and 'buy-in' *see* MAKE OR BUY

staff relationships, with customers *see* PARTNERSHIP TRIANGLE

stakeholder communications *see* CORPORATE PUBLIC RELATIONS

stakeholders The tradition used to be that only those individuals (or organizations) who had a direct ownership relation to an organization were considered in any decisions taken by its management. These were the 'shareholders'. It is now often considered that all those others having any relationship which is affected by the organization's actions might also be considered – these are the 'stakeholders'. In practice this usually means the workers/staff, who are now recognized to have a very direct interest in what happens to the organization; but it can also be expanded to include customers and suppliers, who are also dependent in various ways on it, and especially the local community (which can sometimes be almost destroyed by a decision to, say, close down a plant).

stalemated businesses As represented by one quadrant in the Advantage Matrix (from the Boston Consulting Group), here there is the opportunity for neither differentiation nor economies of scale; examples are textiles and shipbuilding. The main means of competition, therefore, has been reducing the 'factor costs' (mainly those of labour) by moving to locations – indeed, to different countries in the developing world – where these costs are lower.

stamps, promotional *see* PROMOTIONAL PRICING

standard deviation *see* NORMAL CURVE

standard industrial classification (SIC) The national system which codes all industries into categories. The international version is ISIC.

standardization versus adaptation In the literature, this whole debate has now been condensed down to a dichotomy between 'standardization' (that is, global marketing, the standardization of products across all markets) versus 'adaptation' (the classic marketing approach to the individual needs of markets/consumers). Henzler and Rall (1986) ask three critical questions:

1.   Is our business suited to globalization? . . . What might peak demand for the product in the major markets amount to, and what factors will affect it? Realistically, how uniform are customer needs from one country or region to another? . . . What further performance potential in the value-added chain could be realized by a shift to a global orientation? . . .

The two further questions, assuming the first test is passed, are:

2.   What is our best strategy? . . .
3.   Can we implement this strategy? . . .

If the company has no significant competitive advantage and the market is already occupied by global competitors, a globalization strategy may make little or no sense. In such a situation, the wise course may well be to retreat into a specialized niche or a customer segment with extremely high service requirements. More obviously still has been the decision to actually rename brands in various countries, in order to have truly global brands. Thus, the UK Marathon brand (chocolate count line) was very expensively renamed, by Mars, as Snickers – to bring it into line with other countries.

In this same context, Warren Keegan (1989) illustrates a commonly held approach to international marketing: 'The international product life cycle is basically a "trickle down" model of world trade and investment. First, products are introduced to the home market, then to the other advanced countries, and finally to developing and less developed countries.' He does add that an alternative is the 'shower approach': 'This strategy is to develop a product and simultaneously introduce it in world markets'. On the other hand, Kenichi Ohmae (1985) makes the point:

Most large companies grow by building dominant positions in what turned out to be huge markets, not by mastering the ins and outs of a wide range of businesses. Think how many leading companies are largely monocultural, in my sense of the term. GM is 88 per cent automobiles; Royal Dutch/ Shell 88% petroleum; Exxon 87% petroleum; Ford 93% automobiles. Much the same is true of IBM, Toyota . . .

See also COMPARATIVE ADVANTAGE, GLOBAL; ECONOMIES OF SCALE, GLOBAL; GLOBALIZATION; GLOBAL MARKETING; TRIAD POWER

References: Henzler, Herbert and Rall, Wilhelm (1986) Facing up to the globalization challenge. *The McKinsey Quarterly*, Winter.
   Keegan, Warren J. (1989) *Global Marketing Management* (4th edn). Englewood Cliffs, NJ: Prentice-Hall.
   Ohmae, Kenichi (1985) *Triad Power: The Coming Shape of Global Competition*. New York: The Free Press.

standard reorder quantity   *see* PRODUCTION DECISIONS, LOGISTICS MANAGEMENT

standout test   A test to see how the product stands out against its competitors when on the shelf in a store.
See also PRODUCT TEST

Stanford Research Institute   *see* INTERNATIONAL MARKETING RESEARCH; PROACTIVE PR

Stanislavsky's Method   *see* COARSE MARKETING; SYNTHESIS AND ASSIMILATION, OF MARKETING RESEARCH DATA

stars   In the popular application of the Boston Matrix these are those products in the quadrant with high market share and high market growth rate. These are probably relatively new products in the growth phase. Because they have high market shares, however, they may be generating sufficient gross profits to cover their current investment needs (demanded by their fast growth). A few such products can even be so successful that they generate some net profit at this stage; but usually the predominant strategy is to grow them to the next stage, the 'cash cow', where the most profit is made.
See also BOSTON MATRIX

starter brand   *see* INVESTMENT MULTIPLIER

statements of purpose   *see* CORPORATE OBJECTIVES

static or dynamic models   *see* MODEL CATEGORIES

station break   *see* BREAK

statistical models   *see* MODELS

stepped saw   Unlike the competitive saw, which looks at the impact of on-going, relatively minor changes, this form of the diagram looks at the effect of major inputs, or major investments (such as new products or significantly increased promotional spending). These may have the effect of raising the average level of the 'saw teeth'; though, as shown below, later neglect (or a comparably strong competitive response) can just as easily result in a step down to a lower average level.
See also COMPETITIVE SAW; PRODUCT LIFE CYCLE (PLC)

Steps to Quality   *see* CROSBY, P. B.; SUGGESTIONS SCHEMES

step-wise advertising models   *see* BUYING DECISION, ADVERTISING MODELS

stereotyped enemies   *see* GROUPTHINK

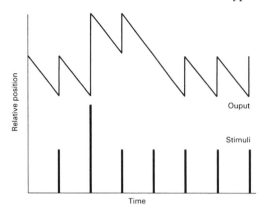

stereotype of salesman   *see* SALESMAN
STEREOTYPE

stick to the knitting   *see* NEW PRODUCT
INNOVATION

St James model   *see* SAINT JAMES MODEL

St Michael   *see* CORPORATE PROMOTION VERSUS
BRAND PROMOTION

stock control   *see* COMPUTER INVENTORY
CONTROL; INVENTORY CONTROL

stock decisions, logistics management   *see*
PRODUCTION DECISIONS, LOGISTICS MANAGEMENT

stock forecasting   *see* FORECASTS INTO BUDGETS

stockholding   *see* INVENTORY CONTROL

stockholding cost   *see* ECONOMIC BATCH
QUANTITY

stocking filler   A small, cheap item which can be
used to help fill a Christmas stocking.

stock level   *see* PRODUCTION DECISIONS, LOGISTICS
MANAGEMENT

stock pressure   *see* TRADE DISCOUNTS

stock recording   *see* COMPUTER INVENTORY
CONTROL

stop motion   A (frame-by-frame exposure) movie
technique used to animate cartoons, or to very rapidly speed up other events thus photographed.

stop-press   *see* FUDGE

store traffic   The number of customers entering a
store.
See also RETAILING

storyboard   *see* ADVERTISING PROCESSES; CONCEPT
TEST, NEW PRODUCTS; CREATIVE DEPARTMENT,
ADVERTISING AGENCY

straight rebuy   *see* BUYGRID ANALYSIS;
ORGANIZATIONAL BUYING SITUATIONS

strange familiar   *see* SYNECTICS®

strategic alliances   *see* PURCHASING

Strategic Business Unit (SBU)   One extension
of the planning process (pioneered by General Electric in the 1970s, and adopted by many other large
organizations in the 1980s) was to split the largest
organizations into smaller units, the SBUs, which
(as effectively 'autonomous' units) could be more
directly controlled by their immediate management
(and could have all the important strategic functions
under their own 'decentralized' control). From the
point of view of marketing (as opposed to the corporate strategists) there is, however, no significant
difference between an SBU and an equivalent
independent business of the same size. Igor Ansoff
went rather further, to describe SBAs (Strategic
Business Areas) – a somewhat more positive approach to market segments (which are the equivalent
of his SBAs) that the SBUs address – thus linking
the SBUs firmly with a marketing approach. Unlike
many of his other ideas, though, this terminology has
not entered into widespread use.
See also CORPORATE PLAN; MARKETING PLAN STRUC-
TURE; PLANNING PROCESS

strategic forecasts   *see* MARKETING PLAN
STRUCTURE; SHORT- VERSUS LONG-TERM FORECASTS

strategic (international) alliances   A positive
approach to using 'third parties', especially used by
the larger corporations (who are often already multinationals in their own right), is very deliberately to
build strong marketing links with other organizations
– 'strategic alliances'. As Kenichi Ohmae (1989) says:

Companies are just beginning to learn what nations have always known: in a complex, uncertain

world filled with dangerous opponents it is best not to go it alone . . . But managers have been slow to experiment with genuine strategic alliances. A joint venture here and there, yes, of course. A long-term contractual relationship, certainly. But forging the entente, rarely . . . Alliances mean sharing control . . . Globalization mandates alliances, makes them absolutely essential to strategy. Uncomfortable – but that's the way it is.

He goes on to explain: 'Alliances are not tools of convenience. They are important, even critical, instruments of serving customers in a global environment . . . Few companies operating in the Triad of Japan, the United States, and Europe can offer such topflight levels of value to all their customers all the time all by themselves.' He also highlights the problems of finding the resources needed: 'To compete in the global arena, you have to incur – and sometimes find a way to defray – immense fixed costs. You can't play a variable cost game any more. You need partners who can help you amortise your fixed costs . . .' Such strategic alliances are, therefore, created to engender monumental economies of scale; truly global undertakings!

David Lei (1989) makes the same point: 'The higher costs and risks of R & D, production, financing and market penetration brighten the prospects for expanded strategic alliances between global companies as top management believes that no company can manage all of the high risks associated with world-scale ventures'. But he goes on to add the caution: 'Yet joint ventures raise several questions of great corporate strategic importance since this vehicle for cooperation can also seriously undermine the company's long-term competitiveness if management is not careful in defining and implementing its "foreign policy"'.

Michael Geringer (1988), however, points out the amount of effort and investment involved in such a process:

Because of the presumed long-term nature of most joint ventures and the costs associated with premature dissolution, there tend to be relatively high financial and human costs associated with the selection of partners for successful ventures. Firms must be willing to incur substantial search costs, including those associated with developing selection criteria and evaluating partners, as well as the extensive resource expenditures typically involved in the negotiation stage. In addition, the process

needs to be approached with considerable patience and realistic expectations.

See also MARKET ENTRY TACTICS

References: Geringer, Michael J. (1988) Selection of partners for international joint ventures. *Business Quarterly*, Autumn.

Lei, David (1989) Strategies for global competition. *Long Range Planning*, 22(1).

Ohmae, Kenichi (1989) The global logic of strategic alliances. *Harvard Business Review*, March–April.

strategic screening, new products After the new product concept has been generated, the next stage is that of the initial screening of these idea(s). The contexts for this screening process are the corporate and marketing strategies. The potential new 'products' which have been found are now simply matched against these requirements. This can be handled as a two-stage process:

Qualitative screen
This simply looks qualitatively at the ideas to examine, at the broadest level, whether they are in conflict with the overall corporate or marketing strategies. This examination need not demand major effort, since the key characteristics of the new 'product' will usually be obvious, as will those of the relevant parts of the strategies – always assuming that the organization takes notice of its own planning documents. A match or mismatch should thus be fairly obvious. It may be simple, but it is an absolutely critical step in the new 'product' process.

Make or buy
This is also the stage at which the decision either to 'make' or 'buy-out' is likely to be taken. Traditionally, organizations only offered the products or services which they themselves 'manufactured'. In recent years, on the other hand, many organizations have adopted a wider perspective, and have marketed products (either in part or totally) made by other organizations – because those other organizations had the special expertise necessary or simply because their costs were lower. Occasionally the key characteristics may not be so obvious, so care should, in practice, be applied to the examination.

Financial analysis
If the qualitative screen reveals no significant problems, the acid test, at this early stage, is to forecast the financial performance of the new brand. The best way to achieve this is to prepare a dummy profit-and-loss statement, together with the associated balance sheet and the traditional further analyses such as cash

flow. With the advent of spreadsheets on personal computers this should now be a relatively simple process – especially if a skeleton, a standard framework, is already available. The great potential benefit of such spreadsheets, but one which is rarely capitalized upon, is the ability to very easily carry out 'what if' tests. For example, it can literally be a matter of a few seconds to change the price, adjust the projections of volume and have the resulting complete financial performance of this new set of assumptions printed out. This means that there should no longer be any excuse for not examining all the alternatives. *See also* NEW PRODUCT SCREENING, ORGANIZATIONAL FACTORS; NEW PRODUCT SCREENING, PRODUCT FACTORS; PRODUCT CHURNING, NEW PRODUCTS; PRODUCT DEVELOPMENT PROCESS

strategies for intent buyers Purchasing at times can take on an aspect which may be inadequately covered by the marketing literature. In this case, a buyer may find him- or herself facing an unresponsive seller, in the private or public sector, who simply does not want to meet that buyer's needs – either because of 'limited supply' or because he or she has a 'preferred clientele'. An 'intent buyer' may set out to overcome this lack of response. According to Kotler and Levy (1973) the main strategies could be:

- *Coercion* – through force or authority (by judicial means, for example, or at the other extreme by illegal means!).
- *Inducement* – offering something in return which will overcome the supplier's normal resistance (including paying a premium, the equivalent for a seller of cutting price, or even perhaps bribery!).
- *Persuasion* – by 'selling' the 'seller' into supplying the goods (using the means of 'promotion' available).
- *Education* – and, over the longer term, changing the seller's beliefs or values!

The priorities here can be very different to those of the average marketing programme, where the salesperson, say, can move on to the next prospect. Here, obtaining the supplies may be a matter of survival; and this, understandably, colours the whole process!
See also PURCHASING

Reference: Kotler, Philip and Levy, Sidney J. (1973) Buying is marketing too. *Journal of Marketing*, 37.

stratified sample In this form of (marketing research) random sampling, the original 'population' is 'stratified' (that is, categorized by some parameter; age, for example) and random samples are then drawn from each of these strata. This ensures that there are adequate numbers in each of these subsamples to allow for valid statistical analyses.
See also CLUSTER SAMPLING; DATA COLLECTION; QUOTA SAMPLES; RANDOM SAMPLES; SAMPLES; SAMPLING STATISTICS

Strengths Weaknesses Opportunities Threats analysis *see* SWOT ANALYSIS

strikes *see* MARKET ENTRY DECISION

structural barriers *see* REGULATORY CONSIDERATIONS, FILTERING UNSUITABLE MARKETS

structural unemployment Unemployment due to a mismatch between the skills required (job vacancies) in the economy and those which the unemployed actually have.

structured interview *see* SURVEY RESEARCH

structure of international marketing The most important factor in any organization's relationship with the various national markets is its own structure. The stereotypical relationship is that between a purely national company, such as Dole Pineapple, and its 'overseas' markets; in which case the company will see almost all its relationships as those of exporting. These relationships are, in many important respects, different from those applying in the rest of marketing. At the other end of the spectrum are a few giant transnationals which can afford to almost disregard national boundaries, or at least are able to consider them merely as unavoidable nuisances.

There are various definitions, and matching terminologies, offered by different commentators, but the main types of structure, in terms of handling international business, are:

- *Transnationals.* These are the truly global organizations, such as IBM or Shell, which operate in most countries; they have marketing organizations in all of these, and production units (and even development laboratories) in a fair number. These organizations can afford to view national markets as purely regional affairs, with each region having its own marketing characteristics but otherwise with no special marketing problems.

- *Multinationals.* These organizations, such as Unilever and General Mills, also operate in many countries. On the other hand, they tend to have individual operating companies in each country, which market to (and 'manufacture' for) that market. Country organizations are therefore subsidiaries which control their own country operations largely independently of the other country organizations. The marketing process is thus almost a purely national operation, with the parent only controlling the operations at the group level (and then typically in terms of the flow of funds).
- *International traders.* These are organizations, like Renault and Cinzano, which are typically based in one country and produce most of their output there. In other countries they have sales subsidiaries (and sometimes limited production, often assembly, operations). They are largely in the business of export. On the other hand, they already have the international structure which addresses these problems and compartmentalizes them – so that they may be largely dealt with as normal marketing activities.
- *Exporters.* These represent the majority of those trading internationally. Their main base, often overwhelmingly so, is their 'domestic' (home) market.
- *Domestic producers.* These comprise the largest number of organizations in any national market. They do not involve themselves in overseas markets; perhaps wisely so, as many small export operations are loss-makers, though the formation of 'international' groupings such as the EU or NAFTA may force them to widen their operations.

See also GLOBALIZATION

style modification   This is, perhaps, the most frequent 'product' modification; at least in style-conscious industries (which covers a very wide range, from Coca Cola through to IBM PCs). An 'old-fashioned' product may be unsaleable in some markets, although it may find a niche in more conservative ones.

See also PRODUCT (OR SERVICE) MODIFICATION

suasionetics   Techniques, used in the USA, for persuading people to adopt behaviour patterns.

sub-assemblies   *see* MATERIALS MANAGEMENT; MATERIALS REQUIREMENTS PLANNING (MRP)

subcontracting   *see* TRANSPORT DECISIONS, LOGISTICS MANAGEMENT

subcontractors, marketing research   Within the market research community itself there are now a host of specialist organizations serving the needs of the commissioning agencies. Thus an agency which has itself been commissioned by a client will typically plan and design the research itself, but it may then appoint a subcontractor (based on a specialist database) to provide the sample, another organization to pilot the research with group discussions, another company to conduct the main series of interviews in the field and yet another to undertake the computer analyses of the results. The client company does not see these subcontractors, and does not need to; all it needs to see is the outcome (and to be happy with the validity of this).

See also CONSULTANCIES, AND MARKETING RESEARCH; CUSTOM RESEARCH; MARKETING RESEARCH; OMNIBUS SURVEYS; PANEL RESEARCH; RETAIL AUDITS

subcultures, influences on the purchase decision   Within the overall culture there will be smaller groupings which have their own distinctive values. These are perhaps most obvious in ethnic or religious groupings, which attract their own specialist suppliers. They may also be as diverse as City 'yuppies' or football hooligans. Each of these groups holds a very strong set of cultural values – and each may be targeted by specialist marketers, supplying Porsche cars or team colours.

See also CULTURES, INFLUENCES ON THE PURCHASE DECISION

subhead   *see* SIDEHEAD

subliminal suggestion   Advertising which (flashed on the screen very quickly, say) operates at below the viewer's conscious level. It is generally disapproved of (and there is little evidence that it has any significant effect).

subscribed circulation   That part of circulation which is paid for, as opposed to that which is free.

subscription marketing   The generation and retention of subscribers to both paid and unpaid circulation magazines.

See also DIRECT MAIL ADVERTISING

subsidiary/branch office   *see* LOCAL SALES
ORGANIZATION

subsidiary brands   *see* DEDICATED FOLLOWERS

substitution curve   Where a new technology is
substituted for an old one, it has been shown, for
instance by Fisher and Pry (1971), that (once the
substitution has progressed beyond the first few per
cent) the substitution curve which is followed is very
predictable, with the form $R = M/(1 - M)$, where R
is the rate of substitution and M the market share of
the new technology (such that 'the rate of substitution of new for old is proportional to the remaining
amount of old left to be substituted').
See also DELPHI TECHNIQUE; QUALITATIVE FORECAST-
ING METHODS

Reference: Fisher, J. C. and Pry, R. H. (1971) A simple
substitute model of technological change. *Technological
Forecasting and Social Change*, 3.

substitution threats   *see* CROSS–ELASTICITY OF
DEMAND

subversives   *see* SKUNKWORKS

suggestions schemes   These are schemes which
have, in the West, had a variable degree of success.
Employees are able to submit suggestions, typically
through a suggestions box located in their department, about ways of improving the activities of
the organization. Successful suggestions are usually
rewarded (with cash). The importance of such
schemes, however, is maximized in their rather different use in Japan. As developed by P. B. Crosby
(1979) as one of his Steps to Quality, it was given the
rather complex title of Error Cause Removal (ECR) –
which explains why the Japanese (rather confusingly
for the West) simply called it a suggestions scheme.
The difference from the Western version is that
the employee is not required to submit a solution
but only to identify the problem. Thereafter it is the
management who must find the solution and implement it (and in Toyota, for instance, more than 95 per
cent of problems identified in this way are rectified).
From the employee's point of view this makes it
much easier to make a 'suggestion' (and they are still
rewarded for identifying the problem). From the
management's point of view it means that there are no

barriers to the identification of problems: as soon as
an employee notices one, he or she puts a note in the
suggestions box. It is an extremely powerful approach to all aspects of operations management (and
is one of the most important aspects of Toyota's
success in the area), and is one which is very simple to
implement in theory. In practice it needs careful
planning, since the 'suggestions' must be implemented and, as Toyota alone receives several million
of them each year, it demands very sophisticated
management to cope with this (for, if the suggestions
are not implemented, the workers are demotivated).
It is for this reason that Crosby put this step late in his
series (usually not being implemented for at least a
year – until the basic management structures are in
place).
See also CROSBY, P. B.

Reference: Crosby, P. B. (1979) *Quality is Free*. New
York: McGraw-Hill.

summary close   *see* CLOSING TECHNIQUES

summary, of research reports   The first element in a research report will usually be the summary. This provides the context for understanding
the detailed results. It should, though, be read in that
spirit – not as a list of proven facts, and certainly not
(if the research is important) instead of the detailed
material!
See also RESEARCH REPORTS, USAGE

Sunday colour supplement   *see* MEDIA IMPACT

superfluous words   *see* KISS ADVERTISING

supermarkets   *see* LOCATION, RETAIL; RETAIL
PRODUCT OR SERVICE CATEGORIES

supermarkets, precision marketing   *see* DATA
MANIPULATION, PRECISION MARKETING

superordinate goals   *see* VISION, CORPORATE

superstores   *see* LOCATION, RETAIL; RETAIL
PRODUCT OR SERVICE CATEGORIES

supplier evaluation   The supplier should ultimately be evaluated against the specific order. It is
sometimes suggested that this should be by an impersonal 'rating' system (based, say, on quality and
service as well as price). This allows for some very
fancy mathematics but, one suspects, relatively little

practical use! It does, however, avoid the excesses at the other end of the scale – where business is placed solely on the basis of personal relationships (sometimes maintained on the back of rather dubious entertaining and other considerations – which might have a rather debatable ethical, and even legal, foundation!). Beyond the suitability of the product or service offering itself, the choice of supplier should also take into account the suitability of the supplier overall: its financial position (will it be able to 'guarantee' its survival long enough – and will it have the resources – to deliver what it is promising?), its facilities (does it have what is necessary to meet the quality and volume needs? A plant visit may well be the best, and easiest, way of determining this) and the ability of its management to cope (again, the plant visit may be the best approach). From the above comments it would seem that on-site (plant visit) evaluation is often worthwhile. In any case, this starts the second stage of any buying process: the post-order maintenance of relations with the supplier – in particular, with the 'production' management who are going to produce the goods. A sound selling job on these managers in the supplier's organization will work wonders – not least because most other customers will never think to even contact them (except to complain), let alone flatter them with their personal attention. Such personal contact is likely to work more wonders for quality than any specification!

See also PURCHASING

suppliers The culture of buying is still largely dominated by the 'master/servant relationship', deriving from the days when houses had separate entrances for 'tradesmen'. The supplier is seen to be the servant of the buyer – and very definitely subservient! The reality should be that it is very much in the buyer's interest to treat the supplier with all the courtesies which would be accorded to a customer. Again, almost all the marketing techniques apply. In this case, though, the justification is not to maximize sales but to optimize purchases. Knowledge of the supplier's needs allows the purchasing to be matched to these, thereby benefiting the buyer as much as the seller.

Almost all of the conventional marketing techniques relating to the handling of customers can be applied. Even desk research has its place, in terms of finding new suppliers and keeping abreast of developments in general; though, it has to be admitted, few suppliers are likely to go to the extreme of employing market research agencies! The 80:20 rule applies even more forcefully – concentrating attention on the needs of those few suppliers who provide the bulk of the input. Much can be learned, however, from trying to apply even the apparently more esoteric elements of marketing. Thus, for instance, 'segmentation' of suppliers into groups (and on dimensions which relate to the needs of the suppliers rather than those of the buyer) may offer an effective pattern for buying.

Perhaps the most important 'technique' should be that of involving suppliers as (equal) partners: relationship management. In essence, this says that the buyer should try to involve the key suppliers in the organization's operations exactly as if they were in another department within the organization.

Lyons et al. (1990) go further, to specify the trends leading to improvements in these relationships:

Cross-functional teams. Increasingly firms are using teams to co-ordinate development and improvement across functional areas and these reduce development times. These are . . . also instrumental in the co-ordination and integration of cross-technological components . . . the team is increasingly likely to include supplier representatives.

Supply base rationalisation. Firms today are aggressively reducing their total number of suppliers . . . with an increased reliance on the suppliers that remain . . .

Longer term contracts . . . accompanied by substantially longer contract periods . . . contract negotiation processes are also changing. Adversarial (win–lose) bargaining is being supplanted by mutual benefit (win–win) bargaining . . .

See also PURCHASING

Reference: Lyons, Thomas I., Krachenberg, A. Richard and Henke, John W. (1990) Mixed motive marriages: what's next for buyer–supplier relations? *Sloan Management Review*, Spring.

supplier selection One aspect of buying which is, arguably, different from marketing is that of selecting the supplier. This activity clearly requires judgement as to the suitability of the prospective suppliers, including their ability to meet requirements over the longer term. The stages involved are:

1. *Supply sources.* The starting point for this element is the equivalent of desk research. It does, however, go beyond that point to actively evaluating the suppliers (by reference visits to their customer sites, by using personal contacts, etc.). It may even go as far as a formal 'inspection visit', where a technical team checks that the proposed supplier's production, quality control facilities, etc. meet the standards of the buying organization.
2. *Approved list.* The formal outcome of the above stage may be the inclusion of the supplier on the 'approved list' – with the tacit implication that they will stand a chance of receiving business at some time in the future!

There are two extremes to placing business:

1. *Single supplier.* The most efficient approach, making the best use of any economies of scale, is that of concentrating all the purchases on a single (optimal) supplier. This also allows the best chance of a close 'seller partnership' developing.
2. *Multiple suppliers.* At the other extreme, several suppliers may be chosen to ensure continuity of supply. At its most extreme a buyer may place business in several countries, in case a national strike, for instance, closes down supply! Multiple suppliers are also supposedly expected to recognize the existence of their competitors, and accordingly offer keener prices; though the impact on 'supplier partnership' may be problematic in that case!

See also PURCHASING

suppliers, new   *see* ORGANIZATIONAL BUYING SITUATIONS

suppliers of marketing research   The starting point is the organizations which offer market research services, for it is a very large, and unusually sophisticated, organization which will have the resources to handle all aspects of its own research. The suppliers can be grouped into three main types:

- syndicated research
- custom research
- subcontractors

See also CUSTOM RESEARCH; MARKETING RESEARCH; SUBCONTRACTORS, MARKETING RESEARCH; SYNDICATED RESEARCH SUPPLIERS

supply and demand   Much of the theory of pricing has derived from that of economics. The basic idea, according to such theories, is that 'demand' will be different at each price which might possibly be chosen. In one of the leading economics textbooks, Begg et al. (1987) define it as: 'Demand is the quantity of a good [which] buyers wish to purchase at each conceivable price'.

Demand is normally, but not always, assumed to fall as price increases. Thus, a 'demand curve', showing the demand at each price, can be drawn:

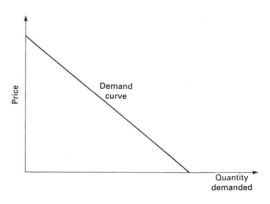

For convenience, the demand curve is here shown as a straight line, but it could follow other paths; and, indeed, is often shown as a smooth curve which is concave towards the origin, since demand is normally expected to be inversely proportional to price (that is, the higher the price, the less the demand). One point to note is that, perversely, as economists seem to be in many such matters, the 'input' (price) is shown on the y axis and the 'output' (the demand) on the x axis – the reverse of the normal scientific notation – perhaps in recognition of the fact that much of economic theory seems to turn scientific method on its head!

Much of economics was, and still is, traditionally taught on the basis of graphical representation, and hence the 'demand curve'; and the graphical approach does make the theory easier to appreciate. In recent years, particularly with the wider availability of personal computers and the presumed increase in numeracy, this approach has been complemented by the equivalent mathematical representation; in this case it is the 'demand function'. For an explanation, see a recent economics textbook – such as that written by Richard Lipsey (1983).

Similar concepts apply to supply. Begg et al.'s definition, not surprisingly, is: 'Supply is the quantity of a good [which] sellers wish to sell at each conceivable price'.

Supply is, not unreasonably, expected to increase as price increases – giving the 'supply curve':

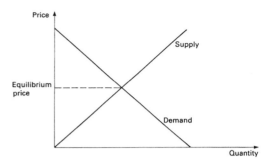

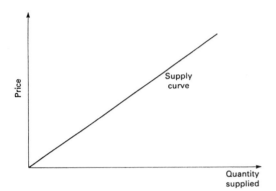

The supply line is conventionally assumed to be straight.

The problem posed by this traditional 'economic' approach is that the 'demand function' is usually almost impossible to determine. As the eminent economist W. J. Baumol said in 1972:

We have seen, then, how difficult it is to find actual demand relationships in practice. These problems are, to a large extent, a consequence of the very peculiarity of the demand function concept itself – the fact that it represents the answers to a set of purely hypothetical questions and that information is taken to pertain simultaneously to the same moment of time. Unfortunately, this odd demand relationship turns out to be indispensable to sophisticated decision-making within the firm. We simply have to learn to live with it, and to face up to the difficulties in its empirical determination. An essential part of the process is knowledge of the pitfalls which await the unwary investigators who set out to beard the function in its lair.

However, if we assume that the function is known, and if the two curves (of demand and supply) are superimposed, we get:

This is the conventional graphical representation of the theory of supply and demand.

At the 'equilibrium price', the quantity demanded by consumers matches the quantity supplied by sellers; there will be nothing left to sell, nor will there be any shortage – and it is said that the market has 'cleared'. This is the price which will therefore be set by the market.

See also DEMAND CURVE ESTIMATION; EQUILIBRIUM PRICE; NEOCLASSICAL ECONOMICS; PRICE ELASTICITY OF DEMAND; PRICE FACTORS; PRICES, CUSTOMER NEEDS

References: Baumol, W. J. (1972) *Economic Theory and Operations Analysis* (3rd edn). Englewood Cliffs, NJ: Prentice-Hall.

Begg, David, Fischer, Stanley and Dornbusch, Rudiger (1987) *Economics* (2nd edn). McGraw-Hill.

Lipsey, Richard (1983) *An Introduction to Positive Economics*. London: Weidenfeld & Nicholson.

Support Success Forget Failure (SSFF) This very simple rule, which follows from the (Pareto) 80:20 rule, has much the same message but in a more specific context. It asks only that you abandon the tendency of managements to throw good money after bad, by trying to rescue projects which can never succeed – in the process ignoring the opportunities offered by those that are a success.

See also PARETO, 80:20, EFFECT

surging *see* KANBAN

survey research The marketing research most familiar to the general public is survey (or questionnaire-based) research. Typically, this may be designed to find out, descriptively, what are the participants' habits, attitudes, wants, etc. It is based simply on asking the participant, or respondent, a number of questions. The classic device used on such surveys is the questionnaire – a preprinted form on which the interviewer or the respondent fills in the answers to a series of such questions.

See also DATA COLLECTION; MARKETING RESEARCH; MARKETING RESEARCH STAGES; QUALITATIVE RESEARCH; QUESTIONNAIRE DESIGN; WALKABOUT

susceptibility *see* ENHANCED AIUAPR MODEL; THREE PILLARS OF THE PURCHASING PROCESS

swatch A small sample of material (or colour).

switch selling A bargain is initially offered with a view to switching the customer to something else which is more expensive. It is illegal in certain countries.

switch trades *see* COUNTERTRADING

SWOT analysis One technique which is particularly useful in the analysis of the material contained in the marketing audit, is that of a SWOT (Strengths Weaknesses Opportunities Threats) analysis. It groups some of the key pieces of information into two main categories (internal factors and external factors) and then by their dual positive and negative aspects (Strengths and Opportunities, as the former aspects, with Weaknesses and Threats representing the latter):

1. *Internal factors* (internal to the organization, its strategies and its position in relation to its competitors)
    (a) Strengths
    (b) Weaknesses
2. *External factors* (presented by the external environment and the competition)
    (c) Opportunities
    (d) Threats

The internal factors, which may be viewed as strengths or weaknesses, depending upon their impact on the organization's positions (for they may represent a strength for one organization but a weakness, in relative terms, for another), may include all of the 4 Ps, as well as personnel, finance, etc. The external factors, which again may be threats to one organization while offering opportunities to another, may include such matters as technological change, legislation, socio-cultural changes, etc., as well as changes in the marketplace or competitive position.

The technique is often presented as a form of matrix:

Strengths	Weaknesses
Opportunities	Threats

But the flowchart by Lusch and Lusch (1987) shows the relationships rather better:

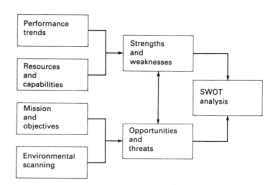

You should note, however, that SWOT is just one aid to categorization. It is not, as many organizations seem to think, the only technique. It also has its own weaknesses. It tends to persuade companies to compile lists rather than think about what is really important to their business. It also presents the resulting lists uncritically, without clear prioritization; so that, for example, weak opportunities may appear to balance strong threats. The aim of any SWOT analysis, rather, should be to isolate the key issues which will be important to the future of the organization, and which subsequent marketing planning will address.

See also MARKETING PLANNING, ANALYSIS; MARKETING PLAN STRUCTURE; PLANNING PROCESS

Reference: Lusch, Robert F. and Lusch, Virginia (1987) *Principles of Marketing*. New York: Kent Publishing.

symbolic analogy *see* SYNECTICS®

symbolic inputs *see* HOWARD AND SHETH MODEL, OF CONSUMER BEHAVIOUR

symbolic moves   *see* LOGICAL INCREMENTALISM

symbol retailer   Also called a 'voluntary (group) retailer', this is an independent owner who is part of a voluntary group originally formed to obtain better bulk purchase prices, but now commonly providing a range of shared services and promotional activities.
See also RETAILING; RETAIL ORGANIZATION

symposia   *see* CONFERENCES AND SYMPOSIA

symptoms   *see* COMPLAINTS

synchromarketing   The aim of some marketing activity may be to 'redistribute' existing sales (which are already at optimum levels) so that they occur at times, or in places, which the supplier prefers. Thus, for example, organizations which have highly seasonal sales (which make inefficient use of resources) may want to increase non-seasonal sales. Walls achieved this by balancing its summer sales of ice-cream with pies and sausages, demand for which peaks in winter. The suppliers of central-heating oil offer special deals for those customers willing to re-stock their tanks in summer.
See also CORPORATE OBJECTIVES; COUNTER-MARKETING; DEMARKETING; PLANNING PROCESS

syndicated research suppliers   These are suppliers of shared marketing research services. They usually offer the easiest and quickest service. They typically have on-going or *ad hoc* research programmes, the results of which they sell to a number of clients. Some of this can be standard research, such as the A. C. Nielsen store audits, which provide information on retail purchases by consumers, or the TGI (Target Group Index) of MRB, which has followed the fortunes of some 5000 brands in the UK for more than 20 years. Shared cost is one advantage of such an approach, but another (even more important) one is the quality of the research – such research is usually sold on the basis of quality, rather than (and unlike much other research) only on the basis of price.

Ad hoc syndicated research will be undertaken when a research company (often specializing in the industrial field) sees a topic which it believes will be of interest to a number of companies; it will then conduct the research and sell the results 'off-the-shelf'. Finally, some researchers with on-going programmes (especially those conducting opinion polls, such as NOP or MORI) will sell 'space' (or, more

accurately, interviewer time) on the back of their omnibus surveys, so that their clients, in this respect, can ask one or two simple questions – which will be added to the end of the main survey, and will thus be asked of a large sample (at a relatively low cost).

As already suggested, apart from the ease and speed of obtaining the research information, the great advantage of all these approaches is usually that of cost. Because the overall cost is shared between a number of customers (and even if the research companies' profits are higher), the cost to any one client can be that much lower. It is thus quite cheap (a few thousand pounds) to ask one or two key (but simple) questions of a large sample. At the other end of the spectrum it allows research (such as store audits) that few individual organizations could afford by themselves.

In most cases, as already stressed, it is also quick, and certainly easy to organize; so that sometimes a few simple questions are asked in this manner as a pilot (to establish the critical proportions of the population to be involved, say) for more complex studies.

The main areas of syndicated research are:

- retail audits
- panel research
- omnibus surveys
- consultancies

See also CONSULTANCIES, AND MARKETING RESEARCH; CUSTOM RESEARCH; MARKETING RESEARCH; OMNIBUS SURVEYS; PANEL RESEARCH; RETAIL AUDITS; SUBCON-TRACTORS, MARKETING RESEARCH

Synectics®   As practised by Synectics, this method of idea generation is a complex process (using sophisticated psychological techniques), partly based upon analysis of the existing situation – leading to model building to find alternative solutions ('making the strange familiar') – and partly by inverting, transposing and generally distorting the existing situation to see if viable new ideas emerge from the process ('making the familiar strange'). It is most widely known, however, for its use of analogy. For example, it looks to see how other organizations have solved similar problems. Alternatively, are there any scientific analogies? According to Vincent Nolan (1989), chairman of Synectics, 'The richest source of analogous solutions seems to be the natural world'. Are there any solutions to similar problems in other countries or other industries? Less widely reported is the use of 'symbolic analogy', focusing on the use and meanings of key words associated with the problem, as well as the use of fantasy. This approach is often combined with carefully structured group discussions, where the participants are carefully chosen from a wide spectrum of backgrounds – and possibly also screened for 'high creativity' ('divergent' or 'lateral' thinking, in the terms of Edward De Bono (1970)). In practice, if not conducted by experts, this may be a very scientific sounding name for simply looking to see if someone has already solved the problem in another context! In the right hands, however, it also encompasses a wide range of other approaches to 'creativity' and can represent a major source of new product ideas.

See also GENERATING IDEAS

References: De Bono, Edward (1970) *Lateral Thinking.* London: Ward Lock Education.
    Nolan, Vincent (1989) *The Innovator's Handbook.* London: Sphere Books. (Synectics® is a registered mark of Synectics Inc., Cambridge, MA, USA.)

synthesis and assimilation, of marketing research data   For many, if not most, managers, marketing research data remains as so much impersonal data lying in hundreds of pages of tables in dusty files. Just a few managers, however, bring it alive by assimilating it into their everyday view of their business life. They build an inner model of the customers they are dealing with by using the data they have received to synthesize a multidimensional picture of their customers, and then they assimilate it into themselves, almost as if absorbing it by osmosis through their skin. Needless to say, the technique of walkabout is the most useful of all in this process, because it gives the best 'feel' for what the key elements are. It is rather like the actor who uses Stanislavsky's Method to bring the character he is to play into himself; he does not play the part, he lives it. Thus, the synthesized manager can live the part of the customer. The great benefit of this is that the manager does not have to search through the vast collections of data to know what the customer's reaction would be to any of the several dozen deci-

sions which may be made in a day – that would be unproductively time consuming, and is precisely why the research results gather dust. Instead, he or she can draw upon their inner model to instinctively 'feel' what the customer's response will be. This is a difficult process, especially when there are a number of different customer groups to assimilate in this way, but like the actor the manager can, after considerable effort, usually achieve success. Perhaps, though, the analogy should not be to Stanislavsky but to Bertolt Brecht. His acting technique, of 'alienation', used the former's approach as the starting point but then forced the actor to extract the essence of the character – for this simple essence was more powerful in communicating with the audience. The most skilled marketer will similarly extract the essence of the customer; for the most powerful marketing, too, uses the simplest messages.

See also ANALYSIS OF MARKETING RESEARCH DATA; MARKETING RESEARCH; WALKABOUT

systematic samples   *see* RANDOM SAMPLES

systems approaches   This is a holistic approach to problems (contained within a specified systems boundary), developed by the Rand Corporation from operational research work (based on the application of mathematical and statistical techniques to production processes) during World War II, typically employed by technologists. It usually revolves around the use of systems diagrams, including relationship diagrams (which show how the elements of a situation relate to each other), input–output diagrams and flow diagrams (which show the flow of product, for instance, through the system). Two main approaches are used: the hard systems approach, where the problems and opportunities can be clearly defined, and the soft systems approach – where there is little or no agreement about the problem.

See also LOGISTICS MANAGEMENT

T

tabloid   The small-format (size) newspaper, typically used by the popular press, as opposed to the broadsheet (large) format used by the quality press.
See also MEDIA IMPACT; MEDIA SELECTION; MEDIA TYPES

tachistoscope test   A method of pack testing whereby the respondent is allowed to see the pack for a series of controlled (short) lengths of time and is questioned on his or her responses (observations) for each of these.
See also MARKETING RESEARCH; PACKAGING; PRODUCT TEST

tactics   *see* MARKETING PLAN STRUCTURE

takeover bids   The attempted acquisition of a company by the purchase of (a majority of) its (voting) shares. Some of the terms which may be used in this situation are:

- *Concert party* – a number of investors who buy shares separately, to eventually pool them.
- *Dawn raid* – buying as many shares as possible on the stock market over a short period of time before bidding.
- *Golden parachutes* – very expensive severance terms written for directors, possibly to make a takeover prohibitively expensive.
- *Greenmail* – a bidder whose share purchases are bought by the company being taken over at a premium.
- *Reverse takeover* – a bid by a smaller company for a larger one.

See also ANSOFF MATRIX; WHITE KNIGHT

tamper-evident packaging   A form of packaging in which a seal is incorporated which clearly shows if the pack has already been opened. This works as a deterrent to fraud and, more important, sabotage (such as happened with the Tylenol brand).
See also PACKAGING

tangibility, services   *see* PROMOTION OF SERVICES

target audience   *see* ADVERTISING PLAN; AWARENESS, ADVERTISING; INTEREST, ADVERTISING; MEDIA BUYING, ADVERTISING AGENCY; MEDIA SELECTION

Target Group Index   *see* MARKETING RESEARCH, PRECISION MARKETING

target marketing   Philip Kotler (1988) suggests that there should be three stages which clearly separate the various activities:

- *Market segmentation* – this is the basic activity.
- *Market targeting* – Kotler suggests, however, that knowing the segments is not enough. Considerable effort has to be put into selecting the segment(s) which best meet the needs of the organization. This involves consideration of the resources available as well as the consumer segments and the competitive positions.
- *Product positioning* – the separation of this step makes it clear that, even having decided upon the optimum segment(s), the supplier then needs to choose the optimum position within that segment (as shown on the brand positioning maps etc.).

See also PRODUCT (OR SERVICE) POSITIONING; SEGMENTATION; SEGMENTS OF MARKETS

Reference: Kotler, P. (1988) *Marketing Management* (6th edn). Englewood Cliffs, NJ: Prentice-Hall.

target pricing   In this approach to pricing, the intention is not just to obtain a 'profit' over costs, but also to obtain a reasonable 'return on investment'. The price, therefore, has to be based on both the variable costs (as in 'cost plus') and the capital employed (related to the sales value!). As Russ and Kirkpatrick (1982) say, 'The process of trying to consider investment decisions and pricing decisions simultaneously is a very complex one, requiring accurate information . . .'. It is not surprising that this is one of the less popular pricing policies (except where it is used in a theoretical rather than practical

context, as part of – usually as a justification for – a large capital investment programme!).
See also PRICING POLICIES, PRACTICAL

Reference: Russ, Frederick and Kirkpatrick, Charles A. (1982) *Marketing*. Little Brown & Company.

tariff barriers   *see* MARKET ENTRY DECISION

tariffs   *see* REGULATORY CONSIDERATIONS, FILTERING UNSUITABLE MARKETS

Tate, Sheila and public relations   *see* PUBLIC RELATIONS

TAT (Thematic Apperception Tests)   *see* OPEN QUESTIONS, ON QUESTIONNAIRES

team scanning   Even on a limited scale, the resource demands of scanning imply the necessity for a team approach. One of the most interesting suggestions for handling this came from an organization which asked all of its employees (shop-floor workers as well as managers) to clip any news item (found in the newspapers and magazines they regularly read) they felt might be relevant to the future of the organization. All of these clippings, from the most sensational tabloid newspapers as much as from the serious press, were then 'scanned' by the environmental analysis group. When a pattern emerged, of a phenomenon being reported across a number of such sources, it was reasoned that these particular 'weak signals' possibly indicated an important underlying trend, which was thereafter tracked in more detail. This seems to offer a particularly comprehensive approach to such coverage. It may be beyond the culture of most organizations, but it could be adapted to work across a smaller group (say, those in the marketing department – but including a range of personnel, such as secretaries as well as senior managers). This process will, in any case, benefit from the advent of increased computerized communications – where the extraction of multiple occurrences of data might be detected automatically by computer systems.
See also SCANNING, AND MIS

tear sheet   Page, torn from the publication, sent by the publisher to the advertiser as proof that the advertisement has appeared.
See also ADVERTISING AGENCY ELEMENTS

teaser   An advertisement which says little about the product in order to tease the reader into finding out more.

See also ADVERTISING PROCESSES; CREATING THE CORRECT MESSAGES; CREATIVE DEPARTMENT, ADVERTISING AGENCY

technical buyer   *see* DECISION-MAKERS AND INFLUENCERS

technical press   *see* PRESS MEDIA

techniques of selling   *see* SALES TRAINING

technological change   *see* EXISTING PRODUCT CHANGES; SWOT ANALYSIS

technological development   *see* GLOBALIZATION

technological forecasting   This series of techniques is associated with the plotting of very long-term trends and, in particular, with changes in technology. The estimates are typically based upon a plot of the previous changes over time – showing the increasing performance or decreasing cost, say. These plots will, however, usually have to cover the results over several decades. Spyros Makridakis (1989) states his own position as: 'Such data must span a period of more than 100 years' and then adds the caution that: 'The fact that a long-term trend has been identified does not mean it cannot change'.

In the 'vector approach' (sometimes referred to as 'growth curves') the average growth or development rate is calculated. As with many conventional short-term approaches, the 'line of best fit' is used for this calculation. This plots the historical developments and tries to fit (usually visually) a line (normally a straight one) to these points.

A special form of growth curve is the 'logistic curve'. This S-shaped curve (sometimes called the 'Pearl' curve after Raymond Pearl, the American biologist and demographer who first described it) describes a rapid initial increase followed eventually, after a period of relatively linear growth, by a progressive slowing of growth at 'saturation'. A variation on this curve, which differs only in that it is not symmetrical, is the Gompertz curve.

None of these 'vector' approaches can, however, forecast the 'breakthrough'.
See also QUALITATIVE FORECASTING METHODS

References: Makridakis, Spyros and Wheelwright, Steven C. (1989) *Forecasting Methods for Management* (5th edn). Chichester: John Wiley.

technological life cycle   Perhaps the greatest justification for life cycle theory lies in the area of technological change. Strangely, this is a topic relatively little discussed in the most influential life cycle literature, even though there are a large number of markets which are subject to technological change. The humble washing powder market has, in recent years, passed through new blue whiteners to biological to fabric softeners to deodorants to non-biological to tablets. The personal computer market now seems to pass through a life cycle in less than a year!

These changes happen in a cyclical fashion, and an awareness of what this means is important for all those involved. However, the processes are somewhat removed from those classically described in life cycle theory. They are those of cash flow balanced against the competitive advantage offered by having the very latest fashion in technology.

This sounds like a conventional life cycle, but it is different in many important respects. The most important is that the 'brand' never changes its place in the market; it is only the version of the product which changes. The sales volumes do cycle, with peaks following the new launch and (perhaps unexpectedly) again at the start of the end-of-life price reductions, but these are not the patterns predicted by conventional theory. Almost as important is that the cycle is under the control of the supplier, not the market. As such it is not a stable cycle; for example, IBM found, to its concern, that in the course of the 1980s the 'life cycle' for mainframes fell from around seven years to as little as three years. This had dramatic impacts on cash flow. It also demonstrated the dangers of assuming that life cycles are predictable!

technologically deficient strategy   *see* NEW PRODUCT INNOVATION

technologically driven strategy   *see* NEW PRODUCT INNOVATION

telemarketing, inbound   *see* INBOUND TELEMARKETING/COMMUNICATIONS

telephone order-handling teams   *see* INBOUND TELEMARKETING/COMMUNICATIONS

telephone sales   *see* CHANNEL DECISIONS

telephone surveys   In this form of survey research the interviewer uses a telephone to contact respondents. It is a very fast survey technique; results can be available in a matter of hours, and hence it is often now used for those opinion polls where time is of the essence. It is also relatively cheap (and hence often affordable even in industrial markets). On the other hand, it limits the sample to those with a telephone, though this is now much less of a drawback as more than two-thirds of households have a telephone (and these represent the more affluent, who are usually the most attractive to marketers). More fundamentally, the interview can last only a short time and the types of questions are limited (particularly where the interviewer cannot check visually that the question is understood). Even so, Prout's (1973) comment that 'telephone interviewing is the Cinderella of the three major types of field research' probably still holds. Certainly his subsequent comments are valid: 'a properly organised telephone survey can be a very cheap and efficient way of gathering information . . . one expects a much higher success rate . . . a greater degree of flexibility . . . ideal where the researcher wishes to probe . . .'.

See also DATA COLLECTION

Reference: Prout, T. P. (1973) *Industrial Market Research Workbook.* Aldershot: Gower Press.

teleprompter   *see* AUTOCUE

telesales   Somewhere between direct mail and the face-to-face sales call lies 'telesales'. This is, to a degree, personal, and it certainly can be interactive – whereas a mailshot cannot. It is a medium most often used in the industrial goods sector (where the relatively high cost per call can be more easily justified), but some consumer 'capital goods' suppliers (such as those offering double glazing, and Ford, in the USA, which once made 20 million calls to produce leads for its sales personnel) also use it. On a more typical scale, a Midland Bank teleselling campaign in the UK at the end of the 1980s required close to 40 000 outbound calls, together with the handling of 7000 inbound calls.

Advantages

Its great advantage over face-to-face selling is the rate at which calls can be made. It is quite realistic for even untrained sales personnel to make more than 50 such telephone calls in a day (compared, say, with perhaps as few as 300 face-to-face calls in a year). Where specialist telesales personnel are used the call rate can rise to hundreds per day. The great advantage over direct mail is the success rate, which is estimated to be as much as ten times as high. It is not unusual to achieve a 10 per cent 'response rate' – where, for instance, the intention is to invite contacts to a suitable 'seminar' as a preliminary to face-to-face selling – and Edward Nash (1986) states that it can be 'as high as 25 or 30 percent of all calls made.'

Disadvantages

The clear disadvantages are that it is limited in comparison with face-to-face calls: there are no visual stimuli (for either side), and the calls have to be much shorter. It is considerably more difficult to be persuasive as a disembodied voice, which is why the technique is often only used as a means of obtaining the first step towards a face-to-face call (either as a direct appointment – 'bird-dogging' in the jargon – or indirectly via an invitation to a 'seminar'). It is also a relatively expensive technique, costing several times as much as direct mail (but possibly up to a hundred times less than a face-to-face call!). Moriarty and Moran (1990), for instance, quote a rate of $17 dollars per hour (compared with $300 per hour, 'loaded' face-to-face, for direct representatives).

See also CALL TARGETS; PRECISION (DIRECT) MARKETING, RETAIL; TELESALES AGENCIES

References: Moriarty, Rowland T. and Moran, Ursula (1990) Managing hybrid marketing systems. *Harvard Business Review*, November–December.

Nash, Edward L. (1986) *Direct Marketing: Strategy, Planning, Execution*. Maidenhead: McGraw-Hill.

telesales agencies   It is expensive to maintain your own telesales team. Accordingly, many organizations use specialist telesales agencies. These are specially set up to handle the difficult task of controlling and motivating their teams of telesales personnel; for most sales personnel nothing could be more soul-destroying than spending all day making 'cold' telephone calls – which means that these agencies have to recruit special personnel, and work very hard to keep them motivated. The basis for such calls is usually a 'script' (which will be produced in cooperation with, and agreed with, the client). This needs to be written by very skilled 'authors', since it takes the telesales staff through the various levels of 'conversation' with their contact. As such it has to handle all the various alternatives they may encounter. Equally, though, it means that the call can only deal with very simple matters – which is one reason why it is often best used as an introductory device. The telesales personnel will not be product experts, so the call has to be superficial, but the people they contact usually recognize that such telesales personnel are 'administrative staff' and do not expect a high level of technical expertise (which they might normally expect from sales personnel). This script can

be handled, with 'branching questions', as a folder. Increasingly, though, the most sophisticated agencies are using computers to present the script (and to take them rapidly through the questions).

Appointing an agency

All the rules for appointing any external agency apply. It is a decision which should not be taken lightly, however. It may appear a peripheral activity, but (since the telesales personnel will seem, to those contacted, to be working directly for you) if badly handled it can seriously damage the reputation of your organization. At the same time, there are a range of telesales agencies which employ different techniques, some of which may be more suitable to your organization's needs (and some of which, operating at the lower-quality end of the market, may be very unsuitable indeed!).

See also TELESALES

television   This mass medium is normally the most expensive medium, and as such is generally only open to the major advertisers (though some regional contractors offer more affordable packages to their local advertisers). It offers by far the widest coverage, particularly in the peak hours (roughly 7.00–10.30 p.m.) and especially of family audiences. Offering sight, sound, movement and colour, it has the greatest impact, especially for those products or services where a 'demonstration' is essential, since it combines the virtues of both the 'storyteller' and the 'demonstrator'. To be effective, however, these messages must be kept simple – and have the impact to overcome the surrounding distractions of family life. The medium is relatively unselective in its audiences, and offers relatively poor coverage of the upper-class and younger-age groups, but as it is regionally based it can be used for regional trials or promotions (including test markets). The price structures can be horrendously complicated, with a 'rate card' (the price list) offering different prices for different times throughout the day; and this is further complicated by a wide range of special promotional packages, and individual negotiations! It is truly the province of the specialist media buyer.

After a slow start, satellite television audiences have now grown to the point that they are on a par with those of the largest ITV regions. Cable television was similarly supposed to represent the future a decade ago. This promise has been largely fulfilled in the USA, where the average household can now tune in to 31 channels (and 1000 or more interactive channels are promised). It has yet, though, to achieve comparable levels of penetration in other countries. The future of both media may or may not subject to dramatic expansion. In any case, it will still require much the same media-buying, as well as creative, rules as the more earthbound channels – until the time when 1000+ interactive channels are widely accepted, and personalized delivery is in effect achieved, when it will become much more like precision marketing (and that time may be less than a decade away!).

The recent launch of digital television will significantly expand the number of channels, but it is not yet clear how this will affect the use of the medium for advertising – apart from reducing audiences for individual stations.

See also MEDIA TYPES; PRECISION (DIRECT) MARKETING, RETAIL

television commercial *see* CREATIVE DEPARTMENT, ADVERTISING AGENCY

television commercial testing *see* ADVERTISING RESEARCH

television rating (TVR) The measure (usually as a percentage of total households) of the popularity of a television programme as measured by survey or, more typically, panel research.

telex *see* ELECTRONIC DIRECT MAIL

tender pricing *see* PROJECT PRICING

tenders *see* MARKET ENTRY TACTICS; PRICE, PURCHASE

tension, customer *see* PARTNERSHIP TRIANGLE

territory management The most important decision of sales management is how responsibilities are to be allocated within the sales team. The now-traditional basis for this uses the building block of the individual territory. In fact, the concept of sales professionals being entitled to their own territory is a relatively recent one. It was only just before the First World War that John Patterson instituted the concept of territories as a fundamental aspect of the NCR sales operation. Shortly afterwards Thomas J. Watson, then at NCR, took it to IBM – and there used it as a basis for building that company's legen-

dary sales force. Prior to the time of these pioneers there had been no territories. All prospects were fair game for all salesmen; their main competitors could just as easily be from the same company as themselves! Fortunately, since this anarchy destroys the foundations of territory management, territories are now an established practice.

Although such territories are normally thought of as geographical areas, there can be a number of bases for the way they are structured. Examples are as follows.

Geographical territories

Most territories are based on a geographical area, ranging from a whole country down to a single postal district. One advantage of such an approach is that they are relatively easy to define, and hence should avoid unnecessary contention – since it should be obvious what are the physical boundaries of these territories. On the other hand, very few sales professionals rigorously check what their territory is, and this situation is often complicated by the fact that such territories are often split along main roads – with one sales professional calling on the businesses on one side and another on the opposite side of the same road! An alternative geographical approach may be to explore what parts of these purely geographical territories have the most potential and allocate the 'territories' on this basis. This potential may be immediately evident, for example, in the form of large factory estates, shopping centres or office complexes. But it may also require considerable research in terms of searching the various lists and directories to determine where individual large prospects are located. However, no such system can beat the exploratory eye of the individual salesperson walking (or these days more probably driving) every street of their 'patch' – particularly as this is the only way of finding the new businesses that are just moving in (who are normally some of the hottest prospects). For this reason, as well as that of simplicity, most territory allocation is on the basis of simple geography. There are, however, other factors which can considerably complicate the picture. For example, traffic patterns can mean that physical distances are much less important than travelling times, and it is the latter which must be allowed for in plans (drawing 'contours' of equal travelling time).

Industry territories

A territory split which is used much less frequently (than geography) is that by industry. But this can be a very powerful choice. For many years IBM split its main business by industry, and this had the great benefit for IBM that the sales professionals dedicated to each industry were steeped in the knowledge and folklore of that industry – though at the price of having a wider geographical spread of their territories.

Product territories

This approach is often necessary because to understand the products in sufficient depth to be deemed an expert may be time consuming, and sales personnel may not have the personal resources to apply this to all products in the range. IBM, for example, also traditionally split its sales force into categories, each of which specialized in certain ranges of products. Even so, this was usually in terms of a relatively wide range of products – with large mainframes and their associated products in one group (Data Processing Division) and intermediate systems in another (General Systems Division). On the other hand it could be very specific – so that the copier sales force sold nothing else.

See also CALLS AVAILABLE ANNUALLY; MANPOWER PLAN, SALES; SELLING

territory plans

territory plans Once the typically 'geographical' decisions about sales territories have been taken, management should be in a position to plot those areas of highest potential on their 'map(s)' to give the true 'shape' of the territories. Against this potential they will also need to determine what resources will be required to tap it and what is actually available. The essential resource is, of course, 'sales manpower'. In order to manage this resource plan, sales management first of all needs to know how much its sales personnel cost per hour. This is usually far more than sales management think! Sales activities are very expensive!

Most managers who have little practical experience of selling are surprised by just how short a time is actually spent with the customer. The table below, which is taken from Malcolm McDonald's (1984) book, shows a breakdown of a salesman's daily workload in one consumer goods company. It indicates that less than one-third of his time was spent on customers' premises and almost four-fifths of even this short time was spent waiting for the customer to see him! McDonald's understandable conclusion is that it is important for a salesperson to plan their time effectively.

Breakdown of a salesman's daily workload

	% of time spent
Travel	50
Making the call	24
Selling	6
Administration	20

See also CALLS AVAILABLE ANNUALLY; MANPOWER PLAN, SALES; SELLING; TERRITORY MANAGEMENT

Reference: McDonald, Malcolm H. B. (1984) *Marketing Plans.* London: Heinemann.

territory sales plan The sales plan for an individual sales territory should, either formally or informally (where it has to be recognized that most sales professionals are loathe to ever commit pen to paper), be focused on the customer and prospect sets. Indeed, this is the stage at which the customer and prospect database will usually be built since each category of these will, to a greater or lesser extent, require individual attention.

Customers

Without any doubt, the most important split on almost all territories is that between customers and prospects. Customers are almost universally more productive than prospects; and, indeed, more productive than many sales professionals (or their management) allow for. What is more, assuming that the organization has previously offered good customer service, they are already tied to it; competitors will have to justify breaking these links before they can even begin their selling process. In such customers the organization already has an existing base on which it is natural to build. It does not have to sell over the psychological barrier caused by their not wanting to bring in new ideas (justifiably so, because new installations often are painful). Yet many, if not most, sales professionals devote disproportionately less time on customers. The 'macho' image, the stereotype, persuades them to spend their time unproductively touting for new business, when common sense should tell them to spend at least adequate time defending, and growing, their customer base. This problem was particularly evident in the earlier days of the personal computer market. All the research showed that the one group who were almost guaranteed to buy a system was that group of existing customers who had already bought a system –

typically within the past year. On the other hand, cold prospects were unlikely to show a better than 10 per cent chance of buying a system. Yet most sales professionals still sadly neglected their customers, giving the industry an appalling reputation of poor service. So the first priority of any sales professional must be to allocate resources to the customer set, but differentiating between customers according to their worth. Some will be '*bankers*' and will bring in a large part of the easy 80 per cent of business – and these investments must be cosseted. Some, on the other hand, will be totally unproductive, demanding resources for little return – and in these cases the plan must be to contain the 'bleeding'.

'A' prospects
The sales team should know their customers well enough to be able to predict the sales performance of each. But the real skill comes in being able to separate out the sheep from the goats amongst the prospects. They need to decide which are the 10 per cent or so of prospects who will bring in 50+ per cent of the new business. This is partly a function of their size (in terms of potential business) and partly of their probability of closing. These are the prospects that should take first cut of the resources left after the planned support of customers.

'B' prospects
Similarly the sales team will have to determine the 50 per cent or so of the remaining prospects who will bring in the remaining 50 per cent of new business. Even so, it needs careful planning, and a ruthless determination to control resource exposures in order to ration out the small amount of resources remaining after customers and 'A' prospects have been catered for. Determining which are 'A' and 'B' prospects is unfortunately just a matter of experience; it is a skill the best sales personnel learn. There are no easy guidelines. But (obviously) size of company is a good indicator. An effective sales management will, though, learn the types of companies that are more likely to be productive prospects.

Losers
All others have to be treated as outcasts. No matter how much they plead, the productive sales force will have to be ruthless and refuse to fritter away resources on unproductive areas. The main danger is that they allocate some of their precious resources, only to find that the prospects are 'tyre-kickers' (in the jargon of the sales discipline – which does not always hide its questionable origins in the used car industry!) after all – happy for the sales professional

to spend considerable time talking to them, indeed demanding this, but never really likely to buy (despite their loud promises). So the true professional must be ruthless and insist they prove their good intentions. It sounds the reverse of good salesmanship – but at times good salesmanship is as much about managing scarce resources as it is about winning friends and influencing people.

Husbanding resources, for the 20 per cent of accounts that will bring in 80 per cent of business, is a critical aspect of all territory and account planning. It is one of the 'management' aspects of professional salesmanship that many sales professionals find most difficult to implement; they more naturally 'shoot from the hip', rushing to the account that immediately demands attention without considering the long-term implications. Planning is essential to the sales professional, and is often the activity that distinguishes him from his less professional juniors.
See also CALLS AVAILABLE ANNUALLY; MANPOWER PLAN, SALES; SALES PROFESSIONAL; SELLING; TERRITORY MANAGEMENT

tertiary readership   Casual readers, such as those seeing the publication while in a waiting room.

testimonial letter   *see* REFERENCES

testing advertisements   *see* MESSAGE SELECTION

testing direct mail   *see* RESPONSE RATES, MAILING

test mailing   *see* MAILING LIST

test market   The ultimate in new products (or promotional programmes) testing is a test market, which is sometimes used by the more sophisticated marketers. This is used to limit risk, as well as for optimizing the marketing mix prior to a national launch. It ideally aims to duplicate everything – promotion and distribution as well as 'product' – on a smaller scale. It replicates, typically in one area, what is planned to occur in a national launch; and it very carefully monitors the results, so that these can be extrapolated to projected national results. The 'area' may be:

• *Television area.* In this case, the complete campaign, including television commercials and the use of distribution channels, is tested in the area covered by a single television station. This approach should result in the closest approximation to the results of a national launch.

- *Test town.* It may be possible to duplicate most of the activities in a test town, rather than a complete TV region, at considerably less cost. Clearly, television cannot be used, and the local press available will have different characteristics to those of the national press; typically it carries less authority, and its readership patterns are different. But, as mentioned above, it can be much cheaper to run and, if the test is a final test of the viability of the product rather than one of the promotional support, it may still provide most of the information needed.

- *Residential neighbourhoods.* Sometimes just a local area, served by one supermarket, perhaps, can be selected. Here the promotional coverage must be almost exclusively restricted to door-to-door, though this may be supplemented by some local press. As a result, such tests move even further away from the realities of a national launch. They can, however, prove to be a useful vehicle for very sophisticated 'product' tests, or for workable tests of promotion or pricing alternatives.

- *Test sites.* In the industrial sales (capital goods) environment the test may consist of recruiting pilot installations with individual customers. These are sometimes referred to as 'field trials'. This is probably the most suspect of all, in terms of grossing the results up to national projections, since it is likely that these will in practice be the best customers – who are unlikely to be typical of the range of customers and prospects as a whole. Even so, it is a very useful device for 'debugging' some of the potential problems in advance of the launch – and is a device which computer manufacturers use extensively (often then called, more esoterically and rather inexplicably, 'beta testing').

There are a number of decisions to be taken about any test market:

- *Which test market?* Where is the test to be run? Is it to be, economically, in a test town; or, more comprehensively, in a television area? Which area will be most suitable for the specific needs of the test? Some areas have specialist facilities (such as retail audits and promotional discounts) to support tests; but, then, are the consumers in these test areas exposed to more new product launches than elsewhere, and are they still typical of consumers across the whole market?

- *What is to be tested?* There is a tendency to view test markets as just a 'mini-national launch'. This aspect has to be taken into account, of course, but each 'product' has certain factors which are most critical to its success, and special emphasis will need to be placed upon measuring these factors.

- *How long?* A major decision is how long the test will need to run before the 'repeat purchase' patterns can be observed – and the all-important long-term future of the product predicted.

- *Success criteria?* What are the levels of performance to be achieved before the test is judged a success, and the product deemed suitable for national launch? Part of the design of the test should include 'controls' (similar markets which are not exposed to the test 'stimuli') to ensure that other factors are not responsible for the results observed.

The decisions so far have revolved around a simple go or no-go decision, and this (together with the reduction in the risk factors) is normally the main justification for the expense of test markets. At the same time, however, such test markets can be used to test specific elements of a new product's marketing mix – possibly the version of the product itself, the promotional message and media spend, the distribution channels, and the price. In this case, several 'matched' test markets (usually small ones) may be used, each testing different marketing mixes. Clearly, all test markets provide additional information in advance of a launch and may ensure that the launch is successful; however, it is reported that, even at such a late stage, half the products entering a test market do not justify a subsequent national launch.

All test markets suffer from a number of disadvantages:

- *Replicability.* Even the largest test market is not totally representative of the national market, and the smaller ones may introduce gross distortions. Test market results therefore have to be treated with reservations, in exactly the same way as other market research.

- *Effectiveness.* In many cases the major part of the investment has already been made (in development and in plant, for example) before the 'product' is ready to be test marketed. The reduction in risk, therefore, may be minimal and not worth the delays involved.

- *Competitor warning.* All test markets give competitors advance warning of your intentions, and therefore time to react. They may even be able to go national with their own answer before your own test is complete. They may also interfere with your test, by changing their promotional activities (usually by massively increasing them) to the extent that your results are meaningless.
- *Cost.* Although the main objective of test markets is to reduce the amount of investment put at risk, they may still involve significant costs. It is likely that such costs could easily exceed $1 million. The cost may be much higher where the initial capital demands for the launch cannot be scaled down – for example, where a minimum size of production plant is required, which will also meet national levels of demand. Under these circumstances the costs of a test market may not be too different from those of the national launch; and, as mentioned above, there is therefore no justification for it (except that it might still optimize the marketing mix – and might just avoid a very costly mistake in terms of image!).

See also PRODUCT DEVELOPMENT PROCESS

TGI   *see* MARKETING RESEARCH, PRECISION MARKETING

theatre style   *see* PRESENTATION STYLE

Thematic Apperception Tests (TAT)   *see* OPEN QUESTIONS, ON QUESTIONNAIRES

theory of marketing   Marketing theory, like much of management theory, is characterized by the wide variety of theories which may apply – often to just one situation. Thus, there are probably several tools which are equally applicable to the situation, each of which offers a different framework for your own individual analysis.

Yoram Wind (1982) states that 'Marketing as a discipline can provide few generalizations, "principles", or "laws". The major contribution of the marketing discipline is in its approach to problem identification and solution'. Unfortunately, rather less than half a century after its birth as a widely used practical tool of management, too many marketing theorists appear to be hungering after the (academic) respectability of scientific accuracy, and are begin-

ning to adorn their work with esoteric mathematical approaches – where the subject, as practised, remains just as determinedly 'fuzzy'.

Quinn et al. (1988), in the introduction to their splendidly eclectic handbook on strategy, also make the point: 'We do not apologise for contradictions among the ideas of leading thinkers. The world is full of contradictions. The real danger lies in using pat solutions to a nuanced reality, not in opening perspectives up to different interpretations. The effective strategist is one who can live with contradictions, learn to appreciate their cues and effects, and reconcile them sufficiently for effective action.'

Marketing theory is, in the main, derived from observation of practice. It thus describes what is most likely to work, for much of marketing practice is very pragmatic – based solely upon what has been shown by experience to work rather than what abstract theory would prescribe. Lilien and Kotler (1983) report that 'Marketing people often say that marketing experience is the best teacher, that planning and performing a diversity of marketing activities – selling, pricing, advertising, servicing – create sound judgement about what will work and what will backfire'. The acid test of any tool is whether it works in the specific situation which faces you, whether it helps you.

References: Lilien, G. L. and Kotler, P. (1983) *Marketing Decision Making.* New York: Harper & Row.

Quinn, James Brian, Mintzberg, Henry and James, Robert M. (1988) *The Strategy Process.* Englewood Cliffs, NJ: Prentice-Hall.

Wind, Yoram J. (1982) *Product Policy: Methods and Strategy.* Reading, MA: Addison-Wesley.

Theory *X/Y*   *see* PLANNING PROCESS

think tanks   Government-funded institutions (such as the Rand Corporation) set up (mainly in the 1960s) to explore alternative answers to problems experienced by government.

See also NEW PRODUCT CREATION

Third World countries   *see* EXPORT MARKET ELIMINATION

threats   *see* SWOT ANALYSIS

Three Choice Box   A simpler version of the GE (General Electric) Matrix is just:

For most, relatively unsophisticated users this simpler version (dubbed the 'Three Choice Box')

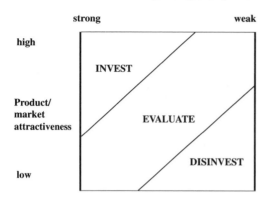

Business strength/competitive position

offers a more immediate picture. It has the great virtue that it surfaces the many subjective decisions which lie beneath the surface of the original (here only you decide where your entry lies within it – you cannot subcontract that decision to fancy mathematics). It also highlights the fact that there is a spectrum of outcomes. To help provide more information immediately to hand, it is conventional to show the chosen position as a circle (whose area is proportional to the size of the market) with a solid (pie) sector within this whose size represents your share of that market.

See also ADVANTAGE MATRIX (BOSTON CONSULTING GROUP); BOSTON MATRIX; CORPORATE PLAN; CORPORATE STRATEGY AND MARKETING; GE (GENERAL ELECTRIC) MATRIX; MARKETING STRATEGIES

Three Pillars of the Purchasing Process　The Enhanced AIUAPR Model can be so complex that a condensed version of this is offered:

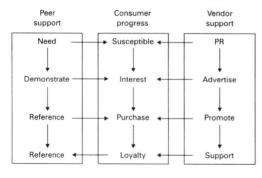

THE THREE PILLARS OF THE PURCHASING PROCESS

thresholds　*see* TEAM SCANNING

throw-away (give-away)　*see* SALES PROMOTION

thumbnail sketches　*see* ADVERTISING PROCESSES

tied indicators　*see* LEADING INDICATORS

tie-in sale　*see* FULL-LINE FORCING

tills, scanning　*see* EPOS AND EFTPOS, PRECISION MARKETING

time-based advantage　*see* RISK VERSUS TIME, NEW PRODUCTS

time buckets　*see* MATERIALS REQUIREMENTS PLANNING (MRP)

time management　*see* CREATIVE IMITATION; EMERGENT STRATEGY; LEAPFROG

time, media　*see* MEDIA BUYING, ADVERTISING AGENCY

time, new products　One of the factors often overlooked in any process of innovation is just how long it may take.

See also NEW PRODUCT SCREENING, ORGANIZATIONAL FACTORS

time preference　The preference, as described in economics, for individuals to consume now rather than in the future.

See also PERMANENT INCOME HYPOTHESIS

timescales　One aspect of conventional marketing theory which has come in for some criticism in recent years is its relative neglect of the timescales involved. There has been a tendency, at least in the theory, to concentrate upon the single transaction. Thus, the archetypal model of consumer marketing is that of the consumer choosing between competing brands on the supermarket shelf – swayed by the advertising messages to which he or she has been recently exposed. It is argued, by some theorists, that the reality is that even purchasing of 'consumables' (FMCG, for instance) should be viewed in the context of a whole series of such transactions. In this context, the buyer is not isolated from historical experience but is well aware of, and possibly dominated by, the habits that he or she has developed over time. This psychological investment in 'brand loyalty' may be high – comparable in influence with the high financial investments involved in some industrial purchases.

Certainly, the longevity of the brand life cycle indicates that there is a high level of investment in the brand itself which is not easily displaced, as conventional marketing theory might hold, by short-term promotional activities in the marketplace. Most marketing may therefore be more realistically viewed in the context of the longer timescales, with relatively high investment levels by purchasers as well as vendors.

See also MARKETING DEFINITIONS, EUROPEAN

time-series analyses To account for the variations due to seasonal trends in quantitative forecasts, as well as those due to long-term trends, more-sophisticated calculations are needed. The 'models' thus built are merely more-complex equations; for, in this context, a model is nothing more than an equation used to calculate what will happen. Thus the exponential smoothing technique, where

new forecast = (previous forecast)
            + (0.1 × actual deviation)

is a model, albeit a very simple one.

Such general time-series models (sometimes described as 'decomposition' models, wherein the overall forecasts are 'decomposed' into the various elements – trend/cyclical/seasonal/etc. – which change) can be built by, for example, arithmetically removing a steady overall trend (the straight line showing the long-term average increase) by measuring deviations from it, to give the underlying average seasonal pattern. Models can also be built by visual inspection (which is what Z charts sometimes may be used for). Whichever means is chosen, the end result will be an 'equation' which allows for the inclusion of the various factors which the forecaster believes have an impact on the variable he is forecasting.

Auto-Regressive Moving Average (ARMA) techniques are the most sophisticated of the 'simple' time series. They filter out (using mathematical 'adaptive filtering' techniques) the various effects of cycle and seasonality (for example) to detect the underlying growth. The most commonly reported methodology is 'Box and Jenkins'. This simply assigns various of these ARMA models to the specific observations being processed and tests them until an optimal outcome is achieved. That model is then chosen.

On the other hand, although widely reported in the literature, 'Box and Jenkins', along with the other more sophisticated techniques, is relatively little used in practice.

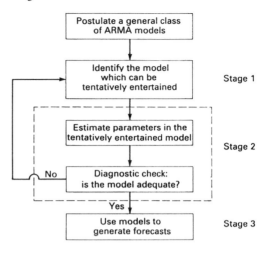

See also MULTIPLE REGRESSION ANALYSIS; QUANTITATIVE FORECASTING TECHNIQUES

timing of mailings The timing of mailings can influence their impact. Clearly, they have to be integrated with the overall campaign. On the other hand, there are some times of year when it is traditionally believed to be unproductive to mail. The summer months (of July and August), when prospects are supposed to be on holiday (or thinking of nothing else), are one such time, as is December (when the letter will be lost in the deluge of Christmas mail). Even the day of the week on which the mailing is sent can have an impact. Riso (1979), for example, reports: 'Care should be taken, they say, to avoid reaching a businessman's desk on Monday, or any day following a holiday, when there is likely to be a large accumulation of letters needing attention . . . . the best day is Tuesday, and Wednesday is next best.'

See also PRECISION MARKETING

Reference: Riso, Ovid (ed.) (1979) *The Dartnell Sales Promotion Handbook*. New York: The Dartnell Corporation.

Timotei shampoo   *see* GLOBALIZATION; GLOBAL MARKETING

tones   *see* LINE DRAWING

top-down planning   *see* PLANNING PROCESS

torture testing Pushing products to their limit, destructive testing, as part of the development process; and sometimes, separately, as part of the quality control of existing products.

total audience package (TAP)   A low-cost package of advertisements which will provide a specified number of impressions – hence the reason it is sometimes called guaranteed home impressions – placed at the media owner's discretion (probably off-peak, so the coverage may be relatively low).
See also MEDIA BUYING, ADVERTISING AGENCY; MEDIA SELECTION

total quality management (TQM)   From the customer's viewpoint, quality does not stop at the physical, tangible, elements of the product (or service). Just because it cannot be measured does not mean that any aspect of the organization's operation is not important, in terms of quality, to the customer. All the elements of the extended 'product package', especially the support elements, are equally important. A growing awareness of this need has led many companies to pursue 'total quality management' drives in which every employee is persuaded to concentrate on providing 'quality' in what he or she is responsible for – on the premise that all actions of employees add to overall quality. IBM is one of the most avid supporters of this movement, but for many years IBM had already employed the philosophy, under the banner of 'customer service' (arguably an even more direct and effective philosophy for ensuring the total quality which matters to the customer). Indeed, the reason given by senior management at Toyota – arguably the world's leading exponent of TQM – for its success is quite simply 'our relations with our workforce.'
See also CUSTOMER SATISFACTION SURVEY; INNER MARKET; JUST IN TIME (JIT); QUALITY SPECIFICATION

Touche Ross, consultants   *see* CONSULTANTS

touting for new business   *see* TERRITORY SALES PLAN

town test   *see* TEST MARKET

Toyota   *see* GLOBALIZATION; KANBAN; SET–UP TIMES; STANDARDIZATION VERSUS ADAPTATION; SUGGESTIONS SCHEMES

TQM   *see* TOTAL QUALITY MANAGEMENT (TQM)

trade agreements   *see* COUNTERTRADING

trade associations, and external data   One of the best sources of data, not least the 'informal' data acquired during conversations at meetings, is that of trade associations. There is usually a fee for membership, but this is frequently very good value in terms of what may be learned from these sources.
See also EXTERNAL DATA; LIBRARIES

trade discounts   In payment for the services they provide to the supplier, members of the distribution chains receive different sorts of payments:

- *Trade discounts.* This is a standard discount, usually a fixed percentage, which is offered to a channel member. The percentage may, though, vary according to the 'category' the producer believes the intermediary falls into.
- *Quantity discount.* This has the advantage that it offers an incentive for all intermediaries to try to sell the maximum quantity and hence trade-up to higher discount levels.
- *Promotional discount.* The producer may also attempt to 'push' the product or service by offering promotional discounts in the belief that these will persuade the intermediary to substitute the brand in question for another, where the end-user will often accept what is in stock. Alternatively, the intention may be to persuade the retailer, for example, to overstock, thus creating 'stock pressure', so that the retailer is then forced to give the brand extra display in order to reduce these stocks.
- *Cash discount.* Most producers normally offer trade intermediaries terms which require payment in 30 days. This is of considerable value to retailers such as Sainsbury, who have managed to get some of their stockholdings down to less than 5 days. The extra 25 days of credit can in effect be used as a free loan, to be used to fund physical assets such as their property and buildings! The producer may, however, want to provide an incentive for retailers, or wholesalers, to pay earlier. Hence, a cash discount, or a discount for immediate or prompt payment, is offered. This type of discount has fallen into disfavour, though. If it does not balance the free interest which would otherwise be obtained, the retailer will continue to take advantage of the 'loan'. If it does represent a bargain, on the other hand, the producer is losing out – unless there is a desperate need for cash flow to be improved. Worst of all, the evidence suggests that the majority of customers will

probably take the cash discount and still pay late (often after 60 days rather than 30)!

See also CHANNEL MEMBERS; CHANNEL STRUCTURE; DISTRIBUTION CHAIN; INTERNAL MARKET

trademarks   These consist of words, symbols or devices which are used to distinguish your products from those of competitors or from generic products. If used properly they may be protected by law, and competitors may not be allowed to use similar marks (ones which consumers might believe were for the same brand).
See also BRAND MONOPOLY

trade-off model   A consumer behaviour model which seeks to explain behaviour in terms of the 'utilities' individuals attach to different product characteristics.
See also BUYING DECISION, ADVERTISING MODELS; MARKETING RESEARCH; MODELS

trade press   *see* PRESS MEDIA

tradesmen   *see* SUPPLIERS

trading down   Reducing prices to increase sales by becoming more competitive.
See also COMPETITIVE PRICING

trading system, world   *see* GLOBALIZATION

tradition   *see* CULTURE, ORGANIZATIONAL; SALES TEAM MANAGEMENT

traffic function   *see* ADVERTISING AGENCY ELEMENTS

traffic, page   *see* PAGE TRAFFIC

transactional analysis   Theory used by market researchers, based on psychoanalytic theory, describing a 'unit' (the transaction) of behaviour between two people.
See also MARKETING RESEARCH; MOTIVATION RESEARCH

transaction cost economics   This is the branch of microeconomics developed from the original work of Ronald H. Coase (1937) which explains organizational behaviour, especially such features as divisionalization, in terms of defects in the market, especially in terms of information. Thus, it assumes that, ideally (as in neoclassical economics), provision of any good or service to an organization is most efficiently sourced by means of the market. The drawback is the 'transaction cost' – the cost of drawing up and monitoring performance against the (usually theoretical) contract (and, in practice, the problems of dealing with external suppliers). Thus, production is often undertaken internally, this being the safest route. Problems largely arise because of a range of defects in the market of which the best known is 'bounded rationality', whereby the actors (the individuals) cannot be considered to be fully rational since they have difficulty dealing with complex problems and have incomplete information.
See also RATIONAL EXPECTATIONS THEORY

Reference: Coase, R. H. (1937) The nature of the firm. *Economica*, 4.

transfer payments   *see* FISCAL POLICY

transient advertisement   *see* INTRANSIENT ADVERTISEMENT

transmission medium   *see* ENCODING

transnational   *see* GLOBALIZATION; INTERNATIONAL PRODUCT DECISION

transnationals/multinationals and exporters   Subject to their decisions as to how they will treat their brands around the world (as global, international or merely, but most frequently, national), the marketing departments of multinationals and transnationals can largely ignore the complexities of international marketing. All they need do is apply the normal marketing practices. Paradoxically, therefore, the theory of international marketing is least relevant to its most significant practitioners! Indeed, the major requirement for international success would appear to be established success in a (strong) domestic market; and usually dominance of that domestic market. Only then do the organizations have the financial and structural strengths to penetrate overseas markets on the scale that is necessary to dominate them, too. In particular, funds flows cross-subsidize the emerging overseas operations (often having to invest very heavily to overcome locally entrenched competitors), until these become self-funding and then, in turn, cash generators. The truly global corporations have their roots, therefore, in very strong national marketing, eventually managing to treat the whole world as one national market (as IBM, Coca Cola and McDonalds have done). It is true, as Hamel and Prahalad (1955) suggested, that 'Global competitors must have the capacity to think and act in complex ways. In other words, they may slice the company in one way for distribution, in another for investments, in another for technology, and in still another for manufacturing.' Thus, for example, IBM has a truly global strategy for its development laboratories, a continental strategy for its manufacturing plants, but a largely nationally based strategy for marketing (though based on globally enforced standards and prices). Michael Porter (1986) succinctly summarizes his view of the whole debate when he says 'Is Ted Levitt right about globalization? Yes. Does that mean that you standardize and homogenize the way you perform marketing in every country in the world throughout the marketing mix? Of course not.'

See also COMPARATIVE ADVANTAGE, GLOBAL; ECONOMIES OF SCALE, GLOBAL; GLOBALIZATION; GLOBAL MARKETING; INTERNATIONAL PRODUCT DECISION

References: Hamel, Gary and Prahalad, C. K. (1955) Do you really have a global strategy? *Harvard Business Review*, July–August.

Porter, Michael (1986) The strategic role of international marketing. *The Journal of Consumer Marketing*, 3(2).

transparencies/acetates *see* PRESENTATION MEDIA

transport contractor *see* TRANSPORT DECISIONS, LOGISTICS MANAGEMENT

transport decisions, logistics management The running of a fleet of delivery vehicles is a major operation in its own right. With large delivery vehicles costing many tens of thousands of pounds, the investment is substantial, but the specialized management of the personnel and resources involved can be just as important. Apart from managing the pure logistics involved (the optimal utilization of the expensive vehicles and drivers), the main tasks of transport management traditionally have been those of scheduling – a balance between the prompt service to be offered to the customer against the cost of providing it most economically – and routing – which demands the classical 'linear programming' test of achieving the minimum distance (and time) to reach all the delivery points. Both, and in particular the latter, are tasks which should be ideal for computers; and, indeed, they are now being more frequently

handled in this manner. Increasingly, though, organizations are subcontracting their whole transport operation to outside operators. This has become the classic 'make or buy' decision (whether it is more economic to provide support, or production, inhouse rather than buy it from outside specialists). On the smaller scale, the operator simply collects the producer's 'parcels' and then sorts and delivers them in much the same way as the Royal Mail does for smaller packages. On the larger scale the operator can, in effect, run the organization's own dedicated, and 'badged', fleet. This way, it looks to the outside world exactly as if it belongs to the producer, but still benefits from the expertise and efficiency of being run by a large transport contractor.

See also FACILITY DECISIONS, LOGISTICS MANAGEMENT; INVENTORY CONTROL; LOGISTICS MANAGEMENT; PRODUCTION DECISIONS, LOGISTICS MANAGEMENT

traveller *see* COMMERCIAL TRAVELLER

travelling time *see* TERRITORY MANAGEMENT

tree-structured approach to long-term forecasting *see* BAYESIAN DECISION THEORY

tree-structured database *see* MATERIALS REQUIREMENTS PLANNING (MRP)

tree structures, forecasting One aid to qualitative forecasting is the use of tree structures. The main factors affecting the organization's environment, for example, are plotted and the possible alternatives (or decisions – hence the sometimes used name, 'decision trees') are shown at each stage, branching at each level like a tree. An example is that of the choices facing an inventor, described by Hull et al. (1976): p. 403 below (top).

At the end of this process all of the various possible contributions (or at least, all that the forecaster chooses to take into account) will have been documented, including some which might not otherwise have been thought of. This is the main value of the technique, though an obvious problem is in dealing with the sheer number of alternatives that then become apparent.

A specialized form is the 'relevance tree', where the approach is used to force a panel of experts to identify, for instance, technological deficiencies or areas where research is needed, and to prioritize these or attach 'relevance' ratings – as illustrated by Makridakis and Wheelwright (1989): p. 403 below (bottom).

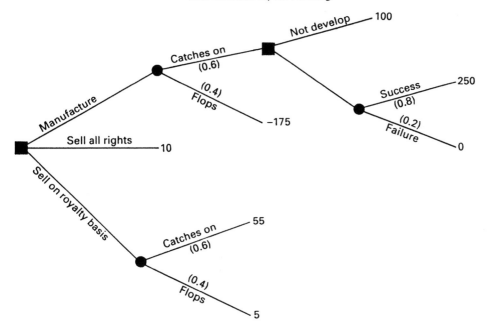

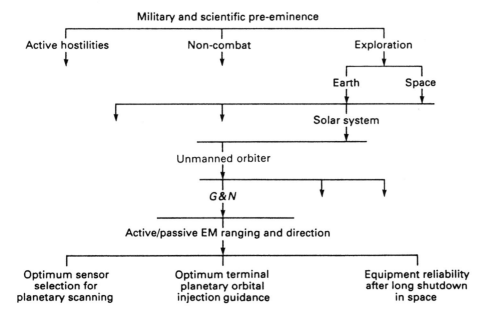

   An even more complex approach also takes account of the fact that each of these 'tree branches'
may be related to decisions being taken elsewhere in
the 'network', and includes these relationships. This
means that not all the tree structure needs to be
included (there is no need to include all factors at all
levels). This makes the larger networks more manageable, but does require a more conscious effort to
decide what should be excluded. The end result of
this process (as well as that of a similar approach, the
'mission flow diagram') is a network which looks like
a critical path analysis and, like that, usually requires
computer analysis to untangle the information.
See also QUALITATIVE FORECASTING METHODS

References: Hull, John, Mapes, John and Wheeler, Brian (1976) *Model Building Techniques for Management*. London: Saxon House.

Makridakis, Spyros and Wheelwright, Steven C. (1989) *Forecasting Methods for Management* (5th edn). Chichester: John Wiley.

trend forecasting   *see* MACRO- AND MICRO-FORECASTS

triad power   'Global' markets are made up of 'national' markets which have very different weightings. The major economies of the developed world account for a dramatically disproportionate share of these markets. Kenichi Ohmae (1985), whilst not denying the importance of other markets, stresses the key role of the three major markets (which he terms the 'Triad'):

> By now, the strategic significance of Japan, the United States and Europe should be obvious. This Triad where the major markets are; it is where the competitive threat comes from; it is where the new technologies will originate. As competition becomes keener, it is where preventative action against protectionism will be needed most. To take advantage of the Triad's markets and forthcoming technologies and to prepare for new competitors, the prime objective of every corporation must be to become a true insider in all these regions.

This view places a great weight upon being a truly 'global' organization (at least in terms of these three massive markets).
See also COMPARATIVE ADVANTAGE, GLOBAL; ECONOMIES OF SCALE, GLOBAL; GLOBALIZATION; GLOBAL MARKETING; INTERNATIONAL PRODUCT DECISION

Reference: Ohmae, Kenichi (1985) *Triad Power: The Coming Shape of Global Competition*. New York: The Free Press.

trial   *see* REPEAT PURCHASING PROCESS; SAMPLING

trial close   *see* CLOSING TECHNIQUES

trial, obtaining   *see* OBTAINING TRIAL

trial purchase behaviour   *see* ENHANCED AIUAPR MODEL; PEER PYRAMID; THREE PILLARS OF THE PURCHASING PROCESS

trial size   *see* SAMPLING

trial use close   *see* CLOSING TECHNIQUES

trickle-down theory   *see* ADVERTISING OBSOLESCENCE; OPINION LEADERS; SOCIAL CLASS INFLUENCES, ON THE PURCHASE DECISION; STANDARDIZATION VERSUS ADAPTATION

trunking   *see* FACILITY DECISIONS, LOGISTICS MANAGEMENT

trust   *see* CONVICTION MARKETING; SERVICE QUALITY

Tupperware   *see* PARTY SELLING

turnkey, bid   *see* MARKET ENTRY TACTICS

TVR   *see* TELEVISION RATING (TVR)

two-bin inventory control   One of the simplest, and most effective, methods of inventory control is to have two 'bins' of a product (or service). When the first 'bin' is empty it is replaced by the second, full one and another bin of the product is put on order. If the requirements of such a 'component' represent a very small part of the overall cost, this approach may be the easiest to implement, and may well be the most effective. A rather more sophisticated version of this simple system, one which (as the 'kanban' system) has been very effectively used by Japanese manufacturers, is to provide a card with each 'bin' supplied. When the bin is empty the card is returned – and automatically generates an order on the supplier.
See also INVENTORY CONTROL

two-step model of advertising   *see* OPINION LEADERS

two-tailed test   A test of significance, as part of statistical testing of marketing research results, based on two possible outcomes. Thus, the hypothesis is that the result is higher than or lower than 50 per cent, say.
See also ANALYSIS OF MARKETING RESEARCH DATA

tying contract   A contract which requires a distributor to take another product along with the one wanted.

typeface *see* FONT

typesetting *see* LINOTYPE; PHOTOCOMPOSITION

typographical error *see* LITERAL

typological analysis Categorization of households by both psychographic and purchasing habit data.
See also SEGMENTATION

tyre-kickers *see* TERRITORY SALES PLAN

U

umbrella advertising *see* CORPORATE
PROMOTION VERSUS BRAND PROMOTION

umbrella strategy *see* EMERGENT STRATEGY

UN *see* INTERNATIONAL MARKETING RESEARCH

unaddressed mailings *see* DOOR-TO-DOOR

unanimity *see* GROUPTHINK

unbundling *see* PRICE INCREASES

uncertainty *see* CONTINGENCY PLAN; VISION,
CORPORATE

uncertainty and marketing research The marketer is often faced with a degree of uncertainty, and
can never be quite certain that even the best laid
plans will achieve their objectives in exactly the
manner expected. Such uncertainty is usually an in-
escapable part of any manager's life. It is normally
greater in those markets which are changing, and
greatest in those which are changing rapidly. Unfortunately, at least in terms of uncertainty (albeit fortunately in terms of the opportunities created), a great
many markets have been experiencing very rapid
change over recent years, especially since the 1970s;
and the 1980s saw the emergence of 'chaos' as a
factor to be managed. Even in mature markets, such
as those of car production and shipbuilding, marketers have been caught out by developments. To help
reduce uncertainty, all management needs a constant
flow of information. In the case of the marketing
manager, the process which provides this information is marketing research. The information
thus gathered may cover: markets; customers and
consumers; competitive activities; the impact of environmental factors such as governments or socio-
cultural changes; or the results of the organization's
own marketing activities.
See also CHAOS; MARKETING RESEARCH

uncertainty reduction, forecasting For most
organizations the view of the future is clouded by a
degree of uncertainty, and this doubt means that
their plans may be that much less productive. The
primary aim of forecasting is thus to reduce uncertainty to the lowest level possible. Even so, it is as
well to bear in mind the problems which this uncertainty will pose for the forecasting process itself. As
Donald Michael (1989) writes:

> Given mounting evidence of societal disarray and
> lack of success in significantly reducing incoher-
> ence, it may become more acceptable, even good
> politics, to concede this in public and make a pro-
> nouncement such as, 'We really don't know where
> we are on this matter or what will work for sure.
> We must discover and rediscover what questions
> are useful and what approaches we might experi-
> ment with. Therefore, we must become a learning
> organization.

Michel Godet (1982) gives a more direct message:
'The economic history of industrial society has been
marked by repeated forecasting errors. What is serious is not so much the existence of the errors, as the
systematic ignoring of past errors when new forecasts
are made.'
Daniel Bell (1974) poses some of the limitations
(on long-range forecasting, in particular) even more
directly:

> Forecasting is possible where there are regularities
> and recurrences of phenomena (these are rare), or
> where there are persisting trends whose direction,
> if not exact trajectory, can be plotted with statisti-
> cal time-series or be formulated as historical ten-
> dencies. Necessarily, therefore, one deals with
> probabilities and an array of possible projections.
> But the limitations of forecasting are also evident.
> The further one reaches ahead in time with a set of
> forecasts, the greater the margin for error, since
> the fan of these projections widens. More impor-
> tant, at crucial points these trends become subject
> to change (and increasingly in modern society
> these are conscious interventions by men with

power) and the decision (to accelerate, swerve or deflect the trend) is a policy intervention which may create a turning point in the history of a country or an institution. To put it a different way: forecasting is possible only where one can assume a high degree of rationality on the part of men who influence events – the recognition of costs and constraints, the common acceptance or definition of the rules of the game, the agreement to follow the rules, the willingness to be consistent . . .

The changes which are taking place in the environment which surrounds the organization will result in the appearance of both opportunities (for its business to increase) and threats (which may destroy the existing position). Another task of forecasting, therefore, is to identify and quantify these changes so that actions can be taken to respectively exploit them and erect defences against them.

See also SHORT- VERSUS LONG-TERM FORECASTS

References: Bell, Daniel (1974) *The Coming of Post-Industrial Society: A Venture in Social Forecasting*. London: Heinemann.
  Godet, Michel (1982) From forecasting to 'la prospective': a new way of looking at futures. *Journal of Forecasting*, 1(3).
  Michael, Donald N. (1989) Forecasting and planning in an incoherent context. *Technological Forecasting and Social Change*, 36(1–2).

uncertain waits   *see* QUEUE

undercutting   *see* COMPETITIVE PRICING

understanding   In the overall personal communication process, listening is not enough. The key to the professional sale (and to questioning by managers) is understanding. This is a process to which the main contribution must, of course, be made by what the person being questioned says; though it should be noted that this may include what he or she said in a number of previous meetings as well as in the current one. But it will also include all the other evidence you have unearthed. Put it all together and, hopefully, you will be able to complete the jigsaw. Understanding, therefore, is a cumulative process that may span several discussions. It is a fundamental skill of the sales professional (and an important one for managers), yet it is almost totally ignored by sales trainers – who concentrate on the single call and the instant reaction. It is the quality of your listening, not just the quantity, that is critical. Analysis is central to this quality. Ideally this analysis takes place as the discussion progresses. But, even when listening, this schizophrenic act takes a great deal of effort, and may divert your attention to such an extent that you miss critical facts. It is almost impossible when you are talking – another good reason for listening rather than talking. The best compromise is to take copious notes (unless you have an excellent memory) and analyse what you have heard after the meeting. At leisure, then, you can (and should) analyse what was said. In practice, missing questions usually do not prove fatal; just so long as you ask them at the next meeting.

See also AIUAPR (AWARENESS, INTEREST, UNDERSTANDING, ATTITUDES, PURCHASE, REPEAT PURCHASE) MODEL; ENHANCED AIUAPR MODEL; NOTE-TAKING; QUESTIONING; THREE PILLARS OF THE PURCHASING PROCESS

understanding, advertising   Once an interest is established by advertising, the message has to explain the product or service, and its benefits, in such a way that the reader can understand them and can appreciate how well the product or service may meet his or her needs – as revealed by the marketing research. This may be no mean achievement where the copywriter has just 50 words, or 10 seconds, to convey everything there is to say about it; which is one reason why complex capital goods sales are the province of the sales professional (who may take many hours, in total, to fully explain the product) and, on the other hand, why there is such a demand for good copywriters who can actually describe consumer goods – in meaningful terms – in such few words in an advertisement. On the other hand, David Ogilvy (1983) advises that 'long copy – more than 300 words – actually attracts more readers than short copy'. This stage of the advertising process is thus a mix of sound marketing research mediated by professional copywriting skills.

See also ADVERTISING

Reference: Ogilvy, David (1983) *Ogilvy on Advertising*. London: Pan Books.

undifferentiated approach to segmentation
see SEGMENTATION APPROACHES

undirected viewing   *see* SCANNING, AND MIS

unexplained waits   *see* QUEUE

unfair waits   *see* QUEUE

unfreezing an organization   *see* PARADIGM SHIFT, STRATEGY

uniform customer needs   *see* STANDARDIZATION VERSUS ADAPTATION

Unilever   *see* ADVERTISING; ECONOMIES OF SCALE, GLOBAL

unique product identities   *see* DIFFERENTIATION AND BRANDING

Unique Selling Proposition   *see* MESSAGE, ADVERTISING

United Nations yearbooks   *see* INTERNATIONAL MARKETING RESEARCH

United States   *see* TRIAD POWER

univariate analysis   Quantitative analysis where each variable is analysed separately, typically in terms of frequency distribution.

unloading   Dumping goods, by selling them at a low price.

unmeasurable outputs   *see* NOT-FOR-PROFIT ORGANIZATIONS, OBJECTIVES

unplanned strategy   *see* EMERGENT STRATEGY

unpredictable strategy   *see* EMERGENT STRATEGY

unrealized strategy   *see* EMERGENT STRATEGY

unresponsive seller   *see* STRATEGIES FOR INTENT BUYERS

untrustworthy huckster   *see* SALESMAN STEREOTYPE

upper classes   *see* SOCIAL CLASS INFLUENCES, ON THE PURCHASE DECISION

upper-class opinion leaders   *see* OPINION LEADERS

usage and loyalty   Whatever the marketing programmes undertaken, what is usually most important is the customer's response to the 'brand'. This can be described in three main ways:

Usage status
Philip Kotler (1988) groups 'users' into a number of categories: 'non-users, ex-users, potential users, first-time users and regular users'. Each category is likely to have a different behaviour pattern and accordingly may require a different promotional approach.

Usage rate
Most important of all, in the context of classification of users, is usually the rate of usage, which is where the Pareto, 80:20, rule applies. 'Heavy users' are likely to be disproportionately important to the brand (typically, 20 per cent of users accounting for 80 per cent of usage – and of suppliers' profit!). As a result, suppliers often segment their customers into 'heavy', 'medium' and 'light' users; and, as far as they can, they target 'heavy users'.

Loyalty
An important dimension, in the context of classification of users, is whether the customer is committed to the brand. Kotler defines four patterns of behaviour:

- *Hard-core loyals* – who buy the brand all the time.
- *Soft-core loyals* – loyal to two or three brands.
- *Shifting loyals* – moving from one brand to another.
- *Switchers* – with no loyalty (possibly 'deal prone', constantly looking for bargains, or 'variety prone', looking for something different).

The categorization by rate of usage is perhaps most evident in industrial markets, where organizations will categorize the 'heavy users' as 'major accounts', and put senior sales personnel and even managers (possibly backed by a team of sales and support personnel) in charge of these. 'Light users' may be handed to a general sales force or (more frequently, perhaps) to a dealer.
See also BRAND VALUE; CUSTOMER FRANCHISE; CUSTOMERS

Reference: Kotler, Philip (1988) *Marketing Management* (6th edn). Englewood Cliffs, NJ: Prentice-Hall.

usage gap   The gap between the total potential for the market and the actual current usage by all the consumers in the market. Clearly there are two figures needed for this calculation:

Market potential
The most difficult estimate to make is probably that of the total potential available to the whole market,

including all segments covered by all competitive brands. It is often achieved by determining the maximum potential individual usage and extrapolating this by the maximum number of potential consumers. This is inevitably a judgement rather than a scientific extrapolation, but some of the macro-forecasting techniques may assist in making this 'guesstimate' more soundly based.

The maximum number of consumers available will usually be determined by market research, but it may sometimes be calculated from demographic data or government statistics. Ultimately there will, of course, be limitations on the number of consumers. In the cosmetics field, for example, the current boundaries may be most women and girls over the age of 12 years, say. But you also have to consider, realistically, if these will be the boundaries in the future as well. Not so long ago the lower boundary was something over 16 years, and who is to say that significant numbers of men will not at some time in the future also take up cosmetics; as they have in recent years taken up the use of perfume, albeit suitably camouflaged as 'aftershave'!

For guidance, you might like to look to the numbers using similar products. Those wishing to sell the newly developed compact disc must have paid great attention to the existing sales of record and cassette decks. Alternatively, you might like to look to what has happened in other countries. It is often suggested, for example, that the UK follows the US patterns, but lagging by a decade or so; though, with the increased affluence in all the major Western economies, the lag may now be much shorter.

The maximum potential individual usage, or at least the maximum attainable average usage (where there will always be a spread of usage across a range of customers), will usually be determined from market research figures.

Existing (market) usage
The existing usage by consumers makes up the total current market, from which market shares, for example, are calculated. It is usually derived from market research, most accurately from panel research such as that undertaken by A. C. Nielsen but also from *ad hoc* work. Sometimes it may be available from figures collected by government departments or industry bodies; however, these are often based on categories which may make sense in bureaucratic terms but are less helpful in marketing terms. Any marketer with aspirations to professionalism should in any case know, at least roughly, what the size of his or her market is, since that is the battlefield!

The usage gap is thus:

usage gap = market potential − existing usage

This is an important calculation to make. Many, if not most, marketers accept the existing market size, suitably projected over the timescales of their forecasts, as the boundary for their expansion plans. Although this is often the most realistic assumption, it may sometimes impose an unnecessary limitation on their horizons. The original market for video recorders was limited to the professional users who could afford the high prices involved. It was only after some time that the technology was extended – initially by Sony, which was already the brand leader – to the mass market.

In the public sector, where the service providers usually enjoy a 'monopoly', this 'usage gap' will probably be the most important factor in the development of their activities; though the 'product gap' should not be ignored. However, persuading more 'consumers' to take up family benefits, for example, will probably be more important to the Department of Social Security than opening more local offices.

This 'usage gap' is most important for the brand leaders. If any of these have a significant share of the whole market, say in excess of 30 per cent, it may become worthwhile for them to invest in expanding the total market. This was IBM's policy overall, though paradoxically not so in the PC market! The same option is not generally open to the minor players, though they may still be able to profitably target specific offerings as market extensions.

Gap analysis is a tool to help you examine as thoroughly and objectively as possible your current marketing position and the strategies which you could follow to improve it in line with overall company strategies. It is very likely to direct you to fresh product/market strategies and to the need to develop new and improved products.

You should be aware, however, that terminology in this area is open to debate. Rowe et al. (1989), for instance, use almost exactly the same terms in a very different way, where the 'product' and 'distribution' gaps are seen as representing growth in overall market sales rather than increasing brand share within current market sales.

See also COMPETITIVE GAP; DISTRIBUTION GAP; GAP ANALYSIS; MARKET GAP ANALYSIS; PRODUCT (OR SERVICE) GAP

Reference: Rowe, Alan J., Mason, Richard O., Dickel, Karl E. and Snyder, Neil H. (1989) *Strategic Management: A Methodological Approach* (3rd edn). Reading, MA: Addison-Wesley.

user buyer   *see* DECISION-MAKERS AND
INFLUENCERS

users   It may be a fine distinction, but sometimes
users are not quite the same as purchasers. It may be
the children in the family who actually consume the
cornflakes – and usually will make their brand preferences very well known, even if it is only because
they want to collect the free gifts in the packets of
breakfast cereals! The difference is most noticeable
in the case of newspapers and magazines, where
readership figures (the number of those who read a
given issue, as determined by market research surveys) can be much higher than those for circulation
(the number of copies sold, from special audits of the
publisher's own accounts). In this case it is the readership figures which are of most interest to the advertisers, who provide most of the income for such
publishers; hence the growth of the so-called 'free'
(or 'controlled circulation') publications. In most
marketing practice, however, such fine distinctions
do not normally pose critical limitations. The important fact is that some of the individuals in the market
buy the producer's brand and some do not.
See also CUSTOMERS; MARKETS; PROSPECTS

USP   *see* MESSAGE, ADVERTISING

utility, pricing   *see* PRICES, CUSTOMER NEEDS

V

VALS (VAlue LifeStyles) In 1983 Arnold Mitchell (of SRI International) developed lifestyle groupings, using four main categories subdivided into nine 'lifestyles', based on consumers' answers to long questionnaires:

- *Need-driven groups* – Survivors, Sustainers
- *Outer-directed groups* – Belongers, Emulators, Achievers
- *Inner-directed groups* – I-am-me, Experientials, Societally conscious
- *Combined outer- and inner-directed groups* – Integrated

According to this framework, the 'Outer-directed' groups – Belongers (conventional, conservative, etc.), Emulators (ambitious, upwardly mobile, etc.) and Achievers (leaders who make things happen etc.) – account for two-thirds of the US population. Thus *The Times* newspaper might expect to target 'Achievers', and to possibly address a larger total market segment than *The Guardian*, which might be looking to the 'Societally conscious' for its most ardent supporters.

In the later development, VALS-2, a rather different set of groupings was proposed: Strugglers, Makers, Believers, Experiencers, Achievers, Fulfilled and Actualizers.

Another, similar approach is LOV (List Of Values), which is based on segments such as self-respect, security, warm relationships with others, being well-respected, self-fulfilment, self-accomplishment, sense of belonging, fun and enjoyment of life.
See also AIO (ACTIVITIES, INTERESTS, OPINIONS); LIFESTYLE INFLUENCES, ON THE PURCHASE DECISION

Reference: Mitchell, Arnold (1983) *The Nine American Lifestyles.* New York: Macmillan.

value analysis One special technique often applied to purchasing, or to the internal design processes, is 'value analysis'. This process, often employing the use of 'brainstorming' techniques, examines the design of parts (or the whole) to see if costs can be reduced (or reliability, say, improved) by changing the specification.

See also PURCHASING; SPECIFICATION

value chains *see* ADDED–VALUE DEAGRAM; PRACTICAL VALUE CHAINS

VAlue LifeStyles (VALS) *see* VALS (VALUE LIFESTYLES)

values, shared *see* CULTURE, ORGANIZATIONAL

variability, services Sometimes referred to, in this context, as 'heterogeneity', this comes about largely as a result of the 'people' content, but because the service is usually produced and consumed at the same time, many services are much more variable than physical products. A hi-fi system or a television can be guaranteed to exactly match the specifications each time one comes off the production line. A service often depends upon who is actually providing it and under what conditions. A performance of 'Antony and Cleopatra' at the National Theatre, starring Anthony Hopkins and Judi Dench, probably had a different feel to the same play produced by a local amateur dramatic company. The most important implication is that services require much higher levels, and standards, of management to ensure that the service actually being provided matches the specification; and, indeed, many ser-vice-based industries have a higher ratio of managers to employees. Training, too, has an important part to play. Japan Air Lines, for instance, give their cabin crew longer etiquette and politeness training than any other airline; and it shows (not least because they now sell the training package to those other airlines!).

variable costs *see* BREAK–EVEN ANALYSIS, NEW PRODUCTS; MARGINAL COSTING, NEW PRODUCTS

variance analysis In this approach to analysing/ monitoring performance, criteria (typically budgets or targets) are set, against which each of the products or customers are subsequently monitored. If their performance falls outside the expected range, this is highlighted. This means that only those items where there are 'variances' need be reviewed. On the other hand, the variances reported are only as good as the

criteria (usually the budgets) set; and setting these is, in practice, a major task. This is particularly problematical where parameters change with time, so new criteria will need to be set on a regular basis. This is usually beyond the capacity of most managements, so this approach is often only used (if at all) on the '20 per cent' of most important items.
See also PERFORMANCE ANALYSIS

variances These are the result of comparing actual results against budget (target) figures or, typically in manufacturing, against pre-set standards.
See also BUDGETS; MARKETING INTELLIGENCE SYSTEMS (MIS)

variety The evidence is that many markets are moving towards significantly increased variety in terms of the ranges of products or services offered. This is a requirement imposed by consumer demand and is the very reverse of that favouring economies of scale – once a viable level of mass production has been reached. As quoted by Hesketh and Signorelli (1988), Benetton in the early 1980s, for example, had a product line with more than 500 colour and style combinations. Also in the 1980s, Japanese manufacturers moved to 'flexible manufacturing', which enabled them to increase the number of varieties they offered without dramatic reductions in efficiency. It is significant, incidentally, that the most influential description of this process was provided in 1988 by George Stalk Jr of the Boston Consulting Group – the main proponents of experience curves!

Woo and Cooper (1988) showed that, at least in the case of stable markets, 'low market share does not inevitably lead to low profitability'. They add the suggestion, for achieving success under these conditions, that 'The most distinctive feature of these strategies is selective focus. They do not copy the strategies of market leaders . . .' This has often been described as 'niche' marketing.
See also ECONOMIES OF SCALE; FLEXIBLE MANUFACTURING

References: Hesketh, James L. and Signorelli, Sergio (1988) In Robert D. Buzzell and John A. Quelch (eds), *Multinational Marketing: Cases and Readings*. New York: Addison-Wesley.
   Stalk, George, Jr (1988) Time – the next source of advantage. *Harvard Business Review*, July–August.
   Woo, Carolyn Y. and Cooper, Arnold C. (1988) The surprising case for low market share. In David E. Gumpert (ed.), *The Marketing Renaissance*. New York: John Wiley.

vector approach   *see* TECHNOLOGICAL FORECASTING

velocity of money   The speed with which money moves from buyer to seller through the economy. It is an important factor in the theory of monetarism.
See also MONETARISM

vending machine   *see* AUTOMATIC SELLING

vendors   *see* PURCHASING

verbal (computer) databases   Specially developed computer programs (such as IBM's STAIRS programs, and the equivalent versions for PCs) for storing and retrieving vast quantities of verbal information are available. Some of these require the originator to specify the topics covered (often using 'key-word indices'). The best, and most useful, index every word in the documents, so that an enquirer on a terminal can ask to be given those documents which mention a given topic anywhere in their contents. Where this may perhaps throw up several hundred references, the search is gradually narrowed by using combinations of words in the search. Thus the first level of search on the word *database* might list hundreds of references. The second level, combining this reference with that of *personal computer*, might reduce the number to several tens of documents. Specifying a further level of *relational* (and hence only looking for documents which contain, say, the words *database*, *personal computer* and *relational* in the same paragraph) may reduce the number of references to a handful – which can then each be examined.
See also VERBAL DATA RETRIEVAL; WRITTEN REPORTS

verbal data analysis   Because verbal data is apparently so approachable, there is a tendency to immediately accept it at face value. The reader's critical faculties are suspended, particularly if the message reinforces his own prejudices. Even if the reader does somehow retain his critical approach, the 'data' is often difficult to analyse, because writers of such reports tend to use the same words to mean different things, and the importance they attach to events more often reflects their own enthusiasm rather than any absolute measure. In addition, collating a number of such reports and distilling these into an overall impression becomes a matter of judgement rather than a simple analysis, and all too often is used to create 'evidence' to bolster the manager's own preconceived ideas. To a certain extent some of these problems may be corrected by a well-designed re-porting system or by the use of electronic mail – the structure of which tends to standardize the format and even the language of replies.

See also DATA ACCESS PROBLEMS; ELECTRONIC MAIL; ROUTING RULES; WRITTEN REPORTS

verbal data retrieval Perhaps the main short-coming of verbal material is in its retrieval. If not filed in the waste-paper basket, memos and reports are consigned to the vagaries of the manager's or department's filing system (both of which usually rely on categories which have long since outlived their creators and are meaningless to their current users). Indeed, managers are notoriously inept at filing and usually leave it to their secretaries, who may have no real idea of what the content is about. The most useful file in many offices is therefore the 'day file', in which copies of everything being sent out are filed in date order (which means that the area of search can at least be narrowed to a range of dates, if not to the subject!). But before even starting such a search, the manager has to remember which docu-ment the specific piece of information was included in – always assuming he has kept it! The general problem will not be resolved until all filing is held on computer, when it will be a matter of asking the computer (rather than the secretary) to search the millions of words to find those that are needed, and the raw computing power is available to do just that. In the shorter term there are a couple of ways of protecting the key data:

* facts books
* computer databases

See also FACTS BOOKS; VERBAL (COMPUTER) DATABASES; WRITTEN REPORTS

verbal proof close   *see* CLOSING TECHNIQUES

verbatim script   *see* PRESENTATION STYLE

vertical circulation Publication designed for readers in one industry or sector.
See also MEDIA BUYING, ADVERTISING AGENCY; MEDIA SELECTION

vertical industrial markets   *see* HORIZONTAL AND VERTICAL INDUSTRIAL MARKETS

vertical integration   *see* RETAIL ORGANIZATION

vertical marketing This integrates the channel with the original supplier – producer, wholesalers

and retailers working in one unified system. This may arise from one member of the chain owning the other elements (often called 'corporate systems inte-gration'); for example, a supplier may own its own retail outlets (in the way that Radio Shack, the Tandy electronic goods supplier, does), which is for-ward integration. More likely, perhaps, a retailer may own its suppliers, as backward integration (such as MFI, the furniture retailer, owning Hygena, which makes its kitchen and bedroom units). But the integration can also be by franchise (such as that offered by McDonalds Hamburgers and Benetton clothes) or simple co-operation (in the way that Marks & Spencer co-operate with their suppliers). Alternative approaches are 'contractual systems', where the members are bound together contractu-ally, often led by a wholesaler or retailer co-operative, and 'administered marketing systems', where one (dominant) member of the distribution chain uses its position to coordinate the other mem-bers' activities. This has traditionally been the form led by manufacturers. The intention of vertical mar-keting is to give all those involved (and particularly the supplier at one end and the retailer at the other) control over the distribution chain. This removes one set of variables, one set of uncertainties, from the marketing equations. Other research indicates that vertical integration is a strategy which is best pur-sued at the mature stage of the market (or product); at earlier stages it can actually reduce profits. It is arguable that it also diverts attention from the real business of the organization. Suppliers rarely excel in retail operations (as even IBM found with its abor-tive foray into its wholly owned personal computer outlets), and retailers in theory should have their focus on their sales outlets – not on manufacturing facilities (the most successful retail operator, Marks & Spencer, very deliberately provides considerable amounts of technical assistance to its suppliers but does not own them).
See also CHANNEL DECISIONS; CHANNEL MEMBERSHIP; CHANNEL MOTIVATION; DISTRIBUTION CHAIN

Vertical Marketing System (VMS)   *see* CHANNEL STRUCTURE

veto power   *see* DECISION–MAKERS AND INFLUENCERS; SAFETY IN NUMBERS

viewer   *see* MEDIA IMPACT; MEDIA SELECTION

virtual monopoly, pricing   *see* BRAND 'MONOPOLY' PRICING; PRICING, PRODUCT POSITIONING

vision, corporate   Perhaps the most important factor in successful marketing is the 'corporate vision'. Surprisingly, this is one which is largely neglected by marketing textbooks, though not by the popular exponents of corporate strategy – indeed it was perhaps the main theme of the book by Peters and Waterman (1982), in the form of their 'superordinate goals'. Theodore Levitt (1986) says 'Nothing drives progress like the imagination. The idea precedes the deed'. Even Robert Townsend (1971) echoes the statement in his comment that 'Things get done in our society because of a man or woman with conviction'. If the organization in general, and its chief executive in particular, has a strong vision of where its future lies, then there is a good chance that the organization will achieve a strong position in its markets (and attain that future). This will be not least because its strategies will be consistent and will be supported by its staff at all levels. What is a worthwhile vision, however, is usually open to debate – indeed, to considerable debate – hence such visions tend to be associated with strong, charismatic leaders. But the vision must be relevant. Townsend adds the very pragmatic footnote 'Before you commit yourself to a new effort, it's worth asking yourself a couple of questions: Are we really trying to do something worthwhile here? Or are we just building another monument to some diseased ego?'! The problem for marketers is also that this vision is often unrelated to the markets. As Peter Drucker (1980) says, 'every "right" product sooner or later becomes a "wrong" product'.

The message for the marketer is that, to be most effective, the marketing strategies must be converted into a powerful long-term vision – if such a vision does not already exist. Drucker, once again, says:

> In many markets one prospers only at the extremes: either as one of the few market leaders who set the standard, or as a specialist . . . What is not tenable is a strategy in between. . . .To make the future demands courage. It demands work. But it also demands faith . . . The idea on which tomorrow's business is built must be uncertain; no one can really say as yet what it will look like if and when it becomes a reality. It must be risky; it has a probability of success, but also of failure.

See also MISSION

References: Drucker, Peter F. (1980) *Managing in Turbulent Times*. London: Heinemann.
Levitt, Theodore (1986) *The Marketing Imagination*. New York: The Free Press.

Peters, Thomas J. and Waterman, Robert H. (1982) *In Search of Excellence*. New York: Harper & Row.
Townsend, Robert (1971) *Up the Organization*. London: Coronet Books.

visualizers   *see* AWARENESS, ADVERTISING; CREATIVE DEPARTMENT, ADVERTISING AGENCY

visuals   *see* ADVERTISING PROCESSES

VMS (Vertical Marketing System)   *see* CHANNEL STRUCTURE

voice-over   The commentary spoken to a television commercial.
See also ADVERTISING PROCESSES; CREATING THE CORRECT MESSAGES; CREATIVE DEPARTMENT, ADVERTISING AGENCY

Volkswagen German Cars   *see* GLOBAL MARKETING

volume businesses   As represented by one quadrant in the Advantage Matrix (from the Boston Consulting Group), in this case there are considerable economies of scale but few opportunities for differentiation. This is the classic situation where organizations strive for economies of scale by becoming the volume, and hence cost, leader.

voluntary (group) retailer   *see* RETAIL ORGANIZATION; SYMBOL RETAILER

volunteers   Some not-for-profit organizations have a different form of 'distribution' requirement. They need to devote considerable marketing resources to recruiting the volunteers which provide important elements of their service. As Kotler and Andreasen (1987) suggest:

> Nonprofits have limited resources. As a consequence they must become experts at securing additional manpower, skills, and financial resources. This, too, is a marketing task. Others must be convinced that the benefits of helping exceed the costs. Nonprofits are unique in needing volunteers to help accomplish their basic goals. Strategies for recruiting and managing volunteers must take into account changes in the environment. Today's volunteers cover a wider spectrum of people. They are more demanding and have different

motivations than they had in the past. More importantly, some groups are challenging the basic values of volunteer service.

See also RETAILING

Reference: Kotler, Philip and Andreasen, Alan R. (1987) *Strategic Marketing for Nonprofit Organizations* (3rd edn). Englewood Cliffs, NJ: Prentice-Hall.

voucher *see* PROMOTIONAL PRICING; SAMPLING

W

waiting lists *see* PRICE AND NOT-FOR-PROFIT ORGANIZATIONS

Waitrose supermarkets *see* COARSE MARKETING

waits *see* QUEUE

walkabout One very practical approach to marketing research, and one which seems to be central to the Japanese approach to marketing research, involves no more than going out and about, where the action is on the product or service in question, and experiencing what is happening. In particular, the sales professionals meet their customers and distributors, and talk through, at length, what is happening. It has none of the statistical validity which survey research enjoys and even desk research can often lay claim to. Yet better than anything else it conveys the flavour, the essence, of what is being studied. If you want to understand Toyota you can spend months of desk research reading the hundreds of papers which have been written about its efficiency, or you can spend half a day watching the confident grace with which the workers on its production lines assemble cars; as, decades before, Mr Toyoda himself learned his lessons by similarly spending time (three months in his case) watching American workers going through their less graceful routines. The essence is experience; assimilating what is happening – what is really important to the product or service.
See also SURVEY RESEARCH; SYNTHESIS AND ASSIMILATION, OF MARKETING RESEARCH DATA

Walls pies and sausages *see* MARKETING OBJECTIVES

warehouse *see* FACILITY DECISIONS, LOGISTICS MANAGEMENT; PHYSICAL DISTRIBUTION MANAGEMENT

warning competitor by test markets *see* TEST MARKET

warranty card, precision marketing *see* DATA AVAILABILITY, PRECISION MARKETING

wastage *see* DATA MANIPULATION, PRECISION MARKETING

Watson, Thomas J. *see* CONVICTION MARKETING FACTORS; TERRITORY MANAGEMENT

wave research *see* PRODUCT TEST

waves of advertising *see* MEDIA SELECTION

waybill *see* CONSIGNMENT NOTE

weaknesses *see* SWOT ANALYSIS

weak relationship models *see* MODEL CATEGORIES

weak signals *see* TEAM SCANNING

web offset A large-scale (25 000+ copies) lithographic printing process.
See also REEL FED

Webster and Wind model, of organizational behaviour Models have been produced to explain the complexities of the organizational buying process. The best known of these is probably that of Webster and Wind (1972a,b). This follows the buying process inwards from the external environment, through the organizational environment, to the 'buying centre' (the group concerned in the buying decision), to the individuals involved and the buying process they go through. It is useful, in terms of illustrating the variables and the complexities which may be involved, but it is difficult to relate to practical decisions.

There are other, competing models in this field. Sheth (1973), for example, concentrated more on the information flows – to achieve a more dynamic model.
See also HOWARD AND SHETH MODEL, OF CONSUMER BEHAVIOUR; MODELS

References: Sheth, J. N. (1973) A model of industrial buyer behaviour. *Journal of Marketing*, 37, October.

Webster, W. and Wind, Y. (1972a) A general model for understanding organizational buying behaviour. *Journal of Marketing*, 36, April.

Webster, W. and Wind, Y. (1972b) *Organizational Buying Behaviour*. Englewood Cliffs, NJ: Prentice-Hall.

weeklies   *see* PRESS MEDIA

what-if analysis   *see* SPREADSHEETS, AND FORECASTING

what-if tests, new products   *see* STRATEGIC SCREENING, NEW PRODUCTS

wheel of retailing   In 1958, Malcolm McNair postulated the idea that retailers moved through a cycle. According to this hypothesis, retailers enter the market as low-status, low-cost enterprises, taking business away from the established retailers. In time, as they grow with success, they too upgrade their outlets and charge high prices – exposing themselves to new competitors entering the 'wheel'. It is a widely accepted concept, despite its relative lack of development – even in the original paper. Yet, on the other hand, there is remarkably little evidence to support it, and much (based on retailing developments in recent years) to dispute it – there are innumerable cheaper hamburger outlets than McDonalds, but few obvious successors! In fact, more recently, even Malcolm McNair himself has concluded that the concept is too narrow to explain all the outcomes – but these later comments have yet to reach many textbooks! A second group of theorists look for a retail life cycle to match the product life cycle, but starting with 'innovation' leading to 'accelerated development' before the more conventional 'maturity' and 'decline'. This seems, as with life cycles in general, eminently reasonable. Like other life cycles, though, it is not obvious what the exact pattern of this life cycle should be for a given retailer, as most retail chains are in the 'maturity' phase (and retaining their position by on-going, incremental developments).

See also RETAILING

Reference: McNair, M. P. (1958) Significant trends and developments in the post war period. In A. B. Smith (ed.), *Competitive Distribution in a Free, High Level Economy and its Implications for the University*. University of Pittsburgh Press.

white knight   A firm, or individual, which makes a takeover (which is favoured by the existing management), on improved terms, in place of a hostile one.

wholesalers and distributors   Between producers and retailers (and between producers and other manufacturing and service organizations) may be a layer of wholesalers or distributors. Their role is to provide a link between the extremes of the distribution chain – where the numbers of independent retailers, for example, make it uneconomic for a producer to have its own sales force and the distribution network to handle these. Organizationally they may take several forms:

- *Wholesalers.* These are mainly service retailers, usually in the independent sector (for multiples mostly have their own 'wholesale' distribution operations which supply their branches). They stock a range of items from different suppliers (varying from a generalized range, which matches that of the supermarket, to specialized ranges, just covering stationery, for example) and market these either by their own sales force or by self-service, 'cash and carry' warehouses which are exclusively for retailers.
- *Distributors.* There is much learned discussion as to what practically differentiates a distributor from an agent, from a wholesaler, etc. In practice, 'distributor' is now most often the name applied to those wholesalers who deal with industrial establishments (business to business).
- *Agents.* The difference in relationship with the producer is important at this level. Agents typically represent one or more suppliers, on the basis of a formal agreement, whereby they operate, to all intents and purposes, as extensions of that supplier (following his terms of business, quality standards, etc.) even though they are independently owned.

In many respects, the function of any wholesaler is the simplest of any member of the distribution chain. The role is simply to distribute, at the lowest cost; though some service elements (in particular availability) also enter the equation.

In this context, the decisions to be taken parallel those of the retailer (with, perhaps, significantly less emphasis on image):

- target market
- range
- place
- price

Promotion and merchandising usually have less relevance.

There is also a further dimension, as follows.

Support
The amount, and type, of service provided will vary depending upon the decision of the wholesaler. For example:

- *Cash and carry*. The most basic level of support (and now probably the most prevalent in the mass consumer markets), this mimics the self-service element of supermarkets. The customers (typically small retailers and caterers) serve themselves (albeit by the case) and pay at a checkout – in exactly the same way as supermarket customers do.
- *Wholesaler sales force*. At the other extreme, the wholesaler's representative can go out to the retailer to take the order, which is then delivered. This is the traditional, but decreasing, form – now increasingly limited to specialist markets.
- *Rack jobbers*. These take the level of support even further, and actually service 'racks' on the retailer's premises (maintaining stock levels, which are maintained by the jobber's own staff).
- *Mail order*. Some industrial distributors, typically those offering a very wide range of infrequently purchased products (relating to stationery or building services, for example), offer these via catalogues – in exactly the same way as do consumer mail-order catalogues.

See also CHANNEL DECISIONS; RETAILING

widow Very short last line of a paragraph left at the top of a new column, which looks odd, so the typesetting is normally changed.

width The number of different (independent and distinct) 'product' lines carried, which is a measure of the number of different markets addressed. Thus, Unilever has a very wide range of product types (covering Birds Eye Frozen Foods as well as Persil Detergent) but Coca Cola for many years had a very narrow one (based on just the one product).
See also PRODUCT (OR SERVICE) MIX

width of retail products *see* RETAIL 'PRODUCT' DECISIONS

Wildlife Trustees *see* MARKETING RESEARCH, PRECISION MARKETING

win–lose bargaining *see* SUPPLIERS

winner brand *see* INVESTMENT MULTIPLIER

winning friends and influencing people *see* TERRITORY SALES PLAN

winning the order *see* SALES CALL CLOSE

win–win Miller et al. (1985) encapsulated relationship management in the concept of 'win–win': 'Those of us who have prospered by using Strategic Selling [the name of their technique and their book] know that good selling is never an adversarial game in which Buyers' Losses are our Wins, but one in which Buyers' Losses are our Losses too, and their Wins always serve our self-interest as well as theirs. We understand that only by enlisting our buyers as partners in mutually supportive joint ventures can we hope to achieve mutual satisfaction over time.' They conceptualize this philosophy in terms of the 'Win–Win Matrix':

Seller (I)

	I win / you win	I lose / you win
Buyer (you)	I win / you lose	I lose / you lose

In practice, this is something of a gimmick since their comments show that of the remaining quadrants lose–win and win–lose tend to be unstable and degenerate into the lose–lose situation. Even the lose–win situation degenerates, since it sets up unrealistic expectations for the future. They stress 'let the buyer know it . . . the most serious mistake you can make in playing Lose–Win is failing to tell your Buyers that they're getting a special deal'. On the other hand, the concept of win–win is a very powerful concept; and the only real alternative of lose–lose serves to highlight this. Partnership, or win–win, is what must always be striven for.
See also COMPLEX SALE; INTERACTION, AND THE ORGANIZATIONAL PURCHASE; INTER-ORGANIZATIONAL RELATIONS; ORGANIZATIONAL BUYING SITUATIONS; RELATIONSHIP (MARKETING) MANAGEMENT; SALES PROFESSIONAL; SELLING; TERRITORY MANAGEMENT; TERRITORY SALES PLAN; WIN–WIN TRIANGLE

Reference: Miller, Robert B., Heiman, Stephen E. and Tuleja, Tad (1985) *Strategic Selling.* New York: William Morrow.

win–win triangle Win–win is a very powerful concept (and the only real alternative of lose–lose serves to highlight this), and partnership, or win–win, is what must always be aimed for. If you substitute a triangle for a matrix, however, the message is conveyed even more forcefully – since it demonstrates how unstable the relationship may become if you adopt the wrong approach:

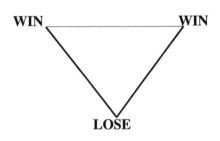

SUPPLIER   **CUSTOMER**

The main lesson of this triangle is the stress it places on sharing the 'win'. If either side loses in the short term then the triangle immediately becomes unstable and topples over – so that, as a result, neither side wins in the long run. 'Win–lose' and 'lose–win' are ultimately unstable and degenerate into 'lose–lose'. The 'win–win triangle' simply shows this more directly.
See also PARTNERSHIP TRIANGLE; WIN–WIN

women's magazines, sampling   *see* SAMPLING

Woolworth   *see* CONVICTION MARKETING TYPES

word association   *see* OPEN QUESTIONS, ON QUESTIONNAIRES

word of mouth   One generalized aspect of communications within the community as a whole is 'word of mouth'. Much of advertising theory concentrates upon the 'direct' receipt of these 'indirect' communications; it assumes that the consumer receives the message directly from the media, and only from the media. In practice the message may well be received by word of mouth from a contact (who may have seen the advertising – or may, in turn, have received it from someone else). Equally, even if the consumer had previously seen the advertising, word

of mouth comments may reinforce (or undermine) what this has achieved directly. An interesting, but very complicated, example of such 'indirect' effects is the 'third person effect', originally described by Davison (1983), which has been most directly investigated in the context of political processes – but is claimed to be just as applicable to the wider scene of advertising. As described a few years later by Diana Mutz (1989):

> The third person effect hypothesis predicts that people exposed to a potentially persuasive communication will expect the message to have a greater effect on others than on themselves . . . The effect that the communication achieves is not due to any direct persuasive influence of the message itself, but rather to the behaviours of persons who anticipate, or think they perceive, some reaction on the part of others, and behave differently as a result . . . The third person effect involves more, however, than simply a psychological tendency to assume that others are more easily influenced than oneself; the hypothesis also suggests that people may take significant actions based on these precautions.

She goes on, however, to suggest (based on her own research) that the effect may be, rather more simply, explained by the fact that individuals underestimate the effect of such communications on themselves!
See also ADVERTISING; BUYING DECISION, ADVERTISING MODELS; OPINION LEADERS

References: Davison, W. Phillips (1983) The third person effect in communication. *Public Opinion Quarterly*, 22.
    Mutz, Diana (1989) The influence of perceptions of media influence: third person effects and the public expression of opinions. *Journal of Public Opinion Research*, 1(1).

workforce communications   *see* CORPORATE PUBLIC RELATIONS

working layout   *see* ADVERTISING PROCESSES

work in progress   *see* INVENTORY CONTROL; MATERIALS MANAGEMENT

world and national economy forecasts   *see* DERIVED FORECASTS

world system risk   *see* MARKET ENTRY DECISION

world trading system   *see* GLOBALIZATION

worst–case scenarios   *see* SENSITIVITY ANALYSIS, NEW PRODUCTS

writer   *see* MESSAGE, ADVERTISING

written reports   Numeric performance data have the great advantage, in terms of analysis, of being numeric. This makes abstraction and manipulation much easier as arithmetical operations are commonplace. Much of the remaining data within an organization is, however, available only in verbal form – as memos or reports. From the marketing viewpoint perhaps the most useful of these are the sales reports. In some respects the reliance on words rather than figures may seem to make the manager's job easier because many, if not most, managers are more at ease with words than numbers. This is something of an illusion and problems occur in a number of areas:

- verbal data analysis
- data access problems
- data overload
- verbal data retrieval

See also DATA ACCESS PROBLEMS; INFORMAL (ORAL) REPORTS; VERBAL DATA ANALYSIS; VERBAL DATA RETRIEVAL

X

Xerox Corporation   *see* JOINT VENTURE

Y

year plan *see* MARKETING PLAN STRUCTURE

yes-men *see* PLANNING PITFALLS

yes/no, on questionnaires *see* CLOSED QUESTIONS, ON QUESTIONNAIRES

yes/no stamps *see* INSERTS, DIRECT MAIL

Z

Z charts The sales data (for one year) can be neatly combined on one graph, to give a Z chart. The bottom bar of the Z is made up of the monthly actuals. The top bar is the moving annual total. The diagonal eventually joining them is the cumulative figure (equal to the first monthly actual at the left and the moving annual total at the end of the year at the right).

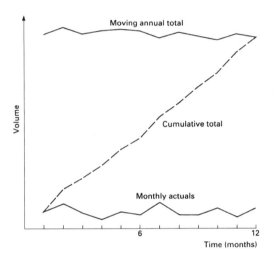

This is a visual representation which allows the forecaster, by comparing the Z charts for succeeding years, to visually determine what, if any, patterns are emerging. It is also often something of an academic exercise, since the attention of most forecasters will be firmly focused on the bottom, 'actuals', line – which is, in the Z chart, reduced to a scale which is barely meaningful. They will, with some justification, prefer to expand this to fill the whole chart (and ignore the MAT line).

See also QUANTITATIVE FORECASTING TECHNIQUES

zero-based budgeting *see* BUDGETS

zero defects The quality concept that an organization should aim for perfection in the quality of its products, with no rejects. This replaced the concept of the Acceptable Quality Level (AQL) which had prevailed previously. It was made possible by a range of developments stressing prevention throughout the production process from quality gurus such as A. V. Feigenbaum, who emphasized that quality was the responsibility of everyone, especially the workers on the production lines, and G. Taguchi (1987), who revolutionized the quality process by identifying that it was in the design of the product that the main contributions to zero defects were made. The concept of zero defects was originated by P. B. Crosby (1979) as part of his work on the US Pershing Missile project, but it was taken up and advanced (as were many of the quality ideas which originated in the USA but were never developed further there) by the Japanese. It is a simple (and powerful) philosophy, but a complex process; it is only introduced as the seventh of Crosby's 14 Steps to Quality, and then only after a year of introductory work (in an overall process which typically takes at least four years).

See also CROSBY, P. B.; JUST IN TIME (JIT); KAISEN; NORMAL CURVE; SUGGESTIONS SCHEMES

References: Crosby, P. B. (1979) *Quality is Free.* New York: McGraw-Hill.
   Taguchi, G. (1987) *Systems of Experimental Design: Engineering Methods to Optimize Quality and Minimize Costs.* New York: Kraus Publications.

zero defects versus AQL For many years quality control was dealt with on the basis of statistics – measuring the 'reject rate' (the proportion of 'products' which failed to meet the standards set in the specification) from samples of batches, and accepting or failing the whole batch of products on the basis of these samples. The 'pass level' was the 'Acceptable Quality Level' (AQL); it was the percentage of rejects which was considered acceptable! The theory behind the application of AQLs was that the cost of removing the last few percentage points of 'rejects' grew 'exponentially'. Thus, the last 0.1 per cent (from 99.8 per cent to 99.9 per cent, say) was perhaps ten times as great as that for the previous 1 per cent (from 98 per cent to 99 per cent fault free, say).

This was the widely accepted philosophy of production. The 'quality' (the percentage of rejects in this case) had to be traded off (exponentially) against the cost, and the chosen balance between the two determined the AQL.

The Japanese, creating a classic paradigm shift, simply decided that they would ignore this theory and instead accept 'zero defects'. It turns out that this requires considerable effort, but is – within limits – not impossible (and certainly does not demand exponential increases in cost). Indeed, the process is now rationalized by organizations which follow this philosophy, such as IBM, with another exponential curve! This new theory states that it costs, say, ten times as much to rectify a problem at each subsequent stage through the whole production and delivery process. Thus, it costs ten times as much to rectify a fault after the customer has taken delivery as it does at retailer level; which is, in turn, ten times as expensive as before it leaves the factory; which is ten times as much as while it is still on the production line; which is, finally, ten times as much as rectification at the design stage!

The exponential nature may, once more, be apocryphal – but the concept of removing faults at the earliest possible stage (especially during design) seems to pay substantial dividends to those using the technique, as well as offering the customer defect-free products – which is invaluable.

The power of the zero defects concept is illustrated by an example, of the improvement in quality of simple electronic components, given by Tom Peters (1987): 'Typical improvements, from 1980 to 1983, measured as defects per million: transistors, from 2,800 to 200, a 14-fold improvement; transformers, 4,200 to 100, a 42-fold rise in quality; and capacitors, from 9,300 to 80, 116-fold rise'.

As suggested above, perhaps the most important new emphasis with a zero defects approach is that the whole process starts with design. As Taguchi and Clausing (1990) say: 'Quality is a function of design. The "robustness" of products is more a function of good design than of on-line control, however stringent, of manufacturing processes.'

They justify the need for quality by the very practical comment, echoing the comments earlier, that 'When a product fails, you must replace or fix it. In either case you must track it, transport it, and apologize for it. Losses will be much greater than the cost

of manufacture, and none of this expense will recoup the loss of your reputation.'

To give a scale to the problem, they quote Taiichi Ohno, the former executive vice-president of Toyota Motor Corporation: 'Whatever an executive thinks the losses of poor quality are, they are actually six times greater'.

See also CUSTOMER SATISFACTION SURVEY; QUALITY; QUALITY CIRCLES

References: Peters, Tom (1987) *Thriving on Chaos*. New York: Alfred A. Knopf, Inc.

Taguchi, Genichi and Clausing, Don (1990) Robust quality. *Harvard Business Review*, January–February.

zero-level distribution   *see* CHANNEL MEMBERS

zero-level marketing   This is a commitment to approach each new activity afresh – a blank sheet of paper – without the prejudices derived from previous exposure to theories. The factors which you write on that blank sheet of paper, therefore, should only be the key factors which are directly relevant to the individual situation in hand. The essence of this process, of zero-level marketing, is the distillation of exactly what is important to the current situation – unencumbered by any academic gimmickry (no matter how elegantly it may be packaged!). Having undertaken this exercise in minimalism, and having achieved this initial distillation, you can then proceed directly to the rest of the 'Analytical 4-Step'.

The theory you choose to help at this stage (and especially at step 4), should also be tested against the eight steps of the 'critic's charter'.

See also ANALYTICAL 4-STEP; CRITIC'S CHARTER

zero philosophies   *see* KAISEN

zero-sum   *see* ADDED-VALUE DIAGRAM; INTER-ORGANIZATIONAL RELATIONS; SALESMAN STEREOTYPE

zip code   US postcode.

zone pricing   *see* GEOGRAPHICAL PRICING